P9-EAX-335

The Western Scientific Gaze and Popular Imagery in Later Edo Japan: The Lens within the Heart is the first full-length study to consider the introduction of Western technology into Japan in the eighteenth century, when, it has been assumed, that country continued to isolate itself from external influence. Timon Screech demonstrates that exposure to such Western equipment as lenses, mirrors, and glass had a profound impact on Japanese notions regarding the faculty of sight. The hugeness of this paradigm shift, moreover, was felt less in the area of Japanese scientific inquiry than in art and popular culture, where these devices were often depicted and used metaphorically, as commentary on prevailing social norms. Based on archival sources here published for the first time in any language, this study also sheds new light on Japanese art and its relation to the West; the relationship of science to art and popular culture; and the autonomy and/or internationalization of Japanese culture.

The Western Scientific Gaze and Popular Imagery in Later Edo Japan

CAMBRIDGE STUDIES IN NEW ART HISTORY AND CRITICISM

This series provides a forum for studies that represent new approaches to the study of the visual arts. The works cover a range of subjects, including artists, genres, periods, themes, styles, and movements. They are distinguished by their methods of inquiry, whether interdisciplinary or related to developments in literary theory, anthropology, or social history. The series also aims to publish translations of a selection of European material that has heretofore been unavailable to an English-speaking readership.

Other Books in the Series:

Reading "Rembrandt": Beyond the Word–Image Opposition, by Mieke Bal
The True Vine: On Visual Representation and the Western Tradition, by Stephen Bann
Deconstruction and the Visual Arts, edited by Peter Brunette and David Wills
Calligram: Essays in New Art History from France, edited by Norman Bryson
The Gothic Idol: Ideology and Image-Making in Medieval Art, by Michael Camille
The Rhetoric of Purity: Essentialist Theory and the Advent of Abstract Painting, by Mark A. Cheetham
The Aesthetics of Power: Essays in Critical Art History, by Carol Duncan
Art and the Roman Viewer, by Jaś Elsner
Art and Text in Ancient Greek Culture, edited by Simon Goldhill and Robin Osborne
Narrative and Event in Ancient Art, by Peter Holliday
Postmodernism and the En-Gendering of Marcel Duchamp, by Amelia Jones

THE WESTERN SCIENTIFIC GAZE AND POPULAR IMAGERY IN LATER EDO JAPAN

The Lens within the Heart

TIMON SCREECH

School of Oriental and African Studies, University of London

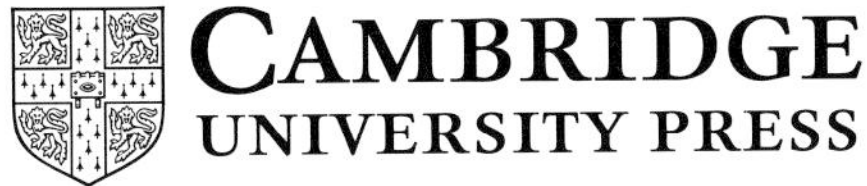

CAMBRIDGE UNIVERSITY PRESS

Published by the Press Syndicate of the University of Cambridge
The Pitt Building, Trumpington Street, Cambridge CB2 1RP
40 West 20th Street, New York, NY 10011-4211, USA
10 Stamford Road, Oakleigh, Melbourne 3166, Australia

First published 1996

Printed in the United States of America

Library of Congress Cataloging-in-Publication Data

The western scientific gaze and popular imagery in later Edo Japan
: the lens within the heart / Timon Screech.

p. cm. – (Cambridge studies in new art history and criticism)

Includes index.

ISBN 0-521-48225-9 (hc)

1. Art, Japanese – Edo period, 1600–1868. 2. Art, Japanese – European influences. 3. Art and technology – Japan. I. Title. II. Series.

N7353.5.S4 1996

709'.52—dc20 95–15643
CIP

A catalog record for this book is available from the British Library.

Erratum
The correct ISBN for this book is
0-521-46106-5

For Zoo

dōgyō ninin

The precision of a microscope is such that if you put just a droplet of water on the end of a pin and look at it, you will see that even the freshest sort has a multitude of creatures within, all of odd shapes and strange types. Forms that have never before been seen in this world are to be discerned, sporting there. . . .

The microscope exceeds even the Buddhas' eyes.

Further, there may exist what is so reduced even the microscope cannot grasp it, and if this is so, no restriction can be placed on how infinitesimal matter can be. Pushing the logic further, we may suppose there to be no limit on vastness either. The universe that we inhabit can be likened to a drop of water, millions of universes piled up together with it.

And how can we be sure something is not out there with a microscope, looking on?

—Tachibana Nankei, *A Record of Pleasurable Travels in the West* (*Seiyū-ki*, 1798)

CONTENTS

List of Plates and Figures viii

Preface xiii

Introduction 1

1 Trade and Culture in the Eighteenth Century 6

2 The "Batavian Temperament" and Its Critics 31

3 Mechanics and Motions 61

4 Machinery for Pictures 94

5 Seeing In 133

6 The Eye and the Lens 166

7 The View from On High 212

Notes 254

Glossary 288

References 290

Index 300

PLATES AND FIGURES

COLOUR PLATES follow page xiv.

1. Kawahara Keiga, *View of Nagasaki.*
2. Suzuki Harunobu, *Tamagawa in Kōno,* from the series *Mu-tamagawa.*
3. Shiba Kōkan, *Serpentine.*
4. Shiba Kōkan, *Tweelandbruk.*
5. Maruyama Ōkyo, *Orange Tree Hall.*
6. Utagawa Toyoharu, *The Bell which Resounds for Ten-thousand Leagues in the Dutch Port of Frankai.*
7. Okumura Masanobu, *Enjoying the Cool at Ryōgoku Bridge.*
8. Unsigned, *Western Figures in a Garden.*
9. Maruyama Ōkyo, *Legs of the Person to the Right,* and *Boy Seen from Above,* from *Jintai seisha sōhon.*
10. Kitagawa Utamaro, *Woman Reading a Letter,* from the series, *Fujo ninsō juppon.*
11. Iwasaki Kan'en, *Franz von Siebold.*
12. Shiba Kōkan, *Mosquito Larvae.*
13. Katsushika Hokusai, *Microscope and Butterfly.*
14. Katsushika Hokusai, *Ryōgoku Bridge,* from the series *Oranda gakyō: Edo hakkei.*
15. Katsushika Hokusai, wrapper to above series.
16. Katsushika Hokusai, *Women with Telescope and Parasol,* from the series *Fūryū nakute nanakuse.*

FIGURES

1. Ichiyanagi Kagen, from Tachibana Nankei, *Seiyū-ki.* 14
2. Shiba Kōkan, *Yoshio Kōsaku with Symbols.* 15
3. Katsushika Hokusai, from Asakura Shijin, *Kyōka azuma asobi.* 19
4. Utagawa Hiroshige, from Tenmei Rōjin, *Kyōka Edo meisho zue* 20
5. Kitao Shigemasa, *Beauties of the Eastern Quarter: O-naka and O-shima of Nakachō in Fukagawa,* from the series *Tōzai nanboku bijin.* 25
6. Takehara Shunchōsai, from Akisato Ritō, *Settsu meisho zue.* 27
7. Kubo Shunman, *Murano's glassware shop.* 29
8. Katsushika Hokusai, from Kanwatei Onitake, *Wakanran zatsuwa.* 35
9. As above. 36
10. As above 37
11. As above. 38
12. Katsushika Hokusai, from *Muna-zan'yō uso no tanaoroshi.* 39
13. Unsigned, *Inspectors Studying Trading Goods,* from *Bankan-zu.* 40
14. Unsigned, *Dutchman Weighing Out Trading Goods.* 41
15. Johannes & Caspaares Luiken,

Balance-maker, from *Spiegel van het menselyk bedryf.* 43
16. Kitao Masayoshi, *Erkiteru*, from Morishima Chūryō, *Kōmō zatsuwa.* 45
17. Unsigned, *Static-electricity Generator* and *Elephant*, from Egbert Buys, *Niuew en volkommen woodenboek.* 46
18. Shiba Kōkan, from *Saiyū ryōdan.* 47
19. Shiba Kōkan, from *Oranda tensetsu.* 49
20. Unsigned, *Foreign-made Barometer*, from Shibukawa Kagesuke (ed.), *Kansei rekisho.* 49
21. Chōkōsai Eishō, from Hekizentei Kunenbō, *Hade mezurashiki futatsu no utsuwa.* 51
22. Shiba Kōkan, *Mt. Fuji.* 55
23. Unsigned, *Camera Obscura*, from Ōtsuki Gentaku, *Ransetsu benwaku.* 57
24. Utagawa Toyohiro, from Takizawa Bakin, *Kage to hinata chinmō zui.* 59
25. Shiba Kōkan, *Dutch Ship*, from *Saiyū ryōdan.* 62
26. Santō Kyōden, *Pestle-pounding Monkey* (detail), from *Komon gawa.* 68
27. Takehara Shunchōsai, from Akisato Ritō, *Settsu meisho zue.* 69
28. Unsigned, *Three Cheers for the Strongman Boy*, from Nishimura Shigenaga, *Ō-karakuri e-zukushi.* 70
29. Takahashi Kageyasu, *Fountain*, from *Kōsei shinpen* 71
30. Johannes & Caspaares Luiken, *Pump-maker*, from *Spiegel van het menselyk bedryf.* 72
31. Unsigned, *Watering the Garden and Tending Flowers*, from *Bankan-zu.* 73
32. Kodera Gyokuchō, from *Misemono zasshi.* 74
33. Unsigned, *Miniature Fountains*, from Morishima Chūryō, *Kōmō zatsuwa.* 74
34. Unsigned, *Minature Fountains*, from Egbert Buys, *Niuew en volkommen woordenboek.* 75
35. Takehara Shunchōsai, from Akisato Ritō, *Settsu meisho zue.* 77
36. Ōhata Giemon, *Imported Automaton Clock.* 80
37. Hosokawa Hanzō, *Tea-carrying Boy*, from *Karakuri kinmō zue.* 83
38. Nishikawa Sukenobu, *Woman with Clock.* 84
39. Japanese clock. 85
40. Jippensha Ikku, from *Shingaku tokei-gusa.* 87
41. Odano Naotake, *Abdomen and Intestines*, from Sugita Genpaku (et al.), *Kaitai shinsho.* 88
42. Shōun, *Ragorā* 90
43. Kitao Shigemasa, from Tsuta Karamaru, *Shintai kaichō ryaku engi.* 93
44. Unsigned, *Rose*, from Rembertus Dodoneus, *Cruydt-boek.* 96
45. Unsigned, *Elephant*, from Johannis Jonstonus, *Theatrum universale omnium animalium quadrupedum.* 96
46. Unsigned, *Vue de la maison royale de Somerset avec l'église de Ste Marie dans le Strand, à Londres.* 99
47. Shiba Kōkan, *Optiques.* 100
48. Unsigned, *Vue de la maison royale de Somerset avec l'église de Ste Marie dans le Strand, à Londres.* 101
49. Shiba Kōkan, *Tweelandbruk.* 103
50. Santō Kyōden, *View of Awa in Kazusa*, from *Shinzō zue.* 105
51. Unsigned, *Lucerna Magica*, from Gulielmo s' Gravesande, *Physices elementa mathematica.* 107
52. Unsigned, *Casting an Image onto a White Wall*, from Sukenari, *Tengu-tsū.* 108
53. Toriyama Sekien, *The Dangler*, from *Gazu hyakki tsurezure-bukuro.* 109
54. Utagawa Toyokuni, from Hekizentai Kunenbō, *Hōtsuki chōchin oshie no chikamichi.* 110
55. As above. 111

56. Torii Kiyonaga, from Santō Kyōden, *Jikun kage-e no tatoe.* 112
57. Unsigned, *Un homme mur à côté d'un jeune garçon*, from Jean Lavater, *Essai sur la physiogonomie.* 113
58. As above. 114
59. Torii Kiyonaga, from Santō Kyōden, *Jikun kage-e no tatoe.* 114
60. As above. 115
61. Santo Kyōden, from *Hitogokoro kagami no utsushi-e.* 116
62. As above. 117
63. As above. 118
64. Shimokabe Ikei, from Akisato Ritō, *Settsu meisho zue.* 119
65. Samuel van Hoogstraten, Peepbox. 120
66. Unsigned, *Peepbox*, detail of *Asakusa* handscroll. 123
67. Santō Kyōden, from *Gozonji no shōbaimomo.* 124
68. Kitao Shigemasa, *Fortune's Great Karakuri*, from Santō Kyōden, *Ko wa mezurashiki misemono-gatari.* 128
69. Santō Kyōden, from Morishima Chūryō, *Shin-Yoshitsune saiken Ezo.* 131
70. Johannes & Caspaares Luiken, *Glasier*, from *Spiegel van het menselyk bedryf.* 135
71. Unsigned, *Glass-blower*, from Mitaku Yorai, *Bankin sangyō-bukuro.* 137
72. Unsigned, *Dutch Feast*, from *Bankan-zu.* 139
73a&b (left page and opposite page). Hosokawa Shigekata, from *Mōkai kikan.* 140
74. Unsigned, *Specimens in Preservative Liquid*, from Hiraga Gennai, *Butsurui hinshitsu.* 142
75. Satake Shozan, *Dragon*, from *Shasei-chō.* 143
76. Morishima Chūryō, *Dragon*, from *Kōmō zatsuwa.* 143
77. Kitao Shigemasa, *Exhibition of Rareties*, from Santō Kyōden, *Ko wa mezurashiki misemono-gatari.* 145
78. Kitao Shigemasa, from Shiba Zenkō, *Ōchigai takarabune.* 146
79. As above. 147
80. Chōkōsai Eishō, *Kadotama-ya Wakamurasaki*, from the series *Kakuchū bijin kurabe.* 148
81. Shiba Kōkan, from *Kopperu tenmon zukai.* 149
82. Shiba Kōkan, from *Oranda tensetsu.* 150
83. Glass float containing human figure. 150
84. Kitagawa Utamaro (attrib.), *'Glass' O-shima.* 151
85. Engraved comb. 153
86. Ichiyanagi Kagen, from Hirokawa Kai, *Nagasaki bunken-roku.* 154
87. Unsigned, *Transferring a Western Print onto Glass.* 155
88. Unsigned, *Woman with Cat.* 156
89. Johannes & Caspaares Luiken, *Mirror-maker*, from *Spiegel van het menselyk bedryf.* 157
90. Morishima Chūryō, *Mirror Stand/ Mirror Shield*, from *Tora no maki.* 160
91. Ishikawa Tairō, *Sugita Genpaku*, title page from Sugita Genpaku, *Keiei yawa.* 161
92. Santō Kyōden, from *Kaitsū unubore kagami.* 164
93. Kodera Gyokuchō, from *Misemono zasshi.* 165
94. Odano Naotake, *The Eye*, from Sugita Genpaku (et al.), *Kaitai shinsho.* 168
95. Ishikawa Tairō, from Sugita Rikkyō (et al.), *Ganka shinsho.* 170
96. Santō Kyōden, from *Akushichi henme Kagekiyo.* 173
97. As above. 175
98. Jippensha Ikku, from *Yome tōme kasa no uchi.* 176
99. Kitagawa Utamaro, *Woman with Pipe*, from the series *Bijin gomensō.* 178

100. Santō Kyōden, from *Akushichi henme Kagekiyo.* 179
101. Pipe case and tobacco pouch. 179
102. Shikitei Sanba, from *Ono no Bakamura uso ji-zukushi.* 180
103. Kitao Masayoshi, from Koikawa Yukimachi, *Sakaemasu megane no toku.* 185
104. As above. 186
105. As above. 186
106. Jippensha Ikku, from *Yome tōme kasa no uchi.* 187
107. Kitagawa Utamaro, *A Canny One*, from the series *Kyōkun oya no megane.* 188
108. Harukawa Shūzan, from Santō Kyōden (attrib.), *Sanshōdayū shichinin musume.* 189
109. Utagawa Kunitora, from anon., *Otome sugata.* 190
110. Utagawa Toyokuni, from Sakuragawa Jihinari, *Fukutokujū goshiki megane.* 192
111. As above. 193
112. Unsigned, *Microscope*, from Morishima Chūryō, *Kōmō zatsuwa.* 195
113. Kitao Shigemasu from Santō Kyōden, *Sakusha tainai totsuki no zu.* 197
114. Jippensha Ikku, from *Mushi-megane nobe no wakakusa.* 197
115. Utagawa Kunisada, from Santō Kyōden, *Matsu to ume taketori monogatari.* 198
116. As above. 199
117. Shiba Kōkan, *Ants* and *Mosquito Larvae*, from Morishima Chūryō, *Kōmō zatsuwa.* 200
118. As above. 200
119. Unsigned, *Mosquito Larvae*, from Jean Swammerdam, *Histoire générale des insectes.* 201
120. Unsigned, *Dutch Microscope.* 201
121. Torii Kiyomasa, from Rinshō, *Kogane yama Fukuzō jikki.* 205
122. Ogawa Yoshimaru, from Shikitei Sanba, *Hara no uchi gesaku no tanehon.* 207
123. Kitagawa Utamaro, from Namake no Bakahito, *Uso shikkari gantori chō.* 207
124. Shunsai Eishō, title page from Nansenshō Somahito, *Hara no uchi nozoki karakuri*, vol. 1. 208
125. Kitagawa Utamaro, *Woman with Mini-Peepbox*, from the series *Bijin sōgaku juttai.* 209
126. Shunsai Eishō, cover from Nansenshō Somahito, *Hara no uchi nozoki karakuri*, vol. 2. 210
127. Unsigned, *Foreign Celestial Telescope*, from Shibukawa Kagesuke (ed.), *Kansei rekisho.* 214
128. Takehara Shunchōsai, *Temple of Kiyomizu*, from Akisato Ritō, *Settsu meisho zue.* 219
129. Maruyama Ōkyo, *Temple of Kiyomizu.* 221
130. Satake Shozan, *Looking Down; Looking into the Distance*, from *Shasei-chō.* 222
131. As above, *Double-spiral stair.* 223
132. Katsushika Hokusai, from Kanwatei Onitake, *Wakanran zatsuwa.* 226
133. Kitao Shigemasa, from Hatake no Dojin Maimosuke, *Kontan teori shima.* 227
134. Shiba Kōkan (attrib.), *Vulture Peak* and *Hot-air Balloon.* 229
135. Hasegawa Settan & Settei, from Saitō Gesshin (et al.), *Edo meisho zue.* 231
136. Santō Kyōden, from Sharakutei Manri, *Shimadai me no shōgatsu.* 234
137. Utagawa Toyokuni, from Shikitei Sanba, *Ningen isshin nozoki-karakuri.* 235
138. Katsukawa Shun'ei, from Ichiba Tsūshō, *Tenjiku mōke no suji.* 239

139. Kitao Shigemasa, from Shiba Zenkō, *Tōsei daitsū butsu kaichō.* 241
140. Koriki Enkoan, from *Hokusai taiga sokusho saizu.* 243
141. *Great Buddha of Kamakura,* Kōtoku-in. 243
142. Hasegawa Settan & Settei, from Saitō Gesshin (et al.), *Edo meisho zue.* 245
143. Suzuki Harunobu, *Motoura of the Yamazaki-ya in the South,* from the series *Ukiyo bijin hana o kotokuki.* 246
144. Katsushika Hokusai, from *Nanasato fuki.* 247
145. Unsigned, *Arhat,* Kita-in. 248
146. Shiba Kōkan, *Orrery,* from *Tenkyū zenzu.* 249
147. C. Lemprière, *The Great Orrery.* 250
148. Unsigned, Copy after Ōtsuki Gentaku & Kimura Kōgō, *Kaikai ibun.* 251
149. As above. 252

PREFACE

This work, I hope, is not an ordinary history of art: it is not a history of ordinary art. We are to be concerned with things that were viewed only lightly in their own time. The project demands retrieval of what seemed fruitless or trivial in its own day, from popular storybooks to fairground goods to brothel memorabilia. But the words of Isaac Titsingh, who was in Japan in the early 1780s, are to the point: if I "lead the reader to suppose the Japanese sink the more important matters in an ocean of frivolities," then, "before he adopts so harsh a notion . . . he ought to consider their present situation, and to acquire a smattering at least of their history." More than two centuries later, the warning could not be more apt. Although our concern here is with the popular, that is things outside the purview of authoritarian institutions, the objects are not vain. My argument is, indeed, that the data furnished here were precisely at the core of later eighteenth-century thought. I make no claims to methodological originality in this position. Yet I do believe that what is offered here has not been attempted before in the field of East Asian art. I cannot, of course, speak for my level of success, but the project, I am convinced, has been worth the undertaking.

Many of the documents presented here have not been studied since they were written, and although I have greatly benefited from the work of other people, there has also been much sailing in uncharted waters. The difficulty of reading some of the materials has been extreme, and occasional citations below would assuredly have admitted of interpretations other than the ones I give them. But as Sugita Genpaku wrote when he published the ground-breaking treatise on European thought in 1774, "Reader, if there is anything here resistant to reasonable interpretation, then come, as long as I am yet living, and dispute it with me."

This book would not have been possible without the aid of several munificent bodies and the companionship of many invaluable friends. Harvard University offered an opportunity to an unproven youth, and it was thanks to the initial confidence shown in me there that what follows came into its first stage of being as a doctoral dissertation. The Japan Foundation sponsored two years in Tokyo, during the which bulk of the research presented here was undertaken; the School of Oriental and African Studies (SOAS) in the University of London, provided generous conditions in which to write; I thank my colleagues there in the Department of Art and Archaeology, and the Japan Research Centre.

My study in Cambridge, Massachusetts, was directed by John M. Rosenfield, whose wisdom was dispensed in a rare atmosphere of calm and wit; other teachers with whom I worked include Howard Hibbett and Haruko Iwasaki; indeed, the germ that became this book first appeared in their classes. In the companionship of Mohammed al-Asad, James Nichols, Mark Oshima, Nicole Rousmaniere, Elizabeth Segal, Stefan Wolohojian, and countless more, I saw through three New England winters.

In Tokyo the great generosity of Mrs. Hattori Toyoko and the Fukuhara family made much possible; my first experiences of Japan were thanks to the family of Akari Shōtarō: they all set me on a course I would seldom regret; any understanding of what it was I hoped to gain by study was fostered by Akiyama Terukazu and Kobayashi Tadashi, who supervised my research at Gakushūin; Tanaka Yūko and Takayama Hiroshi had faith in the project when few else did; Mutō Junko and Robert Campbell helped decipher many intricate texts, and Chino Kaori, Inoue Ryūmei, Kasuya Hiroki, and Kawai Masatomo offered much assistance. To Murayama Kazuhiro I owe everything else.

Tokyo could never have become my second home without Andrew Barnie, Gyōtoku Seiichirō, Hamana Emi, Hanano Gōichi, Hironen, Imahashi Riko, Katō Chigusa, Matsuda Hideo, Nagashima Tarō, Ray Miles, Terada Kuniyoshi, the late Paul Toolmin-Rothe, Ueno Shōichi, Watanabe Yukihiro, and Dodo Yoneyama.

I must also thank those in Nagasaki who showed great kindness, Matsuo Hōdō and the brothers at the Kōfuku-ji, and Nakano Yutaka; Rob and Sally Horton contrived the unlikely services of British Petroleum and Mitsubishi Heavy Industries to give me my first exposure to that fascinating city.

In the end was the beginning: I never expected to terminate this project where it all began, in England. My first tutor in Japanese studies, James McMullen, deserves great thanks for initiating me in Oxford, and Ruth and Andrew Calder and Christianne and Alain Dufour also provided early models, from which I have diverged no doubt at my cost. To my parents and brothers, Mat and Toby, I owe a realisation of the worth of scholarship and the value of love – I hope they accept the interpretation I now give to both terms.

Encouragement has been amply provided by many more: Tamsin Barton, Tim Clark, Frank Dikötter, Evan Davis, David Game, Charles Gant, Neil Hunter, Mark Jeanes, Nicholas Jones, Stephen Nelson, Lorcan O'Neil, Beth Sealey, Martin Stokes, Francis Sullivan, Jane Ware; an early but formative draft of what follows was written on Nicholas Carlisle's dining table, and it is dangerously possible that the ricketiness of his furniture has transferred itself to the argument.

Were it not to smear them with too foul a brush, I would say that there are some who deserve the title of co-authors. All responsibility remains my own, but disaster was averted by timely interventions on the part of Sumie Jones and Tom Rimer. Henry Smith was a cornucopia and provided much material that, if he had only kept it back for his own use, would surely have been adduced to better effect. His seminar group at Columbia University read and commented on the entire manuscript at a stage when (I was informed more than once) it was a thankless task; I thank particularly Chris Hill, Matthew McKelway, and Keith Vincent. Robert Danly and Steve Dodd scrutinised Chapters 1 and 7, respectively, and the keen eye of Mavis Pilbeam fell across all the pages.

Cambridge University Press has proven a model publisher, and Beatrice Rehl, Camilla Palmer, and Brett Kaplan rare examples of ones who actually do temper their justice with mercy; Norman Bryson, whom I knew many years before he knew me, has been benevolent though firm from first to last. Help with the illustrations was offered by Paul Fox, Fukuda Kazuhiko, Oka Yasumasa, and many dealers and curators. Barbara Folsom uncoiled the serpent of my prose to save each reader from having to do so on their own.

Publication of this book was made possible through the generosity of the Japan Foundation, the Metropolitan Foundation for the Study of Far Eastern Art, and the Anglo-Daiwa Foundation, to all of which the author is profoundly grateful.

I am profoundly grateful to all, but feel I must still finish in the Edo manner: *hazubeshi, hazubeshi.*

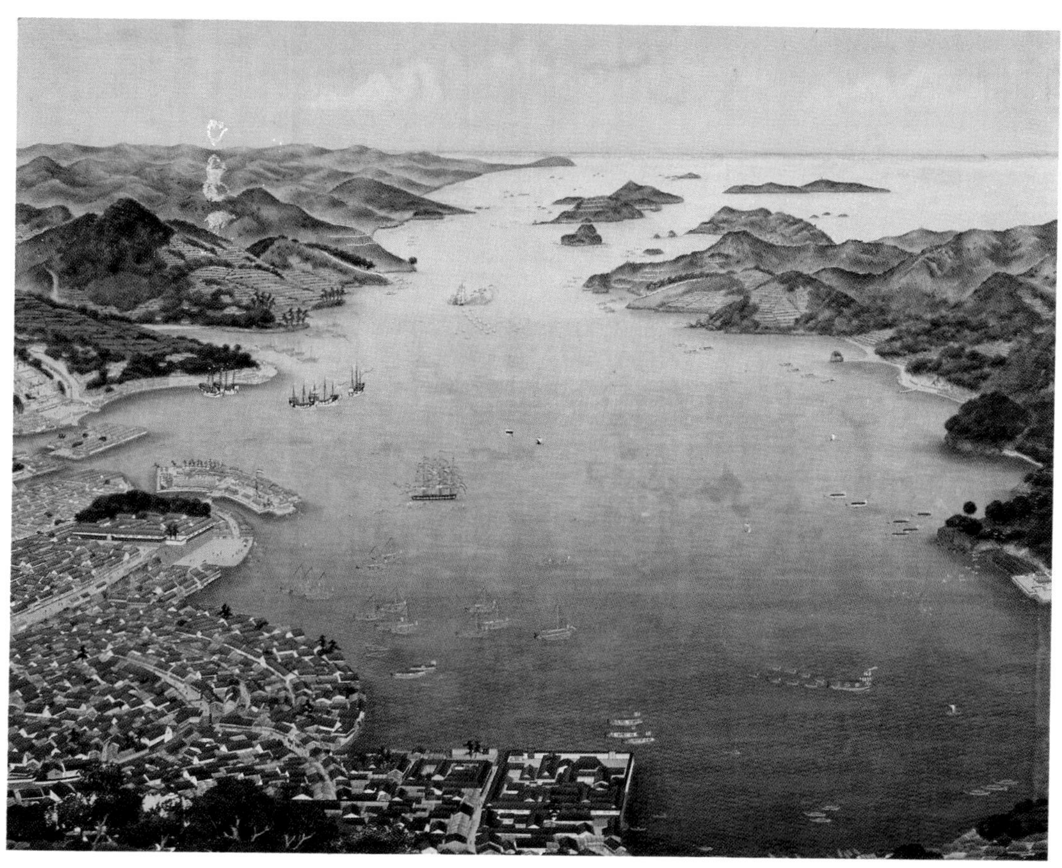

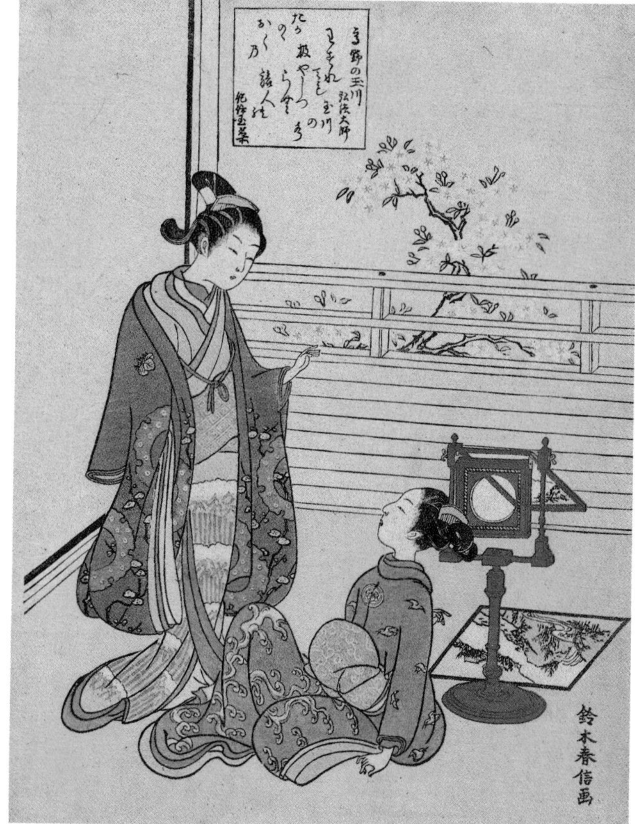

1 (above). Kawahara Keiga, *View of Nagasaki*, single-leaf screen; c. 1825. Kobe City Museum.

2 (right). Suzuki Harunobu, *Tamagawa in Kōno*, colour woodblock print from series *Mu-tamagawa*; before 1770. Kobe City Museum.

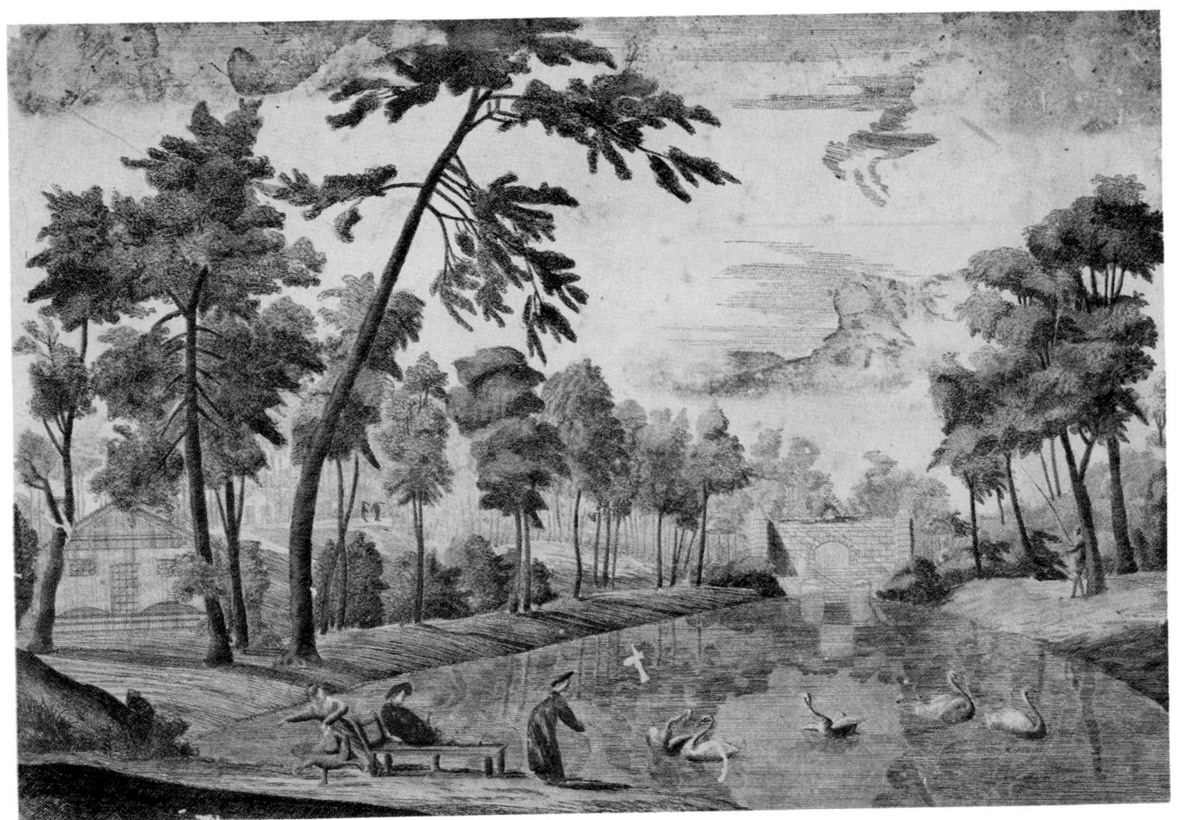

3 (above). Shiba Kōkan, *Serpentine,* hand-coloured copperplate print; c. 1787. Kobe City Museum.

4 (below). Shiba Kōkan, *Tweelandbruk,* hand-coloured copperplate print; c. 1787. Kobe City Museum.

The scene is reversed; compare with Figure 48.

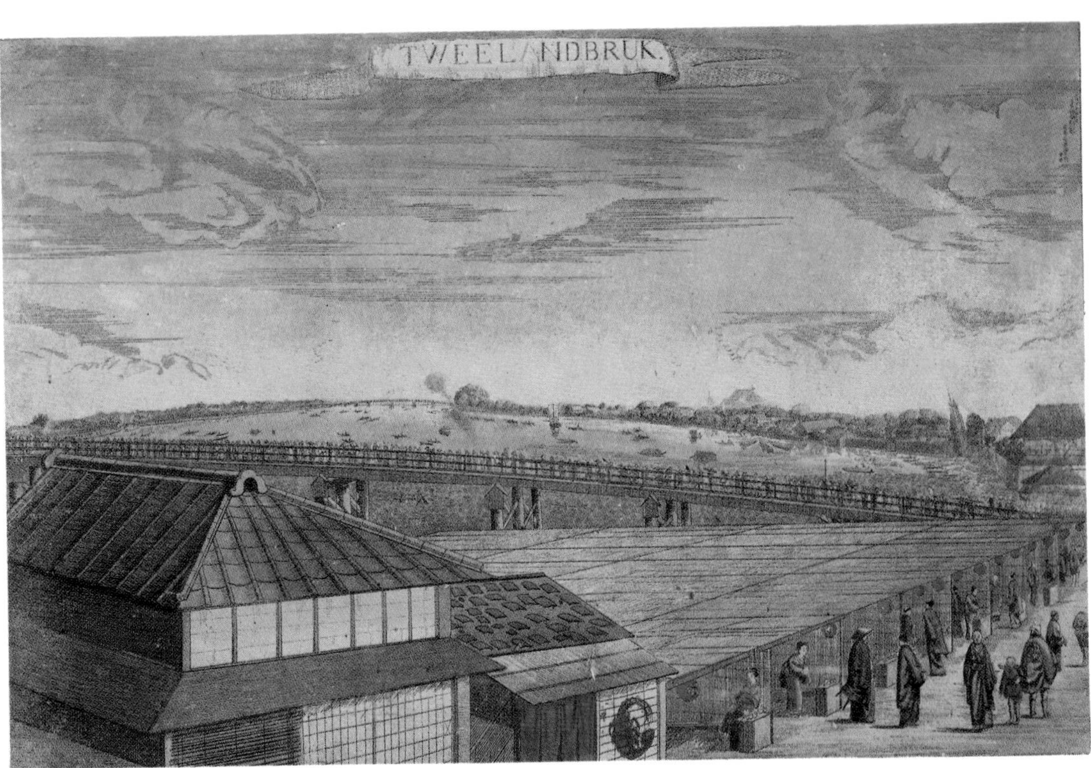

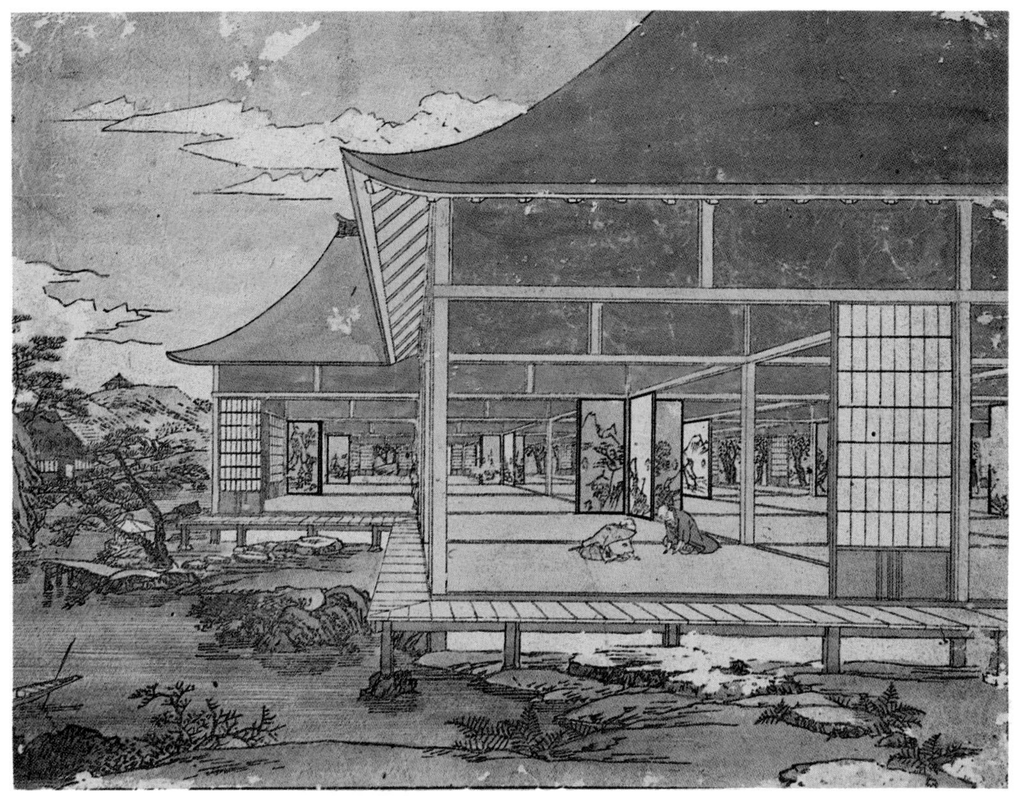

5 (above). Maruyama Ōkyo, *Orange Tree Hall*, single sheet painting; c. 1780. Private Collection.

6 (below). Utagawa Toyoharu, *The Bell which Resounds for Ten-thousand Leagues in the Dutch Port of Frankai*, hand-coloured woodblock print; c. 1770. Kobe City Museum.

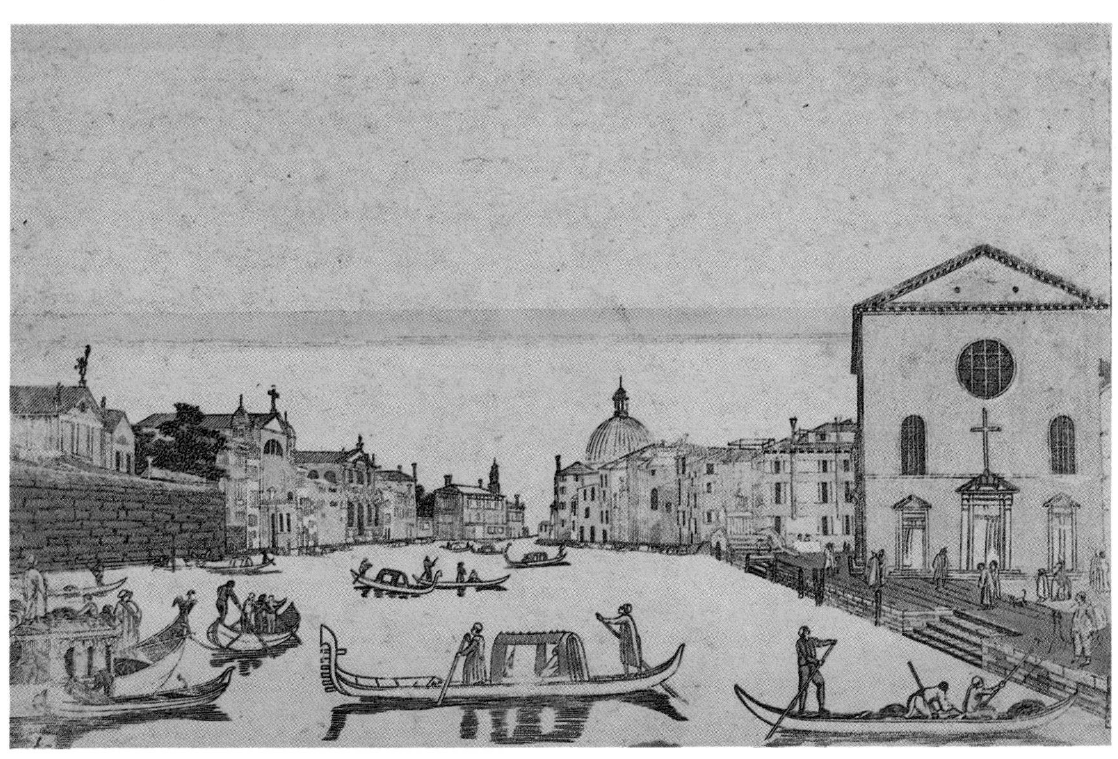

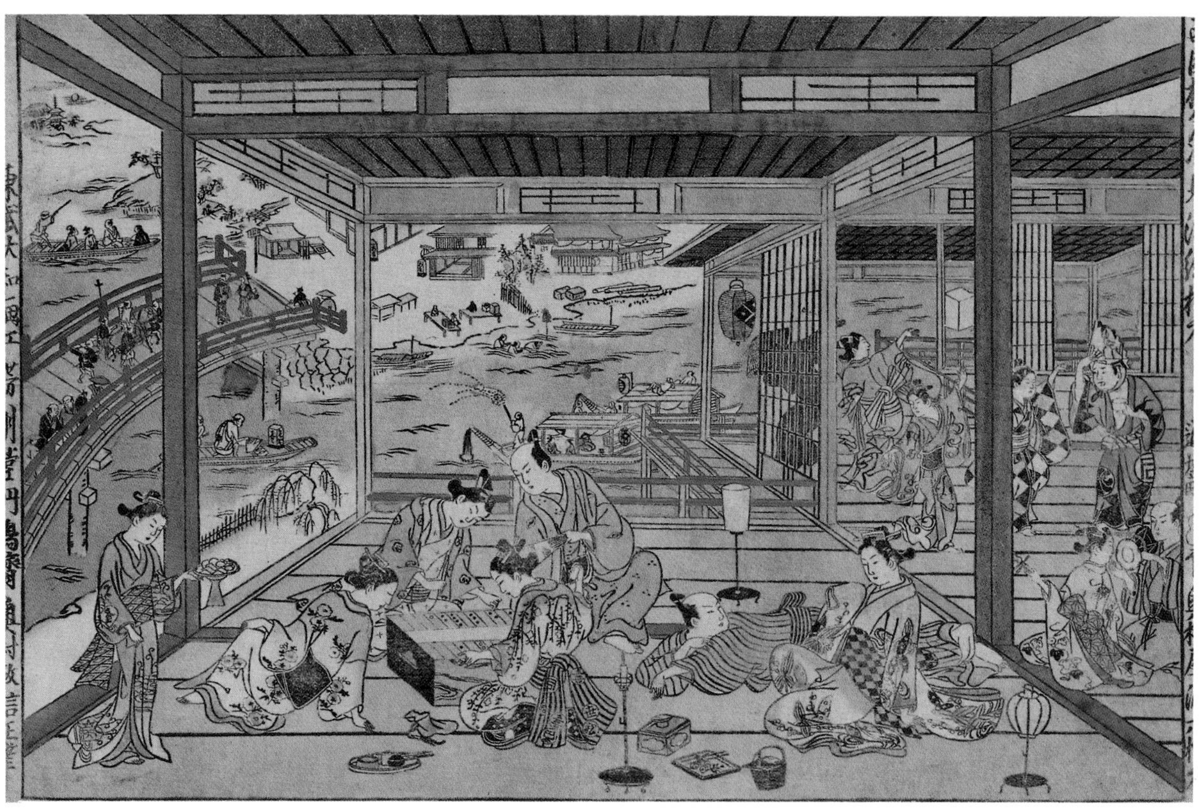

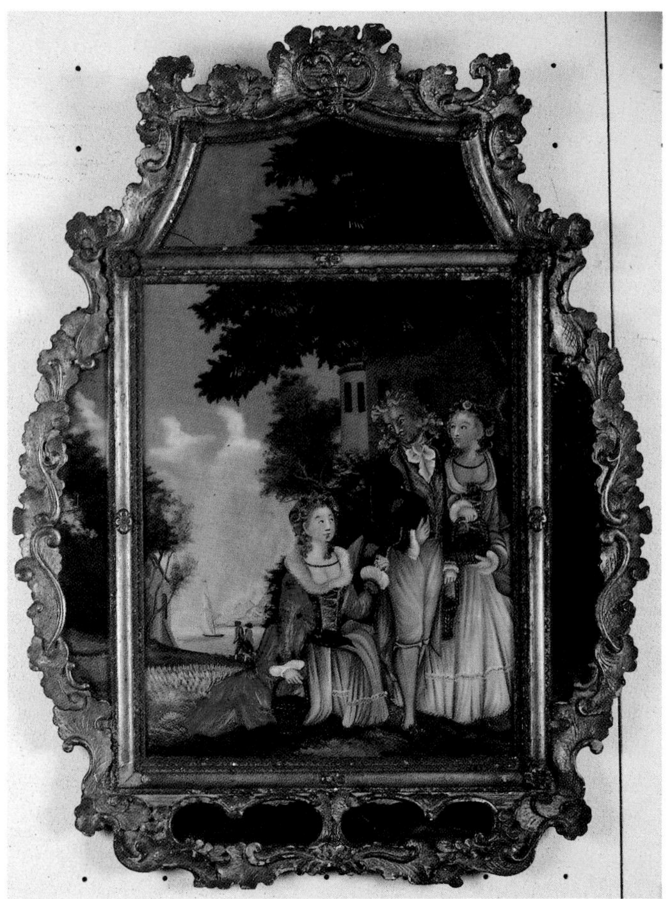

7 (above). Okumura Masanobu, *Enjoying the Cool at Ryōgoku Bridge*, hand-coloured wood-block print; c. 1735. Kobe City Museum.

8 (left). Unsigned, *Western Figures in a Garden*, painting under glass; early nineteenth century. Hamamatsu Municipal Museum of Art.

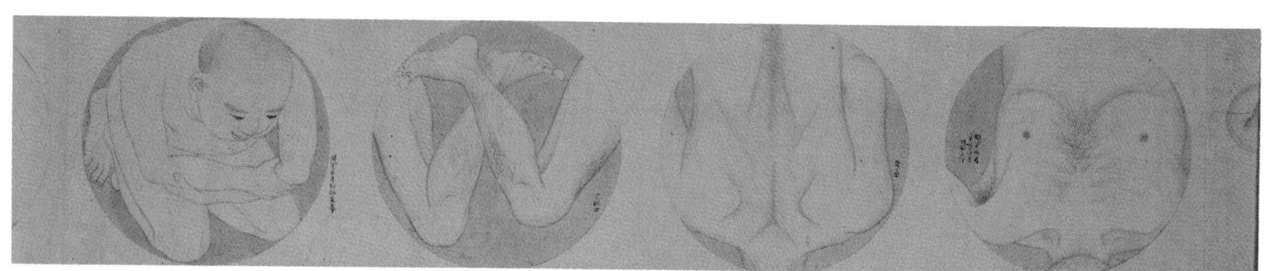

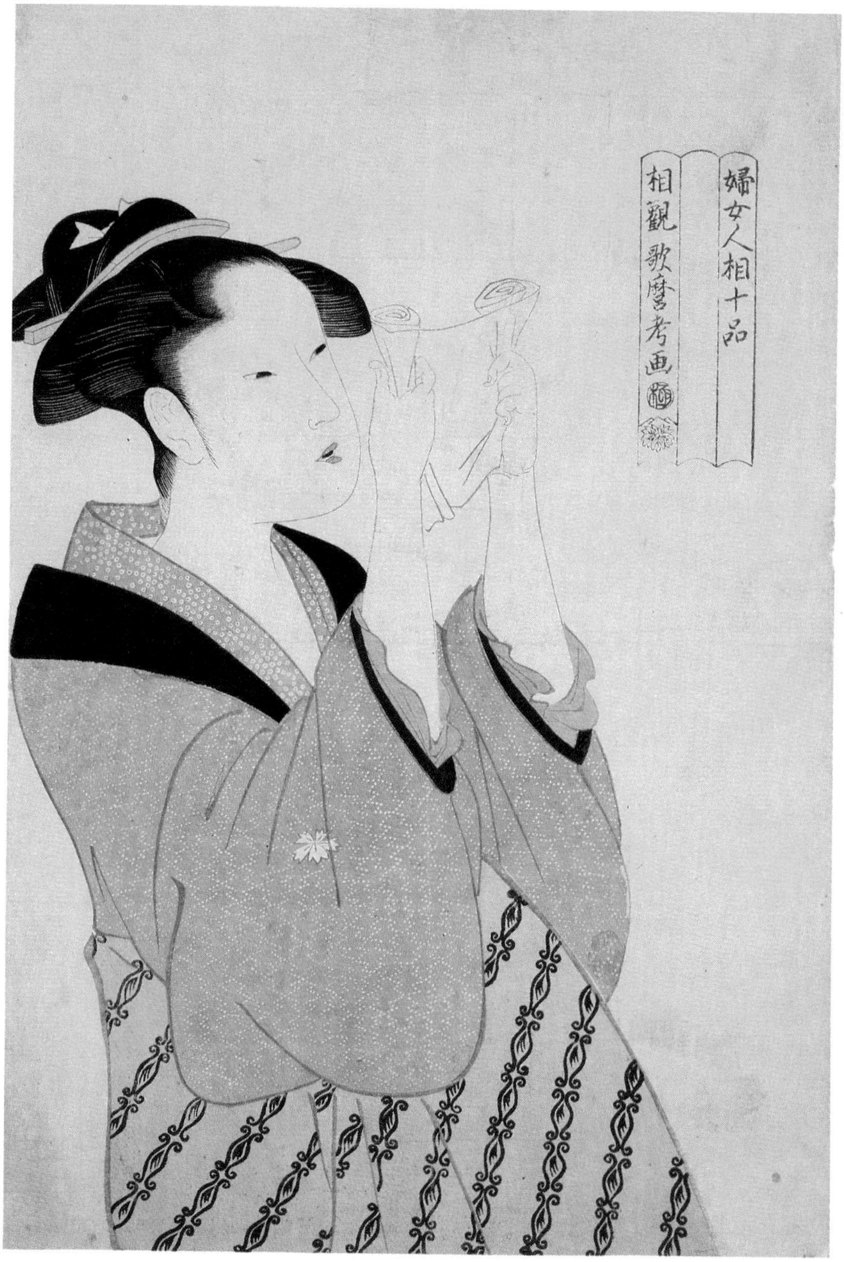

9 (above). Maruyama Ōkyo, *Legs of the Person to the Right* [omitted] and *Boy Seen from Above*, segment from handscroll *Jintai seisha sōhon*; 1770. Tenri Central Library, Tenri University.

10 (right). Kitagawa Utamaro, *Woman Reading a Letter,* from the series, *Fujo ninsō juppon,* colour woodblock print with mica; c. 1792–93. Clarence Buckingham Collection, 1942.119; photo © 1994; The Art Institute of Chicago.

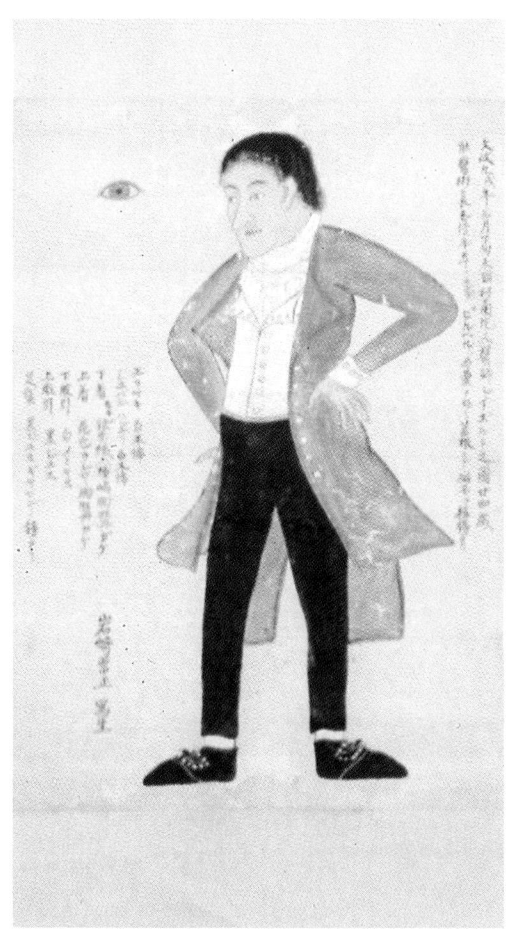

11. Iwasaki Kan'en, *Franz von Siebold,* hanging scroll; 1826. National Diet Library, Tokyo.

The inscription details the date and the colour of Siebold's clothes.

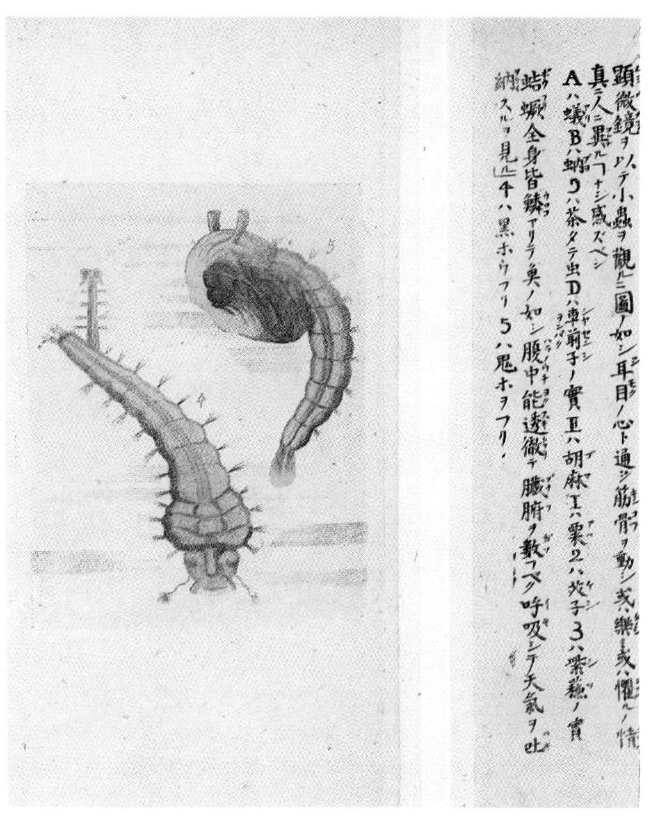

12. Shiba Kōkan, *Mosquito Larvae,* hand-coloured copperplate print from his *Tenkyū zenzu,* 1796. Kobe City Museum.

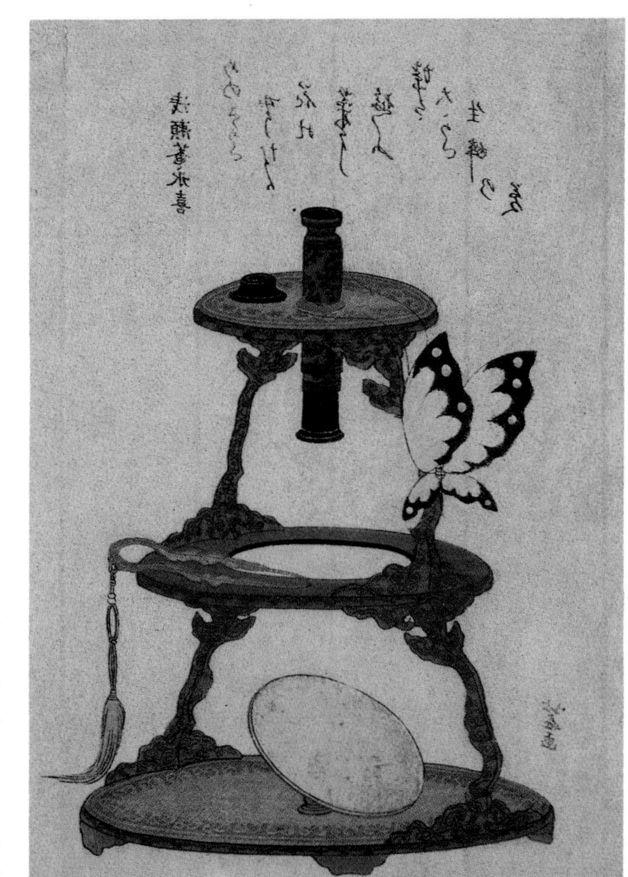

13 (right). Katsushika Hokusai, *Microscope and Butterfly*, private-edition colour woodblock print; c. 1810. Spencer Museum of Art, University of Kansas, William Bridges Thayer Memorial; photo: Robert Hickerson.

14 (below). Katsushika Hokusai, *Ryōgoku Bridge*, hand-coloured woodblock print from the series *Oranda gakyō: Edo hakkei*, c. 1797–1804. Kobe City Museum.

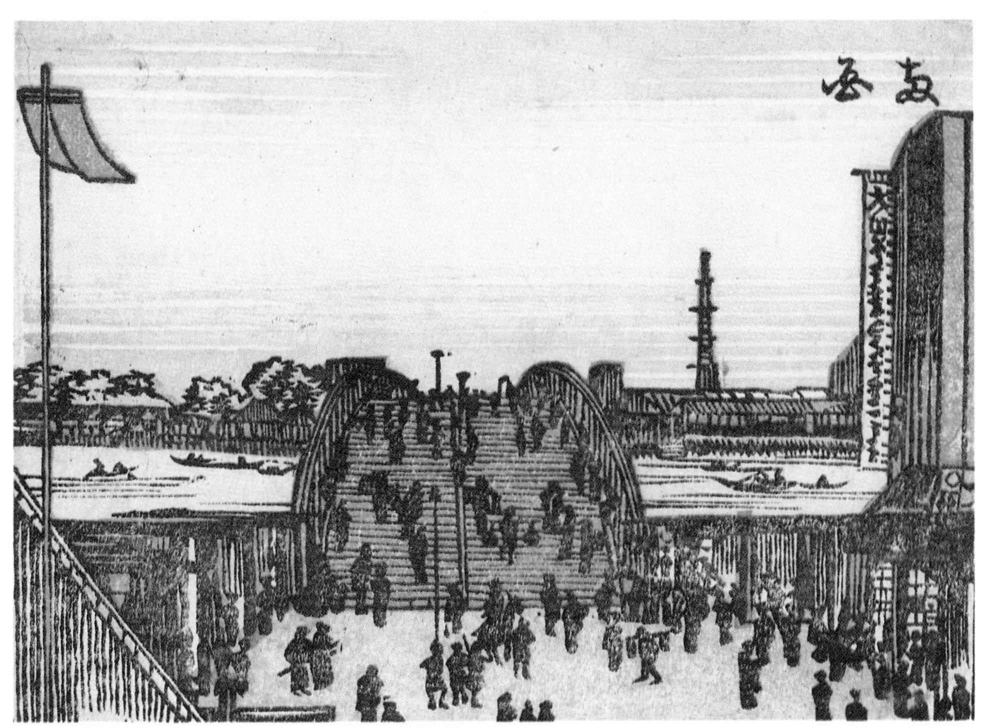

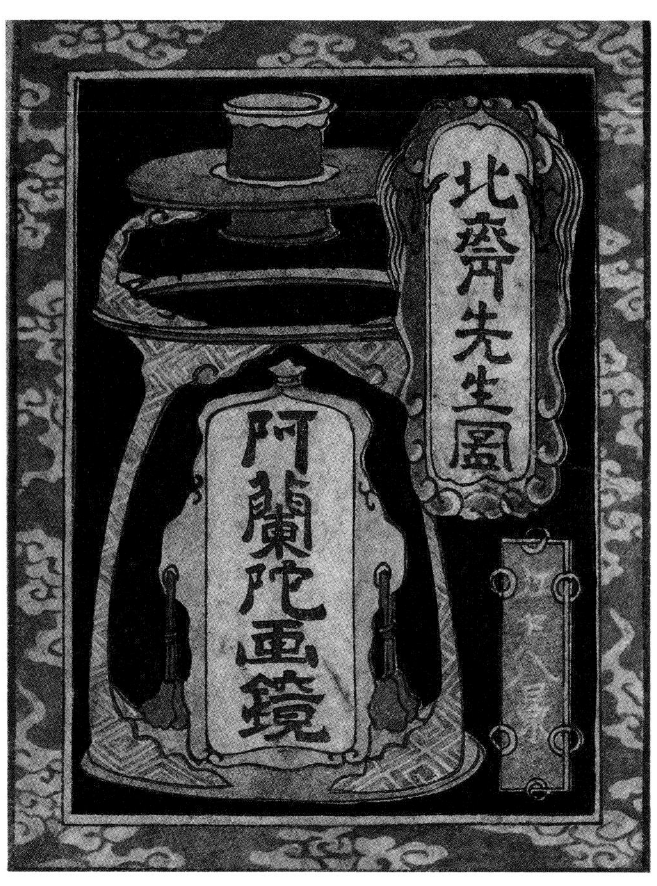

15. Katsushika Hokusai, hand-coloured woodblock printed wrapper to *Oranda gakyō: Edo hakkei*; c. 1797–1804. Kobe City Museum.

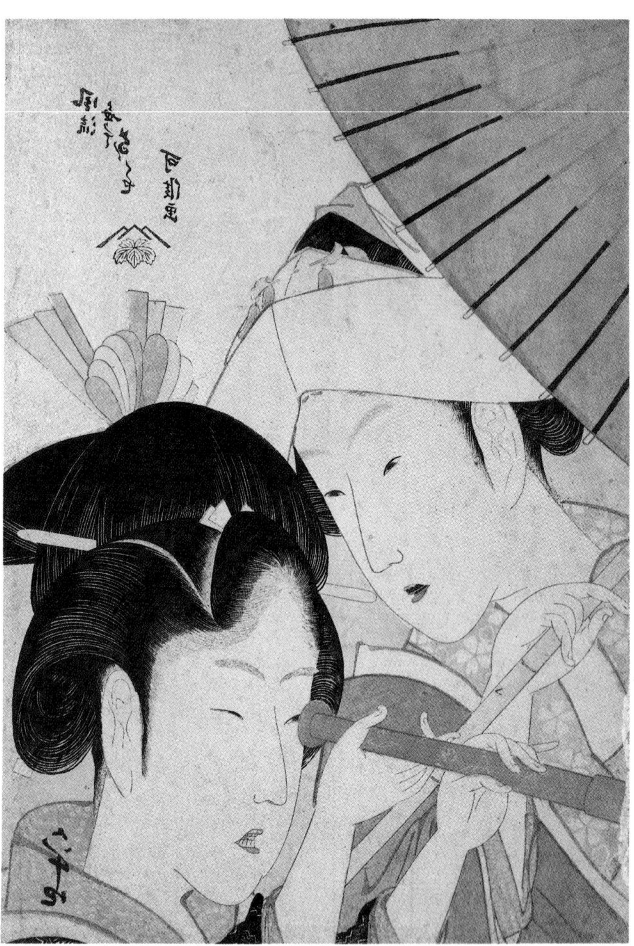

16. Katsushika Hokusai, *Women with Telescope and Parasol*, colour woodblock print from the series *Fūryū nakute nanakuse*; after 1798. Kobe City Museum.

INTRODUCTION

THIS BOOK ADDRESSES a two-fold theme, the one domain lying within the other. Vision is our larger concern: the root issue debated in the pages that follow is what seeing means, and how it can be said to lock into wider cultural concerns. Our inner theme is international encounter – the existence and compulsion of "the foreign" within a native space. We shall consider how one cultural cluster – Japan (federal and disparate as it was at this time) – used another in the building up of its proper self. The case is made that this encounter provoked a change in Japan that particularly related to systems of visual awareness – indeed, to a reassessment of the entire faculty of sight.

Germane to the work is the matter of overseas expansion. The intrusion into Japan of Europe, principally represented by the Republic of the United Provinces (after 1795 the Batavian Republic, though as today usually called Holland), provides the impetus for this study; to a lesser degree, Great Britain and Russia are implicated too. China and Korea, Japan's continental neighbours, had functioned since antiquity as foils against which domestic dispensations could be postulated, and as such were already written into Japanese culture on almost every level; the Continent is of only tangential concern here. From the mid-eighteenth century, the West had a startling immediacy and represented a new alternative.

A myth formerly prevailed that Japan was in a state of isolation during the early modern period (the Edo or Tokugawa period, 1603–1868). This conception of a "national seclusion" (*sakoku*), forged in the nineteenth century, is now substantially discredited. But the nature of Edo-period international relations was nevertheless rather special: the West never invaded Japan nor blockaded it, and it never had the writ to command. Japan, consequently, remained fully independent. This was felicitous for those who lived there, no doubt. It is also happy for the historian, as eighteenth-century Euro-Japanese interaction represents a genuinely unique case study in almost egalitarian cultural collision. As the nineteenth century opened, military threats from the land (Russia) and the ocean (Great Britain) became causes of alarm. That moment, therefore, marks the terminus of this book's concerns. We address a cultural meeting predicated on equal power or, if anything, on an inferiority in Europe's might.

Free from an over-abundance of men and women from abroad and, more pertinently, sheltered from their muskets and cannon, Japan was at liberty to construct its own ideas of what Western culture might be said to be. We thus deal with a process of cooptation rather than "influence," for Japan constructed a "Europe" of its own making. What Europe meant in the shogun's realm and what it meant to Europeans might differ – indeed, the two blatantly failed to coincide – but the distinction is irrelevant to this study, for only the Japanese "Europe" is to our point.

I was tempted to retain the original terminology used for the West (*Oranda, Yōroppa, Angeria, Roshia*) in order to make it clear that these places are fragments from within the space of the Japanese consciousness, not geographical terms with their own normative values. Yet indigenous usages can be fiddly or opaque and I have resisted them wherever possible. I hope the point will be made anyway. The term "Red-fur" (*kōmō*) was the generic label used for Europeans, and that has been kept, for it seemed necessary to stress that these are not "us," but are creatures of a Japanese fashioning. Though used derogatorily at first, Red-fur assumed positive overtones in the later eighteenth century. The term "*Ran*" (from *Oranda,* Holland) was enlisted too, to stand for Western culture in the abstract – a Japanised reading of the European intellectual arena, which term has also been deployed here.

It is not arbitrary that this book centres on vision, for chief amongst the novelties that the Red-furred people disembarked from their ships were goods and ideas that bore on interpretations of the world seen. Vision is a faculty, and barring disablement it may be said to be a given; but this book understands seeing to be something that goes beyond the physiological fact. Encrusting itself within societies like a stone in the gall, vision is accreted over generations, and no two cultures will be alike. This construction overlays the eyes (to change the analogy) like a colouration, or indelible stain. It was held to be true in Japan that vision was the very sphere in which the differences between *Ran* and the home order were most absolute. This book is a contribution to the study of those obscure and complex systems that make and alter artifices of sight, those interpersonal strategies known as the "visualities" of an age.

Sight in Japan had previously been imagined as something discursive or extrapolatory, moving from object to object associatively, or traversing the seen and unseen by passing along links that were historic, artistic, or poetic, but not coordinated by logic. The dominant Japanese fabrication of seeing, simply put, was synaptic, such that objects viewed were attributed meaning by the instant formation around them of a ring of association, drawing the empirically seen into a web of things previously learnt. The "Western scientific gaze" was a regime of visuality incompatible with this. A "gaze" is taken here to imply a fixity of looking – sight held and used to dismantle what lies around; being scientific, this gaze dissected and selected, dwelling on objects and separating them as autonomous and apart, evacuating their cultural ballast. The Western scientific gaze was rooted in close and objectifying observation.

Japanese investigations of external phenomena had not generally been ocular in this way, nor had it been held that evidence seen constituted necessary proof. The nearest term then available for "science" was *kyūri,* literally, the investigation of "principles" (*ri*); principles by definition are what lie behind the seeable, and are rationalisable only cerebrally, being resistant to experimental support or refutation. The word *kyūri* was, faute de mieux, employed by eighteenth-century writers, though some preferred transliterations of Dutch terms. The overriding assumption of Japanese writers, though, was that Red-fur cognition was erected on the double pillars that we can sensibly call "scientific gazing," although whether this was accompanied by plaudits or diatribes depended on the disposition of the critic; there were plenty on both sides.

New notions of seeing impinged on Japan for the first time during the later eighteenth century. Our time span originates, not from the arrival of the West as such (in 1543), but from the popularisation of debate over vision; this event, a transfer from the European Enlightenment, occurred much later, and we may place it in the 1760s. The rapidity with which Enlightenment notions appeared in Japan will, I trust, shock those who still adhere to the isolation theory of Edo history. Our terminal date comes with the breakup of the norms that had made the new visuality a substantive issue, and this we may place in the 1810s: a degree of assimilation had obviated the need for further debate on the subject, on the one hand, and, on the other, feared Western predations were leading to a wholesale revision of that interpretation of European culture that we here call *Ran*.

The writings of many a proto-scientist, Confucian intellectual, medical doctor, government bureaucrat, and art theoretician are drawn upon in the pages that follow. The treatises of the small but important body of self-professed "Dutch studies academics" (*Rangaku-sha*) have been plundered, and the names of the more perceptive, influential, or mercurial dot this book. It was, though, in the field of popular culture that changes most profoundly occurred. Academia under the Tokugawa shoguns was hierarchical, segmented, and classically based. It was not, generally speaking, a fertile bed for engagement with a whole new episteme. But popular thought was less beset by codes of intellectual propriety, and so we will accordingly examine the popularisation of the Western scientific gaze and its utilisation in the public domain. The history of science is less our field than the history of common pursuits, and the documentation of street shows, toys, throw-away prints, and comic illustrated literature features largely.

The Western scientific gaze was often applied metaphorically too, still invoked to stand for a precise looking, but no longer directed at specimens culled from the natural world. The gaze was turned to address facets of the human condition: social norms, personal relations, individual integrity, and morality. This, as everyone knew, was the ethical domain of the Buddhas.

THE NOVEL VISUALITIES that I propose must be proven to have had for those of the time a discernible locus in foreignness, and that means the status of imports. Chapter 1 outlines the extent of purchasing from the West. A full cartography of international trade is not attempted beyond what has relevance to the activity of Japanese seeing. Import patterns, though, are not easy to define because of the high degree of falsification and doctoring of accounts, of smuggling and what was coyly called "private trade" (or *nukeni:* "omitted goods").

Chapter 1 also considers some of the main players in the spreading and discussion of imported ideas and things, and it introduces many of the figures who will people the subsequent pages. Also outlined are the genres and topoi most infected by *Ran,* particularly those associated with the Floating World (*ukiyo*) – that demimonde that existed on the peripheries of the shogunally sanctioned metropoles.

Mathematics and calculation formed the defining grid in which the Western scientific gaze was said to be set, and the rhetoric of "precision" was its overriding base. This is commented on in Chapter 2. We shall investigate how "Dutch precision" balanced with older notions and evince comparisons between *Ran* and Japan, and between Japanese interpretations of Europe and of the intellectual life of China.

The scientific gaze not only severed objects from their cultural contexts. It did more: it demanded admission to the insides of things; it was an *anatomising* stare. Invisible workings were sought out for inspection, whether of human beings, animals, particles, or larger abstract systems. It was proposed as axiomatic that a full reevaluation of the significance of internal workings was necessary for the new comprehension of external empirical wholes.

Working models were imported in quite large

numbers, and Chapter 3 looks at how new driving forces (particularly hydraulics and clockwork) came to be bearers of thought. Instruments of immense complexity belied their clever interior functions with the smooth packaging of their exteriors, and this brought to the fore a sense of the urgency of the requirement to open and inspect if one truly wished to know. Where mechanical devices (automata or games) were in human shape the metaphorical extension of hidden parts was powerful indeed, not least in a Japan that felt increasingly ill at ease with the conditions of social morality.

Coupled with the rhetoric of a piercing, interior vision was a sense of the need to record for good its hard-won findings. Along with the discussions of *Ran,* emerged a discourse on pictures, as is discussed in Chapter 4. It was taken as integral to the Western scientific project that all discoveries must be permanently committed to paper, and that, in such a way looking at a picture replicated as closely as possible looking at an original object; a picture captured what had been opened out, despite resistance, to the gaze, and so it should be true. Western pictures newly imported were said to have an efficiency that older Japanese styles lacked in "capturing reality" (*shajitsu*) or "depicting authentically" (*shashin*).

European pictures (*Oranda-e* or *Horurando-e,* "Dutch pictures") were brought to Japan copiously, usually in the form of monochrome book illustrations or as single-sheet hand-coloured prints, or, less commonly, as oil paintings or paintings on glass. I doubt that many alert people had failed to see a sizeable quantity. Japanese artists took up the style through ad hoc emulation or autodidactic copying, and called their productions *Ranga* (*Ran* pictures).

The later Edo arts are multifarious and rich. It is beyond the scope of this book to address the insinuation of this "authentic" depiction into the totality of eighteenth-century representational practice, but the importance of pictures in capturing and prolonging the gaze of science is a major theme. *Ranga* were, moreover, often *mechanical* pictures. They were made with tools (camera obscuras and pantographs) and viewed with them, too (optiques, peep-boxes). These instruments both eradicated the presence of the artist and also gave the viewer a sense of seeing actual – not depicted – things.

The one material that allowed the visual dispensation of *Ran* to function was glass. Chapter 5 considers glass bottles used for the storage of samples, and the glass window. Glass could set up a wall between the seer and the seen, ensuring distance and safety but without depriving visual access. Conditions on either side of the glass could differ, the viewer's side enjoying a superior or commanding status. Glass conferred privilege. Glass pictures (where the pigment was applied to the rear of a pane) permitted a fictional object to be invested with the same detached objectification of the englassed sample; looking-glasses, too (much imported), subsumed the reflection of the self into the aura of the thing objectively viewed.

Chapter 6 considers a special glass object: ground glass – that is, the lens. Though transparent, lenses adapted sight, bringing the infinitesimal close. Scientific experimentation was dependent on the microscope, and a sense of excitement at the discovery of minuscule life was critical to the popular success that the new visuality of *Ran* can be said to have had.

It was commonly observed that the eye was a natural lens. The validity of *Ran* rested ultimately on the ascendancy of sight over other means of attaining information. The eye, it was said, was the organ of *Ran;* indeed, the extraordinariness of the Red-fur eye (round, blue, and staring) was not without its funny side. But as Westerners were taunted, as they walked through the streets, with cries of "big-eyed Dutch" (*Oranda-ōme*), something profound was being expressed.

Throughout this work it is not the history of science that leads the narrative, but the history of Japanese thought about imported devices. The metaphorical applications are more significant than progress towards membership of any putative modern intellectual community. Social and moral concerns were critical, and very frequently equipment from abroad melted into a rhetoric of precision that was then applied to precisely non-scientific matters – above all, as we shall see, to interpersonal human relations.

Chapter 7 diverges to consider the importance of the epistemology of the downward gaze. Opposite but equal to seeing into the detailed interiors of things was the gaining of a sweeping sight over them. Mechanisms for the levitation of the gaze were invented, introduced from abroad, or discussed textually. The previous general dismissal in Japanese thought (I shall claim) of the downward stare was replaced. In the West, all too often, to look from on high was to look with raw authority. There had been moments when this was also true in Japan, but now, through introduction and local generation of new ideas, downward seeing might also become a means of sustaining a dialogue with the seen thing, the observer being lodged in a detached space, free from bias.

TACHIBANA NANKEI, a doctor from Ise quoted in the Epigraph, drew a smooth continuum between a kind of seeing that was ethically cogent – that of the Buddhas – and the mechanical seeing afforded by the lens of a microscope. Religious and spiritual dimensions in the changes of the visuality are most important. At just this time a popular cult called *Shingaku,* "heart learning," appeared on the streets of Japan's major cities, arguing for a purification by each individual of his or her own mind. *Shingaku* warned that the facades of lies were falling fast, and that vision of what lay beneath would soon come out. This vision within was what the Buddhas' eyes saw, but the interiorising gaze was also known as a feature of *Ran. Shingaku* and *Rangaku* ("Dutch learning" or "study of *Ran*") have to this day never previously been discussed in combination, but they shared at their core an urge to transform a society that by the end of the eighteenth century was felt by many to be twisting out of joint. Both wished to see what was hidden. The gods and Buddhas, ineffably detached, looked, if they looked at all, with a descending vector of sight; and equipped with a lens, as Nankei wondered they might be, and with a reinforced rhetoric of precise vision, how might they consider humankind? When *Shingaku* and *Rangaku* came together, it was as if the Buddhas were looking through microscopes, the ethical realm laid bare by the fine but sweeping Western scientific gaze.

ONE

TRADE AND CULTURE IN THE EIGHTEENTH CENTURY

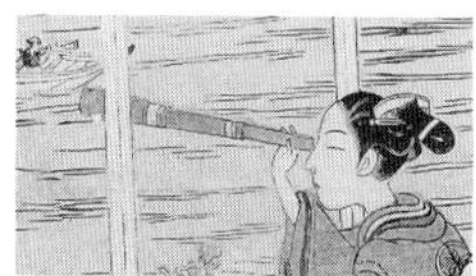

"THE NUMBER OF PERSONS engaged in this study [of the West]," wrote Takano Chōei, "does not exceed one or two in 10,000,000."[1] This statement has about it the hyperbolic glumness of an expert who cannot imagine why others lack excitement for his own small area of concern. But the words suggest something truer of what was generally felt by those who developed enthusiasms for Europe in Edo-period Japan (1603–1868). Chōei was writing in 1839. The situation had fluctuated during the late eighteenth century, and the stock of Western things had risen to a peak in the 1780s; but predominantly the state of affairs remained little different, and certainly offered no cause for jubilation.

Chōei's discipline was called "Dutch studies," *Rangaku* (*gaku* meaning learning and *Ran* being short for *Oranda*). Holland was synecdoche for all of Europe on account of its prominence in East and South-East Asia. Throughout eighteenth-century Japan to talk of the West was to assert the ways of Holland. Those embarking on *Rangaku* had to contend with several factors, most immediately the difficulty of the language; this disincentive diminished from the 1760s with the emergence of a body of published and manuscript commentary in Japanese. Far more confounding and never to be surmounted, though, was the unremitting foreignness of Western matters at a more conceptual level. "Scholars of Holland" (*Rangaku-sha*) inevitably stood apart from the mainstream of academe, which was largely government-sponsored, hortative in tone, and geared to bringing forth good subjects and wise rulers. The materials they handled and the debates they joined were just too discrete from common concerns for ready integration, and the relevance needed proving.

Rangaku experts were amateurs. They might coincidentally be persons of consequence in other walks of life, and some held office, but few men, if any, were raised to positions of note on account of their understanding of Europe. Not until 1855 did the central administration, the shogunate, establish an institution to address *Rangaku* as such.[2] The first private school of Western studies had opened in 1789, the Shirandō ("the Hall of Holland in Shiba" – a part of Edo, modern Tokyo), run by a hereditary doctor called Ōtsuki Gentaku (and about whom we shall hear a good deal); but by the end of the century it had processed only thirty pupils.[3]

Although shunned by established organs, *Rangaku* was not sidelined altogether: it drew sustenance from popular life. The very aspects of its erudition that proved resistant to assimilation within normal educational curricula made Dutch studies immensely appealing to those whose search was only for exotica or thrills. Startling new knowledge and intricate items of overseas make were capable of exerting strong pulls on the mind, once all obligation to defer to understandings rooted in the arcana of foreign settings had been merrily cast aside.

HOLLAND AS DISCOURSE

Historians have written about *Rangaku* scholars before now, and of the role they played in disseminating ideas of the West has received plentiful attention; a generally positivistic approach has been taken, with the underlying assumption that the best work lies in identifying those responsible for the forgotten groundwork that allowed Japan's spectacular modernisation in the nineteenth century.

The thrust of this book is different. Rather than bringing to light the lost archives of "pioneers", I propose to look at what "Holland" meant to the mind of the time and, as a willed construct, what it did. It is precisely the dilatory persons who ignored the overt challenge of *Rangaku* who provide our samples. The focus here is on those 9,999,998 who, according to Chōei, never sought in the West a comprehensive (or even partially coherent) alternative to the life they lived, but who consumed it none the less, for their own ends. Rather than turning *Rangaku* into the centre of eighteenth-century debate, we shall keep it in the margins but consider how, being there, it contributed to meaning and affected thought. In sum, *Rangaku* mutated from being a discourse of assessment of the foreign to a popularised resource operating piecemeal and adduced to answer questions having to do with the self. It is a premise of this book that "Holland" was internal to Japan and detached from the West. For sober *Rangaku* scholars trying to keep the discipline on track, this would not do: "Many know some facts," complained the prolific Shiba Kōkan, prominent for almost forty years from the 1770s, "but few understand the theories."[4] Yet those dilettanti who only really wanted easy tidbits, and lacked concern for categorical disquisitions on far-removed things, are precisely the ones who will absorb us. Imbibing their "Holland" – and this is the point – on their own terms, these people felt a change occur.

The Japanese abbreviation of Holland, *Ran*, is retained here to mean that local reading of the West which was built up from imported ideas and materials. *Rangaku* was an academic pursuit; *Ran*, a patina of foreignness, directed inwards. Our artifice of *Ran* was essentially vulgar. But I maintain it enjoyed vastly important currency throughout the late-eighteenth century.

Ran was a cluster of concepts, not a place. Any attachment to life in the Republic of the United Provinces was quite tangential. The Netherlands, in any case, was chronically unstable at the time: 1795 saw the United Provinces become the Batavian Republic; in 1805 it changed into the Batavian Commonwealth, in 1806 into the Kingdom of Holland, and after 1810 was made a *département* of the French Empire; in 1814 it became the Kingdom of the United Netherlands.[5] This epistemic flux gave free rein to Japan. Yet the realisation that outside the national borders were real people who surrounded themselves with strange and different effects grew, and the sense that persons in foreign lands fathomed lives infinitely unlike those at home, agitated and stirred the status quo.

I take a materialist stance. The argument here is principally for a new mentality culled from imported *things*. Trade was brisk for all that Holland alone among Western countries possessed a supply network in Japan. Import of European goods wavered and changed in type over time: what Europe was pushing into foreign markets in 1800 was not the same as it had been in 1700. But I hold that a steady flow of objects found its way into Japan, and that the range of items to be seen, at least by the people of the larger cities, was not small. It is necessary to stress this, for many still argue for an eighteenth-century Japan closed to the outside world. The greatest conurbations all had their few *Rangaku* experts and their many lay enthusiasts fixated with a notional *Ran* feeding off visible or even purchasable artefacts – those in Edo, the shogunal seat, home to perhaps a million souls, and Osaka, the "nation's kitchen," Kyoto, the cultural heartland, and Nagoya, the shogunal collaterals' Western base, knew the look and feel of foreign goods. Nagasaki was the port of access for foreign vessels and the location of the Dutch trading station (or "Factory").

The Dutch Factory dealt with many mundane items – sugar, copper, cloth – and by these it earned its keep. But such were not the affairs that propelled Edo culture into new domains. That role was played by fringe imports: telescopes, microscopes, spectacles, prisms, kaleidoscopes, static-electricity generators, glasswares, glass panes, projectors, candelabra, clocks, toys, prints, peepshow boxes, scissors, penknives, wine, sweets, flora and fauna, and books. The bulk was known under the generic title of "strange devices" (*kiki*). Spreading far and wide, they were immensely appreciated. All cities saw the public display of objects, often at events where they could be handled or used, and strange devices were not necessarily the preserve of the rich. The custom of putting out oddities on show (*misemono*) long predated the arrival of much in the way of European manufacture, but by the mid-eighteenth century imports were making frequent appearances at exhibitions, and by its end may be said to have abounded.[6] Stalls were set up in vacant plots, behind a temple precinct, in a dry riverbed, or atop a dyke or embankment, and the rarities revealed for a fee by small-time impresarios. It is from the contents of such jerry-rigged huts and from the brushes of those who composed their advertising cant or wrote about what they had seen when they got home, not from academical treatises on heliocentricity, Dutch government, or European law, that what the West was, as we understand it here, is to be discerned. The length of queues at fairgrounds reveals how much "Holland" had to offer on a personal level.

The discourse of *Ran* was popular and detached; it brooked no priority in Holland's own interpretations of itself – indeed, it openly dismissed them. But even so, *Ran* was held in a grip of some firmness through the agency of the materiality of imports. "Holland" did not float quite free, but was moored to the objects encountered. Many *misemono* items were of a semi-technical nature, and this gave rise to a sense of certain innate qualities in all the things of *Ran*. Supreme was the notion of precision. The Dutch, it was said, were close-crafting and adept, and must needs be punctilious and nice to have made such wondrous fabrications. Many goods attested to an impulse to enhance vision. Optical devices were in great evidence, and the West came to be considered as a place where empirical sight was augmented or reformed, and where people used (and abused) their eyes.

THE DYNAMICS OF TRADE

The Factory in Nagasaki was run by the Dutch East India Company. In Japanese it was called *Konpanya* (from *Compannie*). By felicitous coincidence the suffix *-ya* denoted in Japanese a business enterprise, so the function of the foreign entity was easily explained. The Company's own acronym was VOC (*Vereenigde Oost Indische Compannie*), and for brevity that is used here.

The VOC had been in Japan since 1609.[7] In its early days it had been in rivalry with Iberian traders who had arrived some two decades before in the trail of missionaries; the English East India Company was soon to appear as well. But fear of the unsettling effects of Catholicism (the Japanese authorities knew what had happened in Mexico) resulted in expulsion of the Spanish and Portuguese in 1639 – and apostasy or death for local Christians. The English had withdrawn voluntarily sixteen years earlier, unable to turn a decent profit; their attempt to return in 1673 in a ship named *The Return* was thwarted when it was learned that Charles II had married a Catholic queen.[8] From 1639, for the next 229 years until 1868 when the shogunate finally fell, the VOC was in command. But the monopoly was not absolute, for European nations had wrested concessions in China, and produce could arrive via transshipment in privately owned Cantonese junks or aboard bottoms of overseas Chinese from South-East Asia. Chinese trade with Japan was not subject to the same geopolitical limitations as that with Europe, and reputedly thirty or so Chinese vessels were to be seen docked in Nagasaki at any one time.[9]

Japan had been a major international trading nation until the mid-seventeenth century. Thereafter volume shrank dramatically: the VOC sent only two ships per annum. The disappearance of overseas ships was coupled with new restrictions on Japanese travelling abroad and the calling in of residents from the Japantowns dotted through maritime Asia. This was the policy of the Tokugawa family. They had assumed power after protracted and bloody civil wars and founded their shogunate in 1603. It held for fifteen generations. The Tokugawa were keen on trade but disposed to encourage it only in measures that they could keep under their control, directly or through intermediaries. The post-1630s clampdown is to be seen less as distaste for the exchange of goods *per se,* than as the result of a *faute de mieux* acceptance by the Tokugawa that the best way to guard the peace was by preserving mercantile receipts for themselves and not letting a free flow of goods dilute their authority and enrich the regional lords. The nation was terribly friable.

The Japanese archipelago was divided into some 280 domains (*han*) over which the shogun had a federalistic central control; but the *han* were semi-autonomous and ruled by hereditary lords or daimyo, some of uncertain loyalty. It was no more than prudent to deny them access to independent means of creating wealth.

Decades of intensive commerce around the turn of the sixteenth century had seriously depleted Japan's reserves of precious metal. This was significant, as silver had previously formed the bulk of exports. Trade with Japan began to be less appetising to the Western side. It was generally felt in Europe that expansion into continental Asia would be more rewarding than wasting energy on a prickly Japan. The aftermath of the collapse of the Ming dynasty in 1644 made it worthwhile to struggle on in the interim, but within a couple of generations normality was restored in China, and attention turned there again.

Much is usually made by historians of the liberalising activities of the eighth Tokugawa shogun, Yoshimune, who in 1716 attempted to counter general economic depression and the possible withdrawal of the VOC by introducing a series of measures known as the Kyōhō Reforms. Relaxation of import rules was part of the package, and the kinds of goods permitted to be imported were expanded. Western books and small-volume finished equipment, previously discouraged or actually banned, began to be welcomed.[10]

How genuinely different the Kyōhō Reforms made the overall situation remains unclear. The VOC continued to mutter for the rest of the century, and the new imports were not such as earned vast profits, though they made excellent sideline items. In 1735, the VOC board in Amsterdam, the "Gentlemen Seventeen," sent word to their Factory in Japan to "take measures to abandon this trade and strike camp there"; this was to be delayed only until commencement of direct sailings to China.[11] The outlay required to keep the Factory going seemed to have become unwarranted. As the Gentlemen put it in 1734, they would have to see if "a large part of the goods which we now have to pry loose from the

Japanese, could not be procured in the Chinese Realm."[12] They did not in fact pull out.

The first Japanese history of the Dutch Studies movement, published in 1817 and not to be accepted uncritically, has it that Yoshimune consciously initiated study of the West. The shogun perused a Western book, we read in this account by Sugita Genpaku, *The Origins of Rangaku* (*Rangaku kotohajime*), and was impressed. The volume was the Dutch translation of a natural history treatise by a Pole of Scottish descent, Johannis Jonstonus, entitled *Naeukeurige beschryving van der natuur der vier-voetige dieren* (*Natural History of Quadrupeds,* in the English version), and Yoshimune remarked the pictures were so accurate that the text must surely be of value too (Fig. 45); Yoshimune decreed that someone should learn the "horizontal language."[13] This smacks of myth, and it seems far more likely that Genpaku, himself a *Rangaku* expert but distinctly jaded by the time of writing, sought to dignify his career by appealing to a start to the field at orders from on high.

The Kyōhō Reforms were about practical study. But they failed to reap rewards. Yoshimune's retirement in 1745 in favour of his indolent son Ieshige marks the end of whatever official flirtation with *Rangaku* there might have been; a few isolated instances of interest by regional potentates continued, but generally they were not sustained.[14]

But the arrival of new kinds of goods after Kyōhō set the pattern of how the West appeared as provider of "strange devices." The conception that European works were primarily intended for practical application was there to stay. The items were "strange" in the jobs they did and the shapes they took; the countries of their fabrication were also entirely odd. But the devices were clever nonetheless.

The import of strange devices had a modest impact on the history of Japanese science. But failure to engage systematically with the problematics of the Western Enlightenment contrasted markedly with the enthusiasm for instruments once taken down from the philosopher's shelf and diffused among the populace. Functional aspects of devices were often subordinated to other roles – gaming or mere amusement. Metaphorical extrapolations were found in the objects procured which had little to do with the task for which they had originally been built, and the pieces served more as springboards for imagination. Imports were popularised; by popularisation I mean precisely this: the objects were uprooted from their intellectualised schema and recontextualised in another space, that provided by Japan. The objects were used to address concerns relevant to the new site; and often, rather than scientific or phenomenological, these were social or picaresque, and always primed by an immediate sense of strangeness. In the slang of the time, Japan had been overtaken by "Dutch love" (*Orandazuki*) or, in more extreme cases, "Hollandomania" (*Ranpeki*). A critical condition, perhaps, but one owing nothing to Western psychic categories.

The popularisation of *Ran* extended across every social level, comprising the unschooled as well as daimyos. The idea of an academic *couche* and a delirious commonality below is wrong. An example is to be seen in one of the chief ministers of state (*rōjū*) under the tenth shogun, Ieharu. Tanuma Okitsugu showed little inclination for the scholarly discipline of *Rangaku* but was obsessively keen on *Ran*. Okitsugu made moves towards trade liberalisations too, but they stemmed from a diametrically opposed sense of what was to be had from international contact to Yoshimune's. Okitsugu amassed imports until his forced resignation in 1786, and probably most were strange devices. Okitsugu's Hollandomania was projected by his political adversaries as yet another dimension to his famous venality:

> Between the four seas there was no one but quaked before this illustrious lord's dignity, and all day and all night people went in and out of his gateway as

> if it led to a bazaar, kneeling and bending and knocking their heads on the ground. He did everything he chose, inferior to none, and he bought up rare and valuable things irrespective of price. Not stopping at gold, silver, jewels, and precious stones, he stuffed his house with an exhaustive range of valuable items from abroad, too.[15]

These are the words of the disgruntled *Rangaku* expert Sugita Genpaku. Okitsugu was deposed when his son Okitomo was assassinated in the shogunal castle, to stop the chief minister (the VOC believed) from throwing the whole country open to unfettered world contact.[16]

Scholars like Gentaku might object to the levity with which tools that ought to be put to practical ends were stowed away as "treasures." But here is the root of an ambivalence that threads through the eighteenth and nineteenth centuries: though finely wrought and applied, the mechanics of Europe were put, in Japan, to nonfunctional uses. This is what *Ran* was all about – a science directed inwards. Because the pieces were so often of an optical nature – lens-based or glassy – the discoveries bore upon the gaze.

OBJECTS OF TRADE

The location of the VOC Factory in Nagasaki was convenient for sailing to China and Jakarta (Batavia), the capital of the Dutch East Indies. Nagasaki also has one of the finest natural harbours on earth, free from the buffets of typhoon and wave that made many ports unsafe. The VOC was lodged on the artificial island of Dejima, a stone's throw into the bay, a displacement that sheltered their costly merchandise from the ever-present danger of fire (Japanese architecture being at the time wooden, with cooking and heating at open hearths; Pl. 1).[17] Despite the benefits of this pleasant ordering of their business, the VOC was out on a limb as far as the Tokugawa political topography was concerned, and it knew it. Rulers in Indonesia, they did not see why they should be so restricted in the next country. As with the European concessions in Canton (which it resembled more closely than the colonised Indies), Dejima was deliberately removed from the body of the host nation. The foreign and the native were not supposed to fuse. Nagasaki was about as far from the shogunal capital, relatively speaking, as Skye is from London or Anchorage from Washington, and Edo was some six weeks' journey by normal transport (palanquin and coastal sloop); even the nearer conurbations of Kyoto, Osaka, and Nagoya were still at considerable distance.[18]

It is often deduced that Euro-Japanese encounter was crucially hobbled by the siting of the Factory and that genuine cross-semination was precluded. Certainly the VOC was voluble in complaint. But it is important to go a little further in the analysis. Unless the situation in Nagasaki is properly understood, the problematic that this book addresses, which requires a healthy influx of goods, will be misconstrued. I take the view that there is a subtext to the relentless tales of privation and maltreatment that run through the Dutch records sent back to Jakarta or Amsterdam. The ledgers of trade, I suggest, and the bills of lading, give no indication of the genuine volume or type of goods that were actually exchanged. In a word, distant Nagasaki was ideally suited to smuggling. This book begins with smuggled things.

Two forms of malpractice were routinely perpetrated. First, VOC officers might syphon off a percentage of the items from their regular commercial dealings and retail them back home independently; they then justified absence of the same by complaining that the Japanese had palmed them off with goods that were "rascally" and "trash" and that fell apart, or were packed so sloppily they broke *en route*.[19] Creative accounting, the bane of all the East India companies, could cover up disappearances in the stock. It was normal for on-site directors in Asia to accumulate fortunes at their masters' expense. The English East India Company's Japan office, for example, had omitted to submit *any* audited books for three years, and massive fraud to the tune of £4,000 may have been a cause for the recalling home of the outfit (the leader, Richard Cocks, was arraigned for fraud, but he died on his way back to London[20]).

Stealing need not have affected the substance of trade, but the second malpractice did: officers might import goods of their own, conveying them on VOC ships. This was the so-called private trade (*nukeni*). Rare cases, which fortunately allow a comparison of the Dutch and Japanese documents, reveal a failure to square that is almost comical: in 1711, for example, the Factory announced it had purchased 9,000 pieces of porcelain; but the Japanese records give a figure of 179,246 items sold; over 17,000 pieces evidently went missing.[21] The following year the VOC supposedly bought no porcelain at all, but the Japanese side logged a sale of 153,003 individual items and 5,580 crockery sets. Nicolaus de Graff, stationed in Jakarta at the beginning of the eighteenth century, wrote how he observed the Nagasaki ship unload, and when the seamen's personal chests were disembarked, it rose a full metre in the water.[22] So rife was abuse that in 1753 the VOC began to tax rather than attempting to ban the "fruits, barrels of sake and soya, porcelain and other trifles" brought back to Europe by "Japan-sailors."[23] "Trifles" brought out were paid for with "trifles" taken in. Charles Thunberg, physician to the VOC in 1775–6, estimated that during his tenure on Dejima the captain made a profit that "might amount to several thousand rixdollars," and his staff collectively about the same.[24]

Some rigour (though not much) had supposedly been introduced into the proceedings in 1772 when a VOC ship, *The Burgh*, had been abandoned shortly after leaving Nagasaki in a storm; not sinking as was expected, she drifted back and was discovered. The shogunate subjected the vessel to minute inspection – the first time they had had the opportunity to pick a ship apart in this way. "On discharge of the cargo," wrote Thunberg, "was found a great quantity of prohibited goods, which chiefly belonged to the Captain and the Chief."[25]

Economy with the truth is manifest on both sides, for as the entry into Nagasaki bay is long and winding, with the island of Takoboku-jima (Papenberg to the Dutch) lying near its mouth, there was an ideal place for pre-sale of goods before formal arrival. Vessels would heave to for a surreptitious striking of contracts. A simpler eventuality was to fling goods from the side of the ship in motion to be caught by local merchants tipped off and rowing beneath to pick them up.[26] This "and a hundred more artifices have been applied," wrote Thunberg; for example, "some years ago a parrot was found hid in the breeches of one of the petty officers of the ship"; and, on the Japanese end, "[smuggling] they have often endeavoured to do with so much art, as to hide smaller articles under their private parts, and in their hair."[27]

Thunberg, as a Swede, was freer to report than the Dutch among his fellows. As physician he was also less beholden to the Company than were its formally employed staff. Independently wealthy and in Japan more for experience than enrichment, Thunberg was not inclined to stoop to fraud. He was equivalently free from the need to hush it up. On his return to the West he published his memoirs, from which the above are taken, and they appeared in English in 1795 as *Travels in Europe, Africa and Asia performed between the years 1770 and 1779*. But for them, the real state of affairs in Nagasaki would scarcely be known.[28]

Once the military and bureaucratic class (samurai) were involved, an altogether higher level of probity was expected, but the Nagasaki administrators cannot but have been complicitous in what went on. The waterfront district that led to the factory on Dejima was known as Edo Ward, reminding people of the shogun's city, and hence who was (theoretically) in charge;

Nagasaki was indeed under direct rule from Edo to ensure that all proceeds were funneled back unimpaired, and the town had been carved out of the surrounding *han* as a government enclave. But if the system was designed to diminish monetary haemorrhage, it actually did the opposite; for, unlike most Japanese towns, Nagasaki had no resident daimyo and fewer than average samurai. Two pairs of magistrates (*bugyō*) rotated between there and Edo semi-annually, supposedly to lessen corruption, but conversely this ensured a degree of discombobulation in the administration that worked entirely in favour of privateering.[29]

The newly arrived captain would parade down the companionway for a ceremonial disembarkation and to greet his senior Japanese counterparts. As Thunberg recorded, he wore a formal blue coat,

> trimmed with silver lace, and made very large and wide, and stuffed and furnished in front with a large cushion. This coat has for many years been used for the purpose of smuggling prohibited wares into the country . . . [the captain] was frequently so loaded as he went ashore, he was obliged to be supported by sailors, one under each arm.[30]

To match the jacket there were "large and capacious breeches in which he carried contraband ashore." The samurai official in the year of Thunberg's arrival was more astute than most, for the ruse was discovered and the captain humiliatingly stripped: "it was droll indeed to see the astonishment which the sudden reduction in the size of our bulky captain excited in the major part of the ignorant Japanese, who before had always imagined that all our captains were actually as fat and lusty as they appeared to be."

GOODS AND IDEAS

From the above information, anecdotal and haphazard though it is, we must aver that no amount of scrutiny of the ledgers will ever entirely indicate what came and left through Nagasaki. The scope of material exchange between Europe and Japan has accordingly been sorely underestimated. Yet I would not imply that encounter was through goods alone. Many of the finer imports, especially the smuggled kind, or those intended as gifts and bribes, were self-evidently intended for speculative ends, and it is entirely to be expected that they raised questions as to their intended use and purpose. To come across a microscope, a sextant, or an orrery was to wonder how they fitted into their original cultural worlds. Answers to such perplexities were sought at the door of the European residents on Dejima.

The previously unknown purchases were gained on phenomena through instruments, lenses, or pictures and this prompted people to ask why Westerners felt the need of such tools and how they understood the knowledge derived through them. Trade could not have been conducted without personal relationships being formed, and as the Dutch made friends with their overseers, or fell in with local women, ideas were necessarily broached and differences discussed, at whatever degree of elaboration. Suspicion on the part of the Nagasaki people was overcome with presents of cane sugar (previously unknown), while the upper echelons were regaled with stronger stuff: "they don't do much," wrote one leader of the Factory, "but a fast filling up with distiled waters, *vinho tinto* and Spanish wine."[31] At such moments a flavour of cultural otherness would be conveyed. Engelbert Kaempfer, like Thunberg a non–Dutch Factory doctor of independent means, recommended "a cordial and plentiful supply of European liquors" to lubricate social intercourse. The German doctor "went all about," as his biographer put it, "herborising and observing what was remarkable in nature and art," and he wrote a dissertation on Japanese medicine on his return to Europe.[32] Kaempfer was also able to secure enough information to write one of the first serious books to tackle Japan. Published posthu-

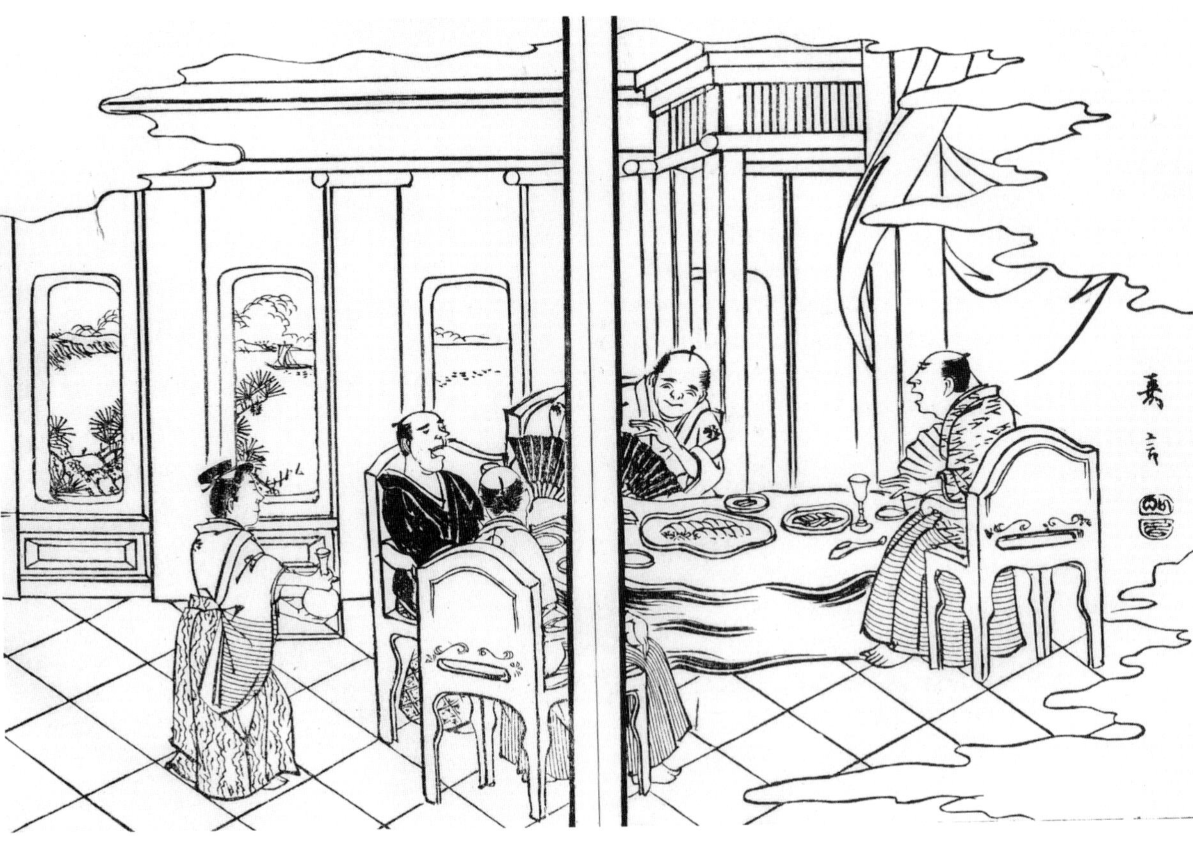

1. Ichiyanagi Kagen, from Tachibana Nankei, *Seiyū-ki*, 1799. National Diet Library, Tokyo. *Nankei is entertained in Yoshio Kōsaku's Dutch Room in Nagasaki.*

mously in 1727 as *The History of Japan together with a description of the Kingdom of Siam,* Kaempfer's writing was dedicated by its translator to Charles II. The book described, the King was told, "a valiant and invincible nation, a polite, industrious and virtuous people, enriched by a mutual commerce among themselves, possessed of a country on which nature hath lavish'd her most valuable treasures" – what Kaempfer himself called "populous and wealthy Nipon."[33] Japan was taken seriously, and it was worth spending the time on. Kaempfer's work was found cogent by contemporary Japanese readers, one of whom remarked, in 1804, that "someone who has not been to the Western part of the country [around Nagasaki] need only read what Kaempfer wrote about the subject to be fully informed."[34] In the course of all this he could hardly have avoided giving out a great deal about the West too, its institutions and its patterns of thought.

Some senior VOC members spoke a smattering of Japanese or knew written Chinese characters (enabling them to communicate with the Japanese on paper). Isaac Titsingh, leader of the Factory twice in 1780–4, could both read and write with a fluency applauded by Tachibana Nankei, the physician who first talked about the Buddhas' eyes.[35] Malay was the lingua franca of the China seas, and Dutch seamen spoke it, as did many among the populace of Nagasaki.[36] Ideas could be verbally exchanged.

The more solid linguistic skills necessary for communication of complex thought were found among the five families of hereditary translators retained in Nagasaki by the shogunate to deal with the VOC (a similar number were employed to negotiate with the Chinese community). The Dutch translators were responsible for vetting imported books against unsuitable materials (especially Christian doctrine), and for keeping the shogunate abreast of Western political affairs.[37] Their reading was necessarily wide. They had samurai status and met and grilled the senior Europeans on a regular basis as equals. Occasionally translators devoted their leisure hours to diffusing what they had learned. The head mediator from the 1770s until the end of the century was Yoshio Kōsaku, who had been Sugita Genpaku's old *Rangaku* teacher. A notably prolific scholar, Kōsaku is perhaps to be reckoned the most knowledgeable person about the West in his day; he penned thirty-nine works, mostly on European subjects, and ran a Dutch-style medical school that enrolled six hundred students.[38]

Kōsaku was a singular enthusiast for Western things, and those who made the trip to Nagasaki invariably solicited one of his heady talks of foreign lands, readily conducted in the Dutch-style house he had built: Kōsaku had a lie-down tub (Japanese baths being cuboid) and a flight of stairs up to the second floor with green-painted woodwork (Japanese stairs being more like ladders, and timber elements always bare; Pl. 5). The place was, wrote Nankei after a visit, "exactly like entering a real Dutch house," although, being used only to mats on the floor, he found sitting on the chairs "gruelling"; the illustrator of Nankei's travel journals drew a picture of the room and the harbour down below, incorporating swirling drapes that come right from the conventions of Western portraiture (Fig. 1).[39] Shiba Kōkan, down from Edo in 1788, spent a few nights sleeping in the Dutch rooms and was so delighted with the reception that Kōsaku laid on for him, including a trip to Dejima itself, that he extemporised a portrait in thanks, drafting it as a Western-style apotheosis with cloud-borne angels trumpeting above the elderly book-bearing translator's head (Fig. 2).[40]

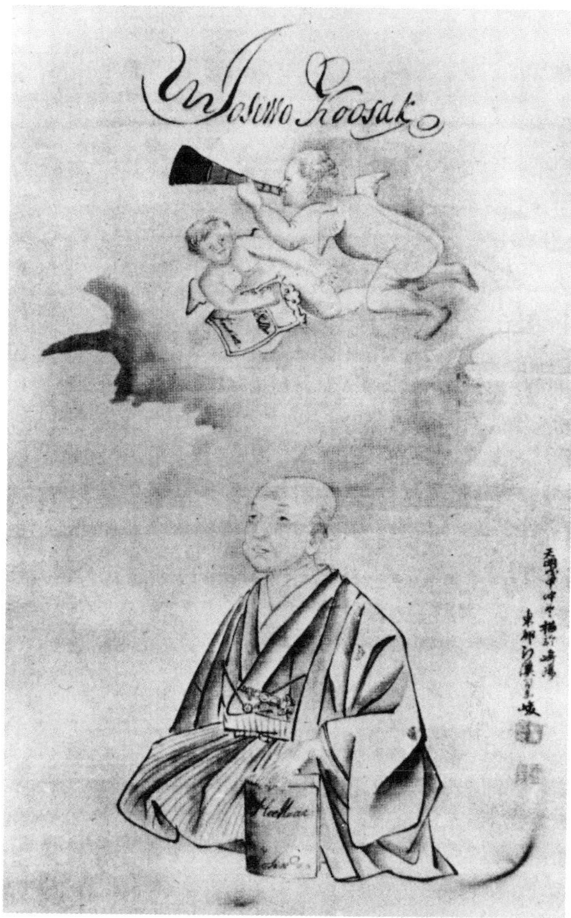

2. Shiba Kōkan, *Yoshio Kōsaku with Symbols*, hanging scroll, 1788. Private collection.

As many as one in five of the Nagasaki population may have been Chinese. Yet for all the internationalism of its demography the town was a rather cut-off sort of place.[41] The spread of ideas was better served by the annual trip made by the three senior members of the VOC to Edo to offer their respects at the shogunal court.[42] The Dutch considered this ambassadorial in function and called it the *hofreis*. To the Tokugawa it was a tribute mission. The journey took the leader of the Factory (*opperhooft*), the physician, and scribe clean across the country, and the people of Kyoto, Osaka, and countless smaller towns along the way had a yearly opportunity to see living Westerners. Kōkan recorded meeting the entourage in Kyoto, crossing them by chance on his way back from Nagasaki, and he seems to have enjoyed fairly open chats.[43] The business pressure was off during the *hofreis*, and the Europeans used it as a moment to unwind. Osaka seems to have been the most appreciated, if Thunberg is to be believed, and he characterised it as a place where "an incessant round of amusements is to be had."[44]

Leaving Nagasaki shortly after New Year, the retinue and its baggage train arrived in Edo (if the timing went right) on the first day of the third month.[45] This was the beginning of spring by the lunar calendar and an appropriate juncture to congratulate the shogun on the fluorescence of his benevolent rule, in step as ever with the natural order. The great haiku (properly haikai) master Bashō put it:

> The Dutch leader too,
> Bends his knee –
> Spring time for my Lord.[46]

The third month was when the cherry blossoms appeared, long hailed as an aesthetic highpoint in the yearly cycle; hence another verse from Bashō's pen invoking also the sound of leather,

> The Dutchmen too
> Have come to view the blossoms.
> Horses' saddles.[47]

The burden of meaning of the *hofreis* was symbolic, and the Tokugawa used the event to bolster themselves in the eyes of their citizenry. Drawn inexorably to the beauty of the shogunal seat, the VOC is thought to have harboured longings to live under glorious Tokugawa sway.

The Dutch, for their part, did not miss an opportunity to argue out practical matters (usually fruitlessly), such as permission to send more ships. But there was not much onerous to the proceedings. As Thunberg put it, "Our whole business consisting in eating and drinking, or in reading and writing for our own amusement, in sleeping and dressing ourselves, and being carried about in norimons."[48] As politics, this was an empty event, but the loose diplomatic schedule of the fortnight's stay allowed for considerable socialising and intellectual interchange on various levels. The first meeting was in the castle, and the VOC was entitled to an audience with the shogun. Not all Tokugawa progeny were of an equally inquiring bent and some forewent the fatigue of a meeting altogether, but many had a genuine desire for clarification on all manner of subjects. As one hard-pressed leader remarked of Yoshimune's intensive question-and-answer sessions, "to satisfy the Emperor [shogun] one would have to be a *homo universalis*."[49] The VOC had to be circumspect in their responses, for blurting out inopportune nuggets on the situation in Europe might redound badly (the French, Dutch, and American Revolutions all took place during the period we consider here). Yet much was transmitted: in terms of this book's span, from the earthquake of Lisbon in 1755, to Napoleon's invasion of Russia in 1812, the shogunal court was made aware of significant European events pretty much as they occurred.[50]

The leader of the Factory was the centre of attention. Occasional efforts were made to locate him at an appropriate point in the Tokugawa pecking order: some reckoned him equivalent to a *hatamoto*, or a high samurai in the shogun's direct employ (of which there were some six thousand). More often he was accepted as *sui generis* and given the title of "Kapitan," a designation that will be retained below (not the same as a ship's captain).[51] Some kapitans had intellectual clout. Titsingh, his biographer assessed, was "a man whose faculties are [*sic;* he was already dead] not wholly under the dominion of the plodding spirit of commerce," and he attracted a number of Japanese admirers.[52] But it was the Factory physician who was best equipped to answer queries on in-depth matters. As the doctor Thunberg said, "it is the physician of the embassy that is considered by the Japanese as learned; and consequently . . . they look up to him as an oracle."[53]

The Dutch were lodged outside the confines of the castle in an official residence kept exclusively for them called the Nagasaki-ya. The building was located right in the centre of the city, near Nihon-bashi. Admission was restricted, and this being Edo, rules were more strict than in Nagasaki; but the VOC was able to host a steady stream of visitors.[54] A Dutch official in 1740 had found the Nagasaki-ya "delapidated and depressing," although it had been rebuilt in 1772 after a fire; by the time of *Ran* fixation, the structure was, Thunberg thought, "tolerably neat, though not such as expected for an embassy from so distant a part of the world."[55] At least the residence amounted to considerably better accommodation than Dejima, which Titsingh thought "extremely crazy." People could be comfortably received.[56]

The Dutch journals record lengthy and informed conversations with many people, and clearly access was nowhere nearly as difficult to contrive as was frequently pretended. Numerous *Rangaku* experts came, especially those of samurai class, although lower-status persons were welcomed too, such as Hiraga Gennai, something of a father to *Rangaku,* who abandoned his rank to pursue Dutch Studies unimpeded. Gennai met Kapitan Jan Crans in 1769, ten years before his untimely death deprived the field of one of its luminaries.[57] The artist Hokusai was invited to the Nagasaki-ya, though of modest rank, to undertake commissions for the kapitan and physician; he also made a drawing of the hostel in 1789, providing one of only two extant indications (neither very helpful) of its general architectural form (Figs. 3 and 4).[58] Yet Thunberg told of "a great personage" who, "came to us incognito, accompanied by only two of his gentlemen," and although "he stayed until late at night discoursing with us on different things . . . not only on the affairs of Japan but also on those of Europe," and proved to be "as curious and inquisitive as he was friendly and engaging," the Nicodemus-like manner of his approach suggests that over-close associations with foreigners were not recommended, particularly for government figures, and especially in Edo.[59]

As for the levels of conversational speech, there were those who regretted the absence of adequate language-learning tools.[60] Titsingh had probably picked up his knowledge of writing in China, for it would have been hard to learn in Japan, where few had protracted tenure. Thunberg wrote acidly that "a Japanese and Dutch vocabulary might, it is true, in the space of two centuries, have been thought of . . . had not incapacity in some and idleness in others laid insurmountable obstacles in the way."[61] And the Swede concluded that the whole opportunity for East–West understanding had been hopelessly vitiated by being entrusted to the Dutch, for whom he had no great love – "the tobacco-pipe has too great charms for them."

More energy was expended from the Japanese side. The year 1788 saw the publication of the first Japanese-Dutch dictionary, which appeared not in Nagasaki but Edo, and was entitled *A Lexicon of Primitive Words* (*Bango-sen*). The compiler was Morishima Chūryō, aged thirty-two, scion of an important samurai house and a former pupil of Gennai. The *Lexicon* works from Japanese to transliterated Dutch and was evidently intended as an aid to speaking directly with Europeans for those not formally taught. It includes several hundred words in twenty sections for easy reference (plus place-name addendum) and was issued in a handy pocket-sized format.

Certain Japanese officials learned to speak Dutch with a degree of ease. One was Chūryō's older brother, Katsuragawa Hoshū. In 1783, following his father's death, Hoshū took the eminent position of private physician to the shogun (*oku-i*), a job that, like most at the time, was hereditary.[62] By virtue of his family connexions Hoshū had right of access to the Nagasaki-ya, and he used his privilege to the full, often bringing his mentor, Nakagawa Jun'an, with him. During the two weeks of Thunberg's residence, Hoshū frequented the hostel daily and proved "inexpressibly insinuating and fond of learning."[63] Much liked, Hoshū was capable of communicating directly in tolerable Dutch and was found "very young, good-natured, acute and lively." Like his brother, he became a prolific writer on the West, compiling works ranging from geographical and political studies to a guide to correct use of the microscope, and not neglecting his real subject, Dutch medicine.[64] Both Hoshū and Chūryō were unapologetic popularisers.

Thunberg and the soon-to-be shogun's doctor developed a deep attachment in the spring of 1776. The thirty-three-year-old Swede called his Japanese partner, his junior by eight years, "my much-beloved pupil," and after returning to Europe he "kept up intercourse . . . during a period of several years."[65] Beyond a testimony of close friendship, the bonds between the two men was of enormous significance, for Thunberg was a considerable cut above the ordinary ship's physician. He had studied at Uppsala University, and worked there with the great Linnaeus on the binomial system of nomenclature (still the standard in species classification). Thunberg was a modern man of science, a botanist of distinction, and someone who commanded a hearing in the academies of Europe; he later assumed Linnaeus's chair. Hoshū, too, was a person of deep thought, and no less endowed with a brilliant mind than Thunberg. Their discussions in the Nagasaki-ya, though inadequately recorded, provided a one-step link from the world of *Rangaku* to the forefront of late eighteenth-century Western science.[66]

POPULAR RESPONSES

"At first," wrote Thunberg of his days in Edo, "we were visited by the learned and the great of the country; afterwards even merchants and others were numbered among our visitors."[67] These nameless "others" would no doubt have been members of the mercantile classes. In addition, lesser enthusiasts, who could neither force nor talk their way in, contented themselves with shouting or staring from outside (Fig. 3). The Nagasaki-ya was near one of the principal bridges over Edo's many waterways and was at a major urban node. The site was not prohibited; indeed, its prominence within the Edo cityscape was deliberate. A massive signboard announced the place as "The Nagasaki-ya: Official Travel Lodge of the Red-furred [*kōmō*] People," as can be seen in a depiction of the place by Utagawa Hiroshige, published in 1856 (Fig. 4). The hostel was a prop in the Tokugawa diplomatic pageant.[68] People scarcely needed encouragement to wander over and look, for they were unerringly agog at the springtime sight of the "red-furred" men and their exotic goods.[69] The throng raised such a hubbub the Dutch felt marooned indoors. As Thunberg wrote, "The view is towards the street, which was seldom free from boys, who constantly called out and made an uproar, as soon as they caught the least glimpse of us, nay, and sometimes climbed up the walls of the opposite houses in order to see us." [70] A love of novelty and an arrant rubber-necking were acknowledged features of the Edoite. But the showiness

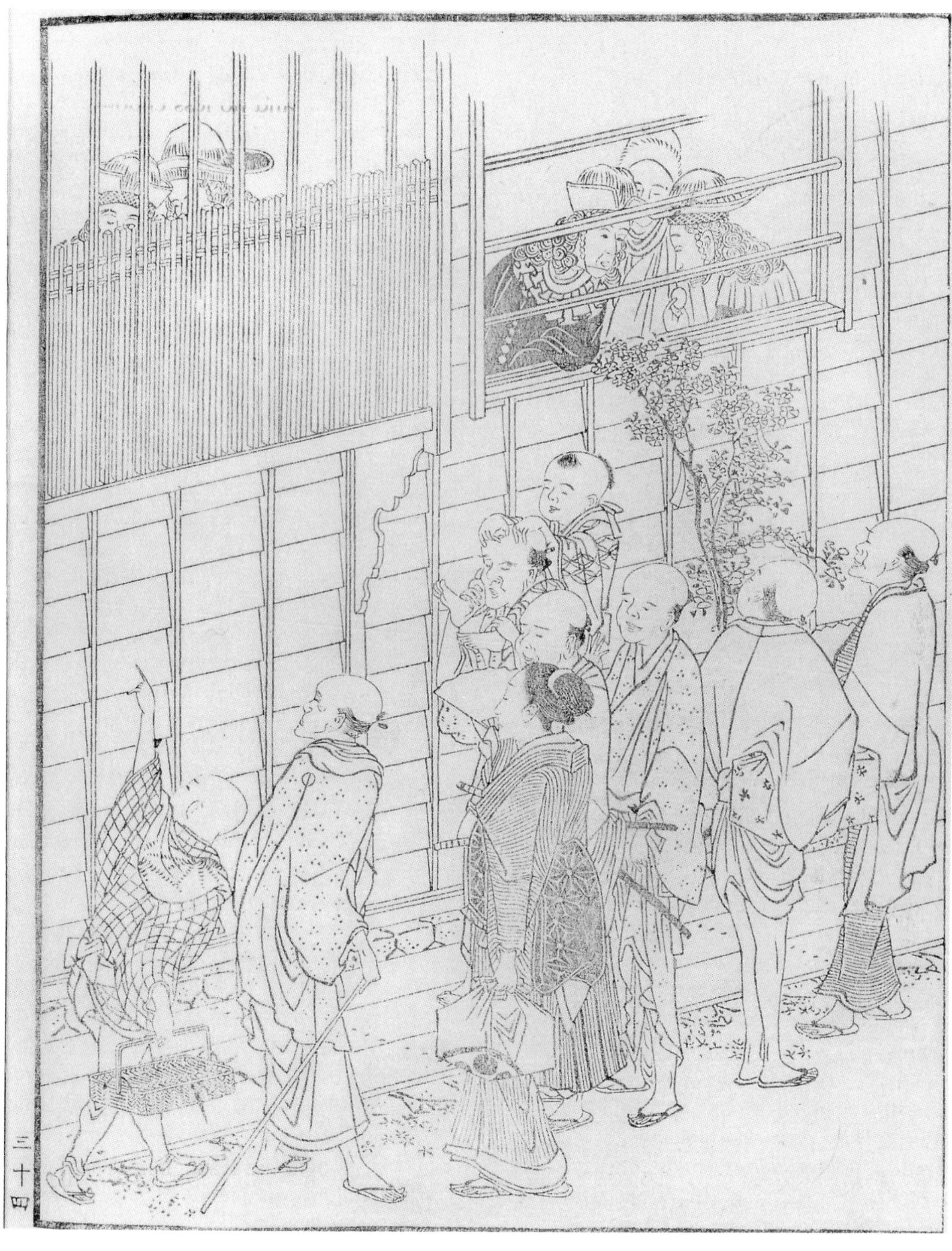

3. Katsushika Hokusai, from Asakura Shijin, *Kyōka azuma asobi*; 1799. British Museum. *The Nagasaki-ya, hostel for foreigners in Edo.*

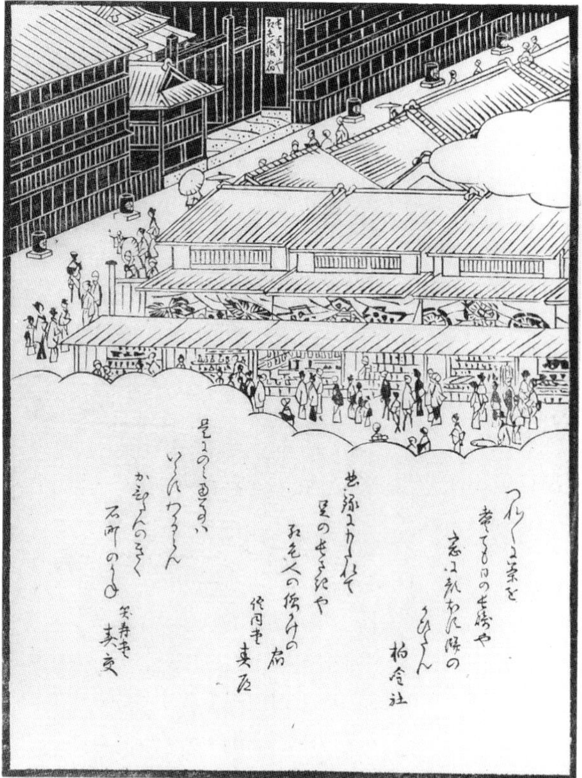

4. Utagawa Hiroshige, from Tenmei Rōjin, *Kyōka Edo meisho zue*, 1856. Courtesy of Arthur M. Sackler Museum, Harvard University Art Museums, gift of Mrs Henry O. Taylor.

Edo streets, and at top centre, the VOC hostel with sign reading, 'Nagasaki-ya: Red-fur Travel Lodge'; three verses are inscribed below.

of the VOC visit translated into a general interest in *Ran* that carried down to genuinely common levels.

If some *Rangaku* experts devoted themselves to writing books the stringency of which was calculated to earn them space alongside scholars in more established fields, not all maintained acerbic relations with the milling populace who loved the "strange devices." Chūryō and Hoshū did not. Some of the more perceptive specialists recognised in a commoner audience their true constituency, and wrote with the townsperson in mind. Educated and possessing some spare cash, the urban classes were denied access to the decision-making processes of state, and they consumed with a vengeance. Hooking with the bait of novelty, *Rangaku* authors might seek to draw curious urbanites into an understanding of what were, after all, baffling and heterodox conceptions.

The Japanese language makes strong distinctions between spoken and written forms, and this can soon take high-flown prose beyond the ken even of those formally able to read. But it is a recurrent feature of a certain type of late-eighteenth-century *Rangaku* to stick close to the spoken vernacular and to shun the dense, sinicised prose of normal scholarship. Shiba Kōkan, for example, not an academic by training but a painter, had no truck with obscurantist phraseology and was scathing of those who employed the pseudo-Chinese (*kanbun*) textual style beloved of proper scholarship but which, he correctly estimated, "the young and the simple have a terrible job trying to understand, for the sentences just get too difficult to fathom."[71] He directed his criticisms towards samurai *Rangaku* writers like Sugita Genpaku, Nakagawa Jun'an, and a senior colleague, Maeno Ryōtaku, none of whom showed any interest in breadth of readership. Kōkan was determined that his own books on the West must be in a lucid prose permitting engagement by those not motivated to study hard.

Satake Yoshiatsu, "Hollandomaniac" daimyo of Akita, held similar views, despite his rank. Lord Satake wrote two treatises on Dutch painting after he had been introduced to the subject by Gennai in 1773. One is couched in the dignified pseudo-Chinese that his status demanded, but he simultaneously composed another version, covering almost identical ground but communicated in natural Japanese.[72]

Much of the popularised writing on the West can be shown to have gained considerable influence. A publication of 1765 entitled *Red-fur Talks*, or *Talks on Holland* (*Kōmō/Oranda-banashi*), was among the first of this accessible breed, and it set the tone for readability. Little is known of Gotō Rishun, its author, except that he derived the bulk of his information from conversations with Hoshū and Chūryō's father, the then shogunal physician Katsuragawa Hosan. Rishun embedded a sense of person-to-person intimacy in the text of his book, and the short paragraphs with occasional illustrations guide the reader through a job-lot of Western matters, as a friendly (if somewhat rambling) speaker might.[73]

A recognised genre in middle-brow publications of the Edo period was the edited transcript of dialogues held between distinguished masters and their pupils (*mondo*). These proceeded by the adept asking questions, which were then answered, and they provided the commonality with aperçus into real scholarship. Some *Rangaku* writers took advantage of the mode; one of the most widely read results was by Ōtsuki Gentaku, founder of the Shirandō Dutch school in Edo and pupil of both Genpaku and Ryōtaku (whose names he synthesized to form his own, Gen-taku). Although a samurai held in high esteem by the shogunate, Gentaku favoured popularisation, and he permitted publication of exchanges he had had with a pupil called Arima Genshō, a samurai in the service of the Hollandomanic lord of Fukuchiyama, Katsuki Masatsuna. Genshō put the work together in 1788, offering the reader his own rather wide-eyed questions followed by patient replies by the master. Clearly directed at a lay audience, the work's title might be paraphrased *Correcting Errors about the Dutch* (*Ransetsu benwaku*). Genshō died before the work was completed, and an even more casual alternative title was assigned to the final publication, *Bansui's Evening Talks* (*Bansui yobanashi*) – Bansui being another of Gentaku's names.[74]

Morishima Chūryō similarly dedicated himself to exposing *Rangaku* to all. Ten years before his *Lexicon* came out, he had published the *Red-fur Miscellany* (*Kōmō zatsuwa*), a selection of information in the form of quick paragraphs to be rapidly interiorised and brought out impressively among friends. Topics were diverse enough to keep even the most fainthearted reader gripped, running from the geographical and maritime affairs of Europe and its neighbour the Ottoman Empire, to "strange devices" like microscopes, loud-hailers, or the newly invented hot-air balloon, and from these to burial customs and New Year's rituals, and then more venturesome matters, such as the extent of prostitution in the West and the criminalisation of gay relationships (a source of perplexity to Japanese writers, not least to Chūryō who, like his teacher Gennai, had a personal stake in the matter).[75]

THE MESHING OF *RAN* WITH THE POPULAR: THE CASE OF EDO

Popular aspects were probably fostered out of pessimism over *Rangaku*'s chances of integration into regular academic debate. For whatever reasons, this put Europe into a special position: the Tokugawa ideological machine mapped out much of how the experience of life was, or ought to be. The role of the shogunate was equated with heaven, adamantine and inconceivable to replace, while the people were the upbearing earth. There was no room for comparative sociology in Edo. This left *Ran* to slide about somewhere not quite definable in regular terms.

Edo, modern Tokyo, was the shogunal capital and one of the hugest cities in the world. It was there that life was kept on its tightest rein. Edo comprises the topographic focus of much of what is discussed in this book, and its flavour should be mentioned briefly. The 280-odd daimyo who ruled the country's regional *han* had High Commissions (*hairyō-* or *kami-yashiki*) in Edo as well as two official mansions there apiece. The city was punctuated with nearly one thousand official compounds and their associated stores and offices. The samurai and retainers who staffed the mansions were extremely numerous, and Edo was full of military hardware. When Shiba Kōkan took a painting student from the milder region of Kyoto, he remarked with amusement how flabbergasted the young man was by the rather choreographed bravura of the Edo street: "he thought," remarked Kōkan, "from all the daimyo and lesser lords with their swords and pikes that he was back in the times of civil war in ancient China!"[76] The populace, packed into the insalubrious corners of the city, forged its tools of self-fashioning and respect from a bricolage of elements melted down from the detritus of this ideological metalwork. *Ran* was so much pig iron.

The Tokugawa state was realistic enough to accept that pressures could be most rigorously placed on its citizenry if release was also allowed in small degree. The shogunate tolerated a fracturing of orthodoxies around the outer skirts of thought. The mental spaces of leisure activity are often billed as mere drollery, but they are more than that: beyond flight from life, or ludic reenactments of it, the Edo sense of play (*asobi*) was a full rescripting of experience. Ideas and manners not formulated by government dictate spun at the peripheries like orbs, but with gravitational pulls of their own. Neither revolutionary nor fully accepting, these lay athwart the division between contestation and compensation, unable to impinge on the centre, nor yet quite distant from it.

The classic of such demi-mondes was the Floating World (*ukiyo*). Ironically enough, this hub produced much of what modern taste finds most amenable in eighteenth-century culture, from the comic storybook to the celebrated Japanese woodblock print. But the Floating World was no orthodoxy in its own time; rather, it was a psychic habitat of alterity. The Floating World was associated with designated zones of relief, or pleasure districts (*yūkaku* or *kuruwa*), established just outside many cities. These were licensed by the government. Edo had the Yoshiwara, Osaka the Shinmachi, Nagasaki the Maruyama, and Kyoto the Shimabara.[77] At root they were brothel areas, but had prostitution been their only point, little would need to be said about them here. Actually, sex could be had more easily and cheaply elsewhere.[78] The Floating World was really a space where the normal strictures of living dislodged or melted away. It was a profoundly important constituent of the mentality of the Edo-period urban classes – whether the disenfranchised merchants unable to buy into power, or the frustrated samurai brought up on a cult of arms but working as paper-pushers. Far more of a forbidden fruit than sex was the opportunity to converse freely with people of another social level whose company one might enjoy, to flout directives on cut and quality of dress, or to over-spend in defiance of sumptuary laws. The Floating World was where alternatives became, for a moment, possible. And *Ran* streamed directly in.

Many of the figures that appear at the more popularising end of *Rangaku* were prominent in the licensed quarters too. An interest in "floating" and *Ran*, in many cases, went hand in hand in a way that cannot be coincidental. Katsuragawa Hoshū, for instance, was not only the shogun's diligent physician and a student of Dutch medicine, but a rake in Edo's Yoshiwara of such legendary proportions that he was reckoned among its "eighteen fashion kings" (*jūhachi daitsū*).[79] A step too far in 1785, during the unrest that preceded Tanuma Okitsugu's downfall, temporarily cost him his job. Hoshū's brother, Morishima Chūryō, did not lag behind in extravagant entertainment, and was on close terms with many spendthrift devotees of pleasure.[80] Hiraga Gennai was as well known in the Yoshiwara as at the Nagasaki-ya, and his case demonstrates how the escape represented by the Floating World was not, paradoxically, about brothels, for his sexual proclivities were exclusively for other men. Gennai is certainly the most famous of *Ran*-sybarites today, but their list was long in its own time, and many will appear below. Some experts actually wrote light works for Yoshiwara consumption as readily as they wrote their serious pieces, and it is not uncommon to find a sober scholar emerging from the pseudonym of a popular author. Gennai wrote puppet plays and popular fiction under the name of Fūrai Sanjin, as well as *Rangaku* treatises on mechanics and botany, and after his death Chūryō assumed the mantle, adding Fūrai Sanjin II to his other pen-names (Shinra Manzō, Manzōtei, and Tsukiji Tsūshō).

Some writing from the Yoshiwara deals directly with *Ran* themes. A couple of instances may be mentioned here as a foretaste of what is to follow. A classic play of about 1748 told of revenge by a group of samurai after their master's disgrace (it was based on a real judicial quandary). This work, *A Syllabary: The Treasury of Loyal Retainers* (*Kanadehon chūshingura*), was parodied by Chūryō in a foreign setting and renamed *A Foreign Handbook: The Treasury of Overseas People* (*Karadehon tōjingura*). A cast of up-to-the-minute foreigners sport European "strange devices" from mirrors, loud-hailers, and telescopes to anatomical charts. Decked out equally oddly are mainland Asians, with their own rare effects.[81]

Kurahashi Ra'ichirō was a samurai and a hereditary retainer to the daimyo of Ogasawara. In his Floating World manifestation he took the name Onitake, "Spook Knight" (probably in reference to his scarred appearance, as he had lost his nose to syphilis).[82] In 1803 at the age of forty-three, Onitake spoofed the latest imported goods (hot-air balloons, static-electricity generators, diving bells) in *A Sino-Japano-Dutch Miscellany* (*Wakanran zatsuwa*); the lapidary title, if read fast, sounds like "I haven't a clue, it's all such a mess" (*wakaran zatsu wa*).

The name Hekizentei Kunenbo was taken by someone clearly of education, though nothing is known for sure. Though a plausible cognomen, the name means "The Monk who Spent Nine Years Before a Wall," a reference to Bodhidharma, the founder of Zen Buddhism; but the holy man, called Daruma in Japanese, was also used as a euphemism for low-grade prostitutes. Kunenbo had it both ways. In 1789, he parodied the great Ōtsuki Gentaku. Kunenbo wrote *A Short-Cut to Understanding the Teachings of Ōtsuki Chōchin* (*Hōtsuki Chōchin oshie no chikamichi*), but glossed the title to make it read, *A Short Cut to Understanding the Magic Lantern* – referring to another import from Europe. Gentaku was ripe for satire, for his *Rangaku* school in Shiba had opened that year and the manuscript of his *Correcting Errors about the Dutch* recently completed. These three books will all be discussed in more detail below, but even brief mention demonstrates a cross-referencing of the Floating World and *Ran* that is more than a fortuity of personal predilection. They are proof presumptive (to be made positive, I hope, as we proceed) of an interconnectedness of the alternative culture of the pleasure districts and the consumed Japanese Holland.

The eighteenth-century entertainment areas were fashion-conscious and quick-paced. Any novelty was likely to be taken up. It was soon possible in the Yoshiwara, for example, to drink sake from a twisted-stem European wine glass, or even to quaff *vinho tinto*, to interlard one's conversation with "Dutch" words like *gorōto* (great), *uein* (wine), *furou* (woman) or *rōdo gekkuto* (an alcoholic flush) – all while being waited on by a woman wearing a kimono closed with a sash of imported stuff such as Dutch velvet or Indonesian batik (Figs. 5, 107).[83] The chance similarity of the word *Oranda*, sometimes abbreviated to *Oran*, with *oiran* meaning a top grade of prostitute, provided an unending source of laughs.[84] Perhaps some savoured the odd experience of luxurious Westernness vicariously by stopping at a brothel in the Yoshiwara called the Nagasaki-ya.[85] Through such jokes, Europe was pivoted on a linguistic fulcrum that tilted between the removedness of *Ran* and that alterity to routine obligation symbolised by the women of the pleasure quarters.

Much European knowledge entered by means of the Roman alphabet, or "Dutch letters" (*Oranda moji*). This term sounded like the festival day on which prostitutes paraded through the streets of their quarter (*oiran no monbi*). A witticism was easily coined to project the sum of Western textuality into the floridity of holiday over-statement, flounce, and flourish, and to suggest that the readers of Western writing were embarking on, as it were, a significatory change that cast them loose from established restraints.[86] Unexpectedly shaped, Dutch letters looked quite alien to those used only to Asian scripts. As memorably put by Santō Kyōden, an Edo tobacconist and best-selling Floating World writer, the Roman alphabet resembled bovine blather: "cow flob – oh I see! they're Dutch letters."[87] A simile emerged in the 1780s whereby "looking like Dutch script" came to mean convoluted or confusing.[88] Shikitei Sanba, a townsman brought up in the midst of the Edo publishing world (he became Kyōden's literary rival) poked fun at the horizontality of Roman letters (Japanese, Chinese, and Korean being vertical) and ribaldly suggested, "there is a theory to the effect that they derive from the forms of wriggling earthworms."[89] It was indeed odd for logic to move over the page crosswise, for "going sideways" (*yoko-yuki*) was already common slang for "weird." European orthography meandered obliquely in a way that seemed internally wayward, even before a text was parsed or its contents examined.[90]

But this did not mean that Dutch letters were absurd. They did not nebulate off from all referents – quite the contrary. The Western languages were known to constitute sense as Westerners understood it. *Ran* was a different but nonetheless plausible epistemic scheme. Nonplusment skulked in and out of the tents of scientific inquiry. Again, "Dutch" matters straddled absurdity, on the one hand and, on the other, a rich vein of sense, until they finally eased themselves into position astride through the joint credentials of the Floating World and of *Ran*. Thought, as evinced in Dutch sentences, as Sanba liked to say, "shuffled along like brothel patrons."[91]

QUESTIONS OF GENRE

The types of literature circulating in the Floating World are collectively called *gesaku*. The term is difficult to translate, but it largely refers to a textuality of comedy where the humour springs from a jostling together of discrete and noncongruent concerns.[92] It is the literature of "play" (*asobi*). As this book aspires to study the interchange between the West and Edo urban culture, *gesaku* writings will provide a large portion of our data. A realisation of the extent to which eighteenth-century fiction is permeated with *Ran* is, I believe, one of the contributions this book has to make.[93] Now is an appropriate occasion to introduce some principal genres and some of their notable exponents.

Senryu was the chief poetic form. They are made to mimic the brief 5-7-5 syllabic count of what are now known as haiku. They select as their thematic ground contemporary urban concerns – sights, shops, trends, and modes – frequently with a satirical edge. Senryu commonly start with a concrete fact of modern life and then spoof it, or rather, invert it by disconnecting the object discussed from the sphere of sense to which it normally adhered; the object is then inserted into another space. Whereas haiku work by linking pre-established elements into rule-bound strings, senryu deliberately jar with cultural oxymorons; the greatest haiku masters also twisted voluminous directives and made their verses free, but composers of senryu started out as they ended, in clamorous caprice. To the Edo mind, normal human experience was deemed a coagulation of assorted spheres of sense, and adult maturity was precisely thought to lie in keeping the compartments separate. The involuntary jumble of elements found in senryu renders meaning precarious.[94]

When it came to spheres of sense, Holland and Japan were just about diametrically opposite. The arrival of Dutch things or European people in the Japanese realm constituted the kind of juxtaposition that made for ideal senryu. The two verses cited above (on the kapitan's obeisance and the Dutchmen's flower-viewing) are technically haiku, as the term senryu was not yet in use, but they point in the direction in which the senryu was to lead. The arrival of the VOC among those old icons of indigenous aesthetic awareness, the cherry blossoms, introduced a literary conflict that sparked a mental wince as two parts of a couple were wrongly married. An outlandish European genuflection before the shogun did much the same. Collisions were effective if they were witty but also if they raised serious problems.

Analogous to the senryu, though more root-and-branch in its approach, was the kyoka or "mad-verse," and its prose counterpart, kyobun, "mad-text." Kyoka was to the courtly poetic form of waka what senryu was to the humble haiku; it took the metrical elements of the older form (a prosody of 5-7-5-7-7 syllables, in the case of kyoka) but wrought havoc with its proper generic base. Kyoka went further than senryu in not only bouncing spheres off each other but unlocking the hold that even the wording of the verse had, and twisting words into prongs that poked and teased but never quite grabbed sense. A kyoka goads at representation itself. There are degrees of confusion, of course, and not all verses cause the translator equal despair. A relatively straightforward example by Shōjūdō Shunkō takes the incomprehensibility of language itself as its theme and alludes to this by way of a reference to the VOC's annual visit; his verse was inscribed on Hiroshige's illustration of the Nagasaki-ya (Fig. 4),

Here is one thing
He understands
Without interpreter:
The kapitan hears
The bell of Kokuchō.[95]

5. Kitao Shigemasa, *Beauties of the Eastern Quarter: O-naka and O-shima of Nakachō in Fukagawa*, colour woodblock print from the series *Tōzai nanboku bijin*; 1770s. National Museum, Tokyo.

O-naka wears a sash of European velvet, O-shima one of Indonesian batik.

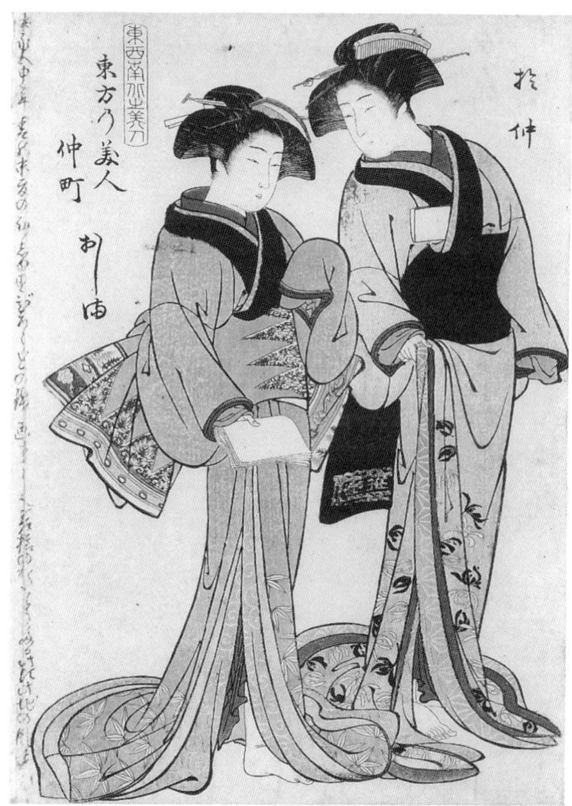

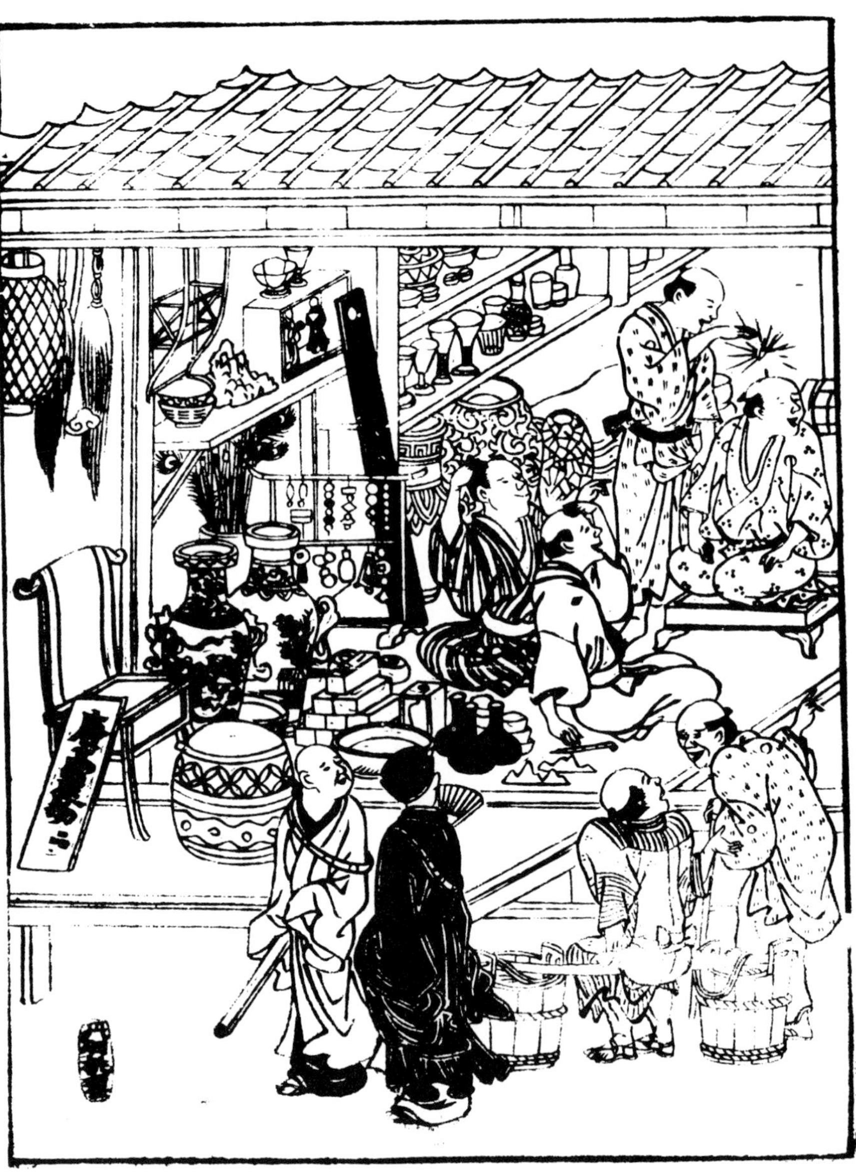

Kokuchō was that part of Nihon-bashi where the "red-fur" lodge was sited. It also boasted one of Edo's many time-bells, this one donated by the shogun in the opening years of the seventeenth century.[96] Surely the kapitan can grasp the meaning of the bell at least, even if Japanese speech defeats him.

The bell allows a glance at clocks, among the commonest of imported strange devices. But European clocks were inept at telling time in Japan as hours there were not measured in even lengths (six hours apiece were given to periods of light and dark so they would seldom all be of equal duration): the ticking Dutch timepiece and the booming Edo bell did not reckon elapse in any mutually comprehensible way. The fatuous

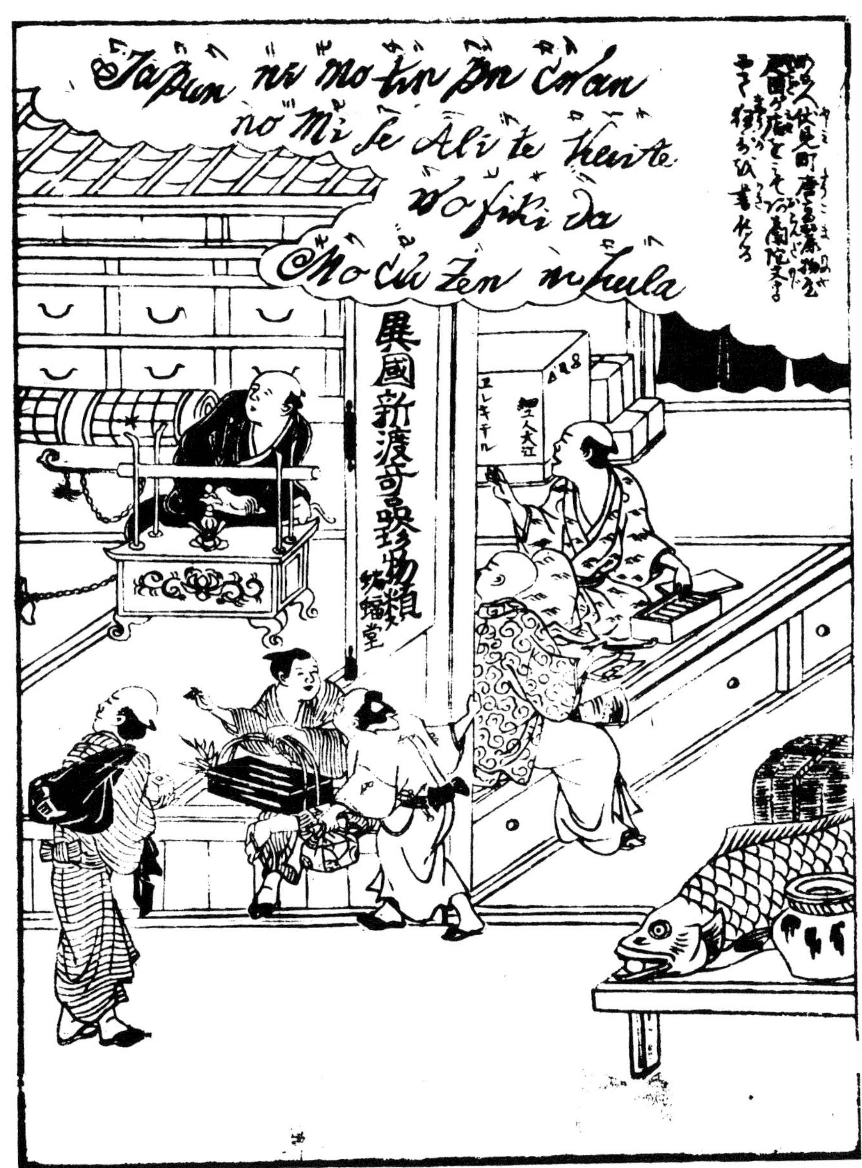

6. Takehara Shunchōsai, from Akisato Ritō, *Settsu meisho zue*, 1796. SOAS, University of London.

Hikida's foreign goods shop, with sign reading 'all manner of strange goods and rare objects, newly arrived from abroad'.

invention of human schemes intended to grapple with abstractions such as time have in fact only spawned incommensurable assessments of what was originally a shared experience.[97]

In citing the bell, Shunkō further recalls the opening of the great medieval battle epic *The Tales of the Heike* (*Heike monogatari*), familiar from the recitations of itinerant narrators. The *Heike* begins with the striking of the bell of the first Buddhist monastery, consecrated in far-off ancient India: "The bell of the Jetavana Vihara reverberates with the impermanence of all things," ran the evocative phrase.[98] The kapitan's bafflement at the Japanese tongue may be alleviated by his partial recognition of the sense of the bell, but that very bell informs the wiser person that nothing can be known with certainty. All is vanity in Buddhism; not just power and glory, but every phenomenon corrodes. The noise of a temple bell dying away to nothing was a standard symbol of enlightenment (*satori*), a state of Buddhist awakening which, correctly defined, is precisely the recognition that no sense or logic is ever fixed, and that all existence is flux. From the reference to Europeans' hopeless attempts to knock at the door of Japanese language Shunkō leads the reader towards a musing on the ultimate inauthenticity of utterance.

Kyoka and senryu rose to prominence in the later part of the eighteenth century. The first major anthology of senryu was the multi-volume *Willow Tub* (*Yanagi daru*), published from 1765. This was also the dawn of the age of *Rangaku*. Senryu, kyoka, and *Rangaku* are three sherds of the broken eighteenth-century consciousness.[99] A fourth may be added: kibyoshi, or "yellow covers" (books so-called for the garish hue of their jackets), and a genre of particular use in the present study. Kibyoshi are short pieces of prose fiction, some dozen or score of pages long, in which text and illustration are intermingled (like a modern comic), with neither the pictures nor the words attaining independent existence. Word and image unite to attack the plot in a sort of scissor action, approaching from opposite angles. Kibyoshi typically hurry the reader through a series of events that can barely be analysed as a story, for they deliberately avoid amounting to anything that constitutes normal sense. The books scatter across competing spheres, picking up random elements and joining them by chance clips of sound association, physical shape and so on, but never by narrative. A joining element (*shukō*) provides the means of movement through a book that is otherwise utterly resistant to placement. Kibyoshi are specious confluences, like a nervous system working with demented synapses.

Onitake, Kunenbō, Chūryō, Kyōden, and Sanba (all mentioned above) wrote kibyoshi often. The genre is said to have been invented in 1775 by Koikawa Harumachi. Harumachi's real name was Kurahashi Itaru, and he was a senior samurai; the following year he became High Commissioner in Edo (*rusui-yaku*) to his daimyo, the lord of Suraga-Ojima.[100] The convivial Harumachi was an associate of another writer, Hōseido Kisanji (they sometimes co-authored). Kisanji's real name was Hirazawa Tsuneyoshi; he was also a High Commissioner, and for none other than the Hollandomaniac daimyo of Akita, Satake Yoshiatsu. Kisanji showered comedy in both kibyoshi and kyoka upon Lord Satake's Dutch inquiries, which far from causing offence, probably led to promotions.[101]

Harumachi and Kisanji were too important to meet merchant-class people anywhere other than in places of removal like the Yoshiwara, but once there, *Ran* provided a shared interest; both knew the lower-ranking circles of Kyōden (whose brother Kyōzan was also a fictionalist) and Kyōden's protégé (Kunenbō's friend), Takizawa Bakin. Kyōden, Sanba, and Bakin, together with a fourth writer, Jippensha Ikku, were to dominate kibyoshi, and, in the nineteenth century, the longer fictional genres of gokan and yomihon.

Kibyoshi were rapidly printed, cheap, and written virtually without ideograms so as to be readable by almost everyone. They are arguably the single largest source of information on the fashionable and popularised culture of the late eighteenth century. Being illustrated, they had an immediacy that propelled, with dartlike aim, matters of elite concern out into the heart of the populace. Kibyoshi illustrations are in woodblock, and many of the names of those who designed them will be familiar to enthusiasts of the Japanese print – or "pictures of the Floating World" (*ukiyo-e*), as they were generically called: the Torii school; Kitao Shigemasa and his followers, especially Masayoshi; Shunshō's pupil Shunchō; Utamaro and his pupil Tsukimaro; Chōki; Hokusai; and the Utagawa school artist

Toyokuni. Many practitioners crossed media boundaries too, and Ikku and Hokusai wrote kibyoshi as well as illustrating them. Kubo Shunman, a samurai and print artist (famous for being left-handed) was also a kibyoshi writer under the name of Nandaka Shiran ("I'm clueless"); he had studied prints under Shigemasa and become close to his fellow pupil Kyōden who was equally famous as print-maker and writer, taking the art name Kitao Masanobu. Even Shigemasa tried his hand at fiction taking the name Hatake no Dojin Maimosuke ("Muddy man from the fields – a real potato"). It is further suggested that Harumachi the storywriter's and Utamaro the artist's official successors were the same person (the two masters having anyway met as students of the celebrated iconographer of ghosts, Toriyama Sekien). Chūryō may also have studied under Utamaro. The figures indeed form a very intricate knot.[102]

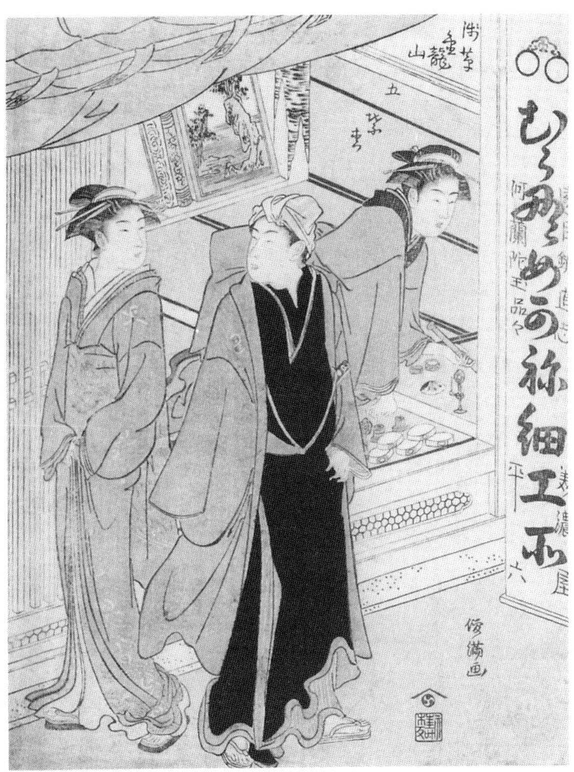

7. Kubo Shunman, *Murano's Glassware Shop*, monochrome woodblock print; c. 1790. Kobe City Museum. *A sign lists the specialities as telescopes and 'Dutch glass items'.*

LET US CONCLUDE this scene-setting chapter with two pictures. Both show imported-goods shops (Figs. 6 and 7). In 1796, the veteran gazetteer Akisato Ritō published a guidebook to Osaka and its environs entitled *Illustrated Famous Places in Settsu* (*Settsu meisho zue*); the images were provided by Takehara Shunchōsai and others. Ritō mentioned a shop in Fushimichō, near the centre of Osaka, kept by a certain Hikida, under the name of the Parasol Hall (Kōmori-dō). Most people called it simply Tōkōmōya, the "Continental and Red-fur Shop." An impressive array of goods greeted the passer-by: glasses and ceramics, pots and furniture, ostrich feathers, and a static-electricity generator. In a cloud-shaped space above the illustration is a kyoka written horizontally in the Roman script. It is glossed phonetically to be readable in Japanese too, and runs:

> In our fair land too,
> Outlandish nonsense –
> And a shop for it.
> Hikida really pulls the custom in
> Foreignness before their very eyes.[103]

The sideways lettering conveys Japanese words. It can be rational after all. But the verse is so full of puns that it is belief in a distinction between sense and its opposite that in fact becomes disreputable. Yet all this, the writer stresses, can be bought if you go to Osaka where "outlandish nonsense," foreign sound and meaning, is rendered material on the Japanese street.

Edo had an import shop too. Murano's Glasswares was located in the Asakusa district. Its appearance was set down in the 1770s by Kubo Shunman. The Murano-ya sold lenses and mirrors (plain and decorated), microscopes and telescopes, glasses, boxes, and pictures; in short, it dealt in the full apparatus of supra-intuitive vision and its record. The shop offered a greatly intensified gaze, calibrated to break apart expectations. A man and woman pause, hesitating whether to buy or to forgo as they read the sign, "All Manner of Dutch Glassware."

This book is about *seeing* the foreign, purchasing it, taking it home, and depositing its claims, to turn new understandings thus reached onto the world around. The Japanese imperative to see was not the same as that familiar to the Western scientist. It was derived from the moral structure of Edo, a system badly cracking by the late eighteenth century. What was to be had through the instruments of vision was once called, by Sanba, the "Red-fur gaze."[104]

TWO

THE "BATAVIAN TEMPERAMENT" AND ITS CRITICS

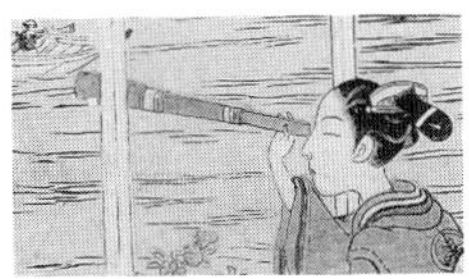

"WHEN IN WU," ran the proverb, "do as the people of Wu." Yet the people of Wu, for their part, will seek to assess the qualities of the newcomers arriving among them. It is an axiom of international encounter that those native to a place will inspect those hailing from outside it for signs of difference. As people speak and write about these things, a sense of foreignness is formed. Commentary, though, is prone to move off along its own lines, keeping in only intermittent touch with its overt points of reference. A recreation of the assessment of Europe by later-eighteenth-century Japan is the purpose of this chapter, and we shall analyse what I here call the "Batavian temperament" (derived as it was from a notion of Holland).[1] The Japanese term was *Ran* – Holland disembodied from its Netherlandish self. The parameters of the sense of *Ran*, and what as a construct it came to signify, solidified, in fact, into a fixed and rather tight set of ideas.

Countries have their mythologies of selfhood; the United Provinces was no different. Japan, too, pillowed its identity in a bed of myth that could be adduced to stand in opposition to supposedly outside norms. This was summed up as "Wa," a purged and abstracted Japaneseness replete with history. But it did not follow that confrontation between native and foreign elements need always be acrimonious. Because *Ran* was a Japanese thing, it was possible to attribute to it notions of a wide scope; features were often selected to bate the local or to move the domestic polity in a certain direction. The definitions might have surprised travellers from abroad. Dutch Studies experts (*Rangaku-sha*), in particular, evinced in their "Holland" a pillar to support their own desires, and their aspirations for the Japanese state and people.

Assessment of the "Batavian temperament" radiated from one central presumed characteristic of *Ran:* a love of precision – *seishō, bisai, sasai, seimyō, komakaki, kuwashiki* – many words were used to denote this.[2] Imported strange devices (*kiki*), arriving in droves, seemed amply to prove that attention to detail, intricacy, and a general closeness of approach were the foremost constituents of the mind-set of the Dutch. The theme of precision constantly reappears. *Ran* ways might be counterbalanced with what was said to pertain in other foreign peoples, the typical comparison being Chinese and Koreans, lumped together under the label of "Continentals" (*tōjin*). How might Dutch precisionism fit with them? And how did it fabricate a larger European world-view? If encouraged in the domestic sphere, how might this *Ran* impact on the Japanese nation? The question came back on itself: was this home-made *Ran* a culture worthy of taking to heart?

THE BEHAVIOUR OF DUTCHMEN

At root were estimations of the representatives of the West seen in Japan. This meant members of the VOC. The comportment of swag-bellied Hollanders has not been the stuff of approval in all lands; indeed, opprobrium greeted them in many parts of the world. Dutch seamen were as likely to be icons of the boorish and uncouth as to exemplify pretty manners, and "as drunk as a Dutch sea captain" was a standard simile in English. But in Japan, most commentators were constrained to agree that the VOC contingent was nice to a fault. *Ran* was proposed as a place of genuine, if alternative, culture.

The annual *hofreis* on which the VOC officers came to Edo provided an occasion when the foreign people could be seen by the elite of the shogunal administration. Dutch and local differences were thrown into relief. It was not always a comforting comparison. The havoc created by the citizenry outside the Nagasaki-ya where the Europeans stayed was widely felt to stand in embarrassing contrast to the order and good sense that reigned within (Fig. 3). The point is not for the modern historian to estimate whether such evaluations are true but to constate their normative force. Sobriety became a token of *Ran*. To the Jeremiahs of public morality the *hofreis* revealed just how far the Edo side lagged in decency and control. Yoshio Kōsaku, the head Dutch translator, accompanied the VOC from Nagasaki and penned remarks in 1774 that are little less than a swingeing indictment of Japanese civil discipline. His point was stark, though his words are surely too abrupt, "In the Eastern Metropolis [Edo] there are large numbers of people, but in my humble opinion their manners are seldom urbane. Since times long gone by, they have delighted in whatever is vulgar and brash. The scope of interests for all too many is pushing themselves forward, and running at cash profit."[3] This was perhaps rich coming from a Nagasaki-ite, for common belief had it that they were the most unmannerly in the land.[4] But the shogunal capital was supposed to set an example for the nation. The vulgarity of Edo as opposed to the effete charm of Kyoto was a standard cliché, but it is important to note the context in which Kōsaku wrote his condemnation: it appears as the preface to the first integral translation of a European book to be published openly in Japan.[5] His new referent for assessment of home is *Ran*.

That Kōsaku was using the VOC as a stick to beat the proletariat of his own day is obvious, and grist to the mill of shogunal authoritarianism was always welcome in some quarters. But the crux of the contrast he drew was far from glib: were the Dutch to be regarded as a "primitive people" (*banjin*) beyond the pale of culture, permanently deprived of the uplifting qualities of finer peoples or, conversely, were they to be followed? It had perennially been true in East-Asian opinion that the Chinese system constituted the only authentic enlightenment, but did the appearance of the people of *Ran* require that definition to be revised? Culture (or lack of it) is notoriously hard to define, but Dutch behaviour was found to be reasonable, even decorous, or at any rate wanting far less often than might have been supposed. Cool heads and an impeccable inter-personal mannerliness were soon identified as the social dimensions of their love of precision.

The mental maturity of the Dutch was subject to intense scrutiny during their time in Edo. Up at the castle they were made to explain the rules of Western etiquette, or even to put on demonstrations, so that their codes of conduct might be evaluated by the shogun and his advisers. The Dutch found these charades demeaning, but then, they never understood the purpose of them; the acts were as important as anything else they did in Edo. The German physician Engelbert Kaempfer, on Dejima in 1692, wrote how in the shogunal city he and his companions had to "walk, stand still, to compliment each other, to dance, to jump, to play the drunkard, to speak broken Japanese, to read Dutch, to point, to sing, to put our cloaks on and off. . . ."[6] and this went on, he said, for two hours, "with innumerable such other apish tricks." Yet even Kaempfer conceded the "great apparent civility" that attended the performance. Had he thought about what was happening rather more, it might have given the lie to his dismissal of the occasion as "perfect farce." Pieter Bockesteijn, a generation later in 1732, was thankful the shows were not required, but a dozen years later again, Jakob van der Waeijen noted how a "shogunal student" had been sent to the Nagasaki-ya in Edo to ask "silly questions" such as "what kind of compliments Dutchmen exchanged on all kinds of occasions" – surely, in fact, a very revealing line of interrogation.[7]

Only the top brass of the VOC came on the *hofreis*, whereas Edo was most readily visible in its mob, so the dice were entirely loaded in the Dutchmen's favour. Comparisons between well-tempered rule, on the one hand, and mayhem, on the other, were just too easy to draw. But even those who saw the run of the VOC team in the Factory on Dejima concurred that behaviour was highly correct and irregularities alien, even down to the lowliest sailors. Tachibana Nankei, the doctor who spent many years in Nagasaki, was impressed by the politeness, not only of the kapitan and his upper echelon of colleagues, but explicitly of the seamen too, and he was favourably struck by the scrupulous attention paid to those two great Tokugawa virtues, neatness and the respect shown to leaders;[8] Hirokawa Kai, physician to Prince Kaihō in Kyoto, and another long-term visitor to Nagasaki said the same, pointing out further praiseworthy aspects, such as the ready Dutch acceptance of death and their absence of fear of the grave.[9] Like Nankei, Kai was converted, and subsequently became an experimenter in Dutch-style medicine.[10] Such *Rangaku* enthusiasts produced the blueprint of what was the Batavian temperament.

The Dutchmen (there were no women) seen in Japan did not amount to the whole story. Morishima Chūryō wrote in 1787 in his best-selling account of Europe, the *Red-fur Miscellany* (*Kōmō zatsuwa*) – named for the vivid profusion of North-European body hair – how the existence in the West of institutions like hospitals, almshouses, and paupers' burials attested to a civilisation built on mutual help and parity.[11] Shiba Kōkan, too, a broad thinker though by all accounts an inimical personality, produced an etching of a European hospital and published it in 1804. The airy grace of the building (in his picture at least) would have put to shame any equivalent facility that Edo had to offer. He also depicted the Sorbonne in Paris, showing how the soft touch might couple with quiet indulgence in learning.[12]

Honda Toshiaki was a low-ranking provincial samurai who eventually became adviser to the Lord of Kaga, the richest daimyo in the land, and he was one of the few to speculate concertedly on how it was that the West bred people of this kind. In 1798 he put the case, at least to his own satisfaction that, "if you consider the system of government used in various European nations, you will find they do not run through military compulsion, but by appeal to righteousness; if you rule by might, you will not be followed from the heart."[13]

All this was ludicrously laudatory in the face of the real problems facing *ancien régime* France, Georgian England, or the sorry rump of the United Provinces. But Japan's *Ran* was a site of desire, not of objective analysis. Yet the barrage of discourse had its effect. The word previously used for Europeans, current since the 1560s, was *nanban-jin* – literally "primitives from the south" – but this disappeared from circulation in the mid-eighteenth century; it was dropped less as a geographical solecism (the colonised East Indies were to the south of Japan) but rather was jettisoned in an attempt to match the now accepted cultural level of the West with the label attached to it. In a rectification of names, *ban* (primitive) was deleted and replaced with *Ran* and *Ranjin* ("*Ran* people"); the new term not only elevated the Europeans from the status of under-developed, it went further by permitting for the first time the Dutch to be called by something approaching their name for themselves (*Oranda*); it also decked them with a garland of refinement, as the ideogram chosen to capture the sound *ran* literally meant "orchid," a flower traditionally thought to be beautiful, and even scholarly. Particularising terms came into being as *Ran* was broken down into parts, and rather than imposing its own labels, Japan again accepted as authentic the toponyms of the West: England became *Angeria,* written to mean "remembering misfortune to advantage"; France was *Furansu,* "religion and good conjecture"; and Italy was *Itaria,* "thinking fecund principles."[14] In a sense, the terms were little more than mnemonics for the odd foreign sounds, but they smothered the places denoted in rich and delightful associations.

"HOLLAND" VERSUS "CHINA"

Old notions of a unity of culture were forced to retreat in the second half of the eighteenth century. The ripple theory of human sensibility that defined proximity to the centre – China – as a chief indicator of worth was substantially eroded. Far up in the north, dark, cold, and unsmiled upon by the elements, Europe was not without merit. As Toshiaki put it:

> Their two lands [Europe and the Russias] are freezing compared with ours, but even so, those who inhabit them are strong, brave and valiant, and also deep-thinking. They are placid before their rulers, perform their labours with due speed, are kindly in disposition; they are academically minded, and make good soldiers.[15]

Perhaps they were and perhaps they were not, but the list offered to the Japanese reader a brimming catalogue of Tokugawa desiderata.

Japan had been uneasy with the hegemony of the geographical middle, and although it still called China the "Middle Land" or the "Middle Flower" (as did the Chinese themselves), Japan saw home as benefiting from its off-centred state. It was there that the sun rose: Japan was the first to be illuminated by the morning rays. Being content to be considered in the far east, Japan did not need to displace the actual notion of centrality. But Yamamura Shōei pointed out in 1802 that both the English and the French considered their countries to be the navel of the world, hence, he thought, the Parisian and Greenwich meridians; other Westerners plotted their world charts from the Azores, and Toshiaki noted the use of Tenerife as a cartographic node.[16] Breaking centrality turned all loci into relative things, and China itself was called into question.

Nagasaki had its community of Chinese, far larger than the score or so of resident Dutch, and this allowed a close comparison of the two foreign groups at first hand.[17] Hirokawa Kai concluded that whereas the Dutch were "very polite," and perpetrated "no rudenesses," the Chinese were the limit, even stooping to egg the Dutch on to misdemeanour.[18] Tachibana Nankei noted that where the Dutch were precise and regulated, the Chinese were chaotic and lax, and he quoted a certain "important gentleman down from the Capital" who had dined at both the Chinese and Dutch compounds, and could confirm that Dejima was "swept clean and fresh," with "not the slightest lapse of propriety to be seen" (he was spared sight of the "blacks and matlos," which, he believed, would have upset him), whereas in the Chinese establishment it was all pushing and shoving, with loud guffaws at authority.[19]

Right or wrong in anthropological method, such *ad hominem* anecdotes coagulated into widely believed notions. On-site observation in Nagasaki yielded startling results as the "primitive" and the "civilised" switched places. Satō Narihiro, a botanist and temporarily in the service of the daimyo of Satsuma (a *han* not far from Nagasaki), recorded that, thanks to the presence of Europeans in the town, the behaviour of "the Nanking people" had finally begun to improve.[20] Far from trickling down westward, culture, like an inverted hourglass, was gentrifying in the opposite direction.

Differences between Chinese and Dutch were argued out in many contexts, but most wittily perhaps in a comic story in the illustrated kibyoshi genre, written by Kurahashi Ra'ichirō, a student of Kyōden, and a forty-three-year-old government functionary in Edo who signed with the pen-name Kanwatei Onitake. The work was entitled the *Sino-Japano-Dutch Miscellany* (*Wakanran zatsuwa*) and published in 1803.[21] Onitake's illustrator was Kakō, already famous under his more widely known name, Hokusai.[22] The pedestrian title is deliberately intended to sound like a *Rangaku* text of the more indigestible sort, but it is entirely tongue-in-cheek. The story is, in fact, a romp through as many *indées reçues* on Chinese and Dutch mental realms as Onitake could muster, liberally worked in with puns and humour. The Chinese are no longer mere pawns to be lost to the Dutch, but are assessed with equal seriousness (if seriousness is an apt description) to determine their own cultural traits. Which is better? If read fast, the title becomes *Wakaran zatsu wa*, "I haven't a clue, it's such a mess."

Hokusai designed the opening page as a mock-up of the then-popular broadsheet genre that showed different types of foreigner lined up to expose their particularities of costume and style, often printed with vignettes above in the native script (Fig. 8).[23] But Hokusai's picture introduces Onitake's three dramatis personae, a Chinese, a Japanese, and a Dutchman. The Chinese's words are mostly illegible through an ineptly placed library seal. The text above the Dutchman is glossed phonetically to be readable as Japanese: "This is the Holland merchant called Snpipyt, 'this year as ever was I'd like to go to Jagasaki,' " he says. The Japanese woman standing between continues the punning introduced by Snpipyt by being described as a prostitute from the "Saruyama" district of "Jagasaki." *Jaga* ("of the snake") is elided with Nagasaki. Mixed in also, perhaps, is the old name for Batavia, Jakarta, while Saruyama joins the red-light district of Maruyama with *saru* ("monkey"). The

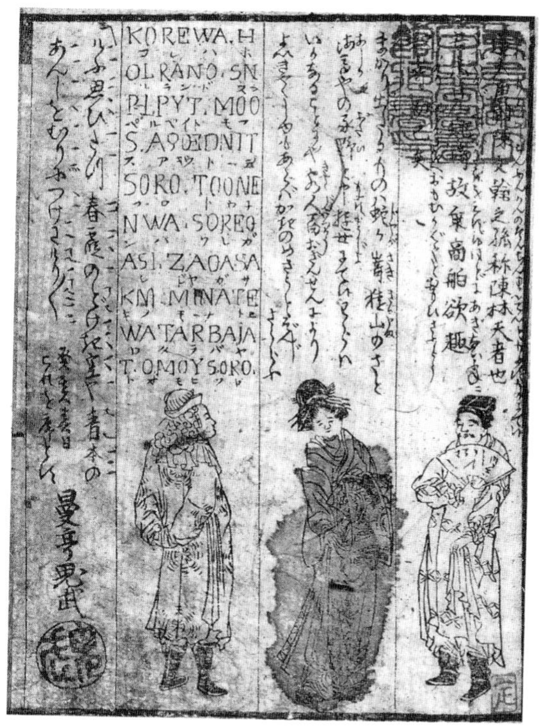

8. Katsushika Hokusai, from Kanwatei Onitake, *Wakanran zatsuwa*, 1803. Tokyo Metropolitan Central Library.

The cast: Chinese man on the right (modern library seal obliterating), Japanese woman and Dutchman.

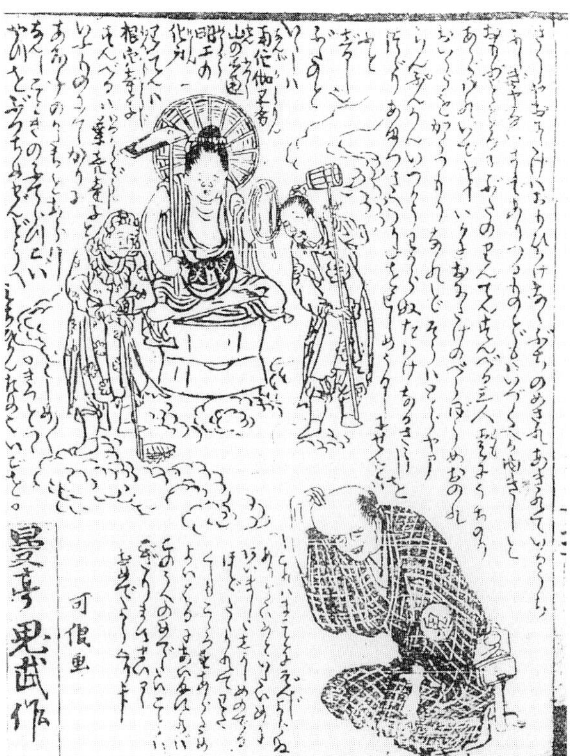

9. Katsushika Hokusai, from Kanwatei Onitake, *Wakanran zatsuwa*, 1803. Tokyo Metropolitan Central Library.

Apotheosis of the Protagonists with the Author beneath.

two foreign men are in love with the Japanese woman: China and Holland are vying for the heart of Japan.

"Snpipyt" becomes "Sunperupei" in the story itself, in a polysyllabic nonsense that would sound *Ran*-like to an Edo ear. But more directly, Sunperupei seems to allude to Charles Thunberg, physician to the Factory in 1775 – 6, whose name was pronounced in Japanese something like *tsunberugu;* squeezed out of the end of this is *hei,* a fart.[24] The Chinese is Chin Rinten, which sounds Continental, but evokes the meaning "dumb smart-arse down on the bottom."[25] The prostitute is hardly a beauty either, and indeed, is so devastatingly ugly that she has earned the nickname Buta ("pig"). Beyond the two foreign clients, characteristically off the mark in their evaluation of Japanese things, she has no admirers. In the end neither man gets her, Buta remains unbedded, and Japan survives unwon. Hokusai's concluding picture shows Buta wisked up to the heavens as a manifestation of the merciful bodhisattva Kannon, the lovesick foreigners assuming aspects of eternal adoration at her side (Fig. 9). Below the vision Onitake butts into his narrative, scratching his head in perplexity at the unforeseen turn things have taken.

The competition between the two love suits constitutes a series of duels between the Chinese and Dutch traditions, which Japan adjudicates. Eventually both are deemed just silly messes. Onitake, however, provides a clear distinction between the orientations of the respective national types: China is sage and mystical, Holland is canny and deft. One exchange is particularly revealing: Rinten avails himself of sage-magic (*senjitsu*), a spiritual capacity acquired through years of austerity and meditation. He has integrated himself with cosmic forces, and now, at one with the natural world, can mollify even the ferocious animal kingdom to make it do his bidding; Rinten goes to meet Buta impressively riding on a beast made friendly. Sages conventionally did this, but Rinten's choice of mount is idiosyncratic – an octopus. He flies to Buta on its back (it flies by word-play: *tako* means both octopus and a paper kite, Fig. 10). Worthy of note as a display of personal unity with stratosphere, as a courting ploy this is a dismal failure. The octopus stinks so abominably that Buta orders it out. Just up from the sea, the fish is already one with humanity and can speak, but it is rude and forward, literally "fresh" (*nama-kusai*), and responds to ejection with a pedantic Chinese philosophical exegesis, annoying Buta further.

Sunperupei next tries his luck. He has the Dutch equivalent of magic – technological skill – and he produces a clever machine, hoping that

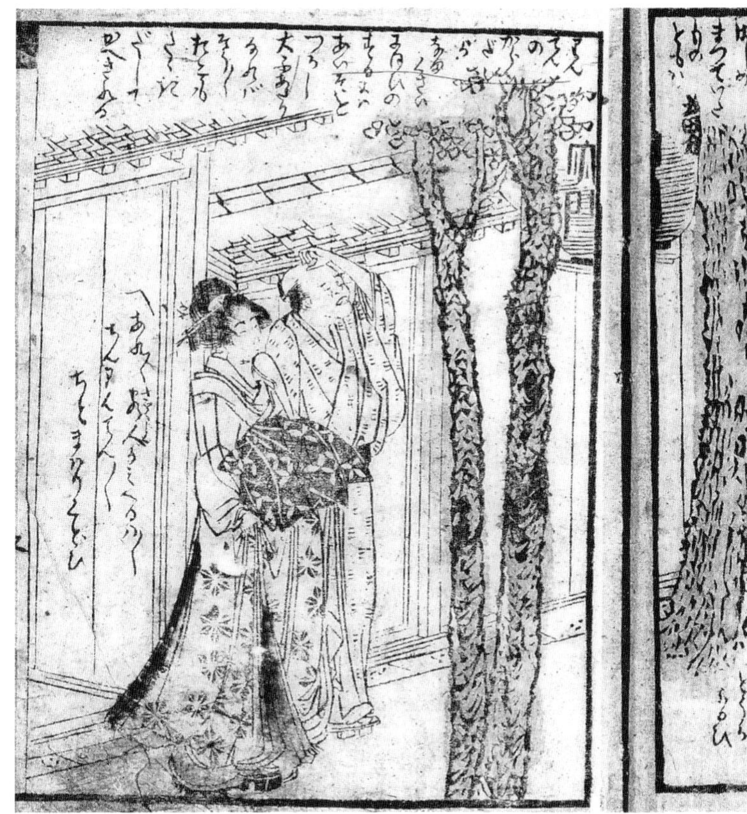

10. Katsushika Hokusai, from Kanwatei Onitake, *Wakanran zatsuwa*, 1803. Tokyo Metropolitan Central Library. *Rinten rides an octopus.*

scientific achievement will twit Rinten's lofty aspirations (Fig. 11). Sunperupei's device is a static-electricity generator (*erekiteru*), and with it he draws fire from Buta's well-coiffed head. But this is as much a flop as the other, for Buta thinks the device "far too common these days," and she vehemently protests as she is rigged up.[26]

There are several similar encounters: Rinten produces an animal from a gourd and subjects inanimate objects to psychic transformation; Sunperupei makes Buta sick in his hot-air balloon and gets carried away with some ill-administered Dutch surgery, lopping off his finger (meanwhile an agile Indonesian – familiar as servants of the VOC – performs acrobatics). By pitting Chinese wisdom against Dutch mechanics in this way, Onitake establishes a difference between East Asian and European epistemologies that were pretty much the stereotypes of his day.[27]

WEIGHING AN ELEPHANT

Onitake's story can be contrasted with another published the previous year, written and illustrated by Hokusai. The book made further humorous comparisons between Holland and

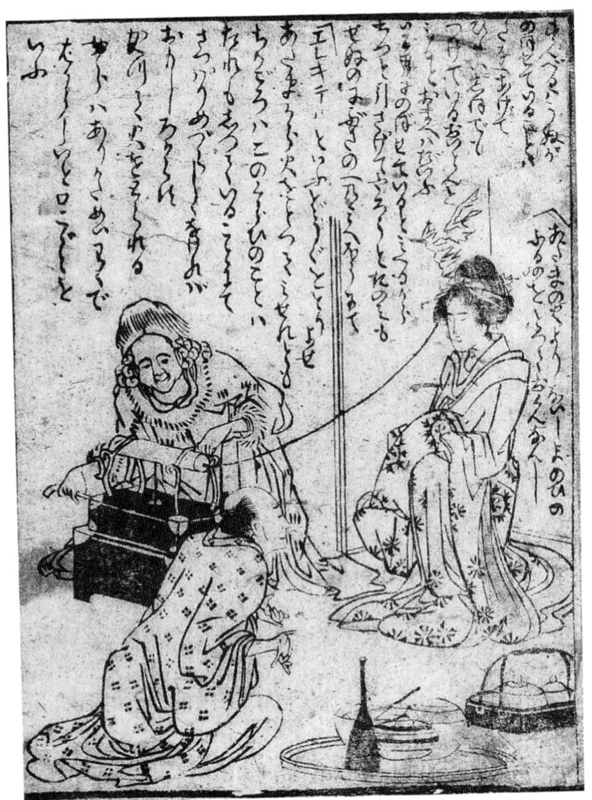

11. Katsushika Hokusai, from Kanwatei Onitake, *Wakanran zatsuwa*, 1803. Tokyo Metropolitan Central Library.

Sunperupei and his static-electricity generator.

China and tackled more closely the associations of the Dutch with precision and accuracy.[28] One episode is based on a parody of a tale in the *Book of Mencius*, one of the classics of Chinese thought, where it is told how Cangshu had weighed an elephant. Elephants are proverbially large, but how heavy are they? Cangshu, precocious son of the huangdi (emperor) Wu of the Tang, at the tender age of five or six devised a method to calibrate the animal. This was a prodigious feat, for just to control so huge and erratic a beast required adroitness, but to weigh it required ingenuity bordering on genius. The pithy one-liner "weighing an elephant" (*zō o hakaru*) was a saw implying resourcefulness. In 1790, the Mencian anecdote had been recalled in Japan in the immediate context of a general encyclopaedia, *The Dust of Ages* (*Jinkō-ki*), a publication adapted from a Chinese work of the same name (*Youjie-ji*) by Shen Xiangmu. This was a dozen years before Hokusai wrote. Xiangmu recounted Mencius's story and explained the child's trick,

> He boarded the elephant on a boat and drew a plimsoll line at the place where the water level came. He then disembarked the beast, and loaded the boat with objects of known mass until the boat sank to the same degree. By this means he was able to calculate the weight. It might be called a brainstorm.[29]

"Weighing an elephant," then, meant having a brainstorm. A versifier in the comic senryu genre alluded to the child's actions in the mid-1760s using what was by then a current expression:

> The last Chinese that gets in
> (With that elephant's big fat butt)
> Had better be good at maths![30]

One man too many and they will all go under.

Hokusai's story is a send-up of precision and calculation. His title makes it clear that Xiangmu's work was the immediate whipping-boy: his kibyoshi is called *A New "Dust of Ages"* (*Shin Jinkō-ki*).[31] This is an extended play on themes of measurement, and on those who invest energy in meaninglessly close analysis. The plot revolves around a fictional Japanese tenno (emperor) who sends two monks to harvest reserves of aromatic wood growing on a neighbouring island. Fragrant timber was an import item and scurrying traders are up for laughs, but there is also a pun, for "aromatic wood" is the literal meaning of Xiangmu's name. The island is called Arithmetic (Sankan) and is charted on a map on the title-page, drawn to look like a coin; its ruler is King Mark-up (Rikan), with his lovely daughter, Princess [Abacus-] Bead (Tama), while the monks themselves are Kazan and Gozan, monastic-sounding enough (*-zan* means a temple) but here written to mean Addition and Miscalculate.

With a theme like this, Hokusai could hardly forebear to touch on the weighing of elephants, and include it he did, with the monks in the role of Cangshu (Fig. 12). The story offered plenty of scope for gags (the elephant gets restless onboard and starts to stuff himself with sticky buns, hence "ship's cookie," says Hokusai),[32] while Hokusai informs the reader of the weight divined with ribald exactitude: 107 *koku,* 16 *shin,* 3 *tō,* 5 *shō,* 5 *gō,* 1 *seki,* 4 *sai.*[33]

The overt target of Hokusai's story may be Xiangmu and his Chinese calculations, but the remoter object is, I think, the Dutch. The Europeans were, after all, the ones best known for loading elephants (and other fauna) onto boats and ferrying them round the world. At the time of Hokusai's writing, elephants had twice been brought to Japan through Western offices, once in 1597 and again in 1726; (there had been an earlier visit, thanks to the Koreans, in 1408).[34] In 1726 two beasts had come, and though one soon died, the other which became the most famous was paraded through the country, causing an unprecedented sensation; pictures and stories were produced, and the elephant was presented to the tenno, who awarded it a peerage; it was then led off to see the shogun. The beast lived on until 1742, when it became too onerous to feed her and she was starved to death. Dead but not forgotten, the elephant bones could still be seen in Hokusai's time by those interested at the Temple of Hōen-ji in Nakano, just outside Edo; many went to pay their respects, including Shiba Kōkan.[35]

Elephant-shipping was a self-ingratiating European ploy designed to curry favour with regional panjandrums. An attempt was made in 1813 (after Hokusai wrote) by a British crew to import a Sri Lankan beast, but given the flag of the vessel, the whole was turned away and the animal not allowed ashore. Ōta Nanpo, a samurai intellectual, littérateur, doyen, and key figure in the pleasure districts of Edo, spent time in Nagasaki that year and memorialised on the non-arrival of the English elephant in a kyoka verse alluding to the foreigners' fond delight in bringing exotic quadrupeds to Japan:

> The first visit in Ōei [1408],
> By Kyōhō [1726] it's, "well come on in through
> the back door!"
> But the third time they come you have to send
> them back,
> These new-fangled elephants.[36]

Nanpo's verse captures the lilt of a brothel madam becoming increasingly familiar with a client, but this is suddenly subverted at the last

12. Katsushika Hokusai, from his *Muna-zan'yō uso no tanaoroshi,* 1802. Tokyo Metropolitan Central Library.

Gauging an elephant.

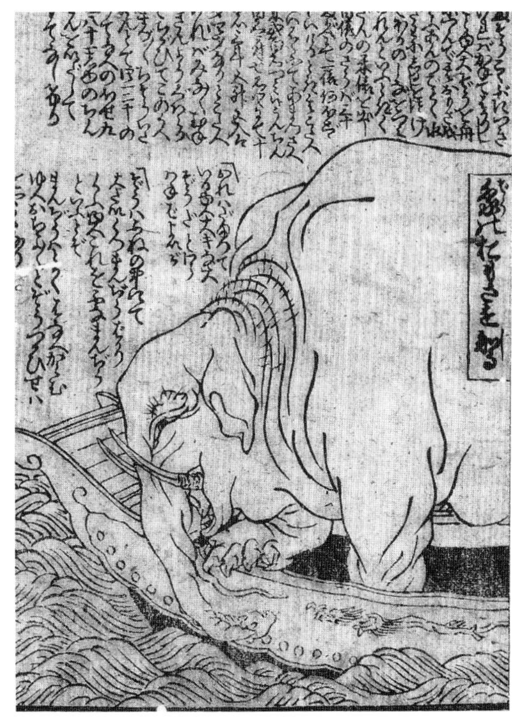

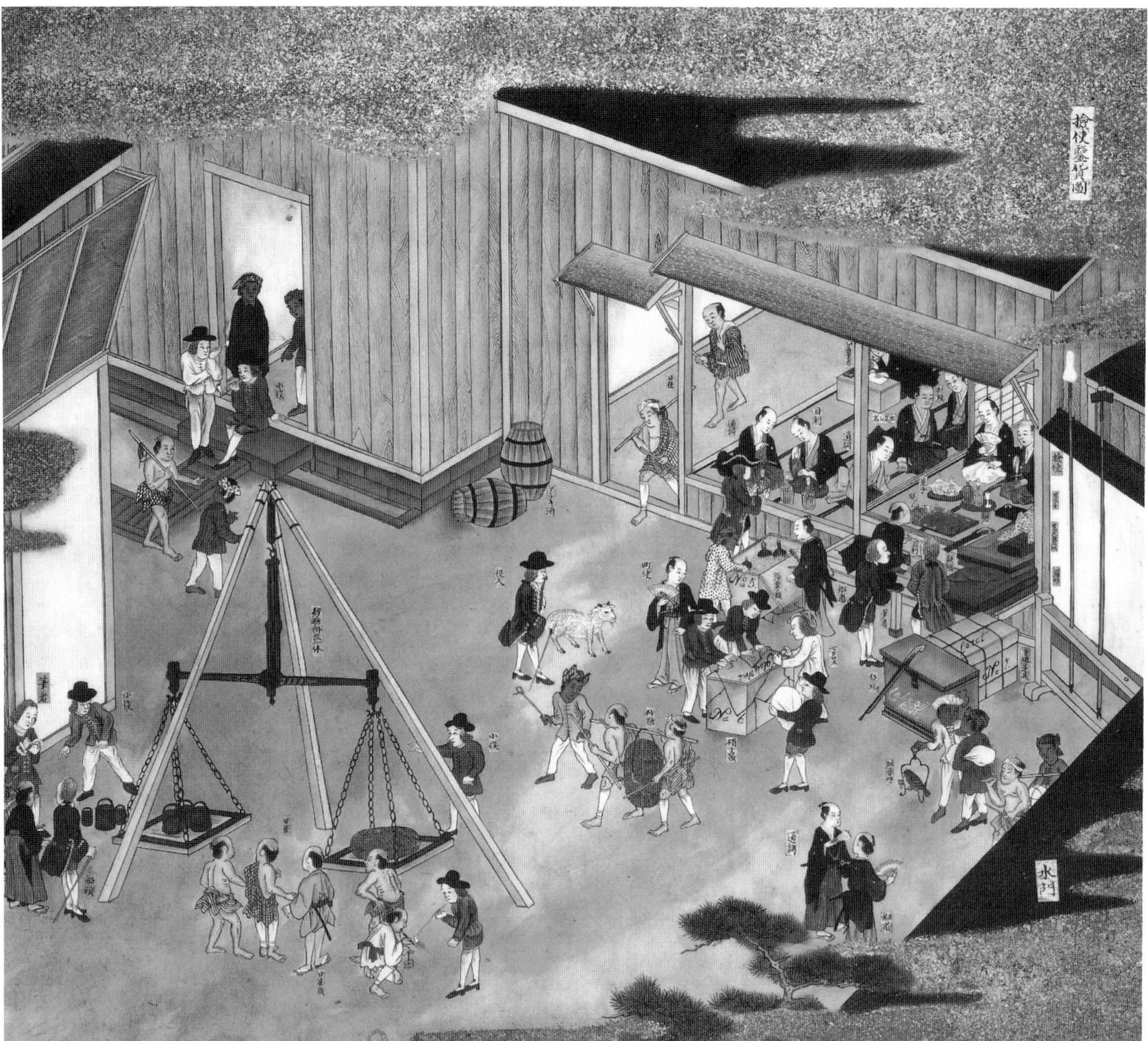

13. Unsigned, *Inspectors Studying Trading Goods*, leaf from the album *Bankan-zu*; 1797(?). Bibliothèque Nationale, Paris.

word, *shinzō*, which means both a trainee grade of prostitute and "new elephant." The Westerners, quite wrong in their assessment of how long they can keep on impressing Japan, are nevertheless brainstorming.

In his story, Hokusai appealed to a more general propensity of the VOC, already known by those who went to Nagasaki, to ship expertly delicate goods, and more generally to maximise the cargo capacity of their vessels. Their skill at loading vast quantities of goods into what were still relatively small East Indiamen was found to be genuinely remarkable. A most exact precision was required to tread the line between wastage of hold space and over-burdening. And when the imported goods were disembarked, the same mental acuity that allowed conveyance of goods safely around the globe was extended to the quantification and inventorising of the merchandise for sale. The Japanese were aghast, recorded one kapitan, at how the VOC scales responded when no more than a handkerchief was laid in the pan.[37]

Pictures of the Factory after the arrival of a ship invariably show the Dutchmen engaged in weighing and calculating, calibrating and balancing, and establishing with minute detail the specifications of their goods. An anonymous set of album leaves of life on Dejima, perhaps executed in 1797, evidently for a wealthy purchaser, includes a scene of unpacking cargo (Fig. 13),[38] this entitled *Inspectors Studying Trading Goods.* A careful rendition includes a fine Dutch balance, being used to weigh sugar and inscribed with the letters JLM and the date 1787. More scrappy, popular prints displayed what may be the same instrument, or at least a similar one; and a quickly produced piece from early in the nineteenth century depicts a balance with a date of "1839," and a title reading, *Dutchman Weighing Out Trading Goods* (Fig. 14). The European figure, with his foreign tool, calculates punctiliously numbered trading items – in this case, not elephants but elephant tusks.

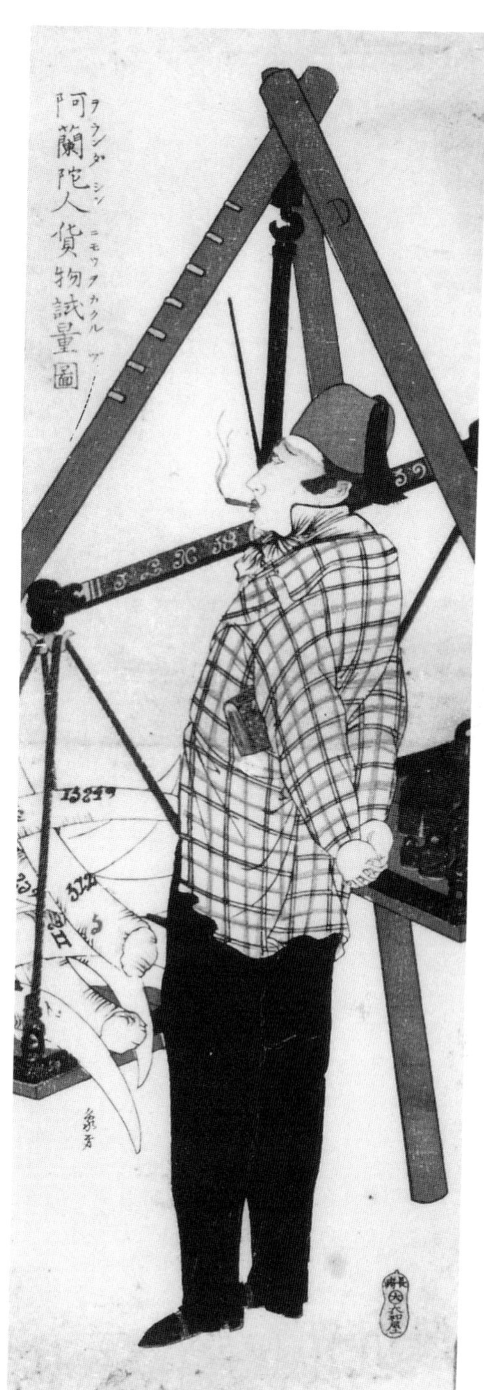

14. Unsigned, *Dutchman Weighing Out Trading Goods*, colour woodblock print; c. 1820. Kobe City Museum.

THE IMPORTANCE (OR OTHERWISE) OF ACCURACY

The Dutch measured closely to enhance the effectiveness of their trade. The activity in itself was thought good. The acceptance of a moral dimension to practical numeracy contrasted markedly with Japanese notions, especially among the elite. Fukuzawa Yukichi, for example, a student of *Rangaku* in the middle of the nineteenth century, recalled his childhood in the small and traditionalist *han* of Nakatsu in the 1830s, outlining the sense of values instilled in him:

> [My father] tried to give his children what he thought was an ideal education. The teacher lived in the compound of the lord's storage office, but having some merchants' children among his pupils, he naturally began to train them in numerals: "Two times two is four, two times three is six, etc." . . . when my father heard this, he took his children away in a fury. "It is abominable," he exclaimed, "that innocent children should be taught to use numbers."[39]

Yukichi had his own agenda (and he was subsequently prominent in opposing the Tokugawa regime), but it is true that mathematics was thought best ignored by the more refined sort of people. Yukichi's father did no more than what any reasonable samurai would have done in such circumstances.

Dislike of numeracy came partly from its associations with the baser realm of cash. But it ran deeper and stemmed from a wider mistrust of step-by-step rationalism and a horror at the creeping limitedness of logic. Calculations and estimates, numbers and measures were not the concerns of a good woman or man, and if countenanced, they would impoverish the mind and, equally heinously, erode the finer Japanese principles of unflinching loyalty and valour. Numbers made people, precisely, calculating. Some *Rangaku* scholars sought to mitigate the concern by stating that even in Holland numeracy was not exclusively fiscal. Honda Toshiaki claimed that Dutch boys were not permitted to handle coin until the age of twelve so as to keep them pure.[40] When Hōashi Banri, a mathematical pioneer of the early nineteenth century, advocated almost for the first time the teaching of numbers in samurai schools, he was regarded with either outrage or genuine amazement, and his suggestion that the abacus should be considered an "important instrument for the samurai," struck no chord.[41] To brand someone as "logical" (*rikutsu-kusai*), was to damn him indeed.

To Protestant nations particularly there was morality in the use of precision measures – "The Lord loveth a just balance." A Dutch book imported to Japan during the eighteenth century, *The Mirror of Human Activities (Spiegel van het menselyk bedryf)*, published in 1694, was a collection of pictures of one hundred employments to be seen around Holland, put together by the celebrated father-and-son team of Johannes and Caspaares Luiken. One page shows a balance-maker; as throughout, the image is accompanied by a (rather awful) tract-like poetic homily attributing ethical value to the craftsman's labour (Fig. 15). The heading reads, "Keep a True Weight and a Close Eye," and the verse runs:

> Oh, thou balancer of our hearts,
> How needful are we to be weighed!
> A temporal and eternal good,
> This is our chiefest guide.
> If our soul tip not the scale,
> Then the scales are untrue, or we are evil.[42]

It was well recognised in Japan that Dutch precisionism was rooted in a grander cosmology of knowledge.

The investigation of external phenomena was much fostered by Confucianism. Serious scholars had been pursuing their researches with diligence, and highly visibly, for generations, patronised by the Tokugawa state and by the regional *han*. But the notion of mathematical science was absent.[43] Despite certain movements towards utility (*jitsugaku*), the sense that investigation ought to be geared towards such practical ends as navigation, quantification, formulation, and commerce remained distinctly foreign. The Japanese word closest to the eighteenth-century Western notion of science was *kyūri* – literally, the investigation of *ri*, or "principle." *Kyūri* was the discipline that sought to search out the purest wellsprings at the core of nature, and it addressed precisely what lay *behind* the empirical and not therefore observationally detectable in it. To suggest an applicability of findings would have been crude, even insulting.[44] Whereas the Enlightenment *philosophe* thirsted for objectivity and an absolute purchase on natural law, the scholars of *kyūri* strove for realisation of the immanent forces that wove together "Creation" (*zōka*) – originally a Daoist term but assimilated into Confucian thought as the outward manifestation of *ri*. The Japanese endeavour was holistic, the European deconstructive.

It was his *Rangaku* pursuits that alerted Yukichi to the folly (as he saw it) of his father's ideological stance. But he swam against a tide. The few mathematical investigators of an applied sort who emerged in the eighteenth century left little trace in the wider community of thinkers, and it was probably to sustain themselves that several pretended to some affiliation with Nagasaki, or directly to the VOC. One of the great turn-of-the-century pioneers, Shizuki Tadao, derived his inspiration from Kaempfer, and he translated part of his *History of Japan*.[45]

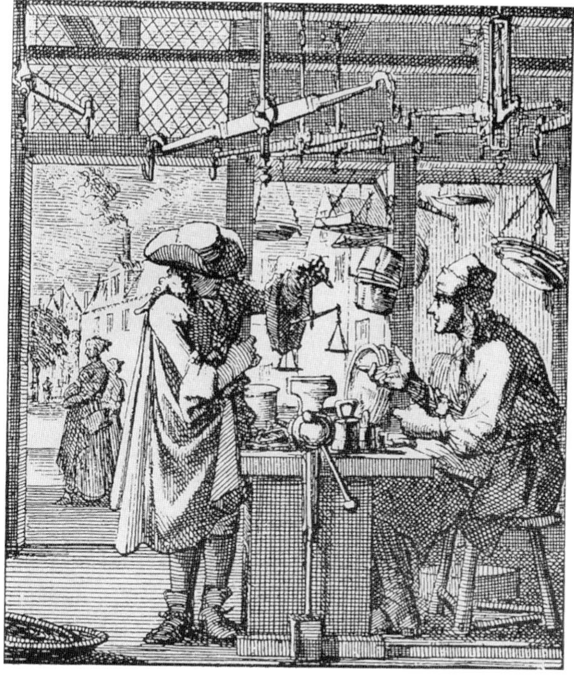

15. Johannes & Caspaares Luiken, *Balance-maker*, from their *Spiegel van het Menselyk bedryf*, 1694. Private collection.

Thunberg made an evaluation of the Japanese situation which, though embarrassing in its arrogance, revealed a valid point from his own perspective: "the Japanese nation shews *sense* or steadiness in all its undertakings, so far as without the light of science, by whose brighter rays it has not yet had the good fortune to be illumined, it can ever be guided."[46] The question was whether externalised objectivity or internal principle was the likelier way to attain purchase on the world as fact. Gotō Rishun, author of the *Talks on Holland (Oranda-banashi)*, drew a succinct comparison between the easy-to-follow down-to-earthness of the methods of European search and the more speculative, traditionalistic East-Asian tradition:

> Unlike in Eastern countries such as Japan, they do not restrict themselves to pondering and applying ancient methods, but consider [evidence] derived from the present as well as the past, and use it all. If a new method is thought up and found superior, then they discard the old in favour of it. Matters do not end there, for they observe the follow-up to the working of their applications. Occasionally they will do things that are only *ad hoc*, providing the method has proven itself in the past. It is on account of this that they have better methods than anyone else.[47]

Kōkan noted that, in Holland, a child was at liberty to correct his father if he erred – a taboo in East-Asian societies that Yukichi might have enjoyed breaching. Hirokawa Kai felt that the generally cool stance he detected in the Dutch towards received wisdom was the necessary prelude to their experimentalism; Honda Toshiaki noted that they preferred, where possible, to argue in numbers rather than words, presumably because the latter could never quite be stripped of their ancestral auras and suasive rhetorical forces. Numbers were open, plain, non-manipulable, and without flourish.[48]

In practical terms, calculation will only yield useful results if the evidence fed into the arithmetical sequences is right. It was reckoned that the Dutch insistence on supporting mathematical work with empirical observation, taking nothing on trust, was germane. The importance of *visual* calculation was repeatedly stressed by *Rangaku* commentators. Seeing allowed the accretion of historical interpretations to be chipped off so that every entry in a sum could be individually assessed before being logged into an overall web of data. Miura Baien, for example, an independent thinker from Kyushu who later became teacher of Hoashi Banri, spent time in Nagasaki in the summer of 1778, and having met Yoshio Kōsaku and encountered the Dutch, he wrote of twin supports upholding Western science – the practical and the visual. Unlike linguistic analyses, he held, visual intellection was universalisable, such that, "Since European sciences entered Japan, by means of observation and experiment, our information has become more exact than before."[49] The epistemology and the data were transferable.

Sugita Genpaku wrote in the first history of *Rangaku* how, when he took up the newly imported medical branch of anatomy, he began like a good Confucianist, using classical books and learning by rote; but he later rejected the procedure, turning to what he considered the Dutch method, "learning by observation" (*minarai*). That sort of study had previously been only the method of workmen, labourers in practical crafts, and not considered right for scholars.[50] Observation, Gentaku contended, was the only way to dispel the error that eventually infested any academic tradition – what he referred to as the "thousand old [notions]" (*senko*). Precision gazing was for him the bedrock of all learning and the sole means of stemming the build-up of falsity over time.

This ocular assessment, in the terminology of Yamagata Bantō, an Osaka scholar of the merchant class, was *menoko zan'yō*.[51] Not a new phrase but one given an emended meaning by him, *menoko zan'yō* signified *precise visual calculation*. It was held to be a feature of *Ran*. After one of his first sorties into reading a Dutch book in translation, Bantō remarked: "the Western approach to knowledge is almost entirely infused by precise visual calculation. In astronomy, medicine, and craftsmanship the Japanese and Chinese do not come close to it."[52]

THE ICON OF *RAN*: THE "*EREKITERU*"

An anecdote concerning the compulsory requirement of vision in all the discoveries of *Ran* may be related here. We may address one device already mentioned above, the static-electricity generator, or "electrostatic cabinet," as it was known in English at the time. The precision aura of machines in general will be considered in the following chapter. Called an *erekiteru* in Japanese, the generator was invoked by Onitake as a quintessential piece of technology, and was also shown prominently in Akisato Ritō's gazetteer depiction of the Parasol Hall foreign-goods shop in Osaka (Figs. 6 and 11). In general, the novel and extraordinary *erekiteru* served as an icon of *Ran*, and most commentators on the West discussed it somewhere.

The purpose of the machine was to educe a spark from a patient's head. This was believed to have the medical value of removing excess heat, though some (like Benjamin Franklin) voiced doubts about the treatment.[53] Tachibana Nankei described how the *erekiteru* worked in his *Record of Pleasurable Travels in the West* (*Seiyū-ki*) of 1795, the journal of his Nagasaki trip:

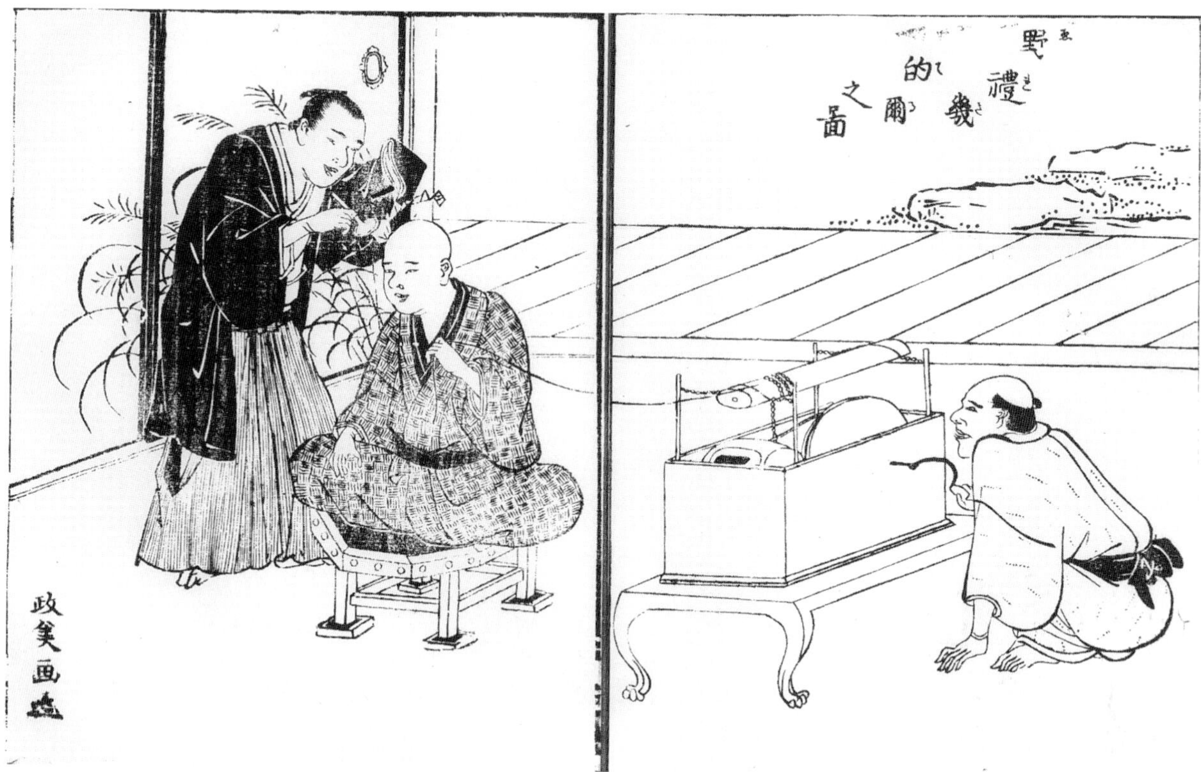

16. Kitao Masayoshi, *Erekiteru,* from Morishima Chūryō, *Kōmō zatsuwa,* 1787. National Diet Library, Tokyo.

> The device called an *erekiteru* came to Japan twenty-three years ago. It is a machine for drawing fire from a person's body. Wheels are set within a box; it is just under a metre and an iron chain, five or six metres in length and ending in a looped handle, leads off. You have someone grasp the handle and then start the wheels rotating, so that power is transmitted along the chain. This provokes a reaction in the person, and little bits of paper brought up to them will move and dance of their own accord; if someone brings their hand close, you can hear a sound like spitting fat, and see a flame flying out. No-one who has yet to see the amazingness of this device will believe in it.[54]

The shogunal physician Katsuragawa Hoshū owned a generator, and he was impressed; a picture executed by Kitao Masayoshi for Morishima Chūryō's *Red-fur Miscellany,* shows the young doctor with the conductor being held near his shaven head, with a servant and other figures, presumably his brother Chūryō, on hand (Fig. 16).[55] An illustration of a cabinet of a somewhat different construction appeared in Egbert Buys's multi-volume encyclopaedia, *A New and Complete Dictionary* (*Nieuw en volkomen woordenboek*); (Fig. 17). Buys's was the latest word in household reference works in the period under discussion; published in 1769–78 and imported to Japan within a few years, it was often cited. The alphabetical arrangement of the entries fortuitously places *electriciteit* next to *elephant.*

Gotō Rishun thought the *erekiteru* a miracle of mechanics, able to make the human body appear like a Buddhist divinity, aflame and haloed in fire. Nonsense, thought Matsudaira Sadanobu, since Tanuma Okitsugu's downfall head of the shogunal administration, and he wrote in 1797, "The love of primitive-made *kiki* in this land really goes too far. Everyone wants to have a play with this machine . . . I can't see how it could be any use to anyone."[56] In Europe, too, scepticism about the clinical value of the generator emerged, but many a gentleman continued to keep an electrostatic cabinet among his philosophical apparatus, and during the latter part of the century the things became (as Buta had said when Sunperupei produced his) quite common. But the first person to achieve the difficult task of fabricating one domestically was Hiraga Gennai, the samurai from Tamatsu *han* who had renounced his rank to pursue his scientific interests. Gennai became familiar with Hoshū and mentor to Chūryō. He wrote in 1771 (the date does not fit with Nankei's chronology): "Even in Holland there are few who understand the device. Koreans, Chinese and Indians have never seen it even in their wildest dreams. Mine was the first of its kind to be made in Japan since this land came into being."[57] Later, other generators were constructed locally, seemingly in large numbers, and the one in the Parasol Hall was made in Japan, as can be told from its packing case, dumped in the neighbouring room and labelled "*Erekiteru* by the Precision Craftsman Ōmi" (a person of whom more will be said in the next chapter).

Gennai specifically contrasted the Dutch mechanical inventiveness represented by the generator with the non-scientific thinking of continental Asians, and he went on to relate what had happened when he showed his machine to a senior samurai and official Confucian scholar, Ishikura Shingozaemon.[58] Although steeped in Chinese learning, Shingozaemon candidly confessed himself at a loss to explain the workings of the generator, and he promised to read up on the subject when he returned home. The typical Confucian answer, suggested Gennai! – and, telling Shingozaemon to ignore his books and avoid paper discussions, he enjoined him to use his eyes: "Look at it if you want to find out the origin of that spark." The ratiocinations of Confucianists, Gennai says, are "fart-theory" (*hōhi-ron*), blown out into the face of scientific inquiry. He advocates a mode that is practical, in close physical contact with material

17. Unsigned, *Static-electricity generator* and *Elephant*, from Egbert Buys, *Niuew en volkommen woodenboek*, 1769–78. Private collection.

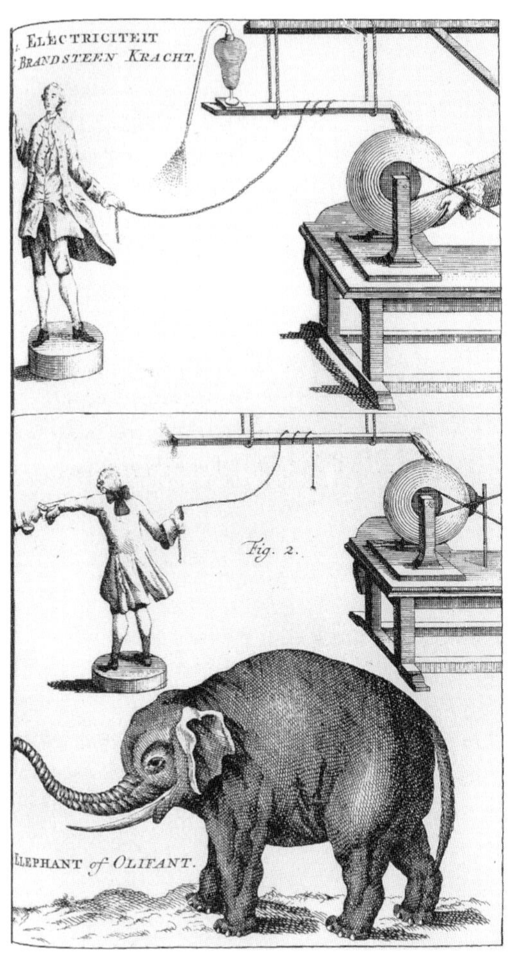

things, and without precedents. Machines guarantee rigour, but vision alone provides the referent in this construction of reason.

PRECISION AND PRECISION TOOLS

Dutch obsessions relied on visual evidence. Where it was not empirically forthcoming, sight was extracted by tools and machines with optical scales or read-outs so that matter not susceptible to ocular affirmation – heat, distance, weight, time – was rendered visual by way of barometers, thermometers, sextants, balances, or clocks.

Everything needed its digital equivalent. The infinitesimal divisions on the scales of imported tools showed with what finicky seriousness this was taken. Nagakubo Sekisui, an official from Sendai who visited Nagasaki in 1765, saw a Dutch thermometer for the first time and remarked on its extraordinary exactitude; "it actually has twenty-four demarcations," he wrote.[59] Shiba Kōkan illustrated the large barometric thermometer that hung on the wall of the kapitan's rooms on Dejima (Fig. 18); some years later, when he obtained a similar piece of his own, he demonstrated the utility of its multiple gradations by carrying it from Kyoto to Osaka, thereby revealing how, contrary to empirical im-

18. Shiba Kōkan, from his *Saiyū ryōdan*, 1794. Private collection. *Rooms of the head of the VOC Factory in Nagasaki.*

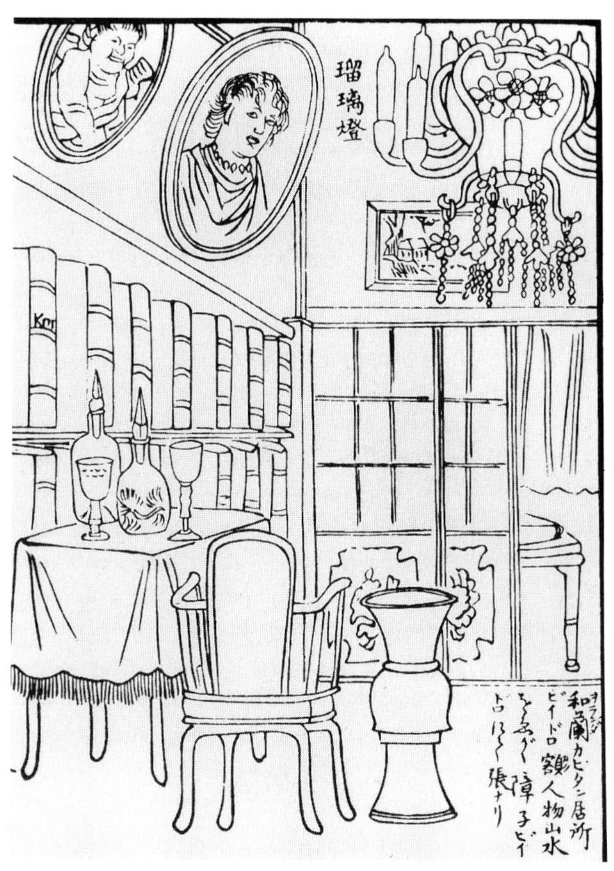

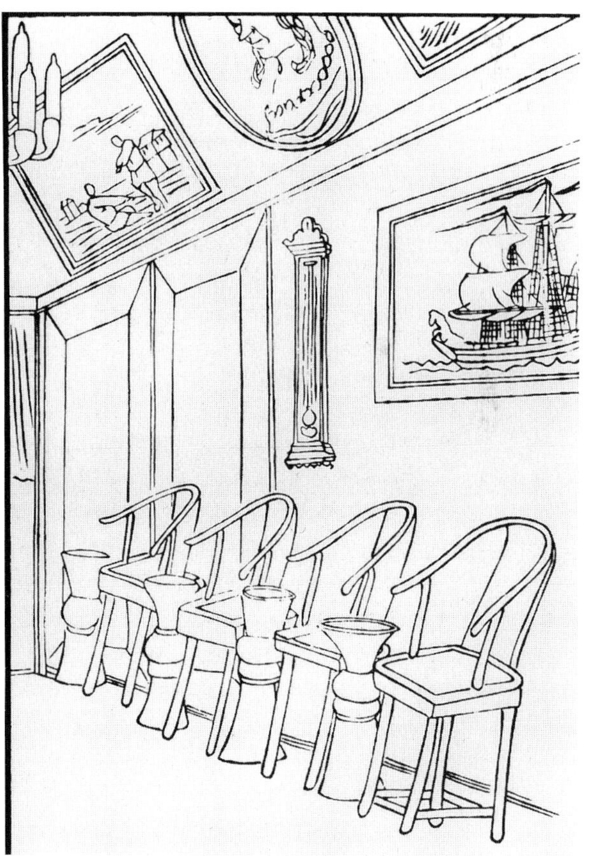

pressions, the temperature was identical in both places – a sweltering 93 degrees, in fact.[60]

Kōkan did not stop at the thermometer, but devoted much writing to discussions of the many precision tools he had either used or seen; he drew a quadrant (*zōgen-ki*) for illustration in his *Dutch Theories of the Heavens (Oranda tensetsu)*, at pains to show the full extent of its complex double scale, and going so far as to provide an inset detailing the minutely accurate markings (Fig. 19).[61] When dials and gauges were numbered in foreign scripts (Roman or Arabic), or additionally labelled in Western languages, the foreign derivation of tool-derived numeracy was rendered abundantly clear: the shogun's observatory checked the weather on a barometer made in England that told pressure on a face reading from "Stormy" to "Very Dry" (Fig. 20).[62]

The proliferation of tools brought areas that had once lain beyond the range of human capabilities within the field of calculation. Tachibana Nankei summed up: "There are things which the naked eye cannot see, and the human body cannot estimate. The Primitive Peoples' [Dutch] instruments are here to address this problem, and thanks to them we can now quantify those things in perceptible ways. . . ."[63]

The eighteenth century was a propitious time to begin the import of mechanical devices. European instrument-making underwent dramatic advances from around the 1750s. Buys's *Complete Dictionary* laid repeated stress on the importance of the "mechanick Arts," and indeed his subtitle claimed that he exhausted all important fields – namely, "art, science, custom, sickness, medicine, plants, flowers, fruit, tools, machines, etc." Readers were given to understand that the making of instruments for empirical investigation, like their sober application, was a genuine social duty.[64] Science was irrevocably machine-based. As the Worshipful Company of Scientific Instrument Makers in London put it in their motto, *Sine nobis scientia languet* ("Without us, science dies away"), and Goi Ranjū of Osaka recorded the centrality of instruments to the whole project of modern science identifying them as coterminous with what it meant to think in the manner of the West: "Unless a fact has been ascertained by what we call precise visual calculation (*menoko zan'yō*), and beyond that, can be gauged with a fixed standard of measurement such as that provided by an experimental device, the Dutch do not offer statements about it, nor do they attempt to use it."[65]

A vast range of "Dutch" equipment was available for the would-be collector and quantifier of evidence. Pieces were generically referred to, as Ranjū did, as "experimental devices" (*kenki*), a word newly coined to emphasise how to cull data directly from external phenomena. *Kenki* fixed findings in recognised units of notation immediately insertable into arithmetical formulations, with no human intervention clouding.[66]

Experimental devices might more generally come under the rubric of "precision craftsmanship" – *saiku* – a term long present in the Japanese language to refer to items of intricate finish, but occurring with astonishing frequency in commentaries on imports from the West. In the love competition for Buta's hand, Onitake had told how Sunperupei matched Chin Rinten's Chinese sage-magic with his own Dutch precision craftsmanship (*Oranda saiku*).[67] *Saiku* became a veritable synonym for *Ran* goods, as involvement with mechanical contrivances became the overarching concern of the *Rangaku* scholar. When a fictionalised biography of Gennai was produced after his untimely death in 1780, the anonymous writer was content to account for blank periods in the subject's life by merely asserting that he had been deep in "Dutch *saiku*" – a thoroughly bland but altogether convincing way of justifying how the legendary experimenter had passed his time.[68] *Ran* and *saiku* rolled off the tongue as a pair. Nankei was emphatic: "when it comes to the marvels of *saiku*, the Dutch outstrip all people on earth."[69]

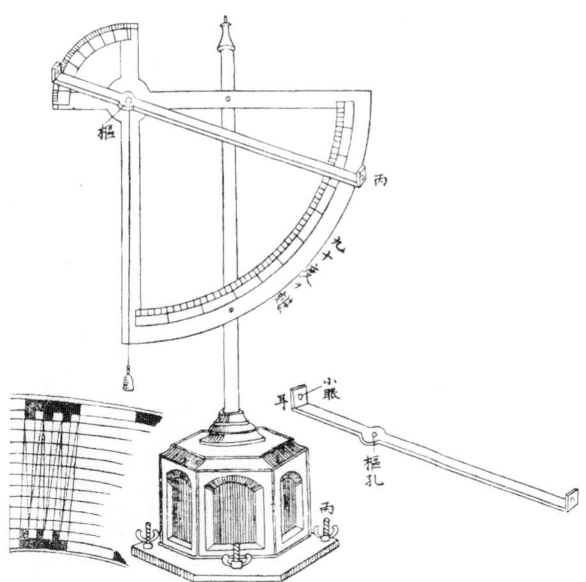

19. Shiba Kōkan, from his *Oranda tensetsu*, 1795. Reproduced from Nakai Sōtarō, *Shiba Kōkan* (Atoriesha, 1942).

Imported quadrant, with details.

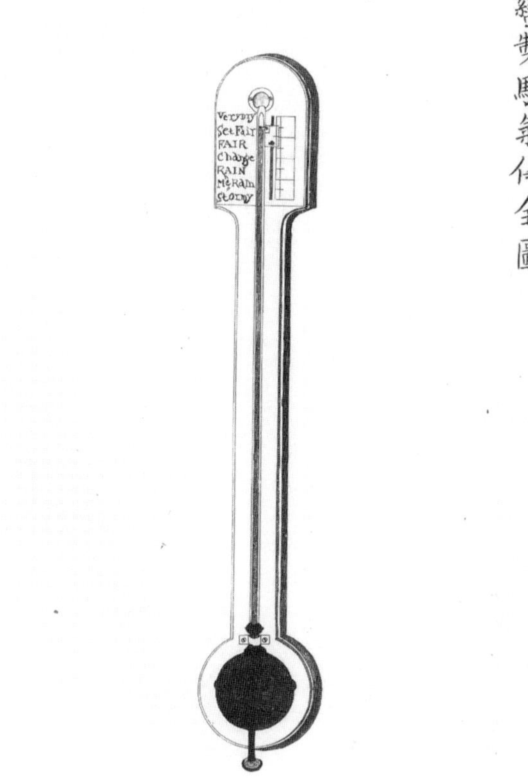

20. Unsigned, *Foreign-made Barometer*, drawing from Shibukawa Kagesuke (et al. eds.), *Kansei rekisho* vol. 20, 1853. National Diet Library, Tokyo.

A host of similar terms emerged, or were revamped, to relieve over-use of *saiku* and *kenki*: *kikō*, "rare skill"; *kihin* "rare goods"; *kiki*, "rare devices"; and *kiku*, "rare craftsmanship." In 1811, the great publicist Kōkan promised a work that would deal with the whole range, to be entitled *Dutch Kiku*, although (as often with him) readers waited vainly for it to appear.[70]

POPULAR PRECISION

Kōkan floated an idea that the government should shoulder the cost of foreign instruments, as no individual could be expected to buy them all alone. As a townsman with no daimyo to fund his studies, Kōkan may have felt financial constraints particularly keenly. But it was important, he thought, for the maximum number of people to have access. He suggested that imports be exchanged with the VOC for the rice the shogunate levied in tax.[71] The government did buy Western instruments, but only ranking samurai had access to them, and even then only if they could demonstrate due reason. *Han* governments provided tools or books for their official scholars; again, circulation was monitored. Those who did manage to use a real rare device, however, Yoshio Kōsaku said, whatever it was, would be overcome by an ecstasy of wonder and disbelief.[72]

Many *saiku* goods were useless until one had the knowledge to work them properly. The kapitan David Brouwer told how in 1743 the then shogunal physician and his students approached him in the Nagasaki-ya and "showed me all kinds of antiquities and mathematical instruments. They asked me the purpose these objects served. It took me until 9 P.M. before I had finished writing a report on how these instruments worked."[73] Such generosity with their time was not often forthcoming, and most of the Dutch were anyway none too informed themselves. The shogun Yoshimune summoned an expert in astronomical equipment from Holland, but no one ever arrived.[74] To the Japanese majority, Western instruments remained bewildering, almost fantastic, and they entered an arena of discourse detached from much likelihood of application. On a popular level, devices were more tropes than tools, constituting the visible parameters of the Batavian temperament, eked out by only the vaguest knowledge of how they were actually used.

Edo, being the biggest city, was also the centre of thrill over the idea of "strange devices." Fascination with the weird was a feature of the shogunal city: "compared with the people of Edo," wrote one kapitan (miffed when back on Dejima that his "telescope with a silver plated machine" did not get the respect it deserved), "the people of Nagasaki do not seem to appreciate outlandish things."[75] So the period of the *hofreis* was when excitement reached fever pitch; in 1783, Ōtsuki Gentaku recorded how Edoites' obsession with Dutch goods was reaching all-year-round proportions, though this did not please him much, and that anything new or unusual had to be marketed as made in Europe, or at least Dutch-inspired, if it was to sell. No doubt this was hyperbole, but he said the populace had taken to hanging up shop signs written in Dutch, even if no one could read them, and advertising their wares as "rare goods" (*kihin*) or "cunning little things" (*sasai no hin*), "and by this means making large amounts of money." Why the canny Edo tradesmen were doing this was simple: "the people of this country adore Dutch strange devices."[76]

The full extent of the European experimental kit was not imported, or certainly not in evidence among the common people. But if insufficient products entered the country at the right price, rather than disappoint, merchants improvised, judiciously supplementing their imported stock with "Dutch" goods that were perfectly fraudulent. This actually aided the diffusion of a *Ran* that was utterly notional. Many items did the rounds in the form of pure hearsay, as ideas spread through the popular domain with reality steaming far behind. Thoroughly fictional levels of instrumental achievement were ever more wildly dreamed up, as the rhetoric of mechanised activity or machine-aided sensory awareness was uncoupled entirely from the real powers of actual objects. Jumbling and mythologising were rife. But in the absence of chances to explore devices in detail, it was unclear where credence ought to stop. Sunperupei's hot-air balloon was said by Onitake to double as a diving bell – but was the fact that one machine could be both intrinsically less plausible than that any could be either? With new innovations – or talk of them – arriving continually (the balloon was known in Japan within months of the Montgolfiers' ascent[77]), gullibility was not readily checked. A senryu writer put it, half in fun, half in earnest:

> How I long to
> Take a telescope,
> And put it to my ear![78]

At the time of his writing in the 1760s, this desire was wishful thinking; but such was the pace of change that within twenty years the longing was realised, as it were, through the introduction from the 1780s of ear trumpets. Kōkan published a study of how these worked and by the end of the century was fabricating his own, probably after a model illustrated in Buys's *Dictionary*.[79]

Mechanics for enhancement of sight and sound (the loud-haler was also known) had a kind of complementarity, and it was probably that which led the senryu writer to compose his little verse. But the association of hearing aids and telescopes was not unreasonable given that the former were called in Japanese "ear-lenses" (*jikyō* or *mimi-kagami*), just as in English the word "auriscope" was also used. In 1798, Hekizentei Kunenbō, the writer whose parody of Gentaku's *Rangaku* academy was cited in Chapter 1, wrote a kibyoshi whose title, *What on Earth!? Two Strange Devices* (*Hade mezurashiki futatsu no utsuwa*), announced the book as addressing the two instruments. Eye- and ear-lenses, in this case a microscope, are accorded semi-miraculous powers. Although designed for their separate purposes, the two are paired and made mutually supportive, for while the phonetic gloss on the title indicates a reading of "two strange devices," the characters themselves say "two strange *male and female* devices." The instruments are paired as *yin* and *yang*, the engulfing ear trumpet and the phallic microscope, joined as if in sexual union and coming together to propagate the brood of never-before-known empirical fact which swarms into the field of awareness. Kunenbō's illustrator, Chōkōsai Eishō, showed the tools in action on the book's jacket – ear trumpet wedged in the canal of a close listener, and lens (which resembles in shape the modern telescope and hence is phallic), screwed snugly in the eye of a scrutinising viewer.

Kunenbō's story tells of how one Mr. Santō (a pun on Santō Kyōden) was visited by his

21. Chōkōsai Eishō, from Hekizentei Kunenbō, *Hade mezurashiki futatsu no utsuwa*, 1784. Tokyo Metropolitan Central Library.

Kabe and Santō use 'strange devices'.

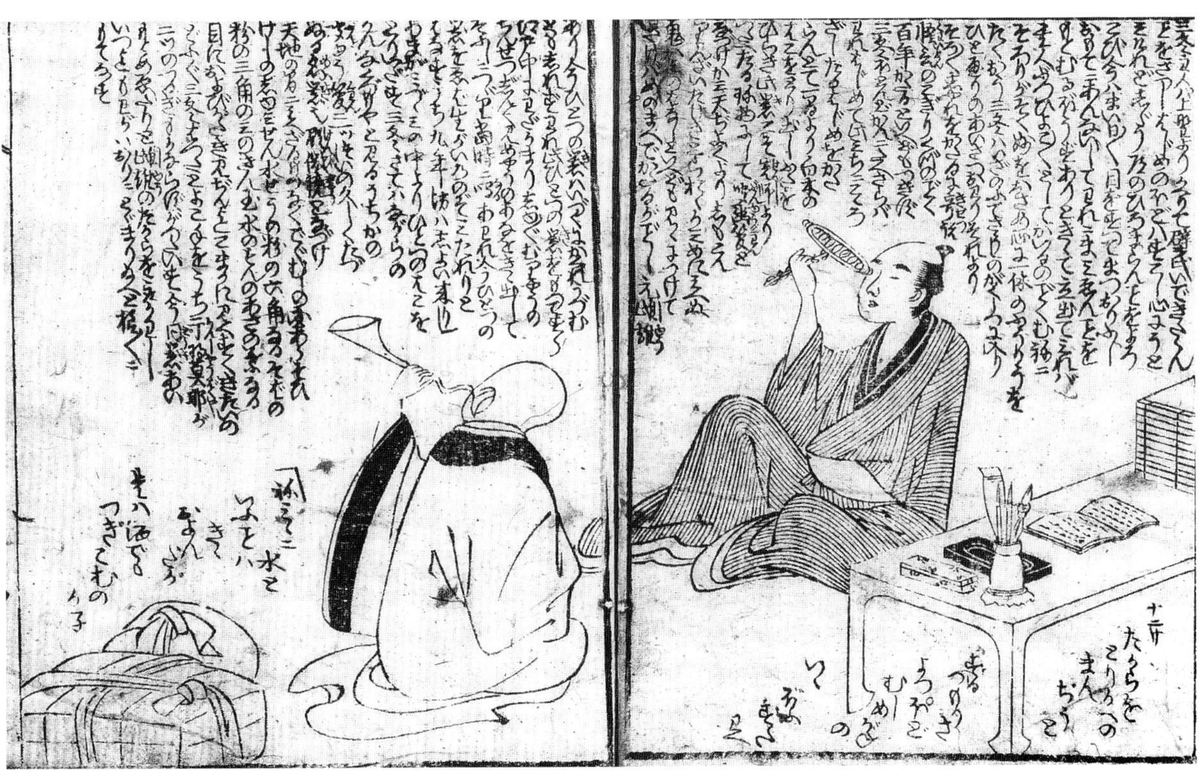

friend Mr. Kabe (a reworking of the author's own name; Fig. 21).[80] Santō is initially annoyed by the visit, but soon warms when he sees what Kabe has brought: "He produced a box of white wood, and lifted the lid; inside was a rare instrument that had been passed to him by his teacher – a mystery-hearing pipe."[81] It may look like having a sake cup stuck in your ear, remarks the author, but once it is properly inserted, you will hear the words of Heaven itself and eavesdrop on the Isle of Devils; better still, Kabe expands, the gossip of all Edo will become audible. Reaching for his second item, Kabe opens a bag apparently containing trash, but rummages out a microscope; this device, he says, will reveal the international wars of insects and show the shapes of crystals and seeds. Excited, both begin the search.

PRECISION AND PRECISION DRAWING

The umbrella term of *saiku* (precision or close-wrought devices) was exceedingly capacious, and more a catch-all for the sum of imported oddities than a genuine category of object. A slew of disparate things was comfortably accommodated. Visual representations could be called *saiku* too. Kōkan, who worked extensively in the Western style, referred to his output as "*saiku* images."[82] The role of imported pictures must be considered. Minutely executed depictions were central to the endeavour of *Ran,* for without it, nothing could be accurately taken down and retained. Ōtsuki Gentaku pointed out in his *Ladder of Dutch Studies* (*Rangaku kaitei*), in a section aptly entitled "Precision" (*seishō*), that "[the Dutch] work in unmatchable detail (*kuwashiki*). This applies to their medical work, and beyond that to astronomy, geography, surveying, calendrical studies, and so forth. In each case they examine the theories and methods of the subject under study with precision, clarity, and exactitude."[83] And he went on to explain the relevance of this to art:

> There are many important studies made by them, but leaving aside the contents for a moment, just consider the pictures they contain. You will see how living things are illustrated to look alive, and dried out things as dried out.[84] . . . Every image approximates exactly to reality both in colour and form.

Gentaku construed the Western pictorial idiom as primarily scientific and concerned with the seizure and transmission of experimental findings. To him and other *Rangaku* experts, European artists strove for (and had achieved) a technique for the exact recording of samples seen.

Western precision drawing and the stylistic features that sustained it (shading, perspective, cast shadows, and the like) were introduced in Japan randomly for no qualified instructor ever arrived, but one fairly comprehensive source was *The Art of Painting in All Its Branches* (*Het groot schilderboek*) a large compilation published in 1707 by Gérarde de Lairesse. Lairesse was a pupil of Rembrandt who defected to follow a high and airy French baroque, and (like Onitake, incidentally), had lost his nose to syphilis; the disease had made Lairesse blind, and no longer able to paint, he wrote, an amanuensis taking down his quite severe discourses on visual representation. The resulting book was massively successful in Europe, and was much studied in *Rangaku* circles, too.[85]

The Western style was identified by various terms in Japan, *Horurando-e* (Dutch pictures) or *Seiyō-ga* (Western pictures). A common word for a picture being *ga,* one label was simply *Ranga,* "*Ran* pictures." The term *saiga* (seemingly a contraction of *saiku* and *ga*) previously existed in the language but was extensively reused with reference to the imported style. More generally, the *Ranga* manner was defined by recoupings from the classical vocabulary of art criticism:

"copying authenticity" (*shashin* or *shinsha*), "copying reality" (*shajitsu*), or "copying life" (*shasei* or *seisha*) – all old terms that acquired an aura of importation. Such language was used in the teeth of dominant beliefs about what constituted quality in art, and *shashin*, *shasei*, and the rest had gone into abeyance because the banner declaration of the authoritative schools was that pictures should "copy ideas," *shai*. "Ideas" were associated with renditions of sentiment in brushed ink. The removal of all traces of brushwork was a startling feature of the Western manner – a point that was repeated *ad nauseam* by Kōkan in particular, a representative salvo offering that, "in distinction to Japanese and Chinese painting, *Ranga* does not have brush dharma (*hippō*), brush energy (*hissei*), or brush thought (*hitsui*)."[86] This continued to be a truism of Japanese interpretations of Western picture-making for decades. Takamori Kankō, writing in 1814, stated similarly,

> The European way of making pictures is different from that of our country. They never enter into debates about "brush energy" or "brush dharma," but rather perfect the laws of "copying authentically"; we would do well to come to terms with the meticulousness (*bisai*) that has been brought over from the West in their intricate (*seimyō*) pictures.[87]

Ruling out the "brush mind" – those contours of aesthetic awareness which since antique times had been said to allow creative genius to flourish – was, by standards of the time, a rash move.[88] The loss of the calligraphic brushstroke in favour of the unaccidented line of *Ranga* might mean loss of all aesthetic claims, resulting in banality.

Gentaku, and later Kōkan, drew attention to a terminology of pictures used in Holland that was different, though equally full. He noted how the word *konst* carried quite different implications from analogous Japanese words (*gei*, *bi*, *gadō*, and so on). As Kōkan wrote, probably referring to Buys:

> The word *konst* is to be found in a certain Dutch dictionary. The term might be translated "skill" (*takumi*), or "careful thought" (*kangae*), or again "to consider" (*omou*). . . . The Dutch call painting *konstschilder*. Unlike Chinese and Japanese artists, they do not theorise about the emotional content of their brushwork, but rather, make "authentic copies." Thanks to this, when you look at their pictures it is like seeing the real thing, or walking through the real place.[89]

Given the state of linguistic affairs, some *Rangaku-sha* preferred to leave *konst* untranslated, only transliterating it as *konsuto*. Western picture-making was, by this definition, not about the creation of what might be termed works of art but only of accurate renditions. This brought two-dimensional depiction into the embrace of scientific accuracy and put art at the service of experimentation. *Rangaku* scholars specifically singled out for praise Western works in which all aesthetic content was subordinate to other imperatives, notably informational, like maps, charts, and diagrams.[90]

Satake Yoshiatsu, the young and enthusiastic daimyo of Akita, was preoccupied with *Ranga* after Hiraga Gennai visited his *han* in 1773, and shortly thereafter wrote the first two Japanese treatises on European representation. Satake is customarily known by his sobriquet, Shozan, and he frequently sealed his paintings in Dutch, *Siozan schildereij* (more poetically he also used, *Segotter vol Beminner*, sea-god full of love).[91] In his treatise *A Summary of the Laws of Pictures (Gahō kōyrō)*, Yoshiatsu stated, "people who make pictures their work have perennially held objectives like the drawing of maps and the recording of watercourses for cities." This opinion was outrageous polemic: such had *never* been the goals in any part of East Asia; indeed, one of the greatest fathers of the artistic canon, the fifth-century Chinese calligrapher Wang Wei, had stated precisely the opposite: "when the ancients made paintings, it was not in order to plan defences of cities or differentiate the locales of provinces, to make mountains and plateaus and to delineate watercourses."[92] But Yoshiatsu was willing to sacrifice historical actuality in pursuit of his goal of rewriting the discourse of visual representation; when he wrote "people who make pictures," he secretly meant pictures of *Ran*.

That the *Rangaku* interpretation of Western pictures seems partial to present-day critics need not be emphasised. In practice, it was accepted even in the eighteenth century that such a reductive definition was not adequate to satisfy the desires of buyers, much less the aspirations of art producers. Dutch-style artists did not, in practice, rule decorative works out of order, so long as they continued to conform to the criteria of precision in line and colour. Kōkan painted many pieces clearly intended for aesthetic delight by the sort of patron who simply wanted a charming landscape or figure. Nevertheless, he did not omit to dilate that the aesthetic response was contingent on the "authenticity" of the image, not on its "idea," and that the real purpose of the picture was to give a sense of being in the place or with the person depicted. Musing or entrancement were not solicited. Lord Satake dismissed the practices of "hiding within pictures" (*gain*) and "meditating on pictures" (*gazen* or *zenga*). Never mind that one of the foremost painters and theorists in the recent history of Chinese art, Dong Qichang, had taken the studio name Meditator on Pictures, Gazen, and was emulated in this in the 1750s by that pinnacle of Japanese literati masters, Ike Taiga; Satake Yoshiatsu would have none of it, and ruled the aspiration "absurd."[93]

Kōkan painted views of that most poetic of Japanese scenes, Mount Fuji, and he confided to a friend, "the people of Kyoto have never seen Fuji so I give out a good number of pictures of it." Fuji was an extraordinary sight ("that miracle of nature Fousini Jama," as the VOC called it),[94] but the sentiments Kōkan wished to provoke relied on the minimal possible discrepancy between the mountain as seen by those who passed by it and the depicted form (Fig. 22). Kōkan went on, "my *Mt. Fujis*, representing the finest scene in all Japan, are drawn entirely according to the Dutch rules of 'copying authenticity.' "[95]

The notion that replicating external likenesses was at least one aim of pictures won currency even beyond the group of *Ranga* painters, and of course it would be foolhardy to suggest that mimesis had never been thought of in the history of East-Asian art. The notion of an accurate "saiku picture" was not universally accepted as the primary driving force in art, but it was still recognised that there was a place for it. Even those generally opposed to the Dutch movement, or who found precision pictures limiting, were ready to grant that the *Ranga* took first place when it came to verisimilitude. Nakayama Kōyō, a painter in the literati style, allowed in a treatise of 1775 that "none can copy from life (*seisha*) better than the Dutch," a generous evaluation, as the manner he practised was predicated precisely on the *un*binding of representation from empirical vision.[96] Literati (*bunjin*) artists produced "mind landscapes" or "scenes from within the heart" and did not wish to replicate the hills and rivers that actually dotted the earth, much less its man-made barbicans and bulwarks.

Those outside *Ran* circles might become temporarily infected with precisionism. It is recorded that Nagasawa Rosetsu, an eccentric painter from Kyoto and a man of no known *Ranga* leanings, drew a magnified flea on a screen, probably several metres across so that it covered the full pictorial surface. The work does not survive and its stylistic features cannot be told, but the motivation must have been *Ran*.[97] Rosetsu seems to have wished to grant the viewer a clear replication of the insect form, now expanded large enough to see, offering to all the new gaze – that which science had newly vouchsafed through

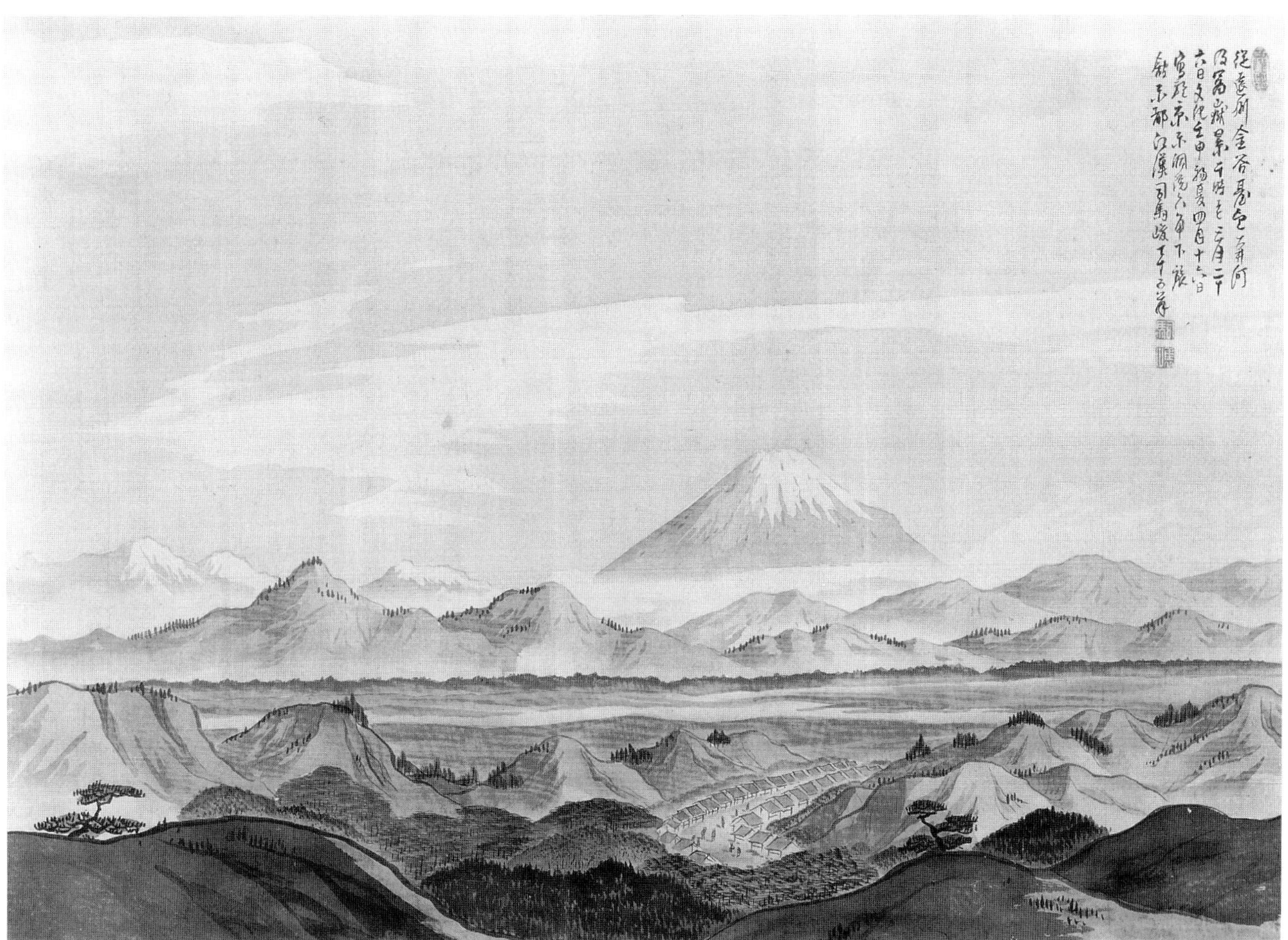

22. Shiba Kōkan, *Mt Fuji Seen across the Ōi from Kanayadai*, hanging scroll, after 1812. Kimiko and John Powers Collection.

imported instruments of vision; indeed, Rosetsu is said to have used a microscope to examine the flea before committing it to such huge delineation. Compare with this the refusal of the celebrated, later seventeenth-century Japanese-style painter Tosa Mitsuoki to depict any object larger than life-size; Mitsuoki would not indulge in magnification presumably on the grounds that to do so would bias the form of an object over its spirit or idea.[98] But that was exactly what Rosetsu must have wished. Motoori Norinaga, a strong critic of imported ideas, wrote in his treatise of 1799, *On Pictures* (*Ga no koto*), "people make depictions of birds and insects, and though there are plenty who do them in punctilious enough detail (*komaka ni kuwashiku*), precious few give them the spirit to take off and fly."[99] And how could a flea several metres across hope to fly?

The date of Rosetsu's *Flea* is not known, but

it may have been executed around the time he came into contact with that singular enthusiast for the microscope Tachibana Nankei; both men were samurai, and had a good enough relationship for Rosetsu to make a series of pictures to accompany Nankei's travel writings of his trip to Nagasaki.[100] All that is known of the *Flea* is a verse composed by Minagawa Kien, a prominent Kyoto intellectual, poetry teacher of Hirokawa Kai and a man who had an almost brother-like relationship with Rosetsu's own teacher, Maruyama Ōkyo:[101]

> He first copied down the insect as seen in the clear lens;
> Then it was just an insect,
> But who would not now think it a bird flying through the woods?
> Who would doubt it to be some heroic beast running over low hills?
> He copied its shape in colour,
> And it fills the entire screen.
> Look at it closely, the downy hairs have become gigantic.
> Now I realise the labour of Creation![102]

Kien conveys his sense of shock at the sudden appearance of an "authentic" insect on the traditional format of the paper screen, and he transfers his arrest to the poetic diction: just as the precisely rendered flea sits sharply in focus, so too the flow of Kien's classical phrase is jarred by the insertion of the non-lyrical (but eminently scientific) words "look closely" (*teishi*).

MECHANICAL PICTURES

An actual *Ran* picture, being a transcription of nature, should betray no evidence of the hand that made it, no more than of the brush that spread the ink. The removal of the personality of the painter was regarded as absolutely necessary and hailed by protagonists as the major advantage of the style. Satake Yoshiatsu disliked the perpetual prioritising of an artist's psychic state over the beholder's acquisition of knowledge, and he attacked the position roundly: "we must not permit ourselves to draw only according to personal feelings and sensations."[103] To traditional-school artists, the physical act of making up the paints and grinding them slowly in water, was a ruminative ritual designed to bring to the fore the artist's inner self, which, having arisen, became *itself* the true theme of the picture, whatever the overt subject. The viewer beheld, and appreciated, no more than that. But Takamori Kankō pointed out that Western pigments did not allow for this mind-lulling exercise, as they were made by boiling gum arabic, a process more scientific than existential, and certainly discouraging of any deep triangular empathy among painter, inks, and brush. As Kōkan wrote, Western painters were "endebted to tools and techniques, and by putting their devices into service, they make their extraordinarily detailed [pictures], without suffering any labour of the hand."[104]

Such was the value placed by *Rangaku* scholars on the *saiku* qualities of spirit-denuded pictures that it might be supposed a machine would do a better job of painting. This was not facetious: there was such a machine, recently invented in the West, and many thought it did outshine the human artist. Kōkan sang the praises of a contrivance able to create automatic pictures, which, he believed, could turn external forms directly into inscriptions on the page. The device was the camera obscura, introduced from Holland at the end of the eighteenth century. The degree of diffusion of the device is unclear, but being the basis of so many optical tools of the seventeenth and eighteenth century, it is unlikely that the camera obscura was not noised about quite widely.[105] Kōkan described the box as "a contrivance to depict scenery so as to make it look to viewers as if they were actually walking through the place."[106] Sugita Genpaku translated the name directly into Japanese, as a "dark-room authenticity-copying lens."[107] Arima Genshō included the object in the compendium of his question-and-answer sessions with Ōtsuki Gentaku, *Correcting Errors about the Dutch* (*Ransetsu benwaku*):

> My question is this: there is a kind of device made from a box and fitted with a glass lens which projects landscapes and people so that they can be copied down. In Japanese this is called an "authenticity-copying lens." Are the original foreign ones called the same thing?
>
> My reply is this: there are several of these boxes to be found in the houses of enthusiasts around the country. The device is extremely cunningly made and is indeed called an "authenticity-copying lens."[108]

Gentaku provided a rough illustration for the benefit of the reader, labelling it with a transliteration of the Dutch, *donkeru kaamuru* (*donkere kamer;* Fig. 23).

It required some little skill to manipulate a camera obscura to good effect, but this was nothing to the time it took to master usual painting styles. With the machine, the artist was almost literally dispensed with, and making *Ranga* pictures became (to those who only knew by word of mouth) almost easy. It is by no means clear how often pictures were actually produced in this way in Japan, but if imported boxes were expensive and scarce, domestic versions could be improvised without undue trouble, the only part difficult to obtain being the lens. A simpler unlensed pin-hole camera could be fashioned, so long as a fuzzy and inverted image was tolerated.[109]

Takizawa Bakin, the fiction writer from Edo and sometime protégé of Kyōden, saw such a camera obscura in Osaka in 1802. He was taken to a literal camera – a room – darkened to blackness and with a hole in one wall. There was no lens and the projected image fell upside-down, but focusing was possible by moving a board that served as a screen backward or forward as needed. The demonstration was carried out in the house of one Fukami Shōbei, a wealthy wholesaler who, with his son, Satarō, an ama-

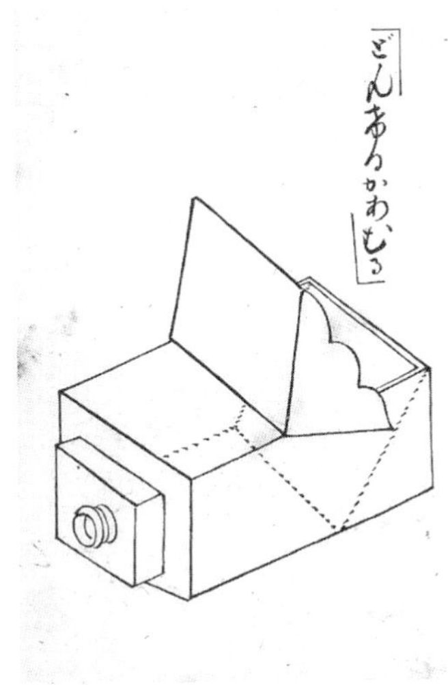

23. Unsigned, *Camera Obscura* from Ōtsuki Gentaku (Arima Genshō, ed.), *Ransetsu benwaku*, 1799. Tokyo Metropolitan Central Library.

teur poet, was obviously in the habit of showing the device off to visitors. Bakin recorded the excitement he felt in the diary of his trip, *Travel Records* (*Kiryo manroku*). Even allowing for overstatement the image sounds remarkably sharp, for Bakin claimed to see a view stretching away over the eighteen metres of garden outside, complete with pond, bamboo grove, and willows; he could even discern some child's practice calligraphy hanging up to dry in the sun, and could actually read its date.[110]

It is not clear whether Bakin or Shōbei knew this effect could be replicated in any darkened location at will. Possibly something magical was believed to lurk about the place that made projections possible. But Shōbei's room was not the only large-scale camera obscura in Japan, and Bakin himself had witnessed a projection in a house in Ōmiya Street in Kyoto belonging to a farmer by the name of Niwa Matazaemon, where a likeness of the fine pagoda of the Tōji, erected in 1644, was to be distinguished; Bakin also cited similar effects in other locations, such as a building behind an unnamed temple in Suwa in

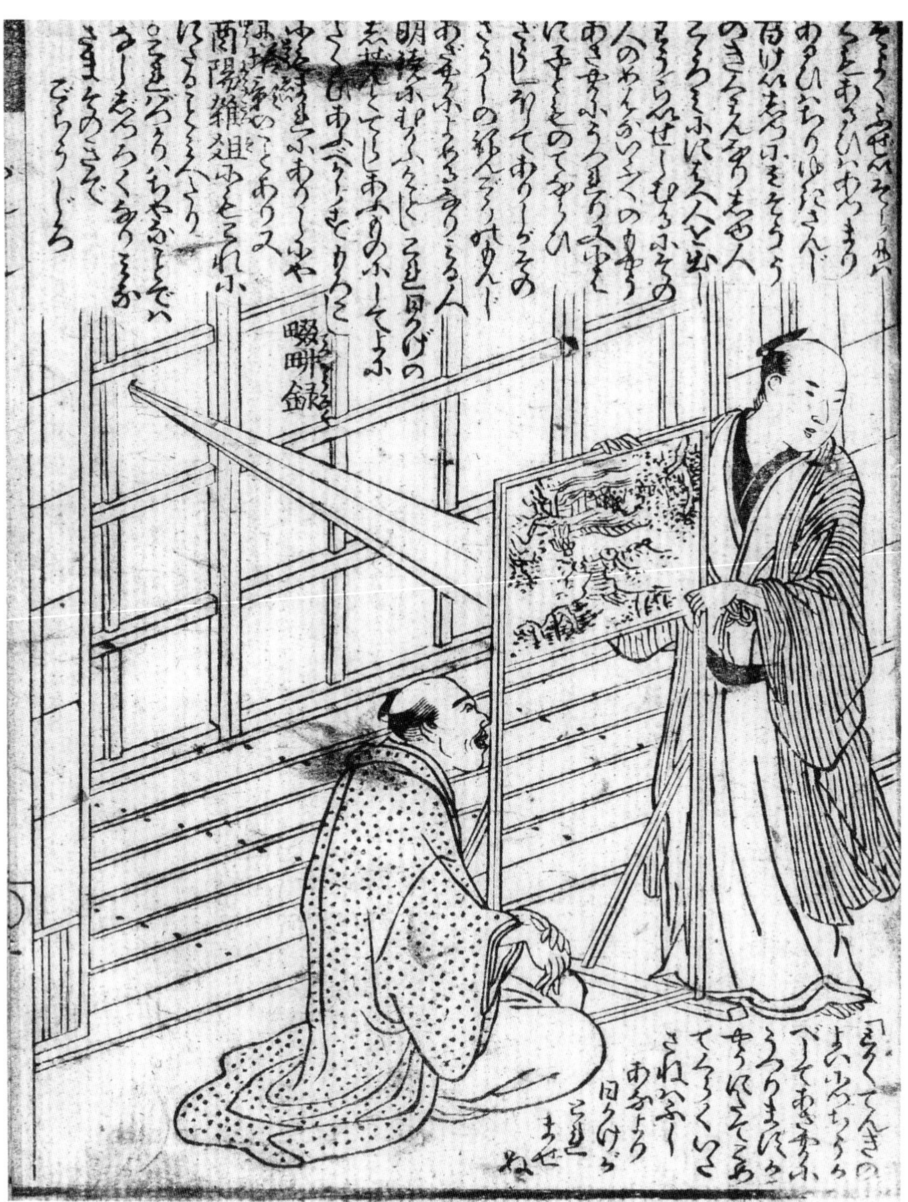

Shinshū, which caught the image of a hall to the Medicine Buddha located just outside.

Bakin's *Records* were published only posthumously, but he circulated news of the camera obscura more immediately by committing it to a kibyoshi published within months of his return, early in 1802. The book, illustrated by Utagawa Toyohiro, was entitled *Rare Designs in Light and Shadow* (*Kage to hinata chinmō zui;* Fig. 24), and other than the opening page on Shōbei's room, it is a collection of rather limp shadow games. The section on the camera in the story is largely identical to that of the diary, although the latter includes an interesting additional observation:

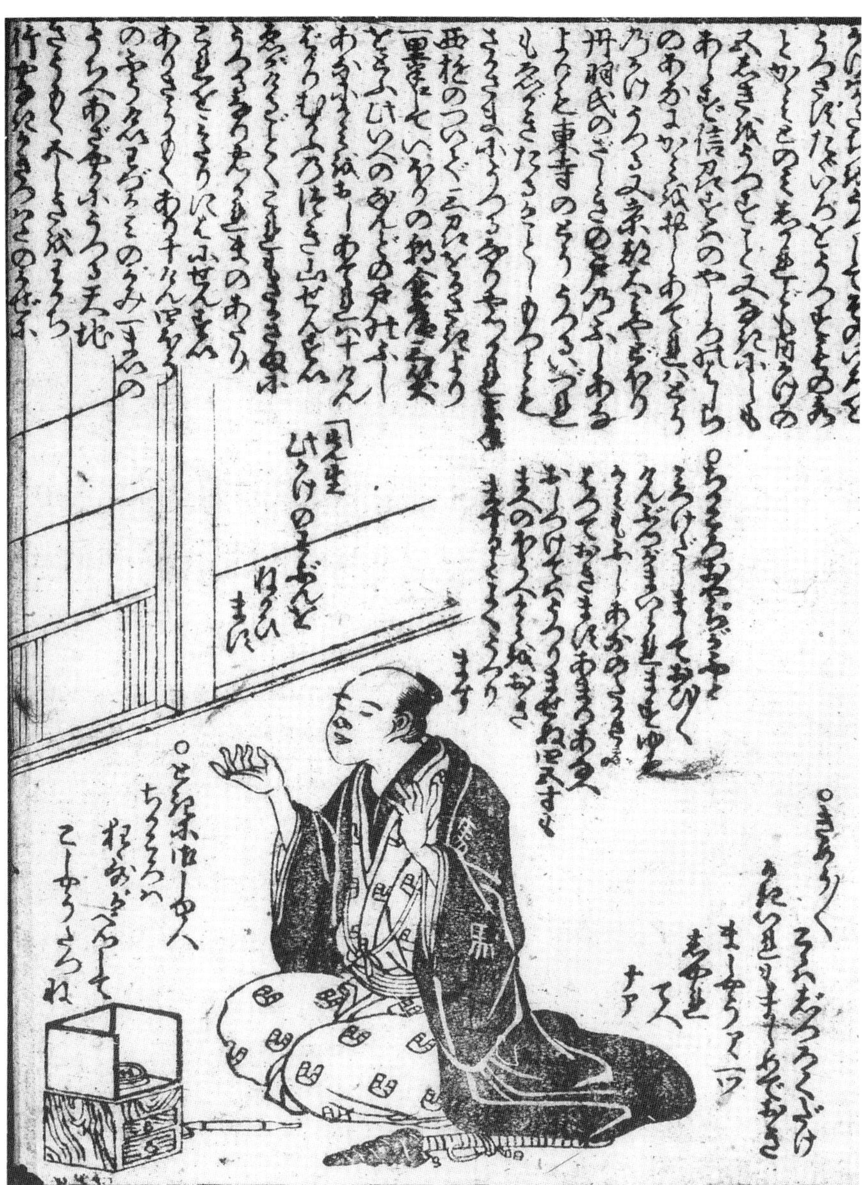

24. Utagawa Toyohiro, from Takizawa Bakin, *Kage to hinata chinmō zui*, 1803. National Diet Library, Tokyo.

A pin-hole camera is demonstrated to the author, seated right.

the projected image, said Bakin, looked like a Dutch picture.[111] How did he gain this impression from a projection that – calligraphy and all – sounds so utterly Japanese? The precision, he said, of the colouring was one feature, and Bakin was struck by the blueness of the sky (skies not being painted in Japanese art); the rendition of the shadows and shading might have seemed European, too. But what was most foreign, I surmise, was the way in which the work was created automatically on the screen in the room, no artistic persona intervening in the fabrication of the picture at all.

No one took the trouble to copy down Shōbei's shadow as it fell on the screen, but had they done so they would have had the perfect *saiku* picture: machine-made, close, impeccably exact, authentic in every degree, and representing an isolated slice of the world, extracted out of the vastness of nature to be presented to the viewer in readable form. The camera obscura was a precision machine that allowed the permanent record of finds. It was a pure piece of *Ran*.

THREE

MECHANICS AND MOTIONS

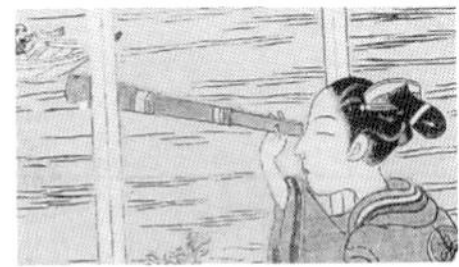

A LOVE OF PRECISION was firmly entrenched as an association of the Dutch. Their meticulous mind-set was said to be aided and extended by the enlistment of machines. The terms for European goods – *Oranda saiku* (Dutch precision work) or *kiki* (strange devices) – stressed the extraordinariness of their mechanical contrivances. A list of "Products of Holland" appeared in the most widely read encyclopaedia of the later Edo period, the *Sino-Japanese Universal Illustrated Compendium* (*Wakan sansai zue*). Originally a Ming Chinese work, it was adapted for Japanese readership (hence the title) in 1713 by an Osaka doctor named Terajima Ryōan. Numerous items of precision type were listed, including clocks, spectacles, magnetic tools, astrological equipment, and surgical apparatus.[1] This sense of the orientation of Holland was thoroughly supported by Tachibana Nankei. In the *Record of Pleasurable Travels in the West* (*Seiyū-ki*), Nankei summed up his whole experience at the VOC Factory in Nagasaki in a section headed simply "*Kiki*."[2]

This chapter will deal with two kinds of strange device: pumps and clockwork. We shall assess how these were used and adapted in Japan – less technologically altered than conceptually transformed. Divorced from practical ends, the new equipment meshed with the Edo system of delight at strange workings, and they often became objects of display, functioning in splendid isolation as *misemono* (exhibits). Out of *kiki* came automata, and out of them came a definite sense of a new role for the hidden and the inner working part. But first we shall consider some preliminaries.

THE DUTCH SHIP

The great foci of Western mechanisation were the VOC ships, two of which would dock in Nagasaki Bay annually. The three-masters were large and staffed by some one hundred men; Thunberg's vessel had 144 aboard (110 Europeans and 34 Indonesians), although it was the biggest ship for thirty years.[3] The "Dutch ship" (*Oranda-bune*) entered Edo-period folklore.

Fantastic in its own right, the vessel traversed the wide seas in safety, if not exactly comfort, and was hailed as the repository of oddities and thrills: Shiba Kōkan drew a picture of the ship he had seen in Nagasaki in 1788, providing smaller inset details of some of its more intriguing accoutrements (Fig. 25); Hirokawa Kai discussed the on-board wonders he knew of in a section of his book on the town, *Things Seen and Heard in Nagasaki* (*Nagasaki bunken roku*), entitled "*Oranda-bune*": he cited charts and instruments, sextants and quadrants for precision navigation, devices for communication at near-impossible distances, like telescopes and loud-hailers, as well as blowers and suction vents for evacuating water and circulating air; there was also a movable mast that slewed from side to side to reap the full force of the wind (presumably he means the boom), and an anchor with chains and windlass to hold the vessel fast or set it free.[4]

In 1786, while the ship-building enthusiast Isaac Titsingh was kapitan, an attempt was made to integrate this foreign technology in a Japanese-made vessel called *The Three Nations* (*Sangoku-maru*). It looked Japanese but had a Chinese keel and Dutch sailing apparatus, but it sank within months of its launch.[5] Those like Kōkan and Nankei who visited Nagasaki sought to make their trip coincide with the arrival or departure of a real European vessel. Chinese junks were more commonly in and out of port, but they were not sufficiently distinct from Japanese craft to merit the same attention. Kōkan reached Nagasaki early in the tenth month, too late for the docking (some twelve weeks earlier), but he found the ship still berthed and stayed around to see it leave on the twenty-seventh. Furukawa Koshōken, a samurai and botanist from Okayama and later official land surveyor to Tanuma Okitsugu's replacement in the shogunal council, Matsudaira Sadanobu, recorded how,

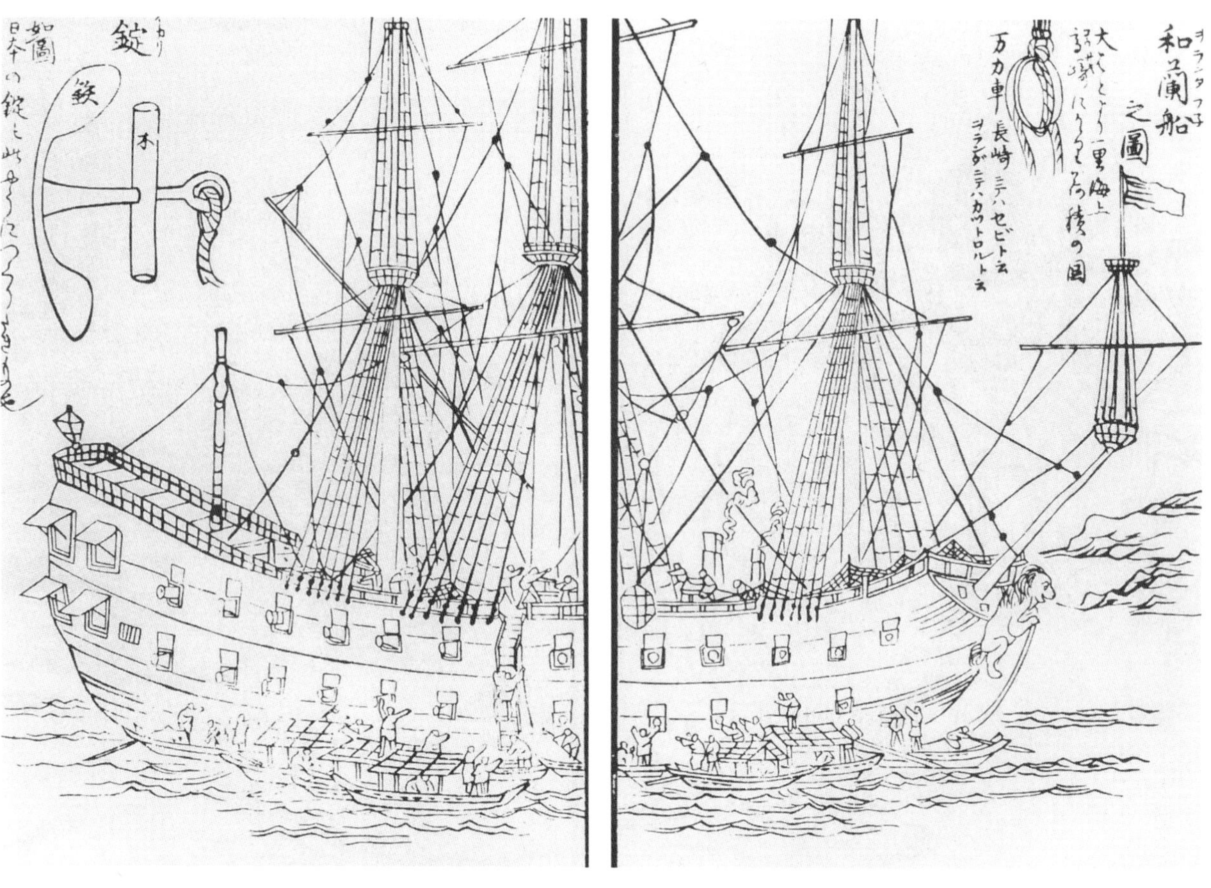

25. Shiba Kōkan, *Dutch Ship*, from his *Saiyū ryōdan*, 1794. Private collection.

when he was still *en route* to Nagasaki in 1783, news reached him that a VOC ship was now due. He began a panic-stricken dash across Kyushu, arriving just in time on the eighteenth of the seventh month, to find the whole town in an uproar.[6]

Like all the best contrivances, ships looked exceedingly complex but were smoothly workable by those who knew the operations. Kai likened the VOC sailors' activities to those of well-disciplined soldiers, as they trimmed the sails, weighed and dropped the anchor, and manoeuvred the ship through the water; he commended their efficiency, "more perfect than the reverberations of a bell."[7] Kōkan thought the deckhands more resembled acrobats or tightrope walkers, as they nimbly exploited their equipment to its virtuoso full.[8] But tomfoolery this was not.

The citizenry of Nagasaki, exposed to four dockings and sailings a year, never entirely grasped how the ship worked. Public rumour had it that wind alone could not propel so large a craft, and though Ōtsuki Gentaku and others remonstrated that wind-power was both strong and harnessable and quite adequate to shifting even very large objects (typically, his example was Dutch – the sails on a windmill),[9] many remained dubious. Nagasaki-ites dreamed up a more outlandish explanation: maritime convention demanded the loosing of a cannonade upon entry into port and, loath to think such splendid thundering gratuitous, the townspeople widely took it as somehow relevant to propulsion. Japanese pictures of Dutch ships entering and leaving the bay invariably show them firing the cannon amid billows of smoke, as if that were a necessary accompaniment to movement (Pl. 1). The fact that shots were also fired when the ship was stationary ought to have given this myth the lie, but it failed to do so. Kōkan wrote: "Each morning, [the Dutch] fire off a blast on their cannon, and on festival days they fire off two or three – this is rather as we use flames in Japan, for the purposes of purification. The belief that firing makes the ship move is pure error put about by the people of Nagasaki."[10] Morishima Chūryō, more on the right track, stated the salvo was a mark of friendly intent, and that by using up the notional last ball, the Dutch indicated that hostilities were not contemplated.[11]

The nature of the cannon remained a matter of confusion, but there was no denying the marvellousness of the event. The shots heralded the sensational arrival of an *Oranda-bune* with its stores of mechanical goods. Tachibana Nankei recorded the electrifying effect this beckoning noise had on the town: "When a Dutch ship enters Nagasaki harbour it always fires off a great stone arrow. The sound echoes around the hills, and the Chinese and Japanese leap from their houses to take a look."[12] Nankei noted that people even failed to agree on a correct transcription for the baffling roar, the Chinese saying it went *biiin* whereas the Japanese heard something more like *doraan*.

It was not possible for many to board the ship or assess it at close quarters. Shogunal officials gained entry to conduct the customs formalities (the Dutch thoughtfully putting beds out on deck so they could sit with their feet tucked up, knowing that Japanese found chairs awkward),[13] but even samurai were not permitted lengthy inspection. How the ship worked was decidedly obscure. The corollary of the benefits derived by those trained to use the in-board equipment was puzzlement for the undrilled. Being unable to fathom how the pieces of mechanics worked, they came to regard them as items of figurative significance.

EDO MECHANICS

The cloud of non-comprehension that hung over Dutch devices was the result of a genuine inability to grasp. But it was not only that: it was also the product of a deeper cultural trope. Though far from being an automated country, eighteenth-century Japan could boast various pieces of equipment that did what humans could not do (or not so fast or cheaply), and the aura surrounding these pieces was not dissimilar from that descending over the *Oranda-bune*. In 1709 Matsumoto Utaguni recorded in a massive gazetteer of Osaka, *Strange Things to See in Shining Settsu* (*Setsu'yō kikan*), how a certain Daimonji-ya Hachibei had set up a water-powered grinding stone in the Yotsubashi district which, by dint of clever workings, allowed one man to do the job of eighteen.[14] In Edo, there was the four-metre waterwheel at Hiroo, built in 1733 on the river Tamagawa and driving one hundred pounding pestles; it was the largest apparatus of its kind, and the oldest, in the city. A tread-wheel pestle at Ōmori in the south-west was also famous, and ground patent medicines for the Wachū-san pharmacy.[15] In 1790, Morishima Chūryō also compiled a (now lost) *Machines for Use in Agriculture* (*Nōkō chikara-guruma*). But the Edo period had a rather special attitude towards these mechanics: their complexity was admired rather than their speeding up of output.

Waterwheels undoubtedly enhanced production, but far more important seems to have been the pull the contraptions had on the potential clientele. Hands and feet were, if anything, cheapening commodities as the eighteenth century progressed, and labour hardly needed saving. But market share was strenuously fought for in the consumer culture of early-modern Japan.[16] Efficiency was not really the point. The apparatuses were always installed somewhere where they could be looked at and admired, and commentaries on them are more apparent in city guidebooks than in technological or business tomes. The things were, in Utaguki's phrase, "strange things to see" (*kikan*). The Wachū-san shop gave on to the Tōkaidō, the nation's premier trunk route that linked Edo with the Osaka-Kyoto region, and literally thousands passed by daily; the scurry of wheels and the thudding of hammers made an otherwise ordinary commercial activity into a talking point, worth stopping off to see. Held captive by mechanics, visitors were easily turned into buyers. Perversely, then, Edo machinery was more noteworthy for its ability to augment demand rather than increase supply.[17]

A cunning machine might enter the realm of the mythology of its locale. The Wachū-san pestle was certainly part of Edo's urban fable. A senryu writer composed a verse on it, likening the wheels to the famous "Battle of the Carriages" described in the twelfth-century *Tale of Genji* (*Genji monogatari*). The verse alluded to the episode in that classic fictional text where aristocratic ladies vied for front-row parking on a festival day and bumped their vehicles against those ahead to jounce them out of place.[18] Since "carriage" and "wheel" were the same word in Japanese, the verse worked well. Redolent of antique courtly cries and a cracking of axles, the short verse nowhere mentions enhancement of the production of pills. All was panache and scintillating flurry:

> The battle of the carriages
> Is taking place in Ōmori
> At a pharmacist's![19]

As mechanical parts were generally fashioned from wood, their construction fell to the lot of the carpenter. Literally the "great artisan" (*daiku*), the Japanese carpenter has always enjoyed a position of prominence at the pinnacle of manual labour. Woodworkers remained firmly artisans, and the names of few are known, but legend surrounded their highest endeavours. One or two masters rose from anonymity to celebrity, if only posthumously. The mid-seventeenth-century Hidari Jingorō was one, and monuments throughout the land were (and are), with varying degrees of probability, attributed to his wondrous chisel. But the finest carpenter of all, it was said, was a man of furthest antiquity, known by a simple toponymic as the Hida Craftsman (*Hida no Takumi*). Hida, lost in the mountains of central Japan, retained ever after an association with agile fingers. The Hida Craftsman featured in such ancient works as the *Anthology of Ten-thousand Leaves* (*Man'yō-shū*) of the mid-eighth century and the *Collection of Writings New and Old* (*Kokon chōmon-shū*) of 1252, in which tales he was said generically to have made fine buildings and elegant statues.[20] One with his trade, the Hida Craftsman became known as Suminawa, literally "ink cord," that is, the snap-line used for measuring and straight cutting, and the primary tool of the worker in wood.[21]

In the later Edo period, Suminawa was not forgotten; indeed, most noticeably the reverse was true: 1806 saw the performance of a puppet play of *The Hida Craftsman,* written by Hōraizan, and there was even a now-lost variant, *The Hida Craftswoman* (*Onna Hida no Takumi*).[22] It was probably in 1808 that Suminawa's life was committed to print in story-book form in its now most well-known version by Ishikawa Toyonobu, a person whose attainments extended from being a hereditary innkeeper in Edo to a poetry writer, scholar on the *Tale of Genji,* and an amateur fictionalist of great popularity.[23] Toyonobu wrote his prose under the pen-name of Rokujūen, and he pioneered the new, novelistic genre of yomihon. Rokujūen's *Tale of the Hida Craftsman* (*Hida no Takumi monogatari*) was illustrated by his close friend, Hokusai.

Rokujūen turned Suminawa into something he had not been before, and reformulated him for the modern audience by according him a crucial supplementary skill: while still the carpenter *par excellence,* Suminawa was now above all a maker of closely working mechanical gadgets valued for the delight of their movements; in short, from craftsman he mutated into toysmith. Suminawa's products were essentially automata; his power drives (as we shall see below) were largely imported. Rokujūen claimed in his preface that the idea for the book had been Hokusai's, and that he had been more or less dragooned into it against his will.[24] If this is true, Hokusai, who five years before had illustrated Onitake's story of Sino-Dutch rivalry and pitted Chin Rinten's sagely behaviour against Sunperupei's "Dutch *saiku,*" apparently wished to thrash out again the issues of mechanical culture.[25]

AUTOMATA

The Japanese term for automata is *karakuri.* The origin of the word is obscure, but popular etymology supported a derivation from *kara,* meaning the Continent (modern opinion holds it to stem from the verb *karamu,* "to twist").[26] But from about this time, *karakuri* took a great leap forward, and associations began to be, rather, with *Ran.* Makers were many, but from the eighteenth century on the motors at their disposal, and with them their position and status, shifted greatly. Some workers began to achieve positions of prominence almost equivalent to Suminawa's legendary standing at court. Early in the century, the great Osaka impresario Takeda Ōmi was awarded the honorific title of *jō* (constable),[27] and a maker from Matsue, Kobayashi Jotei, became so favoured by his lord that traditionalist sensibilities were offended, he being "only" an artisan.[28] Such honours would have been inconceivable in earlier periods. Why the changes occurred must be assessed. We may do so by considering the workings of later-eighteenth-century *karakuri* and the manner of their construction. What follows is not a full analysis – *karakuri* recede into the depths of Japanese history – but an assessment of certain departures.

Denuded of function and working away in emptiness, *karakuri* were part of the world of the strange. They were toys, often in human or other mimetic form, which easily made the machinery tralatitious acquiring extended or metaphorical meanings, standing abstractly for the complex transformation of hidden interiors into outward ends. The apparently inconsistent lines between motion and effect was a good portion of the delight of *karakuri*. As wheels turned the hands of a piece clockwork, or pistons sent jets of water falling into the street, it was bafflement alone that drew the crowds.

To understand and manage a device, the parts had to be made accessible for operation and repair. But for thrill alone, hiddenness was the key. Interiors were kept from view of audiences precisely so that the mechanisms would remain – forever – not understood. It was a small step from installing, say, the Wachū-san wheel at the pharmacy to having an automatic doll *tout court* to draw in custom. It was the mechanical advances of certain kinds of imported machinery – and this is the crux – that allowed the fuller sealing of *karakuri,* the emergence of entirely portable and self-contained apparatuses and hence, the device that was both entirely obscure and fully authentic in its motion (many earlier *karakuri* were revealed as full of deceit if you saw inside).

The master Jotei was alive while Rokujūen was writing. His paramount feat will be discussed below, but one cunning object is worth describing here. Apparently a great drinker (a learned joke on inebriation lies buried in his name), it is said that one day Jotei forgot the money to settle his sake bill.[29] In a quandary, he sent payment to the landlord in kind, handing over a cleverly fashioned wooden terrapin placed in the bottom of his cup. Imagining the toy to be real, the landlord furiously threw it into the nearby pond. When the object came in contact with the water, its machinery sprang into motion, and it began to swim about, to the infinite delight of all. The landlord immediately asked to buy it back.[30] No one knew how it worked but one thing was sure, independently mobile, it was not a fraud.

The charm of *Karakuri* was that, although they did no job, their motions were exciting and viewers though half-fooled at the same time realised that there must be some explanation. The makers played up the wonder of the pieces, and hagiographers further stretched plausibility beyond all reasonable limits. But the *karakuri*-maker was not a magician, only a highly adroit harnesser of established techniques, and a great concealer of workings. Suminawa was said by Rokujūen to have received a tool kit from the gods, but he was still a craftsman – literally, a "person of skill" (*takumi*) – not a wizard.[31] *Karakuri* motions were the result of infinite patience.

Karakuri were surrounded by a passionate secrecy and none were permitted to look inside or see how they were assembled. Trade secrets were vital, and the *karakuri*-maker was a guarded and solitary worker. When the Hida Craftsman made a great flying crane (one of his best successes) the reader was told in Rokujūen's account: "he secluded himself in a small room; people could hear the sound of the hatchet and saw, but only wonder what was afoot; after three days Suminawa appeared and said, 'I have finished, come and see.' "[32] The process of *karakuri*-making did not lend itself to sharing. The logic of the parts had to remain a mystery if the real point of the device – the discrepancy between inside and outside, input and motion – were to be enjoyed. Many *karakuri*-makers were said never to have taken pupils, as even atelier walls have ears; and, in marked distinction to the school orientation of most Japanese crafts, many preferred to die with their expertise than risk exposure. Jotei had no successor and went to exorbitant lengths to protect his privacy, even destroying his tools upon the completion of each object.[33] True, Suminawa has a pupil in Rokujūen's tale, but the fellow is more a narrative device than a real personage, and he spends the whole story struck dumb by the gods lest he divulge what he knows.

The best-known *karakuri*-maker, Takeda Ōmi, did evolve an apprentice structure and by existing over generations his family could monopolise the otherwise fractured field. But even here, secrets were kept within the Takeda group. The name was handed on hereditarily after the death of the first Takeda Ōmi in 1726, and the Takeda *karakuri* theatre, located in the Dōtonbori entertainment district of Osaka, was celebrated far and wide. Akisato Ritō, chronicler of the area, recorded fulsomely, in his *Illustrated Famous Places in Settsu* (*Settsu meisho zue*), that "the theatre is famous throughout the land, and I have heard it said that travellers, whether from east or west, town or country, think if they have failed to see the Takeda *karakuri*, they can't really say they've experienced Osaka at all."[34] The theatre made tours occasionally too, and on one trip to Edo in 1742 the crowd was so great that the doors remained jammed for three days solid; they were back again in 1758, and it may have been to celebrate a tour of 1778 that Torii Kiyonaga produced a kibyoshi on the Takeda *karakuri*.[35] The Takeda Ōmi company appears to have experienced financial problems in the later part of the century, and the theatre temporarily shut down; but it was running again by 1798 when Ritō's book appeared; Takizawa Bakin saw an off-shoot in 1802 in Nagoya, which, he said, had also ceased operation for a while, but was now back on the boards.[36]

Traditional automata worked on strings hidden from the eyes of the viewers. Akisato Ritō stated this and went on to say that the father of the first Takeda Ōmi, Takeda Izumo, "when an old man in Kyoto," had made a *karakuri* without strings.[37] What he did was incorporate imported mechanisms: hydraulics and clockwork. So began the nation's premier troupe.

Export of mechanical items, often clockwork, was a major part of both Dutch and English trade with the East. In 1752, the consort of the Chinese huangdi (emperor) of the Qing, Qianlong, was treated to a display of European automata on the occasion of her sixtieth birthday, laid on by the Jesuit fathers who maintained the vast palace collection.[38] Automata were familiar features of the European urban scene, and most cities had their shows. The Dutch brought not only machinery whose true functions were subverted into metaphor, but actual models too, and gave these as gifts, or sold them. Shiba Kōkan claimed that East- and South-East Asia were awash with toys made in England – a centre of automata production (although Kōkan did not state whether he meant working pieces).[39] No trip to London was complete without a visit to James Cox's "motions" any more than Osaka could be experienced without passing by Takeda Ōmi's. Cox enjoyed tremendous fame throughout the 1770s and became a supplier to the East India Companies; quantities of his products were sent to China. The arrival in England of the Swiss maker Jean-Frédérique Jacquet-Droz in 1776 raised the art of "androids" (as he called them) to new heights.[40]

It is noticeable how many of the eighteenth-century Japanese *karakuri* masters went out of their way to associate themselves with Europe. The town of Nagasaki, home of the Dutch community, was regarded as the hub of manufacture, and most of the best makers were said to have come from there, or else to have visited the town for study. One of the first prominent figures is Matakyūrō, said to have learned his skills from Westerners, and as a result the word *Nanban* (the obsolete term for Europe) was added to his name, together with "precision device," so he became "*Nanban Saiku no* Matakyūrō," or "Matakyūro of the Precision European Devices."[41] A contemporary said of him in 1717: "He could make [a *karakuri* of] anything on the face of the earth. The achievements of all other *saiku*-makers ancient or modern, in all four hundred and more provinces, are as nothing before him."

The rise to prominence of the *karakuri*-maker, and the reemergence of the heroic figure of Suminawa, coincide with the dispersal of the new mechanisms. The exposed and whirling Edo contraption gave way to the enclosed and smooth-sealed body of the automatic toy.

WATERPOWER

Use of waterpower had long predated the emergence of a fixation with *Ran*, but advances in applying it are to be noticed from the early eighteenth century. The first water-*karakuri* had been based on a simple wheel spun around by the kinetic energy of a falling or flowing current. A humble and routine sort (though still to be seen later in the century), was equipped with a model monkey whose arms, attached to the wheel, pounded a pestle in a mortar. This and similar devices appeared frequently at fairgrounds, and the pestle-pounding monkey (*usubiki saru*) is attested in numerous contexts. It became popular at stations on the Tōkaidō highway, where landlords installed them for the diversion of travellers in the hot summer months.[42] Santō Kyōden enlisted the monkey in a book of parody fabric patterns, *Elegant Chats on Cloth Design* (*Komon gawa*), a compilation that took familiar motifs and cut them down into segments like cloth samples in a sort of visual puzzle, to be untangled by the reader (Fig. 26). Kyōden added a capsule history inscribed on the picture: "The first waterwheel was made by Yoshimi no Yasuyo, but this pestle-pounding monkey – operating on the same principle – was initially devised by Sajibei from Shikoku."[43] Yasuyo was son of the tenno (emperor) Kanmu, who ruled in the late eighth century; Sajibei may refer to a person now forgotten, but the name is so common as to be meaningless. Kyōden, in the context of a puzzle, is not really committed to historical record, but it is clear that the monkey is an age-old construction.

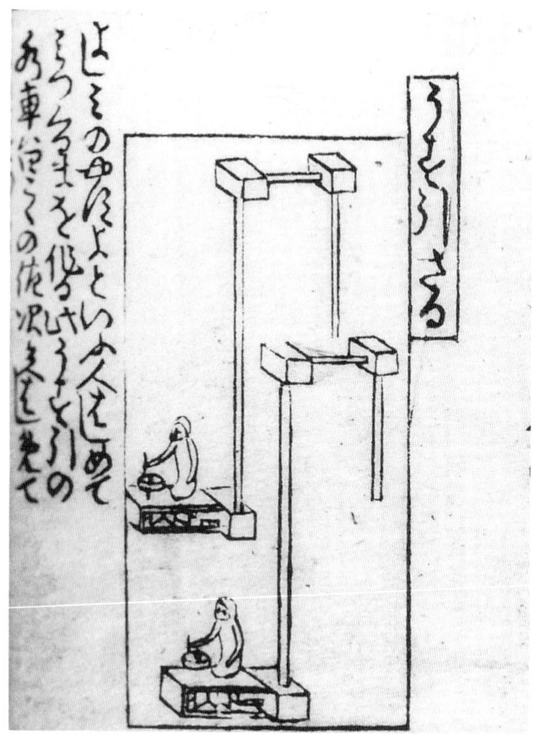

26. Santō Kyōden, *Pestle-pounding Monkey* (detail), from his *Komon gawa*, 1780. Keiō University Library.

Waterwheels were not the only – nor even the best – means of using water to thrilling effect. It was said of one Yamamoto Hida (who may have borrowed the robes of the Hida Craftsman), a late-sixteenth-century *karakuri*-maker, that he was the first person to "understand the art of hydraulics."[44] Nothing is known of Hida other than this observation, but his innovation must lie in superseding the flow of water over a wheel, and I would hazard that he devised a means of conducting pressurised water through pipes. A water-*karakuri* similar to Sajibei's monkey, but with the addition of a sliding block to extrude the water faster, was shown in Ritō's gazetteer, displayed at the Ikutama Shrine (Fig. 27). No text is given, but the complex of tubing may be attributed to Hida's advances; the artist is free in his depiction, and the height of the water that spits back upward looks suspicious. Import to Japan of a Chinese book, *European Waterworks* (*Taisei suihō*), in 1720 introduced the spread of Western hydraulics, and though the work dealt with agricultural drainage and irrigation, it was relevant to all manner of conduit construction and suggested a range of ways in which water might be led along artificial ducts.

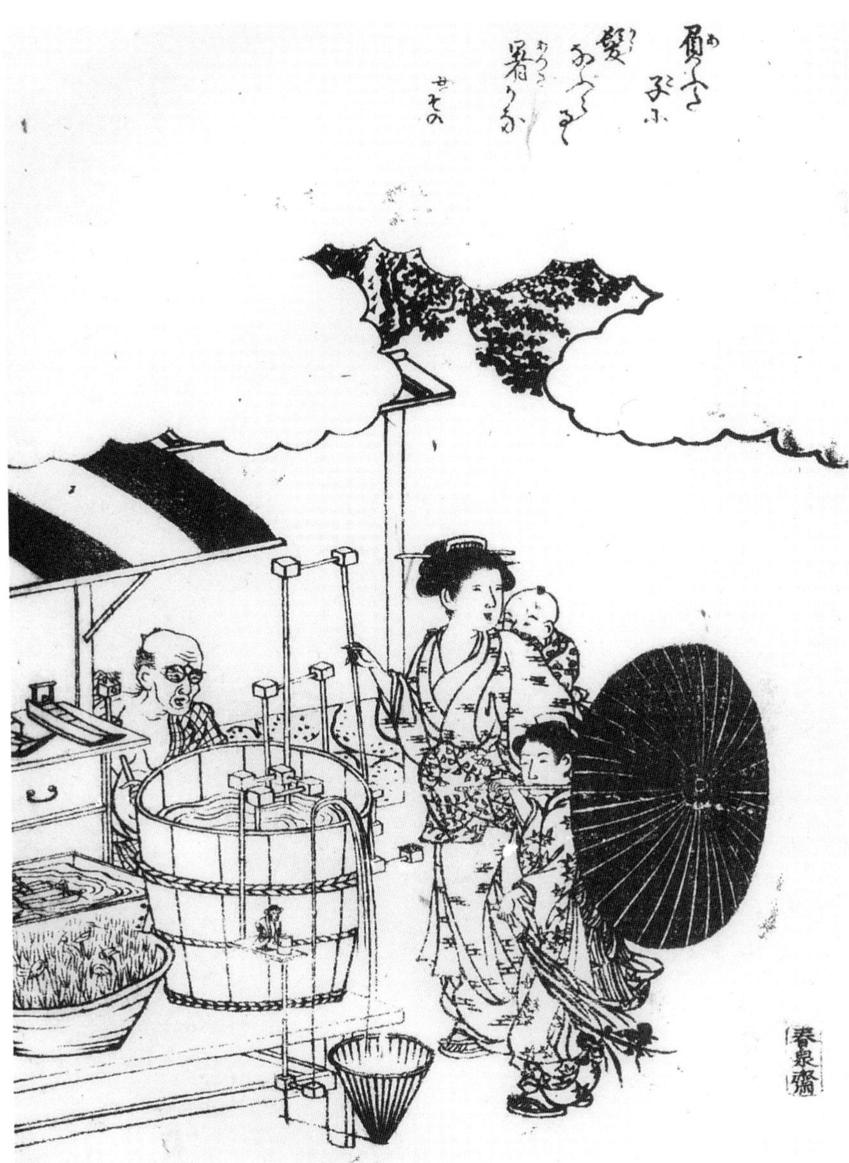

27. Takehara Shunchōsai, from Akisato Ritō, *Settsu meisho zue*, 1796. SOAS, University of London.

Water karakuri in use at the Ikutama Shrine.

In 1798, a shipwrecked sailor from Sendai, rescued by the Russians who look him ashore, saw waterworks in the palace gardens of St. Petersburg. The man, Daikoku-ya Kōdayū, was eventually repatriated (with Isokichi, his sole surviving companion), and debriefed by Katsuragawa Hoshū. Kōdayū was given extraordinary honours in Russia, even meeting Catherine the Great. He told of seeing live peacocks strutting across the palace lawns and swans sporting in a lake "made as though to usurp the art of heaven": more germanely, in it "a multitude of water-*karakuri* had been set up, constructed in waterwheels"; some mechanism must have been included, and these do not seem to have been simple kinetic pieces, for Kōdayū confided,

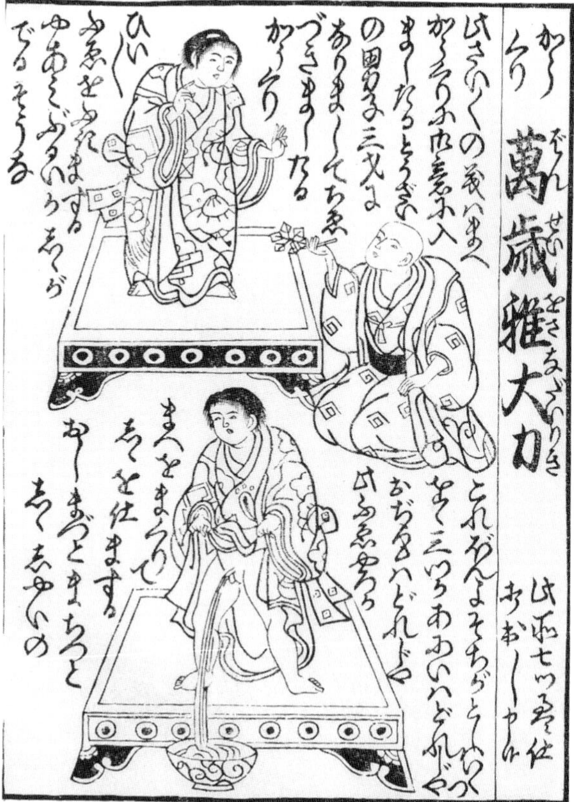

28. Unsigned, *Three Cheers for the Strongman Boy*, from Nishimura Shigenaga, *Ō-karakuri e-zukushi*, 1743(?). National Diet Library, Tokyo.

"truly, my eyes were so bewildered I could not believe this to be the work of human hands."[45] In 1813, the Edo authorities permitted the construction of a water-powered *karakuri* in the Benten Pond in Asakusa; figures of dancing birds and beasts moved to the accompaniment of authentic-sounding roars and twitters.[46] The appearance of the affair is lost, but it sounds rather like what Kōdayū had seen.

In Japan, bamboo tubes were generally used to convey water, but they leaked badly under strain and became inefficient when volume was intense. In the late eighteenth century the leather pipe was introduced. Unlike bamboo, leather had no sensitive joints and was flexible, not rigid. Hirokawa Kai saw members of the VOC using a hose, which "can direct the water in whichever direction you point the nozzle";[47] it was one hundred metres long. Although it required careful maintenance, leather was capable of pretty much infinite extension. The greater distance between vat and outflow allowed reservoir tanks to be kept far out of view of audiences, adding to their perplexity. The continuous pipe also permitted increased pressure and hence speed; all that was necessary was to raise the tank higher up. From the mid-eighteenth century the Takeda Theatre used elevated cisterns mounted out of sight, and possibly the location of their establishment on the Dōtonbori (the embankment of a canalised river) encouraged them to try other aqueous tricks.[48]

One stalwart was a *manikin pis*-like doll, brought onstage to the cry of "Three cheers for the child strongman!" (*Banzai osanai dairiki*). He emptied his bladder to wild applause (Fig. 28). Nishimura Shigenaga's blurb in a Takeda advertising booklet announced the *karakuri* in the manner of the compère's rap:

> This *saiku* is just the sort of thing you expect from a *karakuri*.
>
> The boy is three years of age and extremely intelligent.
>
> "Hey little man, how old are you?"
>
> "Nearly three, and how old are you? How old are you, uncle? Will you play a tune on that flute?"
>
> *Peep-peep*, he plays on the flute.
>
> "Oh, dear, are you feeling a bit trembly? It looks as if you want to have a pee."
>
> Now he's turning toward the front to have a piss. Have a good one then, don't hold back![49]

The raised tank relied on gravitational push, and if the elevation was high, a pressurised jet could even be sent against the expected direction of flow; the illustration of the Ikutama monkey suggests that it had this effect, although the artist there certainly took liberties, for the vat is too low to permit anything like the spray indicated. In effect, the fountain was created. Ho-

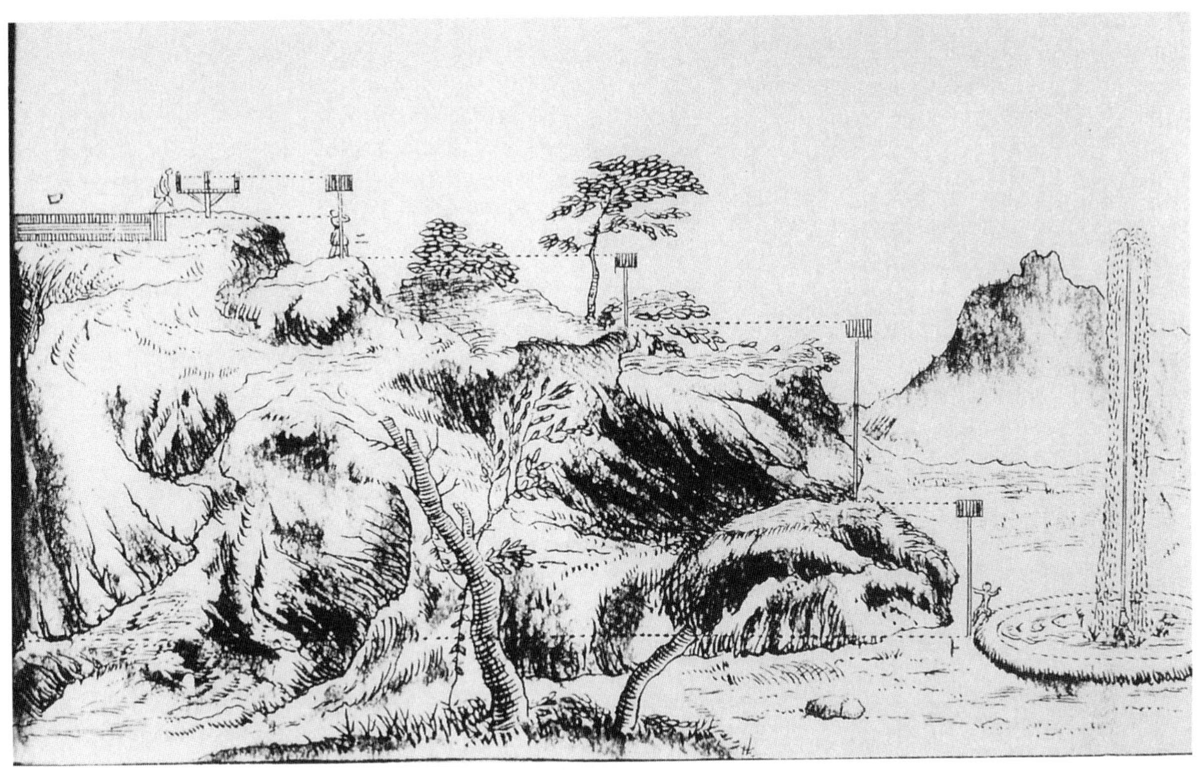

29. Takahashi Kageyasu, *Fountain*, drawing from his *Kōsei shinpen*. Shizuoka Prefectural Central Library.

shū's brother Morishima Chūryō mentioned fountains in the *Lexicon of Primitive Words* (*Bango-sen*), his Japanese–Dutch dictionary of 1798, giving *funsui-ki* ("spouting-water machine") as a translation for *konst fontein;* as his neologism was little known, he glossed the word as "water-*karakuri*." In the 1790s, a shop in Osaka calling itself the "Waterpistol" *(Mizuteppō-ya)* was amusing customers with a "dragon's spume booth," or fountain, fed by long gutters named "dragon's wings." Although more a trickle than a fountain (to judge from depictions), the proprietor maintained that the water could rise up six metres.[50]

The art of the ornamental manipulation of water was extravagant in Europe in the eighteenth century. The *Dictionnaire oeconomique*, a household encyclopaedia compiled by the French curé Noël Chomel and imported to Japan in the Dutch translation of its second edition of 1718, included an entry under "fountain," defining it as "the search for water, and the conducting of it into gardens."[51] Takahashi Kageyasu, an officer at the shogunal Calendrical Office and made official translator to that institution in 1811, undertook in that capacity selection of pages from Western reference books, compiled under the title of a *New Encyclopaedia for the National Well-being* (*Kosei shinpen*). Kageyasu included a section on fountains and supplied an illustration to show how, if several cisterns were banked up the side of a hill, they could produce enough pressure to run a very sizeable spray in a garden laid out below (Fig. 29).[52]

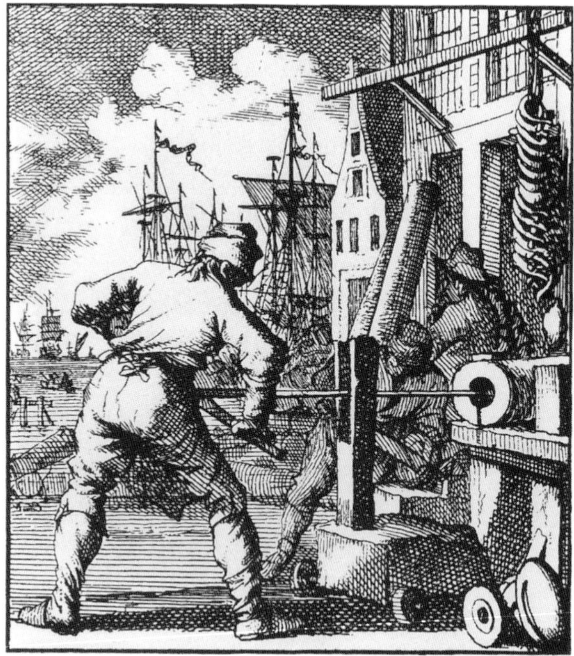

30. Johannes & Caspaares Luiken, *Pump-maker*, from their *Spiegel van het Menselyk bedryf*, 1694. Private collection.

Real fixed-place fountains were known in Japan only from tales or pictures, but the Jesuits had installed some in China in the baroque summer palace built for Qianlong in the 1740s. Carved in the forms of animals symbolising the hours, the fountains were switched on in turn, to mark the passage of time. Suddenly released water spurted out from the appropriate stone mouth and gushed on over the balustrades.[53] Fountains were commonly combined in sculpturesque groups, and Kōdayū was shown a highly elaborate set in St. Petersburg organised to celebrate the feast of the city's patron saint: "In the garden was a large lake in which they had set up beautiful stone fountains, all across the surface. They were in the forms of people, birds, or beasts. From each, water shot out either from the mouth or through instruments held in the hands. There is no way for me to describe what a *saiku* this was."[54] The jets, Kōdayū added, reached a height of five and a half metres.

The full technology of fountain-making was not put into practice in the Edo period, but a second hydraulic advance became widely known: the pressurised jet driven by a pump. In other words, the one-off water-pistol effect of the Ikutama monkey was superseded in the late eighteenth century by the veritable pump that did not need to pause between spurts and could function continuously. Those who had access to the Luikens's book of Dutch craftsmen, *The Mirror of Human Activities (Spielgel van het menselyk bedryf)*, would have seen the picture of the *pompemaaker* labouring over his machinery (Fig. 30). The Dutch had made their country by expelling water, and pumps were something of an obsession with them; indeed, members of the VOC had contrived a two-man spray on Dejima to douse their flower and vegetable gardens during the dry season (the leather hose admired by Kai was fixed to it; Fig. 31).[55] It cast a jet drawn from a pond high up onto the vine trellis. Kai described the equipment as a "water-projecting strange device" *(suiyō kiki)*, adding, "by means of some intricate mechanism it takes up water and propels it out."[56] The pump was ultimately related to the ship, he added, for when one end was dipped in the sea it could be used for swabbing down. Kai sketched the piece, but the workings inside the sturdy wooden case were not to be casually comprehended and he made no attempt at a cross-section.[57]

Piston pumps capable of any degree of projection were probably transferred to *karakuri* at the end of the century. One such was to be seen in Kyoto in 1805, used with a model monkey. Not pestle-pounding this time, the animal held an inoffensive-looking persimmon, and when the gadgetry was worked, the fruit spurted water at the audience, sparkling charmingly (said those who saw it) in the sun and probably soaking those in front, to the hilarity of the rest.[58]

A ball with the same projectile properties was displayed alongside, and all in all the event was so great a success that when the people of Kyoto had seen their fill, the *karakuri* were carted off to Nagoya to be shown there. The quality of pressurisation can be told from the fact that the shower came down some four metres from the automata's stands.

No pictures of these *karakuri* exist, but Kodera Gyokuchō, a resident of Nagoya and a diligent diarist of popular exhibits, sketched some "extremely deftly made *saiku* water-*karakuri*" put on show in the streets of his city one summer after 1819. Neither distance of projection nor mechanism used is stated, but it appears that pumped jets were emitted unexpectedly from seemingly everyday objects – towel racks, sword blades, lanterns, and ashtrays (Fig. 32).[59]

31. Unsigned, *Watering the Garden and Tending Flowers*, leaf from the album *Bankan-zu*, 1797(?). Bibliothèque Nationale, Paris.

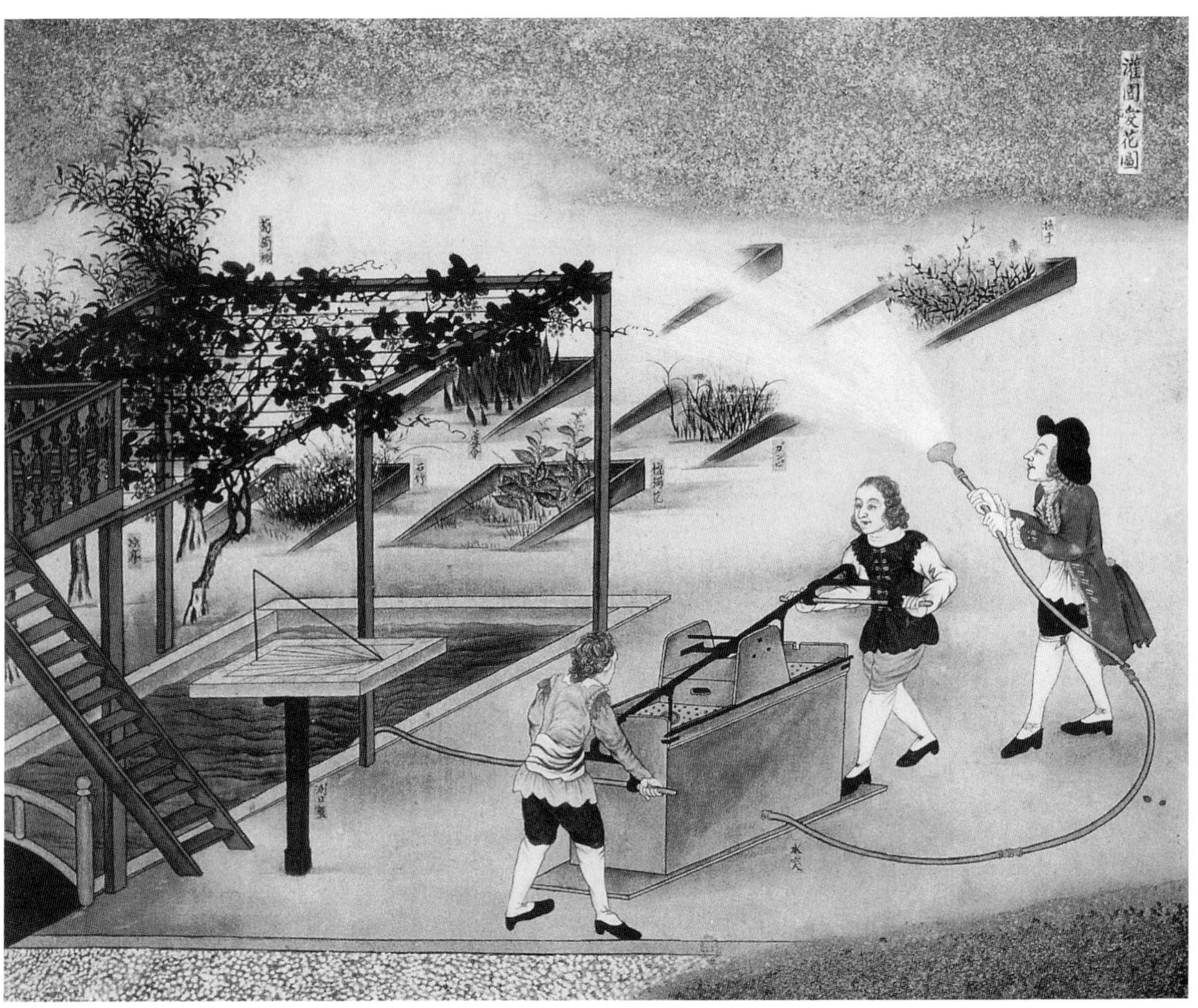

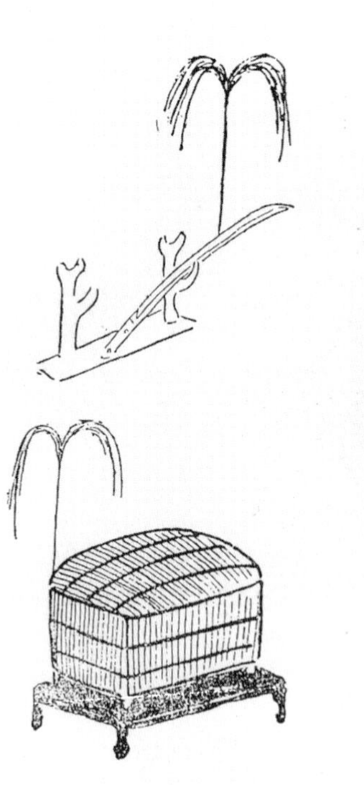

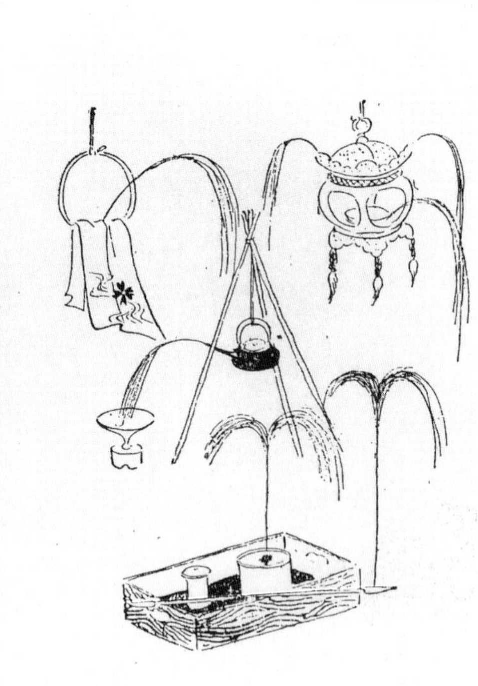

32. Kodera Gyokuchō, drawing from his *Misemono zasshi*, 1828–33. Reproduced from *Zoku zuihitsu bungaku senshū: Misemono zasshi* (Shibundō, 1928).

Assorted trick fountains.

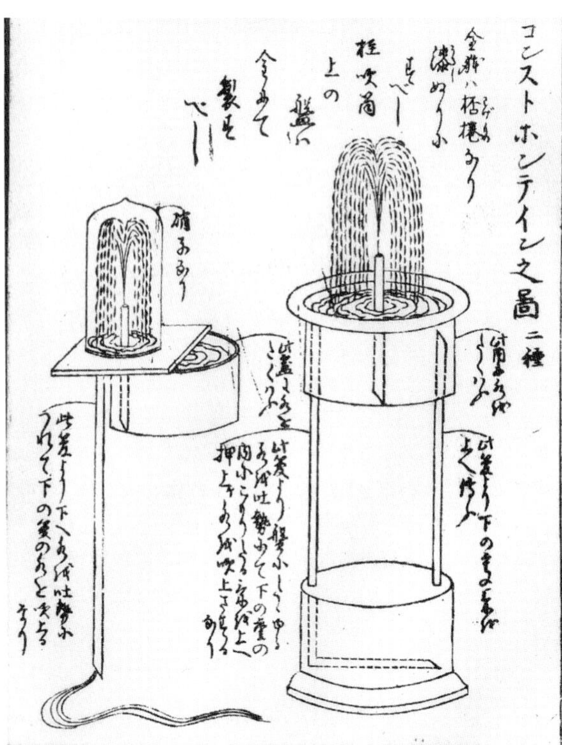

Quite current in Holland in the eighteenth century was a small, table-top water spray known as a *konst fontain,* a word Chūryō had used in his lexicon. This introduced a third new means of manipulating water: the syphon. Chūryō had already discussed the elegant miniaturised spout in his *Red-fur Miscellany (Kōmō zatsuwa),* and he considered the *konst fontain* a departure in water management. He illustrated the device, adding the explanation (Fig. 33):

> The usual water-*karakuri* sends a spout upward by means of pressure from water stored on a higher level. But this picture shows a *karakuri* that takes water up from below. The primitive [Dutch] word for it is a *'konst fontain'* – *'konst'* means technical skill, while *'fontain'* refers to the jets sent out by water-*karakuri*.[60]

33 (left). Unsigned, *Miniature Fountains,* from Morishima Chūryō, *Kōmō zatsuwa,* 1787. National Diet Library, Tokyo.

The device could run for a number of minutes before it required resetting, which compared favourably with the Ikutama sort, though not with tank-worked fountains, which played, as Kōdayū noted of yet another set he saw in Russia, "without interruption."[61] But the power source was now entirely internal and the device could be carried around. Through syphons, hidden apparatuses inside an object could make unexpected events occur no longer dependent on external forces.

Chūryō probably derived his information from Buys's *Complete Dictionary.* The latter had an entire section devoted to the *konst fontain,* together with a page of illustrations (Fig. 34). Chūryō's figures and cross-sectional sketches are not the same as those in Buys, but there is no record of the import of actual instruments and no other pictorial antecedents have come to light. Chūryō may have encouraged readers to attempt their own, and certainly Japanese *konst fontains* appeared in the early nineteenth century. The strange Dutch name was increasingly indigenised; first transliterated to *konsuto hontein,* then truncated to just *hontein,* it was finally corrupted and assigned a false etymology as *honteiki,* written to mean "garden instrument."[62] Although Chūryō's diagrams were not adequate for very successful emulation, one Kawano Yōji gave quite accurate drawings in his *Miscellany Recounted Beneath a Lantern (Tōge zakki),* together with a full description of the syphon's functioning (although he confusedly claimed *konst* to mean "fountain" and *fontain,* "skill").[63]

Water was a part of the world of *karakuri* in assorted ways, and it might serve in many stage effects. The Takeda Company seems to have made a special feature of automata that were cushioned on or propelled through water. A brochure probably issued for their 1758 Edo tour, *Dancing to the Tune of Both Drums: The Great Takeda Karakuri (Nichō-tsutsumi: Takeda Ō-karakuri),* announced how the show would offer an automated rendition of part of the famous nō

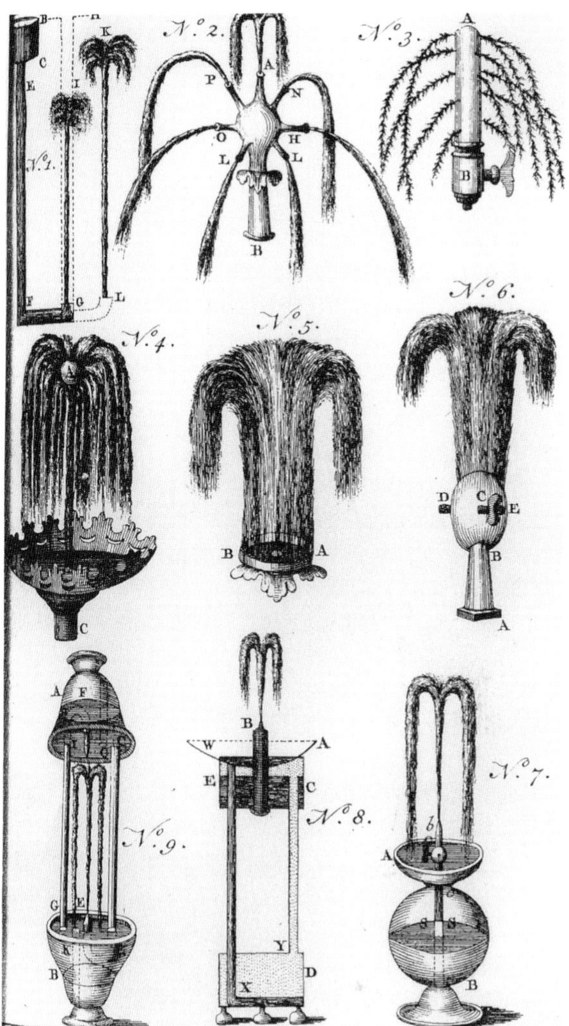

34. Unsigned, *Miniature Fountains,* from Egbert Buys, *Niuew en volkommen woodenboek,* 1769–78. Private collection.

play *Benkei in the Boat (Funa Benkei),* the saga of the tragic medieval heart-throb Yoshitsune, his colossal warrior-monk sidekick Benkei, and his faithless brother Yoritomo (who became shogun in 1185). A fountain was included too. The text ran on, with familiar hype:

> Yes, Ladies and Gentlemen, all the effects in this show are very clever indeed! Firstly there is the

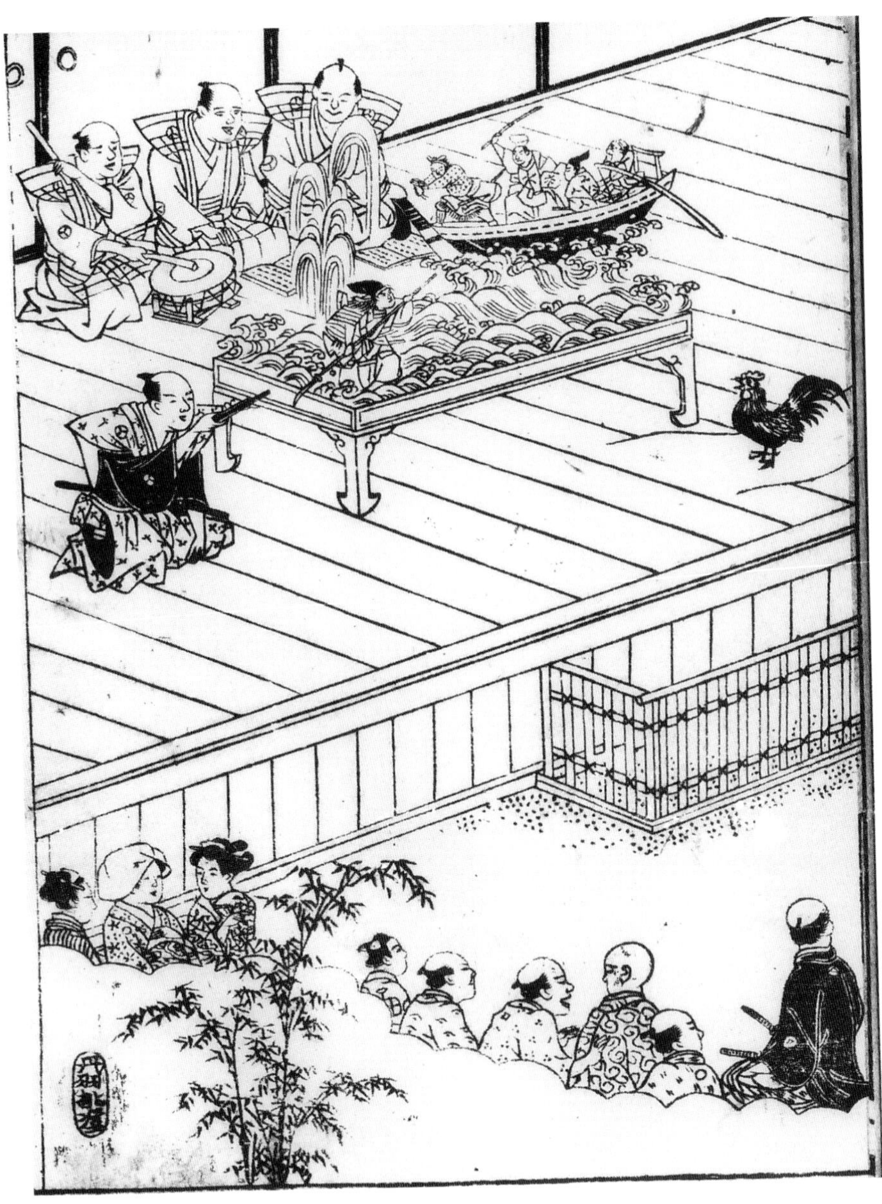

boat itself, then there are the moving dolls dressed up as Chinese lads. The *karakuri* doll of Yoshitsune will draw his great sword – yes! he pulls it clean out to run people through. Benkei is there, telling his beads and praying to malignant spirits.

To start things off, *karakuri* Chinese compare their [swords],[64] then the boys dance. Next, the doll representing Yoritomo appears from beneath the waves and comes up onto the platform. . . .[65]

And the booklet concluded, "this is a most amazing *karakuri*." Later on, the reader is told, an act will follow in which the entire stage is flooded, and afterward, a *karakuri* man will drink real sake and turn red in the face. Such tricks, and so much more, formed the stock of the water-*karakuri* showman at his best.

The *Benkei in the Boat* seems to have been a

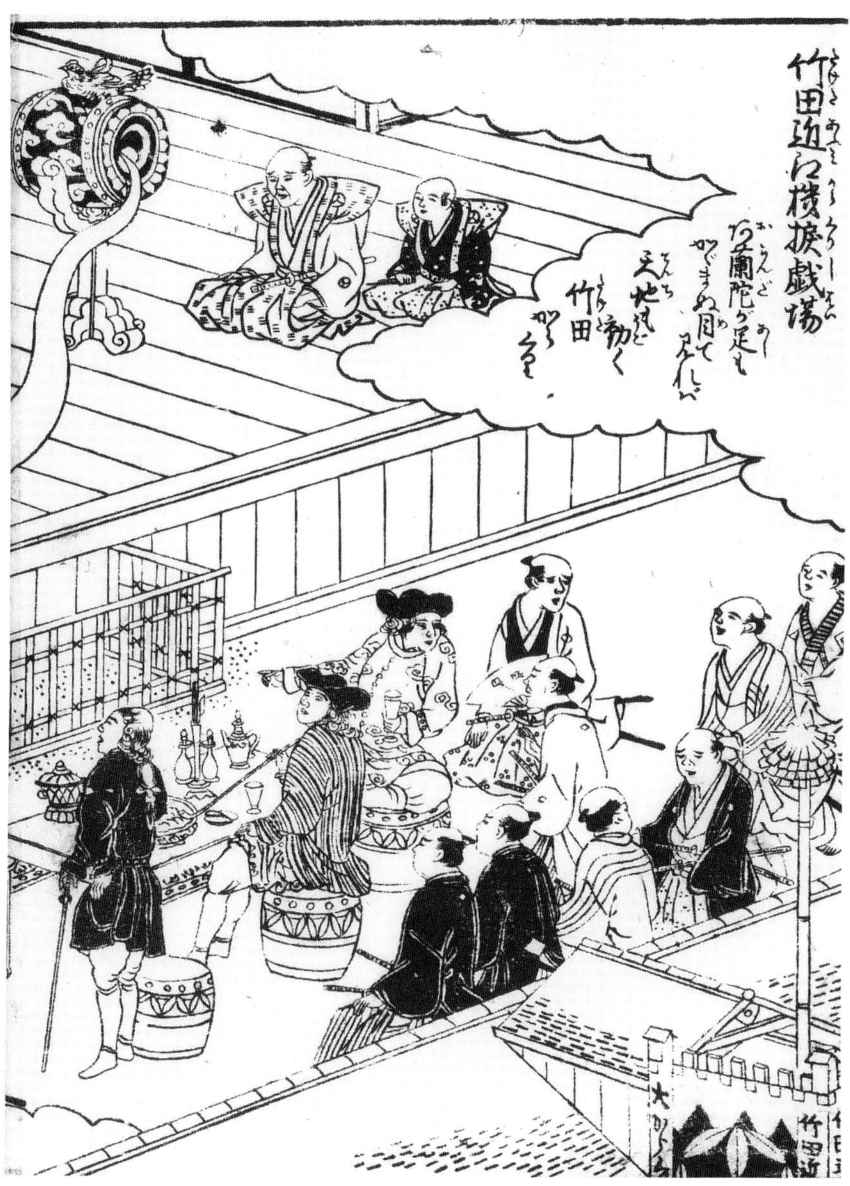

35. Takehara Shunchōsai, from Akisato Ritō, *Settsu meisho zue*, 1796. SOAS, University of London.

Takeda Ōmi's Karakuri Theatre, with Dutch spectators.

Takeda *pièce de résistance.* It is said to have been already seventeen years old when shown in Edo, and it held the stage for another forty years.[66] Akisato Ritō's *Famous Places of Settsu* showed in an illustration of the Takeda Theatre drawn by Takehara Shunchōsai the Benkei assemblage in operation. Supporting the act is another favourite, the *Cock of the Admonitory Drum (Kanko no tori),* the rooster of which has just flown down from its perch (Fig. 35).[67]

The Takeda *karakuri* in Shunchōsai's illustration are the standard pick. But the theatre is shown under rather unusual circumstances: the audience is unwonted, the act being performed for a group of Dutchmen. The text offers no rationale for this. Whether or not a VOC party ever really stopped to see the theatre is unknown, but it is possible that they did. Osaka was a favourite place among Westerners, located between the constrictions of Dejima and the formality of Edo; in the assessment of Thunberg at least, "this town is the most pleasant in all Japan"; he added the illuminating comparison that "it is in Japan what Paris is in Europe, a place where an incessant round of amusements is to be had." Thunberg went with other members of the entourage to various Osaka theatres and was able to enjoy "various other uncommon delights," although automata were not mentioned.[68]

To the side of Shunchōsai's picture a kyoka verse is inscribed noting the admiring Western reactions:

> The Dutchmen cannot even
> Bend their legs,
> Staring with their eyes,
> Heaven and Earth move –
> Takeda's *karakuri*.[69]

Takeda Ōmi's artifices impress, Ritō intimates, those who can best be thought to appreciate the intricacies of cunning mechanics. When it came to hidden workings, *Ran* was to the fore.

Clearly Shunchōsai was seeking to assimilate Takeda's *karakuri* into the rhetoric of Dutch *saiku* cleverness. Even though the stiff-legged foreign contingent marvelled at the display, they would not have been seeing anything they could not have witnessed before, for devices just like Takeda's *Benkei* were known in European cities. Samuel Pepys, earlier in the century, recorded what, *mutatis mutandis*, must have been a remarkably similar sight: an automaton, "with Neptune, Venus, mermaids, and Cupid on a dolphin, the sea rolling."[70]

CLOCKWORK *KARAKURI*

From the middle of the eighteenth century the most appreciated type of *karakuri* mechanism was not hydrobalistic but clockwork. The splendour of clockwork was that its source of power was completely internal and fully hidden, not even needing filling up. This made *karakuri* not only *seem* to run of their own accord but really do so. Many unspecified pieces – from Jotei's terrapin to the dolls in the *Benkei* group – assuredly used clockwork in some form.

To the Takeda, clockwork was the stuff of real automata. A non-lineal pupil of theirs, Hosokawa Hanzō, made this explicit in his *Illustrated Introduction to Karakuri (Karakuri kinmō zui)* of 1796, one of the first works of its kind. Dividing his book into three parts, Hanzō devoted the first (an extended preface) to clockwork in its original form – that is, to run clocks – and only when those vital premises had been adequately put across did he move to his stated subject. Hanzō terminated the first section with the robust statement: "Every *karakuri* ultimately uses rotating parts and escapement mechanisms *(tenpū kyōkarin)*. As such, clocks can be said to be at the root of all technology related to them."[71]

The primary requisite for clockwork is the spring. Displacement of the cords that had worked old-fashioned *karakuri* by the metal coil secured *karakuri* their place in the approved discourse of *saiku*.[72] The Japanese for spring is *senmai*, and Takeda Ōmi took this as his sobriquet, becoming Senmaiken, Master Spring, announcing thereby the crucial piece of mechanics that had allowed him to consign marionettes to rusticity. Understanding clockwork became the one essential qualification for subsequent *karakuri*-makers of the first rank.

When Rokujūen retold the story of the Suminama, he not only turned the ancient carpenter into a *karakuri*-maker, but with sublime anachronism made him into a clocksmith, suggesting it was by employing that mechanism that he had effected his greatest triumphs. In one episode, Rokujūen told how Suminama fabricated a cat so real that a thug, believing it to be alive, lunged at the thing with his sword; he clove the cat into two neat halves and was enormously surprised when "he picked up one half and saw that it was only a contrivance of wood, with innumerable little wheels inside."[73]

The first actual clock is believed to have come to Japan in 1551, brought by Francis Xavier.[74] The first extant piece was donated by the king of Spain to Ieyasu, first shogun of the Tokugawa line, some fifty years later, and was bequeathed to the his mausoleum on Mount Kunō in Shizuoka, where it remains to this day.[75] Terajima Ryōan's *Universal Illustrated Compendium* placed clockwork among the primary imports from Europe, and it remained a significant trade item over the next century and more.[76] As the years progressed, European horology moved in two directions: it became both increasingly extravagant, until massive assemblages of enamel and ormolu were the norm among the rich, and it also tended towards increasing miniaturisation, with the appearance of ever smaller watches, for keeping in the pocket, setting into boxes or trinkets, or hanging from the waist.

The English and French, especially, were involved in a lucrative trade in clocks with China. At the turn of the eighteenth century, the China clock trade was earning London an average of £8,000 annually; Qianlong alone was so avid a collector that in 1784 (not necessarily a typical year) forty-seven clocks were sent to him from Europe; he eventually amassed four thousand pieces, most highly elaborate and bristling with ancillary paraphernalia; it has been poetically said that his summer palace must have echoed to the trilling sounds, until "the gavottes and minuets of London rose strangely in the Chinese air" – accompanied, of course, by the spattering of his fountains.[77]

It is entirely consistent that European dealers should have endeavoured to expand their market to Japan, although numbers can only be guessed at.[78] Improvements in escapement were initiated in England, such as Thomas Tryer's duplex escapement of 1782, able to counter the inequalities of balance-spring motion and recoil. London lost its edge to Switzerland only during the Napoleonic Wars, and in Chūryō's opinion, London was "first in the whole world in the production of clock *saiku*."[79] Pocket watches came to be known in Japan as "London" clocks *(Rondon-dokei)*, and Chūryō wrote, "all the miniature clocks *(netsuke-dokei)* and other types of timepiece brought to this country are made there."

The compact sort were easier to export (and smuggle) and they arrived in Japan in larger numbers. Thunberg recorded how punctiliously the shogunal officers kept an eye on the watches of the VOC men as they went on and off their island on business, fearing they would sell them in town at huge profit and undermine the government monopoly.[80] But records exist of some quite elaborate automaton-clocks being introduced as well. One piece, said to have come from Holland, was exhibited in the precincts of the Temple of Isshin-ji in Osaka in 1821.[81] It was nearly two metres high, and encased in brilliant reddish-gold metal *(ryūkin)*; five cherubs were perched on top and bobbed about playing tunes on Western-style musical instruments to announce the arrival of the hour. The device survives only in report, and its appearance is uncertain, but a similar construction, though somewhat less elaborate, was depicted by one Ōhata Giemon in Nagasaki (Fig. 36). The clock (positioned on an apparently Japanese-made stand) has a panel at the front with moving elements near the base, and at the sides twisted glass rods mounted to swivel in sequence, giving the impression of falling water; on top are figures mounted in a pavilion of chinoiserie taste, ready to pirouette around a globe as the chimes strike.

The connexion between clocks and automata was literal in these highly worked pieces, and the objective of telling the time was all but ousted by the plethora of intricate appendages running off supplementary springs. If the "London" clock appealed through the intricacy of its make, the more rampantly polymorphous pieces thrilled because of their exuberant diversity.

But more can be said: the much-vaunted and regular precision clock was impressive, to be sure, but it had limited direct applicability in Japan, for time there was not told in the same way. Six hours each were ascribed to periods of day and night, and this number remained fixed throughout the year without regard to the relative lengths of periods of darkness and light; this meant the hours themselves had to vary in duration, night and day hours being seldom the same; further, as the months went by, the comparative lengths had to alter, too. A complicated formula was used to determine the distribution of calculated time, and a master of clocks *(tokei-shi)* was employed in wealthy households to oversee the necessary adjustments. Such a system played havoc with a steady Western piece that would be forever running either too fast or slow. A solution was devised by adapting the carriage clock and hanging weights from its gyrating ticker to restrict, and thereby alter, the speed of the mechanism, but it is not surprising that utility was not the supreme feature of the imported chronometer. Perhaps the general sense was summed up by Inaba Tsūryū in a lengthy work on fashion accoutrements, swords, and fabric.

36. Ōhata Giemon, *Imported Automaton Clock*. Private collection.

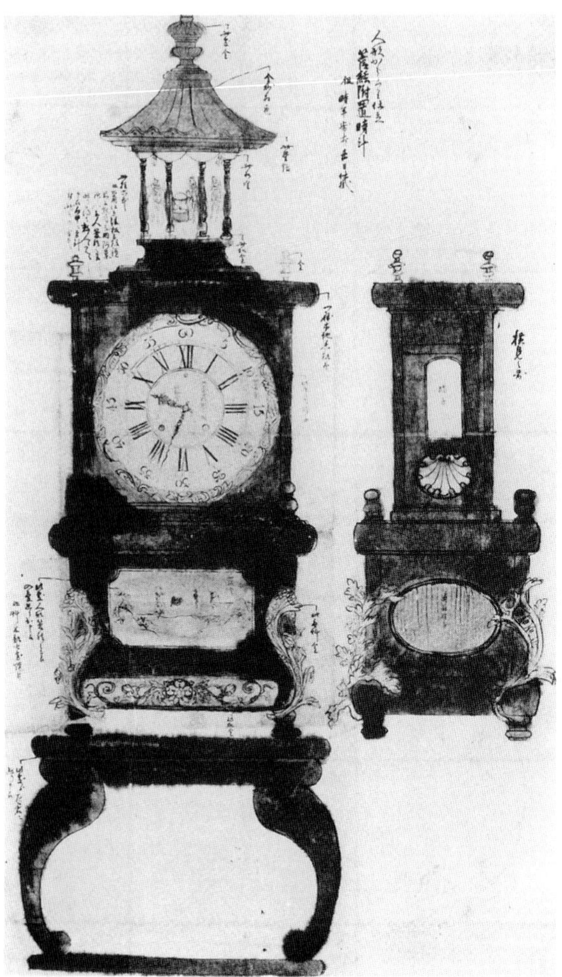

> Because they are offered up by the Red-furs [miniature clocks] are deemed Dutch, but in fact they are made in a neighbouring country called England . . . some also came over from France. In either case, they are wonderfully intricate and skilfully contrived, although it has to be said when they are hung from the waist, you never manage to get through a whole day without them going wrong. It's by far the best to enjoy their mechanisms in a playful kind of way, just turning them about in the palm of your hand.[82]

It made sense to adapt the machinery to working *karakuri*.

Time-telling was not the only point of clockwork. Luxurious display was as significant. The things were disastrously expensive. Isaac Titsingh tried to buy a Japanese-made clock to take home as a souvenir, as "the construction seemed curious," but "the high price demanded for them deprived me of this gratification."[83] Clocks could be positioned in mansions or businesses as a pose to suggest success and affluence, not really to tell the time (Fig. 103). The gentle ticking motion also suggested an order and calm well in keeping with the way in which the great and the good supposedly ran their affairs.

WESTERN INTERIORS, EDO HEARTS

There is no evidence of the Japanese market being as heavily encroached upon by Western timepieces as that of China, but there is ample data to support the position that the new Japanese *karakuri* grew largely out of Western clockwork. As this came to be seen as the quintessential precision mechanism, it bore an increased load of meaning until clockwork stood generically for all cunning and advanced contrivances. Automatic clocks measured that most nebulous of qualities – time – and even if they didn't necessarily do it very well, they could emblematise the bringing out of imponderables and the representation of the opaque in readable terms: an invisible quantity was being calculated by mechanical insides, and then displayed. As clockwork *karakuri* were often in human (as well as animal) form, the springs and wheels became metaphors for the body, with the dials and casings representing the face and skin. But it was notoriously hard to regulate a clock, so how, then, was the heart's metaphorical clockwork to be kept true?

Questions of how the heart and mind might (or ought) to relate to the exterior human aspect were forcefully addressed at this time by the new and popularising syncretic philosophical school of *Shingaku*.[84] Literally "Mind-and-Heart Learning," the term *Shingaku* was coined in 1778 by a veteran roadside preacher, Teshima Tōan, then age sixty. Tōan had set up an academy in Kyoto thirteen years before, and in the next decades his creed spread until there were twenty-two schools in fourteen *han;* by the end of the century the number had mushroomed to one hundred and eighty. *Shingaku* came to Edo in the person of Nakazawa Dōni, a pupil of Tōan, and from 1781 his stentorian voice was to be heard in sermons (*dōwa*) delivered at his school in Nihon-bashi, the Sanzensha.[85] Dōni wrote nothing, but notes taken by students were collected, and provide lively evidence of his colorful (though fearfully repetitive) sessions.[86]

The propositions of *Shingaku* were hardly new, but dressed up in a novel, ready-to-wear guise. Emphasis was placed on an individual's obligations to his or her heart and mind. Tōan used the simile of the mirror, arguing that, like a clouding over of the clear surface of the bronze, the pristine person was easily corrupted and spoiled. It was for each of us to strip off the smear of desire and return to their True Heart (*honshin*). The dusters to be used in the polishing were the meditation and ethics of *Shingaku*.

Dōni held that all phenomena were the creation of Heaven, and that the job of every being was to follow with rectitude and honesty their allotted course, or Way (*dō*), without striving to change it. "We, and all things," Doni stated in his punchy vernacular, "are just so many spooks churned out by phenomena, but if the particular state we find ourselves in seems arbitrary, it must still be adhered to."[87] He went on:

> What is this Way then? Well, it's a sparrow going "chirp-chirp" and a crow going "caw-caw." A kite has its kite-Way and a pigeon has its pigeon-Way, and in just the same manner, a great lord comes into his high rank and carries out what he must. None has any other desire. Heaven and earth cohering in harmony is the Way, and this will come about when things follow their individual Ways.

There was a political message here. Not surprisingly, *Shingaku* endeared itself to the government, and both Dōni and his followers were called in by the chief minister, Matsudaira Sadanobu, to lecture at Edo's penal reformatory.[88] From 1793, Dōni began to expound government edicts directly in his sermons, speaking in support of shogunal policy. But this was no oppression, he held, for all onerous responsibility, all labour and toil, glanced off the True Heart. It was liberation to conform to one's Way: "the unoccluded heart is like a mirror reflecting images but retaining no permanent trace."[89]

Metaphor was the teaching tool of *Shingaku* and there was no limit to what might serve. Morishima Chūryō was caught up in the movement and wrote a proselytising tract in 1795, *Gleanings in Shingaku Metaphor (Shingaku tatoegusa)*; it is interesting to wonder what similes a man like he might have drawn on in the sadly inextant book.[90] Dōni approached *karakuri* metaphors, and it is easy to see how clock analogies could have provided a powerful bolster to his ideas.[91] Machines only function when used for the purpose for which they were built: a tightrope-walking automaton will be poor at climbing ladders; a tea-carrying *karakuri* will not swim in water. Constraints and checks had to be maintained, just as a clock would only tell correct time when its weights were set correctly. Machines relied on an immediate and unbroken link between inner parts and external limbs, free of friction.

Shingaku was the teaching that could return phenomena to their Ways and, locating the heart within, bring it out to view. *Karakuri*-makers, by contrast, refused access to the insides of their pieces, and fooling an uncomprehending audience with false report was just the thing for them. Many *karakuri* were completely rigged. The Takeda Theatre, for example, had a strongman doll that would neck-wrestle for a wager, but anyone who looked beneath its skirts would see it was built into a post sunk deep in the ground and quite impossible to shift. What was special about clockwork was that it was not a hoax. But only constant maintenance could ensure its effective working. Clockwork was indeed like a member of Dōni's wayward congregation, internally complex and capable of diverse things but prone to be put to ends for which its own particular construction had not destined it. Keeping their insides to themselves and laying sweet, smiling faces over devious thoughts was the norm like an ill-set clock dial. A person ought to be his own master of clocks, with good regulation the ultimate goal.

No one wished to reveal his or her heart, just as no showman blew the gaff on *karakuri* tricks. Until, that is, Hosokawa Hanzō published his *Introduction to Karakuri* in 1798. Occasional leaks from *karakuri*-makers' workshops had occurred before, and some devices were well enough established to be open secrets, but Hanzō's was the first complete attempt to offer a thorough airing of his subject, right down to the hidden insides.[92] Hanzō's book smashed the whole *karakuri* world apart by illustrating devices both inside and out, and depicting them over several pages in advancing stages of dismantlement (Fig. 37). Like the cross-sections of Chūryō's and Kageyasu's fountains, *karakuri* interiors were now rendered open to view. To the *karakuri*-master, revelation was devastation. What inclined Hanzō to make his exposé is nowhere stated in his book, but I infer that, for him, clockwork, unlike almost any other mechanism, *was* as clever as it seemed, and did truly control the doll it appeared to, without resort to external aids or jiggery-pokery. Revealing their clockwork parts displayed, in Dōni's vocabulary, that the *karakuri* were in fact, "sincere" or "true" (*makoto*).

To Hanzō, then, his revelatory writing in no way annihilated the interest in the machine. This supposition was in every way one with patterns of popular thought in the late eighteenth century; the proper excitement over *karakuri* had become the system by which inner mechanical constructions related to external functionings. It might even have appeared that the revealing of interiors was a virtuous act, with the unexposed suspect or obscene.

Clockwork required a tedious degree of checking. As early as 1682, Ihara Saikaku, a great fictionalist from Osaka, had remarked, in his story *The Life of a Sex-mad Man (Kōshoku ichidai otoko)*, that it was desirable for a married woman to understand the working of clocks.[93] This was, of course, a utilitarian injunction, as wives must be taught to care for the household treasures. But clock owners were necessarily wealthy and hardly the class for whom home economics was a particularly stringent discipline; rich ladies

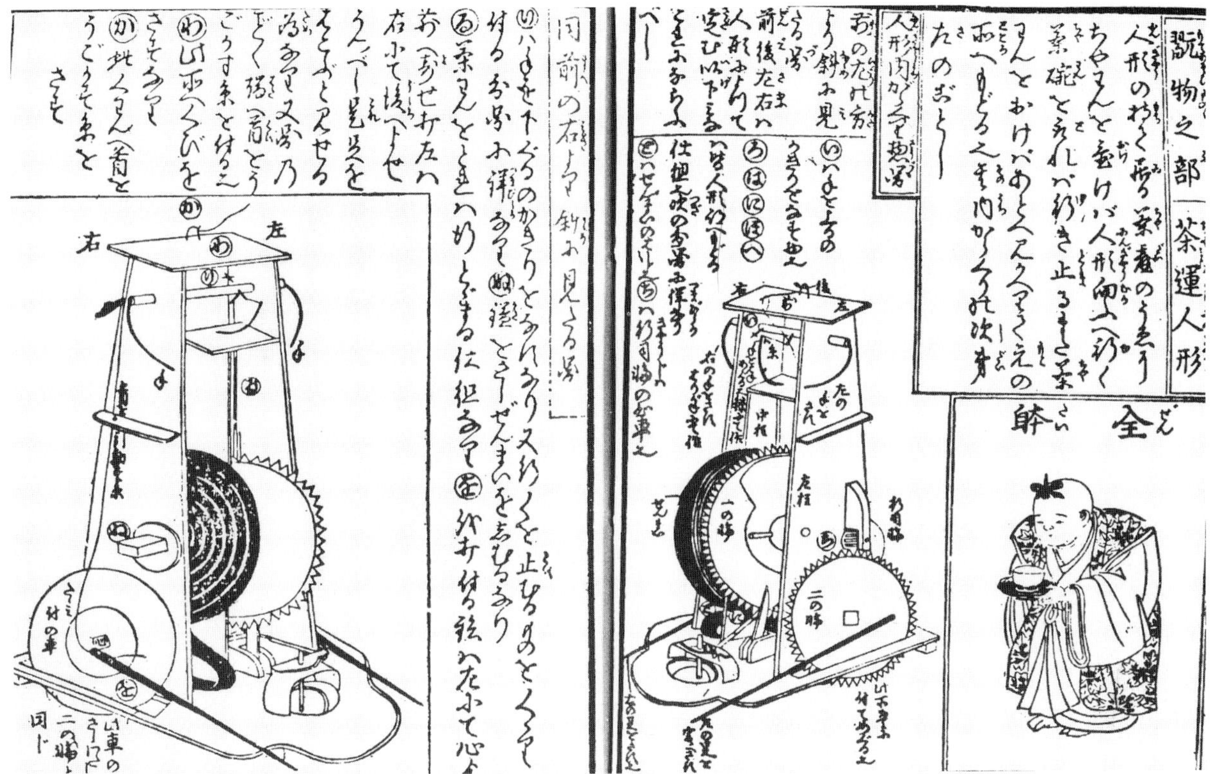

37. Unsigned, *Tea-carrying Boy*, from Hosokawa Hanzō, *Karakuri kinmō zue*, 1796. Private collection.

were seldom called to mundane tasks. Saikaku must include a sense of the insides of the clock as metaphors, the proper regulation of timepieces representing the proper regulation of the self.

Equating a clock's functioning with the human heart became a relatively standard trope. A painting by Nishikawa Sukenobu, datable to the mid-1750s, shows just this (Fig. 38). A lighted lamp indicates that it is night, but a woman is still up (or has risen from bed); her hands stray to the weighted cords of a wall-mounted domestic bracket clock; she is not correcting the mechanism, nor even trying to, but rather knotting the cords to immobilise the workings. Sukenobu's woman is doing the opposite of what Saikaku had enjoined, and she surreptitiously interrupts the correct running to make the clock read amiss. The viewer is left to surmise what is afoot. Perhaps in seeking to detain time, she hopes to defer the arrival of dawn, and we may suppose (given that this is a Floating World painting) the departure of her lover. Her notion is fond but thoroughly erratic, and she wrecks the clock as an obvious extension of her own inner turmoil. She will lie to keep what she wants; being so disequilibrated at heart, she cannot abide regulation in other mechanisms and lashes out to disorder machinery.

A more intelligent understanding of the potentials of clockwork appears in a work in the short and heavily illustrated comic kibyoshi genre, written by Jippensha Ikku and published in the same year as Chūryō's *Gleanings in Shingaku*

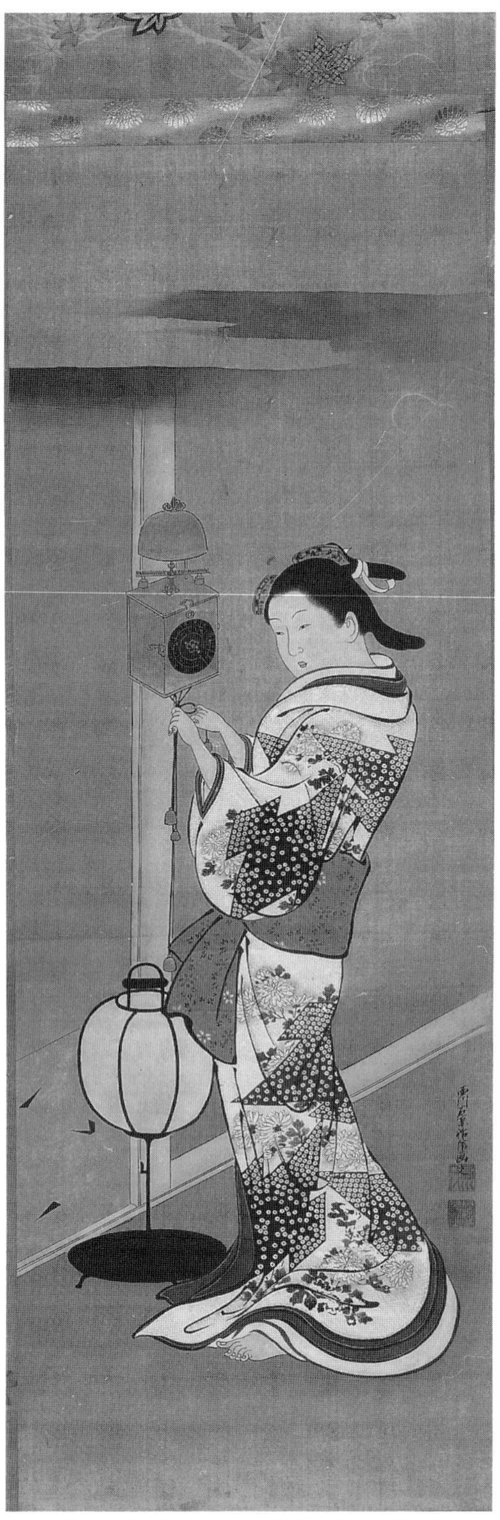

Metaphor. Ikku's title is somewhat similar – he turns Chūryō's into *Gleanings in Shingaku Clock-grass (Shingaku tokei-gusa)* – and punningly slides *tatoe* ("metaphor") into *tokei* ("clock").[94] Ikku had been born into a minor family of country officials and though brought up in a high-ranking samurai house in Edo; he was nowhere approaching Chūryō in social status. But in *Ran* or the Floating World, this was of no regard.[95] Ikku boldly wrote his *Shingaku* story in 1795 as his first effort at fiction, (he was encouraged to attempt it by Rokujūen).[96]

Ikku told of a wise young woman named Kashiwade who worked as a senior prostitute in the Yoshiwara district of Edo; literate and well-versed as well as pretty and alluring, Kashiwade takes advantage of her leisure hours to lecture the women of the establishment in *Shingaku*. Just as a clock runs differently by night and by day, so Kashiwade turns her daylight to mental and her night-time to financial profit. She is the perfect model of the sensible and balanced person.

Ikku extended the metaphor by referring to the specific peculiarities of time-telling, for to keep in trim, like a clock, the human being must temporise, adapting behaviour to suit the moment. Kashiwade expounds to the other brothel inmates how the logic of the night will not be the same as that of the day. Good and evil are not permanently fixed, and an act is judged by situation. With Japanese time, it was indeed the non-adapting clock that read most false. The pleasure districts were proverbially places where night-time truths failed to appear right in the cold light of day, and in the inverted world of brothels, prostitutes worked while other women slept, swore love for money, and made oaths that died with the dawn. But if all took their lessons from the clock and realised the different

38. Nishikawa Sukenobu, *Woman with Clock*, hanging scroll, c. 1730. Tokyo National Museum.

codes, none need ever lie, and night-time truth, like the hours of darkness, needed to be no less true for being different.

Ikku's title as well a parodying Chūryō's allowed for some puns: the ideogram rendered "gleanings" (*-gusa*) meant a published delectus or survey but literally it denoted grass in the botanical sense (read *sō*). The book, then, is both "*Shingaku* clock gleanings" and "*Shingaku* clockgrass." Clockgrass (*tokei-sō*) was a real plant, not indigenous, but imported to Japan from Brazil through Dutch agency in the second quarter of the seventeenth century.[97] It is the passion flower in English, so called because its odd-shaped bloom resembles the instruments of Christ's crucifixion, with nail-like stamens rising from a crown-like arrangement of thorny prongs. Europeans were inclined to see a symbolism in this, and the passion flower was invoked as a natural injunction to live a life of probity and honour so that death would have no sting. The passion flower brought judgment to mind, and in recognition of this it became a much-loved motif for clock decoration. More often the twisting stem was used, not the head, and timepieces with such arabesque designs on dials or facias were imported to Japan. It was in recognition of this that the plant became "clockgrass."[98] Japanese-made pieces adopted the pattern (Fig. 39).

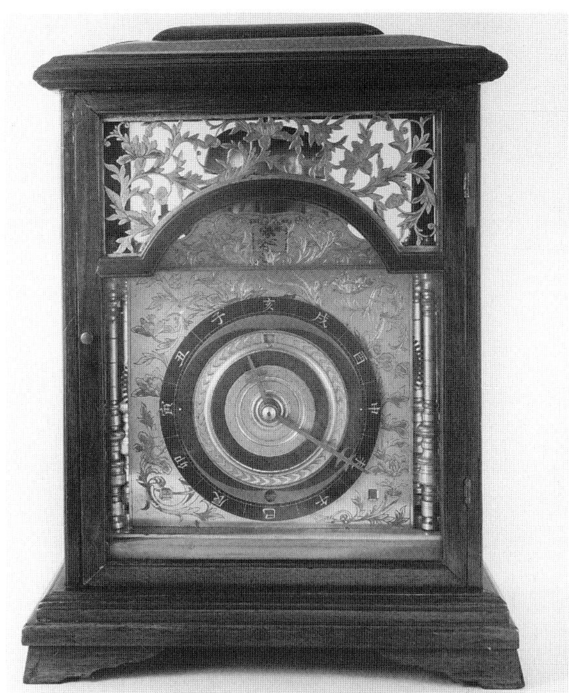

39. Clock with passion-flower motif; c. 1800. British Museum.

Ikku borrowed the rich metaphysical associations of the flower but adapted them to an entirely Japanese context. Gone are Christian referents and in comes *Shingaku*. Clockgrass no longer refers to the hope of redemption, but to the identity of inner workings with outer movements and the requirement to conjoin one's life with the supple demands of one's Way.

Not for nothing is Ikku's reader told that Kashiwade possesses a clock. Much sought-after in the Yoshiwara, she has more clients than she can cope with; but not wishing to cheat any or cut short their stints, she resorts to the clock, apportioning her services at one hour (two modern hours) apiece. Kashiwade takes regulation seriously and adopts timekeeping as her own responsibility (Fig. 40). Tea-house agents blandish and try to secure preferential allocations for the men they represent, but Kashiwade is resolute. Thoroughly unregulated importuners throng her rooms, but Kashiwade will not abandon precision. Ikku, who drew his own illustrations, showed her in the very act of resetting the mechanism of a lantern clock, correcting the movements with unerring rectitude.

The clock door is depicted as open, and Kashiwade is able to secure easy access thanks to the purpose-built aperture. One value of the clock as metaphor was the fact that its inward parts were supposed to be accessed, and ease of entry at time of regulation was one of the aims of the maker. *Karakuri*, of course, were otherwise, and as Hanzō showed, if any rotations ground or

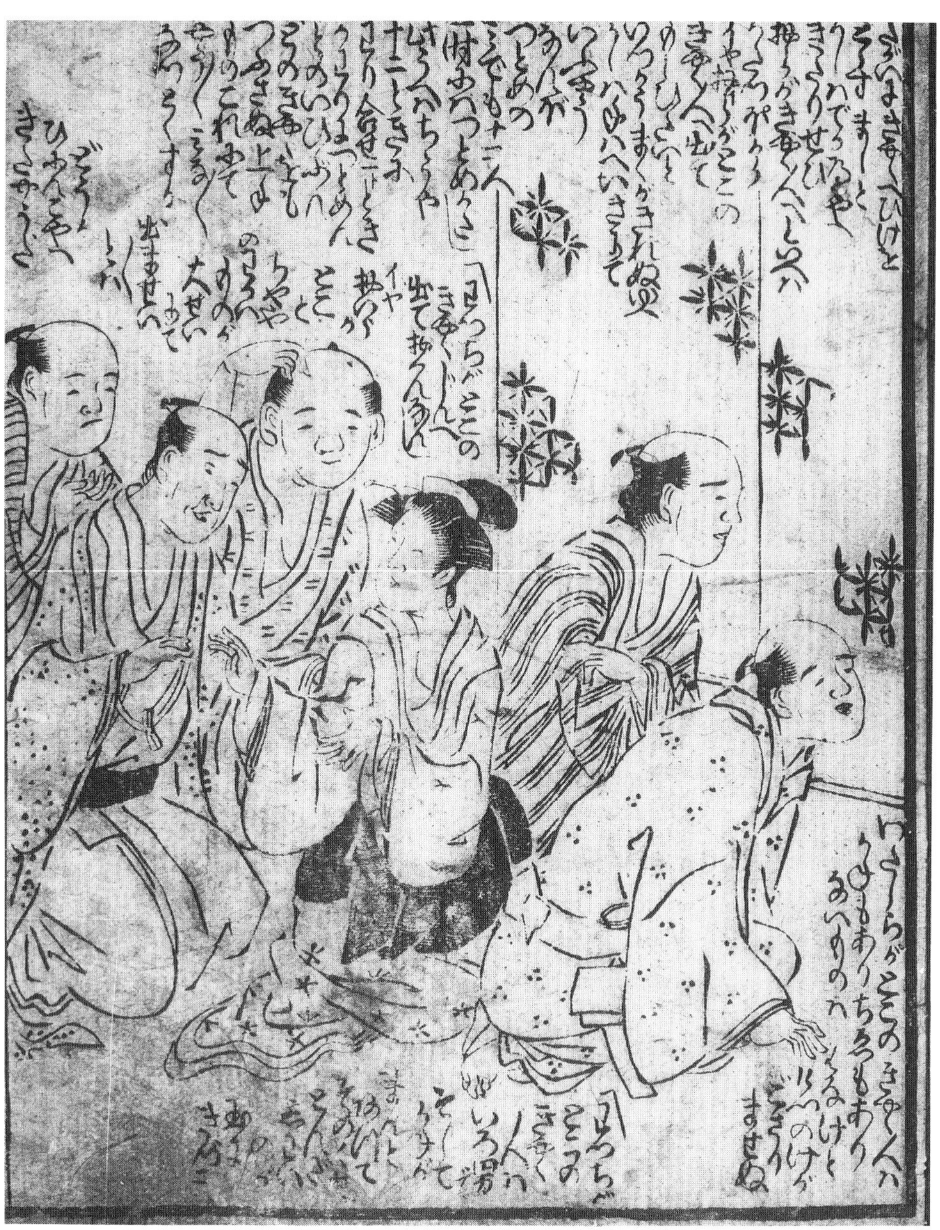

slipped they had to be disassembled for repair. Yet to the untrained eye a clock's workings, even when seen, were nothing so much as a mass of wheels, less enlightening than confusing. A person had to learn how to proceed; a fool approached the heart like an unschooled blunderer before cogwheels and springs, and exasperated at such shambolic disorder might just throw in the towel. As a senryu writer put it:

> No matter how cunningly made,
> A clock's wheels,
> Are just too many.[99]

But there were ways out. The metaphorical mas-

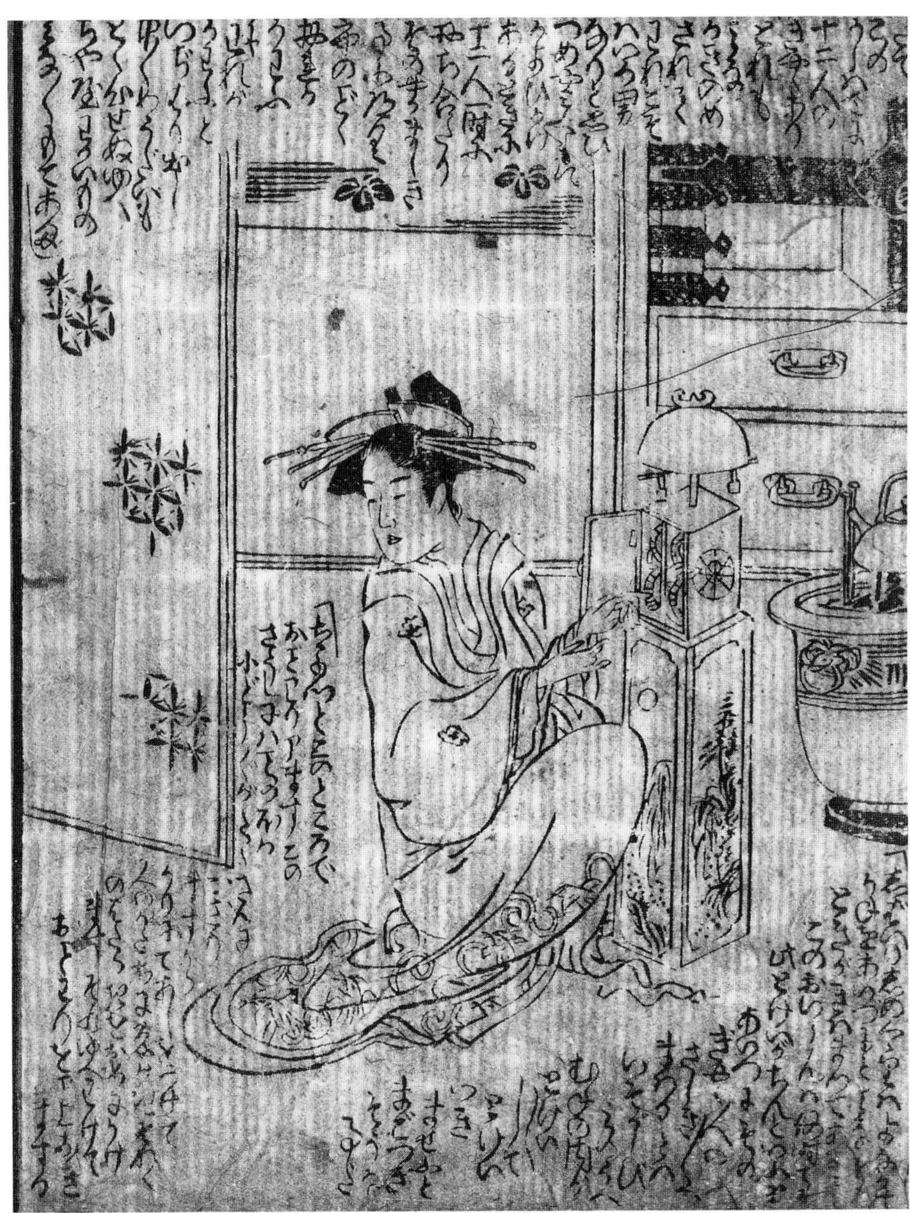

40. Jippensha Ikku, from his *Shingaku tokei-gusa,* 1795. National Diet Library, Tokyo.

Kashiwade adjusts her clock while tea-house agents crowd the room.

ter of clocks was the learned preacher or the wise disciple. Kashiwade's nimbleness of hand is a corollary of her immersion in *Shingaku.*

As clockwork *karakuri* with their wheel-and-spring innards spread across fairgrounds and centres of entertainment, novelists and writers extended the clock/heart analogy more specifically to the automatic model. Authors assumed the role of the master of clocks *vis-à-vis* their fictional characters, explaining and correcting inconsistencies so that the reader would not be abused. A number of stories appear from the 1780s describing the fictional characters' contorted thoughts in phrases such as the "*karakuri*

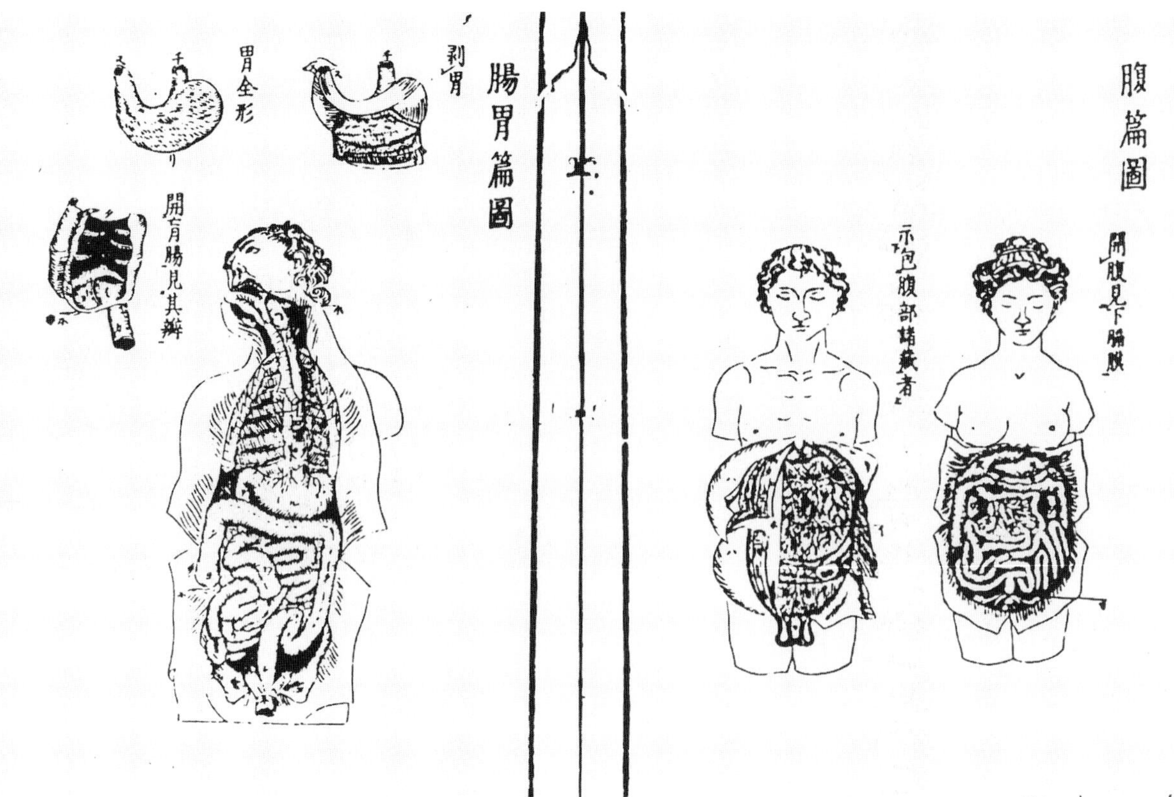

41. Odano Naotake, *Abdomen and Intestines,* from Sugita Genpaku (et al. trans.), *Kaitai shinsho,* 1774. SOAS, University of London.

in the chest" (*mune no karakuri/kyōchū karakuri*) or the "*karakuri* in the stomach" (*hara no karakuri/fukuchū karakuri*). The author will then reveal how they do not rightly connect. Bakin occasionally signed his stories "Bakin, the precision-device operator" (*saiku-nin*) – that is, it was he who set the *karakuri* of the fictional cast.[100]

The actual human interior was accessible to hand and eye by means only of anatomy or surgery. Those two fields appeared for the first time as serious clinical concerns in Japan in the late eighteenth century, and largely as a result of interventions by *Rangaku*-inspired doctors (*Ran'i*). There is no doubt that the extended intellection around the *karakuri* doll owed as much to shifts in medical theory as to the introduction of mech-chanised horology. Sugita Genpaku recorded in his history of *Rangaku* that the first great thrust of Dutch Studies had occurred in 1771, when he himself viewed a dissection. Katsuragawa Hoshū, his friend Nakagawa Jun'an, and Maeno Ryōtaku, were also present;[101] a seventy-year-old unnamed untouchable did the actual cutting.[102] Gentaku claimed the result of what he saw that day inside the dissected frame of the corpse (an old female criminal called Greentea) was so at odds with Sino-Japanese interpretations of the body that he was compelled to take action. The group of like-minded enthusiasts began to translate the Dutch medical book that they had taken with them to the autopsy, the *Anatomische tabellen* of Johannes Kulmus, first published in German in 1725.[103] The translation appeared in 1774 under the title *New Anatomical Atlas (Kaitai shinsho)*. The original copperplates from Kulmus's and other books were painstakingly transferred to woodblock by Odano Naotakė, a samurai from Lord Satake's *han*, brought down to Edo for the purpose by Hiraga Gennai (Fig. 41).

The European postulate of anatomy was that man was made in the image of God and that insides should be studied for theological reasons. Also, of course, an understanding of intestines and bones was held to be a prerequisite for restoring health. Anatomy laid its findings at the disposal of the surgeon, and surgeons opened and reset the malfunctioning body and sealed it again, like clock-masters of the physical flesh.

Neither anatomy nor surgery were much practised in Japan, for cadavers were scarce and few wished to subject themselves to the agonies of surgery, which was still conducted without anaesthetics. Western medicine was a discourse. But pictures abundantly conveyed a sense of the operating theatre, supporting it as a place of quite easy access to the internal areas of a body that, in Naotake's copies at least, was composed of tubes and pouches that looked remarkably akin to mechanical pieces. Some, like Shiba Kōkan, decried the *New Anatomical Atlas*, but readership was extensive, and the notion of a bodily interior available to hand and gaze was purveyed to the many.[104]

Ten years after *The Life of a Sex-mad Man*, Saikaku had penned a story entitled *Social Calculations in the Heart (Seken muna-zan'yō)*.[105] The title deliberately elided the separate notions of mental arithmetic and scheming. The year of the publication, 1692, was well before anatomy had become a topic of interest, but fictionalists of the *Rangaku* era reworked Saikaku's title and extended his conceit to address new discoveries in intestinal manoeuvrings. In 1795, Kyorori (a writer about whom almost nothing is known) wrote *One Heart's Social Calculations (Isshin muna-zan'yō)*, punning on the title of a Buddhist holy text, the *One-Heart Sutra (Isshin-kyō)*; in 1802, Hokusai wrote *Calculations in the Heart – a shelf-ful of lies (Muna-zan'yō uso no tanaoroshi)*; and four years later, Sanba dryly composed *How to Fiddle Short Division Calculations in the Heart (Muna-zan'yō hayawari no hō)*, playing arithmetic against the kabuki technique of quick costume changes where characters were suddenly disguised or unmasked.[106] The trend (as so often) had been started by Kyōden in 1791, with *Extempore Social Calculations in the Heart (Ningen sei muna-zan'yo)*, a title that could also be made to mean *Social Calculations in the Heart of the Living Person:* the double reading in Kyōden's title rendered explicit that his quest was for analysis of the full persona in its aspect of life.

In 1797, Tsuta Karamura wrote a kibyoshi that linked the idea of the machinating heart expressly to anatomy. The prolific illustrator Kitao Shigemasa, Kyōden's teacher, provided the pictures. Karamaru himself is better known as Tsutaya Jūsaburō, the Floating World's foremost publisher. The story begins as the chronicle of an exhibition of sacred statuary. Such events were occasionally held at metropolitan temples for fund-raising, and were called *kaichō*, literally "an opening of the shrine doors." But Karamaru's *kaichō* gets off to a bad start when the monks miswrite their advertising board, giving *kai-* as *bai-*, meaning "purchase"; this is evidently an event for the modern worldly Buddhist. The exhibition is actually a display of Buddhist icons warped to show the folly of contemporary life, and puns *kaichō* with the word recently invented by Rangaku doctors to signify anatomy, *kaibō*. He joins this to another pun, that between "human body" (*jintai*) and "divine image" (*shintai*). The book's title is a patchwork that can be unpicked either as *A Brief History of the Origins of the Exhibition of Divine Imagery* or as *A Brief History of Human Anatomy (Jintai/ Shintai kaibō/kaichō ryaku engi)*.

A number of holy images are on view at the temple, one of the Buddha's son, Ragorā. Sculpted Ragorās were common enough, and usually associated with Ōbaku Zen. Ōbaku was a Chinese school that had arrived in Japan in the mid seventeenth century and still retained strong overseas associations into which exotic Western medicine could be easily intruded.[107] Ragorā had so venerated his father, it was piously said, that his entire inward parts had transmogrified into Buddha-matter; the miracle was iconographically expressed by depicting Ragorā with abdomen riven open and an image of the Buddha inside (Fig. 42). As this *kaichō* is also an anatomical exhibition, the cut-open chest could be amusingly invoked, but Shigemasa reveals a Ragorā of a rather new sort (Fig. 43). This metaphorical anatomy reveals how great are the gaps looming between inside and out, for Ragorā's face and heart diverge. He looks his usual saintly self, but inside is not a Buddha at all but a miserable modern man: grinning out is the form of an Edo shopkeeper, greedy and smug, abacus in hand to tot up his profit and loss. But thanks to anatomy, the discrepancy is plain to see. A label placed before the statue reads, not The Venerable Ragorā (*Ragorā Sonja*), but "Treating People to Things Is a Waste" (*ogoru wa sonja*).

42. Shōun, *Ragorā*, gilded wood; before 1710 (with modern inserted figure). Gohyaku Rakan-ji, Tokyo.

The original face of the Buddha within Ragorā's breast has been replaced with a modern statue.

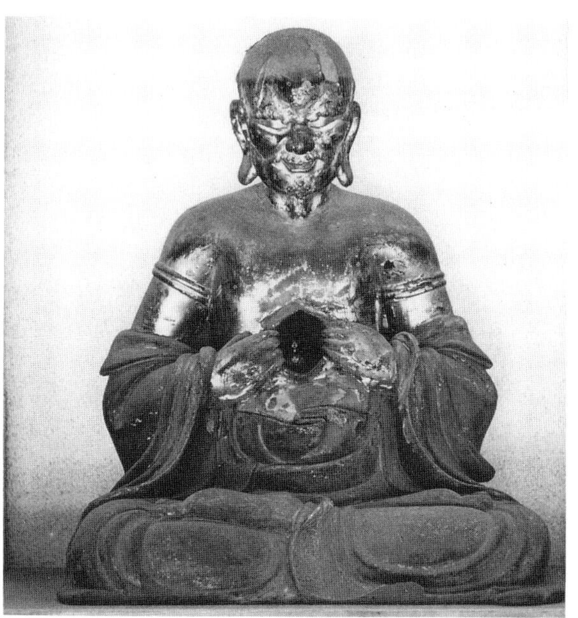

THE *KARAKURI* ASSEMBLAGE

Karakuri were often operated on stage singly, and at such times they might evince truths about individual persons. But machines were often combined into groups so that independent pieces conflated to form a more substantial show. *Shingaku* also stressed how the relative autonomy of individuals was built into a larger social whole: birds, beasts, and great lords following their own Ways accumulated into an overarching harmony of the heavens and the state.

Many of the finest *karakuri*, like the *Benkei in the Boat*, were assemblages, either running on a general governing motor or else with several drives working separately, but coming together in concert. It was the interconnectedness of the movements of such dolls, and the way in which their disparate activities locked into an overall cause, that ensured admiring gasps.

Types were legion, but one *karakuri* grouping was repeatedly assayed by makers – the automated ship. A ship was a very serviceable theme, for sea-bound life was corporate, self-contained, and dependent on each crew member performing his routine with punctuality. Boats functioned symbolically in Japanese thought, as they did in the West, and in times past had represented the human condition, a random mass forced together, adrift on expanses of water.[108]

Tsūdayū, a castaway who, like Kōdayū,

passed through Russia and was entertained at court (in his case by Tsar Pavel) had seen highly intricate model ships, as he informed Ōtsuki Gentaku, who interrogated him over a period of forty days after his return in 1804.[109] The Russian boats were seen in the Imperial Palace in St. Petersburg and could seat five or six people. They were sailed about to practise naval strategy in a pond (the old *Rangaku* scholar interpolated) about the size of Lake Hakone, not far from Edo. In 1809, Honda Toshiaki put the effectiveness of such exercises to the test, fixing up toy vessels for his employer, the daimyo of Kaga.[110]

In Japan it was less the convoy or stand-off of ships that came to be built than a single vessel. As a metaphor, one regulated crew might refer to the general task of communal integration. *Karakuri* boats of many kinds were made, but given the associations of automata with Europe and the wonderment evoked by the *Oranda-bune*, the majority were done to look like VOC East Indiamen, with passengers and crew shown as Dutch or Indonesian.[111] Kōkan's comment that Western sailors behaved like acrobats was germane, as leaping and swinging were among the commonest tricks of *karakuri* dolls.[112] In 1812, Ichida Seishichirō, a Nagasaki-born *karakuri*-maker living in Edo, began work on a fully mechanical Dutch ship some sixty centimetres long and made of glass. It was finished seven years later and put on display in Asakusa, where it became a popular attraction. All decked out it was complete with *karakuri* dolls looking like Indonesians that moved about the vessel, shinneyed up the rigging, turned somersaults, and finally fired off a cannon with a deafening roar.[113] Seishichirō's assemblage was such a hit that it became the subject of a bawdy song:

> The Palace maid and the glass ship –
> You can look at them and heap up praise,
> But I bet you can't get aboard![114]

Other ships followed. Glass seems to have been popular, perhaps because it allowed vision into the interior. In the second month of 1832, Kodera Gyokuchō, the tireless recorder of exotica from Nagoya, saw a "glass *saiku Oranda* ship" set up behind the main hall of the Temple of Daisu-zan.[115] It was, he said, "an absolute must," fully twenty-five metres long and with "innumerable dolls on board." The maker was one Ōmi Yosaburō. Gyokuchō went on (contradicting his remark of a few lines earlier), "the ship is twenty-two metres long, with a fine two-mat palace-like superstructure three metres high; the mast is eleven metres, and the sails six."

Jotei, the alcoholic *karakuri*-master who devised the water-activated terrapin, also made a model ship during the years that Seishichirō's was under construction. It represented a veritable community in miniature, with all parts running on a single power source and meshing in peerless unison. Jotei considered the model the crowning achievement of his glorious career, and he began it only when he felt his death approaching. He consciously devised the ship as his testament, and dedicated it to the Lord of Matsue who had so favoured him.[116] Jotei is said to have disappeared into his workshop for many days and to have emerged at last with a smooth, sealed box; this he entrusted to a retainer of the *han*, Nagao Sakyō, then bound for Edo where the daimyo was residing. The journey from Matsue to the shogunal capital was a long haul, and one of the rigours was negotiating the mountains at Hakone; those crossed, celebrations in the town of Odawara on the farther side were traditionally in order. But on this occasion jollity became excessive: amid the carouses Jotei's box was brought out and, notwithstanding strict instructions to the contrary, opened.

The lid sprang up at a touch of the catch and out popped a perfect replica of a Dutch three-master. A model captain, some twelve centimetres high, appeared on the prow, poised with telescope in hand; upon the turning of a lever, the *karakuri* began to work: the captain withdrew to his cabin, while sailors dressed as Dutchmen

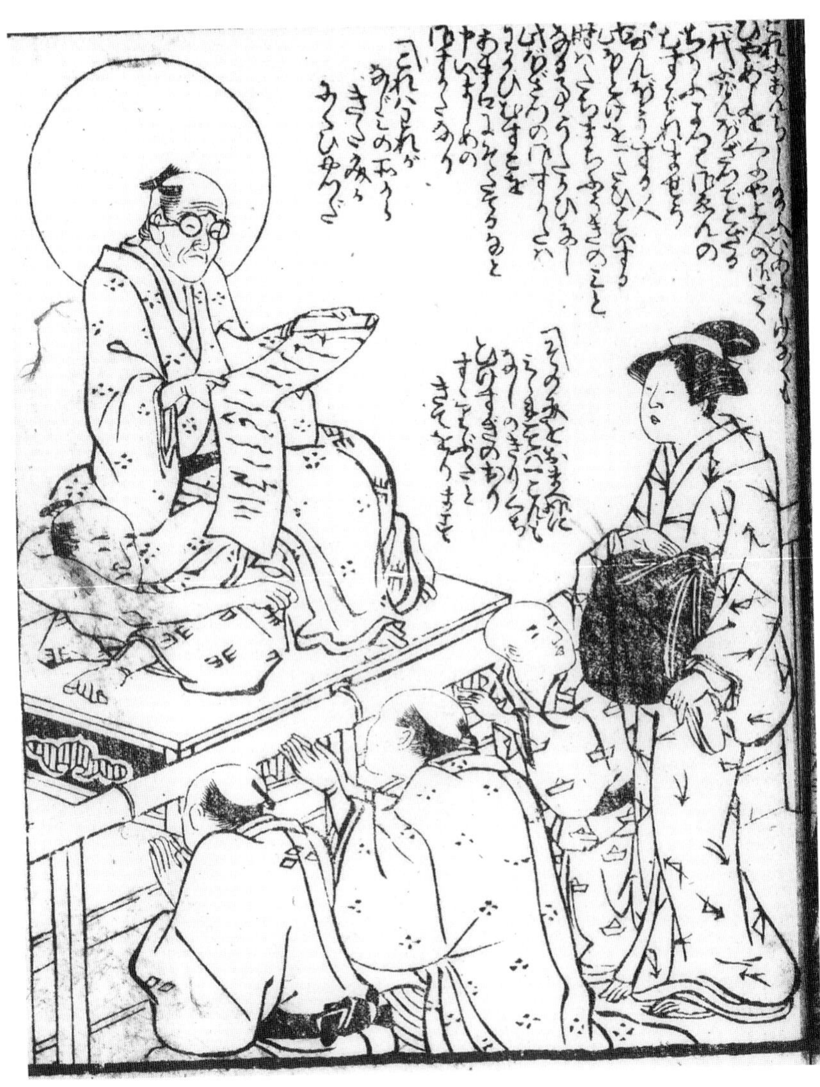

came out on deck; moving forward together to where a miniature cannon was positioned, at a signal from their leader, they fired it off. A ball bearing the markings of Matsue shot from the muzzle. But here disaster struck. Perhaps because the box had not been set on the level, the ball fell short and landed on the superstructure of the ship, crashing through the delicate parts and destroying the model entirely.

The clockwork mechanism had revealed itself in a ballet that was both perfectly timed and (barring *force majeure*) infinitely repeatable. The *karakuri* elucidated in visual terms the mysterious ability of well-run societies to gel, in and out knowing no division. The Tokugawa order was supposed to work thus, unchanged for generations and always true. But by the late eighteenth century the pretence could no longer be maintained. Social disorder was rife, civil unrest was common, and the people lived lives, it was felt,

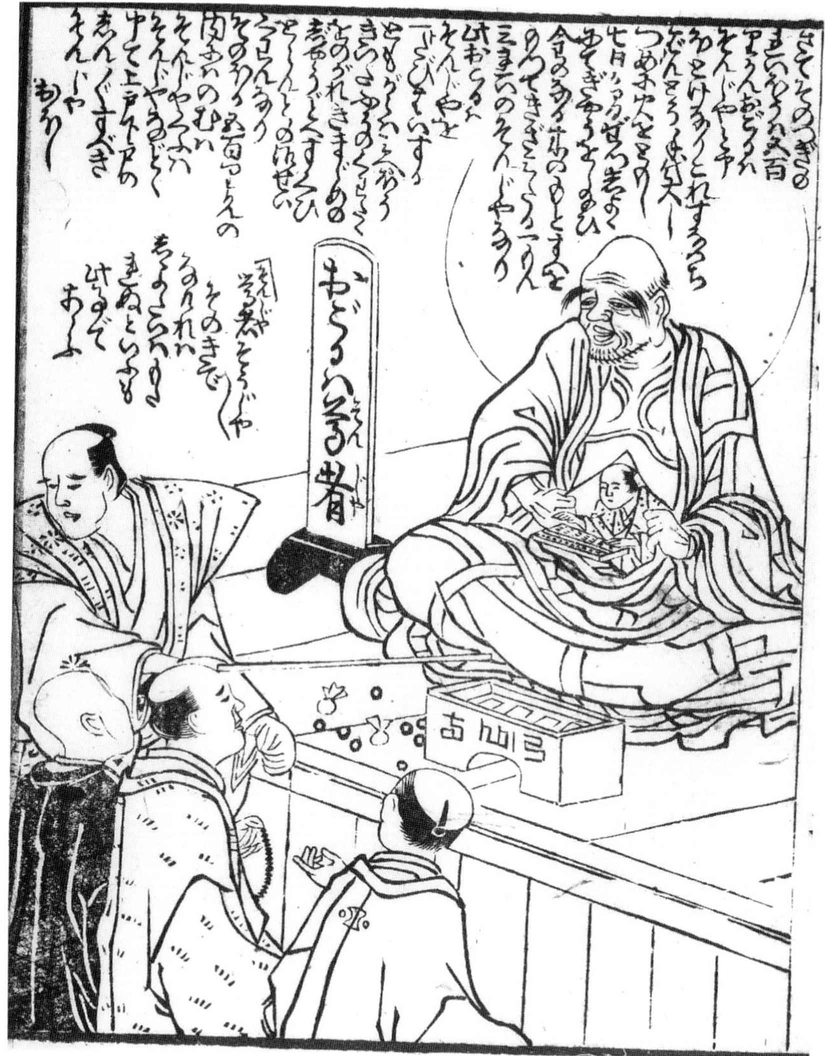

43. Kitao Shigemasa, from Tsuta Karamaru, *Shintai kaichō ryaku engi*, 1797. National Diet Library, Tokyo.

Parodies of riven-breasted Ragorā, and the elephant-riding Bodhisattva Fugen.

of severest reproach. Unless the skills of opening and prying were taught and used, the social contract would fall apart. *Shingaku* – preached in the prison, touted on the street – was the desperate remedy, and its rhetoric came from the moving machine.

If Jotei's ship had proved faulty, that was because Sakyō had been aggressive and grasped a device not destined for him. Such human mischievousness and craving for more than one's entitlement was typical, but always contradictory of the greater good, throwing order into chaos. The perfection of the model ship stood out in pitiful relief against the wayward Sakyō who coveted his master's toy and forgot the Way of the samurai. Actual persons and polities rarely ran as well as motors did. But when he saw what he had done, Sakyō did the decent thing and committed suicide.

FOUR

MACHINERY FOR PICTURES

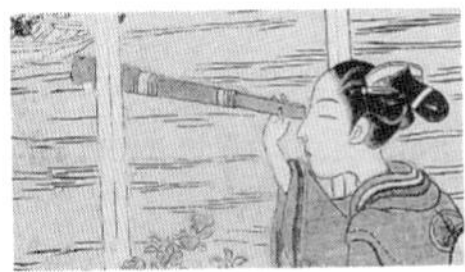

THE ARRIVAL IN JAPAN of Western pictures provoked considerable comment. The rhetoric surrounding imported images, as shown in Chapter 2, was one of accuracy, closeness, and fidelity to the thing depicted. In a word, they were *saiku* (precision works). But imagery did not enter in isolation. It came, in many cases, together with a range of machinery intended for its proper viewing. To look at two-dimensional representation in the Western style (*Ranga*) often began by peering into a regulating apparatus that supplanted the empirical gaze. *Ranga* were, in fact, besieged by the requirements of a thoroughly new regime of viewing. It is necessary here to consider the novel European picture, and its governed gaze, in order to comprehend, in the eighteenth-century Japanese sense, what the Western scientific gaze as captured in art fully came to signify.

THE COPPERPLATE ETCHING

Ranga was first and foremost a style, and Western pictures were seen to delineate with recognisable differences. They dispensed at a stroke, early commentators remarked, with the panoply of spiritual essences by which established forms of painting attributed meaning. It was known that Europeans worked in oils (*abura-e*), which required brushwork as much as a Japanese painting, but imports were largely confined to prints, both book plates and single-sheet sets.[1] There were only two European paintings on open view in Edo in the eighteenth century (and probably none in other cities), both done by a sometime court painter to the Elector of Brandenburg, Willem van Royen; one depicted *Flowers, Fruit and Fowl,* the other *Peacock, Parrot, Ostrich and Tiger with a View of the Rhine.* Both were housed in the Temple of the Five-Hundred Arhats (Gohyaku Rakan-ji) located on the city's outskirts – they were lost when a storm blew out the hall doors in about 1820.[2] Most imports were copperplate prints. Morishima Chūryō included a terminology of etchings in his Dutch dictionary, *Lexicon of Primitive Words (Bangosen).* He translated the Japanese word *gaku* (meaning any framed as distinct from scroll or screen-mounted picture) as "print" (*pureinto*). To Chūryō, the framed Western work and the print were coterminous, and he ignored the phenomenon of the hung painting altogether.[3]

Many imported etchings were of a low aesthetic quality, not the creations of a Dürer, or even the printed reproductions of bona fide Western art, but banausic pieces destined for largely non-aesthetic consideration. In aiming at capturing the visions of the scientific gaze, some felt, *Ranga* delegated its powers to the object depicted and forewent the thrill inherent in depiction. Having lost touch with the higher ideals of aesthetics, such works might have to be banished from serious consideration, surrenderers in the struggle for beauty. The Western work could be termed banal, or simply tedious: *Ranga* might be construed as drudgery, devoid of spirituality and so of depth. Tani Bunchō, sometime teacher of Kunenbō and painter in attendance on Matsudaira Sadanobu, indulged occasionally in the *Ranga* style (he copied van Royen's *Flowers, Fruit and Fowl*), but he finally came to the following conclusion, as his pupils reported in the posthumous *Bunchō on Painting (Bunchō gadan)*: "I used to have a large number of Western pictures in my collection, but I tend to find them like the forms people engrave on seals: they have no meaning (*imi*). When you try to appreciate a Western picture on a profound level, you always find something lacking."[4] Bunchō found such works mechanical and reduced. He felt *Ranga* placed intolerable restrictions on both maker and viewer alike.[5] The opinion was commonly enough shared that in 1799 Kōkan told how he had learned from Gennai that "the other year" a shipment of "several hundred Dutch copper-plates" had all been returned to Europe, having failed to generate enthusiasm in Japan.[6]

Rangaku scholars, of course, lauded this sort of picture. Lord Satake of Akita was an avid collector of imported prints, and other members of the shogunal court might have been so too; there seem even to have been pieces in the Tokugawa's own storehouses (reformatted as handscrolls).[7] The VOC was aware that illustrated compendia could make excellent gifts or bribes to the right recipients, and they came bearing publications that had visual appeal. Some European books achieved fame for the quality of their figures. The accuracy of the specimens in Rembertus Dodoneus's *A New Herball, or Historie of Plants (Cruydt-boeck)* of 1554 was such that the botanist and ex-samurai Hiraga Gennai called them, "amazingly precise" (*hanahada kuwashiki*; Fig. 44).[8] Those in Johannis Jonstonus's *Natural History of Quadrupeds* (*Naeukeurige beschryving van der natuur der vier-voetige dieren*) of 1649–53 sent the mind of the shogun Yoshimune reeling, and he extolled them with the same term, "precise" (*kuwashiki*), as well as "meticulous" (*seimitsu*; Fig. 45).[9]

Copperplate technology underwent significant change in the seventeenth century, and by the heyday of *Rangaku's* popularisation, illustrations of considerably more refinement than Dodoneus's were possible. Shiba Kōkan remarked on how the more recent European efforts were distinct improvements over those he had seen before, and he favourably compared Jonstonus's *Quadrupeds* with Ambroise Paré's *De Chirurgie*, first published in 1592. Once the later had been seen, Kōkan judged the earlier book "remarkably coarse" (*hanahada sōsotsu*).[10]

Woodblock printing had been practised in East Asia since ancient times; indeed, its diffusion there considerably predates that in the West. But compared with copperplate, woodblock is exiguous, its lines thicker and perforce less dense upon the page, and its scope for 'precision' depiction commensurately less. Etchings also had more extended runs, for whereas a woodblock could produce hundreds of impressions, an etching made thousands.[11] Eighteenth-century Japanese prints are today rightly praised for the deftness with which they handle their medium, and they remain esteemed objects in the history of world art; but if a *saiku* picture was sought, the woodblock print was restrictive.

Rangaku experts took up the cause of the copperplate etching. The entire scientific project, with its scrutinising and prying, would be little more than elite time-wasting unless the results could be committed in multiply purchasable form. Copperplate printing was ideal. In 1783, Kōkan became the first person in Japan to resurrect the etching technique, lost after closure of the Jesuit press in the 1610s.[12] Five years later,

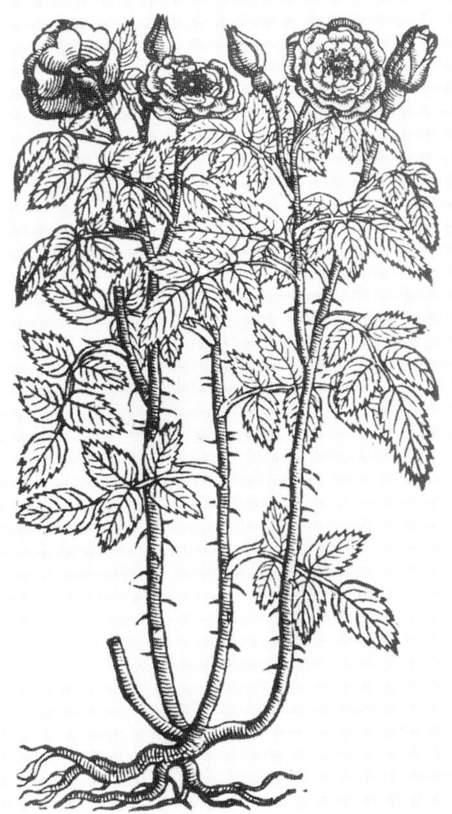

44. (left). Unsigned, *Rose,* from Rembertus Dodonaeus, *Cruydt-boek,* Antwerp, 1644. Private collection.

45. (below). Unsigned, *Elephant,* from Johannis Jonstonus, *Theatrum universale omnium animalium quadrupedum,* Amsterdam, 1755. Private collection. *The later Dutch translation was known in Japan, the author given as Jan Jonston, and entitled* Naeukeurige beschryving van de natuur der viervoetige dieren *(illustrations unchanged).*

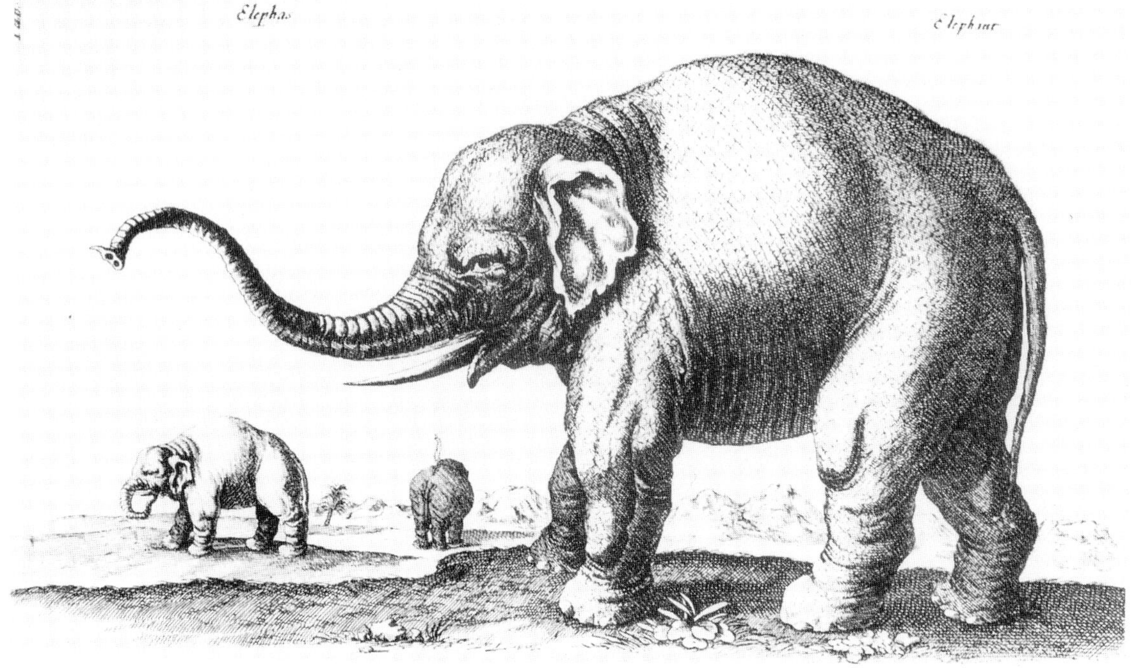

Morishima Chūryō addressed the subject in his *Red-fur Miscellany (Kōmō zatsuwa)* in an entry entitled "On the Western Painting Style and How to Make Copperplates" (*Seiyō no gahō tsuke dōban no hō*); he mentioned a display of the extraordinary properties of aqua fortis laid on at a private medical centre in Edo: "its keen efficacy was demonstrated the other year at a Pharmacopaeic Assembly (*yakuhin-e*) held at the Seijū-kan, and there were those to witness it."[13] Chūryō explained the method by which the plate was bitten and the print then pressed. Kōkan himself remained close-mouthed about his achievement, and as late as 1805 was still teasingly scant in what he would divulge. He remarked in a section labelled "Copperplates" (*dōbanga*) in his large work, *Dutch Navigation (Oranda tsūhaku)*, only, "I shall expose the techniques of etching for the benefit of all the curious in my forthcoming *Dutch Strange Devices (Oranda kikō)*" – a book that never appeared.[14] But elsewhere Kōkan applauded the admirable role printing could play in the exposition of scientific discovery and, further, how routinely illustration was used in Europe to accompany academic texts (a state of affairs quite unlike that in Edo Japan): "writing can convey ideas, but only pictures will serve when it comes to shape and form, and it is for that reason in their lands they expound knowledge through book illustrations."[15]

THE ETCHED VIEW

Probably the single largest body of Western visual data arriving in Japan was not, however, scientific illustrations but single-sheet printed views, or *vedute*. *Vedute* were wildly popular in Europe in the later eighteenth century. Initially a painted genre intended for the wealthy traveller (Canaletto's views of Venice and London achieved the summit of the style), but they soon trickled down the social scale as prints. This was the age of empire and discovery, and the general populace craved views of foreign and domestic wonders. Paintings might be transferred to print, as Canaletto's were, but myriad minor artists headed straight for the copperplate. Small and handy (some twenty-five by forty centimetres), the standard *veduta* could show an arm-chair traveller the delights of far-flung places they would never visit, at a very modest price. Possibly quite huge numbers came to Japan (notwithstanding the "several hundred" Kōkan said had been sent back), and *vedute* may have been the widespread assumption of what Western art most absolutely was. Kōkan identified London as the first centre of European art, an impression that would have been mistaken unless it was the topographical view he had in mind.[16]

Rendering visually plausible an unexperienced site was the goal of the printed *veduta*. It aimed to excite with a sudden sense of "being there" in a place where one had never been. In furtherance of this aim, any number of sleights of hand were permitted. *Veduta* images were not honest, either geographically or topographically, and although verisimilitude was all-important, a bald capturing of the empirical was not desired. Pictures were further intended to liberate viewers from the confines of their surroundings and to give them a plausible sense of access to a new and expanded world. The first artillery piece in the battery of spatial simulation was perspective, and steep lines of recession were wheeled in with unprecedented ostentation. English and French printed views could even be called simply "perspectives," and the vertiginous extremes of the linear recession are indeed the principle feature of the genre (Fig. 46).[17] When Chūryō included the term *seiyō-kei* ("Western scenic view") in his *Lexicon*, he translated it merely as *perusupekuchifu* ("perspective") as if application of that technique were all that need be said of Western landscape depiction. To come upon a place in actuality after growing accustomed to it in a *veduta* was to experience a sad diminution. When such works arrived in Japan, it was the dramatic march towards the centre of the vista and the opening up that this gave into the body of the city depicted that must have appealed.

Perspective was impressive. But to function it required the viewer's physical cooperation: the picture had to be placed at the right level and directly in front, neither too high or too low, neither to left or right. Failure to respect the codes resulted in distortions that vitiated the suspension of disbelief. As Kōkan wrote:

> The Western pictorial manner (*seiyō no gahō*) operates on a highly theoretical level and no one should view works off-handedly. There is a correct way to look, and to this end pictures are framed and hung up. When viewing them, even if you only intend a quick glance, stand full-square in front. The Western picture will always show a division between sky and ground [the horizon line]; be sure to position this exactly at eye level, which, generally speaking, will entail viewing from a distance of about 180 cm. If you observe this, things shown near at hand and things far off – the foreground and the rearground – will all be clearly distinguished and the picture will seem no different from reality itself.[18]

The viewer had a direct role to play and had to concentrate. Gone is the old requirement to engage with the picture in any spiritual way. Espousing the stipulated comportment was enough to manipulate the person into a special visual relationship, whereupon he or she would be automatically ballistered into the interior of the depicted realm.

Stillness of posture was also required. As the eye had to be placed exactly at the point where the pictorial presence obliterated itself – the spot where all lines dropped into the black hole at the end of representation – no movement whatsoever was allowed. To sway even fractionally threw such rigorous perspectival schemes into disarray, undermining the illusion with the absurdity of anamorphosis. The physique of the viewer was subsumed by an event of looking that gave sole authority to the eyes. But if *vedute* were dictatorial in these demands, they were able to be so emphatic thanks to invention of a machine devised to constrain the gaze. This was the *optique*. Kōkan wrote: "[Europeans] represent human figures, landscapes, and everything else in the form of 'perspective views.' Pictures are positioned under an *optique* upside down . . . and are viewed reflected in a mirror. [Thanks to this], landscape and vegetation look just as they do in real life." Kōkan was at pains to stress that the regular Western image is not in fact most typically viewed hanging on a wall but loaded into an apparatus. To clarify for those who had never seen such things, he depicted the two types of *optique* then in current use, adding the simpler expedient of a normal domestic mirror (Fig. 47). The *optique* shown in the centre was the most widely diffused, known in English as a "diagonal viewing machine"; it held its own as standard European furniture until the late nineteenth century, by which time it was marketed under the pseudo-scientific name of a zograscope. In Kōkan's picture, the views (labelled "B") lie flat, and are looked at once removed, as he noted, detached from the page and floating in suspension in a looking-glass (labelled "A"), fixed at 135 degrees to the eye.

Pictures had to be put in the *optique* upside-down because as well as the mirror there was also a lens (Kōkan's "C"). This added another degree of illusionism, for as the mirror pulled the image upward, the lens enlarged it, while at the same time circumscribing the area of vision so that paper margins were cut out and the scene took over all the field of sight. It was a breathtaking effect and, seemingly, perfectly true. But this was no "normal" vista either. The *optique* provided what was quite palpably a construct, utterly removed from any routine experience of looking, and fundamentally unlike deploying an empirical gaze. Eyes were sent leaping through glassware before being allowed to land in the space of a picture which, though precisely drawn and plausible, was in no way checkable against a world outside.

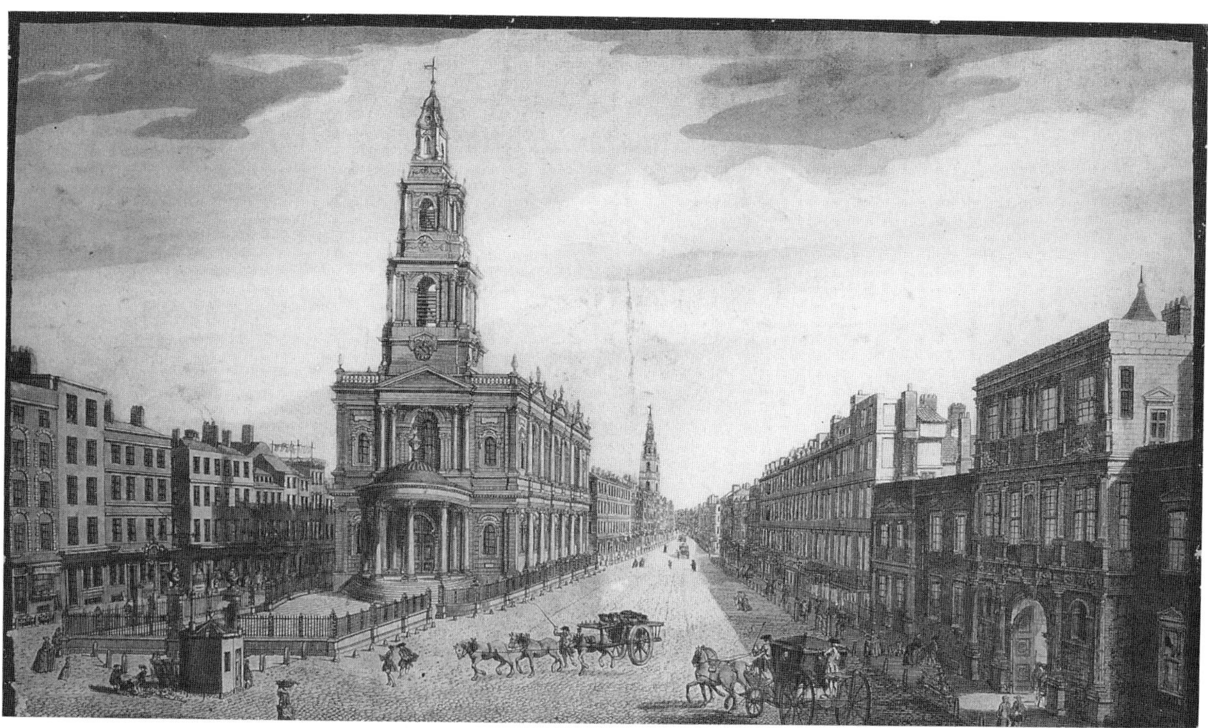

46. Unsigned, *Vue de la maison royale de Somerset avec l'église de Ste Marie dans le Strand, à Londres,* hand-coloured copperplate print; French, c. 1780. Private collection.

Inserting the print upside-down required no preparations, but countering the flipping effect of the mirror was more problematic. In order for the scene not to appear the wrong way round, it had to be printed from the first back-to-front. There was no doubt a broad tolerance of non-reversed images inappropriately inserted into the box and coming out backward – for if the place was far away, minor inconsistencies like swords hanging on the right, or carriages driving on the wrong side, could be extenuated, and perhaps not even noticed. But a kind of picture destined expressly for *optiques* was introduced. These were printed in reverse, and the practice had the important result of making works formally useless at all moments when *not* set in a device. The "realistic" image attained its level precisely by being deprived of value outside the systematics of machines. Yet these de-empiricising reversed renditions were found so assuaging to the late eighteenth-century fact-finding mind that many prints originally intended for straight looking were even reissued a second time, switched (Fig. 48). Reversed prints were known as "optical views" or *vues d'optique,* a term translated literally into Japanese as *megane-e* ("*optique* pictures").[19] The viewing machine was called "Dutch glasses" (*Oranda megane*), injecting it with a feeling of the strange, although an indigenised name, "peeping-glasses" (*nozoki-megane*) was also used.

It was not hard to find access to *optiques* in the late eighteenth century and after. Kodera Gyokuchō recorded that, in Nagoya, "peeping-

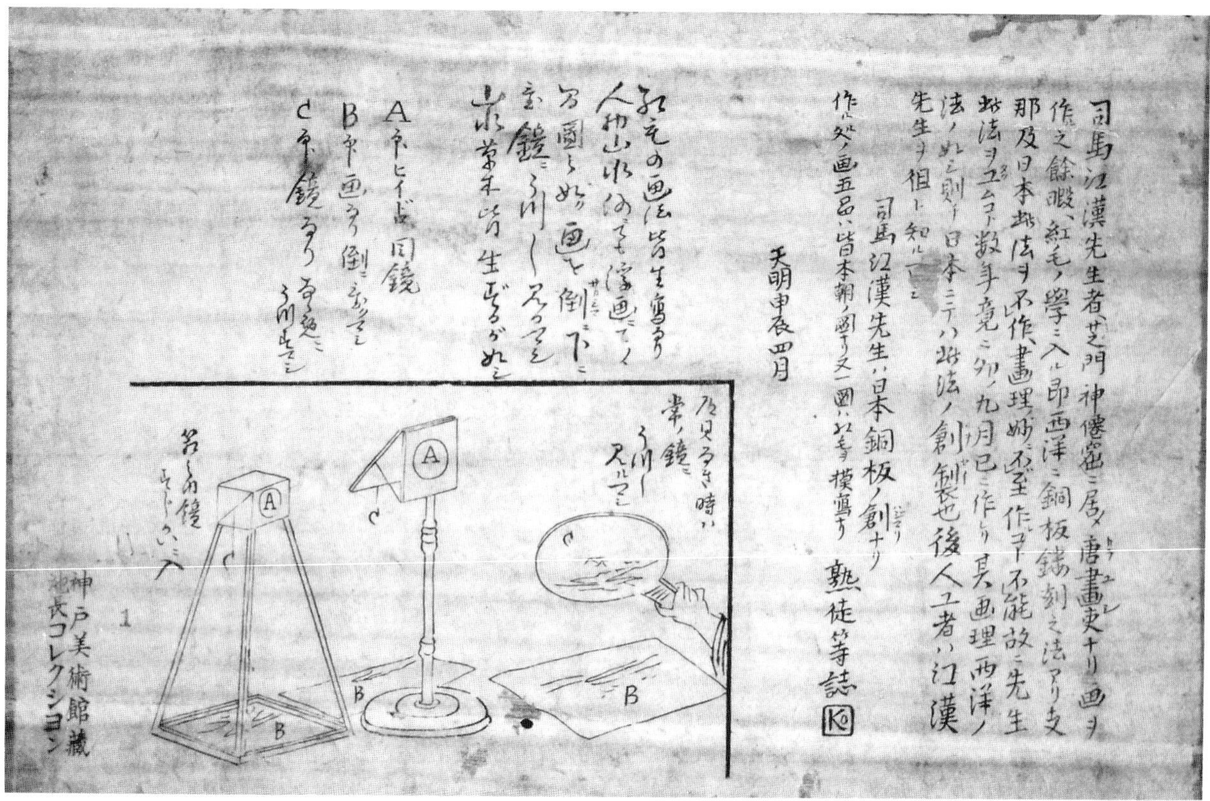

47. Shiba Kōkan, *Optiques*, copperplate print, 1784. Kobe City Museum.

Viewing with two types of optique, and a domestic mirror.

glasses imported from Holland" were on exhibit at the Temple of Daisu-zan one summer around 1813, and that they cost sixteen *mon* – not a large sum – to look through.[20] Some twenty years earlier Kōkan himself had fashioned an *optique* (certainly from imported parts), and he showed it off, charging exactly twice as much – thirty-two *mon* – per peep, although whether he was extorting or the price dropped over time (or whether he had more pictures to use) is uncertain.[21] The rich did not baulk at the fee anyway, and Nakai Hidetake, a wealthy Kyoto rice merchant, considered himself so little swindled by Kōkan that he brought his relatives around for a repeat performance the following day.

DOMESTIC VIEWS

Imported *vues d'optique* were no doubt rare, and surely expensive. Domestic woodblocks could be substituted at a pinch, despite a certain hardness of line (exacerbated by lens and mirror). A print by Harunobu shows a boy and girl using a European *optique* along with a local picture, and though the image is correctly inverted, as it is done in the stark palate of the traditional print and is not printed in reverse, it could hardly have given a convincing sense of the depicted place (Pl. 2). Harunobu shows the interior of a male brothel; as a composition it is not without its enigmas (the inscription above, as well as the peeped-at view, are replete with homoerotic *dou-*

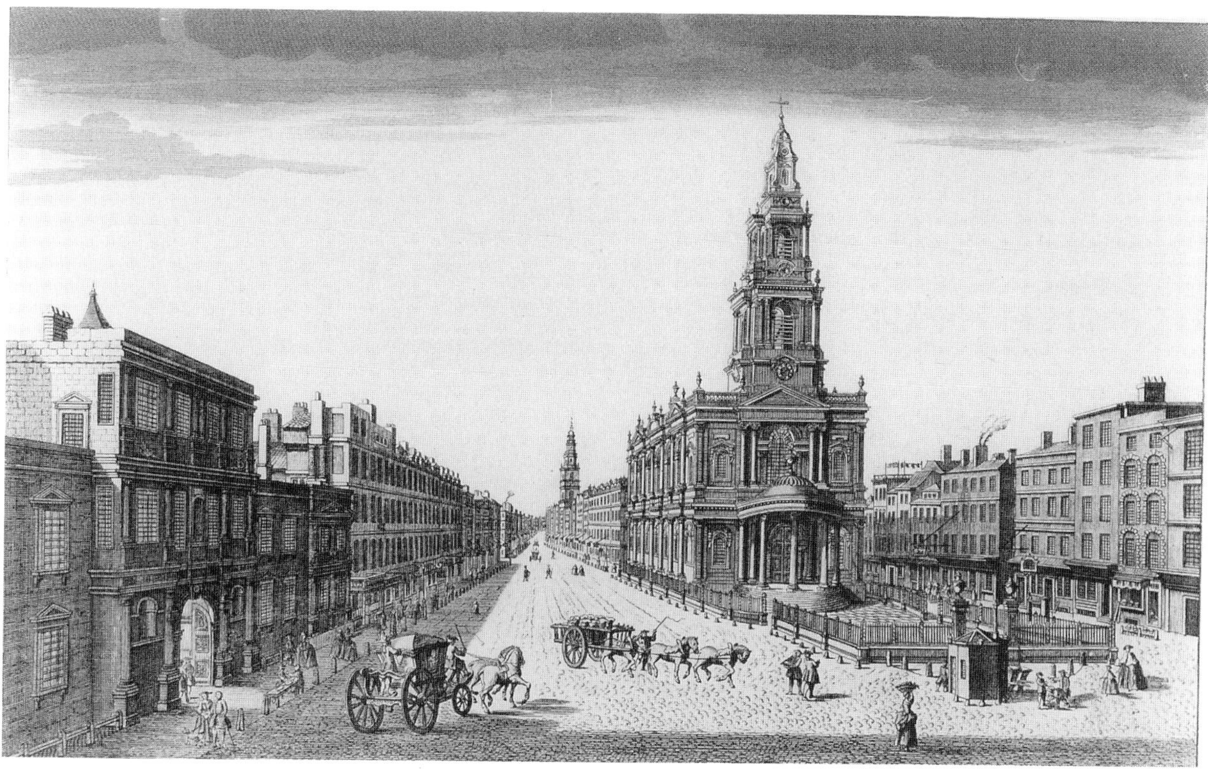

48. Unsigned, *Vue de la maison royale de Somerset avec l'église de Ste Marie dans le Strand, à Londres,* hand-coloured copperplate print; French, c. 1780. Private Collection.

bles entendres); it may be wondered just how genuine a context this is for using Dutch glasses. But it is clear at least that the device was well known by 1770, the year of Harunobu's death and the *terminus ante quem* for this undated print.[22]

Then, in 1783, for the first time, Kōkan contrived to make his own copperplate etchings. He was thereby able to produce the first fully complete domestic *vue d'optique*. The elated artist could now announce, "the principles governing my pictures (*gari*) are identical with those of the West,"[23] and thereafter he sometimes referred to himself as *Nihon sōsei*, "The First Maker [of copperplates] in Japan."[24] It was *vues d'optique*, not scientific works, that constituted Kōkan's initial batches of etchings, and they included views of a hospital in Holland and of the Serpentine Lake in the English country house of Stowe (Pl. 3). These were precisely the sorts of scene that might crop up in a Western portfolio of views; indeed, that is probably where Kōkan found his models, for though the Dutch scene has not been traced, the Stowe was lifted from an English composition of about 1776.[25]

Kōkan was not content to restrict this automated gaze to a survey of foreign places and determined that it should be directed at the local environment, too. He executed copperplate *vedute* of Edo, showing, for example, Ryōgoku Bridge – the hub of the city's popular culture – Mimeguri on the Sumida, Baba's tea-stop in Hiroo, and more.[26] Some scenes he printed right way around, others he reversed for use in the *optique,* some he made both ways (Pl. 4, Fig. 49). Whatever the place depicted, this Red-fur manner remained, by Chūryō's definition, a "Western scenic view." Kōkan labelled several of his etchings in Roman letters, occasionally even translating the name of the Japanese location into Dutch, so the Ryōgoku-bashi (literally, "the bridge of two provinces") became Tweelandbruk. Adapting place-names for inscription was common in Europe (*la Maison Royale de Somerset avec l'église de Ste Marie dans le Strand à Londres,* for example), but the objective there was to render an unknown toponym more comprehensible to the regional viewer; in Japan the opposite occurred, indigenous places being extracted from the pool of known names and put into a foreign tongue. Kōkan evidently wished the Edo viewer to read these pictures as representations in displaced terms, or as scriptings of the known city in a differently formulated text.

Production of copperplates was exclusive to Kōkan for some time, but other artists provided viable alternatives. It was not necessary to put up with the routine woodblock print that Harunobu showed being used. Maruyama Ōkyo, a Kyoto artist and close friend of Minagawa Kien who poeticized on Ōkyo's student Rosetsu's gigantic flea screen, painted scenic pictures in reverse, using wonderfully detailed hand-drawn strokes that would not show up under the lens. Still clinging to the notion of etching as the authoritative medium of *Ran,* however, Ōkyo wielded his brush to simulate the scratchings of a chisel (Pl. 5, Fig. 129). He repeated himself, making the same scene more than once, as a printer might, and sometimes produced the same image frontways and inverted.[27] Though lowborn, Ōkyo attained high prestige and was eventually reckoned as the greatest artist in Kyoto; raised to samurai rank, he was invited to decorate the tenno's palace. Ōkyo's *vues d'optique* are usually categorised as juvenalia although this cannot be chronologically substantiated and is surely on account of modern scholars not wishing to sully his still-famous name with "trivial work."[28] The views have never been satisfactorily dated. It is true that in the late 1760s Ōkyo began his working life at the Owari-ya, a royal appointment toy shop run by Nakajima Kanbei, but there is no evidence that the store dealt in mechanised optical pictures, much less that such imagery was generally conceived as appropriate to such a dealer. It seems more reasonable to propose a date nearer to Kōkan's etchings for the paintings, or even to Ōkyo's death in 1795. Two pupils or emulators, Kokkadō and Fuinsai, went on to paint *vues d'optique* in volume, supplying something approaching Ōkyo's manner to a wide audience.[29]

Painted works, and Kōkan's small-run copperplates, would surely have been expensive; but if a domestic picture was to do service in the *optique,* there were several types available beyond what Harunobu showed. From the second quarter of the eighteenth century – long before the introduction of the *optique* itself – a genre of prints and paintings had come into being known as "floating pictures" (*uki-e*). These sought to replicate, not the medium of the copperplate, but only the perspectival style. Though not reversed, they were very possibly inserted willy-nilly into *optiques,* after the appearance of Dutch-glasses. At any rate, viewers considered *uki-e* highly plausible, and the term "floating picture" may refer to how the image seemed to surge up from the pictorial surface with a stunning absorptive power.[30] It might also said that they were "sunken pictures" (*kubomi-e*), seeming to plunge the viewer downward into the recesses of their illusionistic depths.[31] The runaway popularity of the genre eventually caused Kōkan to warn rather strongly that the full sensations of *Ranga*

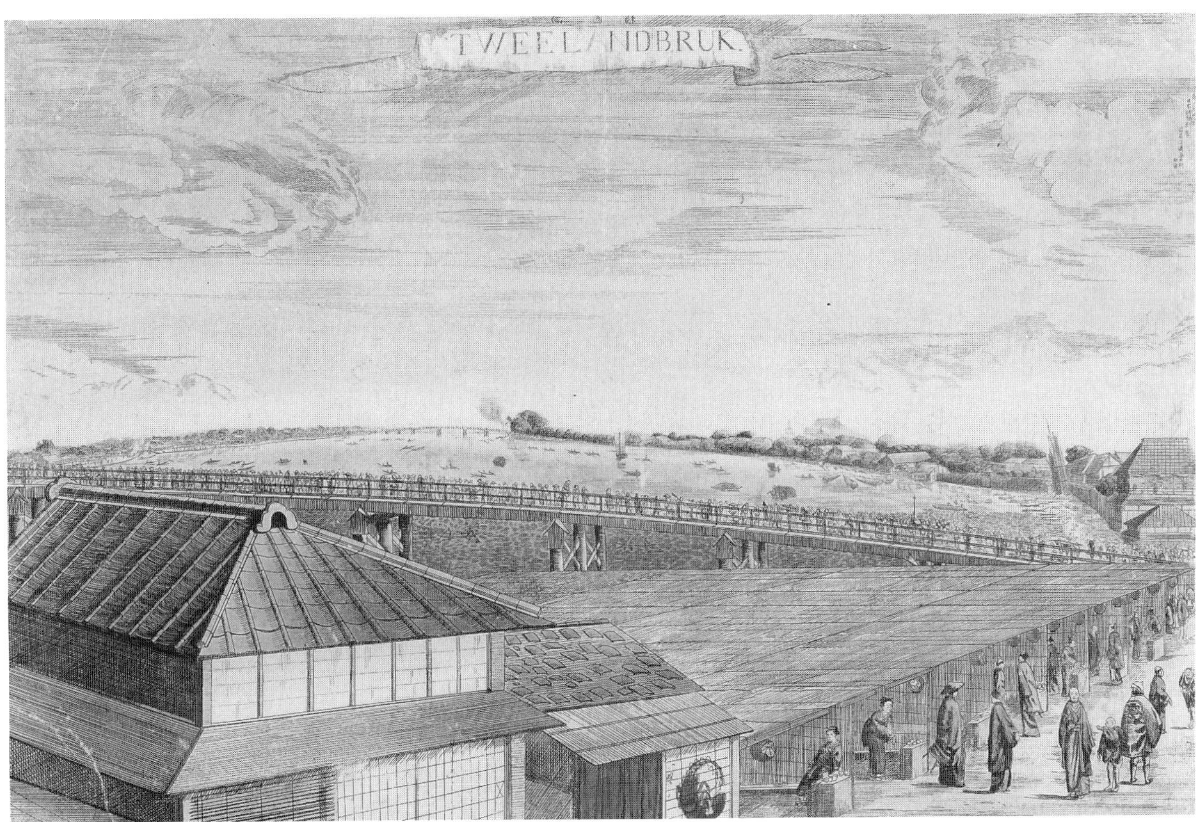

49. Shiba Kōkan, *Tweelandbruk,* hand-coloured copperplate print; c. 1787. British Museum.

were not to be had by *uki-e* alone, and despite all he had done to propagate the *vue d'optique,* he wrote in 1799, "most people believe Western pictures to be no more than perspectives – a risible opinion."[32]

Utagawa Toyoharu, a prominent Edo artist of the 1770s, was a significant producer of *uki-e,* and today the style is often associated with him. Toyoharu made a *veduta* showing the Grand Canal in Venice, and, unusually, the image can be traced back to an original painting by Canaletto, though taken via Antonio Visentini's printed version of 1742 (Pl. 6). This may have been the kind of *tour de force* Chūryō had in mind when he wrote, "when it comes to *uki-e,* Toyokuni's master Utagawa Toyoharu made ones which were spectacular."[33] The label, however, is fanciful: "The Bell which Resounds for Ten-thousand Leagues in the Dutch Port of Frankai." Other scenes by Toyoharu and his peers stem from imported vistas of Fontainebleau, Vauxhall Gardens, Westminster Bridge, and more, though often adapted *en route* to represent Chinese places, giving the outlandish foreign a tinge of the nearer abroad, and very likely owing a good deal in some cases to intervening Chinese copies: *vues d'optique* were making inroads on the Continent too. But *uki-e* were always *Ran.*[34]

Uki-e had been produced for some thirty years already by Toyoharu's time, and Okumura Masanobu is reckoned to have introduced the style

– at least, the earliest datable *uki-e* is his, made in 1743. His production may have spread over many years (Pl. 7).[35] Seemingly, Masanobu took the title of *Uki-e kongen,* "Founder of Floating Pictures" but an extraordinarily precise date, slightly earlier, has been proposed for the emergence of *uki-e,* namely, 20th–25th of the fifth month, 1739.[36] His earliest works are not of foreign vistas, but show Japanese places and tend to be interior scenes, probably through self-restrictions imposed by an artist not yet confident enough to render the more flexed and uneven lines of the irregular outdoors. But, for whatever reason, the tendency of early *uki-e* was to concentrate less on the grand vistas and receding parklands that preoccupied European markers than to identify with interior locations, especially the centres of picaresque urban life. Woodblock prints were already saturating an avid market with subjects like sumo tournaments, actors, beautiful women, brothels, and the fashionable young men of the Floating World, and it was altogether natural for *uki-e* to be subsumed into the ambit of such established pieces. Such an assimilation put the perspective style, however, firmly in the camp of the common person and indelibly associated it with subject matters that were entertainment-oriented. Floating pictures and the Floating World – though the names are co-incidental – overlapped, with inevitable results for the meaning of vanishing-point depiction as a whole. Perspective was enlisted to show precisely what was *not* quotidian, or vouchsafed, but the mimetic space of the stage, the "otherness" of the recreational or escapist worlds, or the pleasure zones beyond the actual. It is common for *uki-e* to depict not only places of flight and alterity but to include within the image a secondary level of representation – dressing up, parlour gaming, dramatics. Always open to the charge of being counter-empirical, convoluted, and outrageous in the liberties they took with actuality, the waywardness of perspective *vedute* was compounded in Japan by its choice of subject and theme.

The association of perspective with a showy brashness outside respected norms (or actually upsetting of them) is hard to gainsay. *Uki-e* were in cahoots with boastfulness and swell. They could be incorporated into narrative contexts; many is the illustrated story which runs comfortably along using traditional spatial configurations, only to switch into perspective (often applied *ad hoc*) when a flashy or insolent space is invoked (Fig. 103). In the first ever kibyoshi, Koikawa Harumachi's *Master Moneypenny's Dreams of Glory (Kinkin-sensei eiga no yume)* of 1775, illustrated by himself, perspective is suddenly used to depict a wealthy mansion appearing in the world of dreams.[37] As Hiraga Gennai put it in 1763 in the context of a run-down of exhibits to be seen around Ryōgoku Bridge, "people who look at floating pictures think of the Wizard of the Jar."[38] He was referring to the legendary Chinese sage, Tsubo Sennin, who had found a huge paradise inside a tiny bottle and had thereby shown that, if the mind was liberated, infinite vastness could exist within tight constraint. The Wizard of the Jar came to feel the enclosed world enjoyed a coherence that the empirical lacked, and took the bottle, not reality, as his dwelling. But this was an eccentric thing to do. Peeping into the lens of an *optique* landed one in a mystery domain of sorts, but for all its credibility, it was only a world of illusion.

Take the case of Sukeroku, eponymous hero of a well-loved kabuki play. A swashbuckler even by the standards of Edo's "rough diamonds" (*otokodate*), Sukeroku was a habitué of the Yoshiwara brothel district. He took *uki-e* as a kind of hallmark. At one point in the play that bears his name, he turns his body into a notional viewing machine and makes the world his perspective view: calling his cronies to gather round, Sukeroku has them look through the queue of his hair at what lies beyond, as if they were using an *optique;* the world beyond, he pre-

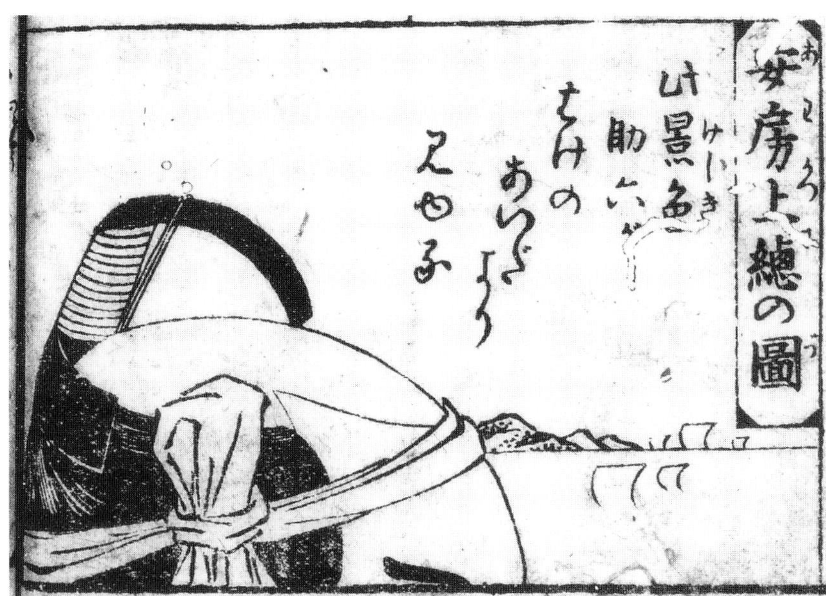

50. Santō Kyōden, *View of Awa in Kazusa,* from his *Shinzō zue,* 1789. Tokyo Metropolitan Central Library.

tends, will be seen as if drawn as an *uki-e* – the hills of Awa captured via his top-knot. *Sukeroku* opened in 1713, but the *uki-e* reference was probably inserted in a later revival; at least, the performance of 1761 mentions *uki-e;* the fullest version though is in a script from 1779. The hero rants,

> All you rough chaps that hang around in these Five Blocks, hear my name right now! . . . My hair is wound in a sweat-band of Edo purple, and look through the gap at the end of the queue, and don't you just know – you'll see Awa in Kazusa looking like a floating picture.[39]

Awa was too far away to be seen from the Yoshiwara (the "Five Blocks"), where Sukeroku uttered the lines, but that is just the point: perspective initiated an exposure of what might pretend to a close marriage with reality, but what in fact was just not to be seen, or not *like that.*

Santō Kyōden, tobacconist, Floating World print-maker, and kibyoshi writer, took up the Sukeroku/*uki-e* connexion and referred to it on a number of occasions. His comic compendium *New Brothel Girls' Illustrated Encyclopaedia* (*Shinzo zue*) – named to parody Terajima Ryōan's *Universal Illustrated Encyclopaedia* (*Sansai zue*) – made Sukeroku stand for all brazen Edo males. The book may be a parody of Chūryō's Japanese-Dutch dictionary *The Lexicon of Primitive Words* (*Bango-sen*) which appeared the previous year.[40] An illustration shows the purported prospect caught through Sukeroku's hair (Fig. 50). The picture is hardly done in real perspective (viz. the ships' sails), but the juxtaposition of a looming banded head and the tiny seascape beyond probably made the point clear enough. The whole is labelled down the side in a space outside the depicted area, as was customary in *uki-e,* "A View of Awa in Kazusa." An inscription is appended on top: "This scene is to be spotted through Sukeroku's queue." The summit of Sukeroku's pate with his purple sweat-band is dressed in a rakish modern hairstyle called the *honda,* and Kyōden's intent is less to pass meaningful comment on perspective prints than to take a dig at trend-setters. But the jibe, whatever its butt, is articulated by allusion to the inflated egotism of the floating picture and its mechanical viewing apparatus. A web of peripheral meanings accrues to the ebullient certitude of the imagery, and the viewing act so irredeemably contrived.

THE DEVIL LANTERN

Before continuing a consideration of perspective views, we may pause to address a different matter. When Kōkan illustrated the two types of *optique* showing how pictures had to be inserted upside-down, he told the reader that this was the same as had to be done with what he called "shadow pictures" (*kuma-e*).[41] Those images went with another new and imported viewing apparatus, dubbed a "devil lantern" (*oni-tōrō*). This was a kind of projector that because of its square shape, could also be called a "bath" (*furo*), Japanese baths being wooden and cuboid.[42] But the peculiarities of the workings more than justified the other designation. The extraordinary capacity of the devil lantern was to produce its weird scenes seemingly *ex nihilo*.

The actual mechanism was simply a box containing a strong light or lights, condensed by a concave lens, and with a hole at the front fitted with another lens; the only escape for the rays was via this second lens, which focused and refracted any image painted on a glass slide loaded between it and the lights. Whatever was depicted on the slide was thrown outward until it hit a place of rest. Rather than tumbling viewers into the space of the picture, the devil lantern made the picture itself jump from its realm to join the human world. The viewer was no longer obliged to pause rigidly, for the projected figures could dance about with them, as the lantern was moved around.

Shadow games had been popular for centuries, and given that Japanese domestic architecture contained plentiful translucent walls, with light sources near to floor level, this was hardly surprising; hand-held cut-outs had long been cast against screens by a lamp or candle to delight or scare.[43] From the middle of the eighteenth century, however, a sudden tendency is seen to associate shadow play with the Dutch. This aura of foreignness might be made by appeal to where the VOC was stationed, and the term "Nagasaki shadow pictures" is attested.[44] The images were common enough to be invoked in 1779 by Koikawa Harumachi, in another kibyoshi, *Pushing Trends to Extremes* or *Useless Vogues (Muda iki)*, a work which ironises several contemporary fads (including the *honda* hair-do). Harumachi cited what he called "*Oranda saiku* shadow pictures," and used them as cyphers for the quick changes of the world of fashion.[45]

Connexions with *Ran* might connote no better thing than novel gimmickry, but there was more than this, for imported shadows had an additional feature: thanks to being caused by images drawn on glass, "Dutch" shadows were coloured; this was new, and glass itself was an imported material. By 1800, a showman in Osaka was exhibiting "coloured shadow pictures of clever Dutch make."[46] The projections had all the qualities of a good fixed picture, and their plausibility was colossal.

Devil lanterns themselves were imported, and the term for the device was in fact a translation of the Dutch *tover lantaarn*. Such things had been common in Europe for a generation or so, and generically called a *lanterna magica*, or magic lantern. The *New World of English Words*, a dictionary published in London in 1696, contained an entry under "Magic lanthorn," defining it as "a certain small Optical Macheen, that shews by a gloomy Light upon a white Wall, Spectres and Monsters so hideous that he who knows not the Secret, believes it to be performed by Magic Art." Gulielmo s' Gravesande included one in his *Physices elementa mathematica* of 1721 (a popularising Newtonian work), giving a cross-section of the device and noting that it was "a phenomenon sufficiently stupifying and peculiar to merit explanation" (Fig. 51);[47] Gravesande called the lantern a *lucerna magica*, but

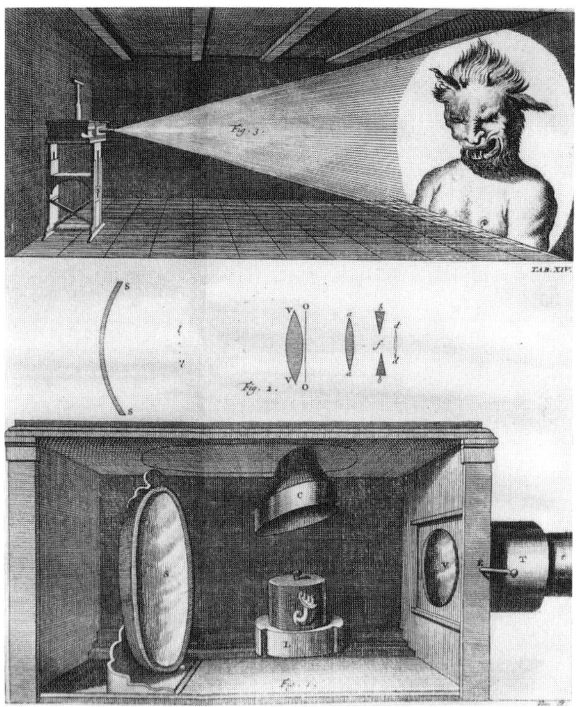

51. Unsigned, *Lucerna Magica*, from Gulielmo s' Gravesande, *Physices elementa mathematica*, Leiden, 1721. Private Collection.

illustration showed how its more lugubrious name became it well. Egbert Buys depicted the device in his *Complete Dictionary (Woordenboek)*, projecting, in that case, a reassuring cross.[48] It is hard for those today who find such optical tricks jejune to understand the compulsion exercised by these images. Ironically, in Europe their strangeness might be evoked by reference to the fiendish Orient, the French term being *ombres chinoises*.

Sugita Genpaku preferred to keep the oddity of the devil lantern in place by retaining the original word, which he transliterated as *tofuru rantaren*. Gentaku discussed the device in the context of routinely imported goods, so that a wide diffusion is suggested.[49] The lantern was also the subject of an exchange in Ōtsuki Gentaku's *Correcting Errors about the Dutch (Ransetsu benwaku)*. It is as if everyone wanted information:

> My question is this: of late Scenic Lanterns (*keiga tōrō*) have come over from Holland. You burn a lamp in a darkened room and place something in front, but there is a trick to them because the shadow that falls on the blank wall opposite will be coloured. If the image is of a human figure it will appear the size of a real person looking completely alive. What is the name of this thing, and how does it work?
>
> My reply is this: in Holland they are called *tōfuru rantaaru*, which we might translate as "devil lantern." Originally they were thought only toys for children. A flame is lit inside a little box in the front of which is a small hole, and you slot a piece of glass with a picture painted on it inside (it must go in upside-down). The shadow image will appear on the wall opposite, right way up and enlarged in size.[50]

This is no longer just a game, Gentaku implies. Strange figures, full-size and with all the aspects of life, can be brought into the domain of the living.

Jippensha Ikku, recently swept to fame as a writer, produced a book in 1811 entitled *Dutch Shadow Pictures: What Fun! (Oranda kage-e otsuriki)*. He deliberately wrote the snappy title in out-of-the-way, scholastic-looking characters so as to give the expression "what fun!" (*otsuriki*) the air of an arcane transcription by a *Rangaku* pedant. But the title also makes a direct link to the imported contrivance, for *otsuriki* sounds like *utsuri-ki*, "projection machine," another name for the devil lantern. The illustrations to the book were undertaken by Utamaro's pupil Tsukimaro, and for the cover illustration he provided a likeness, not of the real lantern, which wasn't much to look at, but of that stand-in for all pieces of cunning Western paraphernalia, the static-electricity generator. The better to thrill with the Dutchness of the affair, Tsukimaro also faked the title-page to look like one to a European work, with a mock-heraldic arch surrounding the wording of the title. One page in again, the fron-

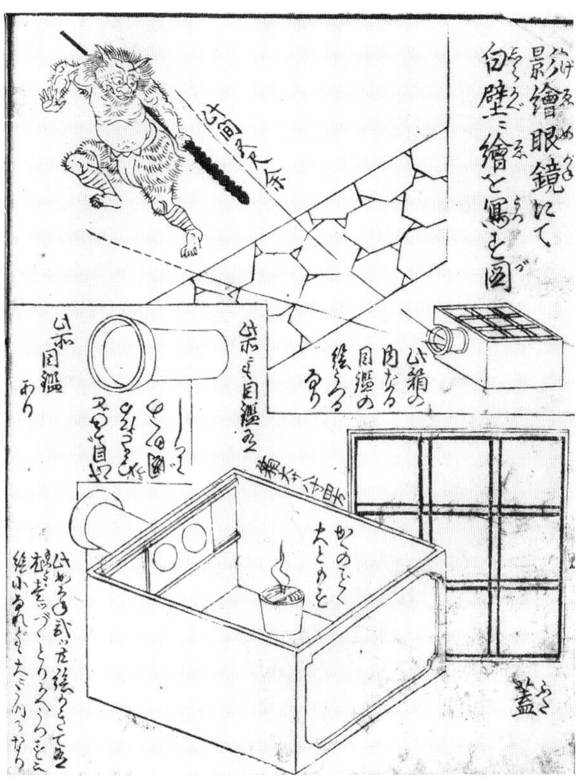

52. Unsigned, *Casting an Image onto a White Wall with a Shadow-picture Lens*, from Sukenari, *Tengu-tsū*, 1799. National Diet Library, Tokyo.

tispiece was simulated to look like a *vue d'optique*, done in perspective and, though printed as woodblock, equipped with imitation hatchwork and shading;[51] the scene shown is the Maruyama, Nagasaki's pleasure district, where (Ikku claims) the Dutch kapitan had spent an evening divulging to him the tricks contained in the book. These are not the usual old games, the author suggests, but are peculiarly baffling, clever, and mechanical – and worth the price of the book.

The mechanics of projection improved, and by the end of the century magic lanterns were being illuminated by Eichman lamps. Chūryō considered the new type relevant enough to be included in his *Lexicon*, and he gave the Japanese for "devil-conjuring lens" in phonetic transcription as *ekiman-kyō*. Chūryō appended an observation that the machine was now widely diffused.[52] Dutch Eichman lamps (*Aranda ekiman-kyō*) were to be seen in the Ueno district of Edo in 1801, where a showman, Ikeda Yūkichi, had taken to projecting pictures painted by himself; a series made up the performance, accompanied by a spiel chanted to the sound of a shamisen.[53] The realism was much admired. These pictures were endowed with the gift of motion, and it was said of one Toraku (who may be the same person as Yūkichi) that he "invented moving pictures by painting coloured images on glass and putting them in a lensed device called an *ekiman-kyō*."[54] Several lanterns might be banked up and used simultaneously, allowing figures to converge or fall apart, or to be superimposed on one another to create a larger scene. Toraku's pictures were reckoned to outstrip the projections, seen in Edo in the recent past, of "nine-tailed foxes and the like."

Chūryō stated in the *Lexicon* that "many books have dealt with the subject" of the projector. What publications these were is unclear. One relatively full explanation appeared in 1799, the year after his writing, in a text by a writer identifying himself only as Sukenari, that referred to the machines as "shadow-picture *optiques*" (*kage-e megane*). The impish title of the work, the *Trendy Goblin (Tengu tsū)*, suggests that the devilish device is all the rage. The author of this compendium of ghosts and conjuring (*keshō*) stated, "The other year the instrument was demonstrated in Osaka on the reclaimed land at Naniwa, but it was difficult to appreciate the tricks fully there, so all is now explained again."[55] There is an apparent intent behind Sukenari's work to stimulate a market in home-sized projectors, for the lanterns he discussed throw their images (very Japanised devils) about two metres (Fig. 52). The text-cum-advertising gush rings out:

> Mirror shops now have this shadow-picture lens in stock. It can make devils and spirits appear – you

> absolutely must have a go with one. All kinds of things are possible, yes, any picture can be painted on the lens inside the box, and whatever it is will be cast exactly right! With this device you can project anything.

Osaka was not the only place of sale, for a shop in Asakusa, the Izumi-ya, was supplying the people of Edo with what were called "newly-invented monster-candles," the exact nature of which is obscure, but which must have been devil lanterns in some guise.[56]

The potential of the machine was wondrous. It might delight or frighten. But it might also take on meanings beyond itself. In Japan, lanterns had perennially been associated with the supernatural, and the lantern-spook (*chōchin-obake*) was a stock character in the pantheon of ghouls and earned mention in the definitive demonology of 1784, *Hundred Ghosts' Essays in Idleness (Hyakki Tsurezure-gusa)* by Harumachi and Utamaro's teacher, Toriyama Sekien (Fig. 53). The devil lantern was the innovative bed-fellow of this ancient ghostly familiar.

Hekizentei Kunenbō, shogunal official, comic writer, and student of Tani Bunchō, issued a kibyoshi the same year as the *Trendy Tengu* entitled *The Devil Lantern: A Short Cut to Its Understanding (Hōtsuki chōchin oshie no chikamichi)*. As with all his fictional works, Kunenbō devised a deliberately boring title to belie the humour of the story. The characters appear with lantern-shaped heads – although Kunenbō's illustrator, Utagawa Toyokuni (much employed by Kyōden and Ikku, too), showed little respect for the actual appearance of projectors, making them almost spherical.[57] Toyokuni may be laughing at Kyōden who made something of a speciality of little metaphysical personalities drawn as spheres that popped up in his kibyoshi to advise or warn the characters. But as Kunenbō's title makes clear, a pun is also intended on the *hōzuki*, a plant customarily used to deck Buddhist alters at the Festival of the Dead (*obon*), an event generally known as the Feast of Lanterns (*chōchin no matsuri*). The *hōzuki* itself resembled a small red paper lantern and indeed in English it is called lantern fruit. The white fruit within was like the Eichman bulbs, and the exterior even had a minute hole (Edo children blew into this to make a whistle). Altogether, lantern fruit went well with an invocation of the realm of spirits.

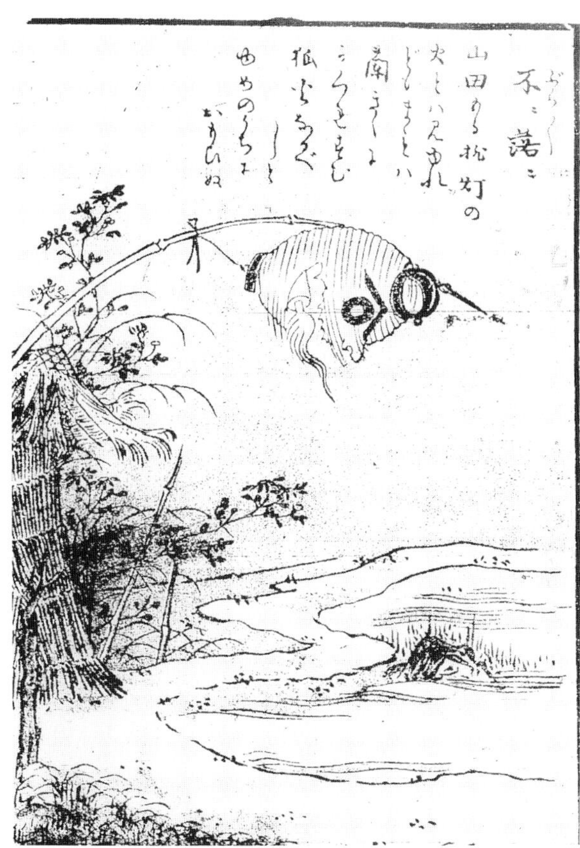

53. Toriyama Sekien, *The Dangler*, from his *Hyakki tsurezure-bukuro*, 2nd ed. 1805 (original, 1784). National Diet Library, Tokyo.

Kunenbō's highly contrived tale is eventually revealed to have been the result of a demonic fox bestowing on a geisha a lantern, the projections from which overrun the intended plot; the story closes as the fox itself is unmasked as a shadow trick.

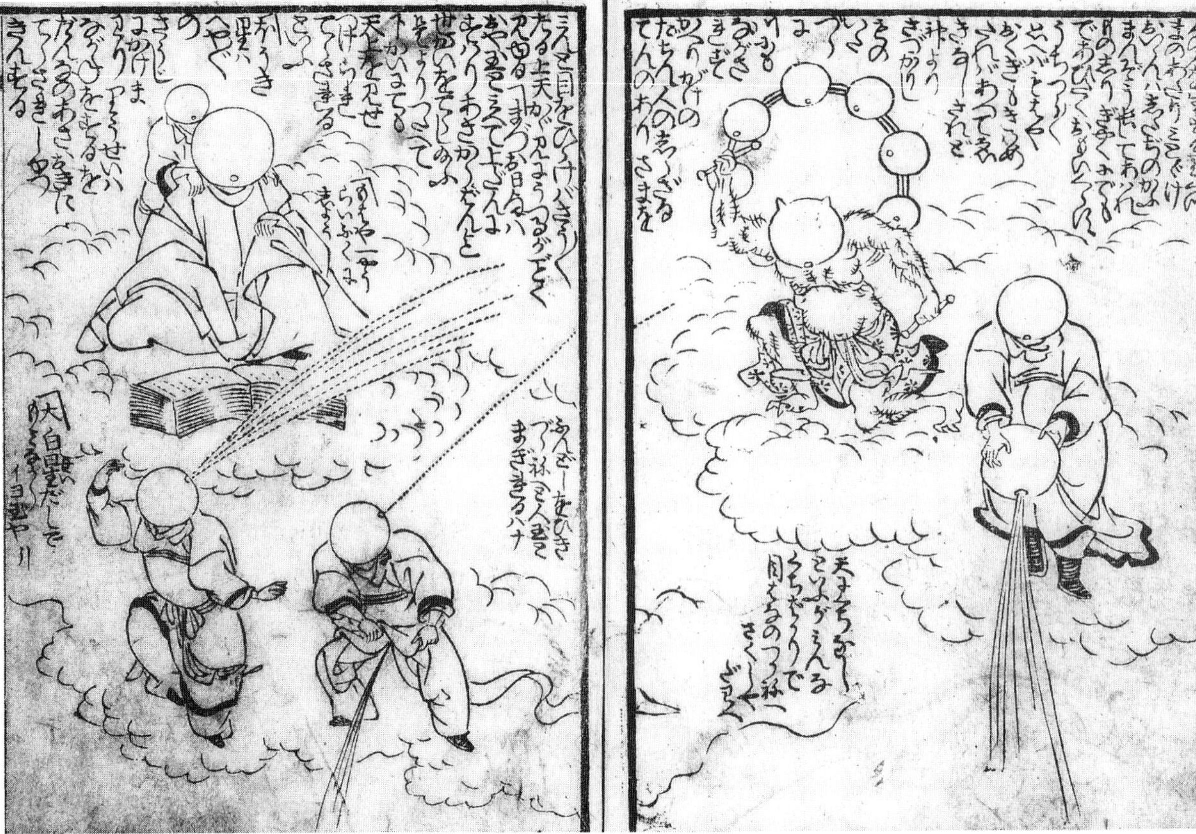

54. Utagawa Toyokuni, from Hekizentai Kunenbō, *Hōtsuki chōchin oshie no chikamichi*, 1798. Tokyo Metropolitan Central Library.

Devil lanterns create rain and thunder.

Foxes were considered unstable in Japanese lore. They had the power to transform themselves – hence the appropriateness of the "nine-tailed foxes" that Toraku had bettered. Like shadows, foxes could roam without trace and indulged in topological mutation; or rather, like devil lanterns, they cast variable outside forms from their unchanging inner selves. Foxes or lanterns sent out into the world a stream that was constant in intensity but passed over unpredictable colourations.

In the Buddhist world-view, all matter is subject to flux; nothing has ontological grounding. Material of the human world can rightly be said to have the qualities of a projection. Kunenbō suggested as much when he had his devil lanterns generate seemingly substantial phenomena: his projectors, now connected to the bodies of the gods, do nothing less than orchestrate the origin of the world and release the seasons' precipitations (Fig. 54). The lamps were the energy of creation; the shadows, elemental matter.

As with many kibyoshi, Kunenbō's book wanders associatively over many themes, letting the reader get perplexed and tangled. To sort matters out, "a certain learned Doctor Devil-Lantern" is introduced, a crusty physician who provides a mock explanation of the vagaries of events thus

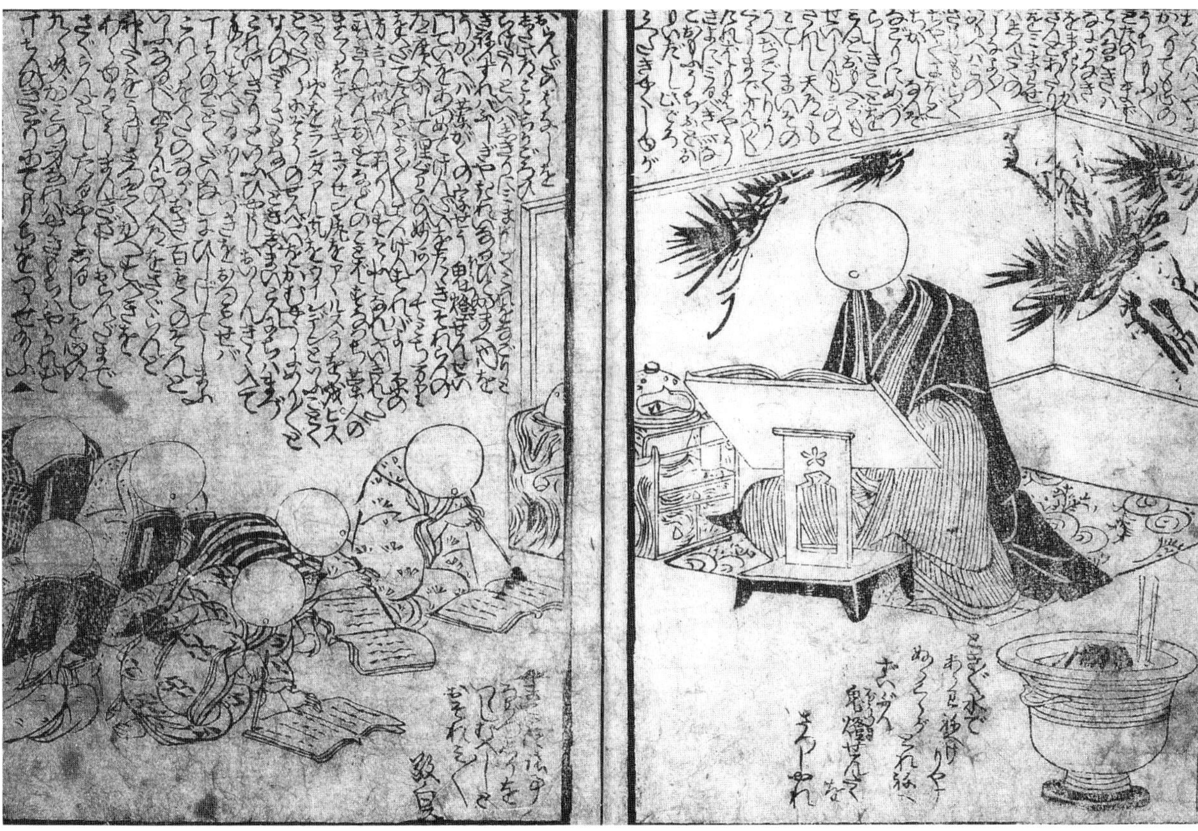

55. Utagawa Toyokuni, from Hekizentai Kunenbō, *Hōtsuki chōchin oshie no chikamichi*, 1798. Tokyo Metropolitan Central Library.

Dr Devil-Lantern instructs his pupils.

far, related to the know-it-all geisha. The doctor's name is written with characters reading "devil lantern," but this is anomalously glossed to be pronounced "Hōtsuki" as in the story's title; an *h* being only minimally plosive in Japanese, the reading readily becomes Ōtsuki, none other than Gentaku's family name. Kunenbō's book appeared in 1798, and Gentaku was ripe for satire: the preface to his *Correcting Errors* had just been penned; and, more publicly, his Dutch Studies academy, the Shirandō (first of its kind in Edo), was to open the following year, and preparations were surely under way (its first pupil was Arima Genshō, compiler of the *Errors*).

Dr. Devil-Lantern is seen dourly propounding arcane truths to six boys, heads deep in books, in a setting that is evidently a parody of how the new school would be laid out (Fig. 55). Teacher and students are now all devil lanterns, and the doctor delivers an elementary *Rangaku* lesson: "In Dutch, you should be aware, they call a pillow an *oorekyussen,* while the word for arse is *aarusu;* for fish they say *pisu,* and a flame is a *rantaaru.*" Kunenbō had an amateur interest in the study of European things, but his story really suggests how the explanations and theories of *Ran,* when they enter local society, come like goblins cast upon a whitewashed wall, to haunt as much as help. But simultaneously they reveal a profounder truth about the status of authentic meaning: as all matter was illusory and vain, the *apparent* concreteness of material things inclined towards false security; the shadow was the truest form.

The sagely cult of Daoism also had things to say about the shadow. Daoism proposed non-initiation of action as its *summum bonum* and extolled the benefits of quietude and stillness. Scorning activity as a petty and feverish struggle, Daoists believed that adherents ought to submerge their personalities in the greater nourishing potency of Creation (*zōka*). The great sage of Daoism, Zhuangzi, had famously used the shadow as an example of the most ideal and rarefied sort of life. Arguing in a tract of the third century B.C., *The Adjustment of Controversies (Qiwulun)*, Zhuangzi stated that humanity should be like shadows, never moving of their own accord, but only in response to superior external forces. Zhuangzi composed a dialogue between a shadow and a penumbra, and although the exchange is elliptical and hard to make clear, it is seemingly based on a pun between "penumbra" (*wangliang*) and a homophone meaning the spiritual presence of deceased natural forms.[58] But the thrust of the case is clear. He wrote:

> The Penumbra asked the Shadow, saying, "formerly you were walked upon, and now you have stopped; formerly you were sitting, and now you have risen up. How is it that you are so without stability?" The Shadow replied, "I wait for the movements of someone else to do what I do, and that something else on which I wait waits further on another to do as it does. My waiting – is it for the scales of a snake, or the wings of a cicada? How should I know why I do one thing or do not do another?[59]

The fainter shadow follows at one remove, but that is the right thing to do. The most dependent, or contingent, aspects of phenomena are proposed as the better forms.

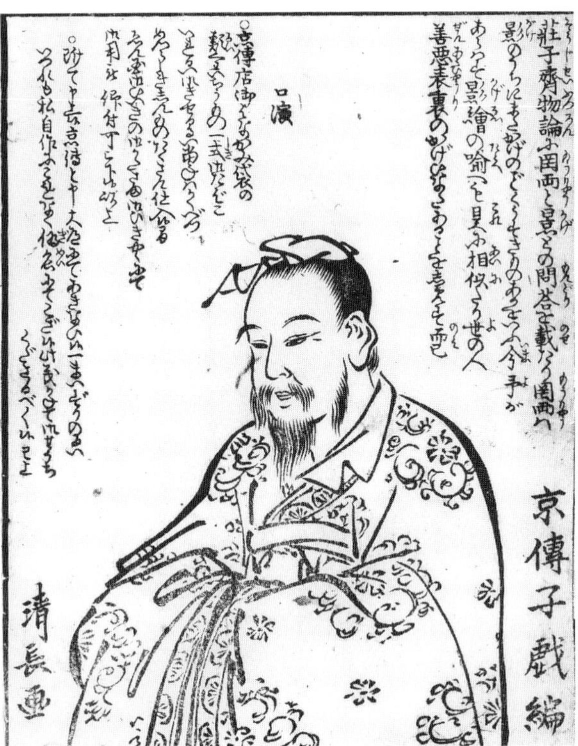

56. Torii Kiyonaga, from Santō Kyōden, *Jikun kage-e no tatoe*, 1799. National Diet Library, Tokyo.

The Daoist sage Zhuangzi.

Zhuangzi's exchange was well known, and in the eighteenth century it was still impossible to muse on the subject of shadows without citing it. Thus, in *Shadow Picture Lessons for Children (Jikun kage-e no tatoe)*, a kibyoshi of 1788, Kyōden invoked Zhuangzi again.[60] The book was illustrated by Torii Kiyonaga, and on the last page the artist provided a portrait of the sage, accompanied by a homily (Fig. 56):

> In Zhuangzi's book, *The Adjustment of Controversies*, there is a debate between a Shadow and a Penumbra. A penumbra is like a further shadow behind the shadow itself, and very thin. I have taken the observations and used them in the metaphorical shadow pictures contained in this book.

> All I hope to do is show that the shape of modern people's shadows is different from what you would see in the cold light of day. There is one form at the back and one at the front, a good one and a bad.

Kyōden adapts Zhuangzi to argue less for the Daoistic honour of the shadow than for its brutal truth. It is the shadow that reveals substances, whereas the outward shows of body and face defraud.

Possibly the genre of the silhouette is relevant here. Satō Narihiro, Lord Shimazu's botanist, wrote of how silhouette images were common in Europe, and he recorded, after a lengthy disquisition on *Ranga* in his *Chūryō's Observations (Chūryō manroku),* that European husbands had black-on-white images of their wives, especially after their deaths, "carrying them in their pockets and never being parted from them." It is not quite clear what he meant, but there was no history of such works in Japan. This was, though, just the period in which the silhouette genre reached its height in the West, and examples may have been imported. Tani Bunchō produced silhouette portraits of himself and his wife, the former made in his seventy-third year, or 1835, five years before his death.[61] Etienne de Silhouette, who had died in 1769, made considerable claims for the outline image, especially of the human head; and far from intending the genre that bore his name as levity, he believed it could depict a kind of truth inaccessible to conventional portraiture. The great Swiss physiognomist Johann Lavater went further in a significantly named book of 1783, *Essai sur la physiogonomie* [sic] *destiné à faire connoitre l'homme et à le faire aimé (Essay on physiognomy designed to promote the knowledge and love of mankind);* Lavater saw in the silhouette all keys necessary to unlocking a human personality (Fig. 57); he produced black-on-white images and went into extended speculation about the persons portrayed, considering, among all types of picture, shadow images to be the "justest and most faithful."[62]

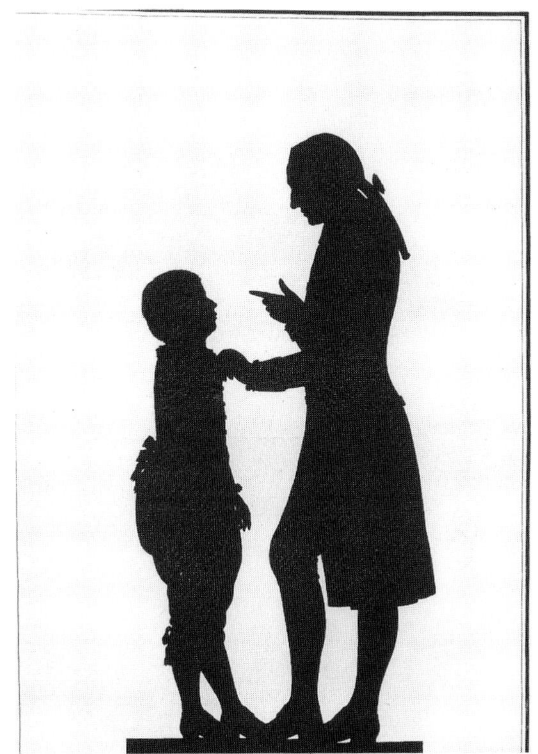

57. Unsigned, *Un homme mur à côté d'un jeune garçon de grande esperance,* from Jean Lavater, *Essai sur la Physiogonomie,* The Hague, 1783. Private collection.

The silhouette was indispensable to the eighteenth-century scientific investigator into character, and in order to render images more precise, and inevitably for the automaticising 1780s, Lavater designed an "unerring and convenient machine," which was "the best method" to fabricate the shadow portrait (Fig. 58). It was a devil lantern to work on the living human face.

Kiyonaga's illustrations to Kyōden's *Shadow Picture Lessons* also reveal the "justest" aspect of the person. For clarity, the illustrator provided direct comparison with the empirical appearance, in a series of double-page spreads. Kyōden extrapolated his eternal principle on the opening page: "Good and bad, sincerity and falsehood, are like a form and its shadow picture" – not now its shadow, note, but its shadow picture.

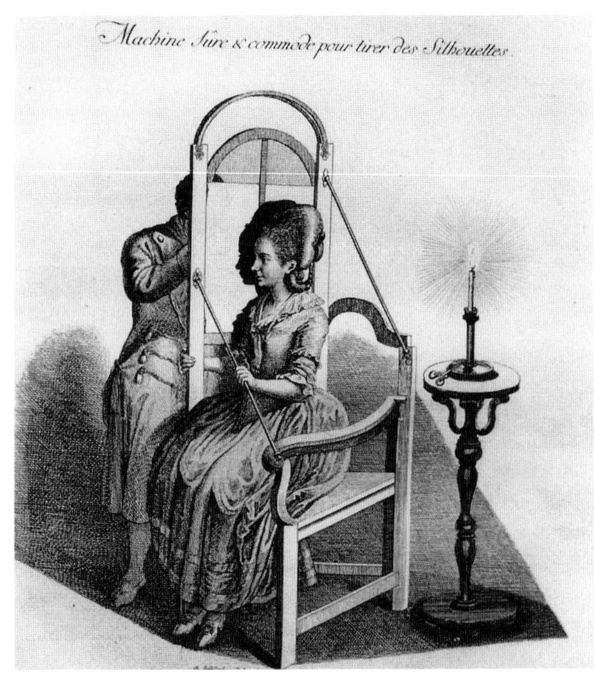

58 (left). Unsigned, *Machine sure & commode pour tirer des Silhouettes*, from Jean Lavater, *Essai sur la Physiogonomie*, The Hague, 1783. Private collection.

59 (below). Torii Kiyonaga, from Santō Kyōden, *Jikun kage-e no tatoe*, 1799. National Diet Library, Tokyo.

A viewer admires an artist, but his shadow tells a different story.

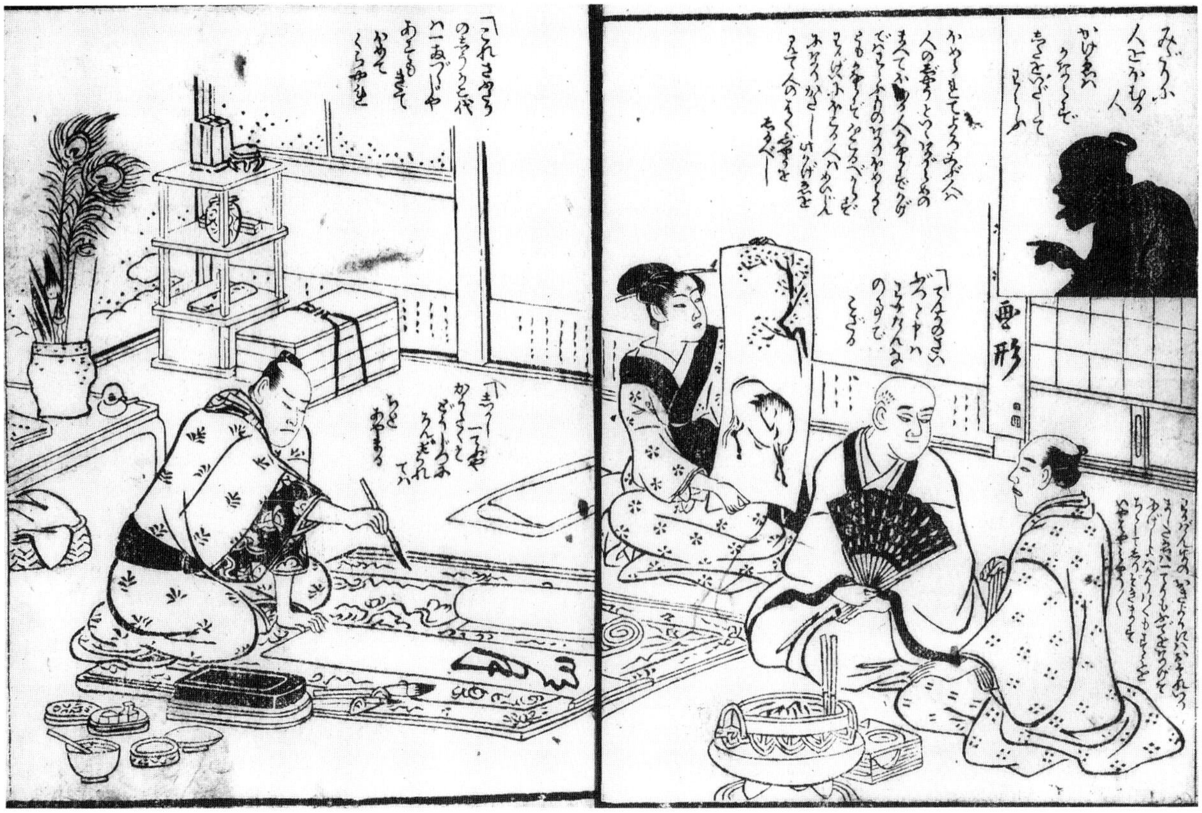

The *Shadow Picture Lessons* is a series of pairs in which a deceitful exterior is exposed by means of a profounder silhouette. One shows a monk and lay couple admiring paintings in an artist's studio (Fig. 59). Praise is flowing liberally, but to understand the truth the reader must look to the inset at the top, where a caption explains, "They're praising the art lavishly enough, but you can be sure that the shadow image will show them with tongues out, jeering." And so it does.

Kyōden billed his book as being just for children, but the readership of such publications was more likely to be adult. The story is for all to learn from. As ever, concerned with the moral unease of the times, Kyōden sought to enhance the urgency of the message by having the reader engage directly with the book, not just in seeing but *doing*. The opening page shows a Shintō priest, serious and devout in mien, but next to him are two alternative half-images (Fig. 60); the reader is supposed to snip one out and remount it as the man's shadow ("gum here," it says on the flap); the options are not happy: a crafty fox and a rustic oaf. The reader makes the choice.

Kyōden has manoeuvred the old theme, and the ethical shadow of Zhuangzi now incorporates the physiognomic picture of Silhouette. It is in casting only the exterior line of the person – something which casual sight will not reveal – that the inner core of signification is revealed. This is to be ignored at peril.

Two years before, Kyōden had already published a kibyoshi on a related theme. The former work linked the silhouette directly to the devil lantern, giving cast images of living people but now endowing them with the motion and clarity of slides, and therefore, by implication, colour (although his book was printed in monochrome). It is the heart itself that is projected. The work was illustrated by the author and no-nonsensely entitled *Pictures Cast by the Projector of the Human Heart (Jinshin-kyō no utsushi-e)*. The term Kyōden took for the projected image (*utsushi-e*)

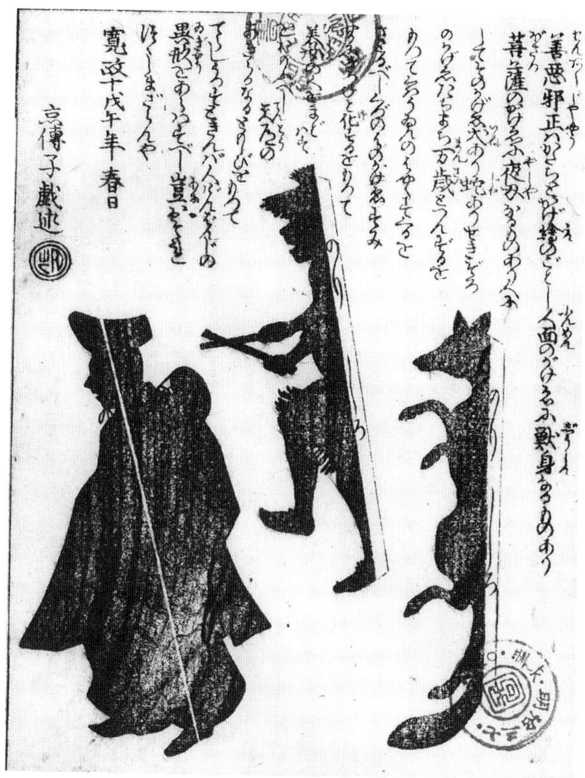

60. Torii Kiyonaga, from Santō Kyōden, *Jikun kage-e no tatoe*, 1799. National Diet Library, Tokyo.

Shintō priest with cut-out shadows of a fool and fox.

was the same as that used by contemporary Edo showmen, and Toraku's "painted coloured pictures on glass" were, the chronicle notes, "shown off under the name of *utsushi-e*."[63] The idea of "heart slides," however, seems to have been Kyōden's own. In the story, the images emanate directly from the person, as their body becomes a brilliant light that throws the contents of their glassy heart outward; the screen they fall on is the chest. As the characters appear on the pages, their interior machinations are perpetually exposed, and the façades of facial feature and bodily comportment can be instantly contrasted with the authenticity below, now seen

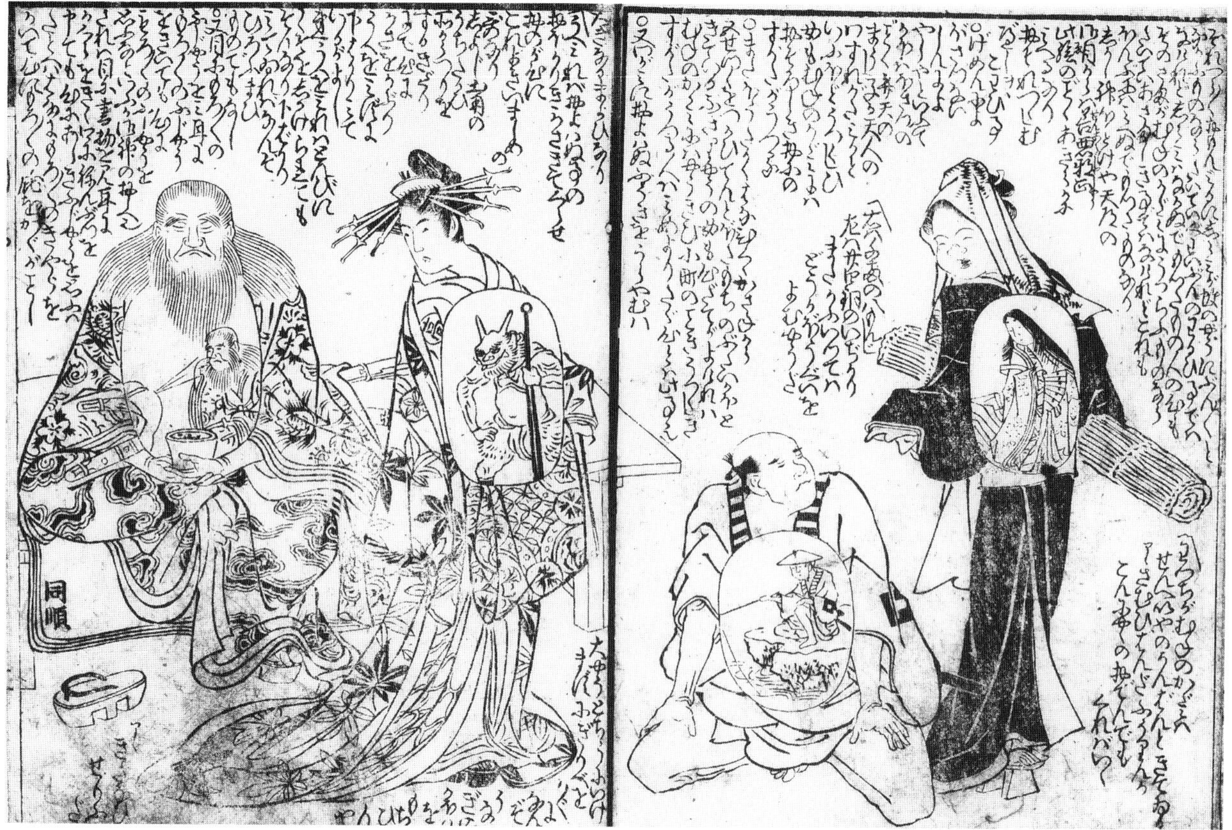

61. Santō Kyōden, from his *Hitogokoro kagami no-tsushi-e*, 1796. National Diet Library, Tokyo. *Street-walker, servant, courtesan, and the pompous samurai Ikyū, their hearts revealed.*

welled up on the surface. In Kyōden's assessment, they are sadly at odds with each other, and few are veracious.

One page shows a balance of the good and the bad. A beautiful woman appears, but her heart is a bludgeon-wielding demon – just the sort that real devil lanterns threw out (Fig. 61); beside her is a lowly servant, but his heart is away in the purifying countryside, line and rod in hand, and he looks for all the world like Tai Gongwang, the talented fisherman spotted by King Wen and employed, despite his poverty, for his sagacity.[64] A poor "night hawk" (*yotaka*), the lowest grade of prostitutes who performed their services in the street, has the heart of a noblewoman of yore. To the left is the samurai Ikyū (not to be confused with the author Ikkū), Sukeroku's implacable adversary from the Yoshiwara; though Sukeroku had been rough-and-ready, at least he was honest, and his rabble-rousing was really a manifestation of his inability to stop gut responses from rising unmoderated to the surface; he is not shown, but Ikyu is, and he lacks all substance, his heart nothing but an *aarusu* emitting *uinden.*

Another page shows a tightrope walker balancing across a wire (Fig. 62). He looks footsure, and the fan he wields to steady himself fulsomely emblazoned with "packed house"; but his heart shows him come to grief, clinging on

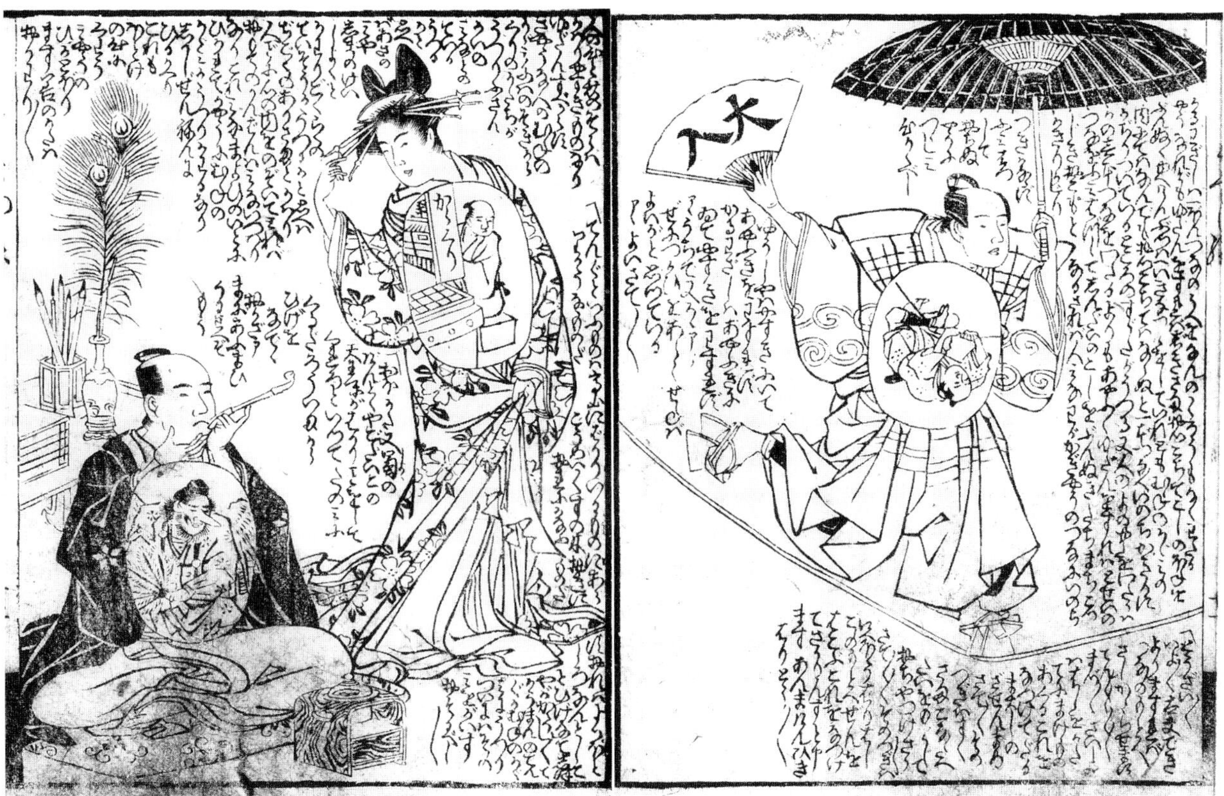

62. Santō Kyōden, from his *Hitogokoro kagami no-utsushi-e*, 1796. National Diet Library, Tokyo. *Tightrope walker, courtesan and trendy youth, their hearts revealed.*

for dear life and wondering, "What if I fall and have to live out my days begging?" Kyōden adds laconically, "crossing through life is harder than walking a wire, you know."

The last picture in the volume shows the author himself, sitting on a dais and haranguing an assembled throng (Fig. 63). Kyōden's heart-slide alone of all those given casts a vision identical to what he seems. His diligence in outward appearance is matched by a projected image of his honest labour, and his tobacconist's shop is seen with its awning and sign-pole, satisfied customers leaving with their sensibly priced purchases (at which point the reader would recall that Kyōden had unaccustomedly signed this book "Kyōden who's waiting for you at his tobacco-pouch shop"). Tongue-in-cheek and amusing, of course, Kyōden suggests that he himself is perfectly at one, inside and out in absolute keeping, rectified in his Way. Under the podium stands Tsutaya Jūsaburō, Kyōden's publisher, recognisable by the ivy leaf and Mount Fuji trademark on his sleeve (see Pl. 10, Fig. 136). Jūsaburō was proprietor of one of the most innovative houses in Edo, he wrote under the name of Karamaru, and sponsored much of the flowering of late eighteenth-century urban popular culture. Some five years later, during Matsudaira Sadanobu's post-Tanuma clamp-down, Jūsaburō was to be attaindered.[65] Kyōden was close to Jūsaburō, and teasingly shows him with a heart of solid accounts as he works out how much this latest creation will earn for him. Truths and appearances have diverged with a most wayward slippage, but there is at least a mechanical tool to find it out.

Kyōden depicted himself on the dais in the manner of a roadside *Shingaku* master, fan and cup of tea to hand, preaching the unification of heart and status, and the virtues of sincerity. The real *Shingaku* master, Dōni, might have done as much. Dōni did not know of the devil lantern (or he never mentioned it), but he was not averse to using toys as ethical metaphors. He invoked the puppet box (*kairai-bako*), a simpler contrivance and much inferior to the lantern in mechanical ingenuity, but equally susceptible to intellectual extension. The puppet box was an apparatus that hung suspended at the chest by a cord around the showman's neck: the puppeteer hid his hands inside, bringing out surprise figures, one or two at a time. Shimokabe Ikei drew one for Akisato Ritō's *Famous Places in Settsu (Settsu meisho zue)*, appropriately, as they were said to have originated near Osaka in Nishinomiya. Ikei showed the appearance of the "mountain cat," the stock final character to appear, that scattered the cast and terminated the show (Fig. 64).[66] Shows ran the gamut of mirth and tears, but as a senryu writer put it:

He won't make me laugh!
He won't make me cry!
That *kairai*-master.[67]

63. Santō Kyōden, from his *Hitogokoro kagami no-utsushi-e*, 1796. National Diet Library, Tokyo.

The author and his publisher, their hearts revealed, and by-standers.

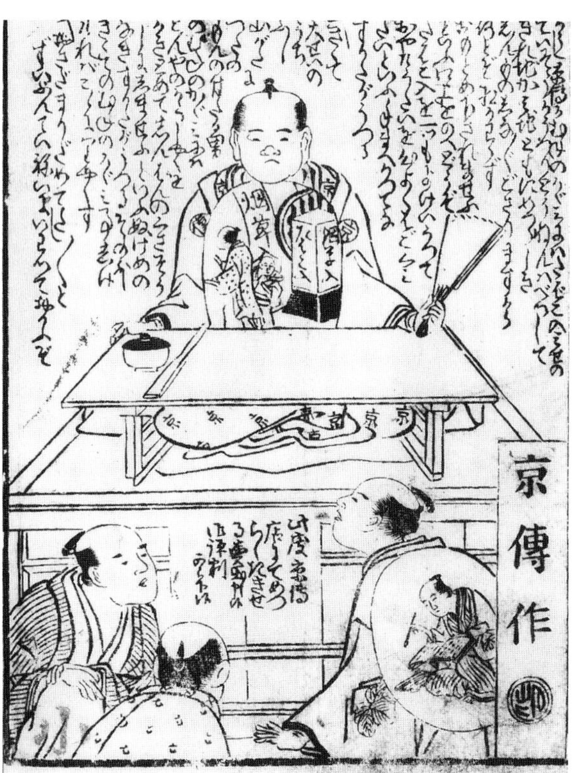

The verse implied no ethical brief, but clearly the show dealt in opposites (beneath the attention of the snooty composer, who nevertheless accepts the polarity). Demonic and heavenly dolls were standards, particularly the generic *oni* demon and the merciful bodhisattva Kannon, so it was not long before someone of Dōni's disposition began to equate the puppets bounding about, poised above the showman's chest with the emergence of good or evil from the heart. Dōni emphasised reformability and choice, and more than once in a sermon he quoted a poem:

Doll-box hanging
At the puppeteer's chest:
"Shall I pull out a Buddha, then?
Or shall I pull out a devil?"[68]

Both were possible, for although each person's real self (*makoto*) was different, all were equally endowed with refined and debased characteristics, to be brought to the fore or neglected in proportion to the degree of moral cultivation. Returning to prose, Dōni thrust home his point with blunt, unadorned eloquence: "Will it be a Kannon that springs from the real you, or will it be some scary old crone? All depends on your desires, doesn't it – it depends on what you want."

THE PEEPING-*KARAKURI* BOX

Optiques and shadow lanterns lent themselves with considerable cogency to metaphor in argumentations about sincerity and its opposite, fraud. A regular shadow always clung beside its originating form and could be immediately compared with it. But a devil cast on the wall like the landscape hovering in the mirror had to stand alone, more akin to the half-visible moral maze of real life. For all Kyōden's conceptualisations, Dutch glasses and projectors did not, in fact, permit any cross-referencing between authenticity and empirical appearance. They were taken on trust. And they much abused it.

We may now turn to the last imported instrument to be considered in this chapter, a device that exposed sequentially and in visual terms both inner reality and outer deceit, exhibiting successive images to illustrate precisely the divorce of interior from surface, of good from bad, and reality from bluff. The machine was called a "peeping-*karakuri*" (*nozoki-karakuri*). Viewing boxes of various sorts had been known in Japan for some time, and already in the mid-seventeenth century there is reference to the import of what may be a progenitor of the peeping-*karakuri*. The diary of the VOC Factory states that in the winter of 1646, a *perspectieff cas* arrived.[69] Perspective boxes were made in Holland, and Samuel van Hoogstraten, for example, was fabricating them at just the moment when the VOC brought their box to Japan (Fig. 65); unlike *optiques*, these were fully enclosed affairs with pictures drawn on several or all of the six inner sides so that the viewer peered into a sealed container through a small hole (or holes) to see a living, three-dimensional interior. Domestic settings were the commonest subject. The box brought to Japan does not survive, and it may have been more modest, possibly with just a single image painted opposite the viewing hole; it is possible that the scene was pasted onto a moveable board to be inserted and taken out, thus allowing other views to be substituted, as desired – such, at any rate, became typical in the Japanese peeping-*karakuri* of the eighteenth century.

64. Shimokabe Ikei, from Akisato Rito, *Settsu meisho zue*, 1796. SOAS, University of London.

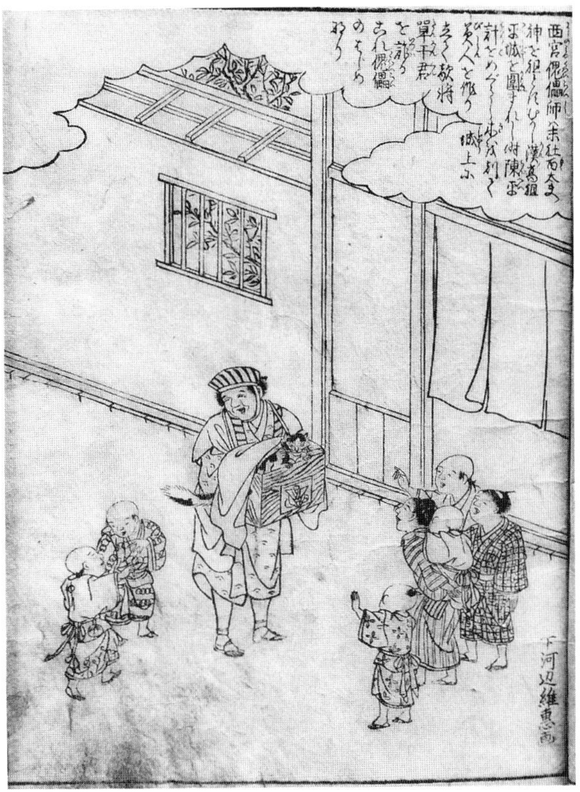

The VOC register goes on to note that the Japanese referred to the novel box as a *gocracq-baco*, presumably *gokuraku-bako*, or "paradise box." The illusory vastness of the space within was apparently considered to be like the Wizard of the Jar's heaven inside a bottle. With replaceable imagery, it is possible that, taking the lead from the puppeteer, scenes of bliss were alternated with scenes of torment, so that "paradise box" was not only a figurative term for the expansiveness of the view but a description of what was inside – and might change later to a "hell box." Certainly subsequent Japanese boxes

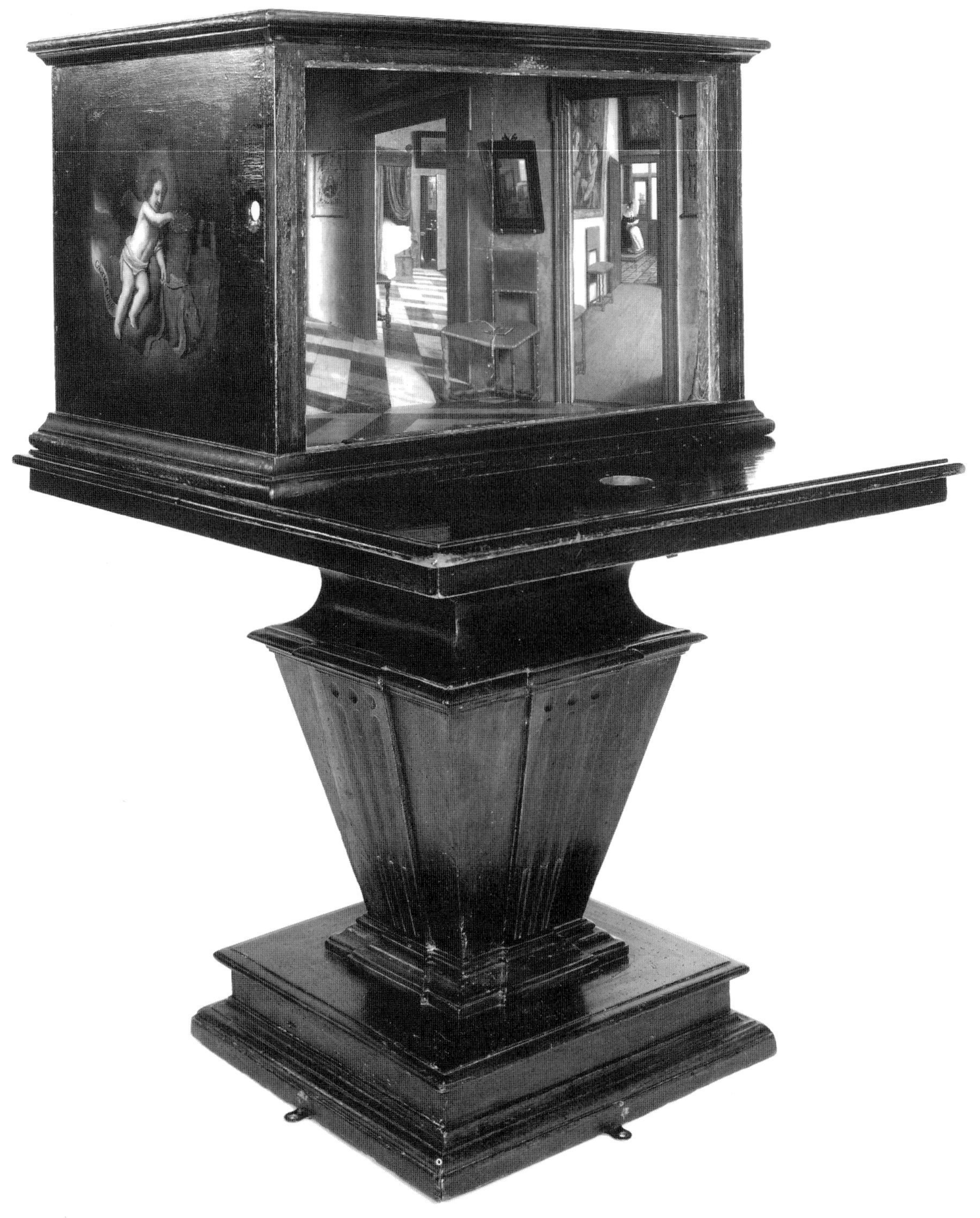

65. Samuel van Hoogstraten, Peepbox, with *Allegory of Fame*; domestic interior within painted on five sides, c. 1656 (stand modern). National Gallery, London.

flipped pictures in this way, offering the user not just a sequence of pictures but a meaningful succession. Either heaven or hell loomed as people's final lot, and, in the same way, one or other awaited the viewer's apprehensive gaze. As we shall see below a metaphysics of the "paradise box" emerged.[70]

There were many types of this *optique*-in-a-box, and the peep-box also has a morphology. The first domestic ones appeared in the Kyoto-Osaka area at the end of the seventeenth century, and the earliest evidence of their arrival in Edo is a painted handscroll executed around 1720, showing a box set up in the grounds of the Temple of Kannon in Asakusa, in a section of the precincts turned over to civic amusements (Fig. 66).[71] Young and old look in, no doubt for a fee through holes pierced in the front. A brightly painted signboard is perched on top to advertise the event, while a merry-go-round twirls above, encouraging passers-by. The showman seems to be operating hidden gadgetry by pulling cords coming from the side, and what is within cannot quite be told; to judge by the number of strings, it may be marionettes rather than pictures, set to swing and dance in response to the twitching of the cords – such puppet boxes (called raree-shows) were current in English fairgrounds of the period.

The standard peeping-*karakuri* of the late eighteenth century, though, was definitely for pictures. Its appearance can be understood from an illustration by Kyōden in his kibyoshi of 1782, *Trade Goods You Know All About* (*Gozonji no shōbaimono;* Fig. 67): a jack-in-the-box replacing the gyrating whirligig, has just sprung from behind the shade of a lamp used to illuminate the signboard announcing commencement of the show. The peeping-*karakuri* still retained its patina of foreignness after a century and more, for the wings of the backboard read "Great Dutch *Karakuri*" (*Oranda ō-garakuri*). The sign also emphasises that this is a Red-fur gaze, for the picture is executed in the perspective manner, and depicts a Westernised waterfront villa receding into the distance with European figures, three in the foreground walking a dog. It is clear that the whole package of visions within is accessible only through the idiom of *Ran*. Ordinary floating pictures would work well in a peeping-*karakuri,* as it had a lens but no mirrors, meaning reversal was not required, and Kyōden shows the operator seated on a chest marked "*uki-e.*" A quantity of sets were to be seen in the optimum sort of box, and the signboard was used to conceal a flytower that stored the pictures out of the way until they were dropped down one by one at the pull of the cords.

"This is the device," wrote Ikku in an anthology of Edo street memorabilia published in 1818, "which they say delights children's eyes more than anything else" (two are seen in Kyōden's picture, profiting from an indulgent grandfather). An anonymous print from the series *Eight Views of Tōei's Foothills (Tōeiroku hakkei)* – that is, of the area around Ueno – illustrates a booth labelled "Great Dutch *Karakuri,*" and "*saiku-nin* Takeda," now with a crowd of adults in front and the holes occupied by two men. An inscription reads,

> One peep in the *karakuri* costs three *sen*
> And 10,000-leagues-off Holland
> Comes before your eyes.
> Look at it together – those before never knew
> On the wide, wide seas
> Sailing ships returning.

Three *sen* was not much, but it was not all puerile. Hasegawa Mitsunobu of Osaka had stated as early as 1730 that "the ones looking in are supposed to be young lads, but in reality you'll find it's servant girls, eyes popping behind their hats."[72] Mitsunobu included a picture of the device he was talking about, showing a machine very like Kyōden's, but with an exotic elephant, like the one that had passed through Kyoto two years before, adorning the sign above.[73] Peeping-

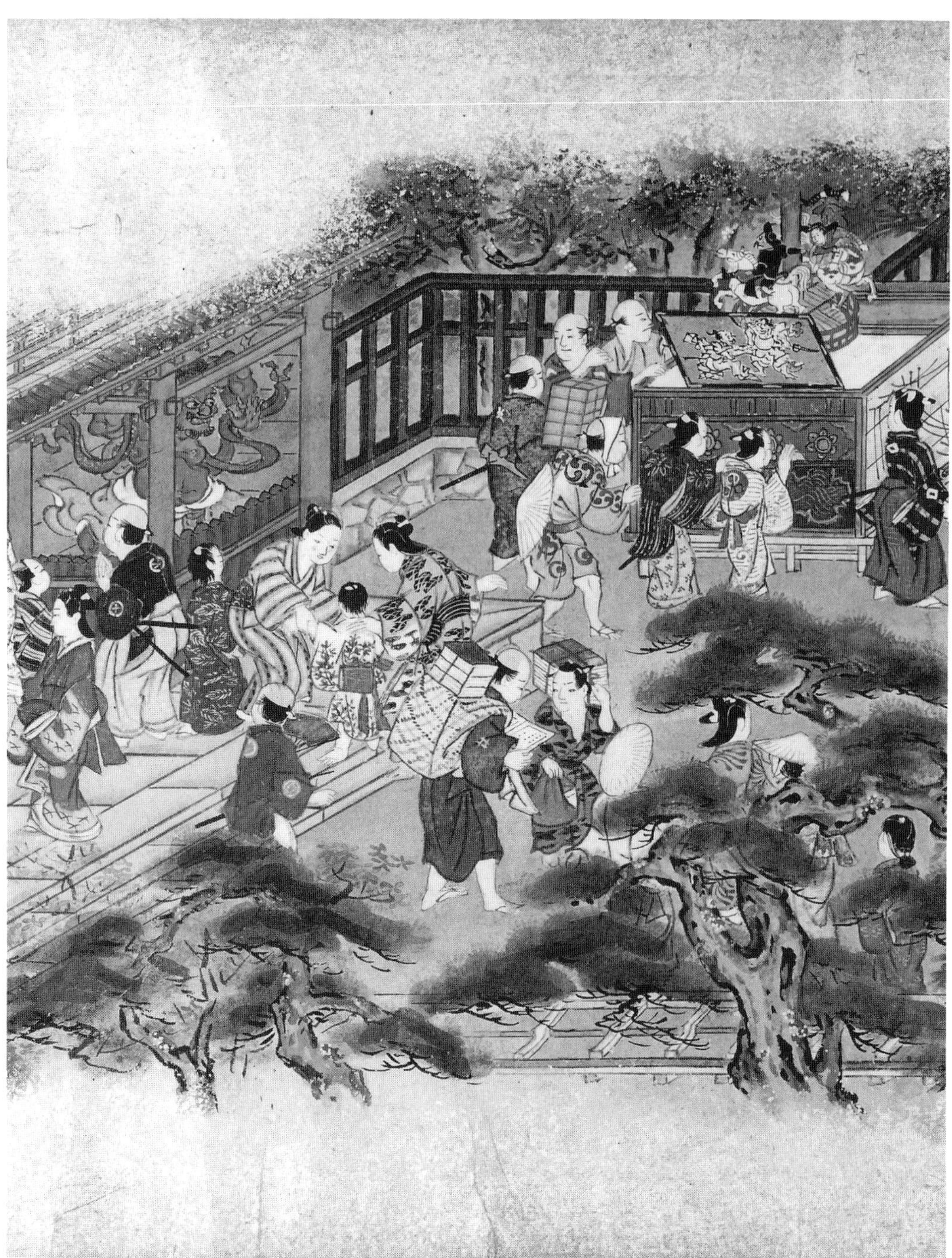

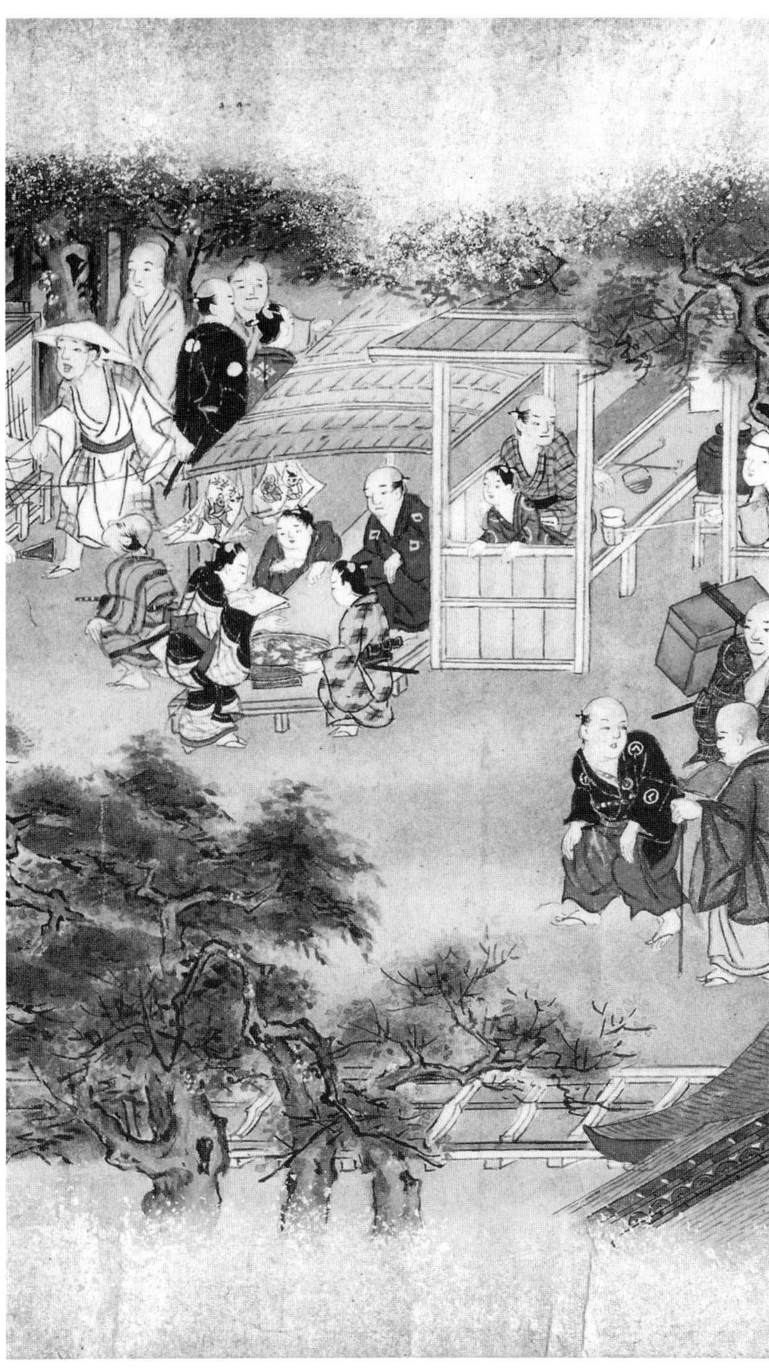

66. Unsigned, *Peepbox*, detail of *Asakusa* handscroll from the series *Amusements in Edo*; c. 1730. British Museum.

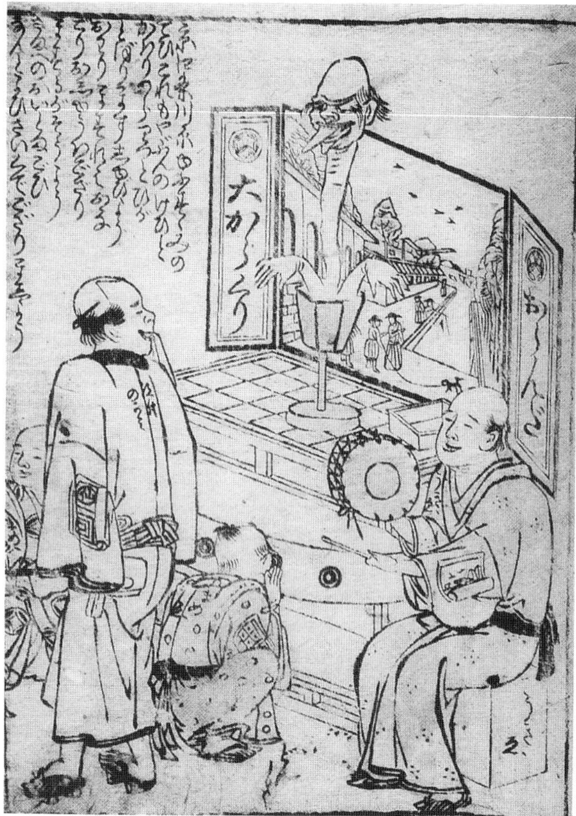

67. Santō Kyōden, from his *Gozonji no shōbaimomo*, 1782. Department of Literature, Kyūshū University.

The peepbox is inscribed on the wings, 'Great Dutch Karakuri'.

karakuri were about interiors, hidden ones, and about obtaining a gaze onto the covert and the not normally seen. Whether or not the reader is to infer from Mitsunobu's words that something shocking was in the box is unclear, but the women hiding behind their hats seem to be aware that they are enjoying a peep into something seldom exposed. As a senryu from a collection of 1765 had it:

> "I wonder if
> It's really that interesting,"
> They say peering in.[74]

Perhaps the usually unseen included the downright unseemly – pornography and the like. An anonymous work of 1735, *The Ways of Love (Endō zukan)*, discussed the peeping-*karakuri*, and although it provided no illustrations, some intriguing possibilities emerge. The text is so shot through with puns that what is most clear about the box is that it twists and turns and will not let things be what they appear; everything is sent inside out. The passage can be read in two completely different ways:

> Covering their tracks and pretending to be constables, the town villains look into the peeping-*karakuri*. It has no glass in the apertures so they see the scenes, drawn in the manner of Ōtsu pictures, with nothing interposing.[75]

This sounds innocent enough. The box is primitive and lacks lenses in the eyepieces, and the images, too, are executed in the naive style of pilgrimage pictures from Ōtsu, a temple town near Kyoto. Yet this reading is utterly demolished as the enclosed subtext wells up:

> Having sex from behind, the cheap prostitutes sell what they've got. At the peeping-*karakuri* the men don't actually use their pricks, but they do look most vulgarly at a picture of a woman's vast entry covered with hair.

The booth thus slides from piety to obscenity; as if to match the displacing transformations of the transient images in the box itself – now heaven, now hell – the text plummets from the lofty to the base. On every level, the box inverts.

Unlike domestic *optiques*, peeping-*karakuri* were set up in public as business ventures, and so the view through the multiple holes was shared. Within the personal and absorptive regime of the perspective gaze there was also a social dimension. Eccentric or rude behaviour was not tolerated, hence another senryu:

> "Hey! Give your nose
> A proper wipe!"
> They say peering in.[76]

The showman's disciplining of the clientele was intended to ensure good order and keep a swift rotation at the holes, but his plentiful injunctions served to fashion a peep that, for all its engrossing qualities, was also quick and breathless. Kyōden included a peeping-*karakuri* design in his spoof pattern-book, *Elegant Chats on Fabric Motifs (Komon gawa)*, published in 1780, showing common objects puzzlingly arrayed in the manner of the recurring imagery on rolls of cloth. A series of peep-holes is billed as the "peep-stripe" (*nozoki-jima*); a pun, as *shima* means both "stripe" and "booth." Kyōden added, with reference to another of the operator's familiar injunctions, "This pattern can also be called the, 'do-pass-along-at-the-front-there-please!'-stripe."[77] The gaze was snatched, obtained with difficulty, perhaps surreptitious, but luckily prized out.

The peeping-*karakuri* was a multifarious device. It showed scenes that changed in swift succession as the views dropped down. But it showed them in the plausible draughtsmanship of perspective. It also offered both a protracted, disembodying gaze and a rapidly taken glance. To look inside was to know the oscillation of contradictions. Diffusing throughout the country, the box carried with it assorted meanings and associations. In Kyoto *nozoki-karakuri* (admittedly rather a mouthful) was abbreviated to just *nozoki*, making it the quintessential "peep," whereas in Edo the word was truncated the other way, becoming simply *karakuri*, turning the box into the automatic device *par excellence*.[78]

More concretely, the nature of pictures to be investigated in the device is problematic to reconstruct. The range that this *Ran* gaze overflew is difficult to trace. Shikitei Sanba's celebrated novel, *The Barber's Shop of the Floating World (Ukiyo doko)*, identified some of the views. Such textual accounts are valuable, as extant floating pictures are relatively few and the scope available to the later Edo-period enthusiast much diminished by time. Sanba's book was published in instalments between 1813 and 1814, and was draughted as an amalgam of rapid-fire stories told during a gossipy afternoon at the barber's. In one passage the three heroes, Seikichi, Tokutarō and Kenzō, all rough lads of Edo, launch into a verbal triple act on the theme of things foreign. Seikichi discuss two actors who have taken up Westernised names as publicity stunts ("Jakarta" Kinokuni-ya and "Oranda" Otowa-ya[79]) and then mentions the peeping-*karakuri*. Kenzō responds by mimicking the rap of an operator as he encourages customers to inspect the series of images inside. No heaven and hells are mentioned, but the box contains a good smattering of topographical perspective views:

> Now then, everybody, come and have a look! Here's the branch factory of the [Dutch East India] Company in Jakarta! There's the look-out post where they use their telescopes, with its two pine trees, and you can see as far as those three girls over there. All is contrived inside the little box! And there's more: a Chinese is standing to greet someone at his window. Then there's a maple tree and a big fat pine. Well? How is it? Oye! You there, have a look too. These lenses will give you a ten-mile Red-fur stare.[80]

Foreignness was not accorded by the subjects of the scenes alone (though that is apparent enough), nor even by the perspectival manner of depiction. It was inherent in the nature of the gaze itself – the ten-mile Red-fur stare (*kōmō no jūri kan*). Looking into the interior of the booth, viewers attained an exotic ability to perceive the unseen, whether the remotely distant or the deliberately concealed, as they probed the out-of-ken. Even when the pictures were no more complex than scenic views, this still applied.

The root *karakuri* or mechanical element in the peep-box (other than the jack), was the latch for dropping the pictures down in turn, and the more basic contraption had no more than that.

But a secondary device was sometimes installed to enhance the cleverness, and this locked the box more firmly into the sequentiality of heaven and hell. A line in Kyōden's *Trade Goods You Know All About* runs, "the scene will show people enjoying the cool of the day at Shijō-Kawara in Kyoto, but in a flash it will change to night with lanterns burning," and the showman concludes, "and what a great *saiku* that is!"[81] Lighting tricks began to be incorporated. This allowed a significant improvement, for the pictures could be animated in a mutation from day to night, before being shifted. Shutters mounted beneath the translucent roof of the box could close off the light, while the board behind the picture was pulled out, making the image back-lit. When doors and windows or lanterns and stars depicted in the scene were cut out of the paper, they seemed suddenly to illuminate from within. Scenes of evening revelry looked good with the treatment, and as *uki-e* had from the first shown nightspots like the Yoshiwara or Shijō-Kawara or such stalwarts of evening entertainment as the annual firework display on the river Sumida at Mitsumata, these were perfect for insertion into the box. Famous events that had unfolded at night could be shown, too, and Bakin recorded seeing the Night Attack from the eleventh act of *The Treasury of Loyal Retainers (Chūshingura)* in a peeping-*karakuri* when he passed through Nagoya in 1811.[82] When Ikku mentioned the operator in his compilation of street memorabilia, he continued with the cry given as a gallop through day and night scenes, beginning with the same one Bakin had seen seven years before:

> Well now, well now! Next comes the eleventh act of *The Treasury of Loyal Retainers*, and after that, it's the suicide of O-shichi, the greengrocer's girl; next there's the tragic journey after the Battle of Ichi-no-tani [in *Tales of the Heike*]. Then you'll see Asukayama [in Edo] far off in the distance, and Itsukushima in Aki shown near at hand. Then it will change to night-time scenes, with lanterns, flaming torches and stars; there'll be the *battue* held [by Yoritomo] on Mount Fuji, and the [Mitsumata] firework displays laid on by the Tama-ya and Kagi-ya.[83]

Ikku continued with more details then ended with the usual, "Will the people at the front pass along please!" One obnoxious child insists on seeing the whole show again through a different hole.

These lighting tricks were common in European shows, too, and *vues d'optique* were often made with cut-outs not noticed when illumination fell on the front, but coming into their own when a candle was placed behind. But in Japan, it was recognised that the best potentials of the technique were realised in the realm of symbolic meaning. The change from light to dark lent itself to a bipolar reading moving from good to bad, or cause to effect, the literal switch from front-to-back lighting fitting in with the reality/falsehood rhetoric already established by other mechanical devices. One scene might be exposed under two conditions, or else successive views, one bright and clear and one dark and fell might form a pair; or, again, there might be series of each as front-lit heavens melted into torturing crepuscular hells, illuminated by the sparse glowing flickering bonfires.

No heaven and hell sets executed in perspective survive, but by changing even a pair of more everyday topographical scenes from day into night, the showman could make manifest a similar transformation, and in a more subtle way. The shift revealed how the bright order of daytime mutated into the riot of evening play, or how diligence descended to extravagance. This had sound moral impact. Light and dark might signify a mutation less of radiance than of ethics.

Lighting tricks invested the peep-box with considerable metaphysical power. Kyōden, in his fabric design of the peep-stripe, punned *nozoki-ana*, the peep-hole, with *nozoki-bana*, a "peeping nose" – that is, one with upturned nostrils. Snotty noses were the plague of collective viewing machines; nostrils might look like two holes to peep into the head through. But the "peeping nose" was more specifically unpleasant for the theoretical reason that physiognomists took it to be a pointer to baseness of character and breeding. Kyōden himself drew regularly upon this belief by depicting feckless or depraved figures in his stories with pug noses (to the extent that they began to be called "Kyōden" noses).[84] Next to the pattern, Kyōden added, "there is no *saiku* as good as this for revealing a person's integrity and standing."[85] It was a joke, of course, but one that gave the peeping-*karakuri* the strange and deep capacity to make revelations of human character; by virtue of a duopoly of vision, the device sought out the uncivilised or immoral and exposed them.

THE MECHANICS OF THE MIND

Kyōden examined the tandem in/out, exposed/hidden *karakuri* gaze more protractedly in 1801 in a kibyoshi constructed as an anthology of showbooths. The stalls selected were used as metaphors, and the ensemble of the book built up to suggest how the amusement of the fun-fair could offer genuine revelations about life. The work was illustrated by Kitao Shigemasa, Kyōden's long-time associate and former teacher, and it announced itself in the title, *Here's a Story of Some Pretty Remarkable Displays (Ko wa mezurashiki misemono-gatari)*. Each page depicts a particular stall, invoked to expose some identifiable vice or foible, while a small inset in the corner illustrates the signboard such a booth might really have hanging outside, which of course was a very different matter from what was seen after one had parted with one's money and gone in, revealed on the rest of the page. The discrepancy that gaped was that between truth and assertion. Sticking closely to the letter of the strange sights purveyed was famously not a trait of Edo stallholders' advertising boards; indeed, they had a deserved notoriety for the over-generous interpretations they put on their wares. Dean Swift had remarked the opposite of London showmen a generation or so before:

> For I have always lookt upon it as a high Point of Indiscretion in Monster-mongers and other Retailers of strange Sights, to hang out a fair Picture over the door, drawn after the Life, with a most elegant Description underneath. This hath saved me many a Threepence, for my Curiosity was fully satisfied, and I never offered to go in.[86]

Kyōden, by contrast, said in his preface that those who stalked the booths of Ryōgoku or Asakusa knew well enough how they contained nothing like what the signs had promised, and the pictures were more potemkins erected over mediocrity. If an operator hung out too modest a sign, of course, people walked right by, and excessive exaggeration might invite reprisals and demands for refunds; most showmen worked on the principle of augmentation of deceit to the maximum unchallenged level. So it was with the human person, who hung signboards over their hearts, anxious not to undersell and to get away with all they could.

One page of the *Pretty Remarkable Displays* gives a peeping-*karakuri* (Fig. 68). The inset shows the usual backboard sign, looking very like what Kyōden had illustrated nearly twenty years before in *Trade Goods*, and what the three *sen* box had displayed: the psychic workings of the booth still came via the interiorising gaze of *Ran;* Dutch and Chinese figures stand before a deep perspectival recession representing a Western scene. But the body of the picture transfers this firmly to the Edo setting. The box itself is complex and made with triple tiers. An apparently affluent merchant house is the theme of the show, but the scenes will reveal what lies behind. A sequence of peep-show views could not be captured in the space of a single image; so one is described textually, while another is shown as a three-dimensional assemblage above the box's ceiling, while a third is represented as if hocked up over the booth. The family shop,

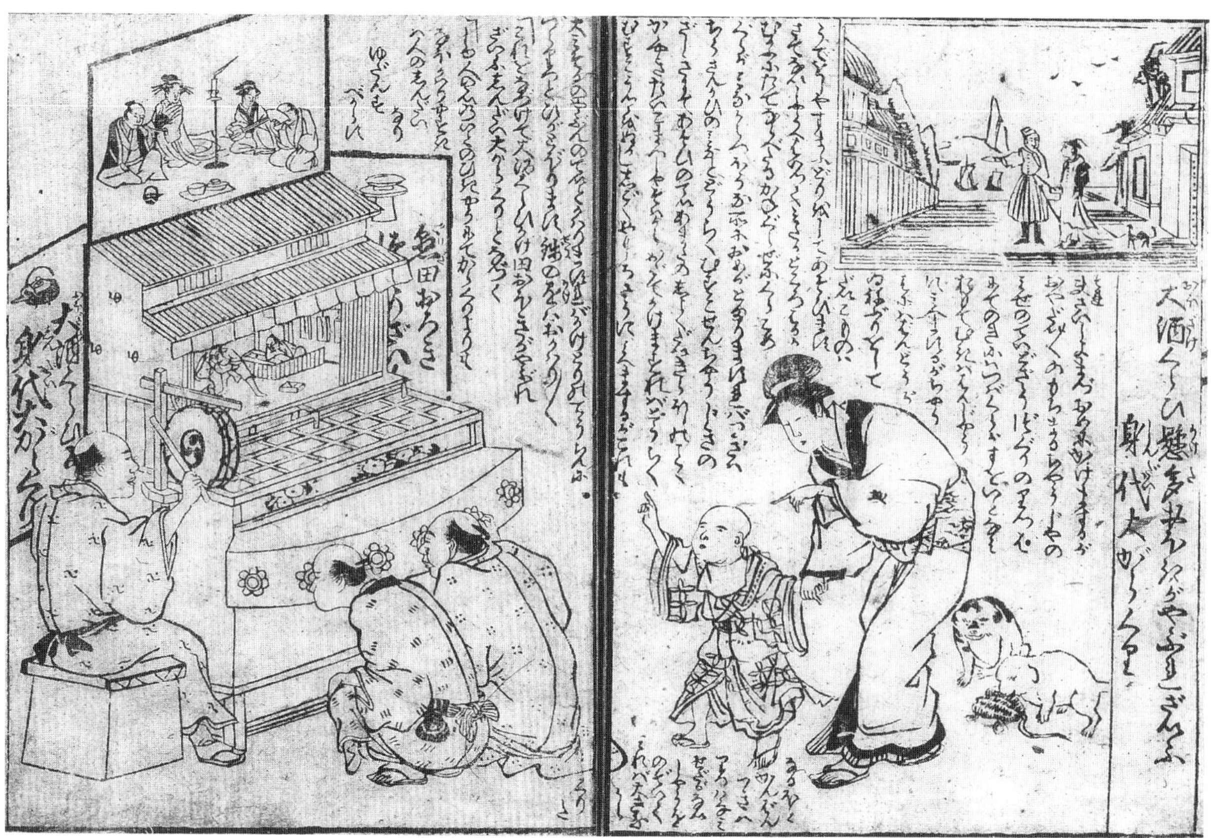

68. Kitao Shigemasa, *Fortune's Great Karakuri*, from Santō Kyōden, *Ko wa mezurashiki misemono-gatari*, 1801. Tokyo Metropolitan Central Library.

announces Kyōden, is five storeys high (an impossibly lavish scale) with bird's-nests lodged in its ancestral eaves and storehouses built in rows outside. Godowns receding into the distance was a common theme in *uki-e*, but the truth here is other than it seems: in the second scene the chief clerk is shown asleep, while his assistants pass their days in horseplay and sumo; the third scene represents the inheritor of the firm engaging in night revels in the Yoshiwara, male and female geishas on call, and a prostitute to sit beside him as a candle burns until morning. This wastrel life-style beckons ruination. It is New Year's Eve, Kyōden explains, and tomorrow the annual settling of debts. Can the necessary payments be made?

This box is overt in its metaphysical claims: labelled down the right-hand wing is the pseudo-trade name, "Kaketa Ōki" – an obvious dig at Takeda Ōmi of Osaka, who did indeed make peeping-*karakuri* booths as well as running his automotive theatre.[87] But a second pun is intended, for the verb *kakeru* (of which *kaketa* is the past tense) means to conceal or impose, while *ōki* means great. This is a booth of great deceptions; but in its series of images, sincerity will eventually out. The left-hand sign furthers this reading, for it identifies the box as "Fortune's *Karakuri*" (*shindai karakuri*). As the sets thump down, the rewards of lethargy and lies are shown, and good and bad bring in their inevitable returns of profit and loss. The slipping of the latches in the flytower, like the turning of Fortune's wheel, brings all into alignment in the end, and façades of lies cannot prevail for more than the span of a fleeting vision in the box. Kyōden went on with the generalisation: "If you were to pull the cords on the human heart, you'd see its appearance change even swifter than [the pictures in] a *karakuri*. This is the wages of Fortune. Let no one lower their guard!"

Kyōden was in fact returning to a theme he had articulated five years before in a kibyoshi mentioned above, *Pictures Cast by the Projector of the Human Heart*. On the page with the timorous tightrope walker had appeared a fashionable youth with a beautiful courtesan (Fig. 62). The man's heart projected as a *tengu* goblin (appropriate for the devil lantern referent), but hers had no substance at all. The woman is nothing but a quick succession of images, amounting to nought, for her inside is as a peeping-*karakuri;* her emotions and feelings shift with the proverbial quickness of the sets inside a booth, her probity reduced to a moving toyshop. Each façade of lies will be stripped away only to be replaced by another, as a new falsehood slams down to begin the cycle again. There is perpetual deferral and instability, and this woman has lost the sincerity of her Way; so tarnished that there is nothing left to be sincere to. Kyōden explained:

> People's hearts change as fast as the autumn skies. Let all be on their guard! The projector shows how the heart of the woman is like a peeping-*karakuri* booth. Just when you think you see Pusan Harbour [in Korea], there it goes, and it's changed to Miyajima in Aki [the same as the Itsukushima Ikku mentioned]. "That's a picture of Paradise!" you tell yourself, and then it shifts to Hell.

If the woman is typical, implications for the human condition are depressing indeed. The Buddhas' hearts, Kyōden offers, do not change; but that is barely grounds for easing circumspection, for, as the preface had already alerted the reader, even Buddhas and bodhisattvas cannot be identified from their exteriors, as an angel face may obscure a devil heart.

Some years later, in 1814, Kyōden's rival Shikitei Sanba drew on the peep-box, making its existential powers further explicit in a longer work with the pregnant title *The Peeping-karakuri for Showing the Human Heart (Hitogokoro nozoki-karakuri)*. The booth does not appear among the (scant) illustrations that Toyokuni provided for the text, but the whole conceit of the narrative is predicated on peeping-*karakuri* mechanisms. Sanba divided his chapters into two parts, giving first the "front" (*omote*) and then the "back" (*ura*) of events, as if they were front-lit images changing to back-lit ones. He showed how bluster and cant give way to a calling to account. One is "a proud doctor who's really a know-nothing: front and back." Sanba's preface warned the reader what was in store with a stream of *karakuri* allusions, mixed with Dōni-esque Buddhology:

> The Creator's great *saiku* divided off heaven from earth in a split that could not be seen even with "Dutch glasses." The workings of humankind are controlled by the Gods, Buddhas, and Sages like dolls of a sort which even Takeda Ōmi could not contrive. Joy and sorrow, pleasure and pain are all manipulated by strings, and wealth and honour, poverty and baseness run on clockwork. Waxing and waning, flowering and withering, it's all like a [peeping-]*karakuri*. One minute you see Pusan Harbour, and the next it's Ryōgoku Bridge. You can look at a picture of brilliant cherry-blossom viewing, but if you linger a little, it will change to a night-time scene. . . . And what of the *karakuri* in your heart? Read on![88]

A rhetoric of *Ran*, with its probing, mechanised dispensation of knowledge, is never far away as imports take their place beside *Shingaku* in a commentary that is, after all, about entirely indigenous concerns.

We may conclude with the treatment of a peeping-*karakuri* by Morishima Chūryō. Chūryō's life straddled many of the competing spheres with which this book engages: *Rangaku* expert, he was also an experimenter and populariser, a lexicographer, public moralist, and patron of the Floating World; born a high samurai, he became an urbane wit and comic. Chūryō was a veritable weave of the of multiple strands of late-eighteenth-century culture. In 1785, he published a kibyoshi and enlisted his close friend Kyōden to do the illustrations. Chūryō, here writing under the pen-name Manzōtei entitled the work *New Yoshitsune's Close Look at Ezo (Shin-Yoshitsune saiken Ezo)*. The title needs unpacking. Overtly it refers to the legend of the glamorous mediaeval warrior Yoshitsune (whose brother Yoritomo's *battue* and whose own tragic journey after the victory at Ichi-no-Tani were standard scenes in the peeping-*karakuri* repertory). Yoshitsune, it was popularly believed, had not been slain by Yoritomo as the historical records said, but had escaped to Ezo (modern Hokkaidō) and thence to other fantastic islands, where he lived out a life of mythical peregrinations among people and places strange.[89] The young hero's event-filled romance was often told, but Chūryō used it on this occasion as a trolley to introduce a pun: "Yoshitsune" sounds similar to "Yoshiwara," which, since it had relocated just beyond Asakusa in the mid-seventeenth century, was properly called the "New" (*Shin*) Yoshiwara. Further, Ezo sounds like *ezu*, a picture-book, whereas *saiken* properly means a detailed guide. With a little imagination, then, the title can be reread as *An Illustrated Guide to the New Yoshiwara*. Such a vade-mecum of the pleasure district was indeed put out by Tsutaya Jūsaburō, supplying information on the latest fads, the habits and qualities of the more popular prostitutes, and other necessary information, updated twice annually; Chūryō's associate, Lord Satake of Akita's high commissioner in Edo. Hōseidō Kisanji usually wrote the preface for it (a job from 1790 taken over by Kyōden). Chūryō's story addresses the ironies and follies of the brothel zone, not its superficial charms, with a critical, under-the-skin "close look."

The reader is taken on a tour of various amusements to be had in the quarter as if they were places on Yoshitsune's island-hopping adventure. The conceit is justified by the fact that the same word, *shima*, which meant a booth and a stripe also meant a brothel and an island. One *shima*, inevitably, is a peeping-*karakuri* (Fig. 69). A group of Chinese boys play around a box from which the jack (in the form of a cyclops) has just sprung; the signboard is of the common sort showing a Dutch-like scene with foreign figures walking a dog, now joined by someone carrying goods on a yoke. A partially visible panel to the left claims the booth as a manufacture to the familiar Osaka automaton master "*Karakuri* Takeda, clever-device maker" (*Saiku-nin [Ka]rakuri Takeda*). The child on the left offers the opinion: "This peeping-*karakuri* is just like those old things that've been turning up in stories recently. I think they're pretty boring." Certainly booths were becoming established literary symbols, although the specific reference here may be to Jūsaburō's publishing rivals, the Tsuruya, who in 1782 had featured peep-boxes on the dust jackets of all their kibyoshi for that year (one of which was Kyōden's *Trade Goods*).[90] But no reader would be fooled by the feigned dismissiveness, and here was nothing boring at all.

The viewing holes are not the unadorned apertures of most, but have been made to look like gaping openings in the chests of caryatids drawn along the front. Like Sanba's peep-box for the human heart, this booth must show some kind of personal interior beyond, within the hidden space. This is better than the "peeping-nose," but lest it appear gruesome, Chūryō notifies the reader that these are men from the legendary

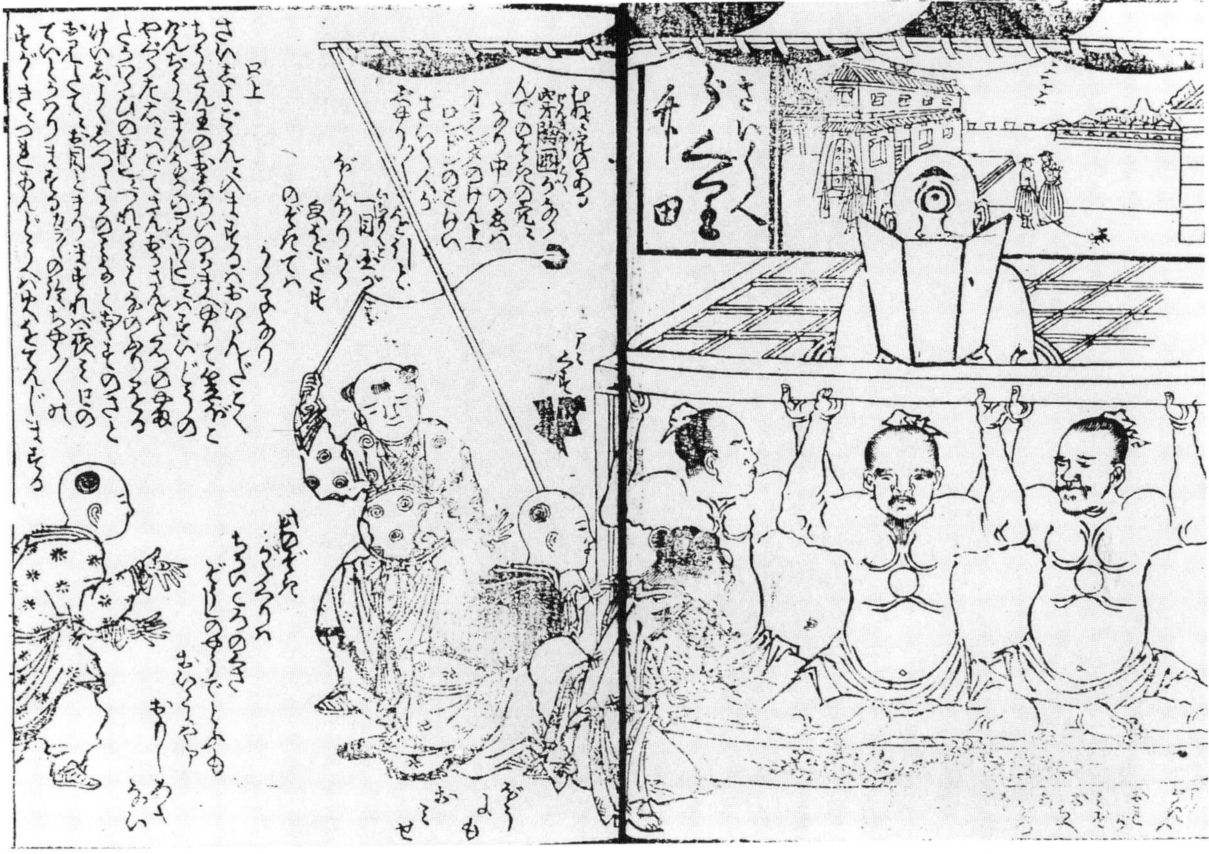

69. Santō Kyōden, from Morishima Chūryō, *Shin-Yoshitsune saiken Ezo*, 1785. Private collection. *Children approach a peepbox made by the Takeda company.*

Land of the People with Pierced Chests (Senkyō-koku), a place still regularly included in Edo-period geographies.[91]

Several interior views are referred to in the text, mixing the foreign topographic with the illicit world of pleasure:[92]

> First of all, Ladies and Gentlemen, we see the luxurious structure built for King Chūsan of Holland[93] – his temporary residence, decked out in all its festival bunting; in the centre of the prospect is his water-turret; to right and left are the hills of Gote and Oka. Then there's a hilarious storm, yes! paper flowers will shower down over the scene. The harbour of Shittaka and the village of Okusū will also delight your gaze. If you tarry, we will change to night-time scenes showing the establishments [of the Yoshiwara] with the tok-tok of their wooden bells and the plinky-plonk of brothel tunes. We'll even make light appear in the lanterns!

This sounds like the normal sampling of peepshow delights, though falling flowers (released at the pull of a cord, perhaps) seem new, and pictures of Dutch skills in hydrotechnology (though readily imaginable) are not otherwise attested.

But there is another image: "One picture inside shows the London clock presented to the shogun by the Dutch";[94] no illustration is provided, but inside the peeping-*karakuri* is the piece of Western mechanics most famous for its ability to run in a complex of wheels and springs, working at a steady and perpetual pace. This tiny "London" clock, small enough to fit into a pocket or box, was just the size of a human heart (Fig. 86). Its regulatory ticking was emblematic of how the well-tempered individual should be. Some years later, the fourteenth shogun, Iemochi, was to take his London clock (made by F. W. Benson of 25 Old Bond Street) to the grave for he was buried at the Temple of Zōjō-ji in the centre of Edo with it, the mechanism coming to a standstill at precisely 8:27.[95]

FIVE

SEEING IN

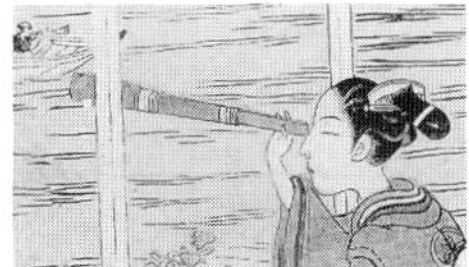

THE LAST TWO CHAPTERS investigated mechanics – those which by their workings suggested the importance of intricate and covert insides, and those which displayed interiors through a direct optical route. We now turn, in this and the following chapter, to a consideration of the new material that single-handedly secured the interiorising gaze. The material was glass. It allowed inspection without dismemberment or invasion.

The view through glass was felt to convey dispassionateness, maintaining a special autonomy for the object seen and not compromising it. Viewers were prevented by glass from pushing beyond themselves. The one who gazed via a pane was bent on discovery, to be sure, but was kept physically distant from the object of inquiry. Seer and seen were discrete. Unlike surgeons who inserted hands and scalpels, or the clocksmith who tinkered with driver and wrench, the viewer through glass only beheld. Its introduction occasioned upheaval in the world of seeing.

THE VIEW THROUGH GLASS

Glass, in being something more to be seen through than looked at, was unique among eighteenth-century materials. Its clear, self-abnegating qualities encouraged the belief that it was, epistemologically speaking, not even there. The gaze suggested untinctured study. This "absence" of glass was entirely a construct, for though the better the material's make the more nearly invisible it was, the novelty of glass ensured that its presence was, on the contrary, always strongly felt. To look through glass did decisively colour what was seen for it was to see in a novel way. The viewer was newly empowered whereas the seen things were caught and thus, zones on either side of the see-through wall were never equal: there was an outside and an in, a liberated and a captured. The non-reciprocality of the stare was a fact of which the user can hardly have been oblivious. Glass set up power structures.

Glass was a foreign material. Although domestically produced in small quantities since the mid-seventeenth century, it remained a major import from Europe throughout the eighteenth (Fig. 13). Glass was integral to the notion of seeing in the manner of *Ran*. Edo-period makers stressed that what they were doing was fabricating a substance of otherness on the native soil. The better class of glassware shop always identified its stock as in some way "Dutch," regardless of whether it had really been imported from there or not.

Ancient Japanese tombs were known to contain sherds or even whole objects of glass, and Tachibana Nankei pointed out that the tumulus of the sixth-century tenno Ankan had recently yielded a glass bowl – as he could attest, having seen it himself preserved in the Temple of Sairinji.[1] Nankei speculated that glass had been widely made in Japan in historic times, but that its technique had been forgotten over time, not to be revived until the inroads of European Catholic missionaries. Modern scholarship holds that even these historic finds are imports, some from as far off as Sassania. Ōtsuki Gentaku offered the assessment that the first "proper" glass had appeared in Japan "two hundred or more years ago," which would give a date of about 1600, precisely the period when trade with the West began. Gentaku conceded that quondam substitutes had been assayed before, but concluded, "antique ways of producing glass were simple makeshifts, the proper technology having only now been learned from Dutch books."[2] Lexically at least, glass became firmly established as foreign. Chinese words for various translucent stone – such as *rūri*, literally beryl, or *aitai*, a rock crystal – might be used to describe it, but the correct vocabulary announced glass as Western, with terms taken from the Portuguese, like *gyaman* and *biidoro* (from *diamante* and *vitro*), or from the Dutch, like *garasu*.

Perhaps the most compelling usage for the material (though not the most widespread) was the glazed window. The technology required for making large panes was just beginning in Europe, too, and in England (a country much cited by *Rangaku* scholars) the first plate factory opened in 1773, rather after that in the Netherlands. In Japan it was not until the second half of the nineteenth century that windows were commonly glazed, and they remained as they always had been, entirely opaque, covered with wooden shutters or translucent *shōji* (in China cloth was used). Charles Thunberg noted after his visit of 1775 that "there are no glass windows here," and he felt "the semi-transparent paper windows . . . spoil the look of the houses."[3] But for all this absence, it was known that Europe had devised a marvellous material to seal the gaping holes in walls without depriving those within of their views of the outside world. The Luikens's book of Amsterdam trades, *The Mirror of Human Activities (Spiegel van het Menselyk Bedryf)*, in Japan by the mid-eighteenth century, illustrated a *glasemaaker* and his mate setting panes into a leaded window (Fig. 70). The ideal Dutch house fulfilled, as the inscribed couplet emphasised, "the human quest for light and air." Glass was relentless in its bisecting of inner and outer spaces, but it also allowed the healthy and unimpeded flow of sunshine or, when opened, wind.

Daikokuya Kōdayū, the castaway from Sendai who found himself meeting Catherine the Great in 1791, described to his interrogator, Katsuragawa Hoshū, the windows he had seen in St. Petersburg: "The *shōji* are made from sheets of *kira* or *biidoro* so that the wind is completely shut out, while you can gaze through exactly as if they were open."[4] The window was dwelt upon by Shiba Kōkan too, who wrote that in London they had buildings "five and six storeys high – or even seven or eight – all with glass in the windows, just as we should use paper." Elsewhere he expressed embarrassment that English visitors to Japan had concluded from the absence of glass even in aristocratic residences, that Japanese architecture was miserable and inferior.[5]

But it was not in fact necessary to go abroad to study the appearance of such windows. Those who journeyed to Nagasaki and came across the VOC Factory on Dejima saw panes installed by, according to Thunberg, "some people who have of late years brought with them from Batavia either a few small windows, or else some panes of glass, in order to throw more light into the rooms, and to enjoy the view of external objects."[6] Glass lit the indoors more fully, but it was even more desirable for vision outward. It was required for any comprehensive environmental seeing, according to the European definition, where houses were, as they were not much in Japan, valued for the loveliness of their external prospects. Kōkan gained admission to the kapitan's lodgings in 1789 and recorded with admiration how not only were the outer windows glazed, showing Nagasaki's spectacular harbour, but even the internal partitions, permitting sight into what lay in the room beyond (Fig. 18).[7]

The first emergence of glazing in Japanese building is not recorded, but one fine structure was erected by the daimyo of Kaga, Honda Toshiaki's employer and master of the richest *han* in the land. At an uncertain date, probably in the early-nineteenth century, the lord built himself a Glass Room (*gyaman-no-ma*) in the Seison-kaku, a private pavilion set in the pleasure grounds of Kanazawa Castle.[8] Whether the room was all of glass as the name implies, or only partially windowed is unknown, but in either case the daimyo must have been able to gaze out into his famously beautiful garden, the Kenroku-en (a century later to contain Japan's first outdoor fountain).

China was easier of access for lavish Western goods, and the Qing ruler, Qianlong, was always among the first to receive objects of exotic delight. In 1758 he versified on glass windows that Jesuit priests had recently fitted in his Summer Palace:

> In Europe, they lack for nothing in amazing goods!
> My glass windows are bright and shining, clean and thick.
> Whereas most around our little courtyard gape,
> So that wind blows in, piercing the gauze drapes.
> I can see both outside and in,
> And how happy I am! . . .[9]

Qianlong looked out over his baroque mini-Versailles, with its maze and parterres, stone sculptures and fountains. The foreign derivation of this newly derived sight hardly needed emphasising. Qianlong went on to outline the sense

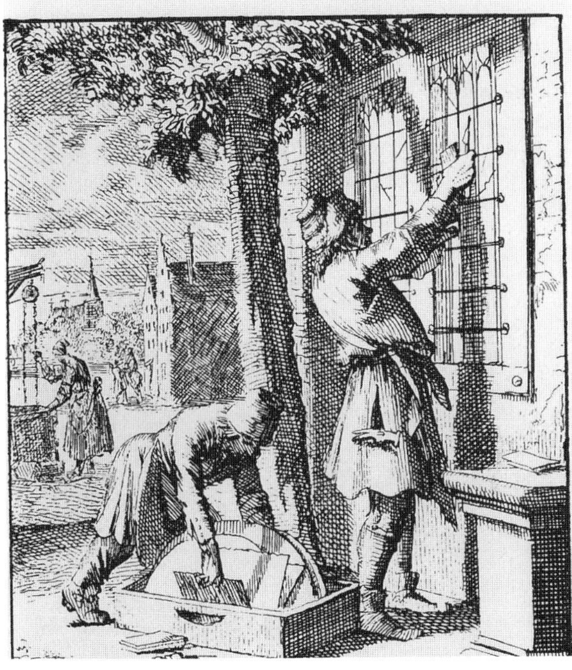

70. Johannes & Caspaares Luiken, *Glasier*, from their *Spiegel van het Menselyk bedryf*, Amsterdam, 1694. Private collection.

of distancing that the material had on him, as it both opened up, and also closed off the outside:

> Though bright in themselves, they are neutral substances,
> And show things through.[10]
> Wind, clouds of dust, and the sun's rays may fall on them,
> But they remain impenetrable,
> So that the tables and seats within stay free from specks of dirt. . . .

Discrete and undiscomfited, he was nevertheless at no stage deprived of view:

> On a bank of the small stream outside
> A bird that had alighted on a high branch is flying off;

Before the gate on the pathway, functionaries walk.
In autumn, I see the chrysanthemums on the steps,
And they add to the melancholy of the season;
For news of the spring, I can rely on the willow. . . .

The glass did not falsify, and interposed nothing of its own, revealing the properties of things exactly as they were and as they transformed over time:

All these things enter my field of vision, becoming clear and distinct;
All phenomena display themselves to me in their beauty and ugliness.

And Qianlong concluded, "in pure appreciation/ I write this verse like an inscription, to keep at the side of my seat."

Any educated Japanese read Chinese, and the huangdi's poetry was among essential texts. On hearing Kōdayū's comments on the windows of Russia, Hoshū addended the marginal note, "they sound like those in that poem in Qianlong's anthology."[11]

Myth had it that the Dragon King of the Sea lived in a crystal palace beneath the waves, his eyes free to rove in all directions. The legend was conjured up in the semi-miraculous new substance by a group of "clever glass workers" (*biidoro saiku-nin*) who, in the summer of 1776, mounted an elaborate model of the Dragon King's palace on the island of Nakazu in the Sumida, right in the centre of Edo. Apparently constructed entirely of glass, the exhibit was open to all comers for a fee and displayed as a spectacle (*misemono*). Such events allowed even those on a more modest level to experience the idea of dwelling in glassy halls. Details are scant, and the Nakazu affair may have been more strings of dangling beads than puttied panes, but the event provoked appreciative comment: "the eyes of both young and old were thrilled and excited," wrote a captivated visitor, "and everyone thought they had really entered the legendary palace; we half expected to see the Dragon King's young daughter come swimming up the river!"[12] Later, in 1836, a real full house of glass (*gyaman no ie*), possibly all window, was displayed at Ryōgoku Bridge, viewable for 31 *mon*.[13]

The workers who fabricated these marvels were probably jobbers of the kind already known for a century, and who set up at fairgrounds and exhibitions to sell their wares – usually little globular objects, performatively blown on the spot. Hiraga Gennai, in a list of entertainments at Ryōgoku, mentioned the glass artist moulding his viscous mass, which buyers thought looked like dripping icicles.[14] Mitaku Yorai, in a book of regional trades published in 1732, included one of the earliest illustrations of a more formally employed glassworker, showing a single man with an apprentice producing spheres, bottles, and cups (Fig. 71). For most people, the experience of glass was restricted to lumpish objects and containers.

Larger receptacles were imported. But even wine and beer glasses came from abroad (those for "malt alcohol" could be told, stated Ōtsuki Gentaku, as they had gold bands around the top); decanters and even the occasional glass salt-cellar made their way into Japan (Figs. 1, 6,13,107,108).[15] Tsūdayū noted that in Russia they could make glass bowls of over a metre, and if necessary a second or third blower came to the assistance of the first.[16] More malleable than ceramic, glass was also ideally suited to fashioning the strange retorts, twisting alembics, and variform dishes required by the eighteenth-century scientist. These, too, were introduced, and filtered into the studios of *Rangaku* scholars.[17] Glass also offered a long-term store for objects and was useful for the experimentalist. Because of its see-through qualities, samples that had to be inspected but not disturbed could be conveniently housed in bottles, and monitored or subjected to various conditions. Technical-looking vessels were generically called *furasuko* (flasks),

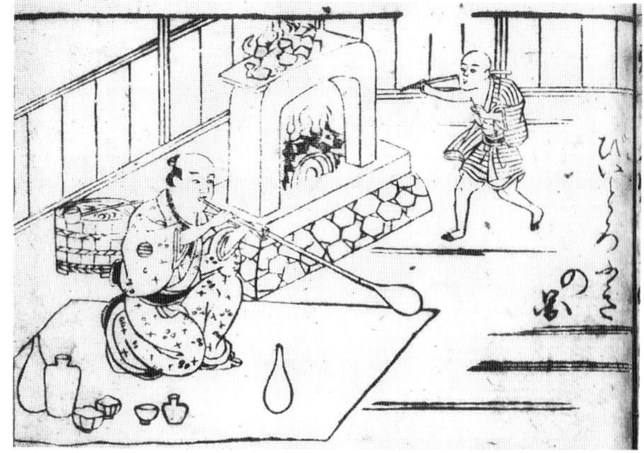

71. Unsigned, *Glass-blower,* from Mitaku Yorai, *Bankin sangyō-bukuro,* 1732. National Diet Library, Tokyo.

whereas goblet shapes were *koppu* (cups). Gotō Rishun stated, in the *Talks on Holland* (*Oranda-banashi*) of 1765, that the Dutch employed *furasuko,* "into which the air cannot penetrate," to keep goods from contamination.[18]

Ōtsuki Gentaku stressed:

> Initially, the material was enjoyed just for its sparkle and shine, but of late it has been recognised that glass ought not to be limited to use in playthings. Jars and bottles have been made, and things stored inside them. When so kept, a material's original characteristics (*honsei*) are preserved indefinitely; medical substances or fragrances can be passed on like this over long periods.[19]

Glass isolated objects from the atmosphere of the outside. Gennai praised the quality of imported stoppers that allowed an air-tight seal to be created but when necessary also released, and he drew attention to a newly introduced material intended for the purpose – cork.[20]

FORMS ON GLASS

Foremost among the pursuits of *Rangaku* scholars was the collection and study of exotic flora, fauna, or minerals. Increasing import of specimens, from ostriches to tulip bulbs and from narwal horns to cobalt, was coupled with a more thorough scouring of the local environment. The natural world exploded into a previously undreamed-of welter of matter and form. Gennai was prominent in promoting exploration, and from 1757 he took advantage of the spare time he gained after surrendering his samurai status, to organise annual colloquia for natural-history enthusiasts, which he called pharmacopaeic assemblies (*yakuhin-e*). The meetings were held at the Seijū-kan in Edo, a private institute built at his own expense that year by Taki Angen, a physician to the Tokugawa; findings were discussed and displayed.[21] Six years after the first assembly, Gennai published a selection of highlights entitled *Varieties of Matter (Butsurui hinshitsu)*. A magisterial array is found: rose-water, soap, Armenian boris, diamonds, saffron, aromatic rosemary, oil of Ulay, fragrant Thai rats, and so on for 200 pages.[22]

Botanical or animal samples were of most value to the investigator when some means of preserving their appearance was devised. The Thai rats had established a colony in Nagasaki and were breeding nicely, but other items might die, wither, or be lost. Permanence was required. Picture-making was one solution, and the "authentic" *Ranga* style was much used for the purpose. Gennai's *Varieties of Matter* was accompanied by figures (Fig. 74). Kōkan thanked the wit of an unnamed Dutchman who had taken down the likeness of a mermaid he had captured before it had passed away, fallen apart, and had to be discarded before ever being seen in Japan.[23] Bottling in glass was a more comprehensive resort. Even cork leaked eventually, so to bottling was added the practice of pickling. Terajima Ryōan's great reference work of 1713, the *Sino-Japanese Illustrated Universal Encyclopaedia (Wakan sansai zue),* listed "preservative spirit" (*yakuyū*) among Dutch imports.[24] But the bottling option was only available for smaller samples even though, technically, anything was susceptible to the treatment if a capacious

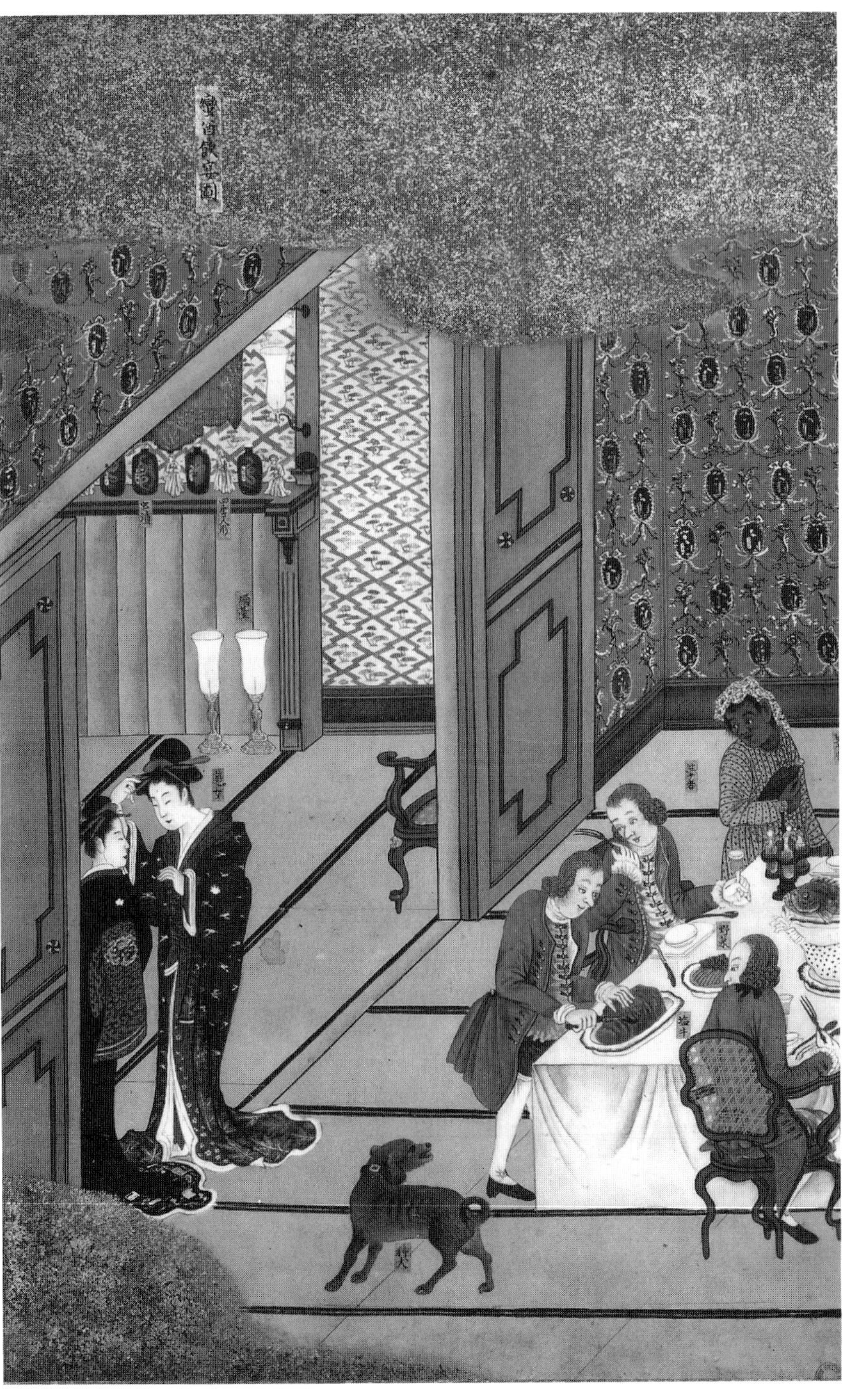

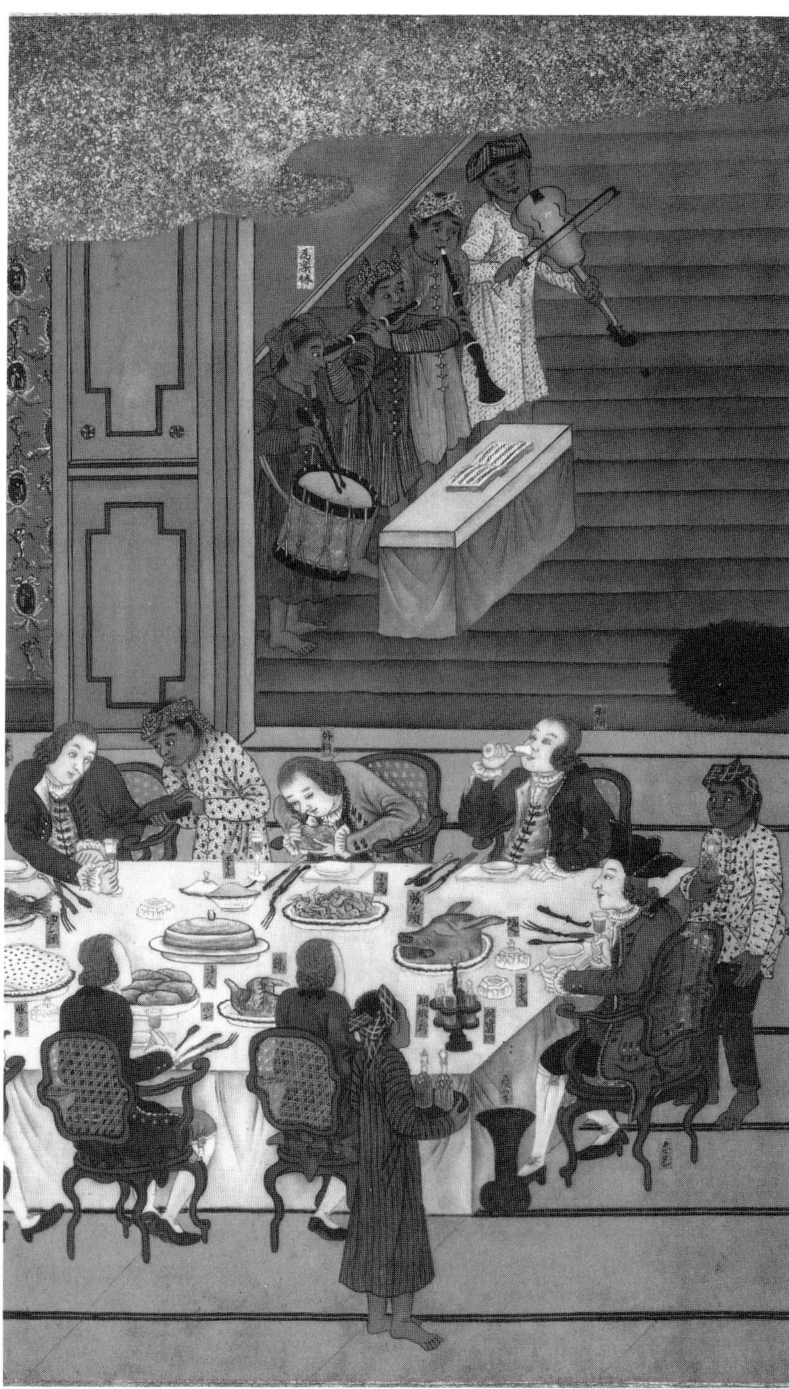

72. Unsigned, *Dutch Feast,* leaf from the album *Bankan-zu;* 1797(?). Bibliothèque Nationale, Paris.

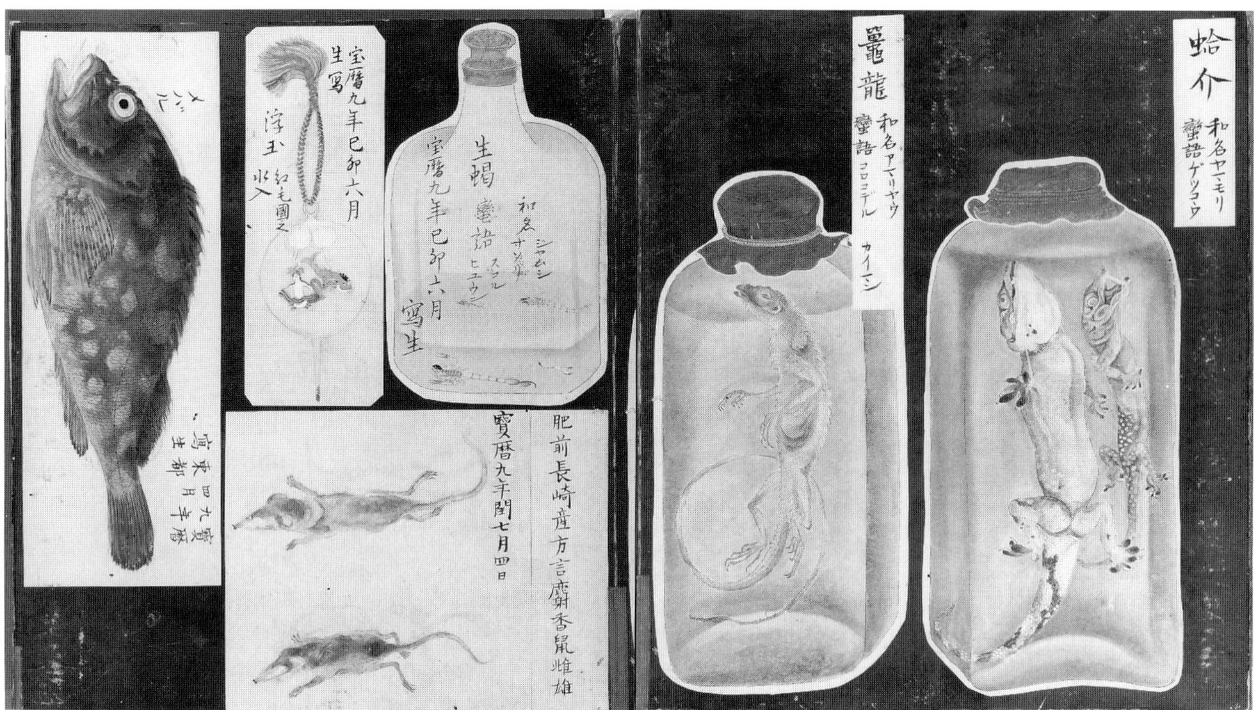

73a&b (above and opposite). Hosokawa Shigekata, paintings from his scrapbook, *Mōkai kikan*, 1760s. Eisei Bunko, Tokyo.

enough glass vessel could be found. So lesser animals, in particular, impregnated with alcohol and firmly ensconced, were kept virtually forever, at the disposal of the enquiring gaze.

Those who made the trip to Dejima saw how adept the Dutch were at pickling specimens, and how, far from consigning the rather unsightly crew to their workrooms of scientific experimentation, the men set them out in their living quarters. The VOC decked its domestic interiors with bottles of fauna, and the glance fell on them often, for the sheer edification of seeing the twisted forms. As early as 1721, Kapitan Diodati had been forced to part with his three favourite bottled animals, demanded from him by the Lord of Hirado. He had not been happy with the situation and "could hardly part with them," but nevertheless "would give the bottles to him since it was a request from the prince [daimyo]."[25] The set was replaced, and in 1746 Nagakubo Sekisui, a samurai from Sendai, noted that liquid-filled flasks were once again lined up on the kapitan's desk – Johannes Reijnouts being in charge that year – with specimens inside that "looked as if they were swimming."[26] The anonymous album of life on Dejima that showed the VOC balance and the two-man water cannon, and made some fifty years or so after Sekisui's visit, recorded several preserving containers, now transferred to the sitting-room and enjoying pride of place on the saloon mantelpiece, interspersed with dolls of the seasons (approved of and sketched by Hirokawa Kai when he visited the compound; Fig. 72).[27]

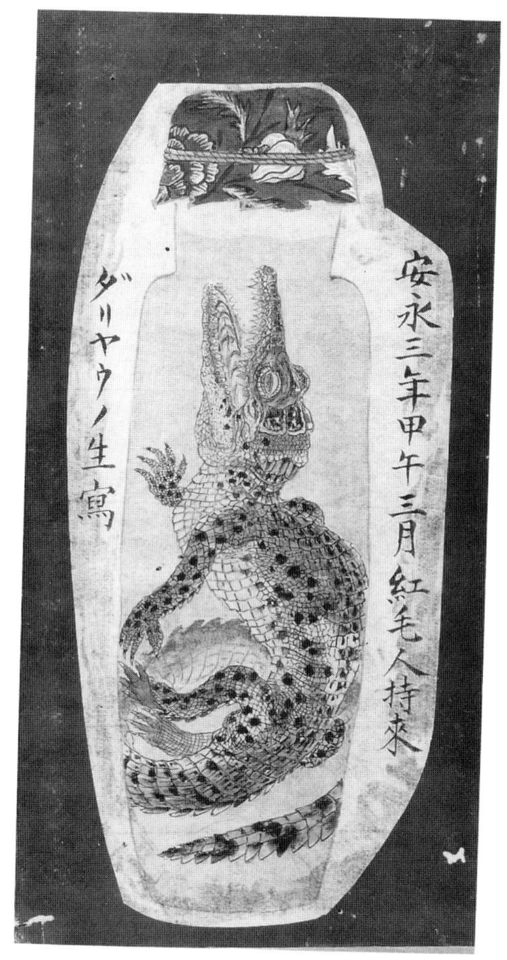

Tsūdayū was taken to the imperial cabinet of curiosities in St. Petersburg. It included a taxidermic pet dog with glass eyes (formerly the tsar's pet) and several pickled animals; more gruesomely, the womb of a woman who had died in childbirth was also exposed.[28] As glass bottles, with their murky contents, began to adorn many a European collection, the amassing of specimens became a craze in Japan as well. Hosokawa Shigekata, daimyo of Kumamoto, a *han* that bordered on Nagasaki and was not far from Hirado, was enviably placed for acquiring foreign goods, and he bought or received a number of liquid-filled bottles with interesting specimens inside. Lord Hosokawa was closely involved with Dutch studies and participated in Gennai's pharmacopaeic assemblies. Not only a fanatical but also a scrupulous collector, Shigekata sketched his samples, pasting the pictures into scrap-books. One volume, *The Strangeness of Beasts and Shells (Mōkai kikan)*, includes annotated illustrations of his bottles, which apparently were numbered in four (Fig. 73a-b). On the left is "a *shamushi* or *sasori*, called in Dutch a *sukoruhyūn* [scorpion], sketched from life in the sixth month of 1759"; next to this is "a *tolong;* Japanese name: rain dragon; primitive [Dutch] name: *korokoderu* [crocodile]" – it is, in fact, an iguana.[29] On the right is a pair of *yamori* – that is, gecko, or wall lizards. Another page shows a further rain dragon, now spelled out in the Japanese pronunciation (*tolong* being Chinese) as *daryō*. Apparently this was "brought by the Red-fur people in the third month of 1774" (the leader of the *hofreis* that year was Arend Freith, whom Thunberg accompanied to Edo two years later).[30] Blind within their glassy tombs, our gaze is free to linger over the reptilian forms, measuring and analysing their features; for optimum visibility the smaller creatures have been suspended by the neck from the stopper so as not to lie crumpled like the *daryō* at the bottom of the flask.

Two of Hosokawa's earlier-acquired specimens were included in Gennai's selection from the pharmacopaeic assemblies, although their provenance is not stated. They were evidently exposed in Edo between their import in 1759 and publication of the *Varieties of Matter* in 1763 (Fig. 74). The pieces are described simply as "animals in glass bottles of preservative liquid." The rain-dragon is there, as is one wall lizard, but the smaller spotted pair has disappeared, perhaps swapped with another collector. The scorpion is absent too, either not sent up to Edo for the event, or else, like the *daryō,* not yet imported.

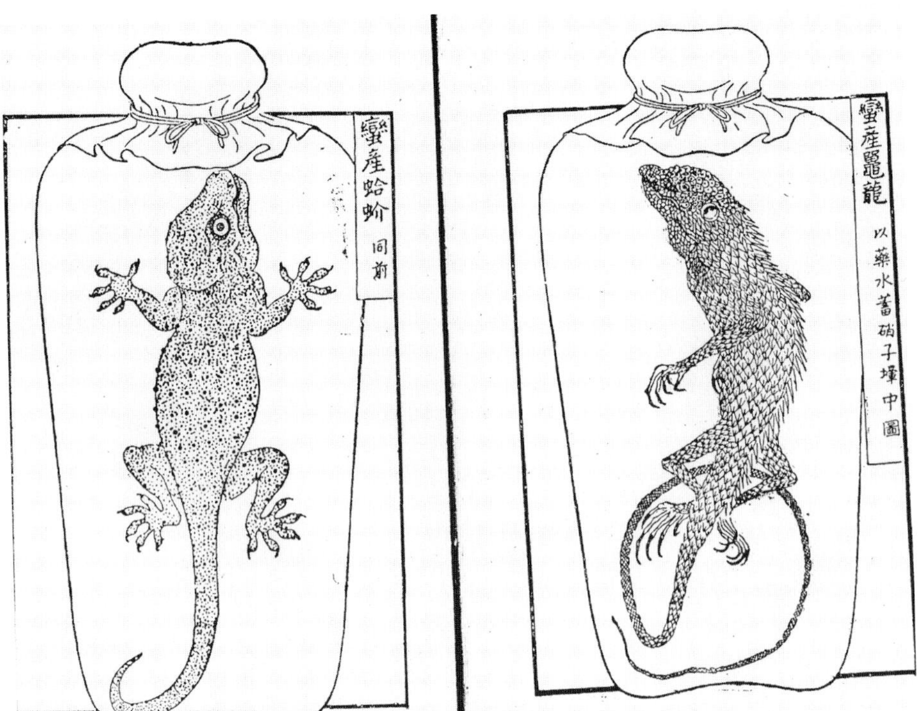

74. Unsigned, *Specimens in Preservative Liquid*, from Hiraga Gennai, *Butsurui hinshitsu*, 1763. National Diet Library, Tokyo.

Satake Yoshiatsu, daimyo of Akita, was too young to have been directly involved in the assemblies (he would have been only seven when the group first met), but he grew to share their interests after being introduced to Dutch matters by Gennai in 1773. Satake's and Hosokawa's *han* were at opposite ends of the country, but they would have had opportunities to meet during periods of compulsory attendance at the shogunal castle; it seems likely they discussed *Ran* at such times.[31] Both men formed part of the coterie of "Hollandomaniac lords" (*ranpeki-daimyō*), and their relationship may have been that of master and pupil, Hosokawa Shigekata being thirty years the senior. Not surprisingly, when Shikekata's bottled fauna began attracting attention, Yoshiatsu sought access too – Gennai noted that dragons were "very occasionally brought over by the Red-furs."[32] There was some confusion in the terminology, as the kapitan, Jan Crans, disputing with Gennai in 1762, told him flatly, "I do not accept the existence of dragons." But Gennai noted that other Dutch talked about dragons as either *draak* or *slangerstein* (the latter animal being still accepted today).[33] Somehow Yoshiatsu found a pickled "dragon" and, being an accomplished painter and gifted in the *Ranga* style (he used the studio name Shozan), he sketched it in a work that, like Shigekata's, stands as an extraordinary testimony to the incisiveness possible to achieve by protracted observation through glass (Fig. 75). Satake Yoshiatsu annotated the drawing in strict academic prose:

> DRAGON: in the Japanese pronunciation, *tatsu;* in the primitive tongue, *daraaka*. Many are to be found in Rimia [Africa].
>
> In the Third Month of 1779, the Dutch brought this one to the Eastern Capital [Edo]. It is stored in preservative liquid kept in glass, and can last a thousand years or more without putrefying.
>
> The Shogunal Physician, Katsuragawa Hoshū, has established the above to be correct.

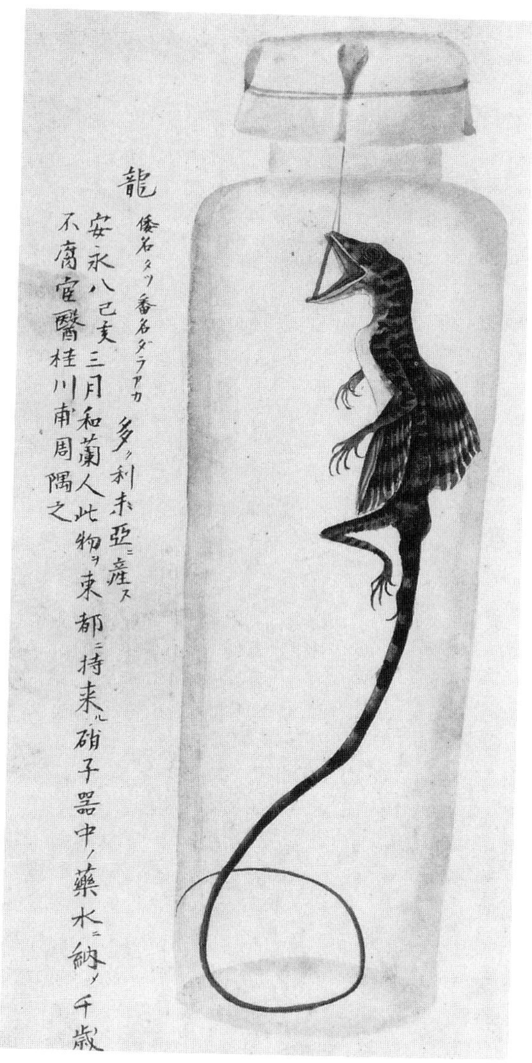

75. Satake Yoshiatsu (Shozan), *Dragon*, drawing from his sketchbook, *Shasei chō*, 1778. Senshū Museum of Art, Akita.

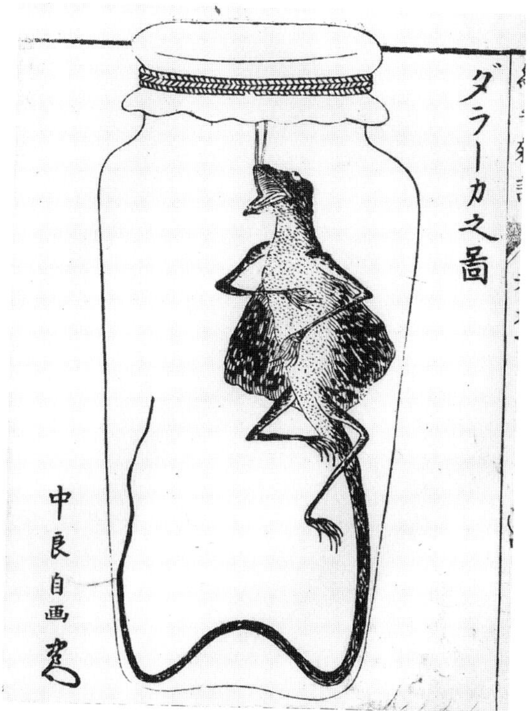

76. Morishima Chūryō, *Dragon*, from his *Kōmō zatsuwa*, 1787. National Diet Library, Tokyo.

The specimen, permanently safe, is also eternally visible.

Lord Satake did not say how he came by his dragon, but a plausible chain of intermediaries can be reconstructed as an illustration of the same bottle appears in Morishima Chūryō's *Red-fur Miscellany (Kōmō zatsuwa)* (Fig. 76). Chūryō, Hoshū's younger brother, published the compendium in 1787, that is, eight years after Yoshiatsu stated the piece had been imported. Chūryō found the object important and executed the picture of it himself (unusually for him, as he generally farmed out the illustrations). It is signed "depicted personally by Chūryō" and labelled in the Japanese-phonetic script *daraaka*. The origins of the bottle are discussed in the text: "In the primitive tongue dragons are called *daraaka,* there are many of them in the Cape, which is located in the South Seas. Sizes vary, but they can reach up to ten or twelve metres in length. Many years ago a Primitive named Thunberg sent a baby one preserved in liquid to my brother, and it looks as illustrated here. From head to tail it is forty-five centimetres."[34] Thunberg and Hoshū met frequently at the Nagasaki-ya during the Swede's tenure as VOC physician. But there is a discrepancy, as Thunberg arrived in 1775, came to Edo the following spring and left Japan for good in the autumn of 1776; this was three years before the year Yoshiatsu himself gave for import of the bottle. Either date or name is wrong, unless Thunberg sent the sample as a gift from overseas. This last is perfectly possible, as he and Hoshū maintained their intimacy by post, Thunberg noting how he "kept up intercourse . . . during a period of several years" with Hoshū, during which time they gave and sent "small acceptable presents."[35] Perhaps the bottle arrived in the hold of a VOC vessel, specifically destined for the shogun's young doctor. On account of this attestation of the bonds of friendship in difficult circumstances, perhaps, Chūryō wrote that the dragon was now regarded as "the most prized possession of our house," and he continued, "many indeed are those who have begged to take a look."[36] One such must have been Lord Satake, who may have borrowed, but probably never owned, the bottle he drew. Satake Yoshiatsu died suddenly in 1785 at the age of only thirty-seven, two years before the *Miscellany* came out, and most likely he made his picture in Edo on one of his periods of attendance.

This was not the end of the story. In 1799, the Dutch translator Narabayashi Jūbei, recently reinstated after rustication from Nagasaki as punishment for a translation error, informed a scholar with whom he held discussions in Mito that a pickled dragon was "in the possession of the Katsuragawa family." He also informed him that "some years ago they exhibited it at the Seijū-kan." Hoshū is known to have participated in an exhibition in that hall (site of Gennai's now defunct assemblies) in the summer of 1788, and it may have been then that the beast was displayed.[37] Jūbei went on to correct the general view, stating that it was not a real dragon but "something called a *boom-draak;* they live in the mountains and leap from tree to tree, emitting rays of light." Still not quite at the end of its peregrinations, the sample resurfaced early in the nineteenth century in Takagi Shunzan's massive (though undated) *Illustrated Natural History (Honzō zusetsu).*[38]

Just how these bottles did the rounds – whether physically sent across the country or kept in Edo and seen there, or again, whether circulated in pictorial form – is hard to judge. And how many saw them is also open to question. But thanks to published works like Chūryō's, knowledge of the practice and purpose of pickling would have enjoyed a wide diffusion until many sensed how great were the powers of glass in the quest to preserve and expose.

LIVE BOTTLING

Santō Kyōden was, as usual, alert to serious intellectual trends that could be bent to suit his Floating-World orientation, and in 1801 he picked up the idea of the bottled specimen, injecting into it a popular metaphorical dimension. Kyōden's pickling made an ethical point: samples were scrutinised not for biological but for personal or social revelations. He mentioned a mock exhibition of specimens in the same volume that discussed the varied spoof entertainments, including "Fortune's *Karakuri*"; the kibyoshi was *Here's a Story of Some Pretty Remarkable Displays (Ko wa mezurashiki misemonogatari;* Fig. 77). The page shows a grab-bag of items, half showman's trumpery and half a pharmacopaeic assembly gone wrong. The indented picture at the top shows a signboard of the type that might advertise such a booth, and the collection is billed "Wonders of Natural History" (*chinbutsu no misemono*). There is a mermaid blowing on a glass air-drum (*popin*), a two-headed snake, and living samples brought from the land of Little People. A bottled Edo youth is also displayed for inspection, conveniently reduced to the size of a bottle, to be gawped at like an iguana. But he is not dead, for it is his life-style that is exposed, and he is in the bottle to mend his ways.

The receptacle is not a scientific *furasuko* but a common oil container (though shown made of glass to allow the interior to be seen), and the contents identified as Son Oil; this is all a pun on the expression "to wring the oil" out of someone (*abura o shiboru*), meaning to make them sweat. It was proverbially true of Edo youth that they disappointed their abstemious parents and dissipated hard-earned funds, and this boy is no exception. Having been derelict in the family business, he leaves his father no option but to englass him as an object lesson. Well-sealed, the boy is a specimen of miscreant life. He mops his beaded brow, as the frustrated father, abacus in hand, has just totalled up how much the nightly escapades to the Floating World have cost. The bottled boy is to be meditated upon in the spirit of wonder, not in admiration of the vast diversity of zoological genera, but at the range of moral types.

Part of the justification for Kyōden's conflation of natural-history exhibition and fairground show was that one particular small life form, caught in glass, was indeed frequently put out on festive occasions, often in the rapidly made receptacles of performance-glass artists, and sold. I refer to fish in fish-bowls. Daimyo and the great might contemplate imported samples, but urbanites had their rough equivalent in the goldfish – and these were alive. Some sort of tiddler

77. Kitao Shigemasa, *Exhibition of Rarities*, from Santō Kyōden, *Ko wa mezurashiki misemono-gatari*, 1801. Tokyo Metropolitan Central Library. *Parodies are shown of assorted natural history items.*

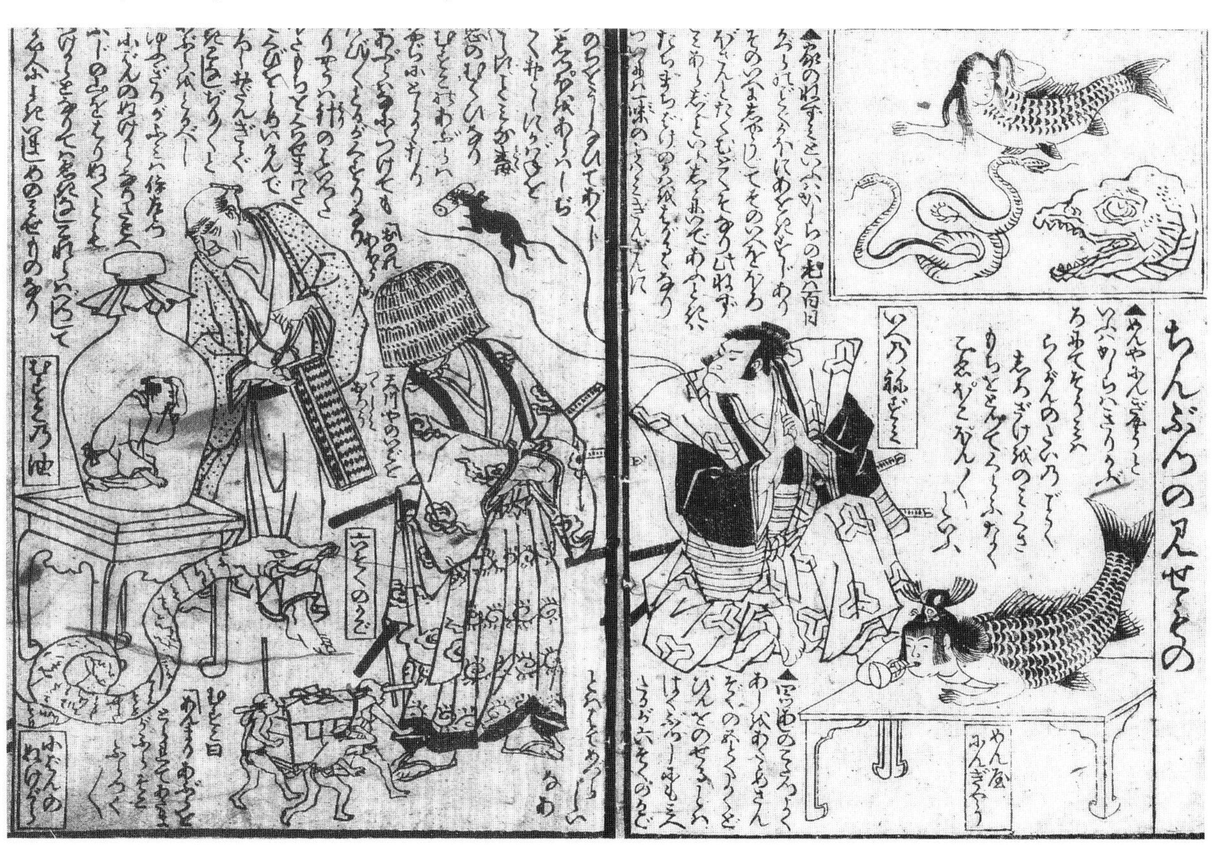

was to be had for small sums (as they are today) at any frolicsome event. The crudely blown spheres came handleless, but they could be carried by a string attached to a wooden peg inserted into the neck (Fig. 80). The fish was in its habitat – or at least in its element – still exhibiting the normal attitudes of life; but, like a sample, it was also selected out from the mass of its peers for particular consideration. The rhetoric of the firm gaze of science, passing through glass, homed in such cases on still-animate life. From the third quarter of the century, flouncing about with fish-bowls became, it seemed, the *sine qua non* of being in with the latest rage, and Gennai observed in 1763, in his longer novel *Rootless Grasses (Nenashi-gusa),* how "wealthy young chaps" (*wakadono*) had taken to encumbering their servants with fish-bowls to carry along beside them for effect. This was still the fashion in the next century for Kyōden depicted the rather ridiculous performance in a story mockingly entitled *Textbook about Comic Literature (Gesaku mondo).*[39] Offering the motions of the twitching fins fully to view, the fish-bowl rightly became the token of indulged Edo youth – brittle containers surrounding complacent, meandering forms. Thanks to the glass, the fish could be always looked at. But it never returned the gaze.

78. Kitao Shigemasa, from Shiba Zenkō, *Ōchigai takarabune,* 1781. Tokyo Metropolitan Central Library.

Tankō receives a fishbowl from the Goddess Benten.

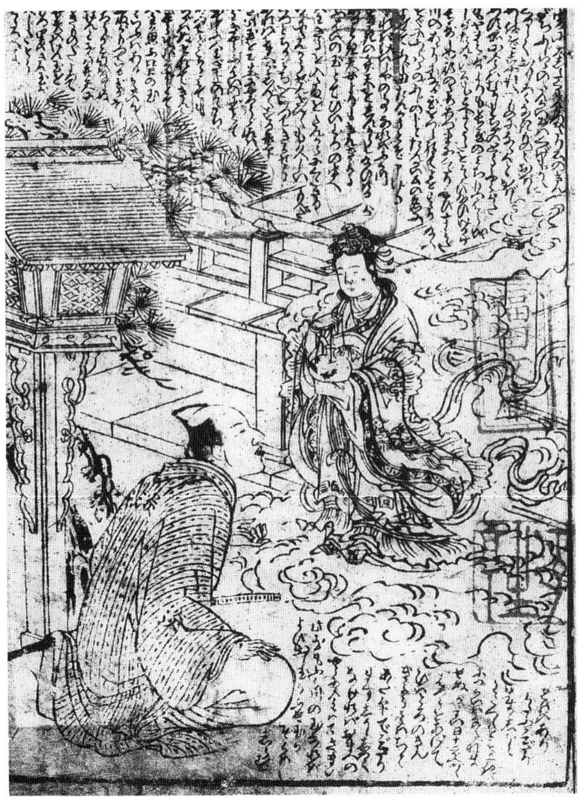

Shiba Zenkō, a hereditary *kyōgen* master from Edo, drew on the idea of the modish fish-bowl in a kibyoshi illustrated by Kitao Shigemasa and published in 1781 as *A Very Different Kind of Treasure Ship (Ōchigai takarabune).* The hero, one Fujita Tankō, was formerly a Kyoto noble, but had moved to Edo in search of a more trendy life-style. Working as a male geisha, he became a devotee of fashionable knick-knacks (*shareta mono*). Tankō prayed regularly to Benten in her shrine in Fukagawa in the hope of amassing the wherewithal to fund his extravagant aspirations; eventually, the goddess responded with a divine visitation. Benten, goddess of the arts, was an object of popular religion and a reasonable recipient of Tankō's invocations, but Zenkō introduced her more for the sake of a pun: her iconographical attribute was a jewel, *tama* in Japanese, a term that had migrated in loose language to mean anything sparkling, and by the end of the eighteenth century often referred to glass. Zenko's story is in fact a general career through themes relating to glass. The first page had prepared readers for typical kibyoshi slippage across domains by leading them through a hilarious (though untranslatable) romp along a string of words incorporating the sound *tama* – thus, *kendama,* a parlour game, *yobidashi-tama,* to call out a prostitute, *kintama,* testicles, and more.

Benten's appearance opens the story. She

comes before Tankō as the *deus* (or rather *dea*) *ex machina* that instigates (rather than ends) so many a kibyoshi plot. But instead of bearing her usual jewel, her *tama* is now a glass bowl with two fish swimming inside (Fig. 78). This she bestows on Tankō. Grateful to the goddess (though a little nonplussed) – he would have preferred money, Zenkō informs us – Tankō starts for home, mumbling, "seems a rather odd return for my prayers." But the bowl is a fashion item and he is pleased enough. Home lies across the Sumida, and as Tankō is being ferried over in the hired boat, what should bolt from the water but the Dragon King, thundering aloft in a shower of smoke and steam (Fig. 79). To the Lord of the Crystal Palace all *tama* is treasure, not least as legend had it that long ago he suffered the theft of his favourite piece, and was on an unending search to get it back. What, the Dragon King wonders, is a mere mortal doing hubristically carrying *tama* about, moreover one imprisoning fish, his own rightful subjects. The king tries to seize the bowl. Tankō mistakes him for a crocodile and protests, "He shouldn't be living in the river!" (escaped from a fairground or a *Rangaku* studio, perhaps). But the Dragon King, immune to such logic, only sheds "crocodile tears" (*wani no me ni namida*), as the fight goes to Tankō.[40]

The bowl was the fashion accoutrement, but it was not complete unless filled with fish. Child

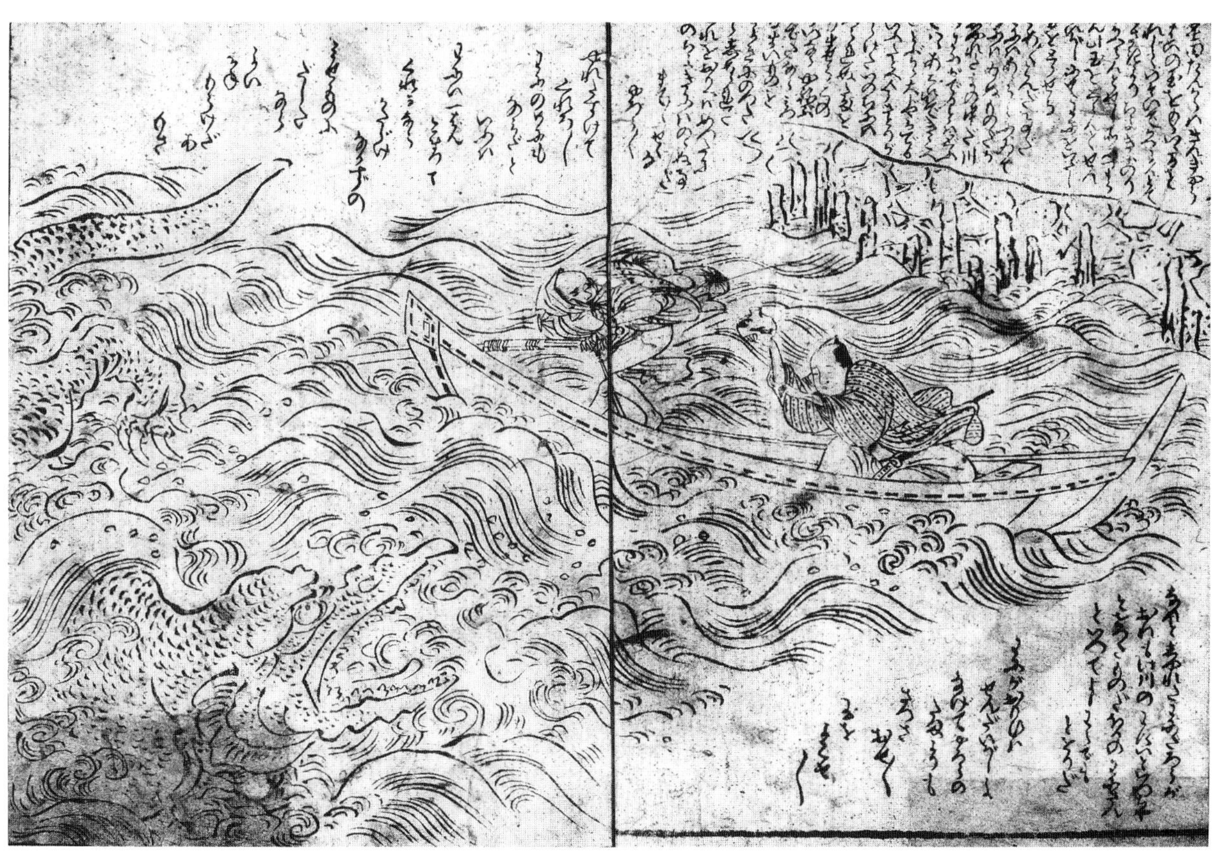

79. Kitao Shigemasa, from Shiba Zenkō, *Ōchigai takarabune*, 1781. Tokyo Metropolitan Central Library. *Tankō heads for home across the Sumida.*

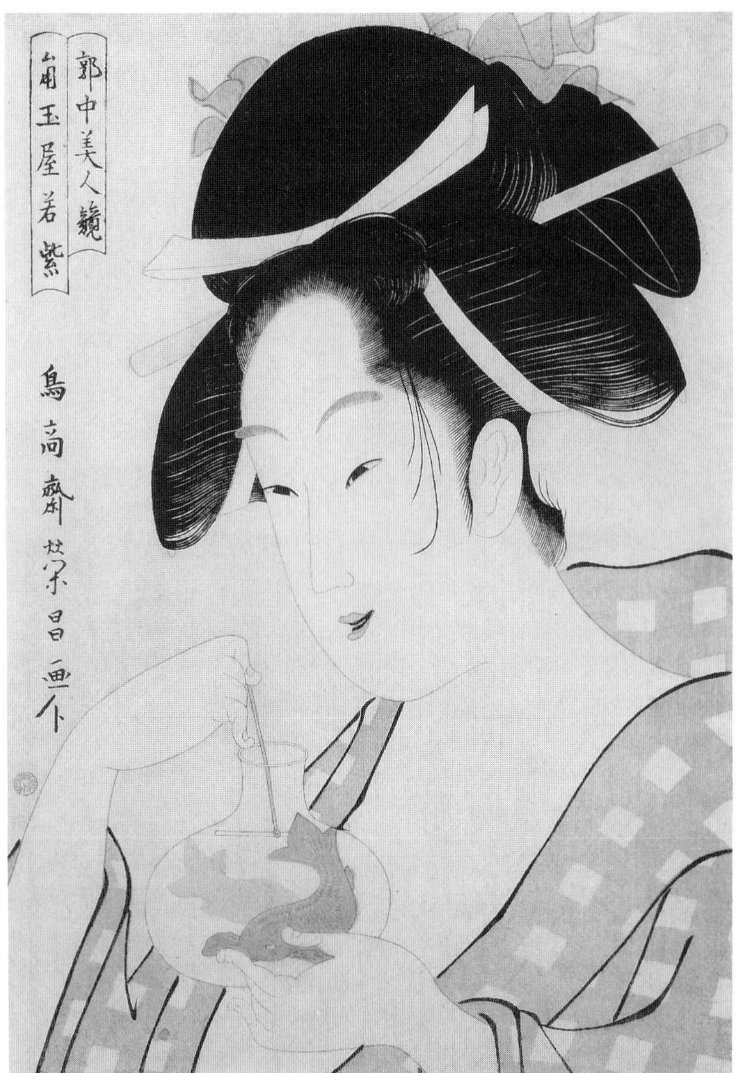

80. Chōkōsai Eishō, *Kadotama-ya Wakamurasaki*, colour woodblock print from the series *Kakuchū bijin kurabe*. Metropolitan Museum of Art, New York, Fletcher Fund, 1925 (JP 1477).

owners probably cherished the swimming creatures, but among adults, thoughts or pathetic fallacies about the captured fish abounded. Scuttling unprotected in the bald light of an empirical stare, the specimens could not but provoke meditation. As a senryu writer put it,

For the fish in the glass –
Its life
Is see-through.[41]

The large number of pictures of bowls attests to more than simply a wide diffusion, and suggests how the image of the sequestered fish spoke for a profounder meaning and pointed to a more speculative stance. It is usually women who figure in the imagery. Poised in stillness, they seem to find a cogency in the eddying movements as the fish goes round and round. Women were in Edo life imprisoned in an immediate sense, especially when they were prostitutes – the frequent subject matters of Floating Words prints. Chōkōsai Eisho, for example, depicted Waka-

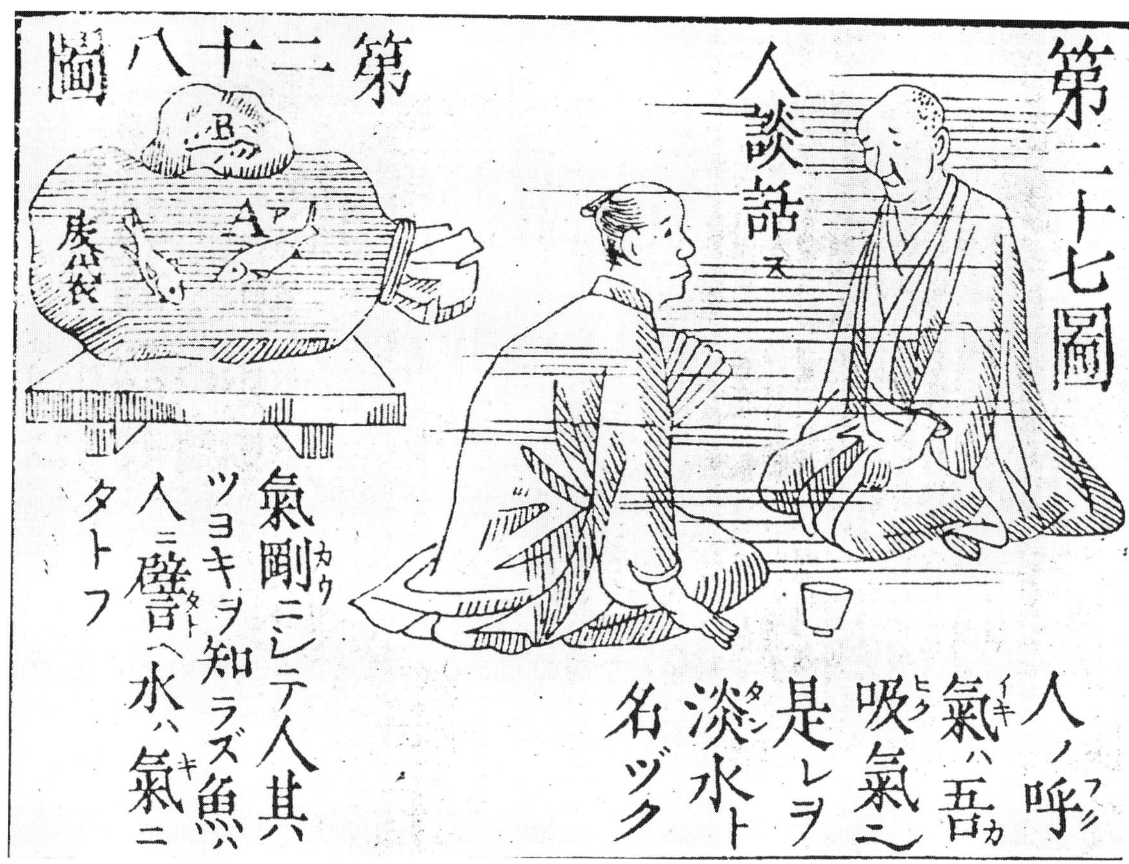

81. Shiba Kōkan, from his *Kopperu tenmon zukai*, 1808. Reproduced from Nakai Sōtarō, *Shiba Kōkan* (Atoriesha, 1942).

People in air are like fish in water.

murasaki, a woman indentured at the Kadotama-ya (perhaps selected because her brothel name includes the character *tama*; Fig. 80).

Thought about more philosophically, all humanity could be said to live in confinement – caught, fretful, upon earth, days spent in a meaningless circle of activity, hemmed in by walls it could not fully see. Incarcerated, in a certain sense, in the bowl of the earth, and living a life of trivial concern, humanity was not, ontologically speaking, very much or greatly different from fish. Tachibana Nankei, in the words cited as the epigraph to this book, wrote of how the universe looked like a little glob of water when viewed from afar, so the bowl and the earth were hardly dissimilar in the relative scales of the cosmos. Only death and extinction brought release from these states.

Parallels between the glass container and the world could be quite precise. Kōkan argued this in his speculations over the substantiality of air. In *An Illustrated Explanation of Copernican Astronomy (Kopperu tenmon zukai)*, published in 1808, he included as figures 27 and 28 a comparison of humanity surrounded by the atmosphere, trapped beneath the dome of heaven, with fish swimming in water; in both cases the element was definitely there, though quite un-

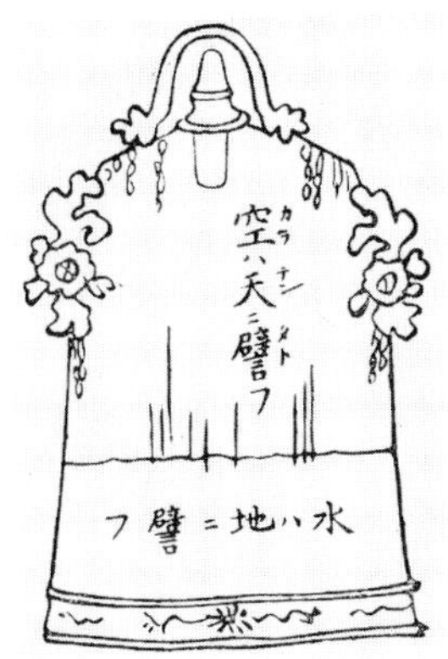

82. Shiba Kōkan, from his *Oranda tensetsu*, 1796. Reproduced from Nakai Sōtarō, *Shiba Kōkan* (Atori-esha, 1942).

Climates replicated in a glass jar.

beknownst to those within it (Fig. 81). Kōkan illustrated "people having a casual talk," showing a student with his fan and tea confronting his master, enveloped in the gusting air every bit as much as a fish in the swirling water of a glass fish-bowl. Kōkan expanded: "The air that other people exhale is what you breathe in; it is as with fresh water. Make the air concrete and people will still not realise the materiality of it; similarly, it might be said that fish are like people but with water in place of air." The glass that kept the water in was analogous to the more elusive membrane retaining the air.

Kōkan had made a similar case in 1795 while conducting experiments into weather.[42] Those tests were written up and published as part of his popularising explanation of *Rangaku* tenets, *Dutch Theories of the Heavens (Oranda tensetsu)*. Kōkan enjoined his readers to conceive of the world as being contained in a glass jar, the heavens enveloping like an upturned bowl, and the various climatic systems operating within (Fig. 82). His experiment simulated the human terrain within a bottle. Partially filling the vessel with water, he subjected it to temperature changes to see how the humidity permeated. "Let this stand for the earth," he wrote on the area of water, and in the space above, "Let this stand for the heavens."

Kōkan made no attempt to reconstruct the physical lie of his metaphorical land, much less to people it; his interests were in the circulation of air and cloud. But more specific glass worlds, water-filled and destined for populations, could be, and were, fabricated. Lord Hosokawa owned one. The object in his collection was shaped like a sphere elongated at the ends. He drew it in the summer of 1759 (Fig. 73a). Two models were set within, a mermaid and a whale. The piece was imported. Shigekata identified it as "a floating

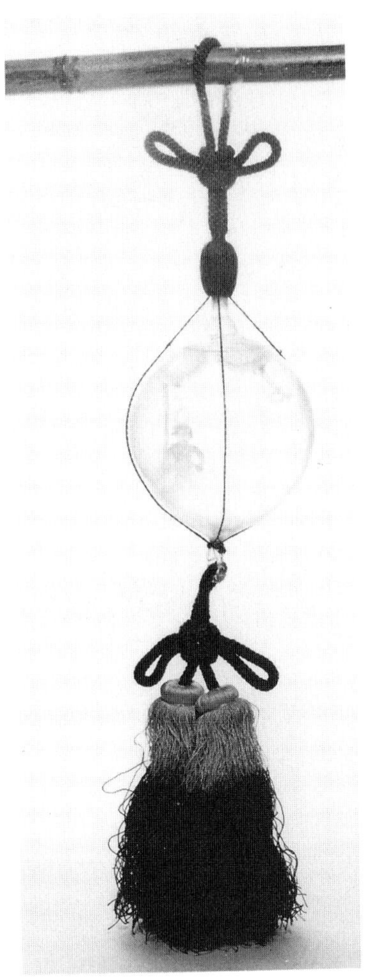

83. Glass float (one of pair) figure inside representing a European boy; early nineteenth century. Kobe City Museum.

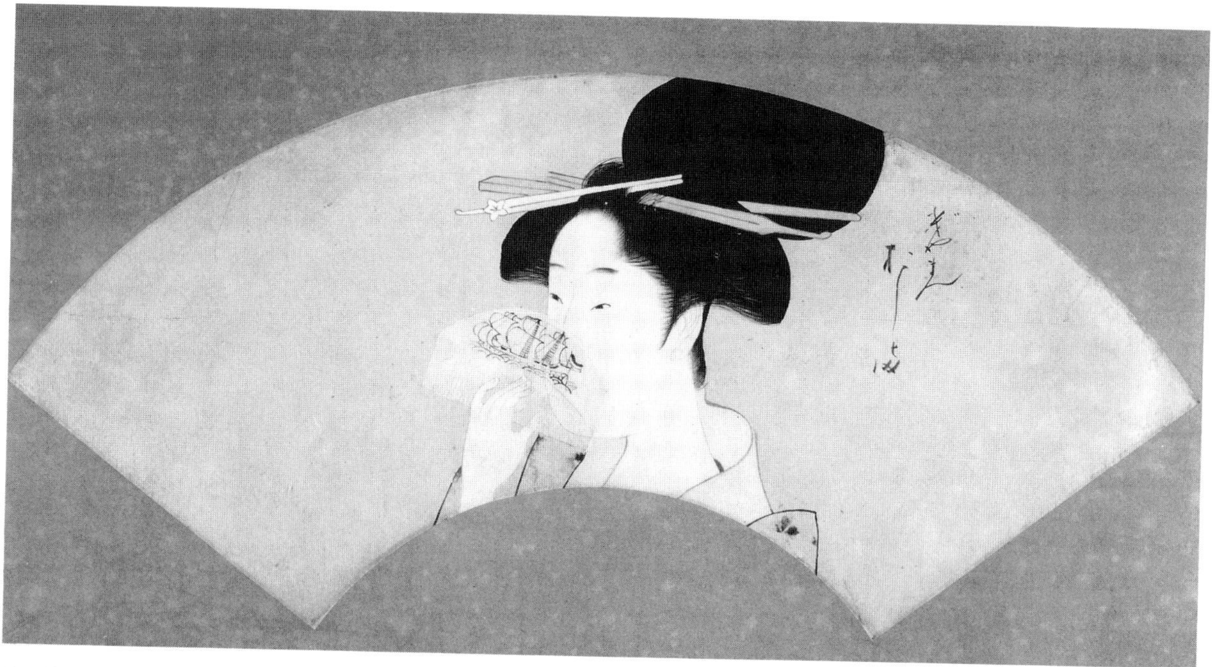

84. Kitagawa Utamaro (attrib.), *'Glass' O-shima,* fan mounted as hanging scroll; 1790s. Private collection; photo: Sumishō Gallery, Tokyo.

glass ball: a Dutch water container." The daimyo considered his toy somehow meaningful and also cognate with his bottled reptile samples, for he pasted the picture next to the pickled animals, as if, uncannily, like them, the mermaid and the whale stuck in the water also offered some meat of epistemological enlightenment. It must have been by virtue of the enclosing glass that he considered the models appropriate to sit beside his dragons, scorpions, and lizards. Spurious as natural history, the toys were nevertheless replete with significance on which an assessment of human life might rest, as they bobbed in their silent world.

A pair of glass balls similar to that in Lord Hosokawa's sketch survive. Some seven or so centimetres across, they contain model boys (Fig. 83). Water is not their real home, but the equation with air holds, and they can reasonably inhabit it; the boys float in their glass-bound realm oblivious to those outside but always observable from without. Viewers gaze their fill, as they watch and learn, but are precluded, for good or ill, from interfering with the model forms. A spiritual extension was not hard to devise. To subject the miniature boys to ethical investigations from a privileged space outside the float was to see them most keenly with a now scrutinising transformation of the Buddhas' psychic eyes.

FORMS ON GLASS

Utamaro, one of the circle of writers and artists that included Kyoden, Chūryō, and Shigemasa, was highly attuned to Edo fashion. He is credited with executing an unsigned fan-shaped picture showing a woman flaunting a glass comb; the ornament is, to say the least, extravagant (Fig. 84).[43] The subject's name is recorded on the picture, O-shima, but she has contrived to have herself nicknamed "glass" (*gyaman*), and she becomes in the inscription "Glass" O-shima, proclaiming her elegant up-to-dateness. But *gyaman* sounded like *jiman*, meaning pride, and a pun is surely intended. Glass was a personal adornment, and often the stuff of self-inflation. A deliberately tongue-in-cheek work of 1752 masquerading under the title *Educational Booklet (Kyōkun zatchōmotsu)* made the point in discussing various types of show-off to be encountered around town, one of which was called the "blown-boaster" (*fuki-miso*). That was, there was a type of person about who fancied him- or herself for their (blown-) glass objects. The anonymous author explained: "In Edo these days it's the slang to call the things people fancy themselves for '*miso*' (not that people in Kyoto or the countryside lack '*miso*' as such). . . . Thus, the many jewellers sell 'bead-*miso*,' while glass shops sell 'blown-*miso*.' "[44] O-shima is self-obsessed, and her comb abets her. The use is brazen but also coy, for she does not obscure the ornament in her hair, but pretends shyly to hide her face with it. Glass functions as a kind of screen to separate O-shima from the viewer. But at the same time, as with a window, it draws the gaze, more to invite than ward off. In *seeming* to hide behind glass, O-shima actually solicits attention. She makes herself, as it were, a would-be specimen for other people's sight.

O-shima's comb is etched with a line drawing of a VOC ship in full sail. Gotō Rishun noted how skilled the Dutch were at etching glass, a technique, he said, made exceptionally difficult owing to the hardness of the material.[45] The Lord of Kaga's windows installed in Kanazawa Castle had also been etched, carrying, in that case, the forms of auspicious birds. Glass aspired to be invisible, so when pictures were etched upon it, they bore upon what lay beyond, enhancing the actual view with the supererogatory overlay of the artist's iconographic choices. The lord's panes turned his garden into a virtuous paradise, the birds seeming to be settled *in* it. As the daimyo looked out at his garden, he saw it as if perpetually flocked with omens of his benevolent rule. O-shima's comb had a similar effect, but rather than rendering her richeous, it rendered her "foreign." She was to be admired through that symbol of supply of the lavishly exotic, the East Indiaman, which hailed the arrival of rare treasures from distant lands to deck out the rich, or the simply smart. "Glass" O-shima is inspected through a haze of *Ran*. Whether such a woman ever lived is unknown, but it is not preposterous, nor is Utamaro's picture just a fantasy, for a comb almost identical to O-shima's still survives (Fig. 85).

Etched objects were scarce. A far easier and more common substitute was to paint directly onto the glass. Although this meant loss of the section of pane covered with pigment, painted glass became a prominent rococo fancy. Colours were applied from the rear of the pane so that they showed well from the front, and the layers had to be built up in reverse order in a technique that was quite challenging to effect. The glass painting was both looked through and looked at. In an age when pictures were not ordinarily glazed, the shimmer was thought charming, as the whole subject matter was briskly enlivened with a glossy sheen. The non-painted parts of the glass might be left to look through. Another option was to partially coat the vacant spaces with mercury, or even entirely cover them, to reflect; in the latter case all transparency was lost, as the glass panel was turned into a mirror. The user was both inside and outside at the same time, for they looked at the glass to see the painted realm beyond, but also found themselves reflected back, embedded within a fantasy space.

A simple example of such a picture was put on show in Nagoya in 1820. Kodera Gyokuchō recorded this, telling how beneath the glass "was a little pocket mirror and, in it, the picture of a peony." The mirror behind the paint gave the

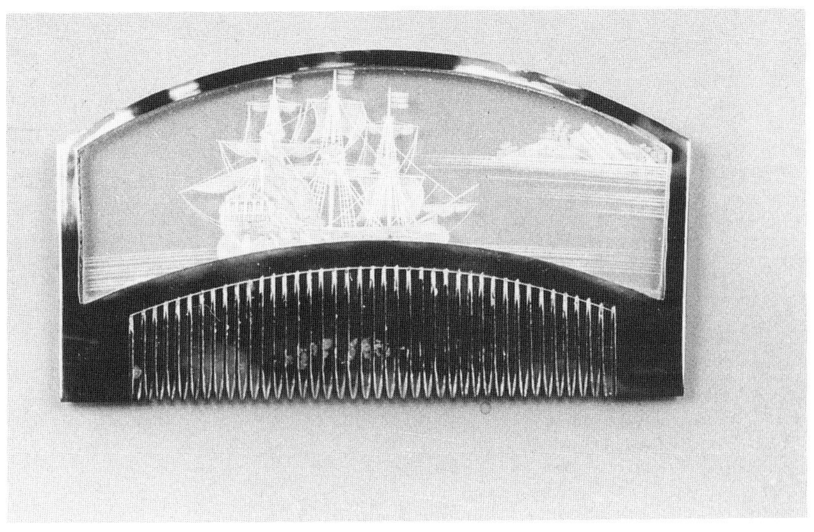

85. Comb, tortoise shell and glass; c. 1800; Kobe City Museum.

impression that the flower was (as he put it) "in" the mirror. Although he did not say so, peering down he would have seen his own eyes in there too, looking back. The poet Minagawa Kien, who had written on Rosetsu's magnified flea screen, came across a similar imported item and compose a verse entitled "The Blossom Enclosed within a Mirror."[46] The curios were typical of their kind, being in effect a picture with a mirror relieving the extraneous space.

The practical benefit of glass and mirror paintings was that, although they were vulnerable to cracks and chipping, they were resistant to damage from grime or flaking; if anything was spilled over them, or they grew dusty, they could be easily wiped clean. For those engaged in the seafaring life, these were sensible as on-board decorations. Glass preserved the pigments from salt air that would otherwise have been the ruin of them. Not surprisingly, mirror pictures were to be seen in fair quantities around the Factory in Nagasaki. When Kōkan described the kapitan's room (only metres from the swell of the harbour), he told how it was hung with several glass-based works on diverse themes; and if his illustration is accurate, there was a good sampling of portraits, sea-, and landscapes (Fig. 18).[47] Miniature mirror pictures were popular among travellers, whether nautical or not, for they enabled those far from home to carry with them likenesses of those they loved, or places they missed, as convenient and durable remembrances, less at risk from rubbing or general wear than the usual painted roundel would be, and cheaper than enamel. As the face of the beholder could be reflected, hovering beside that of the sitter, parted couples seemed momentarily to reunite. Satō Narihiro, natural-history adviser to the daimyo of Satsuma, recorded what he saw in 1798 when he met the Dutch: "The kapitan brought a portrait of his wife to Nagasaki. The picture was only some five centimetres square, and set in a mirror which made her look truly alive. The kapitan always has it hanging at his waist."[48] Narihiro opined that the woman was "something over twenty," and added, "when I told him she was beautiful, he looked pleased and smiled – people have the same weak spots the whole world over." What the kapitan's strange dangling portrait may have looked like would already have been conveyed to the reading public the year before when Tsutaya Jūsaburō put the image of an oval Western mirror (complete with hook at the top and the VOC trademark beneath) on the cover of his kibyoshi for the year – one of which was his own story of the mock-anatomy exhibition with the modern-day Ragorā, an accountant lodged within his riven breast (Fig. 43). On a less conjugal note, Narihiro also noted that Europeans gave out their portraits in miniature to the Maruyama prostitutes they had struck up with, although it is not clear from the context whether these were mirror pictures or not. Yoshio Kōsaku had at least two mirror paintings produced in Holland showing foreign friends who had left Japan, and they hung on the walls of his famous Dutch-style room (although not in the illustration commemorating Nankei's dinner there [Fig. 1]).[49]

Glass images needed not be only of lovers or associates. More generally inspirational or exemplary figures were also depicted, such as sages or heroes of the past, whose features (in a society that believed in physiognomy) one did well to have at hand. Hirokawa Kai recorded seeing a set of tiny portraits fixed inside a portable Dutch surgical desk (it also contained a "London" clock), mounted in positions where regular paintwork would have been swiftly worn away to nothing (Fig. 86). Kai did not specify the identity of the sitters, which from his illustration numbered twelve, but they were probably the likes of Saint Luke, Hippocrates, Galen, and other authors from the recognised medical canon.[50]

Mirror pictures made good gifts, and accordingly were much imported. Properly known in Japan by the literal translation, *kagami-e,* they were sometimes subsumed into the more generic *biidoro-e,* "glass picture"; when the latter term is encountered, it is by no means sure whether or not a final layer of mercury was added.[51] Indiscipline in the terminology bedevils an assessment of the chronology of arrival and assimilation, but non-mirrored glass pictures probably arrived first, and the date of 1663 finds first mention in the Dutch log of imports. Five examples (subjects unspecified) were presented

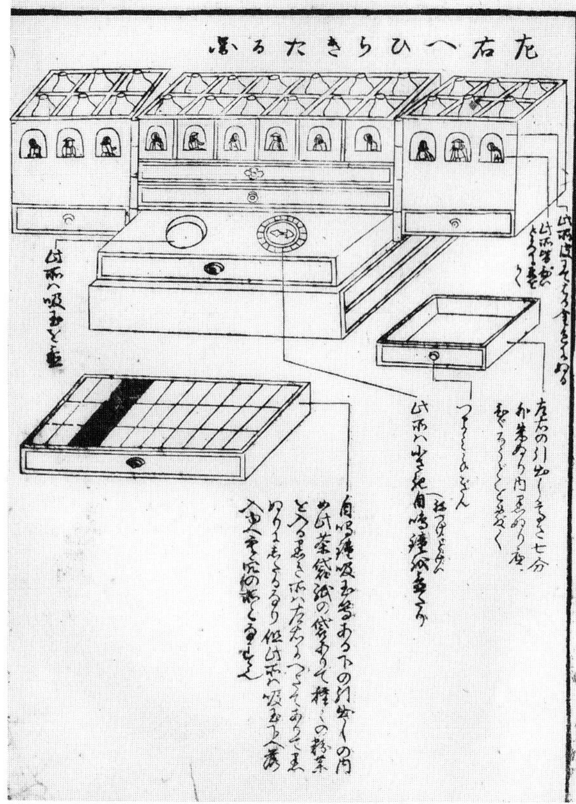

86. Ichiyanagi Kagen, from Hirokawa Kai, *Nagasaki bunken-roku,* 1800. SOAS, University of London.

Dutch surgeon's box, opened to reveal glass paintings, ink-well, and a miniature clock.

that year as gifts to the shogun, Ietsuna, along with a further fifty panes of blank glass.[52] From the mid-eighteenth century, *biidoro-e* attained the status of a "typical" Western picture, and along with copperplate *vues d'optiques* were probably considered Europe's preferred medium.

Narihiro was profoundly moved by the portrait of the kapitan's wife. He referred to its "brilliant conception, and genius-like technique (*kōshi saigaku*)"; Kōkan, too, greatly admired mirror pictures.[53] Many of the examples to be seen were no doubt Dutch, but English ones were also common, and according to Kōkan, Kōsaku had "finely done English framed glass [pic-

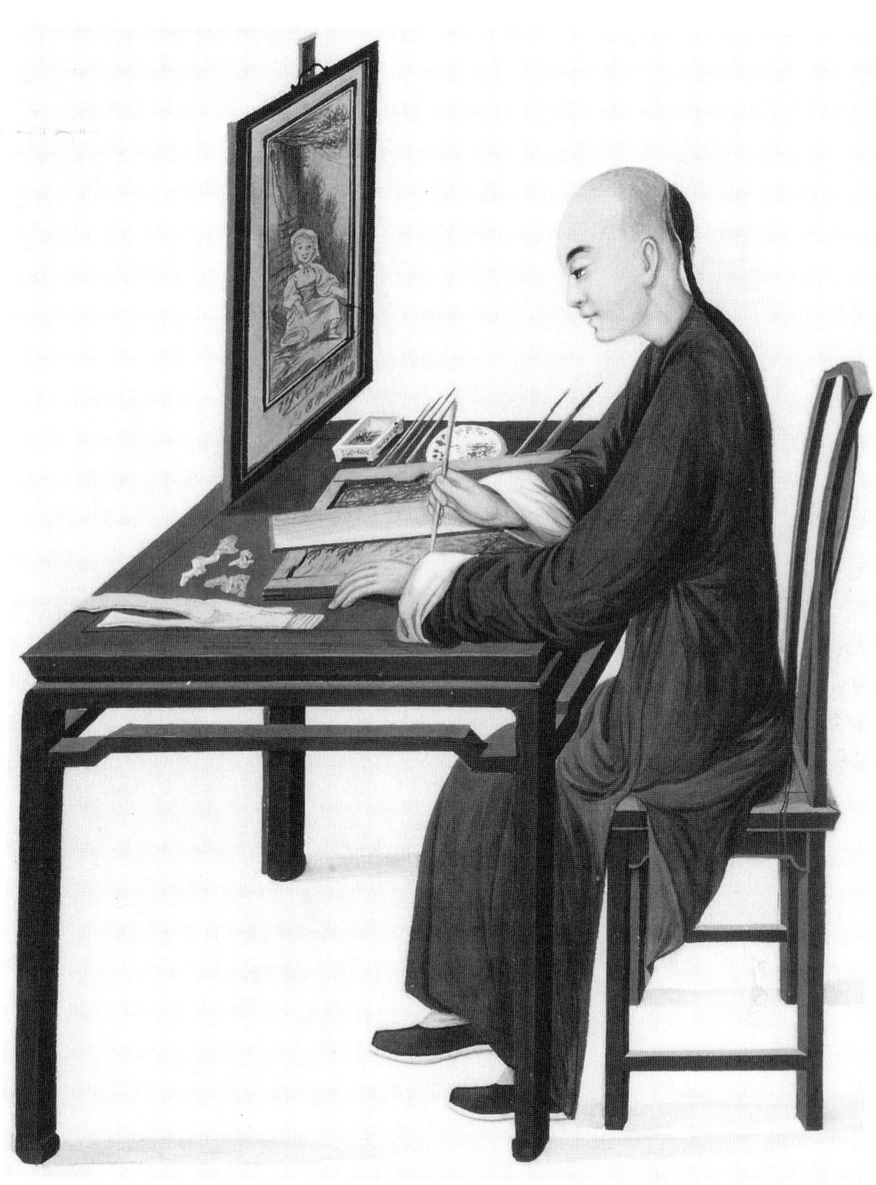

87. Unsigned, *Artist Transferring a Western Print onto Glass*, from the series *Cantonese Occupations*; Chinese, c. 1790. Victoria & Albert Museum, London.

tures] hung in rows below the lintel." Gyokuchō said that the Nagoya peony mirror was made in London.[54] Many apparently Western works came from Canton, where expatriate artists had taught the technique to Chinese people with an eye to producing goods for re-export to Europe; Rococo or chinoiserie subjects were encouraged, often copied from monochrome prints sent out for the purpose (Fig. 87). Some Continental Asian pieces may have arrived in Japan. Attempts to replicate the genre was an obvious next step. Reverse-painting was never systematically taught in Japan, although autodidacts tried their hand. Some became proficient, and by the latter part of the eighteenth century Europeans were buying examples to take home as souve-

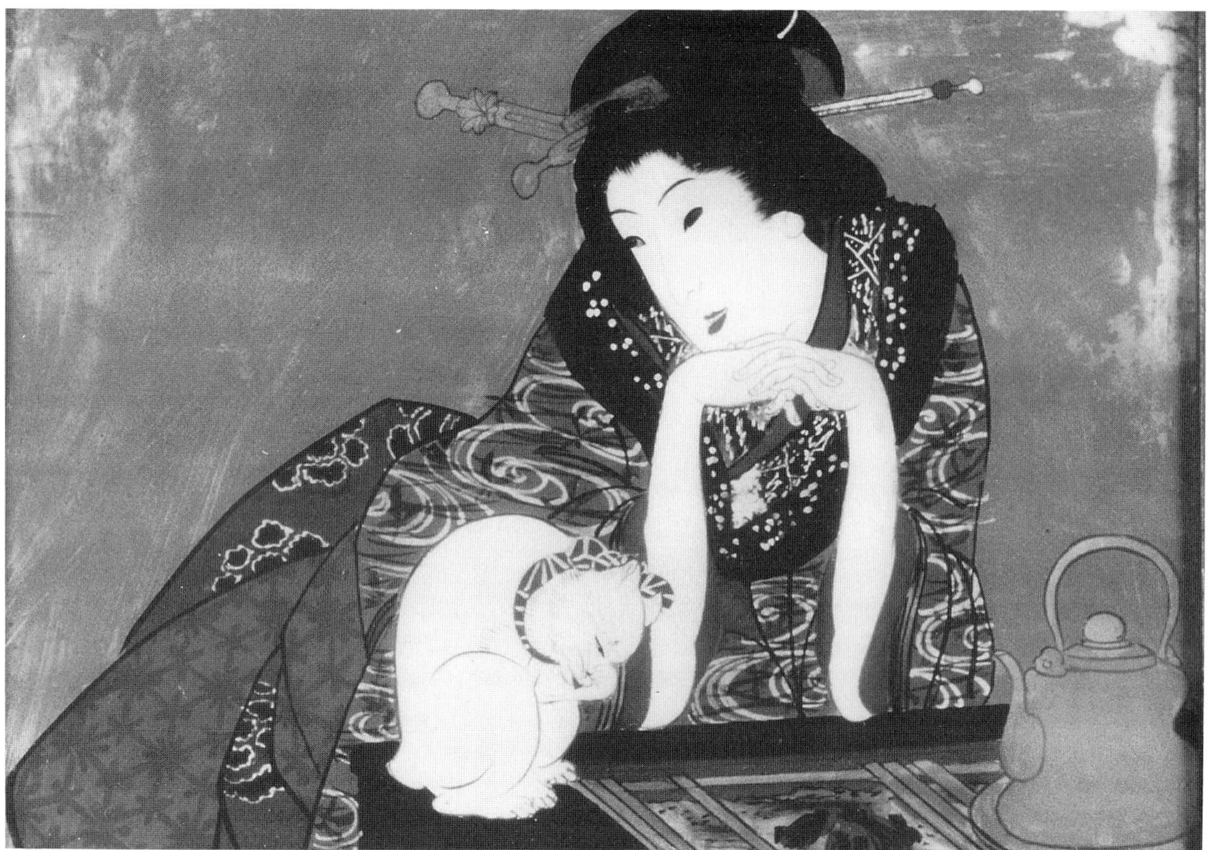

88. Unsigned, *Woman with Cat*, painting under glass; early nineteenth century. Hamamatsu Municipal Museum of Art.

nirs; few survive, but one composite work of six panes remains, framed in richly gilded swirling woodwork, and made to suit the Occidental taste, but seemingly never exported (Pl. 8); figures representing a Dutch couple and another lady, with more people behind, loiter in a waterside garden. In Japan, as in China, domestic subjects were undertaken too. Some were quite racy: in the summer of 1779 grief was nearly caused when an official in charge of the Chinese compound, Ban Kamoike, happened upon a pornographic glass painting when he visited the Factory, slipped in with three innocuous panes; crisis was averted when the Nagasaki magistrate ruled the law did not debar export of erotica.[55]

Because it was not understood how to apply mercury to the rear, Japanese glass pictures did not reflect. They were probably, though, produced by artisans dedicated solely to their production. But more serious artists, especially those inclined to the *Ranga* manner, turned towards the genre. Kōkan envisaged his trip to Nagasaki of 1788 at least partly as a chance to learn how to make glass pictures, and both *en route* and on the way back he visited makers of panes (*ita-biidoro*) in Kyoto and Osaka, presumably to investigate a supply for later use.[56] Kōkan claimed to have made glass pictures on his return to Edo, although none is extant. The medium continued to be practised into the nineteenth century both in Nagasaki and Edo, though generally anonymously (Fig. 88).[57] In 1804, Ishizaki Yūshi, hereditary Censor of Foreign Art Works (*kara-e mekiki*) – who in the course of his business had occasion to study many European manners – cracked the riddle of the application of mercury. He claimed: "I learned the art of making Primitive pictures from my father, [Araki] Gen'yū, and how oil paints are made to shine out from the back of a sheet of glass. I learned from a Primitive person how to apply mercury to the rear of this to make a mirror picture (*e-kagami*)."[58] Who this Western person was (if the story is even true) is lost. Kōkan had met the still young Yūshi in 1788 and characteristically dismissed him as "a pitiful artist." Not all thought him so, and Yūshi, now fifty-eight, said he had several pupils in the "primitive genres" (*banga*), "monastic, lay, women and men," the women being seven in number.[59]

THE MIRROR OF THE SELF

Plain, unadorned mirrors, were also much imported. As early as 1708, a Nagasaki official, Nishikawa Joken, had written that mirrors of all sizes were coming in, the smaller ones 8–10 by 30 cm, and the larger ones up to three times that.[60] Engelbert Kaempfer recorded that mirrors were on the routine import lists by the 1720s, and Thunberg gave "Nuremberg manufactures, such as looking-glasses &c" as major items in the illegal private trade.[61] Regular commercial exchanges dealt in quite large European pieces, and the anonymous Dejima album, of probably 1797, has in the scene of import–export negotiations a fine and highly ornate example lying on the mats of the merchant-house (Fig. 13). At about the same time, Narabayashi Jūbei was able to explain (at least to his own satisfaction) that "glass mirrors have tin foil overlaying the glass, and mercury affixed to it; if you mash the mercury with saliva it will go on well."[62]

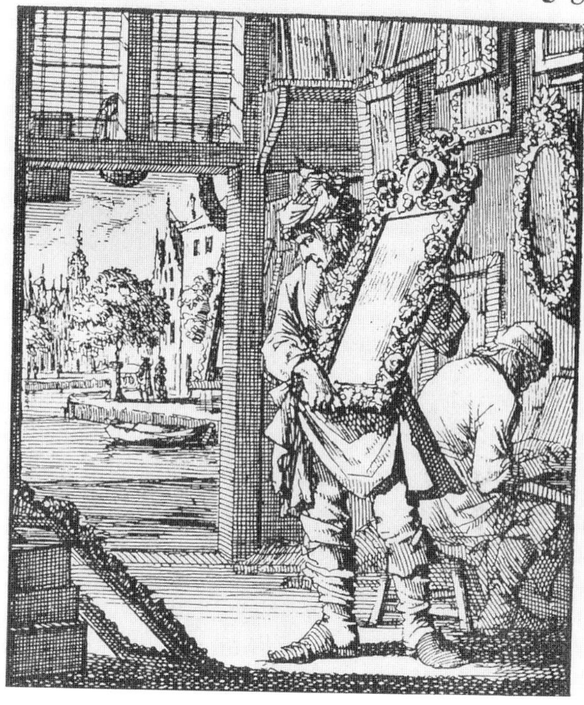

89. Johannes & Caspaares Luiken, *Mirror-maker*, from their *Spiegel van het Menselyk bedryf*, Amsterdam, 1694. Private collection.

The Luikens's book of Amsterdam craftsmen featured the *spiegelmaaker* and appropriately enough as it used the looking glass metaphorically in its title, it accorded special significance to his labours (Fig. 89). The man is said to produce goods of a very singular existential potency, the poem inscribed on the page suggesting how mirrors prompt heuristic meditation. The gazer sees more than the surface of things, as he or she is carried downward to ponder reflections of the subcutaneous self: "likeness depends upon capturing essences," runs the verse, and "whoever searches out first principles will reap fruit." The mirror user probes beneath the surface.

East-Asian civilisations had known mirrors since ancient times, but the material used in making them was metal, usually bronze. Thunberg advised:

> of glass [mirrors] there are none made in this country: but both the smaller and the large sort are made of cast metal, which is composed of copper and zinc, and highly polished. One of these mirrors is fixed on a stand, made for that purpose, of wood, and in an oblique position so that the fair sex may view their lovely persons in it, as well as in the best looking glass.[63]

Well-fashioned bronze offered a very good reflective surface, but it had its shortcomings too. First, the replication of colour was significantly impaired, as everything took on a brownish tinge; a second drawback was the need to polish the metal continuously and vigorously to retain effective quality; metal mirrors tarnished quickly so were covered when not in use to retard, as much as possible, the process. Third, the conventional shape was round with an oblong handle, and this meant that although the face could be fully seen, little of the "person" beyond was visible, a rectangle being necessary for that (Fig. 47). Proximity of the user was also essential, for moving away made the entire image distort into meaninglessness. By contrast, the glass and mercury mirror was true in colour, capable of being manufactured in virtually any size, perpetually bright, and usable from almost any distance. Gotō Rishun mentioned "glass mirrors, large and small," that were "akin to our bronze sort, but retain their sparkle indefinitely"; the larger sort cited by Joken were about a metre and so would show the majority of the body. The writer Bakin used the simile "like a Dutch glass mirror" to stand for an unusually precise capturing of the nuances of hue.[64] These various features reinforced the capacity of the imported mirror to say something momentous. New mirrors provided a thoroughly fresh sense of the figure caught within.

Glass mirrors could enjoy a more prominent role among domestic furnishings, for when tarnishing was not an issue, permanent display was possible; Thunberg had noted how, in Japan, "mirrors do not decorate the walls, although they are in general use at the toilet." But glass need not be hidden away. Hirokawa Kai remarked on a particularly large piece that hung up perpetually in the main room of the VOC compound, and at nearly two metres high by one-and-a-half, he said, it was about as large as a single pane could be made at the time.[65] The bottom portion is just visible in the album leaf of the Factory interior (Fig. 72).

The tendency not to display mirrors for long periods was the result of the metallurgical features of bronze oxidation, but it was also, by dint of long-standing habit, accompanied by cultural assumptions. As the mirror was not always there, its explanatory visions were moveable and removeable, and disinclined the viewer to conceive of a perpetual self unexpungibly present. Once the reflection was put out for continuous observation, the message became emphatic and the self more fixed. Being in glass, the image was also firmly within the discourse of science and perhaps associated with the experimental potentials of the new see-through material. The mirror, after all, hung above the kapitan's collection of bottled fauna. Kai, striving no doubt for adequate language to describe the odd combination of mementos that he saw on the mantelpiece (bottles, statuettes, looking-glass), and the fresh intellectual stance that the mirror encouraged, referred to the area as "a space resembling a Buddhist altar." To Kai, there was something metaphysical, even religious, in these agglutinated elements of *Ran,* discontinuous in themselves but in sum adding up to a new assessment of form.

As the mirror was not (or did not need to be) taken down, it allowed self-visions to come without the prelude of removal from a case, buffing up, and setting on a stand; indeed, glass mirrors permitted, for the first time ever, the chance and unexpected encounter with one's own body, as a person happened to pass in front and saw their frame and features cast unpreparedly back at them. Nagakubo Sekisui identified as a most salient feature of the new mirror the fact that it sent out the fortuitous image of anyone walking by.[66] Bronze mirrors allowed no vision of an off-guard moment. But the mercury kind plumped a person, willy-nilly, inside, viewable from head to toe and in full colour, suddenly like a third person.

Users might not recognise themselves. They would never have seen their particular corporeal idiosyncrasies before – warts, yes, but not gestures, ways of walking and so on. Morishima Chūryō (writing under his pen-name Manzōtei) played on this idea in a joke-book (*sharebon*) published in 1785 as *The Secret Handbook (Tora no maki)*. Chūryō punned the term for the stand on which a bronze mirror rested (*kagami tate*) with *tate*, meaning a shield.[67] A resourceful and modern-minded military commander lines up rectangular body-sized mercury mirrors in front of an attacking army, and the oncoming soldiers, failing to recognise it is themselves they see, are confused by the "mirror-shields" and desist (Fig. 90). Eventually they realise their mistake, but, momentarily transfixed, they stop their advance.

Smaller mirrors probably outnumbered the bigger sort for simple reasons of commercial expediency (and ease of smuggling) and of those imported may have been little larger than the traditional bronze kind, with room only for the face to be visible. But even so, the perpetuity and clarity of the reflection was uncompromised by the lesser scale. Qianlong huangdi, a lover of glass as we have seen, owned a small circular Western mirror set, it appears, in a Chinese-made camphor-wood frame. By force of habit (or for fear that the mystic force of an unpremeditated encounter would be too strong), he kept it concealed in a cloth wrap. Qianlong composed a poem telling how he spent a long evening in meditation on the reflection of his face. Ranking the object together with the finest of marvels of Chinese endeavour, he wrote, "The high price this mirror commands is thought reasonable even in the Capital [where people are urbane]. For it is equivalent to an interlocking ivory ball, or a disc of jade." And he went on:

> Vacant though bright in itself, it responds to all things,
> Such that you ask, "What can it be?"
> Beautiful people appear in their beauty, and the ugly in their ugliness.
> Sitting on my fine bed and gazing at the mirror
> All the multitudinous influences of karma are stilled,
> And then, I commune with myself for a long while.[68]

The huangdi, whose appearance made men sink into the dust, now encountered himself with a piercing sharpness, not as his painters showed or as his scholars eulogised him, but in a fresh and vivid openness. However he defined the "self" (and he was redefining it – that is precisely the point), it was himself whom he saw.

Maruyama Ōkyo, the Kyoto painter regarded as first in that whole art-loving city, made several sketches that relate to visions seen in a mirror (Pl. 9). Ōkyo was adamant about the value to painting of studying reflections seen in the glass. This position had never before been proposed by a senior artist. On several occasions the master advised his pupil and patron, Yūjo, prince-abbot of the Enman-in on Lake Biwa, to use a mirror so as to draw better. Yūjo subsequently diarised: "Maruyama said, 'reflect people's hands and feet in mirrors and sketch them. Do your own too. Fix a reflexion in a mirror, or else focus on an object with a telescope, and copy what you see down.' "[69] By tilting a mirror the artist could see angles and dimensions of his own body not before considered, and he could try out poses and gestures. But it was perspicacity, in its fullest sense, that Ōkyo wished to encourage. He required a gaze directed towards the artist's own body as the prior activity that allowed the authentic depiction of all other forms (telescopes, he said, were for viewing animals that would flee if approached). Many of Ōkyo's studies are drawn within circles plotted on the page, suggestive of the circular mirror. In general, his use of the sketch is significantly greater than that of most artists of this time, and even when the object inspected was not his own body, or even dependent on a mirror, Ōkyo retained a clear sense of the power of the intuitive stare and the need for any picture to grasp the unexpurgated and personal – even private – moments of its sitters. Ōkyo attempted to understand something complete and novel about the identity of the persons depicted, and he drew them in all their states from (in a scroll that accompanies the *Child Seen from Above*) naked old women with sagging breasts and backs, to a masturbating nine-year-old boy and adult sexual organs in various stages of excitement – themes never before addressed in the history of Japanese art.[70]

In 1802, Sugita Genpaku, the first historian of the *Rangaku* movement, wrote of his encounter with the image of himself reflected in a mirror. One night, he recalled, he sent a serving-girl in the place he was staying to bring him a mirror, and in it he inspected his face. What whim it was that inclined the seventy-year-old Dutch-

90. Morishima Chūryō, *Mirror Stand/Mirror Shield*, from *Tora no maki*, 1785. SOAS, University of London.

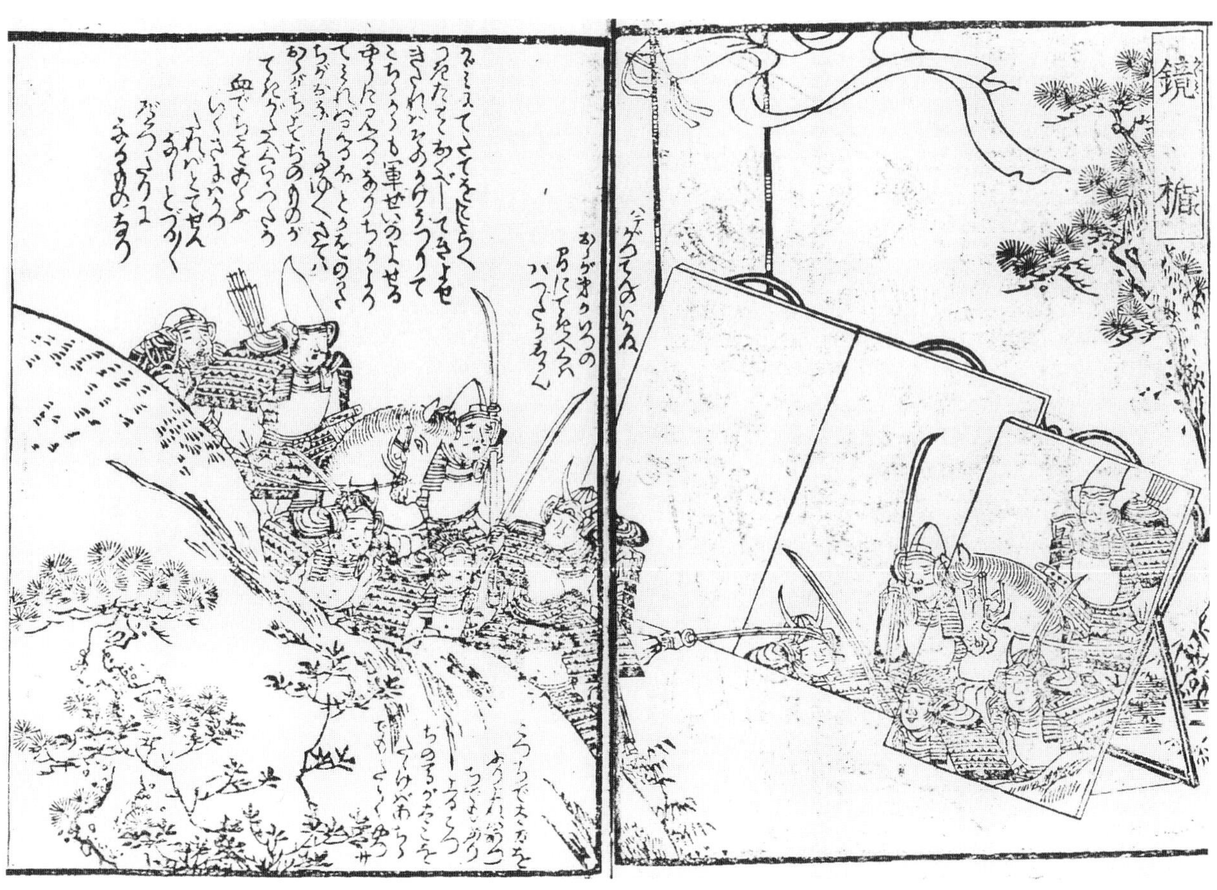

inspired samurai to do this went unstated, but as he gazed he saw something that he had never known before: himself. Genpaku was affected enough to write of his responses in *Night Talks on a Reflected Shape (Keiei yawa)*. When the book was published, he had a frontispiece drawn by Ishikawa Tairō, a high-ranking Edo samurai and a painter who worked exclusively in the *Ranga* style (even taking the Western name Tafel Berg). Tairō presented a portrait of Genpaku's gaunt visage, wrinkled and lined, staring out from the oval form of a mirror's surface set up in a darkened room (Fig. 91).[71]

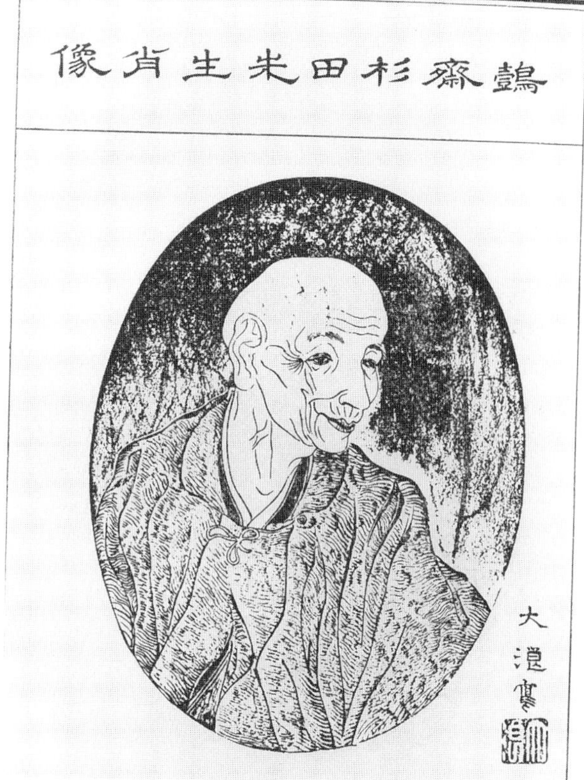

91. Ishikawa Tairō, *Sugita Genpaku*, title page to Sugita Genpaku, *Keiei yawa*, 1802. Keiō University Library.

Many *Rangaku* experts were attracted to the theme of the mirror, and Kōkan brought to light an ancient story attributing heuristic value to the reflected image. He gave no reference for the tale, neither has one ever been unearthed, and it is possible that the story originated with him. A certain Buddhist monk, he recounted, "took a mirror and stared at himself intently in it"; he derived thereby a general principle: "Even good or intelligent people will judge others while neglecting to assess themselves. But if you do not know your own self, how can you understand other things?"[72] Whether or not genuinely taken from a previously existing text, Kōkan's citation is entirely the product of his age. Mirrors had long had a function in Buddhist thought, but their meaning was quite different from that which Kōkan offers: less sources of personal knowledge, they had traditionally been metaphors for the reverse – for how the mind ought to be free from the imprint of fleeting phenomena; the equation was made between how the polished surface of the bronze cast back visions but was not affected by them, and how the heart should be, similarly, impervious to the vanities of insubstantial things.[73] Dōni, in his *Shingaku* preaching, had likened the need to buff up the mirror and remove its marks to the obligation to purge the heart of all excrescence, until every activity coincided with the Heaven-directed Way.[74] The East-Asian mirror taught egolessness; the mercury one outlined a self; and the flashing looking-glass informed a person that they were discrete, autonomous, and affirmable.

THE FALSE MIRROR

The view of one's person in the mercury mirror was to be solicited as an educative experience. But even the smallest kind were expensive. A surrogate emerged that referred to the effect of looking in an all-replicating glass without requiring the extravagance of buying one. This substitute mirror was made of paper, so it totally failed to reflect (though it might glisten slightly) and was similar to a real mirror only in rhetorical terms. Simulation of luxury imports in cheaper media was a ploy of the fly late-eighteenth-century fashion disseminator; Gennai, for example, had devised a way of replicating expensive Dutch beaten leather (*goodleer*, or *kinkarakawa* in Japanese) – much valued for making bags and tobacco pouches – in embossed paper. I propose that the mica-coated prints that appear suddenly in the 1780s are simulations of mercury mirrors. Qianlong had written in his poem how "crystal and mica are shamed" by comparison with the "essence" of mercury, but mica was handy and would do at a pinch. Makers of these pictures did not intend the user to strain to see their own features in the mica surface, for they only wished to convey a *sense* of seeing the self. These false-mirrors form a sub-genre of prints of the Floating World and as such graft the reality of mercury onto the hedonism of leisure life. The fake mirrors were false in every way, flattering the user and contriving an image of them as they wished to be seen. The mirror was subverted into a thoroughly plausible, though egregious, self-representation. The printed subject is always a beautiful woman or a stunning actor, the mica background filling the blank space like the vacant mirror around their reflection.[75] The sheet was thus a kind of surrogate mirror picture, too.

Mica prints were invariably in oblong formats which, though already common in Floating-World prints, also neatly matched the upright proportions of the typical imported looking-glass. The general type was printed as a close-up of the head and neck of the sitter (*ōkubi-e*) or else bust-length (*honshin-zu*) arrangements not at all standard in the history of Japanese composition, but equivalent to the effect of seeing oneself in a glass. Utamaro depicted a letter-reading woman who can become the *alter ego* – the would-be self – of any female onlooker (Pl. 10). She is beautiful in the extreme – poised and dressed with style, rich not gaudy – and (important to note, for it is relatively rare in Utamaro's oeuvre) she is a married woman, not a prostitute, as can be told from her plucked eyebrows. This is a person apt for emulation by a young bourgeois wife of Edo. But it is not a didactic work: still comely, though now in wedlock, the woman furtively reads a letter, surely a billet-doux, unrolled just a little and so as to remain concealed from the prying eyes of the household. This is the woman as she would have herself be, not as the codes instructed her (or as her husband saw her role) having her cake and eating it too. The picture is from the series *Ten Physiognomic Types of Married Women (Fujo jinsō juppin)*, and is inscribed, "Utamaro the physiognomist drew this after careful thought," but the space in the cartouche where the woman's type should be noted is blank. Where Utamaro stands is moot. Dōni had said that the mirror must show "authenticity" (*makoto*), if it was to have real meaning, but this self-serving version throws back delusion as the viewer sees a specimen of female (or male) made after his or her own heart, as if squeezed from the inauthenticity of their private cravings.

The paper mirror was the fond wish of vanity. But the mercury mirror also could all too easily become a pander to self-falsifications. As imported mirrors were predominantly small, they were convenient to carry about, and so suited to the needs of the constant preener. Glass mirrors could fit into the palm of the hand or slip unobserved into the pocket and were lighter than bronze, so that the term "pocket mirror" (*kaichū kagami*) was coined to refer to their new and natty type.

Kyōden, it is scarcely surprising to hear, enlisted the pocket mercury mirror in a kibyoshi. He contrasted the vanity of actual users with the profundity of the image that could be cast, if only they had the maturity to consider it. He offset the insincerity of the self-centered Floating-World wastrel with the authentic readings of character known by those who judged aright.

The book, illustrated by Kyōden himself, appeared in 1788 under the title *Kaitsū unubore kagami*, a phrase that can be read in two ways: *kaitsū* means a thoroughly trendy person, but puns on *kaichū* "pocket (mirror)"; *unubore* ordinarily means "vanity," except that *unubore kagami* ("vanity mirror") meant a mercury glass. The full title, then, can be read as either *The Pocket Mercury Mirror* or *The Mirror of a Thoroughly Trendy Person's Vanities*.[76] The fissure that yawns between the two options is the point of the book. Although put out with the humorous readability of all kibyoshi, Kyōden retains an element of the seriously heuristic search, for he made the protagonist of the tale a foil for himself, scrambling his own business name, Kyōya Denzō, into that of the main character, "Kyōya Denjirō"; the suffix *-jirō* meant second son, so Kyōden splits off a progeny from himself, forging an identity for the main character that is both himself and everyman.

Woefully lacking in social graces but devoid of any realisation of this, Denjirō dreams only of becoming "thoroughly trendy" and raving by night in the Yoshiwara. His budget is hopelessly inadequate and he frets incessantly, until one day the Great Radiant God Brothel Patron (Kyaku Daimyōjin) appears in his lonely room and offers Denjirō a pocket vanity mirror. The piece is described as having been procured from the then-fashionable men's accessory shop, the Koshigawa-ya, in the Ueno district. The glass, then, is both divine and on open sale in Edo. Let Kyōden's readers buy one for themselves.

Reflected in the mystic surface is not the made-up face of the sybarite but the actuality that lurks behind it. The god tells Denjirō, "with the reflections seen in this, you will understand the human emotions that you'll run into in the Yoshiwara – the hearts of the trendy young men, and of everything else too; all people will be shown to you exactly as they are." Denjirō makes straight for the brothel district. He directs the mirror so as to catch the shapes of the people he sees as they engage in their trysts and amorous exchanges. The reflection matches form to reality, and realigns appearance with the heart beneath, as it brings the inner up to the surface (Fig. 92). The Yoshiwara, like all pleasure quarters, was awash with payment in false coin, and as Denjirō casts his eyes on the glass, he becomes aware that the pursuit of pleasure is folly. Awakened, he quits forever the brothel realm, realising how devastating to the individual and to society at large is the ability to paint a face prettier than the substance of the heart beneath. Forsaking all hope of striving beyond his proper walk in life, Denjirō progresses down the path of virtue, identifying himself only with his Way.

Mercury mirrors never failed to throw back images that were clear and precise, absolute in point of pigmentation, scale, and form, but if the user did not peer deep enough, the very plausibility of the image could lead them astray. Paperised mirrors "reflected" total fantasy, and the glass might aspire to equally falsifying ends; it was, after all, the utensil by which one concealed one's blemishes. A badly made mirror warped by accident, but the real one might aid in primping the outer at the expense of the inner – a far more heinous crime. A warping mirror might throw a person into a startled reevaluation, for a bent reflection looked as real as a straight one, until the viewer became aware of the mistake. Distorting glass mirrors were occasionally put out for fair-goers to use, and people might pay to see their faces and physiques transformed, becoming taller, squatter, wider, or slimmer, but still looking fully real. This was fun. But there might also be grounds for serious thinking. Dōni mentioned in a sermon:

> Everything's like a mirror that throws back a reflection, really: if [the one] is clear, [the other] will look clear too, and a laughing face will flash back laughing. The mirror has no volition (*shishin*) of its own – that's virtue in a mirror. But if you look in a soiled piece, that smiling face of yours will become a wraith deriving from the mirror itself. When

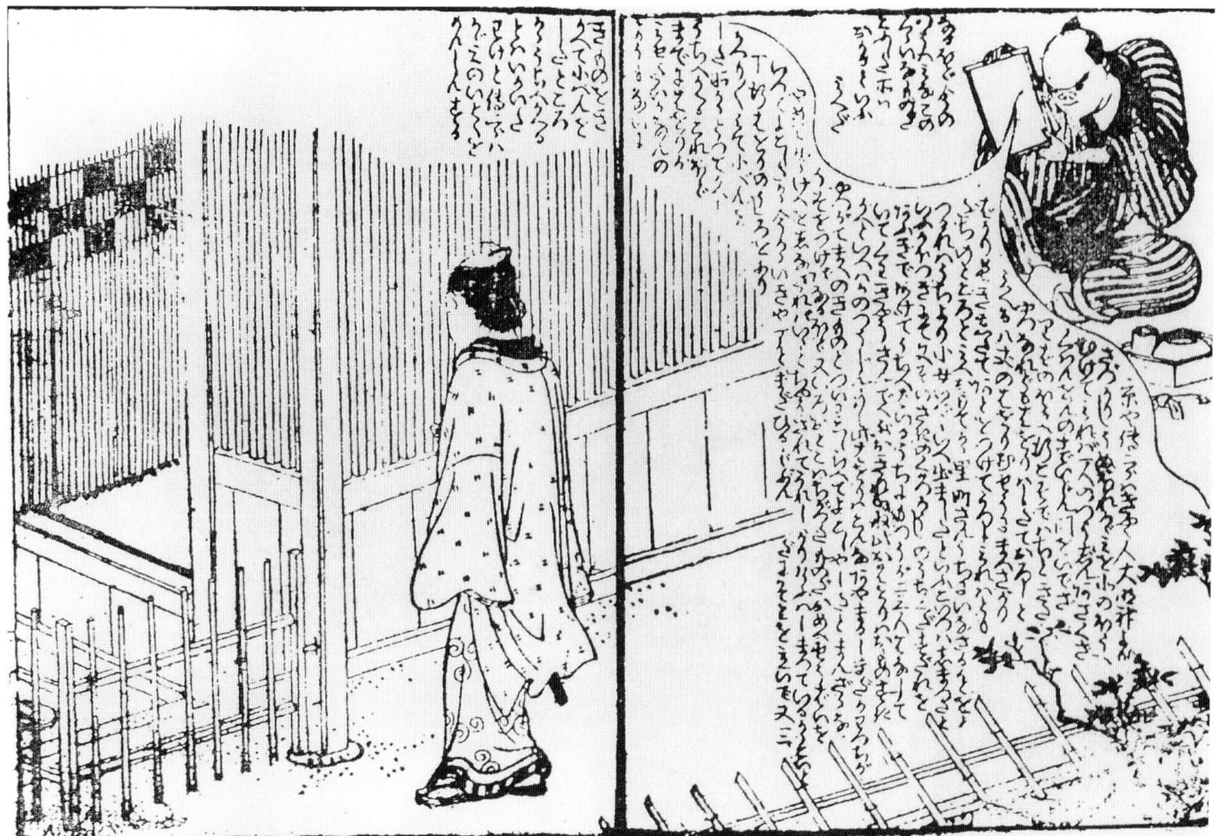

92. Santō Kyōden, from his *Kaitsū unubore kagami*; 1788. British Museum. *Denjirō directs his magical mirror at a youth approaching a brothel.*

> the disloyal and unfilial have a good time, and unscrupulous businessmen flourish, and when the Buddhas and Gods answer prayers for longevity and fortune from bad-livers, these things are all just the apparitions of a faulty mirror.[77]

Clouded bronze, or misshapen glass, turned a charming countenance into an evil one and might make a wicked person temporarily look fair, but what Dōni meant, of course, was that we had better be sure we weren't those silk-draped dandies with the unhallowed grins.

Buddhist legend held that there was a reflective rock set up at the portals of hell which showed the deceased their deeds in life, played back posthumously; quivering corpses watched as a build-up of wickedness consigned them to perdition, or breathed with relief as their virtues released them to the sanctuaries of the pure. This rock, the Floating Crystal Mirror (*Jōbari no kagami*), was depicted on the hell scrolls that hung in temples, and all knew of it. Distorting mercury mirrors had the force to allude to the entrance to hell, for seeing oneself all twisted and skewed was the last thing most sinners would know as the tortures began. Kodera Gyokuchō, in the winter of 1821, went to see seven corrugated looking-glasses set up in Nagoya. Mostly put out for the fun of it ("You look at yourself in them and the result is really hilarious," he wrote), but the visions were not without

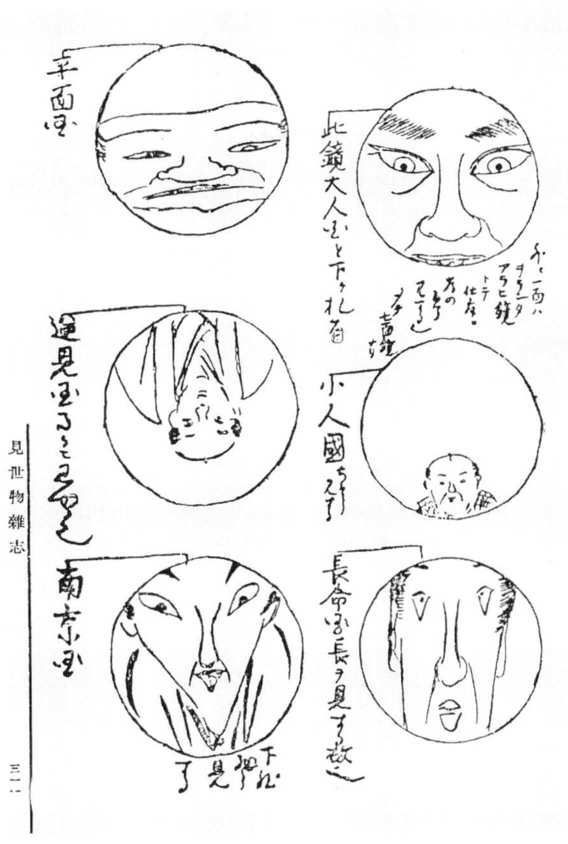

93. Kodera Gyokuchō, drawing from his *Misemono zasshi*, 1828–33. Reproduced from *Zoku zuihitsu bungaku senshū: Misemono zasshi* (Shibundō, 1928).

Six distorting mirrors.

their deeper connotations (Fig. 93). Gyokuchō felt as he looked that he had become suddenly foreign to himself, literally expelled from his local realm into the far and strange, as each glass projected him differently, one to the land of the Broad Faces, one to the land of the Little People, another to the Southern Triangle, and so on. In the mirrors, he adapted and changed without stability, erring from his Way. The venue for display was ominous, for the set was erected, Gyokuchō noted, in the precincts of a Buddhist temple, the Seijū-in. Did the distortions exaggerate, or were they simply showing the ugliness at the heart of all modern men and women? Did those who looked into the glasses see a foretaste of what the Floating Crystal Mirror would one day reveal, their foulness transposed to the face? One visitor to the booth made up the *bon mot*, "What's even stupider than your mug in the seven distorting mirrors?" Answer: "Paying to see it!"[78] But the stupidity was the idiocy of evil, and the hideously laughing form staring back all ugly and coarse kept an uneasy resemblance to the gazer; the connexion of the image could not be denied. This fraudulence writ all over the face beckoned in one direction only: to hell.

SIX

THE EYE AND THE LENS

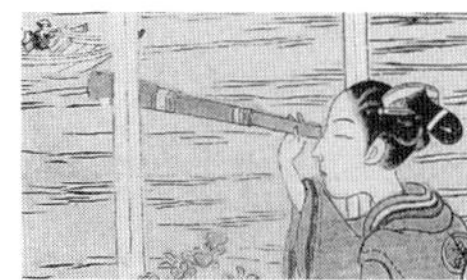

WITH OCULAR PERCEPTION becoming such a problematic area, it is not surprising that argument should turn more generally to issues of the authority of the faculty of sight, the structure and functioning of the human eye, and the anatomy of the organ. How it might work, and how might it work better became points of concern.

THE HUMAN EYE

The importance of sight is evident enough. Ailments of the eye incapacitate perhaps more than any other, and fear of blindness outweighs many another fear. It may have been for this reason that evil spirits were said particularly to attack the eyes. The *Tales of the Heike (Heike monogatari)*, the mediaeval war tale that formed the basis of much history teaching, told in sonorous and classic phrase how politics had been disrupted when the fourteenth-century retired tenno, Sanjō, had been afflicted in the eyes by the vengeful spirit of the court chaplain.[1]

Illnesses of the eye, their causes and cures, were relatively little understood. By the Chinese-derived medical system operating in Japan (*kanpō*), the eye was not considered vital, physiologically speaking, and so was little examined. When Ogasawara Nagashige, a leading lord in the service of the shogun, grew disillusioned with court politics, he retired pleading an eye complaint – an unsuspicious, even generic, means of absenting himself. But in 1716, with a new shogun, Yoshimune, in power, Nagashige returned to court, declaring his eyes wonderfully restored.[2] Perhaps the daimyo intended a metaphor for political perspicacity to be discerned in his actions, but even so he was also taking advantage of the almost uniquely vague position the eye occupied in the medical rhetoric of the day.

Kanpō medicine (literally, the "Chinese technique") concerned itself almost exclusively with those parts of the body identified as the Five Organs and Six Viscera (*gozō roppu*), they alone being central to academic discourse; these were resident within the trunk of the body, and so *kanpō* restricted itself to what modern terminology would call internal medicine. Even there, attention was selective, and corporeal matter unrelated to *kanpō's* chosen parts (the blood, bones, limbs, and nervous system, to name but a few) were extensively neglected, or left to formally untrained doctors (*yabu-isha*) or quack salves (*yashi*), empirics and wise-women, and those beyond the purview of serious medicine. One of the first pharmacies to be opened in Edo when the city was founded in the late sixteenth century dealt in eye remedies and attested to the pressing need for cures, but the establishment, though flourishing, had no links with authoritative sections of the medical world.[3]

This cursory treatment of the eye was castigated by *Rangaku* scholars and their colleagues, the Dutch-style doctors (*Ran'i*). Their sense of the importance of examination and speculation on the eye as the root of the epistemology of *Ran*, led them to locate the organ at the centre of debate. Morishima Chūryō included "oculist" (*ganka*) in his *Lexicon of Primitive Words (Bango sen)* – rendering it as *oog meester* – he evidently deemed the term requisite vocabulary for those discoursing with Europeans, as it would not have been in conversations with local specialists.[4] Sugita Genpaku made a specific comparison between the situation he believed to pertain in East Asia and that in the West:

> Now, for example, the Chinese say, "As the sun and moon hang in the Heavens, even so are there two eyes in the human head" – well, it all sounds pretty lofty, but it does not begin to address the principles that make things visible. The Dutch have discovered that the eye is made up of a liquid film over an eyeball (*tama*) which contains an aqueous fluid; it resembles the white of an egg. All external phenomena, they say, are refracted in the two liquids, being transmitted from the first to the second.[5]

Genpaku is sweeping in his dismissal of Chinese thought, but it is true to note that ophthalmology was the central activity of only one institution in the Edo period, the Bajima School, located in Owari; the institution had a branch in Edo, but the work undertaken there, though valued in its own way, was simply not thought crucial for the general discipline. Eye doctors were consequently low in the professional hierarchy. Medical registers treat them only cursorily. An early eighteenth-century digest, *The Medicine of This Realm (Honchō ikō)*, fails to name a single one in its listing of the nation's famous practitioners, leaving the reader to assume that such oculists were not to be numbered among the great.[6] Medicine was hereditary in all its branches, and so the situation was self-perpetuating, the sons of eye doctors falling afoul of the system and suffering prejudice in admission to schools. At the aptly named August College (Kōgen-in), one of the more celebrated seats of medical learning, the rector debarred progeny of eye doctors from enrolment, stating as the first rule that "sons of eye doctors, even if of the blood line [not adopted], shall not receive instruction here."[7] As a result, oculists withdrew into obscurantism and secrecy, passing on their practices in oral form. In sum, as An Geikin, writer of one of the few treatises on the theme, *A Brief Study of Eye Medicine (Ganka ryakusetsu)* bewailed, eye doctoring was thought to be no more than "small skill and shallow thinking (*tansai senrō*)."[8]

This state of affairs underwent rapid change in the second half of the eighteenth century. Some groundwork had begun earlier: the first book to be published in Japan devoted to the eye appeared in 1689, and was reissued in 1707 under the title *Clear Lessons on the Eye (Ganmoku meikan)*. Trumpeted as the translation of a Ming Chinese text from the pen of one Xing Linan, the book was probably a Japanese work masquerading as Continental to gain a more serious ear for its slighted subject. Most of "Linan's" preface was spent trying to enhance his field of enquiry by arguing for inclusion of the eye as one of the Five Organs of the body.[9] The content of the book itself was basically uninnovative Bajima material.

A surge in the diffusion of matters relating to the eye occurred in 1774 with the appearance of the *New Anatomical Atlas (Kaitai shinsho)*. The *Clear Lessons* had been published in order to raise the place of the eye in the *kanpō* world, but the *Atlas* explicitly linked it to Dutch medicine and to its new experimental foundation, anatomy. Several pages on the eye were unapologetically integrated in an overall treatment of the human body, effectively demanding parity for it with other branches of medicine (Figs. 41, 94).

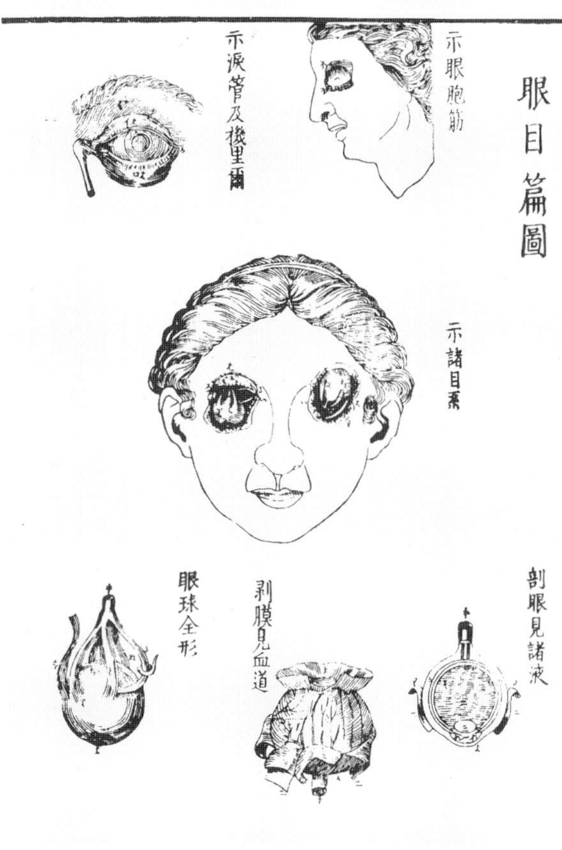

94. Odano Naotake, *The Eye*, from Sugita Genpaku (et al. trans.), *Kaitai shinsho*, 1774. SOAS, University of London.

The *New Anatomical Atlas* was the translation of Johannes Kulmus's *Anatomische Tabellen* of 1725, known in Japan in the Dutch translation of seven years later, *Ontleedkundige Tabellen*. Not so much scholarly as populist, Kulmus's aim had been to inform non-specialists of the structure of the entire body by means of easy discussion and the eye was a natural part. It was the perfect didactic tool for use in Japan. Precisely the reasons that condemned the book to non-acquisition by the supercilious university librarians of Europe, commended it to Japanese readers.[10] Kulmus's admirable lack of pedantry made an immediate impact, and its complete shunning of *kanpō* hierarchies startled readers. A full translation (minus footnotes, which in fact constituted more than half the book) as mentioned in Chapter 3 was undertaken by a team led by Sugita Genpaku, and included Maeno Ryōtaku, Katsuragawa Hoshū, and Nakagawa Jun'an. All were high-ranking stipendiary *han* doctors resident in the shogunal capital. Yoshio Kōsaku, the Nagasaki translator, contributed the preface. Kulmus's numerous illustrations (and several intercalated from other Western studies) were copied out from the copperplate originals for reprinting in woodblock by Odano Naotake, a young retainer of Lord Satake whom Hiraga Gennai had met in Akita in 1773 and brought down to Edo for the purpose.

Naotake's illustrations showed the eye as it had never before been seen: whole, then in various stages of dissection scattered across the page, culminating in total dismantlement. The accompanying text shunned "lofty" theorising, on the one hand, and baldly pragmatic debate on illness or cure, on the other, to address the organ as a bodily structure worthy of attention in its own right. The new status accorded the eye came right from the thick of the world of *Rangaku*.

Hoshū was deeply interested in the new medicine, as his father had been before him. But the Katsuragawa family was unusual in this; most in the exalted position of shogunal physicians (*oku-i*) – there were several – seemingly were not involved.[11] Eye doctors were also retained at Edo Castle for the benefit of the Tokugawa family, but they appear not to have been much concerned with developments in their field.[12] But Hoshū took advantage of his regular meetings with the VOC Factory retinue in Edo to solicit European books, and when he met the Dutch party in 1794, during a prolonged question-and-answer session that lasted two days, he was finally given what he sought: a Western publication devoted exclusively to the eye. He recorded, in a report submitted afterward:

> It was only a small, single-volume work, but it covered cures, medicines, and other things. The whole study seemed very precise, and no quick inspection could do it justice. Many people in my circle have been anxious to learn about Dutch ophthalmology and have been looking for a book such as this for some time. Even with this volume, though, our enthusiasm is not yet satiated.[13]

The work received was by Joseph Plenk, a professor at Basel University, and had been published only shortly before in Latin as *Doctrina de morbis oculorum;* it was the Dutch version of 1787 that arrived.[14] Unlike Kulmus's effort, Plenk's represented the latest word of a considerable expert. Hoshū passed the tome on to Gentaku, who arranged for a student to translate it. They assigned the book the interim Japanese title of *A New Atlas of Eye Medicine (Ganka shinsho)*, a designation clearly selected to borrow weight for the field from the successful pioneering of the *New Anatomical Atlas*. The exacting task of translation came to fruition only in 1815, by which time a reevaluation of ophthalmology had essentially been achieved, and so the title was emended to *The Complete Western Eye Medicine (Taisei ganka zensho)*.[15] Illustrations were provided by Ishikawa Tairō, the senior Edo-based samurai and *Ranga* artist who thirteen years before had painted Ōtsuki Gentaku's portrait in the mirror (Figs. 91, 95).

The translators of Kulmus and later of Plenk encountered a larger hindrance than the rejection of their peers. There was the more immediate problem of how to render European technical terms into the native language. On the one hand, the paucity of the available linguistic pool had to be contended with, and on the other there was an over-abundance of words to describe things the very existence of which Western medicine failed to acknowledge. There were, in fact, sixteen different Chinese characters to denote the eyeball, each with its own nuances and subtleties, and although not all were in current use, Ming texts and their Japanese derivatives were still regularly employing at least half a dozen.[16] The general policy of the *Atlas* was to cut through the web by neologising and combining characters into new words that rendered the meaning of the original Dutch (Chinese and Japanese being ideographic, this was easy to do). Alternatively, phonetic transliteration was used.[17] But there were dangers inherent in this approach. Not all the resulting terms were comprehensible to readers, nor for that matter acceptable to other *Rangaku* scholars who might be devising their own alternative designations. The *Atlas*, for example, used the compound *ganmoku* to denote the eye, combining two separate existing Chinese words. But the Plenk translators disliked this, substituting *gankyū* (which remains the modern word). Given the terminological swamp, it was not surprising that at least one *Rangaku* scholar, Mikumo Kanzen, working in Kyoto in 1798, skirted the issue entirely by arranging for his own illustrated work (some of the pictures in which were by Maruyama Ōkyo's third son, Ōju) to be labelled by a friend proficient in writing Roman letters, and he gave the Dutch as well as Japanese terms, anchoring the tentative home vocabulary in the security of the older originals.[18]

While doctors debated in a learned way, the popular world considered the new-found medicalised eye in a manner more suited to its own needs. On the most basic level, those who thronged outside the Nagasaki-ya in Edo or loitered around Edo-machi by Dejima noticed how the Europeans' eyes looked different from Japanese ones. Charles Thunberg observed how the VOC men continually had to suffer "a considerable number of children, who by their cries signify their astonishment at the large round eyes of the Europeans," as they screamed out, he noted, "Big-eyed Dutchman!" at them.[19] Thunberg appears not to have been irked by this (although he mentions it twice), for he himself accepted, inversely, that "it is by their eyes that, like the Chinese, these people are distinguisha-

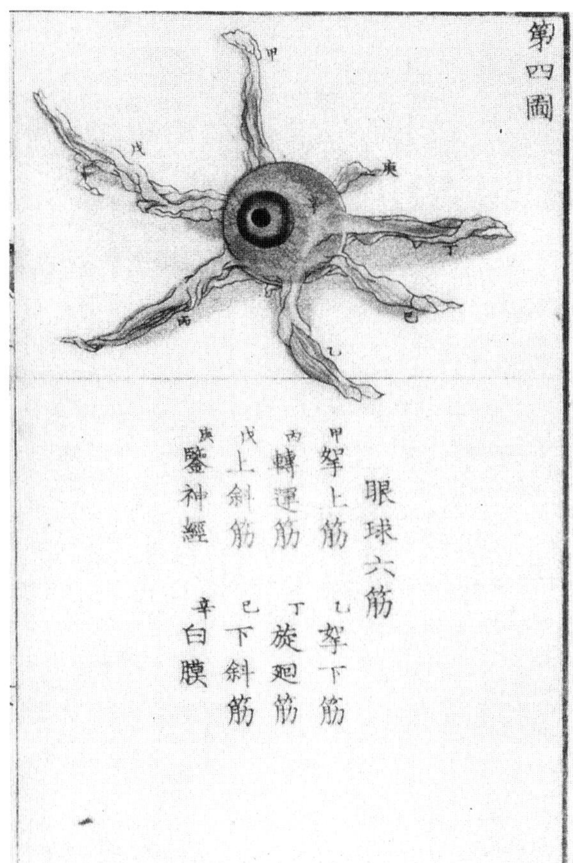

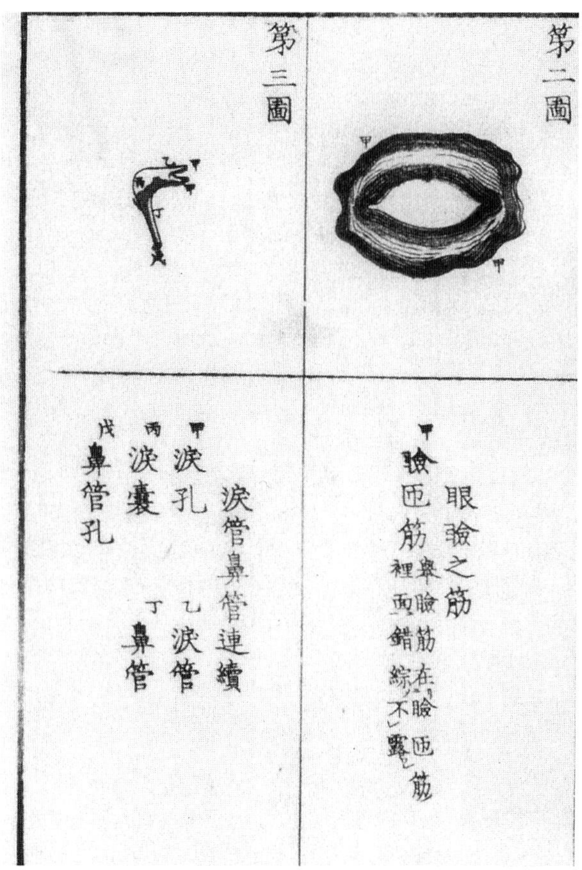

95. Ishikawa Tairō, from Sugita Rikkyō (et al. trans.), *Ganka shinsho*, 1815. Private collection. *Dissection of the human eye.*

ble; these organs have not that rotundity which those of other nations exhibit, but are oblong, small, and are sunk deeper in the head."[20]

There were those who wondered what implications for visual perception structural distinctions might have. In the *Correcting Errors about the Dutch (Ransetsu benwaku)*, Ōtsuki Gentaku is recorded as participating in the following exchange:

> My question is this: They say that the Dutch . . . have eyes like animals, is this true?
>
> My answer is this: how could such an erroneous notion arise? I suppose that it is because Dutch eyes look so different from those of the people hereabouts that they are slandered as "animal-like," but there is, I assure you, no difference in the manner of their functioning.[21]

Gentaku went on to state that the Dutch were not the only ones, as many ethnic groups had eyes of differing shape, the VOC's Indonesian workers being particularized again (a fact corroborated by Shiba Kōkan on his visit to Nagasaki).[22]

THE SOCIAL USE OF EYES

It is understandable how doubts might have arisen. The large, blue, staring discs in the

Dutchmen's heads were indeed remarkable. Gentaku may have insisted that although size and shape could vary, "manner of functioning" never differed (which claim alone could justify the use of Western ophthalmology in Japan), but this was only the beginning of the issue: the social codes of vision and the personal controls placed on the gaze did diverge from place to place. Dutch staring was not just the inevitable result of their oversized, protruding *oogbols* but the outward effect of a culturally encoded visuality that governed and directed their conception of the coherence of sight. Such a gaze was recognised in Japan as being linked to the specific *Ran* epistemology of viewing – to wit, that of science.

In the absence of much knowledge of how Europeans operated in their home environment, it was assumed that a cold, hard gaze that seemed the necessary prerequisite for their precision goods was the universal norm there; this contrasted markedly with the privileged mode of looking in Edo society. The intense stare was uncouth and generally taboo. To look in a scrutinising way was not respectable or seemly, and it also conflicted with that great desideratum of Edo-period fashionable life, *iki* – that is, nonchalance of an elegant, somewhat eroticised kind. The pre-war scholar Kuki Shūzō has written of *iki* vision:

> An oblique look (*ryūben*) was usually a way of showing sensual interest, sending messages to members of the opposite [*sic*] sex by movements of the eye ball. There were several sorts of "oblique look," such as the sidelong, the upward and the downward glances. Looking at a member of the opposite sex head-on but with a sidelong glance was considered erotic too; equally, it was erotic to look upward with the head turned down, while to look downward with the head turned up suggested embarrassment at the thought of a flirtation, which was another sensual trick.[23]

There does not seem to be much left and the frontal stare alone is ruled out. Kuki summed up, "the common feature of all ways of looking was . . . that they broke the direct line of vision." Given this complexity of eye-language, a senryu writer might well versify:

> If you're in the mood,
> Your eyes as much as your mouth
> Will speak your words of love.[24]

Franz von Siebold came to Nagasaki as doctor in 1823 and was a member of the Factory *hofreis* of 1826. While in Edo, he appears to have made the acquaintance of Iwasaki Kan'en, an important botanist, who painted his portrait in celebration of their encounter (Pl. 11). Siebold was uniquely privileged in being permitted to open a private school for Japanese students (one of whom was Takano Chōei), and he married a Japanese woman, becoming the best-known European (he was German, not Dutch) of his generation; Siebold stood as a cypher for *Ran* in the early nineteenth century. Kan'en illustrated the twenty-three-year-old physician, erect in his outlandish clothes;[25] capturing the extraordinary Western physique was clearly the point of the picture. Beside Siebold's form, Kan'en drew in his eye a second time, placing it in magisterial isolation on the page to the left, vast, blue, and staring. Conventions of botanical illustration – Kan'en's forte and Siebold's own amateur interest – allowed for the inclusion of inset pictures within a larger work to endow the salient features of the specimen under discussion with more prominence. Siebold's extra eye has that status. As the Red-furs' most quintessential feature and the distinguishing mark of *Ran*, it deserves its more in-depth treatment.

Siebold's eye, rid of his individuating body, has shed all compromising clogs. This conceit of an externally existing organ operating discretely worked well as a smile for clear vision. Representation of the eye as apart and whole carried a load of signification. Perhaps this was experienced by the *han* doctor of Tokushima in Awa, Kō Ryōsai, who, while studying with Siebold in

Nagasaki, came across a medical model of an independent eyeball mounted on a stand.[26] Ryōsai found the device, imported from London he said, to have the utmost realism; and so great an impact did the model have on the young doctor (he was then a year younger than the Siebold of Kan'en's portrait), that he turned to ophthalmology, becoming Japan's first eye surgeon.

The English model eye was to be probed and studied. Anatomists demonstrated in such products and in their wider discussions, how the tendons and juices of the eye worked to control the gaze. This implied a fabrication of sight automatic and independent of the will. The *New Anatomical Atlas* had noted that the interior of the eye was filled with what it called a "glass-like liquid" (*biidoro-yō eki*), which imparted to the organ the aura of dispassionateness associated with that material. The book went on to discuss how the formation of images in the eye could be equated with the mechanical appearance of forms in Western optical tools, such that the human eye worked "exactly in the manner of a telescope."[27] Other observers made similar associations with the lens.[28]

Kōkan, not himself a doctor, recorded his examination of the mechanics of vision in a manuscript work, *On Heaven and Earth (Tenchi ridan)* completed in 1816; again, the new similes that sprang to his mind to describe the gaze were lens-based, and he compared the eye to both the telescope and the camera obscura:

> The interior of the eye is like a dark room, and the pupil like a pin hole in it, sinews covering it like glass. Thin [at the edges] and thick [in the middle], it is like the lens (*tama*) at the end of a telescope; it is transparent and scratch-resistant.
>
> When you shut a room tightly and make a hole in the door, the outside scenery will transpose itself very clearly inside. This is how the eye works.[29]

Kōkan ended by noting that the coincidence of image-formation methods in the eye and in optical instruments were not chance, for "the telescope, microscope, and star-gazing glass were all fashioned in imitation of the natural workings of the eye". Elsewhere, Kōkan reiterated the point: "Dutch people and other Westerners have dissected the eye and assessed its marvellous natural functioning (*tenkō*), and have thereby devised spectacles, microscopes, and telescopes. All derive ultimately from the eye itself."[30]

A presentation of the eye as detached from personality and bias alluded symbolically to the supposed independence and precision of Dutch ocular science. Such analogies were perhaps picked up from Western claims to objectivity in vision, whose core they formed. Jean-Jacques Scheuchzer, for example, wrote of the eye in his influential *Physique sacrée* of the 1730s as "a camera obscura of an infinite kind, and without which all the beauties of the world would be nothing."[31] Objectivity was strenuously held to be possible in Europe, and consequently also argued for by *Rangaku* commentators, and yet in the Japanese context such a notion might carry rather little metaphysical ballast, and even seem quaint. The very sense of objectivity had few resonances in Japanese thought. "Authenticity" (*makoto*) or the correlation of personal sentiment with the dictates of social position, that is, sincerety, was an emphatic intellectual demand, and the surety, indeed, of harmony between human society and cosmic phenomena. But to extract oneself from oneself and to see without the prescriptions of time and moment would have been a wayward proposition. How (if at all) might a decontextualised, "objective" gaze be restrained by morality?

Santo Kyōden was always ready to turn curious matters of intellectual enquiry into springboards for humorous rescripting of the popular experience, and he wrote a kibyoshi on the theme of eyes in 1786, illustrating it himself. The book, *Kagekiyo and the Seven Bad Eye-opening Tricks (Aku shichi henme Kagekiyo),* takes its lead from the story of Kagekiyo, hero of a nō theatre play culled from the *Tales of the Heike*. Sadly deoculated by his enemy, the Genji, after defeat, Kagekiyo lives out his days in darkened solitude, visited finally by his long-lost daughter.[32] The story had recently returned to prominence in a kabuki version (kabuki being popular and urban in a way that aristocractic nō was not), and in 1778, the great actor Ichikawa Danjūrō V took Kagekiyo's role, publicly dedicating the performance to the memory of his own father, who had died six weeks before.[33] In the original versions, the loss of Kagekiyo's eyes ends his ability for action, and he retires to a life of meditation in a humble hut. But for Kyōden, the gouging of the eyes was where the story started, for the plucked-out eyes, now operating without reference to the body, take it upon themselves to launch a vendetta against Kagekiyo's and his Heike loyalists' foes. These detached eyes never lose their ethical awareness; rather, the whole body's moral purpose is concentrated into their two small spheres. The eyes are both independent and constrained by codes of honour.

The Genji erect a check-point at the entrance to their stronghold of Kamakura in case the eyes try to infiltrate and assassinate the leader, Yoritomo, the future shogun (an oversized official is seen seated in the guard-box; Fig. 96). The barrier is called Eyeblock Point (*Hitome no Seki*), a plausible and military-sounding name but properly the term meant a baffle erected by women around their boudoires to keep out prying eyes. The barrier forms the focus of a romp through every kind of punning jibe on the subject of eyes,

96. Santō Kyōden, from his *Akushichi henme Kagekiyo*, 1786. National Diet Library, Tokyo. *Eyeblock Point.*

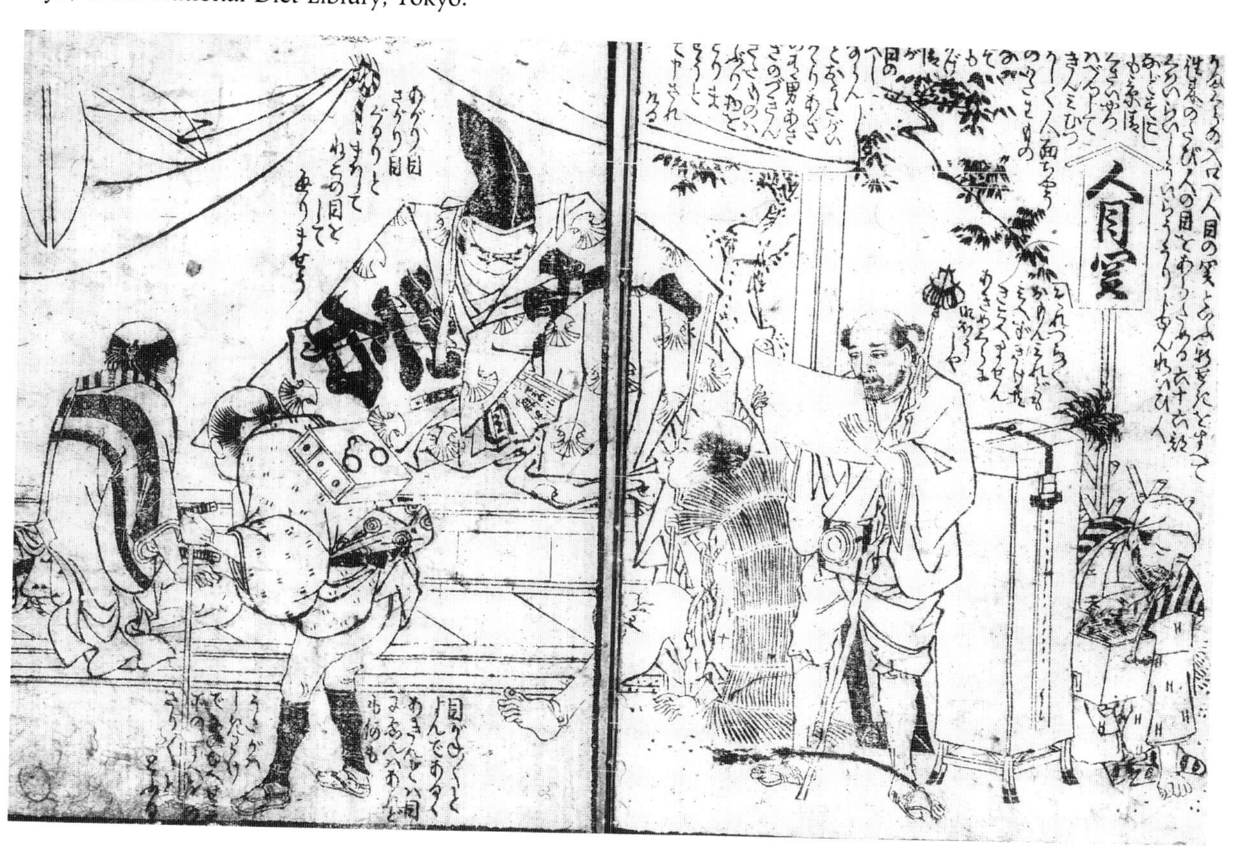

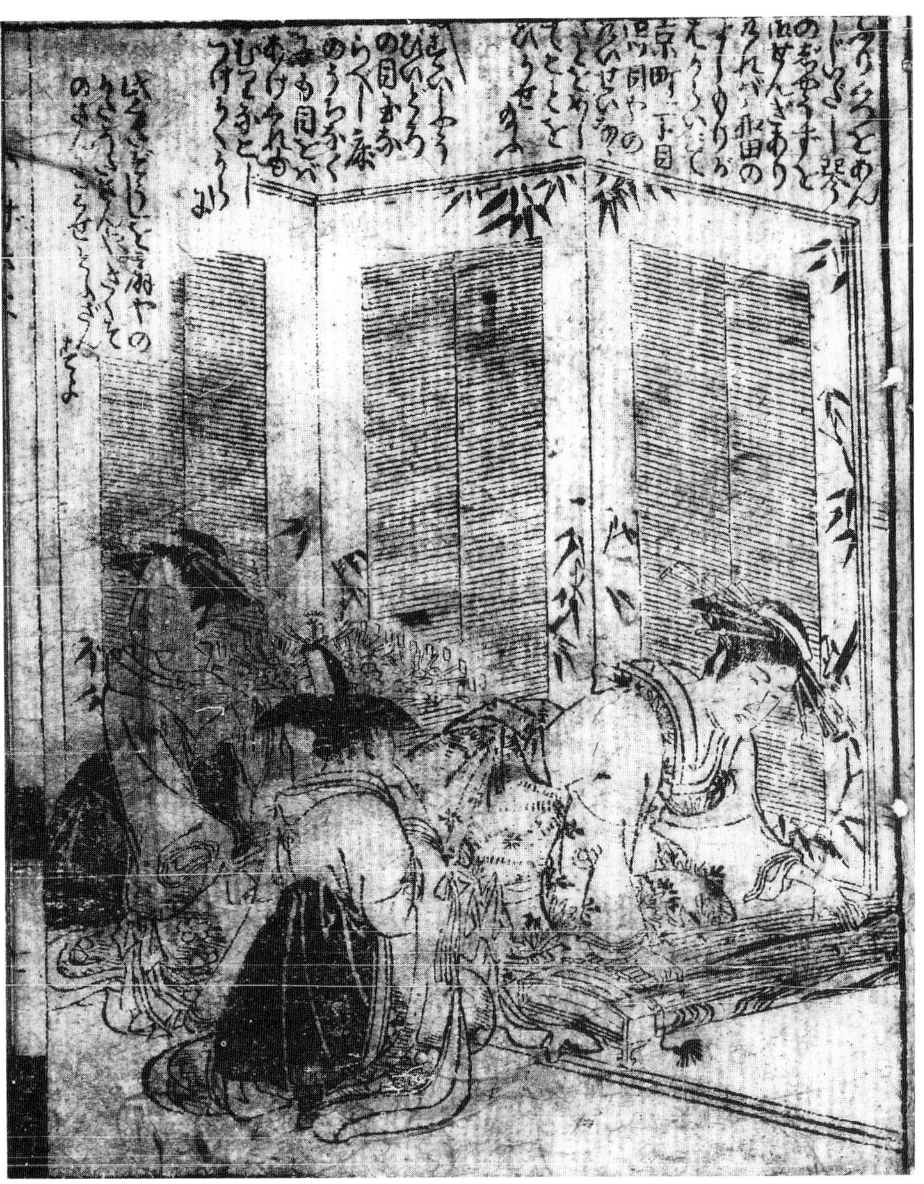

as various people present themselves for admission: Cangxie, the Chinese sage said to have invented written characters and who had double pupils; Oyadama, the three-eyed monster; the Zen patriarch Bodhidharma, whose eyes were those of an Indian. A pantomine horse clops in with eyes resembling Danjūrō V – as his filial performance associated him with the narrative, Danjūrō had to be brought in somewhere, and the characteristic upturned shape of the star's eyes made them instantly recognisable; but Danjūrō was also known for the piercing way in which he glared on stage – a manner he had inherited from his father – and, as Gennai put it, "even to a three-year old child, 'Danjūrō' makes you think of transfixing someone with a stare (*niramu*)."[34] Who more appropriate to batter at the gates of Eyeblock Point?

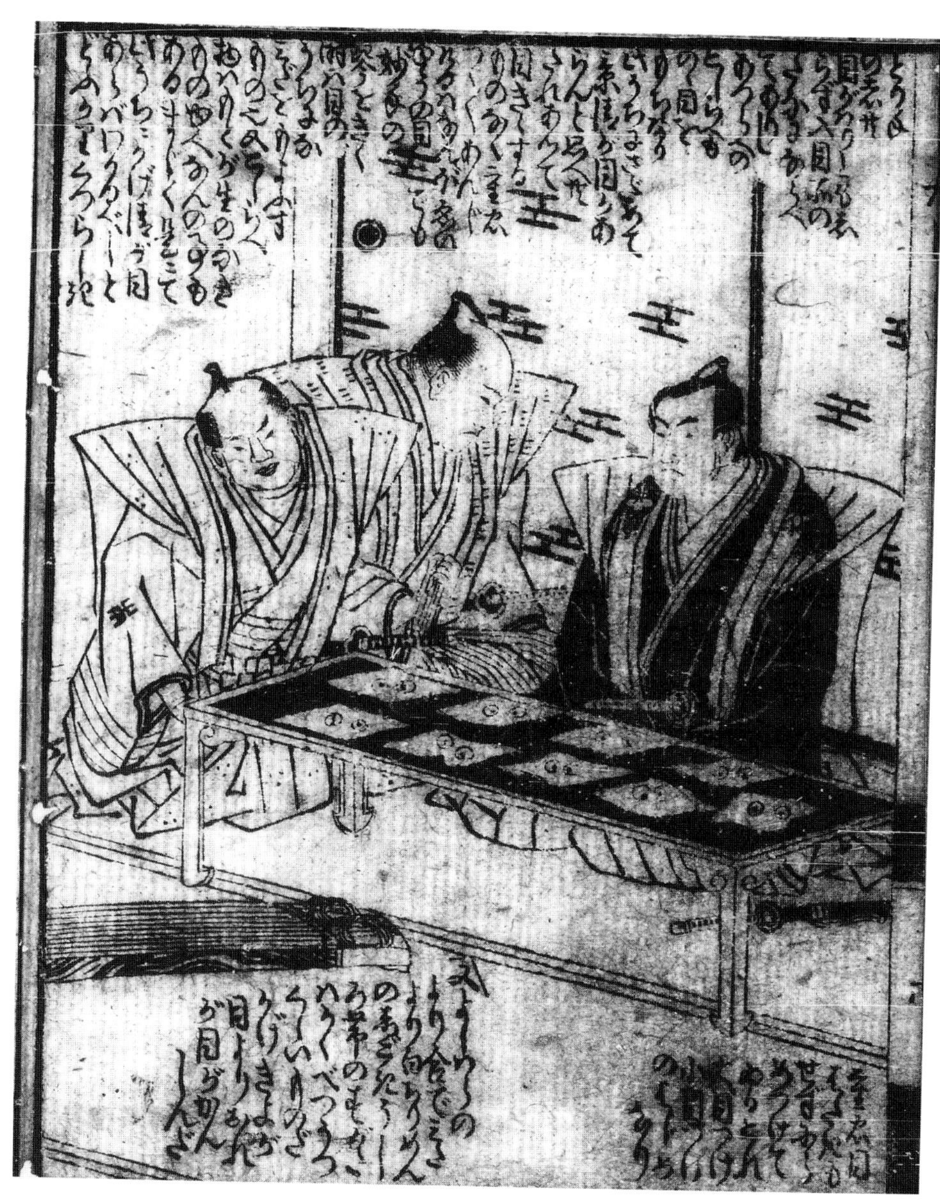

97. Santō Kyōden, from his *Akushichi henme Kagekiyo,* 1786. National Diet Library, Tokyo.

Kagekiyo's lover plays music to real and false eyes.

Another Genji contingent goes out with a "wanted" sign depicting Kagekiyo's eyes (again looking like Danjūrō's);[35] they pause anachronistically outside the sign of Tsutaya Jūsaburō's shop (Kyōden's publisher) and question the locals, who only mistake the troops for wandering medicine-sellers, and offer no help. A third band eventually runs across the offending organs hiding out among some glass eyes in a doctor's surgery. The stock is scooped up and brought before Yoritomo; but telling the real eyes from the glass ones proves difficult, until Kagekiyo's lover (now depicted as a Yoshiwara courtesan rather than a mediaeval lady) is summoned in the hope that, before her, the real eyes will unwittingly reveal their identity (Fig. 97). The woman is made to play music on the *koto,* and as Kagekiyo was a sensitive soul as well as a brave warrior, his eyes

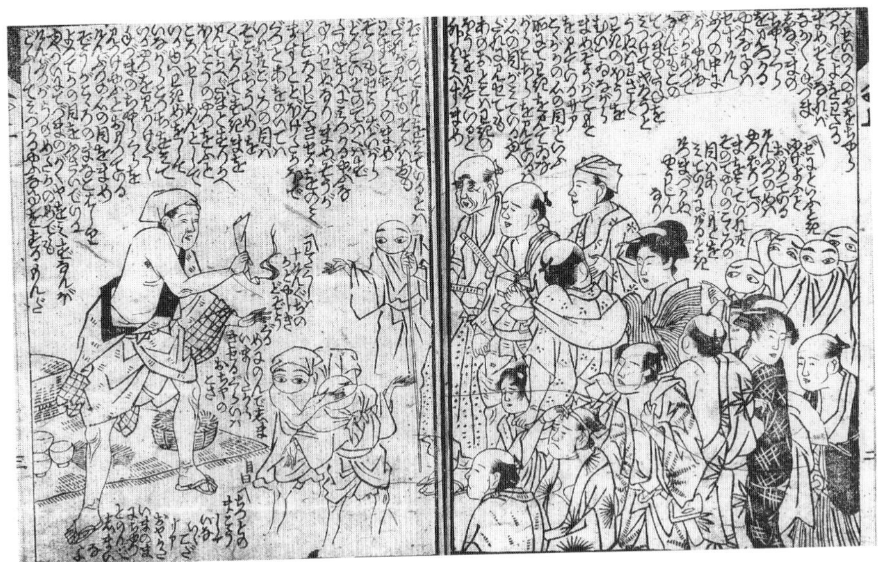

98. Jippensha Ikku, from his *Yome tōme kasa no uchi*, 1797. National Diet Library, Tokyo.

Fire-eater and audience with heart's eyes obscuring empirical vision. Note eye motif on extremities of margin.

break down and weep, giving themselves away. Throughout the story, the independence of the eyes as they pursue their mission serves to emphasise the shining quality of Kagekiyo's character; the metaphor of a "detached" eye becomes a literal parting of company between vision and body, with purpose equivalently strengthened. But these eyes at no stage lose their attachment to the social directives under whose regime they had dwelt before severance.

Jippensha Ikku wrote a kibyoshi on a similar theme some ten years later in 1797, contrasting the depersonalised vision of the eye, vouchsafed by its new-found mechanical composition, with the empirical fact that in actual life people used the organ in encoded ways. His story came out with illustrations by himself as *Night View, Far off and under a Hat (Yome tōme kasa no uchi).*[36] The title refers to the three criteria said to be essential for judging a woman's beauty: she must look good at night, far off, and half-hidden beneath a hat. But Ikku refers to the fact that all three situations are in reality moments of semi-concealment, and he alerts the reader to the fact that within the old expression lurks an assumption that loveliness is primarily a matter of occluding vision. Ikku dwells on the appearance versus reality dichotomy as the characters in the story conspire to compromise sight and keep up semblances. Ikku goes on to postulate humorously two pairs of eyes, the first routine, the second able to see beneath the surface – under the hat, through the dark, or into the faraway, which he calls "heart's eyes" (*kokoro no me*). Objective and moral vision can thus operate in tandem, but in this corrupt world the evidence of the two pairs proves frustratingly contradictory.

Ikku intended this book to stand as his contribution to the emerging debate on the eye, and in earnest of this he inscribed an eye motif on the outside margin of each page in the place properly reserved for the running title (Figs. 98, 106).[37] In preface, the author cited the ancient simile that Genpaku had scorned of the eyes being like sun and moon, but he took the old cliché literally: moon and sun appear in alternation, so that what they see is seldom the same; this matched the discrepancy between empirical vision and sight deep into the heart. Ikku illustrated in his pictures small anthropomorphic "heart's eyes" as moving invisibly among the characters in the story, devoting themselves to orchestrating situations of self-flattery and deceit, massaging egos and spying out openings for advantage. When the heart's eyes are clear, said Ikku, thirty thousand worlds will become visible at a glance – that is, humanity will see with the Buddhas' heavenly eyes, galactic in range and ever true. All too often these gum over and cloud, leading to vanity. As he put it, "there are those who have eyes but see not, and there are those who are blind but see."[38] Ikku told of heart's eyes' vacillation and infirmity in their duties, but how they were also potent enough to intrude upon and subvert the objectivity of vision.

The first illustration shows a roadside entertainer amusing a crowd with fire-eating tricks. He shouts his cant and brandishes a flaming pipe that he is about to swallow: "I've swallowed a twenty-metre storehouse in my time, so a pipe's not going to present much problem!" he boasts as the crowd stares on. But a struggle can be seen taking place in the foreground: the showman's heart's eyes are trying to smother the gaze of the crowd so his cheating will not be spotted; the heart's eyes of the crowd, meanwhile, are lurking at the back and waiting for the performance to draw to a close so they can sprint before the collection bag comes round.

Other scenes show the similarly self-serving actions of contemporary urban people: a monk prepares a corpse for burial while his heart's eyes weigh up the value of the shroud to estimate whether the dead man's relatives are the type to offer a lavish fee, while the corpse's own heart's eyes have gone to check that no one has found his cash box; on another page the faithful forty-seven from the *Treasury of Loyal Retainers (Chūshingura)* are shown blustering about revenging their lord's ignominious fate, while their heart's eyes seek only avenues for appeasement (the good Yuranosuke alone counsels caution, although his heart's eyes have already left to do the noble deed).[39]

What is called for is less "objectivity," and more "authenticity," that is, a matching up of heart and surface pretence. When the Genji soldiers had gone looking for Kagekiyo's fleeing eyes and carried their wanted sign depicting the organs, the reader had been invited to find a pun: the sign was referred to as an *e-sugata*, a "pictorial likeness," but this sounded like *me-sugata*, and "eye-likeness." *E-sugata* normally meant a physiognomist's chart, that is, a way to tell character through facial type. Physiognomy (*sōmi* or *sōgaku*) was part of the baggage of human analysis common to all in the period. Physiognomists inspected clients with the aid of large magnifying glasses before measuring them up against charts for assessment. The term for such lenses was evocative: *tengan-kyō*; "all-seeing glasses" or, more literally translated, "heaven's eye-glasses." They elucidated something more profound than appearances – that is, what was beneath – and allowed the user to see deeply like the heavenly eyes of Buddha.

Utamaro was a physiognomy enthusiast as well as a celebrated print-maker, and indeed he often signed his works Utamaro the Physiognomist (*sōmi* or *kansō Utamaro*; Pl. 10 and Fig. 125). He used the image of the face-inspecting loupe in a set of prints examining various types of woman, and although overtly in the standard *bijin* ("beautiful women") genre, the series aspires in a fairly serious way to depict recurrent traits of female character, identified via particularities in the face; the magnifying glass is prominently drawn on the picture, and the series title written within the lens, *Five Physiognomies of Woman (Go mensō bijin*; Fig. 99). Human type was diverse, and five was a number dictated more by the requirements of a market-oriented publisher (Tsuruya Kinsuke in this case) than of divination. But Utamaro was still able to map out a few parameters. This woman is "apparantly effete and mild-mannered, but she actually forces her opinions through. In general, a physiognomy that at least seems to have a trustwor-

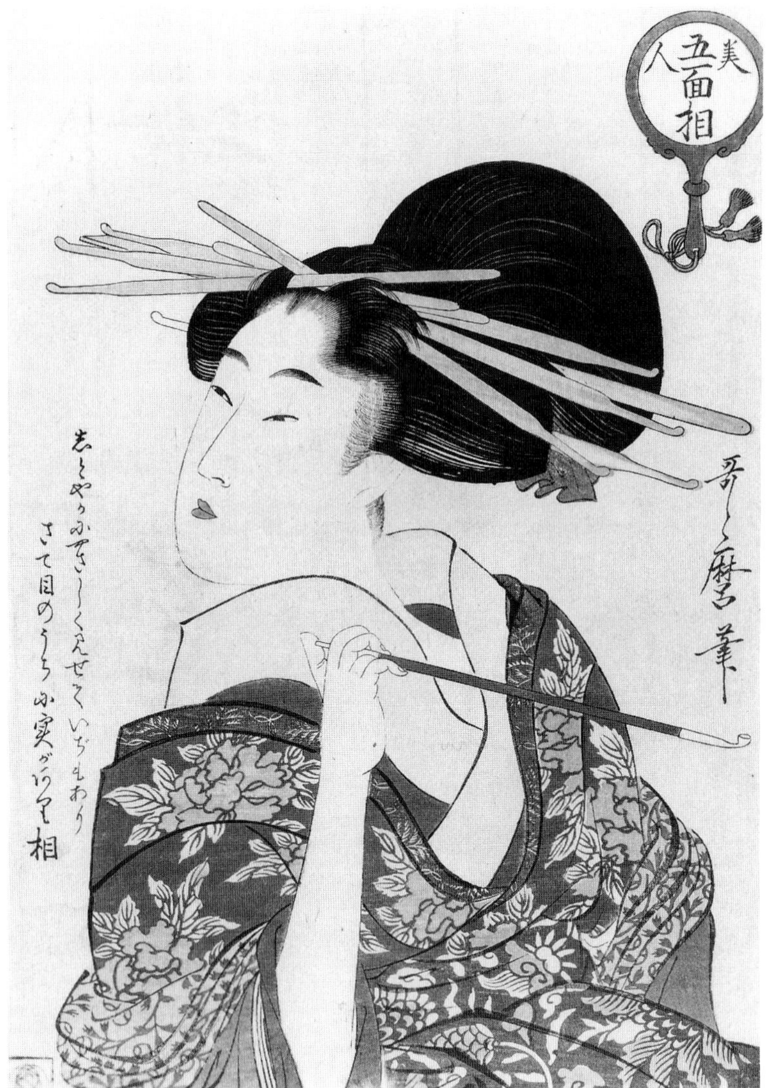

99. Kitagawa Utamaro, *Woman with Pipe*, colour woodblock print from the series *Bijin gomensō*; c. 1800. Print Collection, Miriam & Ira D. Wallack Division of Art, Prints & Photographs, New York Public Library, Astor, Lenox & Tilden Foundations.

thy look in the eye." The eyes are the crux of the analysis.[40]

At the close of his Kagekiyo story, Kyōden had provided a portrait of the well-known male geisha, Mekichi (Fig. 100). The title had prepared the reader for this by alluding to Mekichi's "seven eye tricks" (*shichi henme*), a parlour performance that enjoyed great success in the 1780s.[41] Mekichi (whose name means "eye-joy") had specialised in monologues the narration of which was accompanied by sudden character changes assisted by a swapping of masks known as "eye-wigs" (*me-katsura*). Mekichi wears one in the final picture, and a second can be seen ready on the ground. Seven was an unlucky number, so the seven eye tricks have now become *aku*, "bad," but this also puns on Kagekiyo's family name or style, Akushichibyōe.

Masks were common in the nō theatre and were used to designate stock personae (the good

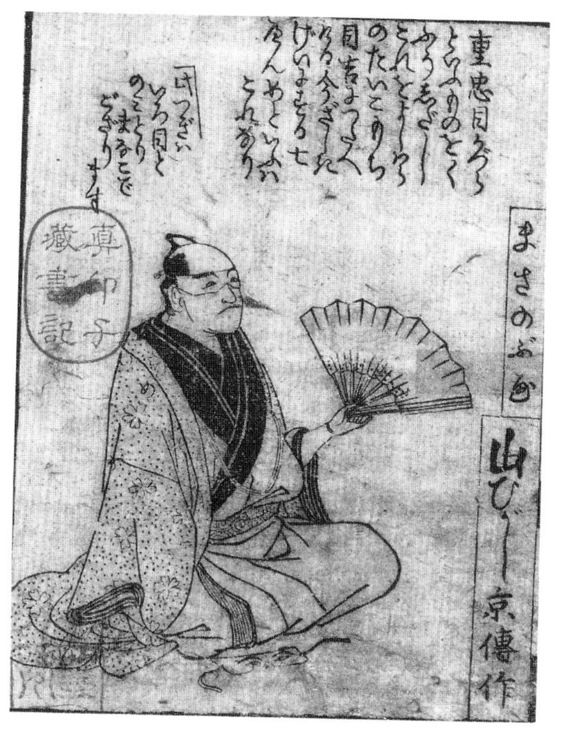

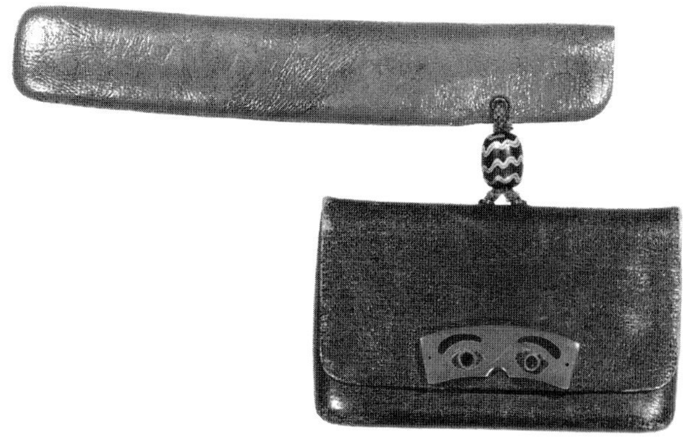

100 (left). Santō Kyōden, from his *Akushichi henme Kagekiyo*, 1786. Tokyo Metropolitan Central Library.

Final page with Mekichi and eye-wigs (with modern library stamp).

101 (above). Pipe case and tobacco pouch; leather and metal; early 19th century. Tobacco & Salt Museum, Tokyo.

wife, the foolish old man, the young hero, and so on), but the idea of covering only the eyes and eyebrows to create character seems to have originated with Mekichi's teacher, Shigetada who, Kyōden said, passed the idea on to him. Some of Mekichi's eye-wigs showed affective mood and were donned to undergo emotional change; others were fixed types – the good, the bad, the old or young – capturing personalities through the appearance of their eyes alone.

Eye-wigs soon became the rage. Kyōden included them in a collection of spoof textile motifs, *New Ideas in Cloth Design (Komon shinpō)*, his first volume, published in 1786, the success of which gave rise to the longer *Elegant Chats on Cloth Design (Komon gawa)* four years later. On one page Mekichi's seven masks are arranged into a decorative pattern such as one might turn into a kimono or towel.[42] Miniature eye-wigs were made for attaching to clothing or pinning onto accessories to show how the wearer was *au fait* with the latest entertainment trends. But such things also suggested an awareness of a certain transformation in the status accorded the eye. By Mekichi's analysis, eyes were the defining characteristics. A reduced-size wig is seen fixed onto a tobacco pouch fabricated from Persian leather (the source of most top-quality hide in Japan) and made probably at the turn of the century. Kyōden, as a tobacconist, may have sold such fashionable pieces. The cut-out eyeholes allow the material beneath to show through like irises; the leather is blue-green so that the eyes appear coloured – as bright as the eyes of a Red-fur, pretending to the precision of *Ran* (Fig. 101).

As Ikku and Kyōden wrote about the eye, it was not surprising that Shikitei Sanba, third in the triumvirate of turn-of-the-century best-selling writers should do so too. As part of a comic encyclopaedia, *Ono no Bakamura's Phoney Dictionary (Ono no Bakamura uso ji-zukushi)*, of 1806,

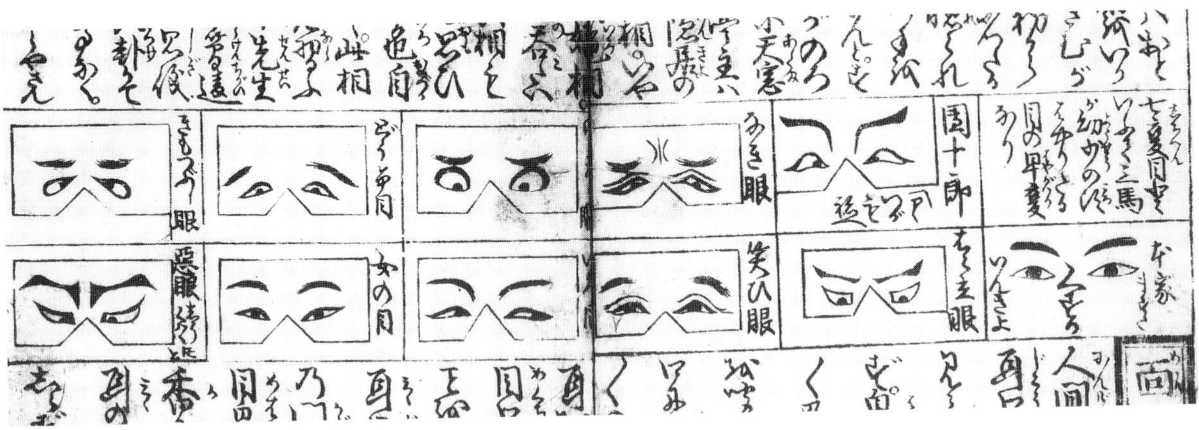

102. Shikitei Sanba, from *Ono no Bakamura uso jizukushi*, 1806. National Diet Library, Tokyo. *Physiognomy of the eye, shown in eye-wigs.*

he reproduced a witty physiognomical chart.[43] Sanba outlined the principle in the preface: "People's hearts are not all the same, as is told in their features. Physiognomy does not attempt to reform humanity, only to discern the heart through the face." In the eye section, Sanba did not show real eyes, only eye-wigs, drawn as if laid out ready for use in a Mekichi-style narrative (Fig. 102). Mekichi stressed the importance of the eye but also, insofar as he had seven different sets at his disposal, he showed how eyes were also falsifiable according to private need. No matter how many parts he acted out as he swapped his masks, it was always him underneath. So, it was the quick-change, falsifying masks that Sanba ultimately made stand for sense not actual eyes; misprision beckons. The Bakamura physiognomist has to cope with deliberate confustication, as the deep signification of the eyes obscures itself beneath an inauthentic veil and people strain to screw up their faces into the most expedient type molding eye-wigs out of their own flesh. Sanba recorded where his whole spoof eye-physiognomy idea had come from: "When the present author was a young lad [he was born in 1776], there was something about called the 'seven eye tricks'; it was the latest thing, and consisted of making transformations quickly with the eyes." Mekichi, with his perpetual mask-wearing, seemed to have no eyes of his own at all and to be just an unstable sequence of other people's. But although seeming to supporting this in his suggestion that no one has any eyes at all, only eye-wigs, Sanba actually provided the reverse: to the scholar or connoisseur, truth will always manifest itelf behind the lies thanks to the science of physiognomy. The first wig shown is the eyes of Danjūrō, distinctively twisting up at the corners. As an actor, Danjūrō assumed many roles, but his ocular trait was unconcealable to those who knew him. In place of the exegesis that appeared with the other examples, Sanba wrote only Danjūrō's name, and under it a fan's cat-call, "absolutely brilliant!" (*aa tsugamon*). All stage roles are played by Danjūrō, but the gallery knows it is him.

Physiognomy was a necessary art in the rapidly expanding early-modern Japanese city, where for the first time people did not know the family lineage of their neighbours, provoking a very modern source of worry. But as an analytical system, was the art of reading the face sufficiently exact? Utamaro had five (elsewhere ten) types of woman. Mekichi had seven masks; most typographies of physiognomy went far beyond. But even the most exhaustive listings could barely be comprehensive enough to deal with all mutations of personality. All people trimmed and tacked contextually, making the permanent isolation of anyone within a fixed category nigh on hopeless, as people were honest one moment and not the next. What was needed was a means of achieving a gaze that evinced meaning across a shifting spectrum, a kind of wandering "heaven's eye-glass." Moreover, as reading the face was a common need, it was dangerous to leave physiognomic analysis to the intermittently appearing specialist. Everyone required permanent access to each other's interiors, and the skill of finding out could no longer be the preserve of academics. As Sanba said, in the closing words of the physiognomy page of his *Phoney Dictionary*, "what we really need is a special kind of magnifying glass implanted in the human chest." Sanba wanted to pierce right through the externals to see the flitting motivations and contingent truths underneath, but with an easy-to-use lens like an open glass window into the innards.

SPECTACLES

When Yoritomo set up Eyeblock Point in the Kagekiyo story, many suspicious characters tried to force their way through (Fig. 96). One was an itinerant glasses seller who approached hawking his goods, calling, "*Megane! megane!*" – "Glasses! glasses!" The man was thought to be suspicious on account of his wares, for glasses are made to help eyes out. Might not he be in league with Kagekiyo's eyes?

Medicine treated ailments of the eye with salves, and *Rangaku* doctors might go further by judicious application of their anatomically based surgery, which could bring the faculty of sight up to its highest physiologically possible level. But if really close scrutiny was required, one had recourse to a lens. The "heaven's' eye-glass" was a specialist instrument; more current were spectacles. Glasses had existed in Japan for some decades, and the first pair were said to have been given to Tokugawa Ieyasu by the Europeans at the turn of the sixteenth century. Glasses sellers began to be a regular feature of Edo-period life only some hundred and fifty years later, although throughout there would still have remained plenty of people who knew them only by repute. An encyclopaedia of regional products published in 1732 gave the main features of the lens in language intended for a still largely unfamiliar public, the author, Mitaku Yorai, explaining in a memorable phrase, glasses "are about 3 mm thick and look like the chopped slices of giant radish."[44] Rough-and-ready spectacles made of crystal and suchlike were constructed in Japan as Yorai stated, and were used by the weak-eyed, the elderly, or those engaged in intricate work (swordsmiths, seal carvers, inlayers) (Fig. 27). But these would not have been pleasant to use, being ponderously heavy while offering a magnification that was not very great. Yorai noted that although glasses were now manufactured domestically, "in former times they came from China." Early crystal ones had, but the lighter glass lensed sort now came, as the *Illustrated Universal Encyclopaedia (Wakan sansai zue)* reported, via the Dutch and were European in origin.[45] "Putting on bits of glass to look at things," announced a miscellany of 1830, "was first of all a Western thing to do."[46] Already by the seventeenth century the import of spectacles was accounting for fully one percent of the total value of the Dutch–Japan trade: in 1636 this represented 19,425 pairs sold, a figure that nearly doubled the following year, to 38,421 (although there were also years when imports fell).[47] When Kōkan fashioned a pair of glasses himself in 1788, he found the most appropriate audience for approbation not in a Chinese scholar but in Yoshio Kōsaku, the person most familiar with European material culture.[48]

The tens of thousands of imported glasses were distributed through a network of urban shops or in country areas by pedlars, such as the one who approached Eyeblock Point. Specialist opticians (*megane-ya*) opened during the eighteenth century, one famous establishment being the Murano-ya in Asakusa, near the Temple of Kannon, the appearance of which was recorded as one of a series of shops in that part of Edo made by an old friend of Kyōden's from his days in Shigemasa's atelier, Kubo Shunman (Fig. 4). Shunman showed the sign outside Murano's identifing the merchandise as "Dutch glass goods" (*Oranda gyoku shinajina*). The stock went beyond simple spectacles to include all manner of glass objects: telescopes, flasks, wine glasses, mirrors, and mirror pictures. It is intriguing to speculate on a possible connexion between the name of the Murano shop in Edo and the great Italian glass-making island identically called in the Venetian lagoon.[49] Despite the claims, though, it is quite likely that many of Murano's goods were domestically manufactured (not the glass lenses which could not be ground locally, the minor affairs) but, as so often, the appeal to *Ran* was made to enhance the curio value of the objects and their aura of precision. To play up Dutchness to the full was not the exclusive tactic of Murano's, for all *megane-ya* did the same; as late as 1824, four out of the seven known glasses shops in Edo were claiming their goods to be "Dutch."[50]

The terminology of lensed instruments was as vague as the products were new. Pretty well all sorts, whether glasses, telescopes, microscopes, loupes, or *optiques* came under the definition of *megane*. Beyond these well-known types was a host of others, many since fallen from use: "scratch-*megane*" (*kizu-megane*) for examining minor imperfections on sword blades; "moon-viewing *megane*" (*tsuki-megane*) for autumn evenings, and "fire-raising *megane*" (*hidori-megane*) for lighting pipes.[51] This range was further expanded by the powerful Edo myth-making machine, and as few owned glasses of any sort or even had access to them on a regular basis, the imagination was free to run riot in devising all manner of additional would-be glasses for the perfection of seeing skills. Some sort of *megane* was said to be available to facilitate every task. Koikawa Yukimachi, the pupil of Harumachi, who had started out illustrating stories for Kyōden and Kisanji, wrote a kibyoshi on just this, blending real and fictional types together in a soup of visual excitement. Yukimachi's concoction came out in 1790 illustrated by Kitao Masayoshi, under the fanfare title of *Great Wealth Made through the Virtue of Glasses (Sakaemasu megane no toku)*. Yukimachi told of one Gyōemon (the reader knows this is the author in disguise[52]), a poor man come to Edo to seek his fortune. Gyōemon's is a modern-day success story, for by diligent application he works his way up in the world, first as a lens polisher and then as an itinerant seller of cheap glasses (ten pairs for three *mon*), until he is able to buy a shop and deal directly, becoming rich – all through the virtue of glasses. The spectacles that comprise his merchandise serve as a metaphor throughout the story and stand for Gyōemon's mature perception of the realities of this world, and his getting on with living regardless of severe initial challenges; he has seen the demands of pursuing his role with "sincerity" (*makoto*), has not shirked, and has reaped his financial rewards.

As time went by, the now-affluent Gyōemon had grown bored with banal sorts of glasses and, striving for access to other truths, invented new types to reveal rarer phenomena: "nearby-glasses" (*chika-megane*) enlarge the wearer's horizons and make close-up objects seem distant ("an ear-swab can look like a rice-spoon," and a lowly hovel appear as spacious as a palace) these *megane* remove spatial limitations, and users can expand themselves in the way they need. Gyōemon lends them to customers to increase the visual splash of his now-flourishing shop, and Yukimachi shows them being worn by a samurai client (Fig. 103) Gyōemon also has "mixed lenses," both microscope and telescope combined, able to assess the vast and the minute within a single gaze; "blindness-curing *megane,*" made by adding medicine to the lens; "literacy *megane*" for those who have never been taught to write, made by mashing up old books; and "scholar *megane*" as an equivalent to help with reading. Particularly useful are Gyōemon's "five-coloured *megane*" (*goshiki-megane*), a word properly meaning a prism but here twisted to imply colourisers; when donned they turn black-and-white pictures into works in full palette (Fig. 104). Harumachi had been part of the circle surrounding Harunobu and Gennai that had invented the technology for multi-coloured print-making some twenty years before; he is also credited with writing and illustrating the "first" kibyoshi (always a monochrome medium) in 1775; Harumachi had died, seemingly by his own hand, just months before the *Virtue of Glasses* appeared.[53] This was an amusing dig. Edo publishers now stock the instruments, Yukimachi says, and let browsing customers wear them, fooling them into thinking the books are of colour plates and charging them accordingly, deriving a huge profit.

The whole array of *megane,* one for every wish, is on sale at Gyōemon's shop. Its advertising awning lists a multitude of available products: lord's glasses, lovely-woman glasses, child glasses, fashion-king glasses, and more (Fig. 105). The shop, as well as being a tremendous joke, is revealing of the ultimate origin of this Edo realisation of the possibilities of mechanically improved perception, for the sign also identifies Gyōemon as a dealer in Dutch precision goods, as he also sells "Red-fur *karakuri*" and "miniature clocks"; Yukimachi informed the reader that customers came from as far away as Nagasaki and even from abroad – perhaps this means the VOC compound and the lands of *Ran.*

GLASSES FOR SEEING THINGS

Ikku's kibyoshi on the heart's eyes had examined how in social life empirical vision might not be enough to comprehend the sweep of experience. His story had not stopped at discussing the naked versus the heart's eye, but had incorporated the theme of vision-enhancing lenses; indeed, Ikku had constructed his whole tale as the narration of a pair of anthropomorphic glasses who mysteriously appear before the protagonist as he dozes off in his study. Empirical vision is insufficient and the chief character is called Chikame ("Myopic"); he only becomes truly sighted when spectacles lend their assistance. Both the jacket and first illustration had shown Chikame at his desk, the glasses having drifted out of the case in which they had been laid to rest, to sit before him, debonairly smoking a pipe (Fig. 106). "It's all thanks to me," they announce presumptuously, "that you can see things as they really are," and so saying the glasses go on to lead both dreamer and reader through the series of empirical versus heart's-eye sequences that makes up the body of the book.

Other writers also told of metaphysical sorts of *megane* that enhanced the moral vision, and Utamaro, for one, produced a series of prints under the title *Educational Glasses for Parents* (*Kyōkun oya no megane*);[54] this set included within the individual designs a running motif printed in the top right-hand corner showing a pair of spectacles, the title written in place of the lenses. One image is of "what's commonly called a canny one" (*zoku ni iū bakuren*), and depicts a woman drinking *vinho tinto* out of a fine imported glass, expensive fresh crab in hand (Fig. 107). As with his physiognomic magnifying-glass series, Utamaro wished to show a profundity elusive to the naked eye; but now no training is needed, for the artist has enlightened all; in the humorous terms of the print, any parent can check instantaneously the disposition of their (no doubt errant)

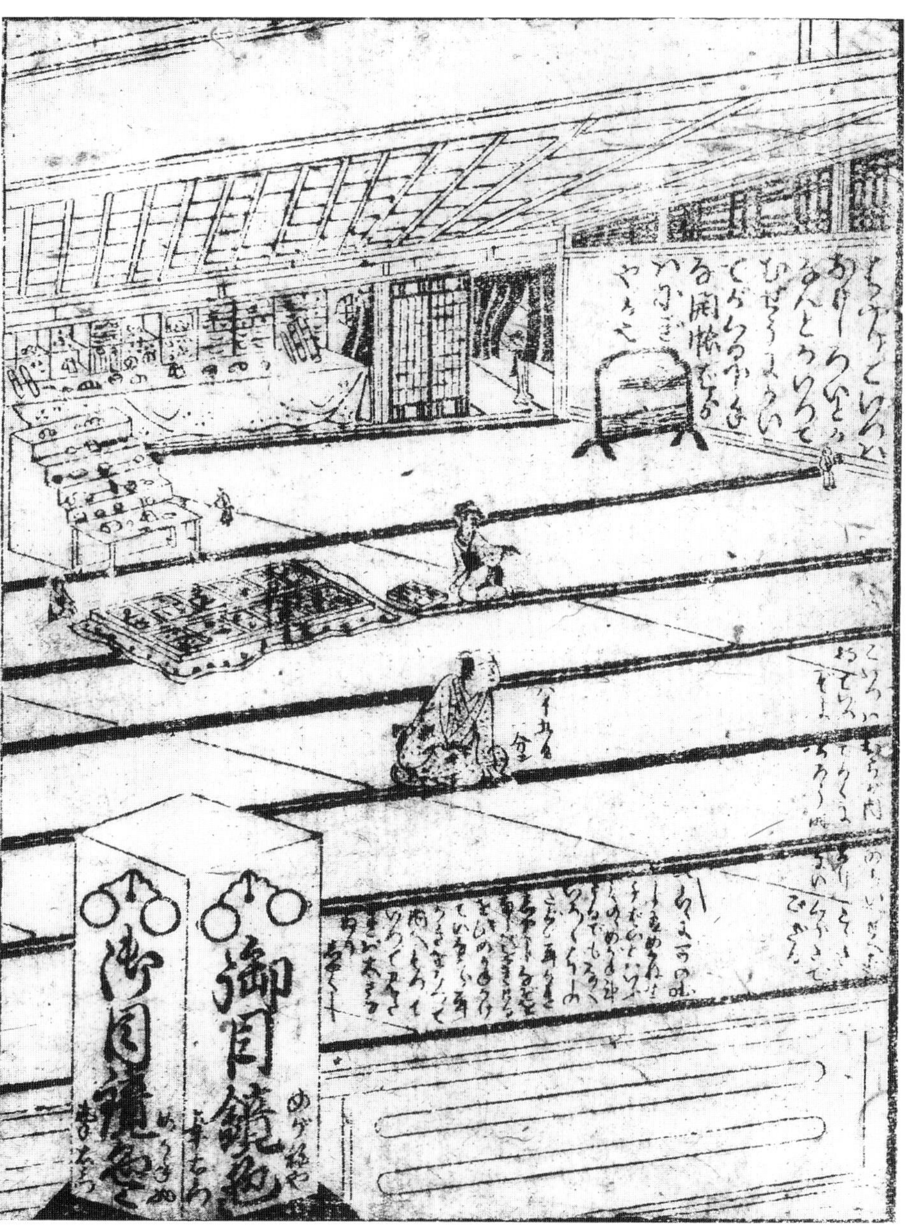

offspring. The inscription defines the feminine object, and informs us:

> Canny: one who seems to regard it as fair not to pay attention to how she is thought of by others, and sees even less reason to avoid talking about what others think is stupid. You might take her to be artless and guileless, but the truth is otherwise. It is not through any lack of social awareness that she ignores what is held to be proper and gives off the impression of being lax. What a waste of time it is to dwell on a woman who cannily writes off her social responsibilities.

Utamaro's viewers can study the type who will assume this insouciant air to ride roughshod

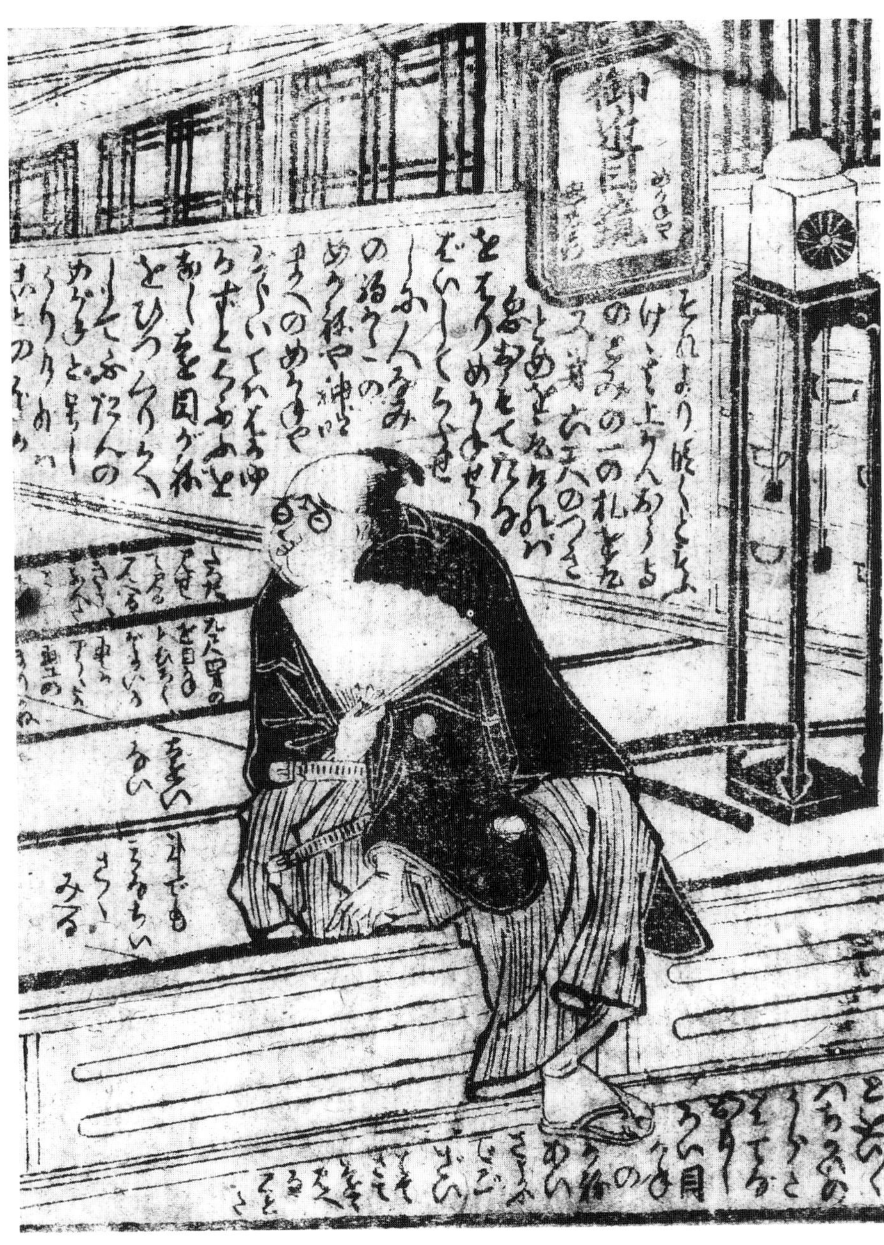

103. Kitao Masayoshi, from Koikawa Yukimachi, *Sakaemasu megane no toku*, 1790. National Diet Library, Tokyo.

A samurai dons glasses and finds his surroundings vastly expanded.

over others, and no longer need they fall victim to false naïvety when they encounter it again.

Glasses, being imported, were not to be had on a bespoken basis but were bought off the peg. They took scant account of individual requirements or astigmatisms. The preponderance were only mildly magnifying and not for regular use, but were donned as required to perform special tasks. Those who kept their glasses always on were rare enough to be worthy of comment; indeed, there appears to have been only one such person in the entire Edo period, Gijsbert Hemmij, kapitan of the Dutch Factory for five years from 1792. Hoshū, who met Hemmij several

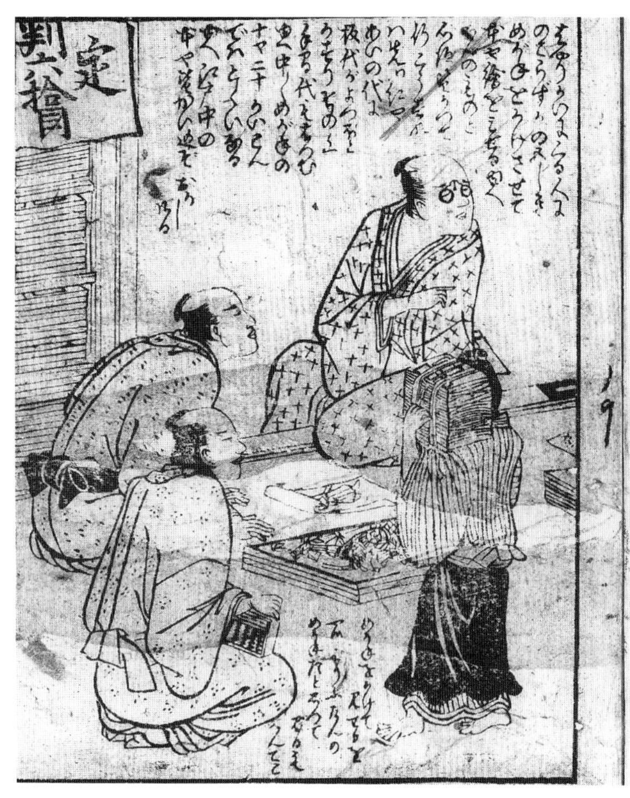

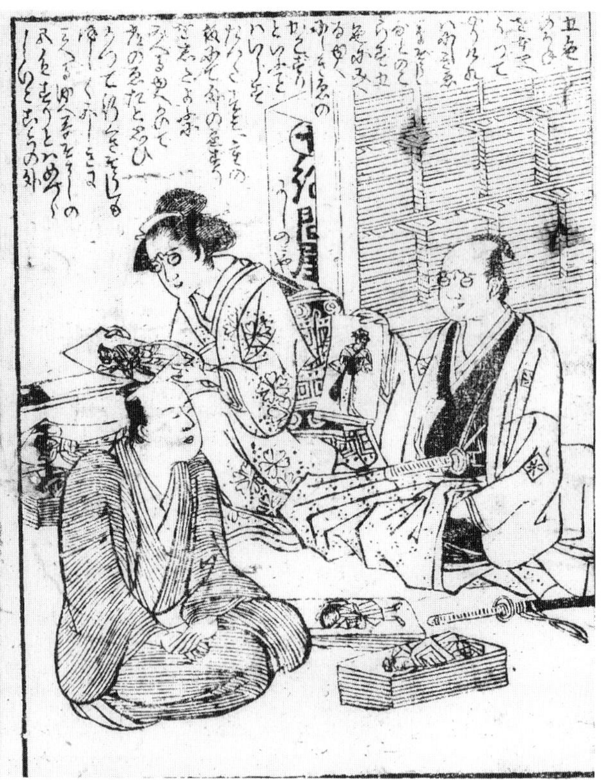

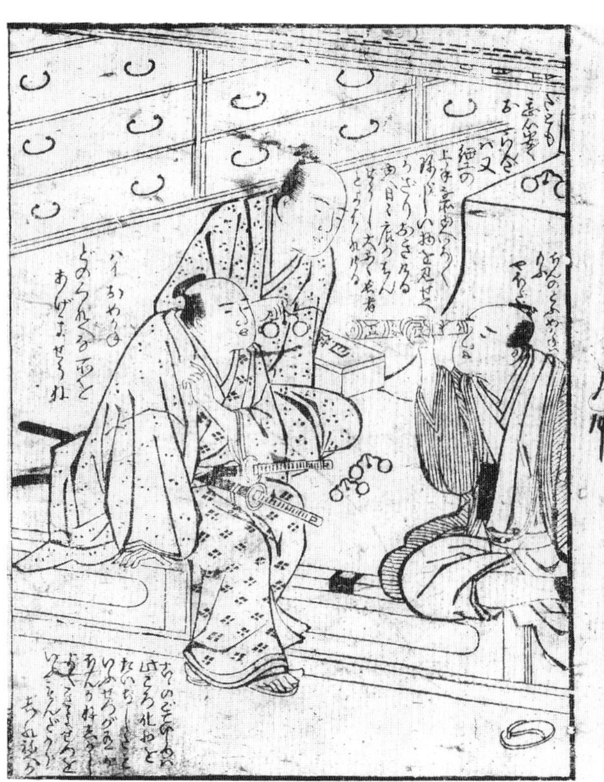

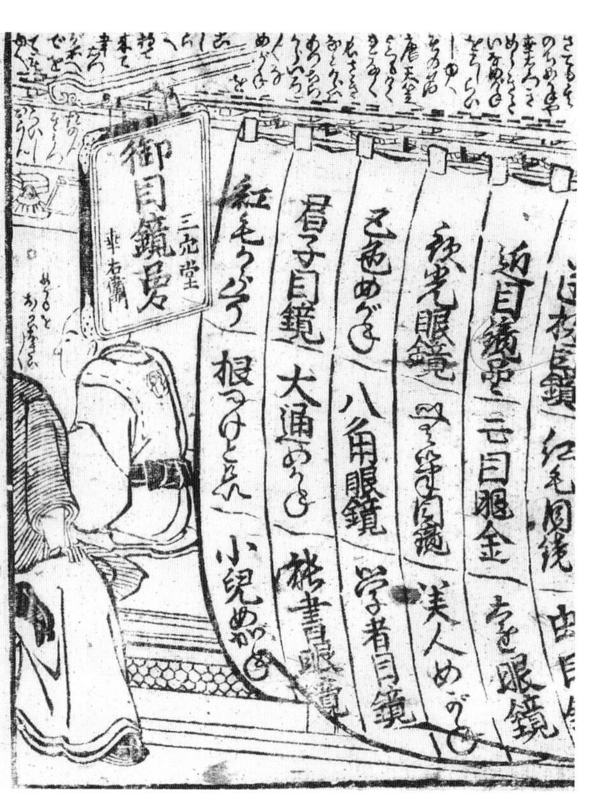
御目鏡屋
三光堂
近目鏡
君子目鏡
大通めがね
八角眼鏡
学者目鏡
美人めがね
小児めがね

104 (top, opposite page). Kitao Masayoshi, from Koikawa Masayoshi, *Sakaemasu megane no toku*, 1790. National Diet Library, Tokyo.

Customers try on glasses and experience monochrome prints in full colour.

105 (bottom, opposite page). Kitao Masayoshi, from Koikawa Masayoshi, *Sakaemasu megane no toku*, 1790. National Diet Library, Tokyo.

Glasses shop with its advertising awning.

106 (below). Jippensha Ikku, from his *Yome tōme kasa no uchi*, 1797. Tokyo Metropolitan Central Library.

Anthropomorphic glasses appear to Chikame as he dozes.

times at the Nagasaki-ya, recorded, "he is forty-four, has missing front teeth and wears his glasses all the time."[55] Hemmij's singularly probing optical hexis befitted his status as senior local representative of *Ran*. Perhaps for the same reason the kapitan himself was looked at askance; he fell into bad odour in Japan, becoming embroiled in accusations of spying and dying on his return from a *hofreis* under suspicious circumstances.[56] Through-the-lens vision was no right-thinking person's normal gaze but, rather, a uniquely eloquent restructuring of sight temporarily directed towards a particular end; lensed viewing would alternate with more prolonged periods of naked vision. The moment users perched a pair of spectacles on the nose, or fastened the securing string behind the ears, they announced that a special viewing was about to begin, and that the object before the gaze was to be scrutinised unusually acutely. Perhaps it was for this reason that eighteenth-century Korean children were forbidden to wear

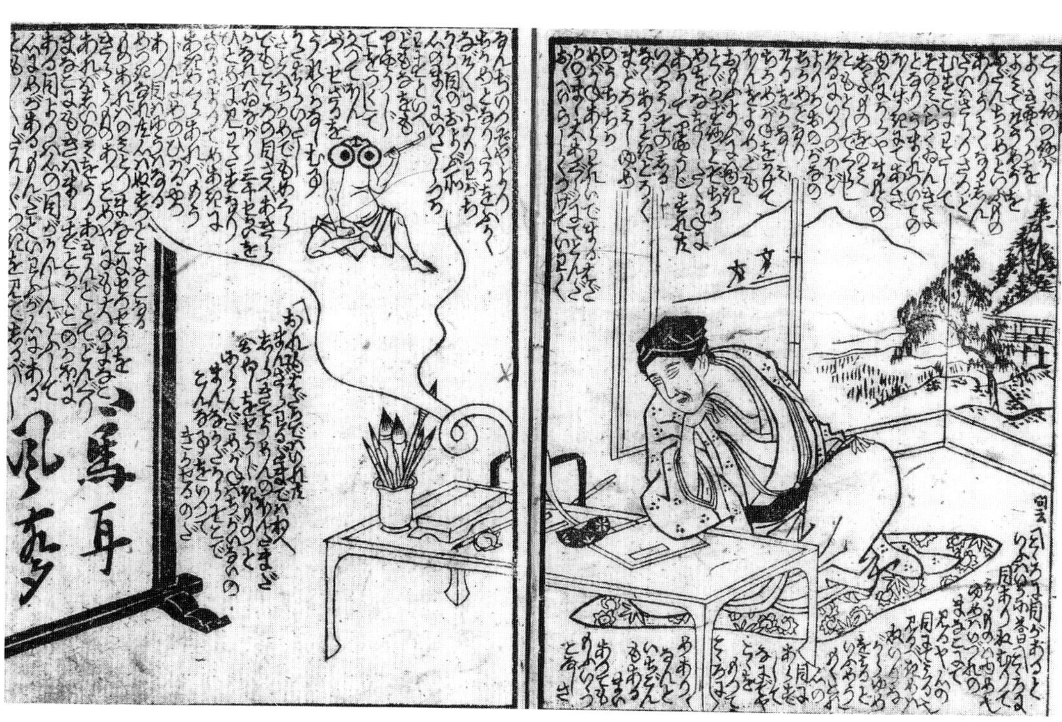

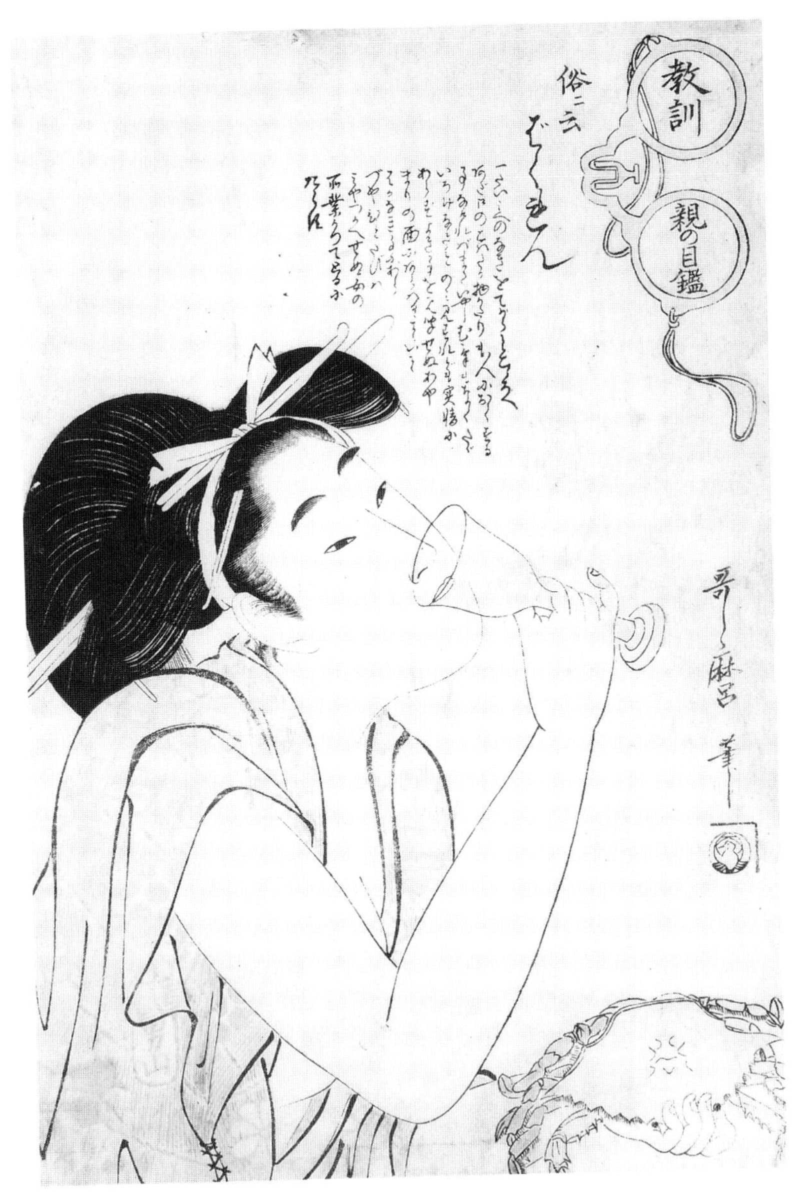

107. Kitagawa Utamaro, *A Canny One*, colour woodblock print from the series *Kyōkun oya no megane*; c. 1800. British Museum.

glasses in front of their parents, the piercing gaze of the wearer being considered simply rude.[57] When eyes disappeared behind lenses it became unclear just what they were perceiving; shielded and immune from inspection, they gave no quarter. English children call glasses-wearers "four-eyes," but in fact they appear rather the opposite, less four-eyed than no-eyed, pupils obscured by chunks of giant radish. As Yukimachi himself had punned, to wear *megane* was not only to see better but also to become oneself suddenly "eyeless" (*me ga nē*).[58] Like wearing dark glasses today, there was something arrogant about being bespectacled and seeing while giving nothing away. Glasses themselves could have a bumptious streak, and thus it was that

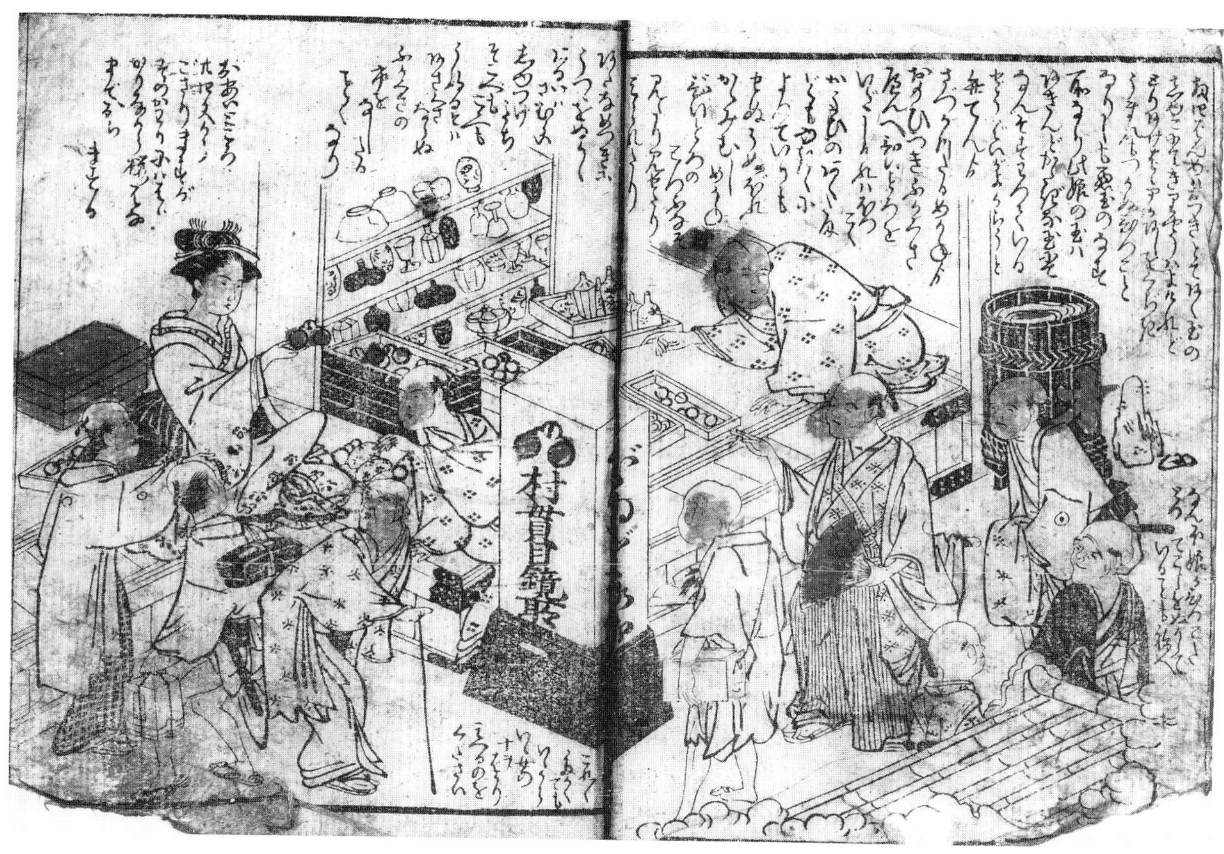

108. Harukawa Shūzan, from Santō Kyōden (attrib.), *Sanshōdayū shichinin musume*, 1794. Private collection. *The Muranuki-ya glasses shop.*

when Chikame's narrator-glasses popped from their case to infiltrate Ikku's story, they were said to appear "stark naked and sitting in a most arrogant posture" (the illustrations show them decently loin-clothed).[59]

Given the bullish mien that was to be had through a pair of glasses, it was worth owning a pair even if only for appearance's sake. The arrogant swagger they gave the wearer, the air of sober scrutiny that covered unleashed eyes, were thought by many to be worth the financial outlay. As if in response to this, glasses were generally considered neither medical equipment nor scientific instruments, but trappings. The *Universal Encyclopaedia* put them in the personal accessories section (*fuku-gangu*), lumped together with fans, back-scratchers, and hanging pockets (*inro*); a poet in 1778 made the point nicely, by listing the three requisite items for a fashionable man in the metrical count of a senryu,

> Braided clothing
> Honda hair with
> Glasses on to round it off.[60]

This being so, glasses could easily lose their precision-viewing role and decline into affected folly. Kyōden suggested as much in a kibyoshi, *The Seven Lovely Mimasu Sisters (Sanshōdayū*

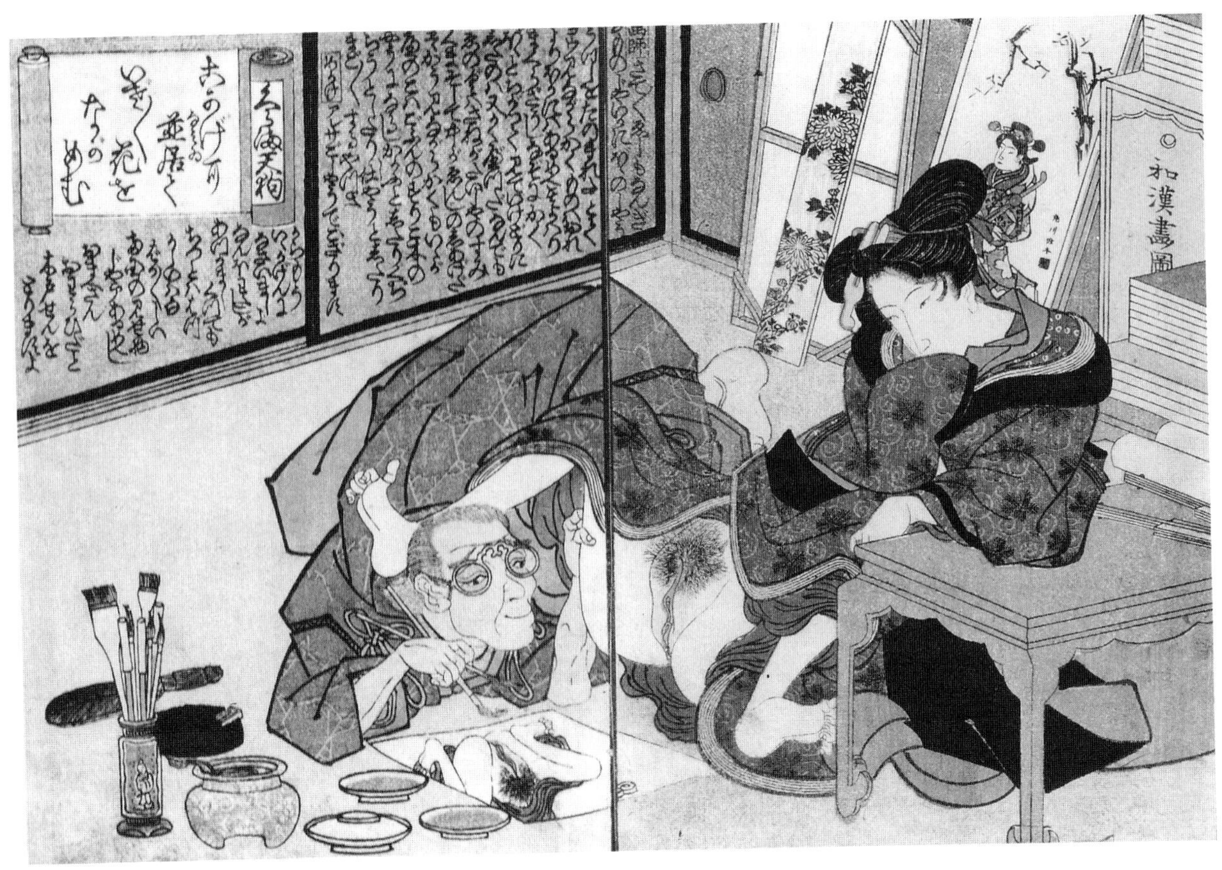

109. Utagawa Kunitora, colour woodblock page from anon., *Otome sugata*, 1826. Photo: Fukuda Kazuhiko.

shichinin musume), published in 1798, the year after Himmij's death and illustrated by Harukawa Shūzan.[61] The fourth of the women, O-tsuki, is said to be pretty but unable to walk, and so she drives a trade, going into the *megane* business and siting her shop in Asakusa (where the Murano-ya really was). O-tsuki uses as raw material a glass ball magically received from the god of success in enterprise, Daikoku, and clients come in droves (Fig. 108). They buy, says the text, "totally unnecessary" pairs of spectacles as an excuse to hang around the premises and exchange a few words, purchasing less in the hope of seeing better than of seeing *her*. The customers, moreover, note the extreme convenience of the location for visits to brothels, as one route to the Yoshiwara began from Asakusa. Even if the glasses are "rather expensive," one patron points out, "if you get to see ten good-looking girls though them, then the money's very well spent." (O-tsuki protests that at twenty-four *mon* apiece they cannot be regarded as over-priced.) All buyers announce themselves anxious to be equipped with precision instruments with which they can go and "rivet a provocative leer" on someone (*adana metsuki*).

Perhaps this kind of looking is what the "beautiful-woman *megane*" of Yukimachi's tale were for. The idea O-tsuki's patrons may have had in mind can be seen in any case in a book illustration by Kunitora, pupil of Kuniyoshi, executed in 1826 (Fig. 109). The picture, blatantly pornographic, is from *The Virgin's Appearance (Otome sugata)*, a book whose content need hardly be recounted, but the title also plays on the academic physiognomist's authenticity-finding chart (*e-sugata*). An old artist is seen smug behind his lenses, with all the paraphernalia of serious professionalism disposed around the room (half-finished works and boxes of copybooks labelled *The Art of China and Japan*); his glasses, too, might at first be taken to imply a close and disinterested vision. But his gaze, though certainly close, is not objective at all, only lustful, and the lenses provide subterfuge for decrepit desire, way out of step with how an old man should be. Much of the output of *ukiyo-e* artists was pornographic, and they were frequently charged with hiding prurience beneath a cloak of study; as a senryu poet noted:

> For artists of the Floating World
> Even looking at pussy
> Is called work.[62]

Kunitora plays the demi-monde Floating World genre against the rhetoric of accuracy derived from the lens and juxtaposes the two to generate an ironic text:

> ARTIST: Hey ho, it's a hard life for the painter! No matter how much I've been told to do the picture accurately from life (*shō-utsushi*), when I look at the thing as I work, I can't help wishing someone else had been given the commission. Accurate life studies like mine, let me tell you, are not to be confused with that filthy porn stuff you find around – oh no! – this work has a different quality entirely.[63]

The female sitter is no more fooled than the reader, and, perfectly aware of the situation, she counters: "I'm not some fairground display at Ryōgoku you know! Stop, sniggering idiot, or I'll charge you per peep." The folly of glasses was attendant (as Yukimachi put it) on their "virtue."

The genuine vision-enhancing sort of lens could turn against sincerity, a state of affairs greatly abetted by this consciously flattering and corrupt gazing. But there were also sorts of spectacles that deliberately fooled the eyes: "all-round glasses" (*happō megane*) were said to be worn by the Dutch on their fingers as rings, and although it is not clear just what these were, they evoke the term for a spineless sycophant (*happō-bijin*);[64] further, a number of types were associated exclusively with play, and specifically intended to subvert: there were "upside-down *megane*" (*sakasama-megane*), incorporating a mirror; and "times-three *megane*" (*yokomitsu-megane*) to give plural images; or, more extremely, "multiplication *megane*" (*sū-megane*). Gotō Rishun gave a reasonably full list of glasses in his *Talks on Holland (Oranda-banashi)*, including the above types and adding the obscure but intriguing "secret *megane*" (*sokai-megane*).[65]

Ikku's bumptious glasses had been aware of this double edge, for they had offered to show Chikame "everything as your heart desires it" (*kokoro no mama*), and if he had creditably asked only for authentic or sincere visions, others would no doubt have had less seriousness of mind. The notion that lenses might not only aid the asininity of their wearers but actually encourage lying was available. The possibility was taken up by Sakuragawa Jihinari in a kibyoshi that appeared the same year as Ikku's, 1797, and was surely intended as its rival. Illustrated by Toyokuni, the book was entitled *Fukutokujū's Prism (Fukutokujū goshiki megane)*. In the preface, Jihinari drew an analogy with *karakuri*, stating that writers before him had used string-controlled dolls as metaphors to suggest the social circumscriptions of human persons, but as such analogies were hardly exciting any more, he would offer a tale of a *karakuri* that controlled vision: his book, he says, is to be a "precision automaton" (*karakuri-saiku*) working on glasses.

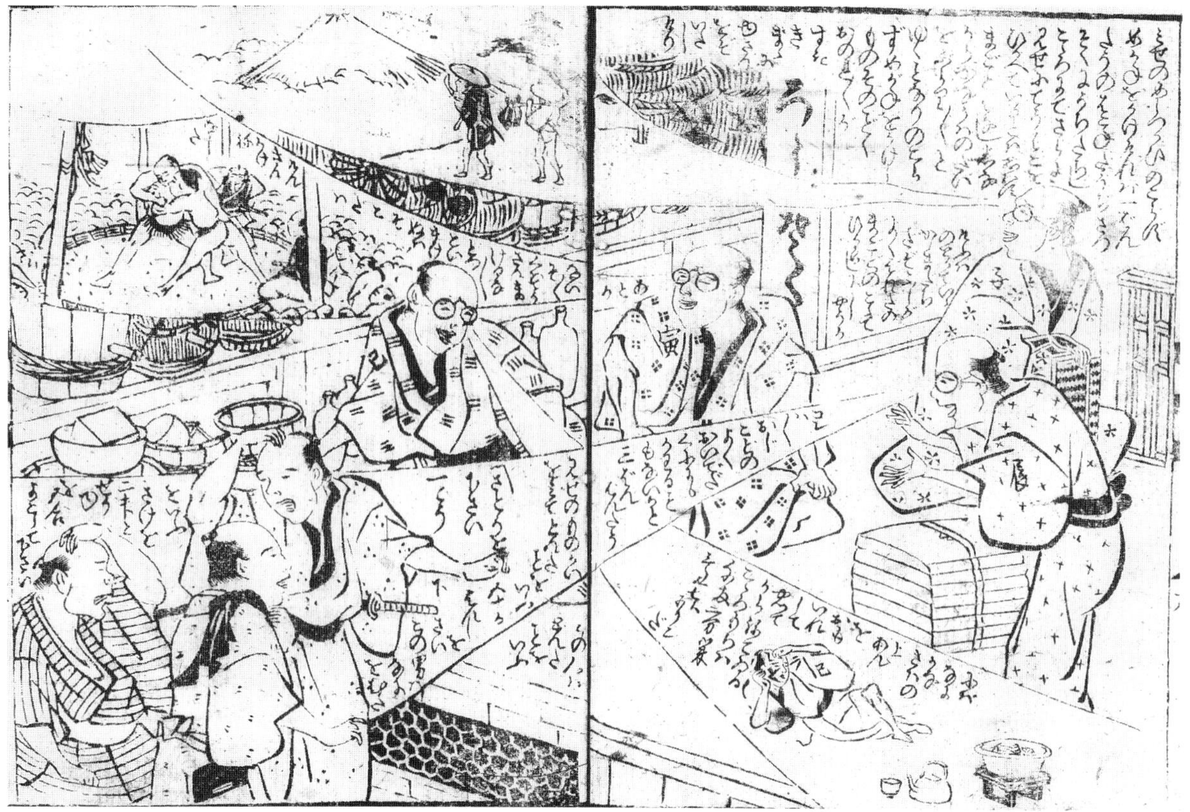

110. Utagawa Toyokuni, from Sakuragawa Jihinari, *Fukutokujū goshiki megane*, 1797. National Diet Library, Tokyo. *Fukutokujū's staff work while believing themselves on holiday.*

Prisms, as cited in the title, are the *megane* which pull phenomena apart and reorder them harshly into their basic component colours, spreading over the spectrum and perfectly lodged in place. In Japanese, "colour" (*iro*) is also a Buddhist technical term for illusion and error, and by extension it also meant sex. The Floating Worlds were also called the places of "colour" (*iro-sato*).

Jihinari's hero is a sake brewer called Fukutoku-ya Tokubyōei (a name with such an overly auspicious ring as to sound alarms); it is abbreviated in the Edo manner to Fukutokujū.[66] Fukutokujū had got off to a good start in life by being given a glass ball by Daikoku (as O-tsuki was to be the next year) with instructions from the god to make a pair of glasses from it. Daikoku promised that the resulting lenses would have magic properties, allowing the wearer to become wealthy without even working. With his new glasses on, Fukutokujū discovers he can see whatever he likes – the cool flow of the Sumida in summer, the cherry blossoms of Mukō-jima in spring – while all the time actually labouring in his shop. Naturally, he has no resistance to work, and he dedicates himself so assiduously to his affairs that they flourish and his shop becomes famous throughout the city. As happens in such circumstances, the workers (who do not know the nature of the glasses) demand their cut

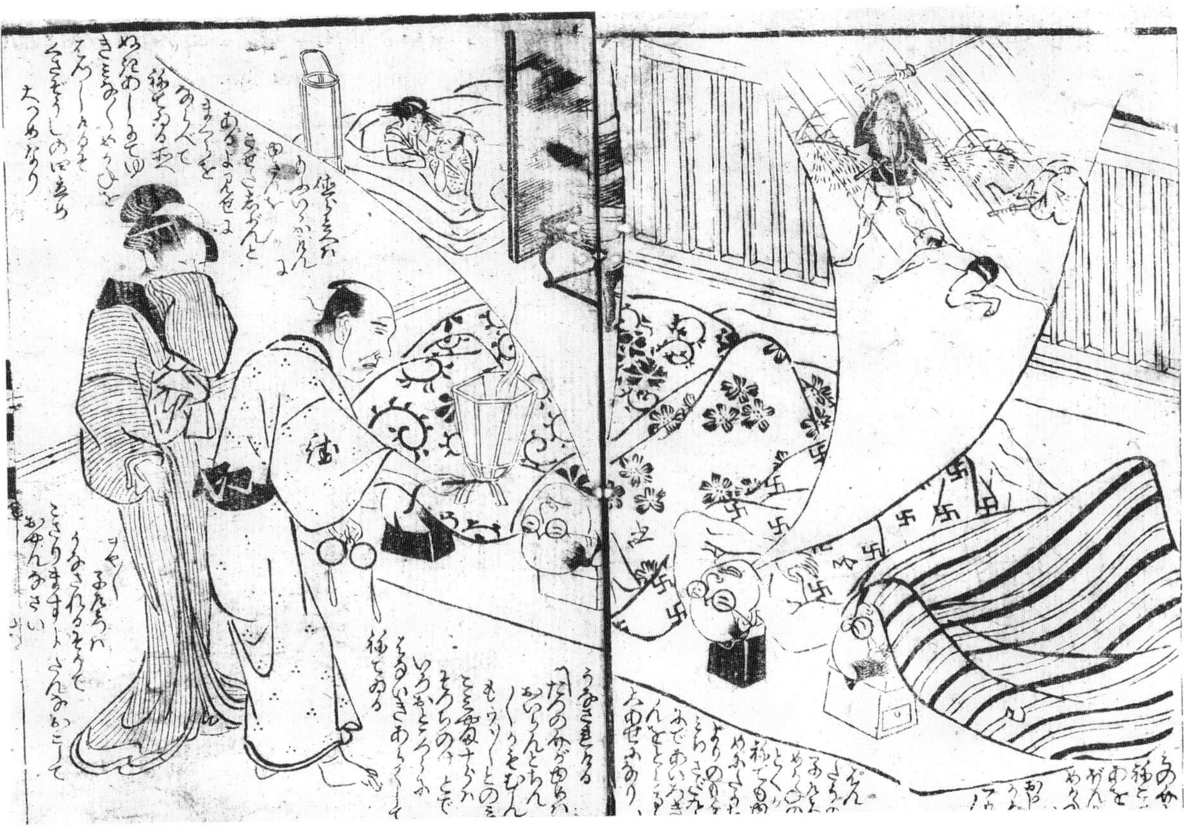

111. Utagawa Toyokuni, from Sakuragawa Jihinari, *Fukutokujū goshiki megane,* 1797. National Diet Library, Tokyo.

Fukutokujū and his wife remove the magic glasses.

and beg for paid leave. Fukutokujū then has the idea of using the remainder of the glass to fashion a pair of spectacles for each member of his staff (plus one for his problem son), so that, like him, they will believe themselves transported to wherever they want to be while really remaining at work (Fig. 110).[67] None of the men had the least intention of going to the places they had trumped up holiday requests for (seeing relatives, visiting temples, and such formalities), and, ignorant of the ruse being played upon them, they wish themselves off to the Yoshiwara, the theatre, or a hot spring. This leads to minor problems when one of the workers (who believes he is lounging at home) addresses the customers as "Dad"; but still, the benefits for Fukutokujū are considerable; at mealtimes, he serves them cheap *chazuke,* and they think it a *de luxe* hamper. The son believes he is finally marrying the woman his father had so obstinately refused to countenance and rejoices at the new-found compliance. After three days (the standard Edo holiday period), Fukutokujū and his wife creep into the staff dormitory and remove the glasses from the workers as they sleep (Fig. 111). At dawn, all "return," effusive with thanks for their master's generosity.

The consolatory force of Fukutokujū's glasses puts them diametrically at variance with the coldly precise lens of empirical use. But be that as it may, Jihinari deliberately links his spectacles to the real world of Edo ware, for the glass ball Daikoku bestowed is said to have been made up for Fukutokujū at a certain "Muranukiya" – an obvious reference to the Murano-ya in Asakusa, but here punned with the noun *nuki,* "an escape." Finding the pun apt, Kyōden borrowed this name for O-tsuki's shop (Fig. 108). Fukutokujū's glasses can be obtained in Edo by fatuous moderns who seek a clear gaze to nowhere. But like all glasses they are pinned into a rhetoric of *Ran* as well, for in Toyokuni's illustration, the "Muranuki-ya" sports a sign advertising the wares as "Dutch and Nagasaki Glasses."[68] Precision is subverted as, *karakuri*-like, the glasses send the eyes through the loop.

THE MICROSCOPE

Unlike spectacles, which were never quite displaced from the orbit of personal accessories and were thus eternally open to charges of pandering, microscopes had a more strict purpose and could scarcely be thought anything other than scientific instruments. The microscope, indeed, was generally recognised as the symbol or hallmark of *Rangaku* scholarship. The translators of the flagship *New Anatomical Atlas* went out of their way to note how several of their explorations into the human body had been performed with the aid of a "large microscope",[69] and when, in 1826, Ōtsuki Gentaku enlarged the work in the *Supplemented Edition of the New Anatomical Atlas (Chōtei kaitai shinsho),* he inserted the design of a microscope into Kulmus's otherwise unchanged original title page.

The first microscopes may have been imported into Japan early in the eighteenth century or even before, but by 1765, Gotō Rishun was writing enthusiastically about the new generation then entering the country – probably they were of the culpepper type – and he praised their experimental utility.[70] Magnification of well over one hundred times was possible with such devices, and Gentaku himself claimed to have experienced two hundred times' magnification with a microscope in the house of the *han* doctor of Tamura, Tatebe Seian, some time before 1782.[71] Gentaku wrote of another *vergrootglas* with the same impressive power in 1795.[72] Katsuragawa Hoshū had a European microscope that he lent to his brother, Morishima Chūryō, to sketch down for inclusion in the *Red-fur Miscellany* of 1787 (Fig. 112). Chūryō discussed the instrument and recorded some of the extraordinary things that could be seen with it:

> Recently a lens for detailed viewing called a *mikorosukopyūmu* arrived from abroad. It looks as illustrated here. We brought several things into focus and inspected them under it. The clarity of the minutiae was quite extraordinary. Salt crystals could be seen to have a hexagonal shape, while buckwheat flour (even the most finely sifted sort) was triangular. A candle wick looked liked a loofah and mould was shaped like mushrooms; water was like hemp leaves with patterning on them; ice had a warp-and-woof design; sake was like boiling water, all seething in bubbles. . . . [73]

The microscope fascinated to a degree that in the blasé late-twentieth century we cannot readily appreciate. The visions were novel to the point of inspiring disbelief. Rather than celebrating the mental unbalancing that microscopic vision brought, it is the project here to see how changes might fit into pre-existing concerns. Access to the minimal in size need not always undermine established interpretations and, on the contrary, it might offer new ways to support them. One case may be cited.

In Zhuangzi it was written how King Yong of Wei and Marquis Tianmao of Ki concluded a treaty of peace.[74] But the marquis broke it. Perplexed, the king called in his councillors, and one introduced a wise man who came forward with a parable, saying: the horns of a snail are two; imagine each a nation, one the Kingdom of Conflict (Chu) and the other the Kingdom of Primitiveness (Man);[75] imagine further that war-

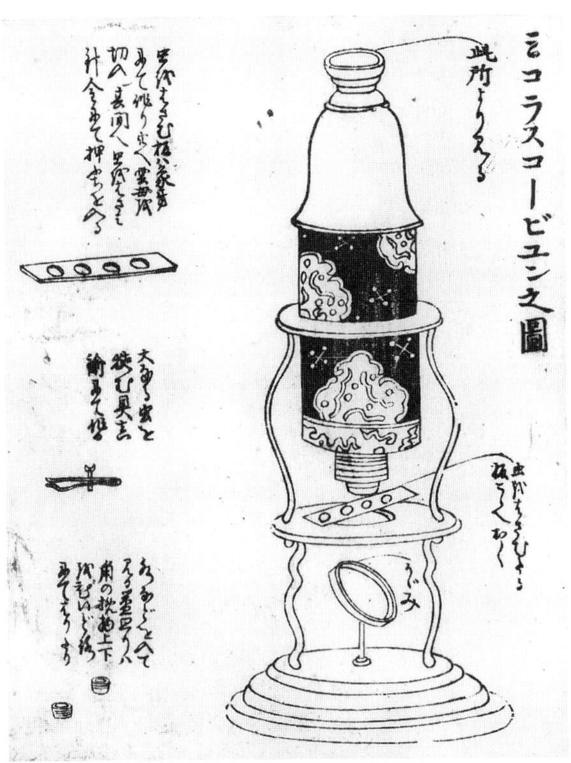

112. Unsigned, *Microscope*, from Morishima Chūryō, *Kōmō zatsuwa*, 1787. National Diet Library, Tokyo.

fare between the two had been incessant and already cost many lives. By this comparison the king was to decide his course of action. The force of the speech was evident: on a human scale, the horns of a snail are not things worth fighting over; equally, in the vastness of space, Wei and Ki did not merit bloodshed either. King Yong abandoned ideas of war. It might be added that a snail's "horns" are actually its eyes, and that if they conspire against each other, like the sun and moon in struggle, disorientation and calamity will ensue.

The Battle of the Snail's Horns was well known in Japan. Shiba Kōkan referred to it in his *Writings of the Wordless Daoist (Mugen dōjin hikki)*, published in 1814.[76] The arrival of the microscope reinvigorated the intellectual force of the parable, transforming what Zhuangzi had written in simile into ascertained fact. By the end of the eighteenth century it was clear that if a wick could be a loofah, then the horns of a snail could indeed accommodate kingdoms – worlds indeed – teeming with life. The parable had taken its impact from the unfixedness of scale, and this was something that microscopy also knew. It was, no doubt, in search of Conflict and Primitiveness that Chūryō put a pair of snail's horns under his brother's microscope. He declared: "On the top of a snail's horns are two domains, one full of conflict and one primitive. With this instrument you can bring them into focus and tell them apart."[77] Chūryō used precisely the language of the Daoist sage, but continued with a phrase intended less to impugn Zhuangzi than to counter expected incredulity on the part of his readers: "what I say is not just Chinese stuff and nonsense (*kōtō*), as anyone who has used the instrument can attest." Nakai Riken, after looking through a domestic microscope in his home city of Osaka, corroborated this: now, he wrote, we know that Zhuangzi spoke the very truth.[78]

The philosopher's story did have an uncanny resemblance to published scientific data. This fortuity led Kyōden, who always operated on the boundary between Westernism and popular culture, into an addiction to the parable. Kyōden hung on his study wall, right behind his desk, a scroll of the *Battle of the Snail's Horns* that showed the animal vast and occupying almost the full space of the picture, antennae protruding to the top of the vertical paper; on the tips, the kingdoms are personified as mediaeval Japanese warriors, armoured and poised to fight the battle of Conflict and Primitiveness (Fig. 113).[79] Kyōden's wife, Yuri (an ex-prostitute he had redeemed from her contract), is sewing in the other room and their dog sits in front as Kyōden has a vision of the bodhisattva of childbirth Jizō (and thereby hangs another tale).[80]

As the minute inflated to the vast, the well-known, earthly phenomena of the seen world like snails or loofahs might be projected down into the microscopic domain to help explain it. *Rangaku* commentators indulge to a striking degree in similes taken from the quotidian. Chūryō emphasised how the stuff of human visual experience could backslip along the scale of magnification into the microscopic: "Among the things I viewed with my lord elder brother, was an old louse. A rift on its side had left the ribs exposed, looking like those of a sardine. The guts were rotting and minute worms were swarming over them, like brown insects."[81]

Invocation of near-at-hand fauna to describe the barely visible became standard practice. Minagawa Kien (see Chap. 2), compared Rosetsu's painting of a magnified flea to larger forms of life: "Who would not now think it a bird flying through the woods?/Who would doubt it to be some heroic beast running over low hills?" he rhetorically asked.[82] Riken likened flies to sparrows; and lice, he said, were as pincered crabs;[83] flies, he went on, wore "purple caps" (*murasaki no bō*) really their eyes – but the simile comes from the kabuki stage, where boy actors wore purple head-covers to hide their shaven foreheads (the government enforced this disfigurement in order to discourage the youths from supplementing wages through prostitution, although the elegant hat ensured the directive did not work).

Physical appearance and scale alone were not implicated in such verbal resolutions, for if a fly might look like a boy (even dress like one), what did this connote in the realm of behaviour? Kōkan's study of 1796, *Complete Pictures of Heaven and Earth (Tenchi zenzu)*, included a note appended to some microscopic studies of mosquito larvae to the effect that "surely they [insects] feel, some of them joy, some of them suffering, with experiences nothing different from those of humans."[84] Nine years later, Shikitei Sanba used this discovery for literary effect, and he composed a tale of "how a weakling insect transformed into a warrior," and like a snails horns, it might well be savage.[85] The advantage of size gave humanity the controlling hand, but when even seemingly trivial objects were realised to sustain the complexity of equivalent larger ones, and when the small were looked at through a microscope and lost their limiting smallness, they could evince an irritability perfectly equal with higher beings. Ikku took the similes presented by the users of microscopes at face value in a kibyoshi of 1796, *Microscopic Young Grass by the Wayside (Mushi-megane nobe no wakakusa)*, in which he told of insects functioning just like humans. Ikku drew the protagonists as actual human beings, the smaller life-forms represented riding on their heads like crowns (Fig. 114). Size was unstable and was certainly no determining factor in organisational or emotional sophistication; as Ikku put it, citing a proverb, "even an inch-long bug can entertain thought in its half-inch soul";[86] and attracted by the appropriateness of this old saw to the modern world, he reiterated it in another story some thirty years later, "even an inch-long bug has a half-inch soul, as even a peppercorn is hot."[87] It was hard to know whether there was any credibility left in a human dimension of value.

Fascination with the world of unseen matter was not confined to those who considered themselves scholars. Microscopes were among the better sort of gift made by the VOC to Japanese officials throughout the eighteenth century, and the rich, whatever their walk of life, also sought

113 (top, opposite page). Kitao Shigemasa, from Santō Kyōden, *Sakusha tainai totsuki no zu*, 1804. Tokyo Metropolitan Central Library.

Jizō appears to Kyoden in his home, a Battle of the Snail's Horns hanging on the wall; the author's dog sits before him while his wife sews in the next room.

114 (bottom, opposite page). Jippensha Ikku, from his *Mushi-megane nobe no wakakusa*, 1796. Tokyo Metropolitan Central Library.

Insect protagonists appear as humans with animal hats.

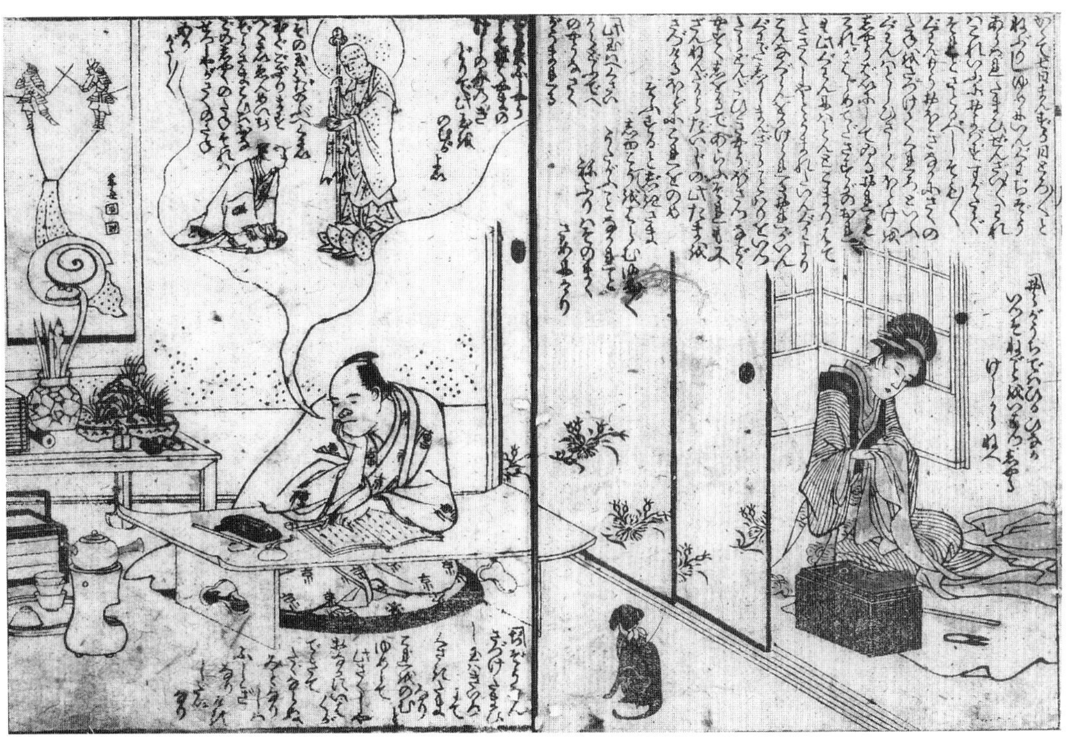

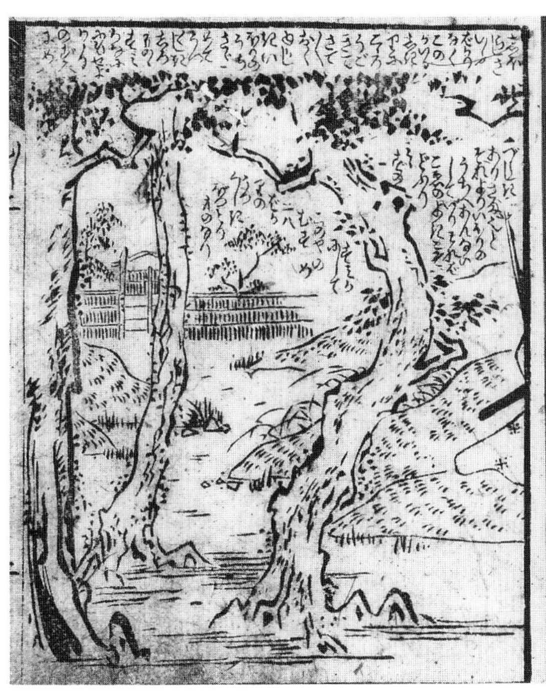

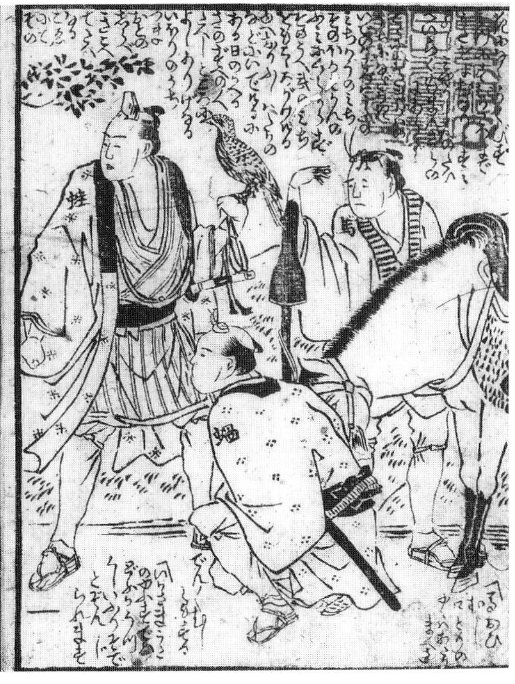

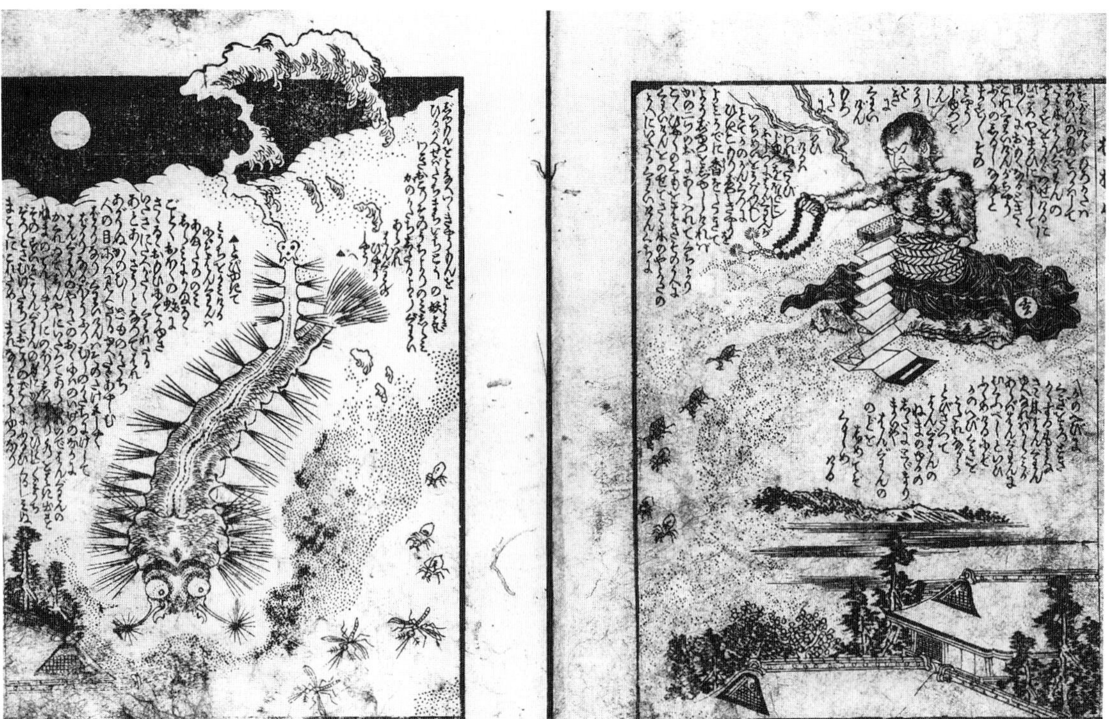

115. Utagawa Kunisada, from Santō Kyōden, *Matsu to ume taketori monogatari*, 1809. National Diet Library, Tokyo.

Kaigen summons demons to descend on Hangan's house.

them out.[88] Yamagata Shigefusa, an Osaka merchant alive in the 1790s, had four, two of which were "small and of Dutch make" and had cost him seventeen *monme* in silver.[89] Ownership became so widespread that a how-to manual was issued for the amateur user, authored by Hoshū himself and published in 1805 with the irreproachably compact title *How to Use a Microscope (Kenbikyō yōhō)*. For those short on silver, microscopes were also set up at roadside fairs, usable by all. Gyokuchō recorded of Nagoya in 1820: "From the fourth month, Dutch lenses (*Oranda-megane*) were on view outside the gates of the Temple of Daisu-zan. All kinds of insect were there for inspection, flees, lice, *shakushi*, spiders, and mosquitoes. Each one seemed as large as the palm of your hand. They were quite terrifying!"[90] Unusually, Gyokuchō took the trouble to include a sketch of the instrument he used and labelled it with arrows, designating "this is where you peep in" and "this is where you put your insect." As if in response to a popular need, the difficult foreign word *mikorosukōpyumu* (from the Latin *microscopium*) was done away with in favour of easier and more memorable terms: Gyokuchō's "Dutch glasses," which stated categorically the imported nature of the magnified gaze, or "insect glasses" (*mushimegane*), which identified the chief objects of observation. Eventually the term settled on as the one Hoshū used, and as it remains, *kenbikyō*.[91]

The appearance of insects at greatly enhanced size was indeed horrific, but the idea that they might possess the volition of larger organisms was more frightening still. Kyōden used this anxiety over insects rendered larger-than-life

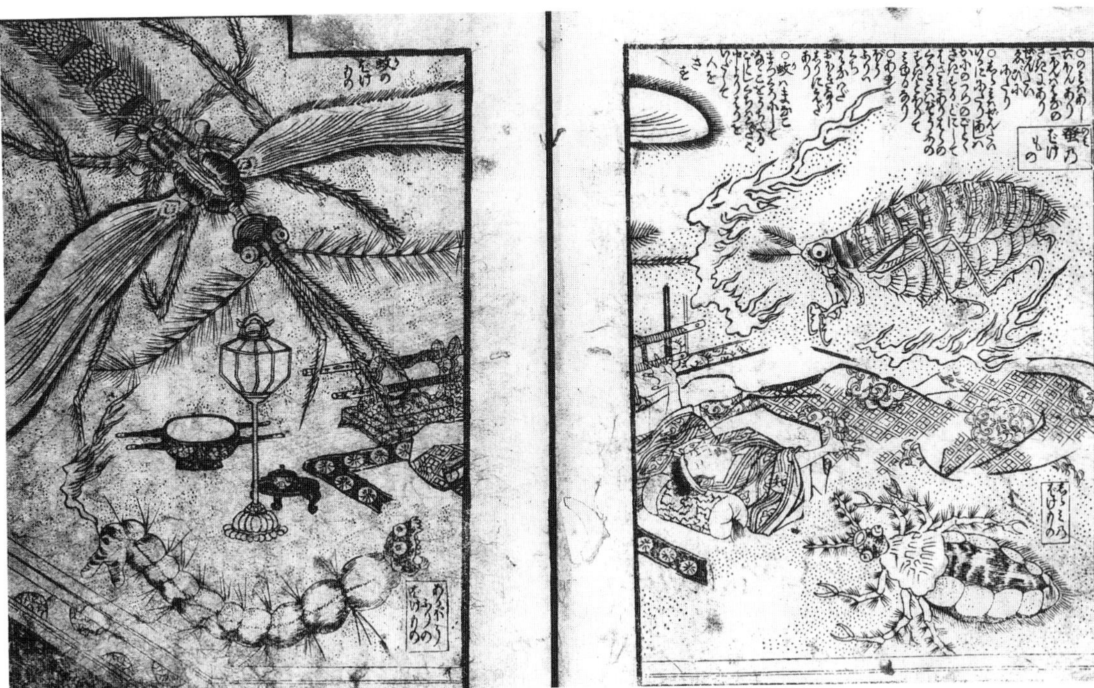

116. Utagawa Kunisada, from Santō Kyōden, *Matsu to ume taketori monogatari*, 1809. National Diet Library, Tokyo.

The sleeping Hangan is plagued by monsters.

in a novel, *The Plum, Pine, and Bamboo-cutter's Tale (Matsu to ume taketori monogatari)*, published in 1809 with illustrations by Kunisada.[92] The story, set in mediaeval times, told of the good hero Sasaki Hangan Tadatomo and his struggles with an evil monk, Kaigen. Kaigen summoned demons to haunt Hangan, but rather than employing the daily consortium of goblins and sprites, the necromancer raised ordinary insects, not hideous in themselves but petrifying by virtue of their new through-the-lens disrespect for scale (Figs. 115, 116). These entirely modern monsters unhinge and inspire terror as they appear as if escaped from a microscope, batheticising the heroic dimensions of antique courage. "Kaigen brandished the sacred text and intoned an incantation. At once a ghostly mist bubbled up, and from it emerged monsters in the forms of flea, louse, and mosquito. Hangan felt as though he were bitten by swarms of fleas and lice and stung by hordes of mosquitoes. The pain was unendurable."[93] These are no longer the "half-inch" souls of Ikku's story; for, as the illustrations show, the insects *are* wild beasts, human-sized, and with an equal capacity for harm.

Kunisada may or may not have used a microscope himself, but in devising his pictures he referred to other writers who had. In fact, he turned to the most ready source of information on *Ran*, Chūryō's *Red-fur Miscellany*, by then a classic of thirty years' standing. Kunisada copied out some of the insect illustrations that had followed Chūryō's picture of his brother's microscope, superimposing them on the image of the sleeping Hangan in his house; Kunisada's only

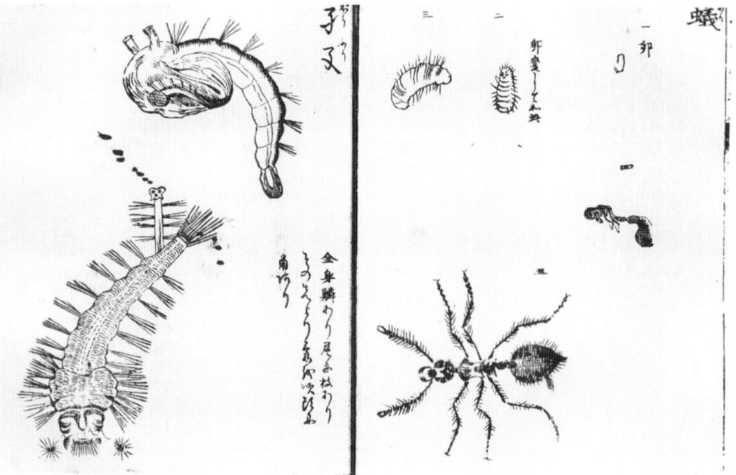

117. Shiba Kōkan, *Ants* and *Mosquito Larvae*, from Morishima Chūryō, *Kōmō zatsuwa*, 1786. National Diet Library, Tokyo.

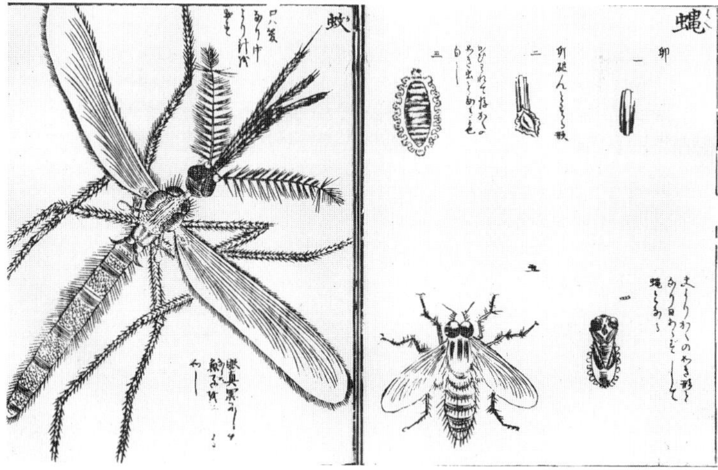

118. Shiba Kōkan, *Flies* and *Mosquito*, from Morishima Chūryō, *Kōmō zatsuwa*, 1786. National Diet Library, Tokyo.

emendation was to enlarge the eyes, assimilating them into the established iconography of horrific beasts (Figs. 117, 118). The first page showed Kaigen's incantations with a mosquito larva descending (not mentioned in Kyōden's text) and a stream of flies around, its air emissions become a jet of spray. In the second picture the insects are labeled as "red" larva, flea, louse, and mosquito; their scientific designations have been left isolated in cartouches, only with the word "monster" (*bakemono*) appended. The transit of these five insects from items of scientific inquiry to instruments of torture is significant and may be traced in detail.[94]

Chūryō had not himself discovered the forms included in his book but had lifted them from a series of drawings by Shiba Kōkan which, he noted in the text, were in the possession of his family.[95] Chūryō gave ten illustrations in all in the *Miscellany*, and the Katsuragawa probably had these together in an album. All have since been lost, but by chance one picture by Kōkan identical to one of Chūryō's survives, and shows the first mosquito larva with a pair. Kōkan prob-

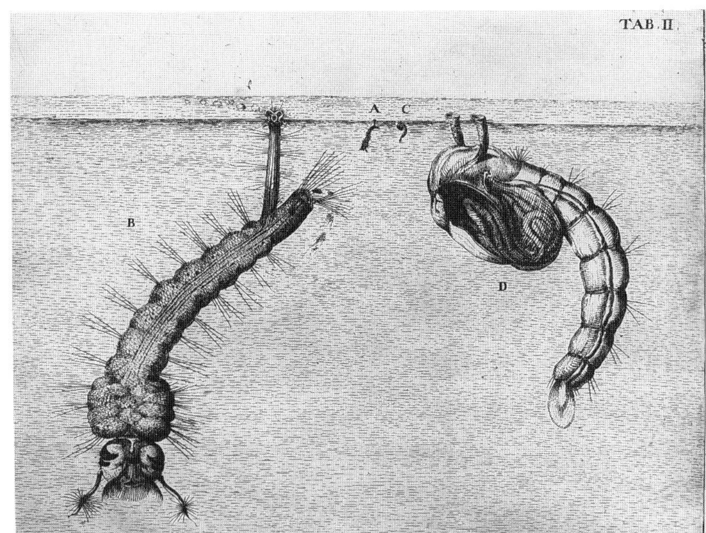

119. Unsigned, *Mosquito Larvae*, from Jean Swammerdam, *Histoire naturel des insectes*, Utrecht, 1682. By permission of the Houghton Library, Harvard University.

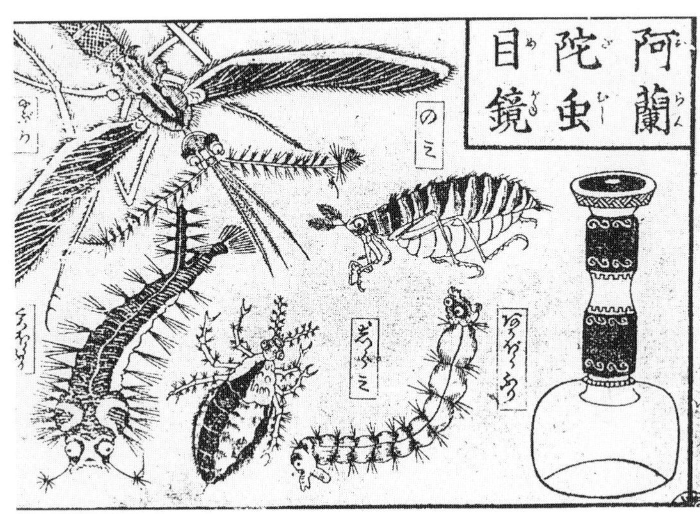

120. Unsigned, *Dutch Microscope*, woodblock broadsheet, c. 1830. Private collection.

ably had several copies of his insect studies, of which he passed one to the Katsuragawa family, keeping another for himself, for these larvae appeared after the *Miscellany* was published, in 1796, in *Complete Pictures of Heaven and Earth* (Pl. 12). Kōkan did not state whence he derived his images, and he left the distinct impression that he had taken them from life in his own surveys, but this was not in fact the case.[96] The larvae can be found in a Western entomological study published over a century earlier in 1682 in French, *Histoire générale des insectes*, the work of Jean Swammerdam, a Dutchman living in Paris (Fig. 119). The large mosquito appears in Swammerdam too, complete with the bent antenna that it still has in Kunisada's picture; the louse is present too. The flea and the worm-like "red" larva derive from some other source that remains to be discovered.

The progress of these insects can be taken one

stage in the other direction as well. A loose broadsheet of uncertain date and lacking all publication data illustrated precisely the same enlarged samples, but now coupled back to the microscope, in an illustration that though ridiculously fictionalised shows an instrument deliberately ornamented in the European manner (Fig. 120).[97] The whole is labelled "Dutch insect-glasses." Given the success of Kyōden's story, the print was probably produced shortly after 1809, restoring Kunisada's borrowings to a pseudo-scholarly context. The sheet seeks scientific plausibility, and the entomological labels now stand alone; the mosquito's damaged antenna is repaired. But the insects' eyes are still immense.

Swammerdam, his English readers were told in an expanded translation of the *Histoire générale* published by Thomas Flloyd in 1758 as *The Book of Nature*, conducted "expensive searches after insects, and . . . experiments of all kinds," they were assured, however, that his veritable "museum of curiosities," though extensive, was kept "without the least confusion."[98] But the sum of questions posed of nature, and the means by which discovery was disciplined into order, were not alike in Europe and Japan. Hangan's house has been thrown into turmoil. It is not science which has collapsed the world around the warrior's ears but ethical wrong, as the enlarged insects are deliberately wafted in by the inflating power of Kaigen's moral morass.

From the pen of a European scholar, to a *Rangaku* study, to a popularising encyclopaedia, and on into the fictional world of monsters in a historic tale, and then reinserted into a spurious scientific print – such a trajectory could be posited as paradigmatic of much of what "Dutch" learning was all about.

LIFE BENEATH THE LENS

If insects' emotions were no different from those of humans, as the evidence seemed to aver, then the fate of the many specimens placed under lenses was not to be envied. Hokusai produced a print in the first years of the nineteenth century showing a butterfly poised on the edge of a microscope, hovering there seemingly aware of the impending destiny of it, or at least its fellows, doomed to become experimental samples, painfully crushed (Pl. 13).[99] A pair of tweezers (clearly imported), are positioned on the shelf beneath, ready to trap and pick the butterfly apart piece by piece and expose all to the prying lens-based gaze. Hokusai's print was issued in a private edition (*surimono*), probably commissioned by the amateur poet whose verse appears inscribed on the page, Asasean Eiki. Written in the popular kyoka genre, it reads:

> Sporting on leaves of colours
> Bright enough to wake you with a start,
> The butterfly is, perhaps,
> A drunkard's reverie.[100]

The allusion is to another passage from Zhuangzi: the philosopher described how he fell asleep and dreamt he was a butterfly; but when he woke, he could not be dissuaded that he might now be a butterfly asleep and only dreaming it was a man.[101] In alluding to Zhuangzi, Eiki was doing nothing arcane, for the conundrum was very well known. But Hokusai's depiction is new, and the purpose to which Daoist thought was put, without precedent. Zhuangzi's point had been that man and butterfly are not fundamentally different, for both are united in the common "principle" of existence (*ri*) derived from Creation (*zōka*). To Daoists, differences are accidental only and inessential. The microscope stands for an alternative epistemology, that of science with its claims to understand by opening up and seeing, and classifying the world into taxonomic plots. Hokusai's pictorial image puts forth no solution to the friction of these two world-views. No indication is proposed as to whether forthcoming lensed investigation will reveal a difference in tissue structure proving the butterfly is not a man or whether cellular make-up is indeed the same. Neither poet nor artist wishes to adjudicate. To the Edo viewer, if a fly can wear a boy's hat, then perhaps a butterfly *can* become a philosopher.

Human beings (at any rate parts of them) were regularly put under the lens too, as the *Atlas* translators recorded. Diagnostic doctors inspected phlegm or fluids in search of physiological truth or symptoms of health and disease. The human under the lens was a powerful conceit. A kibyoshi by a little-known writer, Rinshō, took this up in a work published in 1778 with illustrations by Torii Kiyomasa. The book is a mock-biography of one Fukuzō who hails from Nagasaki; he is a product unique to that town in being of mixed race, the son of an *Oranda kapitan* by a Maruyama prostitute. Fukuzō straddles the Edo-period cultures of the Floating World and *Ran*. Following the medical and surgical bent associated with the Red-fur mind, he becomes a doctor and adopts a "Dutch" name to impress prospective patients: Tsuinaoru Kitenteesu.[102] But Fukuzō has no training and relies for his practice solely on two stand-by instruments left to him by his father before he put back to sea: a mechanical clock and a strange lensed device. The former does not feature in the story, but the latter becomes Fukuzō's principal tool, and when placed in the navel, it can see through to the intestines. Not really magical, just fiendishly *Ran*, the tube reveals all. Inserting the instrument, Fukuzō shouts excitedly, "I can see the whole *karakuri* of the guts from one end to the other!" Then he himself is analysed (Fig. 121). This medical microscope allows inspection without killing the sample, for a good poke in the belly-button will do no harm. Fukuzō is a spiv, but in better hands such an instrument would remove the heavy requirement on the scholar to terminate the life of the item under study. This cleared the conceptual way for examination of a human life *in situ* under the lens while it still functioned as a person. Fukuzō's probe accesses the still-pulsating membranes.

It had been the objection of *kanpō* doctors to Dutch anatomical practice that it based itself on the evaluation of dead samples and so was devoid of real relevance for medicine, which was, after all, about the health and sanity of the living. Sano Yasusada, a *kanpō* doctor and strong critic of practical dissections, wrote a book in 1760 bellicosely entitled *Against the Organs of the Body (Hizōshi)* intended to contradict the pioneering anatomically based study of Yamawaki Tōyō published the previous year, *The Organs of the Body (Zōshi)*. Yasusada ringingly concluded: "What is important about the organs is not their appearance but the divine spirit (*shinki*) that resides in them. When the divinity departs and the spirit falls away, the organs are just empty vessels. I cannot imagine what is to be gained by looking at them, listening to them, or talking about them."[103] Even more forcefully expressed, Fukuoka Sadaaki wrote some years later in *A Doctor's Commonplaces (Ika zokudan)*, with invective that runs counter to the mild title of the work: "There is not one single medical book, from any period of history, that instructs us to open up corpses, look at the insides, and cure people that way. I might say that from of old doctoring has been solely concerned with healing the living; it is not about treating the dead."[104] Fukuzō can view deep inside a life-form, as it remains alive and tightly closed.

The fictional "Dutch" microscope in Rinshō's tale was of little use to the real surgeon, but figuratively its power was colossal. Fukuzō's device was referred to only as *Oranda megane*, and in form it looks like a telescope. But the illustrator Kiyomasa has used this advisedly. The instrument is what was technically called a "tube-type microscope" (*tōyō kenbikyō*), and it was the sort most associated with doctors, and generally the one favoured by the medical profession over the upright sort familiar today (called the "contractible" [*shukushin*] microscope). The tube micro-

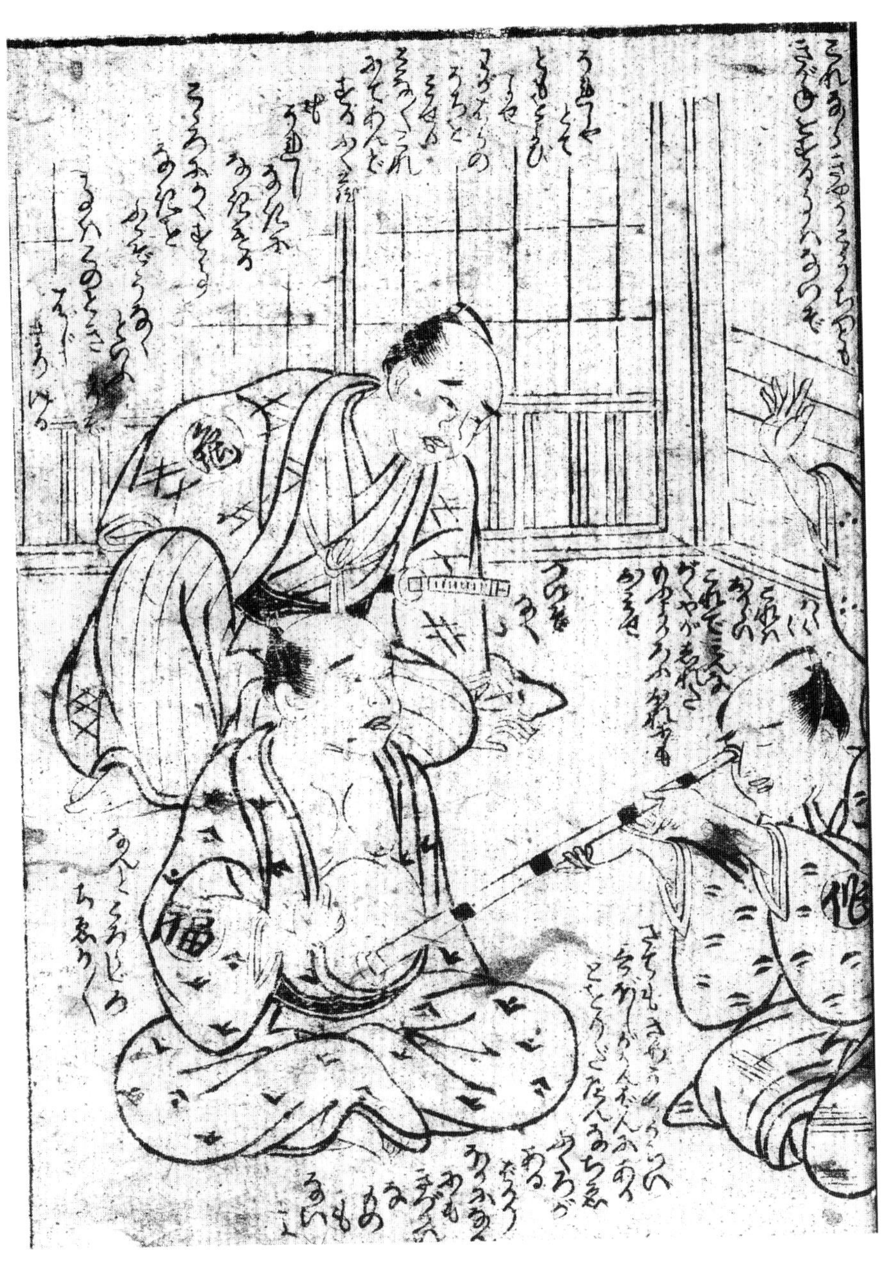

scope was discussed by Nan'a Kō, a celebrated Kyoto investigator (principally an entomologist), and its utility was described in a discussion of various sorts of microscope and what was to be discerned with them. In his *Mirror of Insects (Mushi kagami)*, published in 1809, Kō stated:

> This type of lens is used to tell whether patients have microbes in their phlegm or pus. The tube is fifteen centimetres in length. It has an aperture at the top containing a single lens, with another at the bottom. When used in combination, these reflect

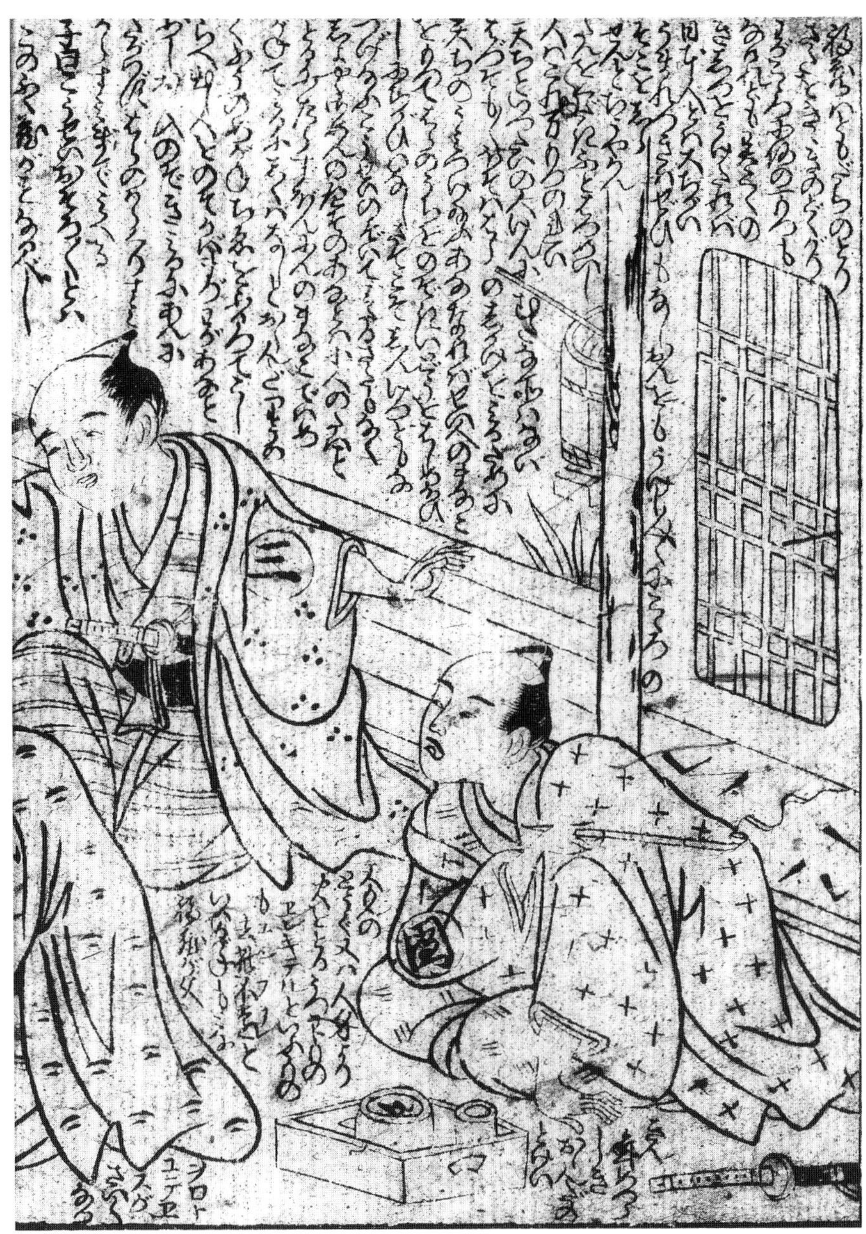

121. Torii Kiyomasa, from Rinshō, *Kogane yama Fukuzō jikki*, 1778. National Diet Library, Tokyo.

Fukuzō is inspected with a 'Dutch lens'.

the form of the specimen. A variant sort has multiple tubes that can be extended and collapsed.[105]

Fukuzō's, then, was the real human-viewing lens, devised by physicians to detect impurities in a person's body. Kiyomasa and Rinshō wish the reader to be aware of this, borrowing the authoritative apparatus of the clinic. More elusive inner workings of the human being, volitions and aspirations, could be pondered as they were submitted to this notional in-life scrutiny. This was comical, but it was also a stern warning that an ability to search the interior would tear off the last concealing place of ambition, lies, and fraud. As Rinshō put it, tongue in cheek, "the navel is an aperture put there by Heaven and Earth for seeing those clever bits in the guts."[106] There is, of course, much punning here: *ana* means either an aperture or a folly or idiocy; *shikake* means both intricate working parts and, by extension, tricks. All is revealed. Rinshō went on with reference to the Dutch microscope, "it peeps into the interior of the stomach using its holy eyes (*shōnin no manago*)." A revelation of flesh would be of use to the doctor, but with Buddhistic eyes the novelist shows a moral persona through the hole bored in the stomach.

Shikitei Sanba wrote similarly of a lensed analysis of still-living humanity – the specimen: himself. The work appeared in 1810 as *The Seed of a Comic Story Inside the Guts (Hara no uchi gesaku tanehon)*. By means of a similar tube-type microscope placed in the navel, a friend inspects the author's stomach (Fig. 122). Sanba teases:

> Well, now you've opened up my insides for a clear view, how does it look? What can you see?
>
> "Lack-a-day, my heart is like a bamboo tree,
> And I would break it ope for thee."[107]

Sanba implies an existential opening, as he jokingly tacks on the idiom of a prostitute promising to reveal her heart to a client. This collides with the more basic exposure of the corporeal body under microscopy. The author wishes for confirmation of what is in the depths of his heart, how inner may relate to outer, and what moral unity or dislocation is evinced under the empowered gaze; his trust in the dispassionateness of the lens is complete, but it is moral vision he seeks. This is a kibyoshi, and deflation of such sanctimonious ideas is bound to be in store: Sanba's lumpen friend replies: "Yes, I can see it! I can see it! That prawn tempura you ate last night has shed its batter and is dangling down inside your stomach! It's seductively tangling itself up with some giant radish. Everything's going into convulsions – there's pandemonium! It's all churning over and over." The microscope is called forth as provider of precise facts, and Sanba himself thinks of these metaphorically – the heart of a lover, now revealed – a lens trained on the human predicament. Taking the interior to be the seat of consciousness, he wishes for guidance on how his guts relate to the him whom others perceive. But the friend remains mired in the literal aspect of science, sight-enhanced, still unable to fathom more than discoveries of anatomical structure, digestion, and the ins and outs of the alimentary canal.

A human looking into another human first saw pulsating organs, but these yielded to matters that touched more profoundly on being itself. Any interiorising viewer was (or ought to be) alerted to compelling dimensions of spiritual meaning in the patterns revealed.

In 1783, an author, whose pen-name meant "lazy fool," wrote a kibyoshi in which he turned to direct observation of the heart. Namake no Bakahito, however, in his working life was Suzuki Shōnosuke, an industrious personal retainer to the shogunate (although he came to an unspecified sticky end).[108] The book was called *Stolen Away by a Goose – What a Pack of Lies (Uso shikkari gantori-chō)* and was illustrated by Utamaro. So as to allow the story to progress easily, events take place in a land of giants. The hero, Kinjūrō, a man of Edo, is one day whisked away by a flying goose and dropped on the strange land. When discovered, he is stripped of his effects, including a love letter he has been carrying from his girl in the Yoshiwara, one Utagiku. Anxious for elucidation about this strange new form of life, the giants bring out a microscope they have at hand (Fig. 123). An inspection takes place, with Kinjūrō relatively speaking now conveniently shrunken to the size of a butterfly or mosquito larva. The illustration shows a giant squinting into a device which in Nan'a Kō's typology is the barrel type microscope (*yōyō*

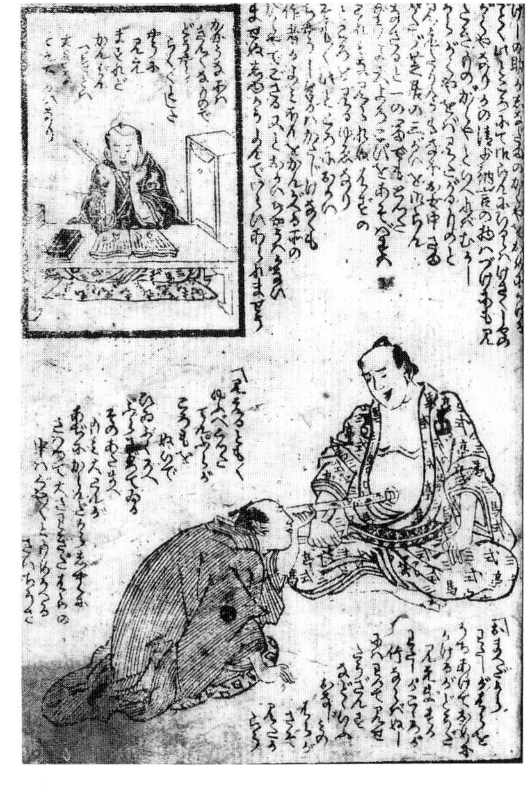

122 (right). Ogawa Yoshimaru, from Shikitei Sanba, *Hara no uchi gesaku no tanehon,* 1811. Tokyo Metropolitan Central Library.

The author is inspected by his friend.

123 (below). Kitagawa Utamaro, from Namake no Bakahito, *Uso shikkari gantori chō,* 1783. Tokyo Metropolitan Central Library.

Kinjūrō's love-letter is read.

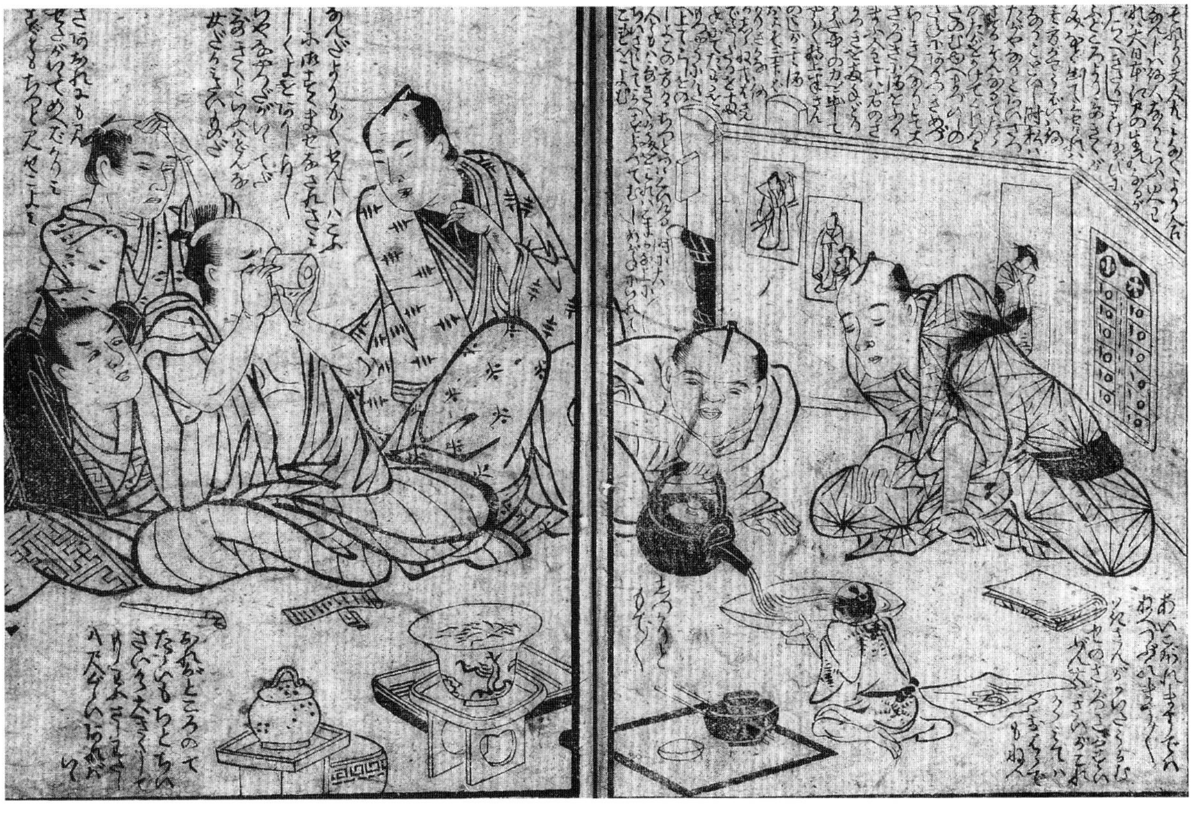

kenbikyō).[109] It is the emotional aspect of Edo life that is up for analysis, for it is not Kinjūrō's body that is looked at, but his letter, and as he is helped to drink sake out of a massive cup the giant reads Utagiku's missive. The secret desires of the two lovers are positioned in the barrel, and their hopes and fears and the whole interplay of their personal lives is caught between the lenses and laid out for decipherment.

The matter was put more directly still in a storybook published in 1826 by Nansenshō Somahito. Shunsai Eishō, his illustrator, placed an upright microscope on the title-page to serve as an emblem of what the book was about: Somahito was professing to sort out and clarify the structure of the human heart. His title (written within the barrel of the device) put the claim without hesitation: this was *A Peeping-Karakuri for Looking Inside the Guts (Hara no uchi nozoki-karakuri;* Fig. 124). The microscope is assimilated neatly into the idea of the heart-revealing peep-box, so that science and fairground mechanics come together to reveal what is beneath. The book is to survey and play via the equipment of the Flowing World and *Ran*. At the bottom of the instrument lies the object to be investigated, cut from the guts like an organ by an anatomist, but now not dripping and putrid, for this is no heart of valve and gristle, but of paper. Not the once-removed heart of Utagiku's gushing letter, this is an actual heart, though with nothing fleshly left – it is the character "heart" (*kokoro*) written on a minute sheet. Anatomy is the metaphor for the seeing, and the microscope the assurance of a disinterested search, but the heart itself is pure social convention: meaning as constituted by language transmitted in text.

Those who used a microscope knew that to gaze within rarely revealed individual entities. However small a sample was, it always broke up into even smaller forms. Anton van Leeuwenhoek, writing in 1683, nicely hypothesised that there were 8,280,000 creatures in a single drop

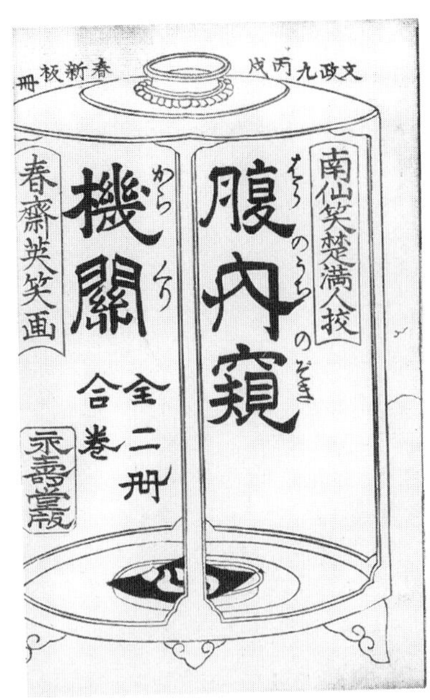

124. Shunsai Eishō, title page to Nansenshō Somahito, *Hara no uchi nozoki karakuri* vol. 1, 1826. National Diet Library, Tokyo.

At the bottom of the microscope is a piece of paper reading 'heart'.

of water, that being more than people in the whole United Provinces.[110] The discovery of swarming collectivities within ostensibly unitary entities was one of microscopy's most salient revelations. This locked well with a morality that called for a recognition of the necessity of social honesty and truth to one's own position. The civilisation created by humanity could be thought of as a throng of small-scale life rooting around in a larger host like scuttling worms. The organisational behaviour of human polities, like any other, could then be the object of enquiry. A city shrunk to the size of a gob of spittle would look no different from maggots in a carcass, and the viewer might see inhabitants with their myriad positions and degrees joining in shared endeavours that, if investigated over long enough time, grew eventually into definite biosocial cultures.

Hokusai produced a set of prints of famous

sites in Edo, probably in the early nineteenth century, and though the genre was thoroughly hackneyed, he breathed new life into it, dramatically raising the stakes and deliberately entwining the traditional selection of cityscapes with the notion of a probing lens; the standard views were there in his series: Ryōgoku Bridge, the Yoshiwara, Sakai-chō, and so on, but he departed from the norm by showing the urban spread, like a seething insect colony (Pl. 14). Hokusai's prints were sold as a set of eight, packed in a wrapper on which was drawn a (rather fanciful) image of a microscope (Pl. 15). The viewer's own city was now their entomological sample, as they stared at the little black forms moving through the very streets that they themselves frequented. The illusion did not end there, for the pictures were actually printed in miniature (just over eight centimetres by eleven) so that they had to be literally peered at closely; indeed, it seems likely that Hokusai intended them to be used with an actual lens.[111] A genre of micro-pictures is attested from the mid-eighteenth century and probably came into being about this time. Looking back in 1823, the novelist Ryūtei Tanehiko wrote that already in the 1750s there was a man at Ryōgoku who "on a single grain of rice draws five geese, or else three Chinese figures, and on a piece of paper two centimetres square he wrote the *Anthology of the Hundred Poets* (*Hyakunin isshū*), and he carved the Thirty-Six Manifestations of Kannon in a gingko nut. In truth, they were all extremely precisely done." No lens in mentioned in those cases, but Tani Bunchō wrote of works where "the viewer uses a microscope to look at them, and not a single brush[mark] is discernible."[112] The minute precision of the lines was something Hokusai was proudly referring to with his emblematic wrapper, but the proper domain of the microscope was minute creatures – the microscope still known as "insect glasses" (*mushi-magane*) – and the thrill of the stunningly detailed depictions relied on a whole rhetoric of the close observation of animal samples. This stemmed from an imported precision gaze. In recognition of this, and of the scientific equipment that supported it, Hokusai entitled his series *The Dutch Picture Lens (Oranda gakyō)*.[113] Further, he executed the scenes in perspective as "floating pictures" (*uki-e*), with the deep recession lines of the foreign style, and with the full panoply of Western representation tropes of shading and cast shadows. The prints are woodblocks, but hatched lines of copperplates are replicated as if they were *vues d'optique*. This "Dutch picture lens" is both microscope and *optique*.

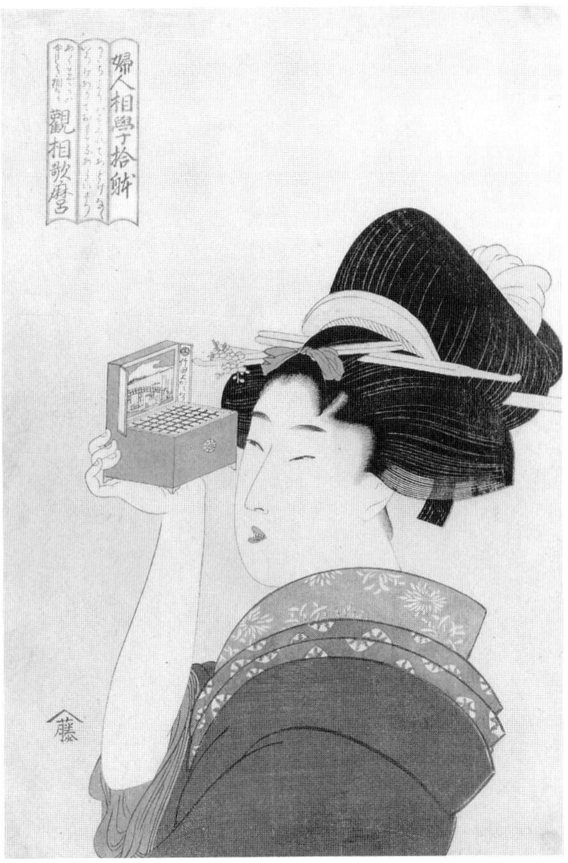

125. Kitagawa Utamaro, *Woman with Mini-Peepbox*, colour woodblock print from the series *Bijin Sōgaku juttai*; c. 1800. Photo: Christie's, New York.

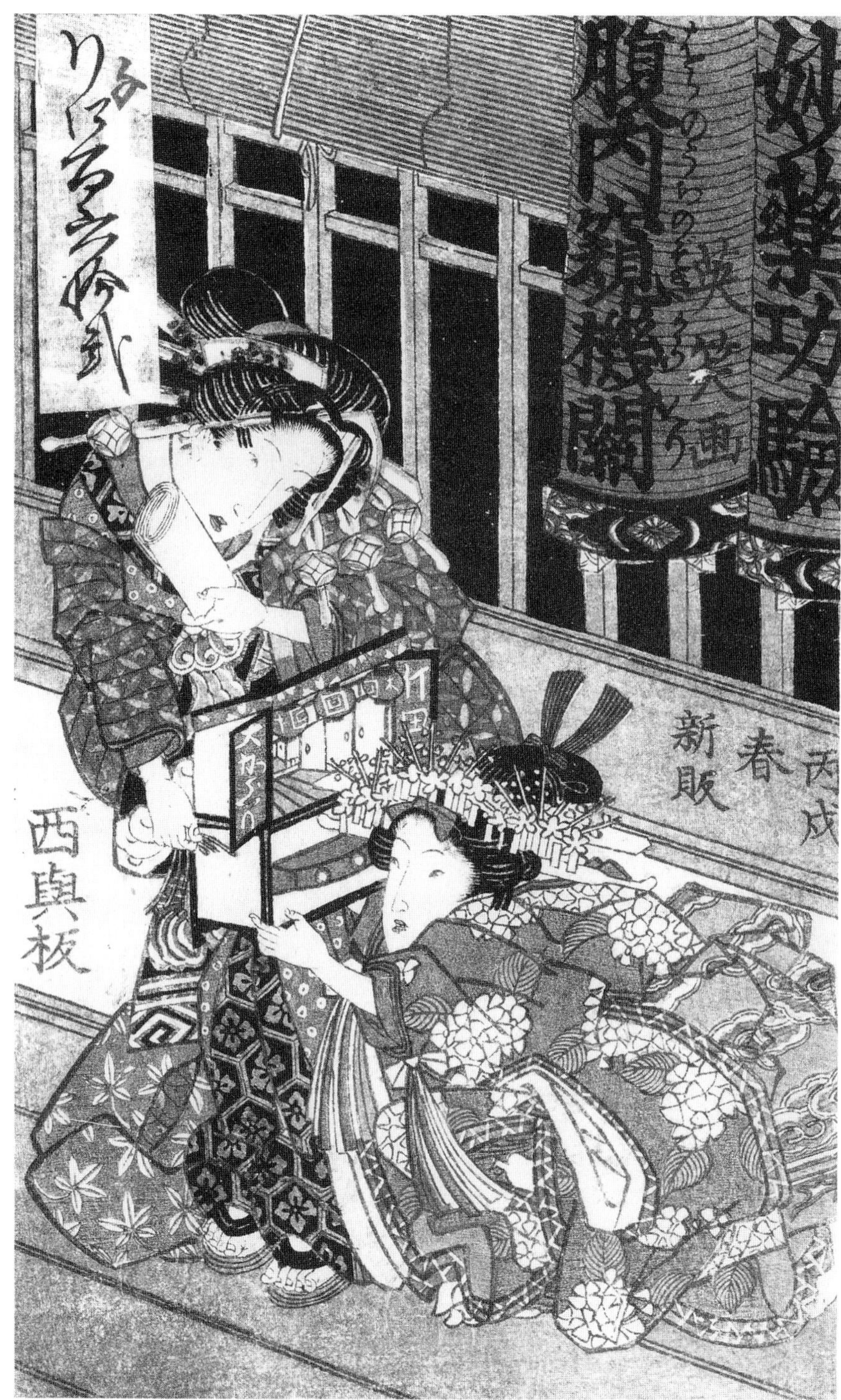

126. Shunsai Eishō, cover to Nansenshō Somahito, *Hara no uchi nozoki karakuri*, vol. 2, 1826. National Diet Library, Tokyo.

The use of professional microscopes with mini-prints was probably rare, and they would hardly have become so popular had there not been a common device that annexed the peeping-*karakuri* to the microscope to make a household mini-viewing box. The peep-hole in such devices was fitted with a magnifying lens so that the miniaturised scene became quite large. The single lens would have had only rather weak magnifying power, but it was the rhetoric that was important: the Western scientific gaze incorporated into the mechanisms of a fair-ground booth and used to capture the personal human world. No such box survives, but a print by Utamaro shows a young woman using one (Fig. 125). The casing is seemingly of dimensions to accommodate pictures just the size of Hokusai's. To judge from the markings on the side, it was made by the great Osaka automaton impresario Takeda Ōmi, and very possibly marketed by him in good numbers.[114] The picture on the backboard shows Ryōgoku Bridge, the binding locus of Edo life and the nation's industrious hub. As the woman looks in, she sees more than pictures on paper, for it is people who cross and recross the field of view, each with energies, motivations, and wills. Utamaro calls for some cogent reading of his print, for it is signed "Utamaro the Physiognomist" and forms part of the series *Ten Physiognomic Types of Woman (Fujin sōgaku jittai)*, issued in the early-1790s as the continuation of the *Ten Physiognomic Types of Married Woman (Fujo jinsō juppin)*; Pl. 10). The space in the cartouche to identify which type this is, reads in the idiom of the scholar explaining the person's face, "Far better than the exterior would suggest, and having a cute kind of allure that does not appear on the surface, this is an incredibly delightful physiognomic type". The woman and the box share their principal characteristics, but coupled to science the visions, unlike those of the peep-box heart of Kyōden's feckless female in the story of the heart slides (Fig. 62), this person is sincere which is rare enough to be "incredibly delightful."[115]

Nansenshō Somahito incorporated the peeping-*karakuri* in his book too, for although the title-page had shown a microscope as such, the outer cover had given a pair of prostitutes amusing themselves with a tiny peep-box (Fig. 126). Sanba's *Peeping-karakuri for Looking into the Human Heart (Hitogokoro nozoki-karakuri)*, it will be recalled from Chapter 4, had come out a dozen years earlier, and it evidently inspired Somahito's almost identical title. They wished for both science and the fairground.[116] To the right, the name of Takeda can be discerned, while three crests of Danjūrō hang along the top. Actors and women of the night – those whose mealy words for professional reasons failed to coincide with their hearts look in at the peep-holes. The women who look are also the objects of the readers' probe, and the instrument used points towards the anatomy theatre with its definitive revealing of parts, but also to the fun of the fair and the exposure of humanity in moments of hedonism in the Floating World. The objectivity so beloved of the Western scientist was not the inspiration of the Edo-period inspector; it was the nature of the moral self and its relation to the polity, the ruptures between in and out and the discrepancies between life-style and Way. If the eyes are to be clarified by a piercing lens, the visions striven for are those of the ethical eyes of the Buddhas.

SEVEN

THE VIEW FROM ON HIGH

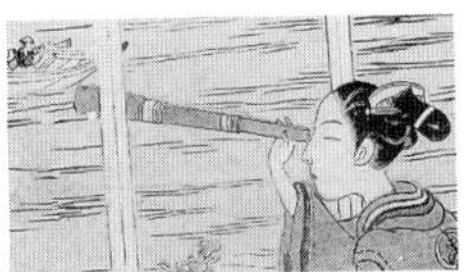

TACHIBANA NANKEI WROTE how when he looked through a microscope, he found himself inclined to thoughts that shook his every expectation. Nankei's words, recorded in 1795, were quoted as the epigraph to this book.[1] The doctor had discovered myriad forms of life inhabiting a single drop of water, and in his amazement he went on to wonder whether the converse might not be true, that vastness was also without measure. The proposition itself was not new. Buddhism was nothing if not sophisticated in cosmological span, and it accepted no limitations of scale in that direction. But Nankei went on to putate something more: the existence of a far-off being, located within the boundlessness of space and staring at the universe as if it were a droplet, through a lens of galactic reach.

Upon probing with the microscope, Nankei proceeded to immediate speculation on matters relating to the intellectual framework that he had inherited ready-formed. His search in water was not for the findings of Enlightenment sciences but for what pertained to himself and his own purpose within the vaster world: the relation of humanity to the sacral entities of heaven, as he conceived them, was the object of Nankei's inquiry. Nankei was a religious man. His thinking ran to the whereabouts of the divine, and how the gods and Buddhas impinged on earth.

THE COMMANDING GAZE

Nankei knew the earth was round and used this information for his analogy. The knowledge had recently arrived, and as Nankei noted, the proof lay in the navigations of Dutch shipping, which "sailing off into the west, came home again from the east."[2] Nothing prevented circumnavigation. The spherical earth hung like a particle suspended in space. Shiba Kōkan likened it to a bauble: "Heaven is vast, and no more can be said of it than that, while the great earth is a lone bullet hanging there."[3] Kōkan adopted the standard *Rangaku* line, identifying heaven (*ten*) with space, and the earth (*daichi*) as a sphere within it. But it was more normal in Japan to see the human planet and its local heaven, adhering above like a dome, combined as *tenchi*, "heaven-and-earth," or the world, beyond which space radiated out. The cosmos was a spilling together of world into world in a slew of objects, now said to be a river of roundels. Buddhas and bodhisattvas presided over one or several of the parts. Nankei equated his microscope with the "all-seeing eyes of the Buddhas" (*hotoke no tengan*) who surveyed his human heaven-and-earth.

In 1825, the by-then elderly Nankei took up the matter again. In a collection of assorted jottings that summed up a lifetime of travel and healing, *Light Chat from a Northern Window*

(Hokusō sadan), he told how, "looking through a precision microscope of foreign make . . ." he found:

> There are places too remote for even the microscope to reach, a fact which must be equivalent for things too vast, and which our minds find it impossible to measure or conceive. This world of ours is a sphere, rolling along in a mass of similar kind, and if a colossal person were to look at this, they would mistake it for water. We cannot be certain there is not such a being out there, holding a microscope and looking on at this aqueous assembly of spheres flowing on and on.[4]

Nankei speaks of a "colossal person" (*kyōdai no hito*). He moves away from the previous theistic to a more neutral terminology, and his notional galactic seeing is brought more into line with the image of the human star-gazer, peering across infinity, telescope in hand.

The telescope was the paramount tool of those who plotted the planets. Aoki Shūrin, a *Rangaku* expert from Hagi, noted in a study of 1825: "Telescopes are the primary instruments of astronomy (*tengaku*). Those who look through them find their eyes reeling off into space ten thousand leagues distant, while remaining all the while where they always were."[5] Telescopes came in two sorts, the celestial and the terrestrial. The former were the more highly regarded, but were necessarily rarer. Mitaku Yorai had recorded as early as 1732 that the celestial telescope needed eight lenses, whereas the terrestrial sort could manage with only two, which made it easier and cheaper to fashion.[6] In common with other optical instruments, telescopes improved over the eighteenth century and by Shūrin's day, the best had up to two hundred-times magnification – a fact of which he was aware, although he knew it only by report, never having encountered such a piece himself. Japanese-made terrestrial telescopes existed, but the quality was uneven. Terajima Ryōan remarked, in the *Sino-Japanese Universal Illustrated Encyclopaedia (Wakan sansai zue)* of 1713, that pieces of local manufacture could reach some 12 km, but that imported ones were superior in range; Yorai cuttingly noted "China has failed to supply any of outstanding quality,"[7] but he implied care was to be taken before purchasing a domestic one, too, as circuitously put, "every now and again an inability to see much with a Japanese one is to be marked."[8] Yorai found domestic glasses generally acceptable for land viewing, but "Nagasaki plays the leading role" in telescopes able to "show the moon up close."

The shogunate preferred imported telescopes for official use, and secured for themselves the most sophisticated and latest sort (Fig. 127). Yet of the public who came across telescopes, most would have seen only indigenous ones. These became quite plentiful though quality is moot. Ban Kōkei, a literary-minded home-furnishings dealer from Kyoto and a friend of Nankei, expressed displeasure at the way the authorities were relying on foreign items rather than stimulating regional craftsmanship.[9] By the end of the century, though Nankei was able to publicise that no thanks to the shogunate, a certain Iwahashi Zenbei from Kaitsuka in Izumi had at last, "with great enterprise and skill," made the first domestic celestial telescope, "said to be able to discern sun, moon, stars, and planets"; an associate, he went on, affirmed the piece to be equal to or better than European equivalents.[10]

Instruments of heavenly capability remained scarce, and the typical telescope secured views only across earthly spaces. In the middle of the nineteenth century, when Matthew Perry led his U.S. navel convoy into Edo Bay to secure a base for blubber-processing, he surveyed the unaccustomed coastline from the vantage of his ship and noticed how the forts that guarded the ridges of the cliffs were only mockups: "the Japanese probably had not calculated on the exactness of view afforded by a Dollard's telescope or a French opera glass."[11] Perry's smugness was ill-conceived. Had his ships arrived in Nagasaki (as the law required), they would have been over-

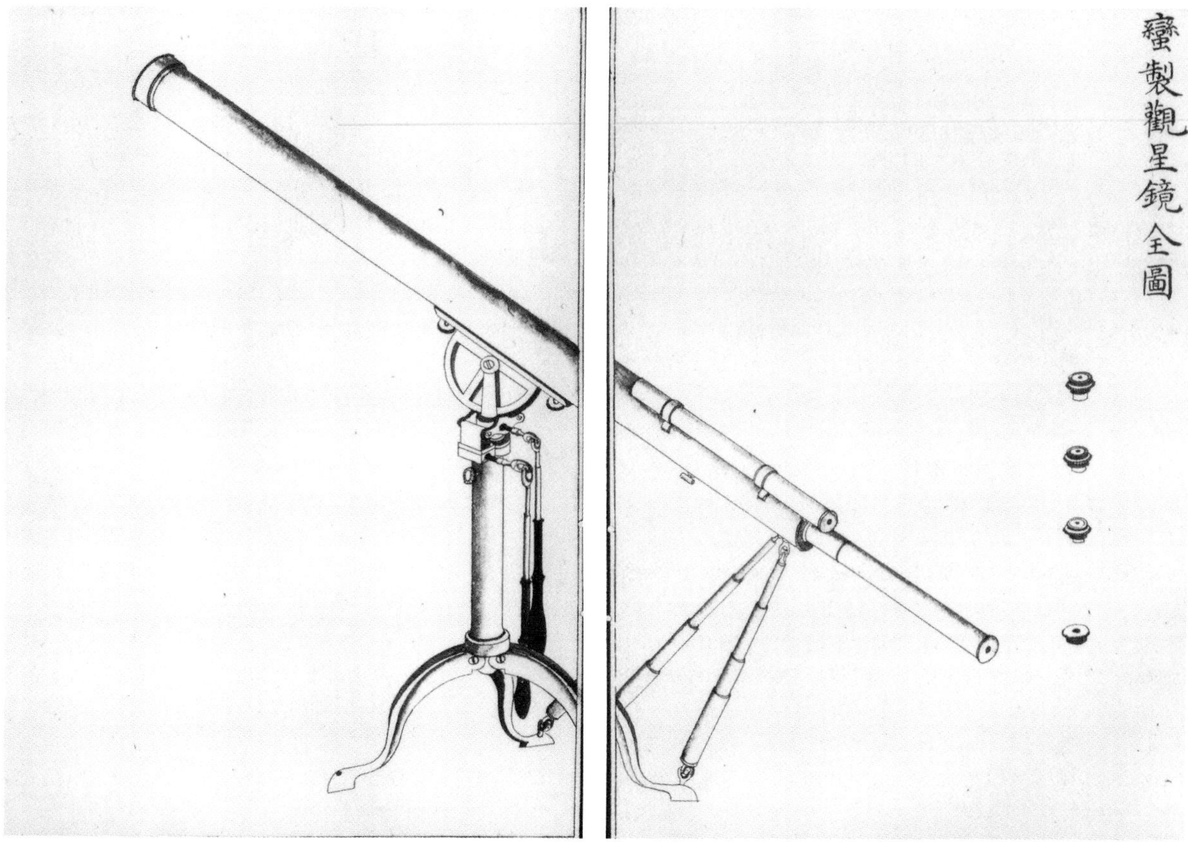

127. Unsigned, *Foreign Celestial Telescope*, drawing from Shibukawa Kagesuke (et al. eds.), *Kansei rekisho* vol. 20, 1853. National Diet Library, Tokyo.

taken by alerts in very real strongholds set at the entrance to the harbour. The VOC knew this, as Charles Thunberg recorded: "on the mountains, by order of the Japanese government, were placed several out-posts, which were provided with telescopes, that the guard might discover at a distance the arrival of ships."[12]

Such telescopes were intended to establish coigns of vantage, places from which to see without being seen, and a forewarning of events. They could pre-empt and so command. The notion of a "commanding gaze" should not be taken lightly, for it had political implications. A telescope required an unimpeded sweep, and ascent to a high place was desirable. The telescopic gazer joined the pre-existing construction of lofty or downward sight, which, in Japan at least, was already dense in meaning. Panoramic seeing had military value, as the 250-odd castle keeps of Japan attested. But it was not the lot of all persons to command. The downward gaze, aided or naked, was fenced around and closed off. It was taboo in Japan for the optical vector to go against the political line of command, and for an inferior to look down on a leader presaged destabilisation. So circumscribed, indeed, was viewing from an elevation that it was dismantled as a meaningful category for many classes of person, who would simply never have known it.

Daimyo castles had mostly been constructed before the cessation of warfare in the 1630s, and many had their look-out towers (*monomi-yagura*) as well as their keeps (*tenshū-kaku*). As the Edo period progressed, these lost their functionality. Still looked up at by those below, turrets became otiose in peacetime, and most fell from service. As the elite surrendered its optical dominance, the downward vision was all but obliterated from the field of thought.

The Tokugawa shoguns and their lords had come to power through force, but they moved towards an ideology based on rule through virtue and merit.[13] The shunning of the surveying gaze was in furtherance of this, for only those fearful of a restive populace required a permanent watch. The shoguns wished it to be thought they needed no such thing, as their goodness alone compelled obedience. Existing castle towers could not be razed without implying a lack of resolve, but when natural disasters took their frequent tolls in lightning, fire, or earthquake, the lofty defensive structures were seldom replaced. In 1657, the main donjon of Edo Castle, thrusting 35 metres into the sky, was lost to fire. It was never rebuilt. A century later, the Tokugawa palace in Kyoto, the Castle in the Second Avenue (Nijō-jō), lost its principal tower, and it too was allowed to remain denuded. Neither latitudinarianism or poverty shelved reconstruction: keeps were public announcements of rulers' fears, and stripped of its panoramic sway a government seemed rhetorically better.

Thunberg visited Edo Castle in 1776 and was permitted access to a subsidiary elevation, "an eminence that commanded a view of the whole town,"[14] he noted, and he extolled the breathtaking sight with, "I shall never forget the delightful prospect we had." But few, even in the castle administration, would have seen the view, or more to the point, few would have considered the experience a dignifying event appropriate as a literary or artistic theme. For generations, English children have played the game of racing to the top of a hill and shouting, "I'm the king of the castle; you're the dirty rascal!" The cry concerns possession of visual command – being the monarch of all that is surveyed. Edo-period children had a similar game, but when they ran up they shouted, "I am the only cedar on this moor; praise me loud!"[15] The cedar is straight and long-living and demands submission, but it has no eyes. By the eighteenth century, looking down had collapsed as a cogent structure for knowledge.

All began to change during the time of enthusiasm for the mechanistic seeing of *Ran*. The downward view was retrieved, but with radically altered meaning, becoming two-way and reciprocal.

LATE-EIGHTEENTH-CENTURY CHANGES

Looking down does not require mechanical equipment. Buildings can be erected to offer elevated sight, and these were generally labelled *kaku or rō* (turrets). Yet it is noteworthy that the history of Japanese architecture is short of examples of genuinely lofty structures. Kyoto had its venerable Golden and Silver Turrets of 1397 and 1482 (now called "pavilions" in English), and there were the independent buildings there identified as the Two Turrets, with the evocative names of the Palace of Lapis Lazuli (Rūri-den, c. 1340), and the Turret of Flying Clouds (Hiun-kaku, 1600) all recommended for the tourist to visit.[16] But the very fact that these four were so effusively celebrated attests to the rarity of examples. None was in any case above three storeys high, and more importantly, the rising up was not associated with anything achieved visually. The turrets had names that did not imply seeing, and levitation was more for enjoyment of the breezes or a feeling of being lost among branches. The Silver Turret was generally called the Turret of Morning Sounds (Chōon-kaku); when the third shogun, Iemitsu, constructed a tower in 1623, despite a spectacular 270-degree vista, he named it the Turret for Listening to Autumn (Chōshū-kaku), appealing similarly to hearing, not to sight.[17]

With such exceptions, significantly raised edifices within the public domain meant Buddhist pagodas. Thunberg admired the "several entities which are not only very lofty, but at the same time very narrow,"[18] and "entity" was an apt description of pagodas, for although admission to them was sometimes possible, they were not really buildings, more funerary stupas than architectural towers. Pagodas punctuated the skyline for the edification of those below, like spires, but were *not* to be ascended. Several of the finest pagodas were highly delicate, or had become so over time, and even when technically climbable, they were so full of supports and struts that entry was barely practicable. The literati artist and samurai Tanomura Chikuden, passing through Osaka on his way to Edo in 1800, was tempted by the late seventeenth-century pagoda at the Temple of the Heavenly Kings (Tennō-ji). The entity was equipped with internal ladders, but Chikuden forewent the opportunity to ascend and, not sufficiently interested, continued on to Edo uninterrupted (when he returned some months later, it lay a charred victim of fire).[19] Chikuden's ambivalence marks him as inhabiting a period of conceptual flux. A growing urge to seize the view was coupled with a nonchalance that militated against expending much energy in the effort. The assumption remained that the high-placed gaze was not particularly to be striven for.

An interesting ambiguity can be noticed in one of Kyoto's chief attractions, the Temple of Freshwater (Kiyomizu-dera); originally constructed in high antiquity, it had been rebuilt after fires in 1633. A three-storey pagoda in the compound was not accessible, nor especially high, but the temple boasted an extraordinary image hall, built with a gantry that jutted over the hillside. The construction was spectacular enough for other cities to imitate it, and Osaka, Edo, and Nagasaki all erected their own branch Temples of Freshwater (Fig. 128).[20] What is most to be noted, however, is that the gantries, though relished, were *not* ascended because they provided panoramas: the Kyoto gantry was orientated sideways so that it did not in any case give over the city, which would have offered the headiest view; the hills beneath were planted with a forest of maples whose foliage was there exactly to prevent clear sight. It was the occluding elements of leaf and bough that beckoned visitors who came mostly in autumn months in search of the crimson expanses that precisely prevented vision of anything further below. The Edo Freshwater gantry, built two years before the reconstruction of the Kyoto one (it was shifted in 1693, though without materially affecting the view), was 150 metres high, but it overlooked cherry trees, and spring was the time to come; beyond the trees was the unincidented sheen of Shinobazu Pond.

The realisation that the Freshwater gantries might provide places for inspection of a visible, even plottable, vista below, was an invention of the latter part of the eighteenth century. After generations of enjoying a *termination* of ocular advance in carpets of red, white, or blue, in the 1780s, Maruyama Ōkyo represented the Kyoto gantry, depicting it as it had not been shown before, as a place of inspection (Fig. 129).[21] Ōkyo had experimented widely with the pictorial manners and mechanical devices of persistent scrutiny, and he showed the stage exaggeratedly tall, emphasising the loftiness, with two figures leaning over, peering at the hills below; the trees are bare and the season is wrong, so that few visitors have come. The draughtsmanship of the picture allows the viewer to see both gantry and view, and all is caught in an image that is a conscious simulation of the best-known Western medium, for though painted, Ōkyo incorporates the characteristic hatched lines of etchings.[22] The image is also painted in reverse, so that the work insinuates itself into the vision-enhancing genre of the copperplate *vue d'optique*.

Ōta Nanpo wrote a kyoka on the Edo gantry in about 1820:

The blossoms everywhere around;
Like a *go*-board;
Mt. Ueno.
Before its Black Gateway,
Such whiteness of cloud![23]

The kyoka counterposes the famous black entrance with the white flowering trees, and Nanpo has ascended for the delight of finding his gaze enveloped by the haze of cherries; and yet as he looks down, he also notices that the trees fit into the crisscrossed and demarcated city, coordinated like the chequered pattern of a gaming board.

The Nagasaki branch of the Temple of Freshwater had perhaps the best prospect of all, for it allowed an unpunctuated view over the harbour. The Chinese and Dutch islands with their vessels in dock, the shogunal compound in Edomachi, and the townspeople's dwellings could all be taken in with a single uninterrupted sweep. The Nagasaki structure was, in fact, the only one erected for the explicit purpose of panoramic seeing and had been built so that no hindrances stood below. But Nagasaki had always been a place of alterity, and stood ambiguously towards the normal space of the realm. Those who stood and overlooked the international encounters taking place in the town below gained access to a novel experience, and they knew it to be foreign. They observed, detached from normalcy, and the vista they saw was all run together in a general unbalancing of scale (Pl. 1).

A clear expression of the thrill of restoration of downward sight may be evinced by another kyoka by Nanpo, written much earlier, in 1773. Nanpo took as his starting point a tenth-century waka by Fujiwara Takamitsu, which, caught in the thought structures of its own period, ran:

In this world forlorn and sad,
Jealous I live
Of the moon.[24]

Takamitsu looks up at the resplendent disk from the despondent position of an earthling. In his composition, Nanpo turned the verse around, making this world the splendid place; and thus it is the moon which looks down from above:

On this world wonderful and great,
Jealously peering in
Is the moon.[25]

The inversion turns a desire for escape to a pristine world outside into a celebration of vision. Nanpo anthropomorphically associates the moon with a man or woman looking on at a place in which they are anxious to participate.

The allusion to Takamitsu may be compared with a chance (though none the less revealing) similarity between two other works: one invokes the person of a fire watchman; Japanese cities were built of wood and heated by open braziers, thus prone to conflagration, so watchmen were stationed in towers about nine metres high to scan the world below. This was an official occupation, and to the average person, the fire-tower encroached more as something to be looked up at from below than down from above (Pl. 14). A senryu published in 1765 perpetuates this visual sense:

Like the joker of the pack,
The fire watchman's face
Sticking out.[26]

An anonymous early nineteenth-century book, illustrated by Toyokuni, also takes the power of the watchman as its theme, but is athwart visual regimes for the man's downward gaze is the subject of the story (it is pornographic and the offi-

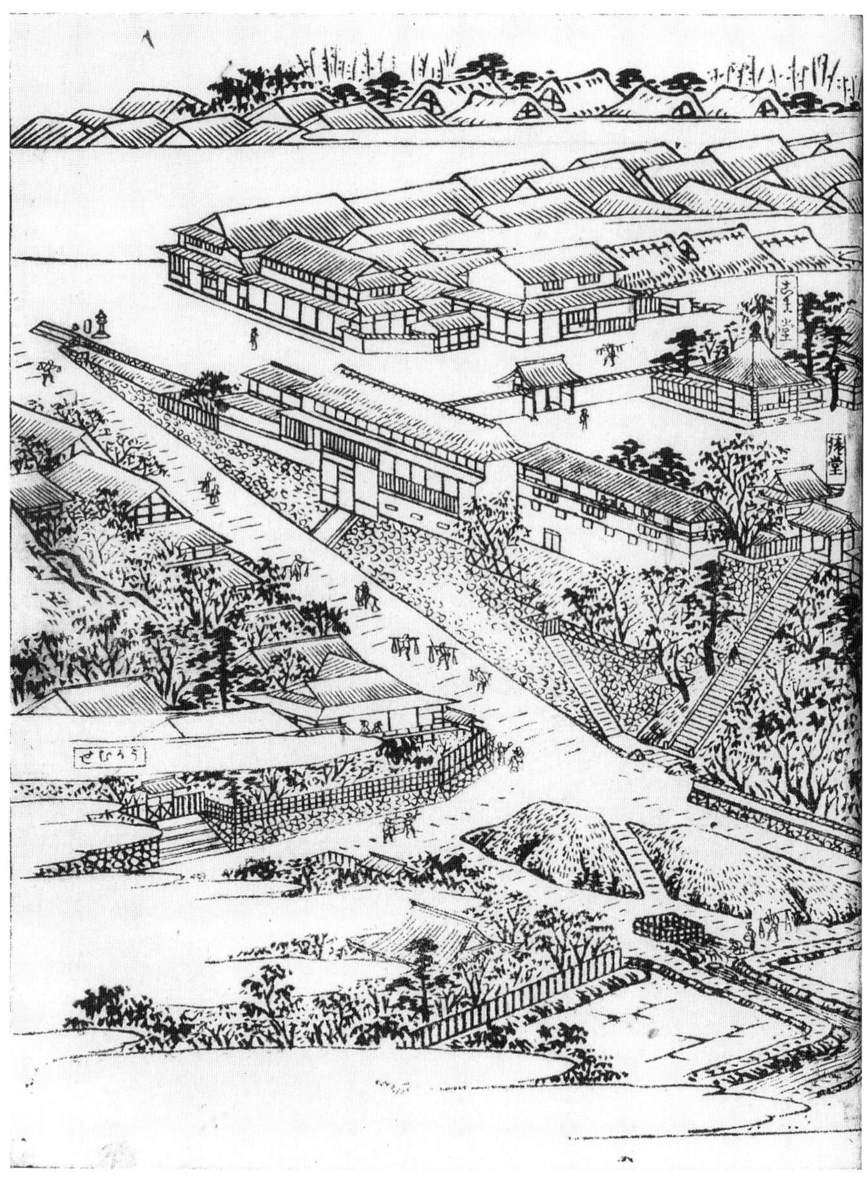

cial pries into bedrooms), yet the work itself is entitled *The Cry of a Goose That Greets the Night (Hōya gan no koe);* the tale speaks of sight from above, but the title addresses the aural effect of the overflying bird on those below.[27] Like Chikuden vacillating at the foot of the pagoda of the Heavenly Kings, Toyokuni hesitates between systems. That the trigger of the change has come from the instrument-based gaze of science is clear, for the watchman is said to have been made suddenly more visually acute by being equipped with a telescope, and Toyokuni's illustrations are drawn within circles, like sightings through a lens.

Late eighteenth-century changes can be further seen in the building projects of Satake Yosh-

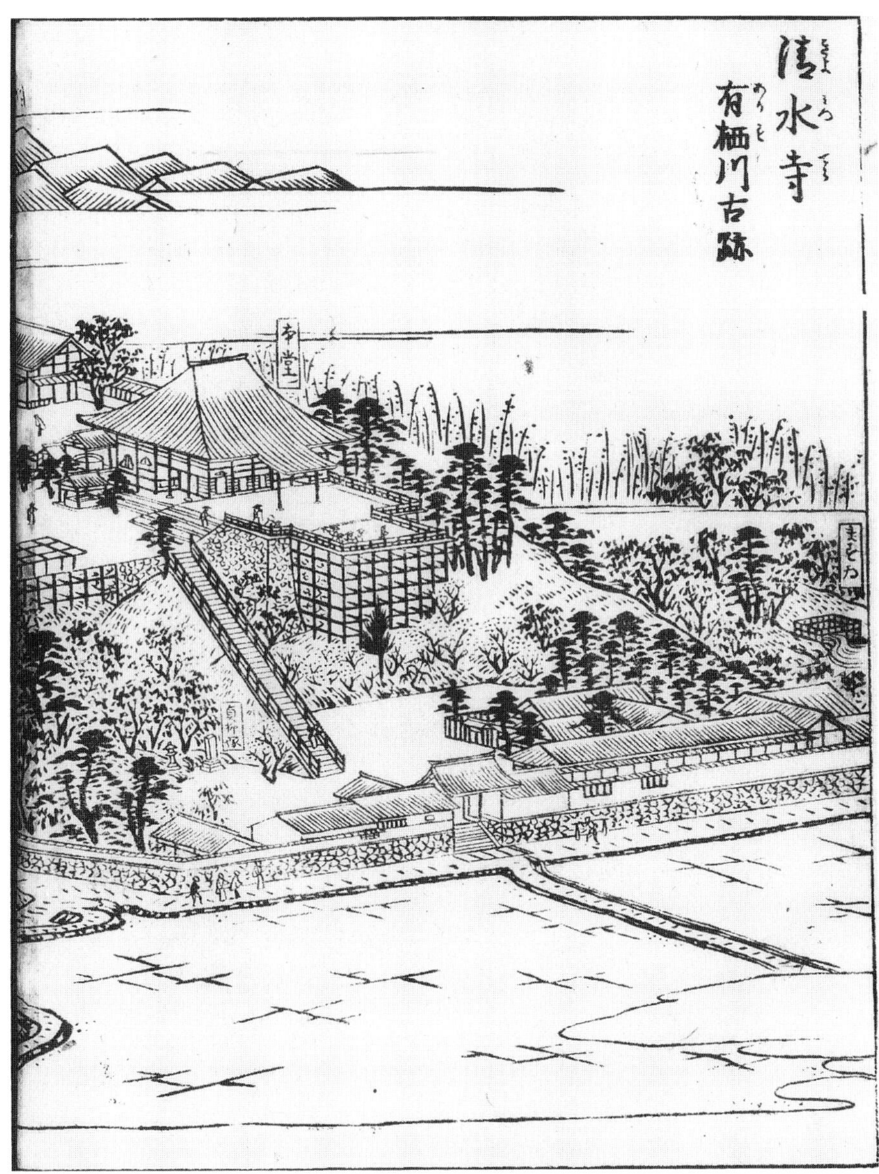

128. Takehara Shunchōsai, *Temple of Kiyomizu and Riverbed of the Former Arisu,* from Akisato Ritō, *Settsu meisho zue,* 1798. SOAS, University of London.

iatsu, daimyo of Akita and great patron of *Rangaku.* The Satake stronghold of Kubota Castle was constructed on an eminence secure against potential attack.[28] But it was without a keep, and apparently had never had one, although there were lesser towers, seven in number, one being as many as three storeys. A pretence of inadvertence in viewing the land was nicely coupled with the requisite military defences. Treasured by successive lords was a part of the complex erected once warfare had subsided, probably in the late seventeenth century, called the "projecting study" (*dashi-shōin*) or the "turret chamber" (*yagura-zashiki*), which was a two-storey private withdrawing room abutting a sudden cliff and securing the finest views.

In 1776, most of Kubota Castle was lost to fire, the study included. Another outbreak inflicted further damage two years later, and Yoshiatsu moved out.[29] It was during his enforced absence that he composed his two treatises on Western pictures appending to them a series of sketches, including plottings of diminution over distance and the effects of looking down on objects (Fig. 130).[30] Yoshiatsu completed his writings late in 1778, and in the fifth month of 1781 he moved back to the resurrected Kubota, with its refurbished projecting study.

Two years later, while in attendance at the shogunal castle, he constructed a three-storey pleasure dome in the compound of one of the Akita mansions by Shamisen Pond in Shitaya. High structures were outlawed within the city, but this was during the administration of Tanuma Okitsugu and profligacy went unrebuked.[31] Nothing is known of Yoshiatsu's tower exactly, but the interests of the daimyo are such as to suggest that a quite direct connexion to *Ran* concerns is likely. Yoshiatsu invited a number of prominent figures to warm the building, and verses were composed. Nanpo was present, and he specifically referred to the new downward vision the hall afforded, alluding also to the name of the locale, Shamisen – a musical instrument the pond was supposed to resemble, but which meant, literally, "three-taste strings" allowing a pun with the number of storeys. The verse can only be paraphrased for the second line is to be read in two ways:

> On the third floor,
> The shamisen is down-fretted thrice, and up-fretted twice;
> The Shamisen Pond is three floors down, from two floors up.
> Looking out as you will, you never tire
> Of this view.[32]

Yoshiatsu's urge to live upstairs was a departure from indigenous norms, whereas the preference for higher-level rooms with views was a well-known feature of the European taste. Nagakubo Sekisui, the samurai from Mito, in Nagasaki in 1765, stressed the prevalence of two-storey buildings in the VOC compound; not used for storage (as below-roof areas were in Japanese domestic architecture), the upper parts were open and intended for recreation and dining. As Sekisui walked about, he saw Dutchmen at the raised windows, decked out, as he said, in their wigs, sleeveless jackets, and *botan* (buttons), and he found the effect of their looking-down "peculiar and rather dubious" (*ayashi*).[33] Tazawa Shunbō recorded, in about 1807, the existence on Dejima of a "two-floor glass-windowed house" complete with a specially constructed "cooling-off platform" (*nōkyōdai*), or balcony, designed to allow enjoyment of the harbour extending below.[34]

The turret-gaze was a feature of Dutch seeing. Dejima was scaled down compared to a real Western city, as those who visited it were perfectly aware, and Kōkan pointed out that, though socialising on the second storey might seem surprising to most of his compatriots, in The Hague people had access to seven or eight floors, with glazed windows right up to the top, maximising pleasurable views. He went on: "the copperplate etchings coming from there show temples and schools, with halls, towers, and balconies rising up scores of metres. In stone blocks, floor upon floor they will never rot away. Some of the towers are round in shape, some square. . . ."[35] Tsūdayū, the returned castaway, gave out the information that Russians used the very top floors of their houses for storage, but that meant units on the fourth and above, buildings habitually being six floors high; receptions, he said, were conducted principally on the third level.[36]

MEANS OF ASCENT

The means of ascent in a Japanese building was by stairs which were ladder-like and steep. The Dutch translator Yoshio Kōsaku, by contrast,

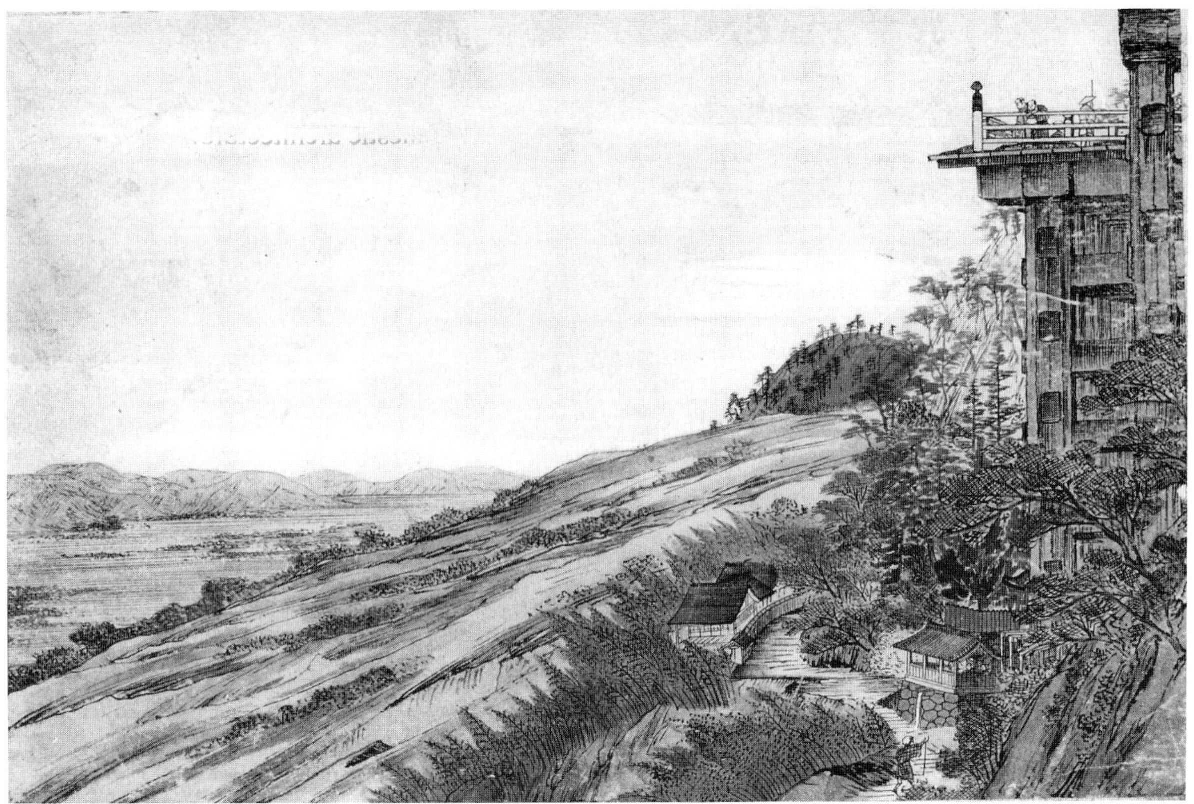

129. Maruyama Okyo, *Temple of Kiyomizu*, single sheet painting; c. 1780(?). Private collection. *The scene is painted in reverse.*

had a Western-style staircase put into his *Oranda* house in Nagasaki (though not visible in the illustration published by Nankei; Fig. 1) and he entertained upstairs. If a climb was expected of guests, they had to be given a means of elegant and composed arrival. Various novel means of ascent were being experimented with at the time, and as the aspiration to regain the raised plane of view gathered momentum, several technologies were essayed. How the top levels of Yoshiatsu's three-story tower were reached cannot be told, but among the daimyo's sketches are cross-sectional and ground-plan drawings of a previously unknown structure – the spiral staircase (Fig. 131). The drawing does not indicate exits for floors, but the twenty-seven steps would be capable of serving a three-storey structure, and it could be continued as far up as desired, providing the joinery was competent. Tsūdayū noted that Tsar Pavel's palace in St. Petersburg had a spiral stair, which meant "you go up on your toes," rather than shinning ladderwise, and "you can't tell exactly how many floors you have climbed"; the building, he said, was five floors high, with a marvellous view from the top.[37]

Satake's represented stair is a double helix. This allowed a greater volume of traffic, by upward and downward lines being free from jostling. Probably of Arab invention, the European double spiral stair was regarded as a creation of genius difficult to erect, and it featured in only a small number of buildings, most famously the

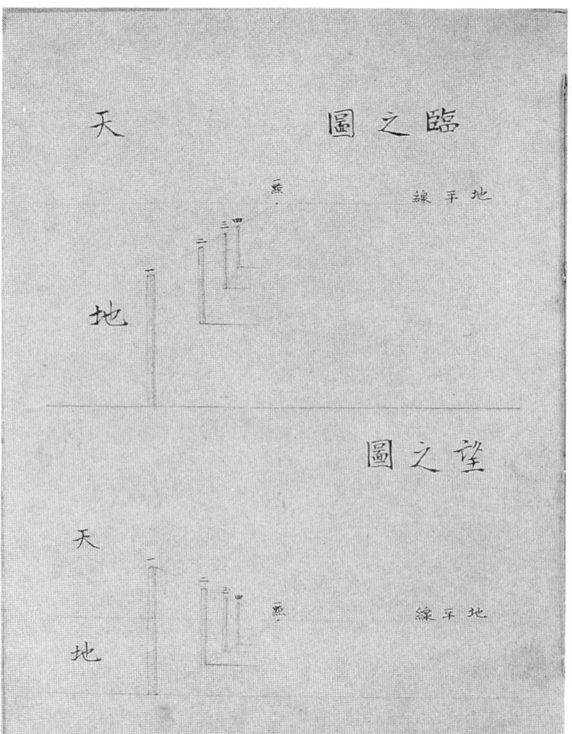

130. Satake Yoshiatsu (Shozan), *Looking Down* and *Looking into the Distance*, drawing from the sketchbook, *Shasei-chō*; 1778. Senshū Museum of Art, Akita.

The following page illustrates the beholder, drawn as a Dutchman, looking across the scenes given.

Château de Chambord. The twin stair was extensively known, however, through inclusion in Giacomo da Vignola's *Due regole della prospettiva pratica,* first published in 1583, and rapidly accepted as one of the classic rule-books of Renaissance building. Yoshiatsu's design is taken directly from Vignola, the work having been imported to Japan, no doubt, in an eighteenth-century Dutch edition.[38] It may seem excessive to speculate whether Yoshiatsu attempted to replicate Vignola's triumph in his Edo mansion, but it is not impossible. The year before Yoshiatsu's tower went up (and while it was probably in the planning stage) his official representative in Edo, Hōseidō Kisanji, used the medium of a kibyoshi to pun *daitsū,* "consummately trendy," with *entsū,* "roundward progression" – the word that came to denote a spiral staircase. His lord's project was evidence of his modern bent.[39] Shortly afterward, in 1796 (by which time Yoshiatsu was dead), a double-helix stair was actually constructed in Japan, also serving a three-storey tower, the Turbo Hall in the compound of the Temple of Seishū-ji in Aizu-Wakamatsu, a flourishing castle town midway between Akita and Edo. No floors gave off, and the Turbo Hall was a free-standing, enclosed staircase, climbed for the pure excitement of going up. Set within the well were images of the bodhisattva Kannon, for the stair was formally used for the rite of Three Circumambulations (*sansō*) so that by the time they reached the top, pilgrims had effected three full circles around the images. Edo may never have had a double helix, but it did have a single spiral stair at the Temple of the Five Hundred Arhats (Gohyaku Rakan-ji), the same temple that owned the van Royen paintings given by the VOC to the shogun. Although its date is unclear, as is its precise structural type, this hall was earlier than the Aizu hall (whose name, Turbo Hall, it shared), and probably erected a few years before Yoshiatsu's tower; Imai Tanito, a gazetteer writing in the context of a guide to the city of Edo in 1792, described completion as "recent" (*konogoro*).[40]

The Turbo Hall of the Arhat temple was three floors, and as at Aizu the stair was so gentle as to be almost a slope. It allowed an easy progress up to seventeen metres. Tanito greatly esteemed the height, "rivalling the clouds," so that when he tilted his head to make out the finial from below, he saw his own eyebrows![41] This would have been the greatest architectural elevation experienced by any user and twice as high as the city's fire watchtowers. If overtly intended for encircling images of Kannon, the Edo Turbo Hall was also prized for a gantry built out above the roof of the second floor, affording views. This

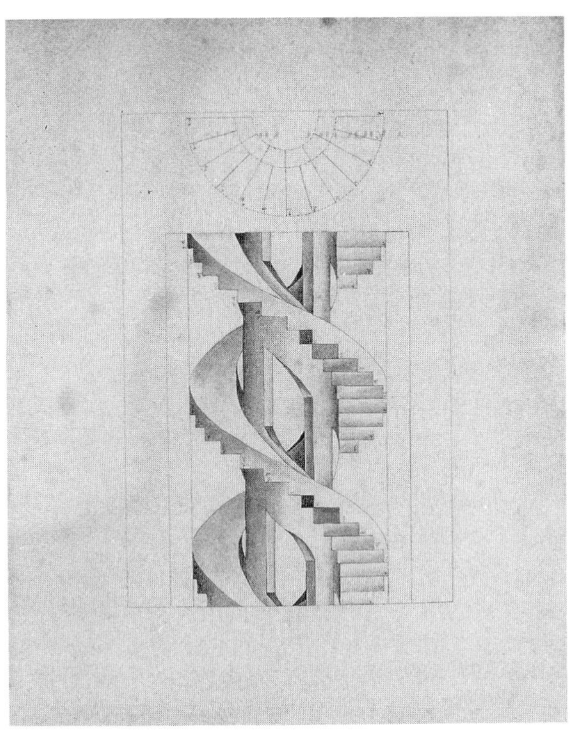

131. Satake Yoshiatsu (Shozan), *Double Spiral Stair*, drawing from his sketchbook, *Shasei-chō*; 1778. Senshū Museum of Art, Akita.

beat the sensation of ascending the Freshwater temple, because that structure was cliff-hanging and not independent, and so less sheer; rather than looking only one way, the Turbo Hall gave prospects in three. Tanito compared the scene from the top with the proverbially finest vistas in China: "Better by a long chalk" was his judgment "than the Eight Views of the West Lake;"[42] a monk named Kakunen wrote in 1813 of a sensation of being raised, all unbeknownst to himself by the winding ascent up to the balcony where "I could take in Sūzaki in Fukagawa way off in the distance, right around to the beach at Shibaura, all in a single sweeping gaze."[43]

The giddiness brought on by the circumambulations seemed to entrance users as they went around, until they were spewed out high up among divine images, awestruck. The prime icons in the temple, as its name suggests, were five hundred arhats, those men who had heard the Great Sermon of the Buddha Sakyamuni, and been enlightened. The site of that famous predication had been Vulture Peak (Ryōjusen), the highest place on earth. Those who ascended the Turbo Hall after having walked through the main hall with its five hundred life-sized statues, must have felt an arhat breaking out within themselves, as they lost their human limitations and entered the holy fellowship high at the pinnacle of Edo.

Vulture Peak was a crucial site to East-Asian Buddhism, and the place had never fallen rom memory, but it surged back into consciousness late in the eighteenth century. Morishima Chūryō announced, in his *Red-fur Miscellany (Kōmō zatsuwa)* of 1787, that Vulture Peak was no pious myth, for it really existed, and indeed the Dutch had found it. The mountain was in Sri Lanka, over seventy-eight kilometres high, still regarded as holy by Buddhists in those parts, and called by the Europeans, Adams Berg.[44] To have Red-furs wandering on holy terrain was an oddity that came inevitably from the shrinkage of territorial space.

The Great Sermon was replicated by the Temple of the Arhats, but in mechanical terms, ascent seemed to hint also at the highest place in Western lore – the Tower of Babel. By longstanding convention, Babel was represented in Europe as climbed by a spiral stair (Brueghel, in the classic depiction, had it so). The Tower of Babel was known of in Japan, and in 1798, Honda Toshiaki explained, "it had a spiral slope so you ascended little by little up to the top, [where] there was a large square platform, affording views beneath of the mountains and oceans of the whole world."[45] The Turbo Hall was exactly like this. All cultural conflict had come from Babel. The widened vistas of *Ran* risked destroying old assurances, as different places with different norms were brought within the purview of one gaze. But the Buddha's Great sermon had been delivered in silence as he simply twisted a lotus flower in his hand, and all had understood.

RECOVERY OF DOWNWARD SIGHT

It had felt to those who ascended the Turbo Hall that their rise was almost automatic. An "urge to soar" uninhibited (*hishō-kan*) has been identified as an impulse of later Edo people.[46] In his biography of the peerless *karakuri*-maker, Suminawa, Rokujūen had interpolated an episode in which he constructed a room that rose and fell in the manner of an elevator. "The house went upward of its own accord," wrote Rokujūen, "and rose to a level of over three metres above the ground; everyone could look down at the tops of trees laid out in the garden below."[47]

The desire to escape constrictions imposed by earth and leap heavenward and, being there, to look back down, is increasingly found from the end of the eighteenth century. The flier stops part-way to oblivion as it were, and speculates on the earth. The first tales of serious attempts at flight appear at the time. There is almost nothing equivalent before, but then in the 1780s, a sudden cluster of narrations appears.[48] About 1785, one Kōkichi, a picture-mounter by trade, invented a flying machine, as recorded in the context of a discussion of automata by the Confucian scholar and doctor Kan Sazan: "[Kōkichi] caught a dove and measured its body weight against its wingspan. He then fashioned a pair of wings for himself, working on the same ratio. He kitted himself out with a *karakuri* strapped to his chest, and setting it working, he flew away."[49] It all sounds simple enough, though Sazan stopped short of explaining the mechanisms. He went on:

> On a certain night, he flew all around outside town, and looking down noticed a group of people having an outdoor party; he wondered if any of his friends might be among them, and came in closer to see. But as he approached the ground, the wind dropped, and before he knew what had happened, he had plummeted into their midst.

The revellers soon overcame their shock and shared the remaining drink with him but the town magistrate got to hear of the event, and passed a textbook Edo verdict: "Doing things that people do not do, even for one's private amusement, is a crime; the wings shall be confiscated and the accused exiled from his abode." The hapless Kōkichi moved from Okayama to Shizuoka, and, familiar with cogs, he set up there as a clock repairer, later shifting to dentistry, an occupation his family continued hereditarily.

About the same time, one Toda Tarōdayū from Mikawa tried to take to the skies: "He was a real eccentric and in his youth was obsessed with inventions. . . . At Goyō there is a seacliff turret, and he conducted his experiments into flying from the top. Coming down hard, he is said to have injured himself grievously."[50] Tokutarō later did better with a pedal-winged apparatus.

Then, in 1794, Hitomi Shōu commented on a farmer from Nii in Akita – not far from the Satake castle where Yoshiatsu's son, Yoshimasa, was now ruling – who studied the form of crows and built himself some wings. Unlike the other aviators, it is not stated that he augmented his strength with a *karakuri,* but his efforts were the most accomplished. "Although he found it difficult at first," noted Shōu, "he gradually improved with practice"; and, the scholar added with no apparent irony:

> He continued to find it hard to fly upward, but when he wanted to descend all he had to do was leap from the ridgepole of some high building on an incline or suchlike, flattening out his wings; he could manage fifteen or eighteen metres, or even twenty, with the greatest of ease and suffering no physical harm.[51]

The historicity of these exploits may be challenged (although there is no reason why gliding could not have been achieved), but recorded and circulated as literary events the flights are important attempts to concretise, even if fictionally, the requirements of the transformed visuality.

A flurry of tales of openly imaginary flights accompany the putative claims of breaking the clogs of earth. Kinjūrō's journey aboard a goose and his subsequent adventures in the land of giants (including inspection of his love letter [Fig. 123]) was discussed above; that story appeared in 1783.[52] Five years later, Rantokusai Shundo wrote and illustrated a kibyoshi of a "Continental umbrella" (*karakasa*) that flew people about at will (including off the gantry of the Freshwater temple in Kyoto).[53] Rokujūen added to the legend of Suminawa his devising a flying machine built in the auspicious form of a crane, and Suminawa said: "It was a wooden crane that I had made a while ago, putting all my energies into it. When a person is tired, they can mount, and the bird will just flap its wings and fly – probably it could go as far as farthest China or India."[54] In other words, they can go wherever the machine is directed.

The list of treatments could be expanded at length, but of interest is how the desire to ascend gradually centred itself around invention of dirigible flying machines. The finest equipment for sharing the high vision of winged creatures was the hot-air balloon.[55] The device had been first successfully tried by the Montgolfier brothers on 21 November 1783 in the Tuileries in Paris, and although this is the story everyone knows today, more celebrated in its own time was the manned ascent of Dr. Charles and the brothers Robert the following month. Chūryō knew of this and recounted in his *Red-fur Miscellany:* "In France they call [the balloon] a *'tuileries'* but the Red-furs call it a *'luftschiff'*. . . . The boat is a few metres in length, and in width about one, with the same draft; two people can fit in."[56] Chūryō fused the pioneers into a certain "Karuresuen-roberuto," but he was as well apprised of the mechanism as any at the time. News travelled fast. Udagawa Genzui, a senior physician and friend of Chūryō's brother Hoshū, learned details from the VOC kapitan, Hendrik Romberg, who read him a newspaper article about the ascent. The information was passed to the shogunate, who received a full report on the fifteenth of the second month, 1784, less than three months after the Charles and Robert flight.[57]

Chūryō reproduced a picture and claimed:

> My illustration comes from a recently published Primitive [Dutch] work in the collection of Lord Ryūkyō, which I have the honour to copy. The picture was imported at Nagasaki last autumn [1786] and offered to Lord Imahashi Ryūkyō. An explanation is written in little letters along the bottom, and I have put the gist across here. I hope to include a detailed pictorial investigation of the device in the next edition.[58]

The "next edition" never appeared, but thanks to Chūryō's book, the plate owned by Ryūkyō, Arima Gensho's lord, the Hollandomaniac daimyo of Fukuchiyama (he was also a keen numismatist of the West and commonly known as Katsuki Masatsuna), reached a wide public. How closely Chūryō copied is unclear, as an original has never been traced; but he showed a water-going boat, with skids, a paddle-wheel, and rudder, flying above puffs of cloud, supported by an inadequately sized balloon, and driven, it seems, by wind caught in a sail. The single passenger is bracing himself against a flagpole. Another imported print, the appearance of which is entirely lost, although it could have been the same one, moved the incumbent magistrate of Nagasaki to compose a Chinese-style verse:

> How clever the Dutch are!
> This thing is floating in the sky with heavy
> weights, like a Chinese ship on the sea.
> It is fixed to a balloon with ropes, and air can be
> let in and out.
> It can travel without meeting any obstacles,
> And I compare it to a crane that flies far in a
> minute.

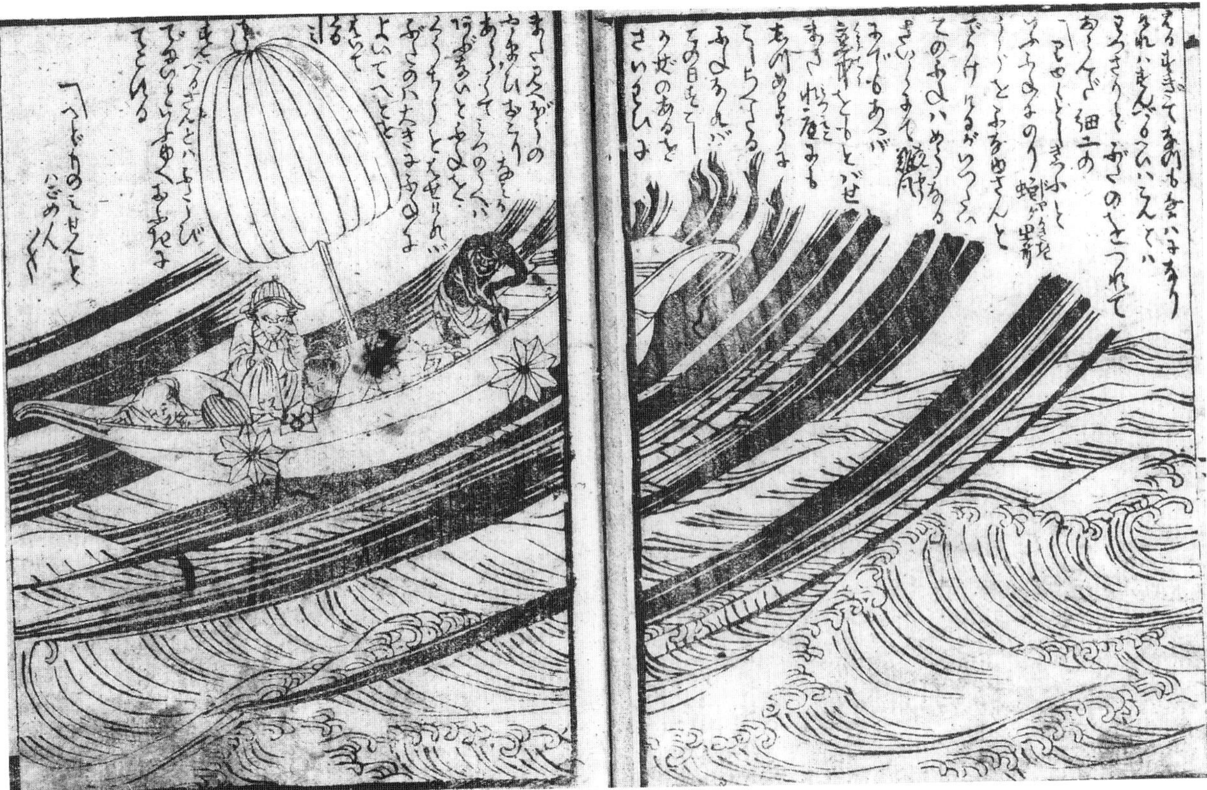

132. Katsushika Hokusai, from Kanwatei Onitake, *Wakanran zatsuwa*, 1803. Tokyo Metropolitan Central Library. *Sunperupei and his Indonesian servant take Buta in a hot air balloon.*

The supernatural powers of the sage, to wander about in air,
Are insignificant compared to this.
I have longed to become acquainted with the stars,
And should like to visit them by balloon.[59]

A balloon craze ensued. Kōkan made plates decorated with depictions, and others produced ceramic objects entirely in the shape of balloons (Siebold bought one to take home).[60] Balloons featured in numerous contexts, detaching themselves from the actual and becoming, as so much had before, "extraordinary devices." The balloon came to be seen as one of the West's most praiseworthy accomplishments, a hallmark of *Ran,* steeped in precision craftsmanship and predicated on the need for ever more extensive seeing. Kanwatei Onitake's story of Sino–Dutch rivalry for the Nagasaki prostitute Buta, included a love-bout in which the Hollander brought out an "*Oranda* precision-made" hot-air balloon to bolster his wooing (Fig. 132). Called a *ryukuto shikippu (luftschiff),* the device was equipped with elegant floral wheels; Sunperupei's loyal Indonesian servant is seen negotiating a hopelessly flaccid air bag, while Buta, annoyed by such showing-off, makes matters worse by throwing up over the side – "I really am mortified at having to depict vomit," admits the author.[61] Other writers wrote similarly. In 1793 the prolific

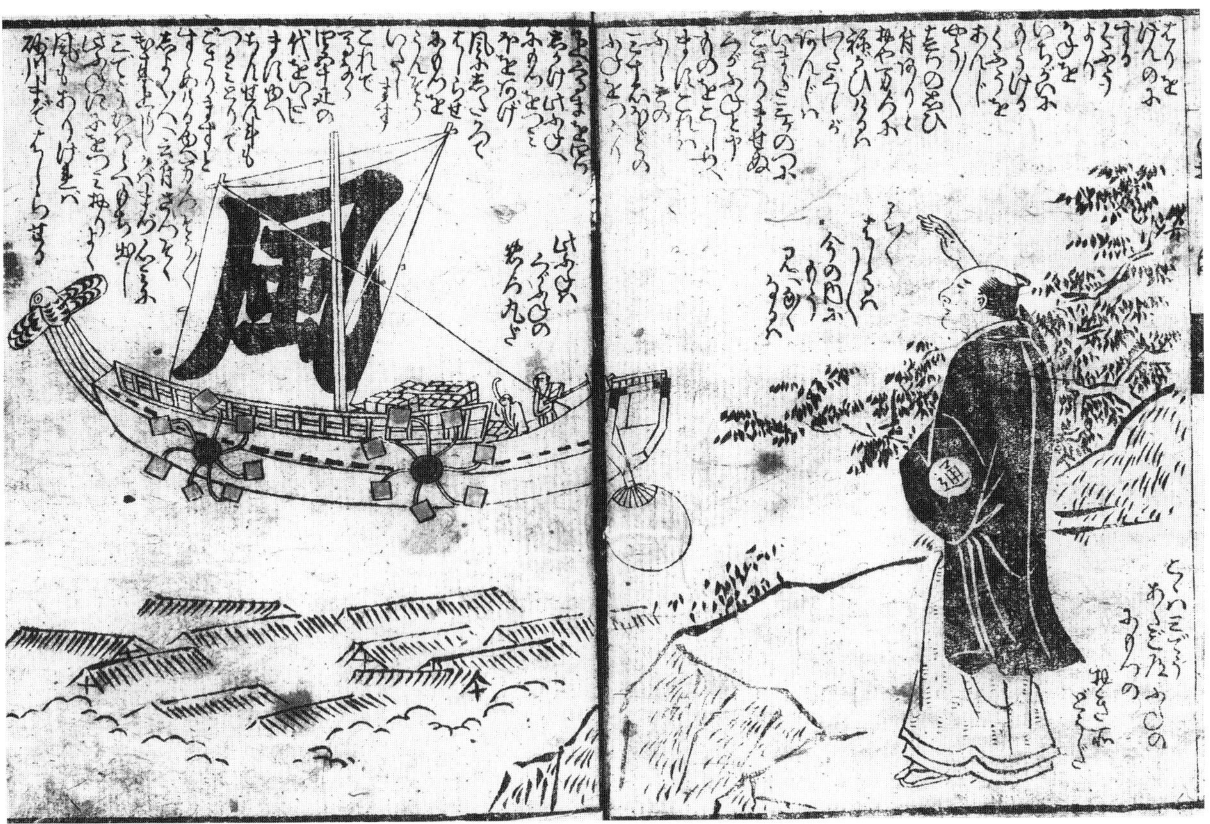

133. Kitao Shigemasa, from Hatake no Dojin Maimosuke, *Kontan teori shima*, 1793. National Diet Library, Tokyo.

The 'landship' flies off Mt Atago, its sail emblazoned with the word 'wind'.

illustrator Kitao Shigemasa tried his hand at a fictional piece, his pupil Kyōden having been so successful in the medium, and told of a "landboat" (*kugabune*) with 5,400-litre capacity, that despite its name is able to fly; an enterprising Edo merchant called Tsūtarō uses it to ferry goods from the Osaka region, flying the apparatus to and from Mount Atago and accruing impressive profits (Fig. 133). One day it drops too low and collides with the palanquin of Lord Muck (Unubore-kō) who ends the money-spinner.[62] Shigemasa's ship is in the now-standard mould, with rudder, wheels, and a sail, although with no balloon at all.

In 1802, stories came back into contact with fact when the castaway Tsūdayū was repatriated. Tsūdayū informed Ōtsuki Gentaku, his interrogator, that in Russia the balloon was called a *shari;* he knew because he had been taken to view one in the company of the tsarina, who had expressly asked for the Japanese to be allowed to attend the "rare event."[63] The basket was big enough for two, measuring 1.8 metres, Tsūdayū said, with a balloon three or four times as large. A man and woman went up, as "there are parts of the mechanism only women can manipulate."[64] A throng watched as the rig flew south: "everyone in every town along the way came out and looked up at the sky and was dumbfounded." The Russians were as elated as Tsūdayū, for "the device was invented elsewhere and being used here for the first time."[65]

Thrill was not the only purpose of the hot-air balloon. It was to acquit itself in military ways too. But Tsūdayū, preposterously, quizzed his hosts: " 'What's the purpose of this device?' I asked. 'And what is the good of it?' "[66] Quintessentially significant was the achievement of a mechanism of elevated observation. Balloon travel brought the bird-like gaze within human capability. The need of visual aids was strongly felt so high up, and most took a telescope along, as Tsūdayū noted the Russian aereostatists had. To ascend unsighted was inane. The first balloon-rider in England, the Italian Vincent Lunardi, reduced the event to a shambles in 1784 when he was so put off by the crowd of 150,000 screaming Londoners that he forgot his "instruments of observation."[67] Increased enginery of flight demanded concomitant care in the accurate scanning and recording of the world.

Chūryō's claimed he took his illustration directly from Lord Rūkyō's print, but it may have come, as other images in the *Miscellany* (like the insects) did, via a Western work used by Kōkan. Kōkan (if the conventional attribution is accepted) has a virtually identical depiction to that in the *Miscellany* as one-half of a diptych, the other half of which appears in Chūryō's book, too (who this time acknowledges Kōkan as his source), and it is one of the *Miscellany*'s two illustrations of Vulture Peak, ultimately derived from François Valentijn's compendium of East Indies history published in 1726: pilgrims perform their ablutions before making the climb (Fig. 134).[68] The balloon is none too convincing, but it floats beside the highest place in the world. The place where the Buddha had propounded his grace-bestowing teaching is now coupled with a foreign mechanism for effortless and free-range viewing. The juxtaposition challenges the beholder, for caught in the gap between the two hanging scrolls throbs an enormous discrepancy of world-views. The mounting of Kōkan's paintings is lavish, and the brocade bears the crest of the Tokugawa shogunal house.

USING A TELESCOPE

Deploying a telescope in air or on high ground increased vision to a huge degree. When the distant drew close, it could only be guessed what might come into sight. As a senryu writer put it:

> "Well fancy that!" they say.
> And look again,
> With the telescope.[69]

Teasingly, the thing seen is left to the reader's imagination; but once used, the device cannot be put aside.

The Japanese archipelago is mountainous throughout, and upland prospects easy to find. Many cities had their hills. Kyoto was ringed by them, and Nagasaki was built like a star creeping into the gullies of surrounding inclines, while Edo was dotted with eminences, such as Mount Atago in its centre. But the tops of hills had seldom been sought for their own sakes. Shrines or temples occupied many elevations – partly, perhaps, from a sense of the sacredness of height, but also because hills were foot-dragging, rocky, and useless, more fastnesses than appealing resorts. The word "mountain" (*san*) doubled as that for "temple," implying a hill was a place far from habitation and keeping unto itself. Access to most religious compounds was free, and no doubt pilgrims to lofty sanctuaries did look down over the path by which they had come, but ascent was more typically a spiritual quest to the summit than desire to obtain a view from the top. Any sights spreading below were incidental to the fulfilling rigour of the effort of climbing up.

Just outside Edo was a hut called Belleview (Nōken-dō), overlooking a vista so spectacular that the ninth-century painter Kōsei no Kanaoka was said to have thrown down his brush in despair at ever being able to depict it; a "brush-discarding pine" still grew at the place

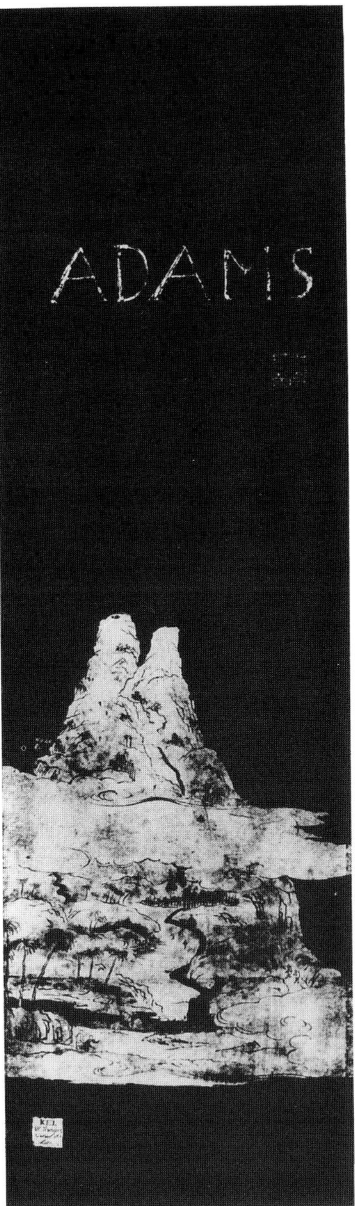

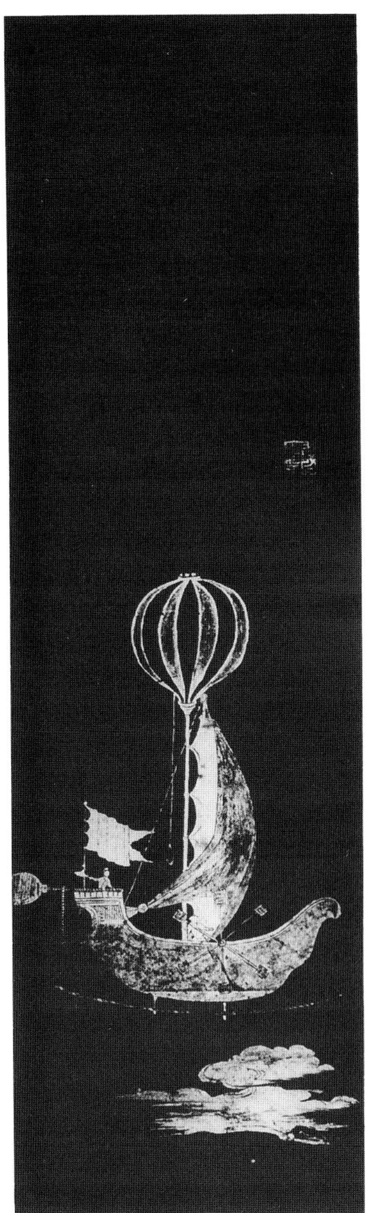

134. Shiba Kōkan (attrib.), *Vulture Peak* and *Hot Air Balloon*, diptych of hanging scrolls; early nineteenth century. Present whereabouts unknown.

The mounting is lavish and bears the shogunal holyhock crest.

where the implement had fallen.[70] The *Illustrated Famous Places in Edo (Edo meisho zue)*, an exhaustive compendium of notable locales published by Saitō Gesshin from 1836, illustrated Belleview and included the tree, luxuriating one thousand years after Kanaoka's visit (surely a successor to the original); an old man looks over the view by means of a long-barreled telescope resting on a horse provided for the purpose (Fig. 135). A haiku by the poet Nishiyama Sokō celebrates the tree, while an inscription informs, "the next pages give a panorama of the beautiful scenery of Kanazawa, as witnessed from this point." Kanaoka has been bettered, for the view,

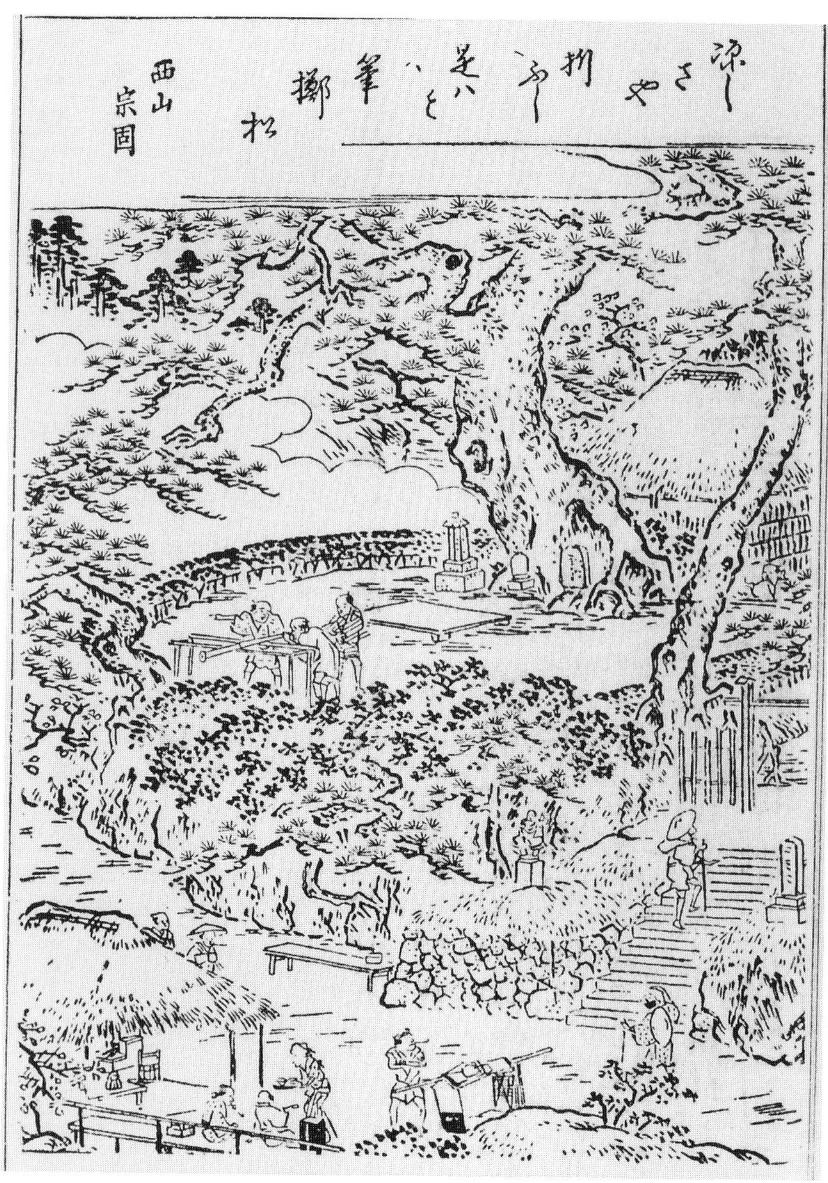

now exposed by the lens, can be copied down. The term used to describe the scene, *heirin*, is literally, a "descending spread view," a neologism unrecorded in Japanese lexicography but only slightly later than the new word coined in 1791 for the English language – "panorama."[71]

Major protuberances in Japanese cities began to rent out telescopes for a small fee, giving the commonality access to far-flung gazes across the land. Improvised observation stations (*mitōshi*) were put up on Mount Atago, for example, and Yūshima, or at other sites where the scenery was fine, offering "Red-fur-like 40 km sights,"[72] as Shikitei Sanba called the view through tele-

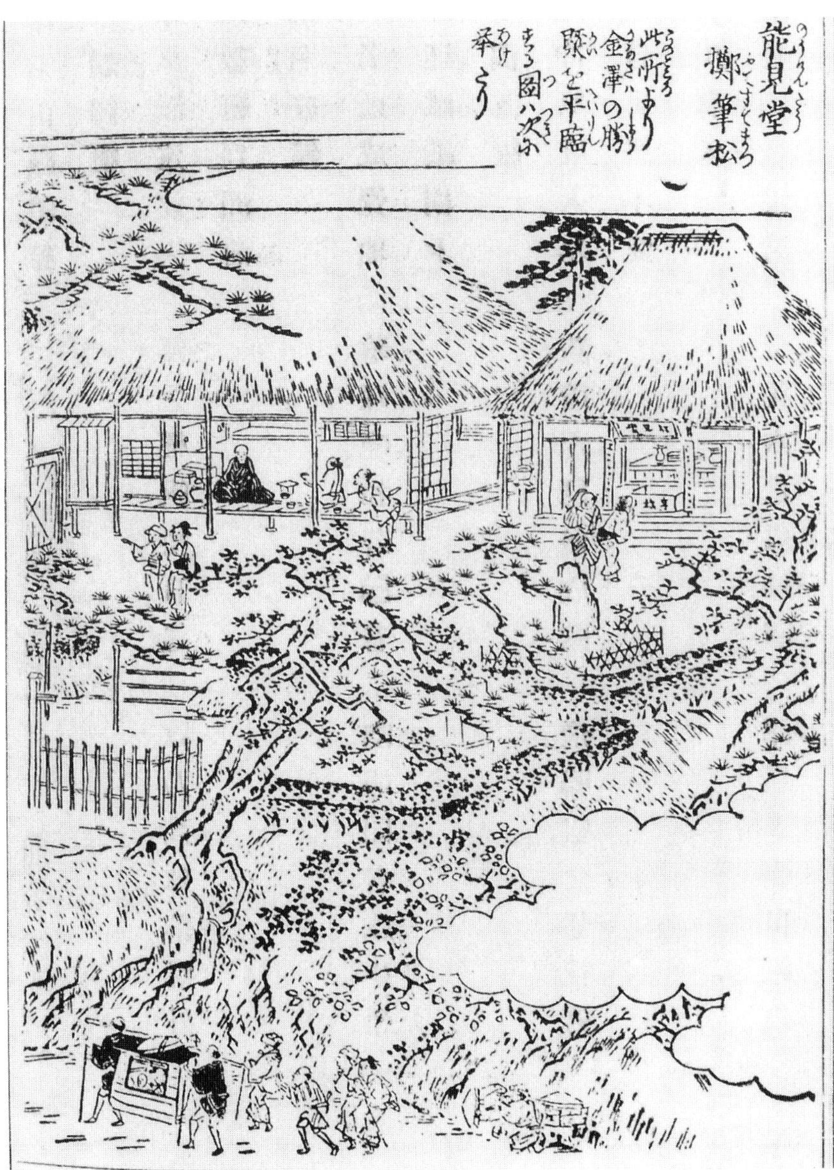

135. Hasegawa Settan and Settei, from Saitō Gesshin (et al.), *Edo meisho zue*, c. 1836. SOAS, University of London.

The Nōken-dō and Brush-Discarding Pine, with tourists using a telescope.

scopes. A senryu writer captured the quiver of excitement that accompanied this as he led a friend to the hill at Yūshima:

> Where we're heading now –
> Yūshima
> And its telescopes.[73]

To look down on the city of Edo exposed something more profitable than expanses of Kanazawa's paddies and mud-flats, for the objects of sight were people. This implicated social codes. But as with Tokykuni's fire-watchman's view into bedrooms, there is a prurience in much of the looking. Yūshima was an illegal brothel district specialising in the supply of boys, and "Yūshima's telescopes" may have an erotic meaning: certainly another word for the extendible telescope, *biidoro* (originally signifying just "glass"), doubled as slang for "penis" and a senryu of 1783 plays on this in what must be a reference to the views at Yūshima,

> Pick out the one you want,
> And then do it with him,
> By telescope.

Exactly thirty years earlier there had been a wilder attempt to capture the swell of the extensible telescope sinking back to size,

> The telescope –
> Such over-confidence,
> Then the eyes go back to how they were.

Such things were not for everyone, maybe, but when the retired daimyō of Kōriyama took his retainers and ladies (seventeen in all) out drinking at the Matsugane-ya restaurant on a bright winter's night only months after the first senryu was composed, they were all rather disturbed by the boy prostitutes next door; they could not really object, this being Yūshima, and in fact the lord took to coming back thereafter, noting in his diary that he liked to frequent the place on account of the telescopes. Interestingly, when he returned from Russia, Daikokuya Kōdayū stated that Muscovite brothels always had telescopes out, as indeed did those Japanese ones (even those intended for heterosexual encounters) when there was anything to see (Fig. 143).[74]

Toyokuni's pupil, Kunisada, mentioned an artist so wedded to empiricism that he took a telescope into a lavatory in search of a model but unable even there to find what he wanted, he stayed for a while anyway with his piece, frustrated, and "what he did next is told in a subsequent volume" – which of course was never written.[75] Floating World pictures incorporating telescopes are far from rare, and they suggest something both coy and lascivious, playing both on the potentials of the gaze and on the shape of the instrument, as charming youths or, more likely, young women, finger it in a manner that integrates the telescopes into the world of that other tubular and erectile object, that eternally hallowed Japanese phallic symbol, the umbrella (Pl. 16).

The number of kibyoshi on telescopes is no less than those on microscopes, spectacles, or mirrors. The stories frequently refer similarly to some additional capacity in the device to reveal the superempirical. The first enlistments of the telescope as metaphor may have been in 1787 by Shiba Zenkō, in *Shiba Zenkō: The Extent of What He Knows (Shiba Zenkō chie no hodo)*, illustrated by Santō Kyōden. Reference is oblique, but the tale tells of a bamboo tube bestowed on the protagonist and used to enhance spiritual seeing. That same year, Sharakutei Manri, a male geisha from Naka-no-chō (the central avenue of the Yoshiwara), published *A Festival Tray: What a Feast for the Eyes (Shimadai me no shōgatsu)*, also with pictures by Kyōden, his close friend. The overt theme of the latter story is the life of one Tsūsaburō, third son of the millionaire Kobayashi-ya, who takes the name Asahina, in reference to the legendary traveller who had wandered far and wide. This fits well, because in Edo literature, rich men's sons always became footloose and went to the bad. But the modern Tsūsaburō saves himself the trouble of absconding to fantastic foreign islands (*shima*), by confining himself to visiting brothels (also *shima*). The pun ripples out, for "island" was also the term for a decorative stand covered with symbolic ornaments positioned in banqueting rooms on festive occasions, and Manri's book was published at New Year when such auspicious items were brought out. The telescope allows the modern man to visit islands in a purely ocular way, without having to step ashore, and Manri introduces the device to suggest how Tsūsaburō can taste his delights ahead of time – which often leads to an awakening, as he realises his errors, and redirects his energies before they are squandered. The author may also be referring to his own name here, for Manri literally meant "ten thousand leagues" – this is better than the telescope, which could be called (as Manri calls it) a "one-thousand-league lens" (*senri-kyō*).

This was all contrived, though amusing too. Kyōden supplied the preface:

> You can use a Dutch telescope to spy out bits of loose change that've dropped in the road, and finding something you think to yourself, shall I go and pick it up or not? Manri of the Yoshiwara slung together this little three-part work only devoting to it the time it took him to have a smoke. Glasses perched on the end of his nose, he peered at "islands," substantial and insubstantial. Lost somewhere in the middle is the matter of the sincerity of those elegant cypress-scented boudoirs on the Naka-no-chō. Read it out with a loud voice![76]

Kyōden refers to the chambers he and Manri knew so well, but it is the "sincerity" (*makoto*) of the brothel area, not just its delights, that is now the object of search by the one- or ten-thousand league lens. In earnest to the reader of this, the publisher, Tsutaya Jūsaburō, had supplied the book with a jacket showing Tsūsaburō receiving a mystic telescope and it is given by a sprightly young god, drawn within the enclosing shape of a vanity-dispelling sacred Buddhist jewel (*tama*).

The god appears to Tsūsaburō at the beginning of the story to make the donation, and Manri jumbles the levels of language to disorient the leader: "Yea, verily, the earth shook and echoed at the divine presence, but the lad had his hair done up in an infantile bob . . . 'I bet he'll make some really slick pronouncement,' " thinks Tsūsaburō (Fig. 136).[77] The setting is a shrine, hand-rinsing basin to the left; it is Yūshima, which had a shrine to Tenjin on top of the hill; the offertory flags are from local prostitutes. This explains the god's androgynous dressing and boyish mien. Nothing is for free, and he warns Tsūsaburō that he wants the instrument back later, as "this telescope I've come with now is only borrowed, and it belongs to the Naniwa brothel on the gentler of the two paths at Yūshima."[78] Naniwa was a name for Osaka, and it was well known that the handsomest boys came from there, just as the most elegant women were from Kyoto.

Manri's *Festival Tray* was reissued in 1794 and enjoyed a second lease of life. That same year Shikitei Sanba, working with Toyokuni, produced a kibyoshi the title of which made more apparent than ever the ethical potential of the telescope: *A Device for Peeping into the Human Heart (Ningen isshin nozoki-karakuri);* the pair found the title felicitous, for they reworked it some twenty years later with reference to the powers of that other wrong-exposing technology, the peeping-*karakuri* booth.[79] In the earlier book, however, a telescope is again bestowed by a divine visitor, this time a mature divinity, Great God Fashion Hairstyles (Ikichon Daitsūjin) – Sanba admits, "It's always happening in these popular stories."[80] The instrument also has psychic power, but is referred to only as "an odd sort of glass affair called a 'gut-revealing lens' (*fukumei-kyō*)." When one peeps through, authenticity is revealed: a mother-in-law is seen with horns, while the father of a dissolute son can be picked out in the distance, incarnadine with rage.

The recipient of the lens is called Mudaya, just about plausible as a name, but which in Edo slang meant "wastrel"; his given name is Umajirō, a pun on Sanba (*uma* and *ba* being the same character, *-jiro* meaning a second son). Mudaya Umajirō "likes sex but had never known real attachment," and, arrogant and shunned, he lives "like a lantern, swinging along aimlessly."[81] But Umajirō's moral fibre is strengthened by the telescope and the inspections it allows him of the deeper emotions of the world; he becomes progressively better, until Fashion Hairstyles reappears and entrusts him with a book that outlines how to be a truly so-

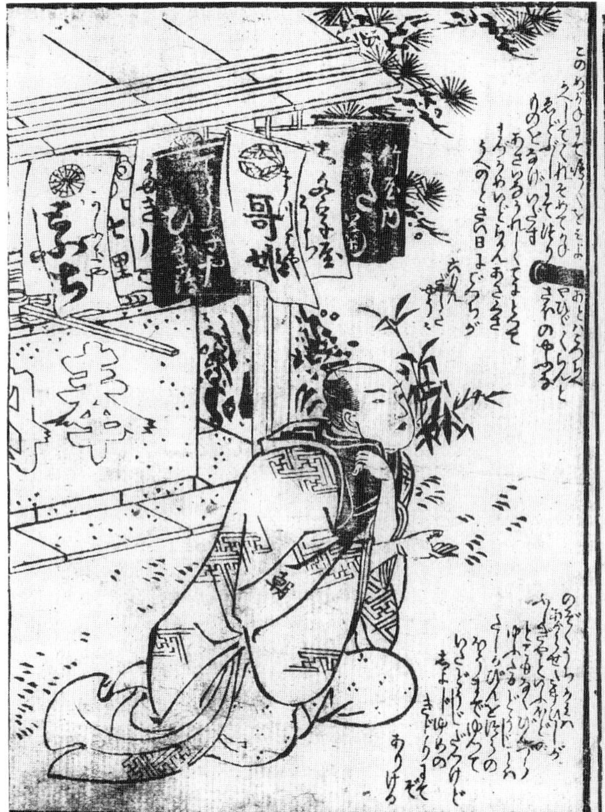

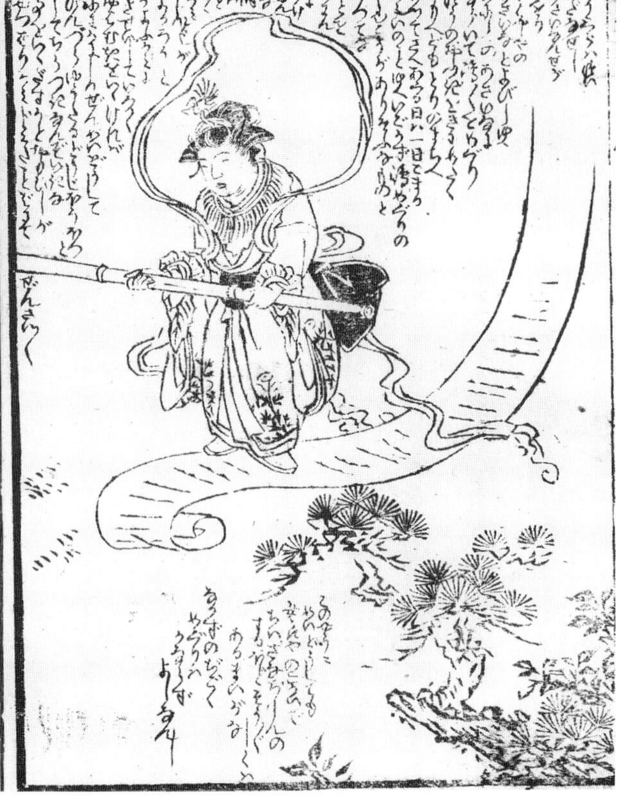

136. Santō Kyōden, from Sharakutei Manri, *Shimadai me no shōgatsu*, 1787. National Diet Library, Tokyo. *A young god, floating on a holy text, presents the protagonist with a telescope.*

phisticated person – a status that includes not only smart clothes and rapier repartee but respect for others, acceptance of one's limitations, and discretion (Fig. 137).

Such views through the far-seeing lens, directed towards the heart of humankind, attributed to the personal interior mysterious revolutions akin to those that the star-gazer saw going on in mobile space. The simile of the human body as earth and the heart as the elusive heavens dictating obscurely above was well worn. The syncretic *Shingaku* master Nakagawa Dōni made use of it in his preachings, stressing that the purity of the human heart is wondrous if pristine, but easily corruptible. He expounded:

> Let's conclude then that the person is a world of tiny scale. Outside their heaven-and-earth combined there is no Way. Take heaven as your heart and let the earth provide your shape – burn the body and it'll reduce to ashes, bury it and it'll go to soil. Lord Gods, noble daimyo, ourselves too, and even beggars and untouchables – it's all a case of "unification of the ten thousand things within one body" (*issetsu banbutsu ittai*).[82]

The potential for heavenliness, Dōni noted, is within all people, but a heart must be ethically schooled if it is to maintain its proper self, just as strictly as the body must be drilled to conform to its role in life, and once done, the personality conjoins with the principle (*ri*) of all phenomena.

The right meshing of the parts ensured attainment of the general Way.

HEAVENLY OBSERVATION

The fundamental similarity of the heavens above and the heart below affected the seriousness with which observation of either zone was taken. There was such extensive cross-referencing, that to view the heart was felt cosmic in challenge, whereas to study the stars had morality at its core. The firmament was structured by ethics. This had to be understood because it was the stars that led people into or out of happiness in the measure that they moved with or against their compelling tugs. Anomalies from heaven – earthquakes, eclipses, tidal waves, bad harvests and famines – occurred when humanity and the cosmos were out of joint. This had political significance, for it was the first role of government to align the state and the stratosphere. In practical terms, social conventions were purified and policed by the state so that immorality did not definitively compromise the land. Human society responded to the motions of heavenly bodies by demarcating their lives in deference to them in months and years, and these (in a lunar calendar) needed much checking, which it was for the authorities to fix. If the stars threw their couplings with earth so that weather went astray from season, and sowing and reaping did not coincide with the times expected, then the auguries for rulers were ill.

It was a matter of horror as the eighteenth century progressed that the official calendar was becoming steadily more erratic. Generous declaration of additional days, or of whole intercalary months, did nothing to ameliorate the grotesqueness of the mismatch or to bring state-designated time back into agricultural step. The calendar had been reset only in 1755 (Nishikawa Joken had been among those who worked on the project), but it was apparent that he and

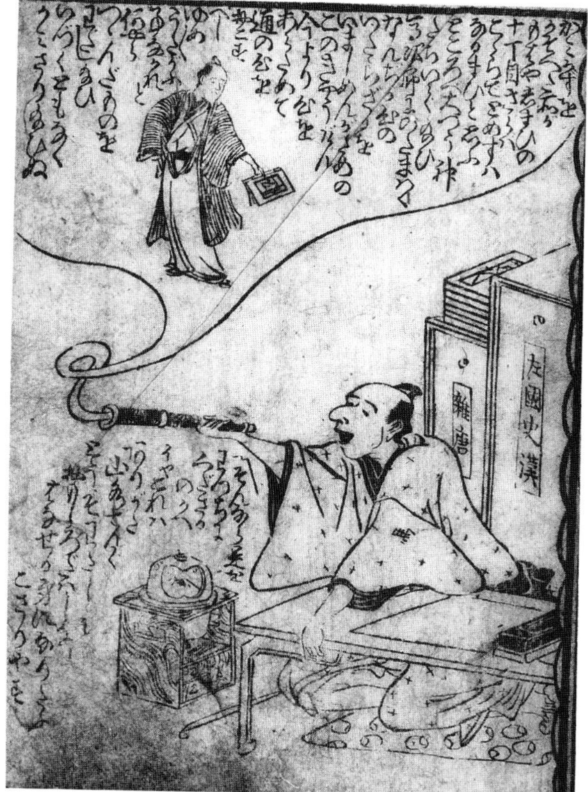

137. Utagawa Toyokuni, from Shikitei Sanba, *Ningen isshin nozoki-karakuri*, 1794. National Diet Library, Tokyo.

The god presents the telescope-wielding protagonist with a fashion guide.

his colleagues had only made the situation worse.[83] A major eclipse of 1763 failed to be predicted, deeply impugning the shogunate. Two years later wholesale revisions were undertaken again.

In 1782, a lavish new shogunal observatory was constructed in Edo, centring on a 95-metre pyramidal platform, tapering to some 5 metres at an apex almost 10 metres up; the whole was bound by a dressed stone parapet and ascended by two flights of steps.[84] Mansions for two of the shogun's senior astronomers (*tenmon-gata*) were connected to observation and study rooms, and when calculations were under way at night, the mound was illuminated by a multitude of candles, given by special gift of the government.[85]

But the considerable outlay was not yielding much. Some *han* gave up, and lest the slippage between season and calendar reflect badly on the daimyo's regional rule, local calculations were devised. Ōta Nanpo applauded the observatory set up by Shimazu Shigehide, lord of Satsuma, whose innovations were to adopt a Western-style seven-day week (over the ten-day *jun*) and to produce a double calendar that logged Japanese moments of importance into European dates. Shigehide also broke with the secrecy that had surrounded declaration of the months, and circulated his conclusions widely in a lucid form that Nanpo found "very clear and perfectly obvious to use."[86]

The national calendar was again reworked in 1798. Certain of the hereditary astronomers were side-lined, and new men brought in, one of whom was Takahashi Yoshitoki, father of the Kageyasu who was to study fountains (Fig. 29) and who was finally executed for giving secret maps to Siebold. This effort was known as the Kansei Calendar, and its results were better.[87] The revolutionary aspect of the Kansei astronomers was their strategic use of Western instruments and imported theories. This was a first in official calendration. Honda Toshiaki expressed the opinion, in a publication of the same year, that now "the root of all calendrical study undertaken in Japan is European tools." Ōtsuki Gentaku noted that this had recently become the case in China too.[88] The Kansei instruments were punctiliously copied down for future reference as an addendum to the voluminous manuscript of the deliberations, edited by the official astronomer Shibukawa Kagesuke as *The Book of the Kansei Calendar (Kansei rekisho)* (Figs. 20, 127).[89] Confidence was largely restored, although dates got out of step again within a generation.

Publication of the promulgated calendars was a privilege of government. Covert versions, however, were made in defiance of the monopoly, for the benefit of townspeople. These listed how the long and short months (twenty-nine or thirty days) were to fall throughout the year – data without which business could hardly be conducted. Being in breech of secrecy laws, the information had to be hidden in rebus-like patterns within a picture, so as not to be apparent on casual perusal. From 1765, illegal calendars began to be works of art as great energies were put into attractive designs. That year saw a consortium of Edo printers and scholars – a veritable sampling of enthusiasts of *Ran* and the Floating World in fact – vying to produce the cleverest and most amusing secret calendar. Looking back in an undated work, *My Wastepaper Basket (Hōgo kago)*, Morishima Chūryō wrote:

> In 1765, the year of the monkey [he is wrong: it was the year of the cock], "long and short" parties (*taishō no kai*) became all the rage. People went to extremes in the charming mini-calendrical compositions they came up with; these were judged and awarded prizes in the manner of picture competitions. It was from this moment that printing in seven or eight colours began to be possible.[90]

Harunobu is reckoned as the first person able to make full-colour woodblock prints, and he produced his ground-breaking piece at this time, as a "picture calendar" (*e-goyomi*). He was helped in the technological feat of multi-block keying (an intricate task) by Gennai, who may have been his tenant at the time.[91]

A calendar was practical. For more abstract or personal inspections of the planets individuals needed instruments. It was *lèse-majesté* to chart the skies as if officials assigned to the task were inept and it was not at all encouraged. But certain *Rangaku* experts went ahead. Tachibana Nankei took to star-gazing while in Nagasaki, going up on the roof with an imported quadrant (Fig. 19); he and his friends became so engrossed that they forgot the need to keep a low profile, and the locals, hearing voices late into the night, thought something was afoot, as Nankei recorded: "We were excitedly commenting on how this star must belong to that constellation and the rest, until the neighbours became suspicious and berated us, asking what we thought we were playing at because it was making them apprehensive. So we composed ourselves and came down."[92]

Where equipment was lacking, inadvisable to use, or too complex, imported maps might be turned to. It was customary for stellar and terrestrial sets to be produced together, laying the world and the heavens out to an impartial gaze in pairs of equal size. *The Book of the Kansei Calendar* included pictures of the "heavenly and terrestrial globes of Primitive [Dutch] fabrication" used by the astronomers, giving two spheres in solid wood rests, heaven and earth taking exactly the same proportions, thus balanced in apparent importance in defiance of the vast differences in size.[93] By definition such plans were overseas products, and they revealed interpretations of the world that were so new as to be quite hard to digest. The year 1774 saw publication of a convenient study, *How to Use Celestial and Terrestrial Globes (Tenchi hikyu yōhō)*, the effort of the *Rangaku* physician Motoki Ryōei, who based his analysis on the much earlier writings of Willem Blaeu.[94] Such autodidacticism was only for the diligent; those who acquired knowledge were much quizzed by others. Shiba Kōkan was called in by the Lord of Kii to explain a globe and heavenly sphere he had obtained but could not yet understand, and Kōkan told how the daimyo confessed to him that "he had thoroughly enjoyed the day's study," which apparently had not been the case when he had summoned the Kansei Calendar officials for enlightenment.[95] Gazing at the human space, and the divine, represented as spheres, the lord was stationed temporarily outside all locations, looking on from a place apart and disenfranchised at the baubles he had received as gifts.

Any invocation of the cosmic in relation to the human led to deep abstraction. Profoundly spiritual evaluations attended on assessments of how man and woman might dwell within a double space which was also populated by planets and gods. Shibukawa Harumi, scion of a hereditary astronomer family and abreast of changes before the majority was, constructed a globe in 1691, and awed at what he had done, he donated it to the grand shrine of Shintō at Ise, for though the axioms of the sphere were modern, the sun was the chief goddess of the animist Shintō cult and not to be mapped lightly.[96] Friction between prevailing religious assumptions and the beliefs underpinning Western postulates was bound to erupt. In China, where Western astronomy was in more widespread use, there were similar stresses. As it was put in a Continental encyclopaedia of 1782: "Assuredly, the Europeans are far superior to our own predecessors in respect of the accuracy of the astronomical calculations and the ingenuity of the instruments. But at the same time, no heterodox sect has ever gone so far where exaggerations, falsity, absurdity, and improbability are concerned."[97] The problem was Christianity. China knew the tread of Franciscan and Jesuitical feet in a way that Japan, within living memory, did not. But a sense of larger implications for the moral order in the new understanding of space was felt in both lands. Articulation of Christian doctrine was subject to draconian punishment in Japan, and even to admit to knowledge of it was dangerous. *Rangaku* writers did well to be wary, and Sugita Genpaku, for example, began his history of the movement with a prominent disclaimer that he was entirely ignorant of Christianity: "I know nothing of that wicked belief and shall say nothing of it" and just to be sure, he terminated the same book with a description (entirely irrelevant) of his pilgrimage to the Buddhist shrine of Ieyasu, founder of the present regime.[98] Notwithstanding such diplomatic pretensions, those who immersed themselves in *Rangaku*, or even only dabbled in the field, were not ignorant. Bibles were to be found in many a lordly collection, kept throughout the period of prohibition or actually acquired during it.[99] Kōkan owned a painting of Saint Paul made in Japan in the mid-seventeenth century, and Morishima Chūryō owned a recent tract by the Swedish theologian Grich Ponteppidous, as well as a fine copper-plate of the interior of a church in France.[100]

Christianity lodged its one God in the empyrean, but Japanese thought identified several species of supernatural entity with varying degrees of separation from humanity. There were the *kami* of Shintō, immanent in earthly things and still of this world. Involving themselves with the production of natural phenomena, and overseeing the unfolding of mundane affairs, Shintō gods were limited to specific roles; many had once been humans, and they inhabited a heaven that was essentially one with earth and clove to it. Buddhas, by contrast, had entered into the extinction of nirvana and could not be reached, nor could they answer supplications. Their space was incommensurable with that of earth. But Buddhism's secondary category of being, bodhisattvas (beings of enlightenment), or those on the point of entry into the extinction who had held back to mediate with earth, could help sentient beings in their strivings towards enlightenment; the bodhisattva Kannon was the most worshipped paraclete.

Many Shintō gods waited on Buddhist superiors, or even aspired to becoming Buddhas themselves, and the two religious strands are far from non-overlapping. There was a looseness of definition. But if humanity poked and pried in the heavenly realm, it was the gods they might find, and only far beyond – if even there – the Buddhas. In 1782, the Iwatoya publishers in Edo provided some of their kibyoshi with a jacket illustration showing a collection of gods and horned demons looking down from their cloud-draped world, making their *riposte* to human intrusions: this was the year the shogunal observatory moved to its new quarters.[101] Tsutaya Jūsaburō went one better and in the same year gave kibyoshi covers showing gods and demons actually spying on earth with a telescope.[102] Iwatoya and Tsutaya were rivals; three years after this spat, a third publisher, the Okumura-ya, produced a kibyoshi with a similar twist. Written by Ichiba Tsūshō, it was illustrated by the twenty-three-year-old Katsukawa Shun'ei (later to influence Toyokuni) and entitled *The Money-Making Pathway of India* (*Tenjiku mōke no tsuji*). India was the home of religion and had been long regarded as a holy land, but Tsūshō has little concern for doctrinal niceties. He built the theme of his book around what Nanpo had articulated a dozen years earlier in his kyoka on the moon looking down to earth in envy: divine aspirations are now to descend and join in the money-grubbing world they see engaged in such aggressive self-enrichment below. The thunder god gets in first, for he habitually does fall to earth, whereas the less mobile divinities and their cohorts are restricted to looking. "The heavens," informs Tsūshō, "are 578,004,000 *jō* 1 *jin* 3 *sun* 2 *bun* in height – ridiculously high in fact – and no-one knows the least thing about them, their being so hard to see with the naked eye, and all that."[103] The gods have the same problem from their angle, so they also resort to aids – a pair of glasses and a telescope (Fig. 138). The illustration provided by Shun'ei almost exactly replicates the earlier Tsutaya covers. The gods are trendily dressed with fashionable accessories to hand – hence their lenses – and attractive women in tow, and, scorning the devout, they home in on more vibrant things, like Edo, with its Nihon-bashi fish market and Sakai-chō theatre district.

Peering and leaning from their banks of clouds, the gods recall to each other the fate of the wizard Kume. Kume, from ancient China, had attained the power of levitation through arduous spiritual exercise, becoming able to fly.

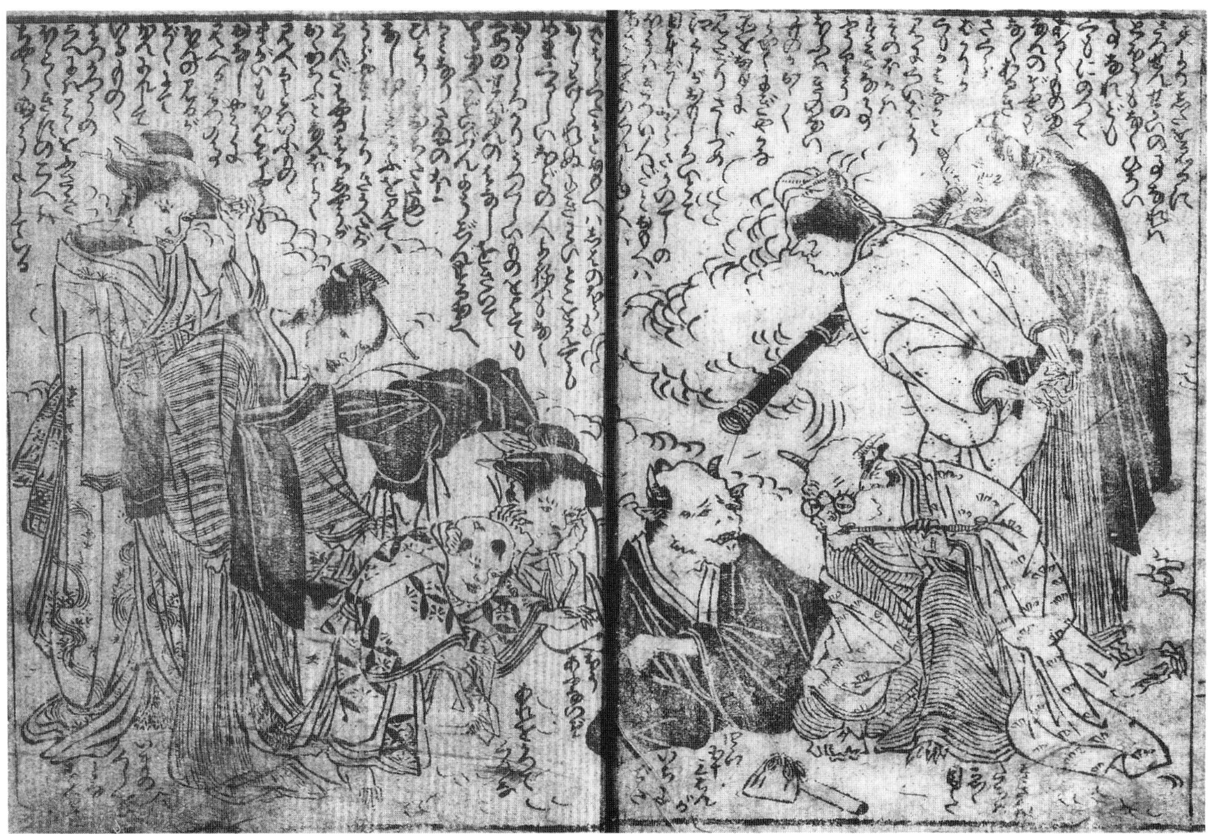

138. Katsukawa Shun'ei, from Ichiba Tsūshō, *Tenjiku mōke no suji*, 1785. Tokyo Metropolitan Central Library. *Gods, demons and their cohorts look down to earth.*

But he had lost his knack and crashed painfully to earth when his poise was shattered by the reflection in a stream of the well-turned female thigh of a young woman treading suds from her washing. Celestial beings must be on their guard, for the separation of gods from humankind is contingent, not absolute.

SEEING AS THE BUDDHAS SEE

When Nankei wrote of how he supposed the existence of a being outside of both heaven and earth and looking on from farther off, it was not these gods he had in mind. However, neither could Buddhas, being in extinction, be understood, in that way, to see. The difficulty of the issue resided in the meaning of sight and the nature of location.

Buddhism believed in the existence of a Pure Land (Jōdō) often called simply Paradise (Gokuraku), a kind of half-way house to nirvana, established by the salvationist Buddha Amida. The place was said to be located to the west, because as the sun set on this life it illuminated the next, but the identification was purely symbolic. Or it ought to be, but simple believers were confused, as Paradise seemed to be geographically determinable. When Kōkan travelled through Hino in

1788, he showed a Western-style globe of his own production, and a woman of thirty-six or -seven came up and asked him: "You have been kind enough to point out India, where our Lord Sakyamuni came from, but where is Paradise? I would like to go there while I am still alive, since after death it will all seem like being in a dream."[104] Kōkan, always ready to browbeat, explained, "You can't get to Paradise when you are alive," and it was not depicted "for the reason that this sphere represents the earth, but Heaven is outside it. There are many worlds like this out in space, and Paradise somewhere with them."

In the context of a more formal discussion, Kōkan spelled out the confusion:

> In the *Amida Sūtra* it is written, "ten thousand million leagues to the west is a world that bears the name Paradise." What this means is that it is limitlessly distant without measure. The sūtra is saying that Amida is in an ineffable vastness. He is not something you can fix on with your eyes and nose as you could a person, and Paradise is farther out than our construction of west.[105]

Prelates exposed imponderables in a language people could grasp, as "expediencies" (*hōben*), and that is why it was said that Paradise was to the west. Similarly, Buddhist statues took the form of human beings in order that people could relate to them, even though the Buddhas did not look that way – or, in fact, any way at all.

The lower members of the Buddhist pantheon were less emphatically removed, and did attend to activities in the human realm with the same sensory faculties of earthly beings. Those who travelled to Nagasaki noted that Chinese halls of worship had statues of two divinities not recognised in Japan, called Thousand-league Eyes (Senrigan) and Prevailing-wind Ears (Junpūni).[106] They were natural objects of devotion for navigating people, as their duty was to protect vessels at sea. The divinities formed an ocular and aural partnership that recalls Hekizentei Kunenbō's pairing of the microscope and the ear trumpet into a copulatory duo in *What on Earth? Two Strange Devices* (*Hade mezurashiki futatsu no utsuwa*; Fig. 21). Divine senses might be very like human ones if it was considered that the roles attributed to the Chinese divinities, in the case of the VOC shipping, were mechanically fulfilled by telescopes to see and loud-hailers to hear.[107]

The degree to which the scientific gaze of mechanised equipment and the moral vision of cosmic order could impart meaningful information for each other was considered by Shiba Zenkō in 1781, in a kibyoshi illustrated by Kitao Shigemasa.[108] Eighteen months earlier, Edo had been transfixed by the exhibition of a celebrated statue of Jizō (bodhisattva of childbirth) brought up from the Temple of Saikō-ji in Shinshū, to the north of the shogunal seat. The display was held at the Temple of Fudō in Meguro, just southwest of the congested part of the city; as Meguro was also famous for its dumplings, it was doubly worth the trip. Zenkō parodied the event, turning the arrival of the Jizō from a rural temple into the rake's progress of a lad up from the country whose orientation is unbalanced by the brilliance of the metropolis. The work came out as *A Modern Person's Voguish Buddha Receipt Book (Tōseijin tsūbutsu kaichō)*; "receipt book" (*kaichō*) is a deliberate miswriting of the homophonous "exhibition of holy icons."

Jizō falls victim to Edo foppery and, taking advantage of the proximity of Meguro to the unlicensed red-light district of Shinagawa, he betakes him there, eventually falling in love with a prostitute by the name of Matsuwaka. Zenkō jokes:

> In the *Holy Scripture of Jizō* in the modern version, it stands written:
>
> "Hurry, hurry off to Meguro,
> Process to the left,
> Process to the right.
> Chestnut dumplings
> Make me puke,
> And rice dumplings too.
> Soba-eating Shinagawa
> That's where I want to go!"[109]

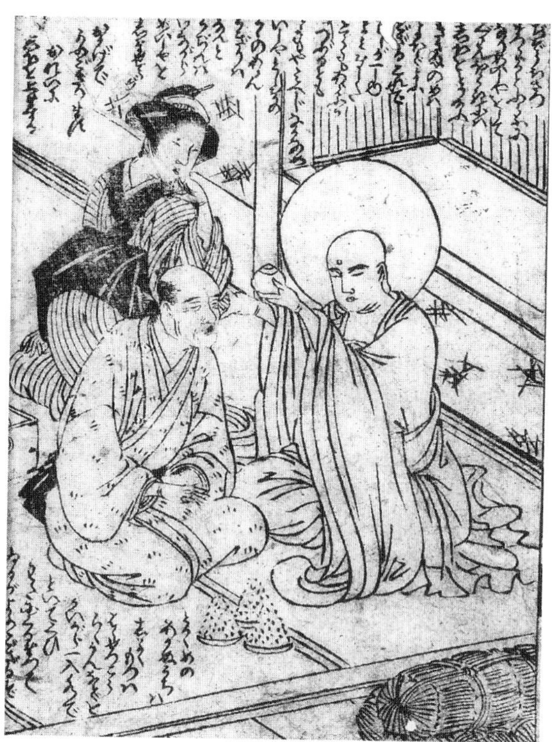

139. Kitao Shigemasa, from Shiba Zenkō, *Tōsei daitsū butsu kaichō*, 1781. Tokyo Metropolitan Central Library.

Jizō anoints a patient's eyes with salt.

No more thank-offering fare, Jizō wants some of that favourite snack over which you traditionally swore love – soba noodles.

Jizō is in good company in the brothel, for he finds there two other statues: a Sakyamuni Entering into Nirvana, brought along by the abbot of the temple on whose altar he normally reclines, and a Medicine Buddha, also from nearby. The three images melt into the Edo urban fabric as playboys, eventually taking up trades to pay their bills. The Medicine Buddha flogs his spiritual unctions as perfume, while Jizō becomes a doctor (iconically he had a shaven head, also a badge of physicians so this works well). He specialises in ophthalmology, and he gives up spirituality for the pursuit of fun, curing the citizenry's empirical shortcomings of sight (Fig. 139).[110] Nowhere is it said that Jizō prescribes lenses for his patients, but this is implied in the justification for Zenkō's specifically allotting eye-doctoring to the bodhisattva: Jizō's attribute is a *tama*, or Buddhist jewel, and in casual Edo parlance the word meant glass.

The Jizō statue from Shinshū was about life-sized – at least it suited Zenkō's purpose to represent it as such, the better to let the corrupted bodhisattva mix with people. But it was customary for important statues to have even more impressive dimensions. Increase of physical scale suggested advanced nobility, but it also meant that the image had an augmented visual range. Sugita Genpaku, Maeno Ryōtaku, Katsuragawa Hoshū, and the other translators of Kulmus's anatomical book had pointed out in 1774 the perhaps obvious fact that animals have eyes at the top of their heads in order to see farther (Fig. 94). The huge Buddhist image could suggest not only collosal spiritual power but a greater field of inspection.[111]

In 1804, Hokusai produced a painting of the founder of the Zen Buddhist school, Bodhidharma, for the Temple of Gokoku-ji in Edo. Neither a Buddha nor a bodhisattva, Bodhidharma was an Indian holy man said to have journeyed to China (crossing the intervening waters on a reed) where he had meditated by a ragged cliff for so long that he lost the use of his arms and legs, which withered and fell off. Limbless, Bodhidharma was known for the power of his gaze. His round Indic eyes had been accentuated when he had sliced off their lids so that sleep would not interfere with his spiritual exercises. Bodhidharma's eyes were the stuff of many an imaginary portrait, and best known for his eccentric efforts in the genre was Hakuin, a Zen monk who produced them *en masse* in his temple in Hara for distribution to travellers passing by on the neighbouring Tōkaidō highway; one representative painting is inscribed with the admonition, "I've got my eye on you."[112] Hokusai had been born a few years before Hakuin's death, and his Bodhidharma portraits, though distinct in style, recall the old monk's work. The point of Hokusai's production of 1804, however, was its extraordinary size. Done on twelve sheets of paper, each large enough for a person to lie down on, the Bodhidharma had eyes that devoured a wide sweep of cityscape beneath.

The image was not supposed to last, and it did not, being lost before anyone thought to copy down its appearance. But a repeat performance laid on thirteen years later at the Nishikakejo in Nagoya left more substantial traces. The whole town was leafleted to advertise the event, and posters, some of which survive, were hawked for 12 *monme* each.[113] A samurai of the *han,* Koriki Tanenobu, helped Hokusai with his brushes, and afterward made a sketch, publishing it as a memento under the title *A Detailed Rendition of Hokusai's Massive Painting, Done on the Spot* (*Hokusai taiga sokushō saizu;* Fig. 140). Tanenobu, using his pen-name Enkoan, shows an eager gathering, including a Buddhist monk (perhaps from the Temple of the Nishi-Hongan-ji next door), milling around in front of the patriarch as he is hauled into place; the image is on the same scale as the Gokoku-ji one, but the venue was more cramped, and the workmen could not get it high enough, so the bottom, Takenobu noted, splayed out.[114] A child on the left is sitting on an adult's shoulders to see better, as Bodhidharma's bulbous eyes bear down on all alike, each one fully 1.7 metres across, as the posters had promised.

The eye played an important role in Buddhist mythology. A principal feature by which Buddhas and bodhisattvas are recognised is the third eye, *usnīsa,* in the centre of their foreheads (Figs. 139, 141). But the perceptions derived from this organ are not those of empirical sight, but precisely the opposite: the third eye pierces with blinding rays into what lurks beneath all form, penetrating with a gaze that the human eye cannot emulate; statues often represent the *usnīsa* as a knob or tuft. The divinities' extra eyes stood for the indomitability of their moral affirmations, and the unswerving and insubornable validity of their assessments. This stood in apposition to the claim of the modern eye of science to seek truth within the structure of the world and expose it.

Shakyamuni, the Historical Buddha, after his enlightenment, was said to have been 16 *shaku,* or 4.85 metres high. Statues of that monumental size were frequently made. But even these were far from the largest. Japan had two colossal Buddha images. Tipping their heads downward, they seemed to inspect the world below, training their physiological eyes on the worshipper, as they meditated upon what was hidden behind form with the extra eye of wisdom. A third vast Buddha image in Kyoto, completed in 1595, had in fact been larger still, stretching virtually to 20 metres from its lotus throne, but this had been temporarily lost to fire in 1622.[115] The remaining two were in Kamakura and Nara. The former image was of the Pure Land Buddha, Amida, built in about 1252, and at 11.5 metres, it dominated the seashore; it had been in the open air since its hall was swept away by tidal waves in 1495, but this made it all the more prominent on the skyline from afar (Fig. 141). Oldest and most venerable was the Great Buddha of Nara, a city that had been capital of the nation when the image was erected in 754, though had since been reduced to a bucolic backwater; the Nara Buddha had been sadly treated, and by the eighteenth century was a patchwork of repairs, but it still loomed over 16 metres; in 1708 it was rehoused in a new structure that remains today as the world's largest wooden building. A pair of shutters high up in the facade could be thrown open to expose the resplendent face within, looking down on devotees as fixedly as they looked up at its benevolent form.

Edo had no Great Buddha.[116] This was a source of disappointment to some, not least as

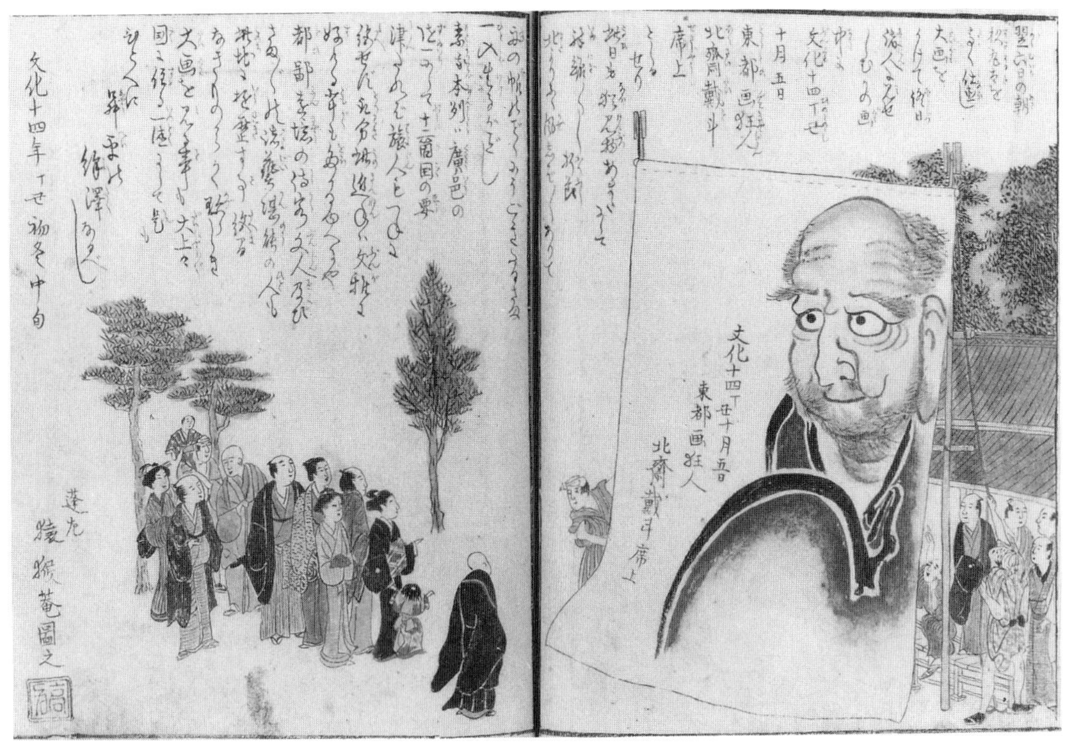

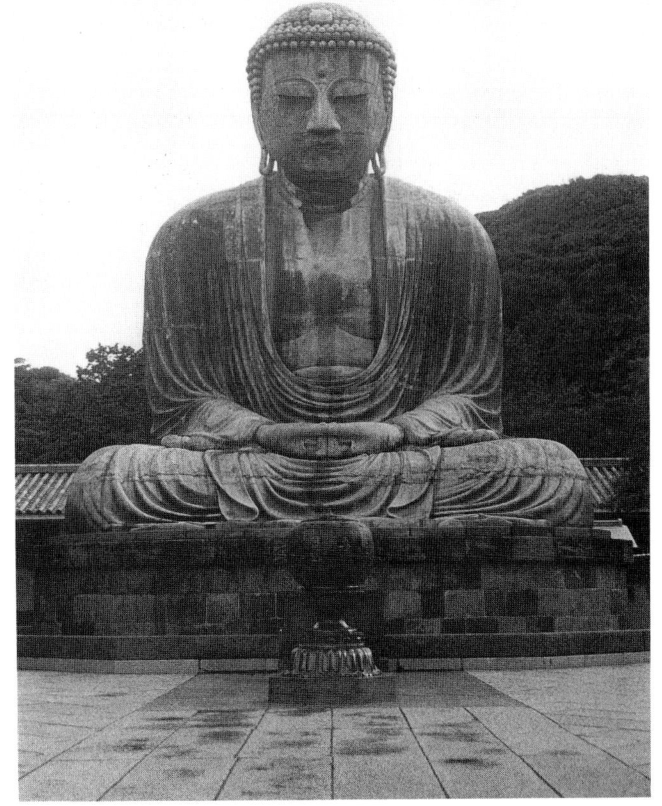

140 (above). Koriki Enkoan, from *Hokusai taiga sokusho saizu,* c. 1817. Nagoya City Museum.

Hokusai's Great Bodhidharma is pulled into place.

141 (right). *Amida, the Great Buddha of Kamakura,* bronze; c. 1252. Kōtoku-in. Photo: Nagashima Tarō.

it was known that even outside Japan other countries possessed gigantic statuary, and Narabayashi Jūbei, the Nagasaki Dutch interpreter, told Tachihara Suiken of a colossal Sakyamuni Entering into Nirvana in Thailand, recumbent (as iconically required) but nevertheless "visible across the sea from over 40 km off."[117]

Edo was not under any material Buddha's all-knowing gaze. Fictional compensations for this blot on the city's pride were attempted. Kyorori told the story of how the Great Buddha of Nara became bored with provincial life and, taking a leaf from the Saikō-ji Jizō's book, came up to Edo for a riotous time. Hakusanjin Kakyo wrote a similar piece, adding that as the Buddha crossed Mount Fuji his head broke through into the realm of the gods.[118]

Then, in 1793, some enterprising monks from the Kaian-ji in Shinagawa determined to remedy the situation in three real dimensions. Shinagawa had grown into a brothel district, for it was there that the Tōkaidō highway emptied into Edo, but it had several major Buddhist establishments too, one of the larger being the Kaian-ji, or Temple of Peace at Sea (Fig. 142). Founded in 1251 when an image of Kannon had been miraculously found in the belly of a shark, the Kaian-ji was denominationally Zen, and boasted the proper complement of icons as well as several lovely stands of maple trees which made its hilly precincts popular in autumn when the foliage was red.[119]

Spring was less good business for the Kaian-ji, and so, on the twentieth day of the second month, the monks unveiled their own Great Buddha.[120] It was an immediate hit, declared "best" of the band of spectacles then on view around town, and mobbed by excited visitors until the hills of the compound looked black.[121] The image became proverbial. When in 1794 Sanba wrote of the morality-seeing telescope given to the arrogant Umajirō, he included the observation that the man's "pride was so way up there he thought he could look down on Fuji or Asama, and trample the Great Buddha of the Kaian-ji under his foot."[122] Despite this, the Edo Great Buddha was erected almost instantaniously, and cheaply made, being neither bronze like the others, nor even wood, but basketwork. Yet it was taller than its metal confreres supposedly, reaching 16 *jō*, or a barely credible 40.5 metres.[123]

Shinagawa was on the waterfront, and this gave the head of the Buddha access to a clear and sweeping panorama. The eyes of the "Basket Buddha" (*kappa ō-botoke*) encompassed all Edo within their gaze. "Divine personages can see through things," noted Sanba, punning *mitōshi*, literally "to look through," with its extended meaning of high places where telescopes could be hired, several of which, as he pointed out, were in Shinagawa.[124] In one of Edo's finer prospects, the Buddha's position boded well for distant viewing. The Tōkaidō left the city to the south-west in a long sweep, the Bay of Edo was to the left. The Kaian-ji was divided from the waterfront by the street lined by a string of brothels. Structurally these establishments were unique and interesting as they had two storeys in the front but gave the effect of three from the rear, because of the way the embankment dropped to the lapping shore below.[125] Clients looking out had the sense of being higher, architecturally speaking, than they really were, and, as in the Turbo Hall, visitors felt as if they were farther up than they had actually climbed. Telescopes were provided by the brothels for time-wasting and delectation of the seascape, as Harunobu showed in a print of the mid-1760s depicting an off-duty prostitute by the name of Motoura and her trainee *shinzō* in the Yamazaki-ya idling until clients arrive, looking at the in-coming evening ships through the lattice (Fig. 143).

Records tell of enthusiasts taking themselves over to the farther side of the Bay of Edo, to Sūzaki and Fukagawa, to look back at the Basket Buddha hanging protectively above the city. It was hard to make the form out so far away,

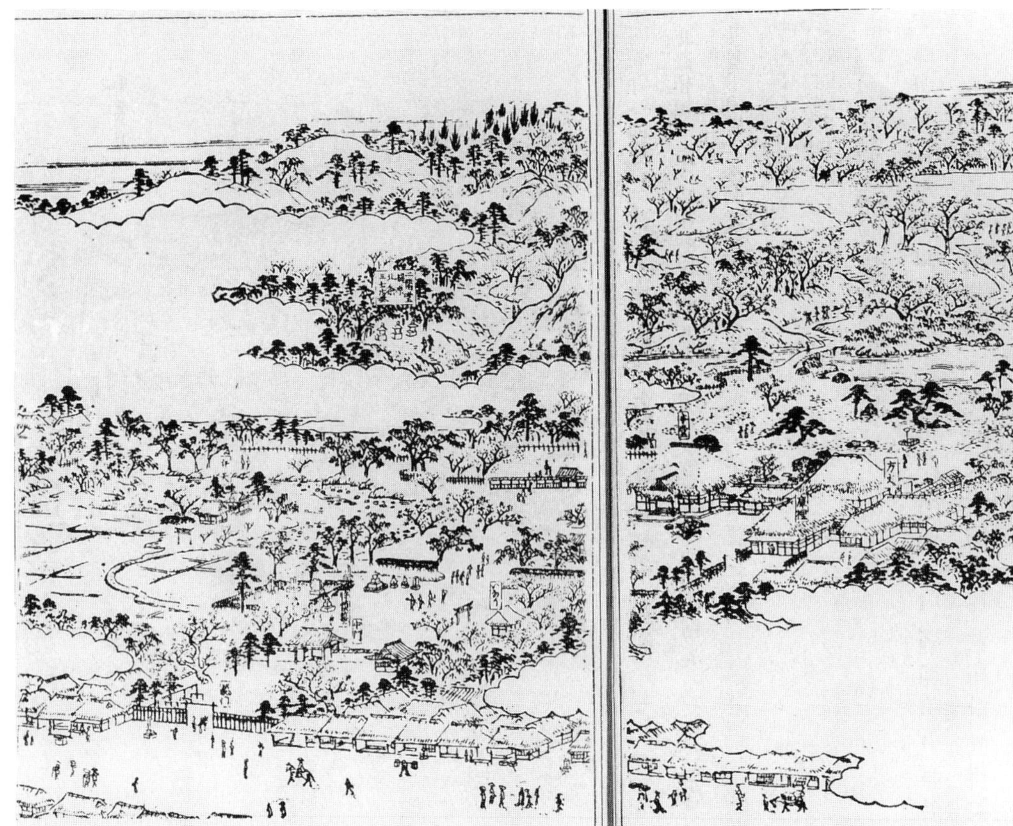

142. Hasegawa Settan and Settei, from Saitō Gesshin (et al.), *Edo meisho zue*, c. 1836. SOAS, University of London. *Temple of Kaian-ji.*

so trippers did well to take a telescope along, too.[126] Hokusai depicted such a group, straining to see the Buddha's head and searching from across the waves in the direction of the shogun's castle (Fig. 144).[127]

Hokusai's picture was partly intended as a genuine depiction of the Edo Buddha and the stir it caused, but it was also a more general call to thought. The image is the first page to a kibyoshi, written as well as illustrated by Hokusai, and published to celebrate another extraordinary event in Shinagawa: the arrival of a whale in the bay in the fifth month of 1798. Other writers dashed off whale-related stories, too: Bakin told of an Edo impresario who wrestled the animal to land and exhibited it for cash; Ikku provided an *August Account of the Bountiful Year of the Great Whale (Taikei hōnen no mizugi)*, linking the event to the legend of the Dragon King's daughter who came to earth; the enigmatic printmaster Sharaku incorporated the whale into a pornographic album of goings-on in the Shinagawa brothels, allowing the animal's spouting to stand for obvious nocturnal ecstasies.[128] Hokusai's writing was more speculative, though nevertheless humorous, and he proposed that the whale was so vast that all who saw it were diminished. The huge sea beast was a physical,

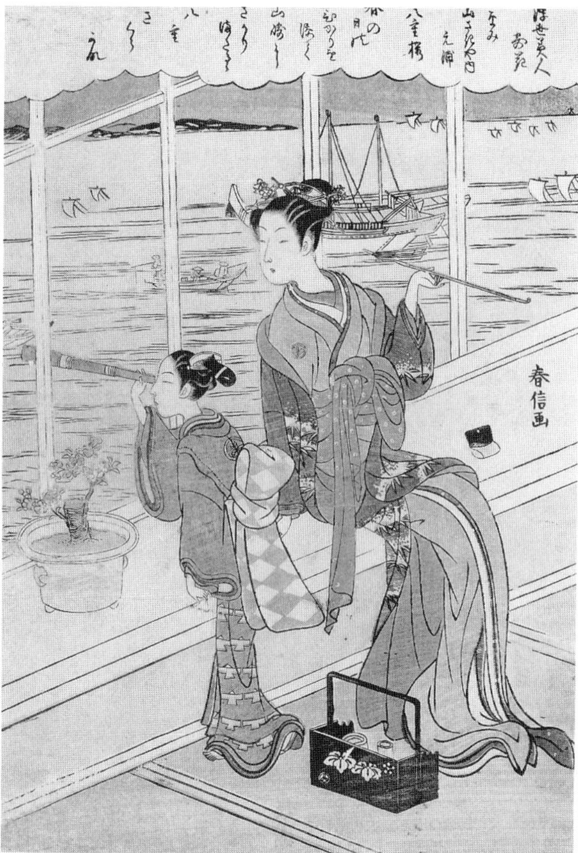

143. Suzuki Harunobu, *Motoura of the Yamasaki-ya in the South*, colour woodblock print from series *Ukiyo bijin hana o kotokuki*; before 1770. Photo: Christie's, New York.

fleshly equivalent of the incredible effusion of religious awe that shrunk everyone who approached the Buddhist colossus.

Hokusai told his tale from a micro-perspective. Edo is reduced to a city of midgets and the fish that swims into the bay a simple tuna, only seeming vast to the ant-like people. The tuna is landed and feasted off for weeks, hence the title of the story, *Plenty for Seven Villages (Nana sato fuki)*.[129] In gratitude, the populace erects a Buddha, great as they understand size to be, but trivial on a human scale (4.5 metres). Significance does not hinge upon measure, and how much can be contrived with the hands depends on a scale relevant only to the individual species. Impressive work is valued by all, but the exhilaration of completing a task against the odds does not depend on any criteria outside the body and mind of the labourer. Tools and machines allowed a disproportionate return on manual strength, but there was not much in the bluster of size alone.

The inanity of appeal to size as a determinant of power or scope, much less of ethical worth, was pointed out in the prefatory salvo to Shiba Kōkan's largest published work, in many ways the summation of his mid-career, though entitled with the misnomer, *Dutch Navigation (Oranda tsūhaku)*. The preface was composed by the seventy-one-year-old Ōta Shukki, a samurai from the *han* of Fukuyama, and dated 1795. It began:

> Now, things do not have absolute largeness or smallness, but only circumstantial size. Scale defines an object in one instance only. What can be relied upon to give this permanent force? Take an ox on one hand and a snake on the other, then the ox is big, but compare it with an elephant and it is small. A mosquito is tiny alongside a snake, but large if measured against a gnat.[130]

Shukki was a Confucian scholar. He was not attributing to Western learning anything he did not already find within his own tradition. Only the lens rendered the prattle of absolutes more fully absurd.

By the time the whale arrived off Shinagawa, the Basket Buddha was gone. It had survived for only sixty days, as a po-faced Magistrate of Religious Institutions (*jisha bugyō*) had commanded its dismantlement.[131] Officialdom found the Buddha a public nuisance, as it crowded the baggage-bearers heading for Kyoto and Osaka. For the Tokugawa regime, order was more important than the frenzy of speculative whim – especially when this proved detrimental to the easy circulation of goods – and in a far-reaching directive, it was declared that all flamboyant and out-sized objects were henceforth banned from

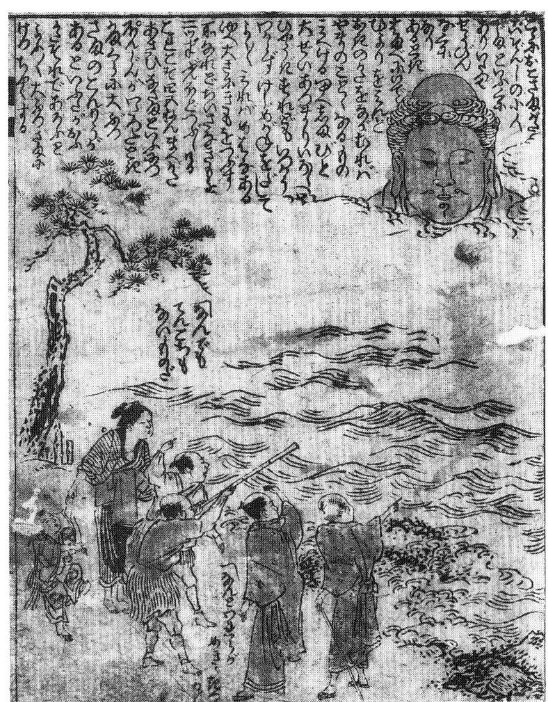

144. Katsushika Hokusai, from *Nanasato fuki,* 1795. Tokyo Metropolitan Central Library.

Trippers view the Great Buddha from across the Bay of Edo.

display. But the scopic regime of the Buddha endured, and the powerful way its woven body had announced to the city that all were under a gaze did not unravel as its slats were pulled apart. The telescopes trained on the plaited staves were lowered, but the palliative of the lens, hoping to answer back to a more directly felt divine sight to attain for humanity some measure of the fullness of cosmic eyes, remained pointed at the stars and planets.

Seven years after the Kaian-ji extravaganza so unfortunately overplayed its hand, a set of five hundred stone images was completed for the Kita-in, senior temple of the Tendai school in the Edo area, located in the castle town of the tiny *han* of Kawagoe, a good day's hike from the city. Each carving was no more than a metre in height, although standing on stone plinths they reached to the chest. The donor of the set was a layman, known only by his subsequent religious appellation, Shisei ("sincere resolve"). He made his first gift in 1782, living to see the ensemble completed just before his death in 1800.[132] The images were of the Five Hundred Arhats and were arranged in two concentric squares around a larger Sakyamuni and attendants, replicating the appearance of the sermon on Vulture Peak. Visitors could wander through the open-air group. Girls sneaked in at night to feel the stones and search for an image that was warm; putting a coin beside it, they would return at daylight to see in the face of the arhat the appearance of their future husband.[133] The unknown sculptor who made the set showed an animated crew, talking to each other, pouring drinks, befriending dragons, and reading texts; he also chiselled one of the arhat brotherhood wearing a pince-nez (*kusabi-megane;* Fig. 145). As an old man, the figure's empirical eyes are weak, but as a divine person his view is lucid. The unexpected ocular feature fuses the compulsion toward enlightenment with the aura of the scientific gaze. The pince-nez, moreover, was never used in Japan until later, so the arhat looks out through mechanisms of sight beyond the reach of the devotee.

MACHINED EYES

In his discussion of Amida's Paradise and its whereabouts, Kōkan had made a comparison with Copernican thought. He stated: "338 years ago, there was a man from Poland called Copernicus; he thought deeply about the Earth, the Five Planets and the Moon's disc, and found them to be spheres; he put forth the theory known as the rotation of the earth (*chiten no setsu*)."[134] Elsewhere Kōkan explained this rotation by reference to an automatic contrivance, specifically devised to demonstrate it: in 1796,

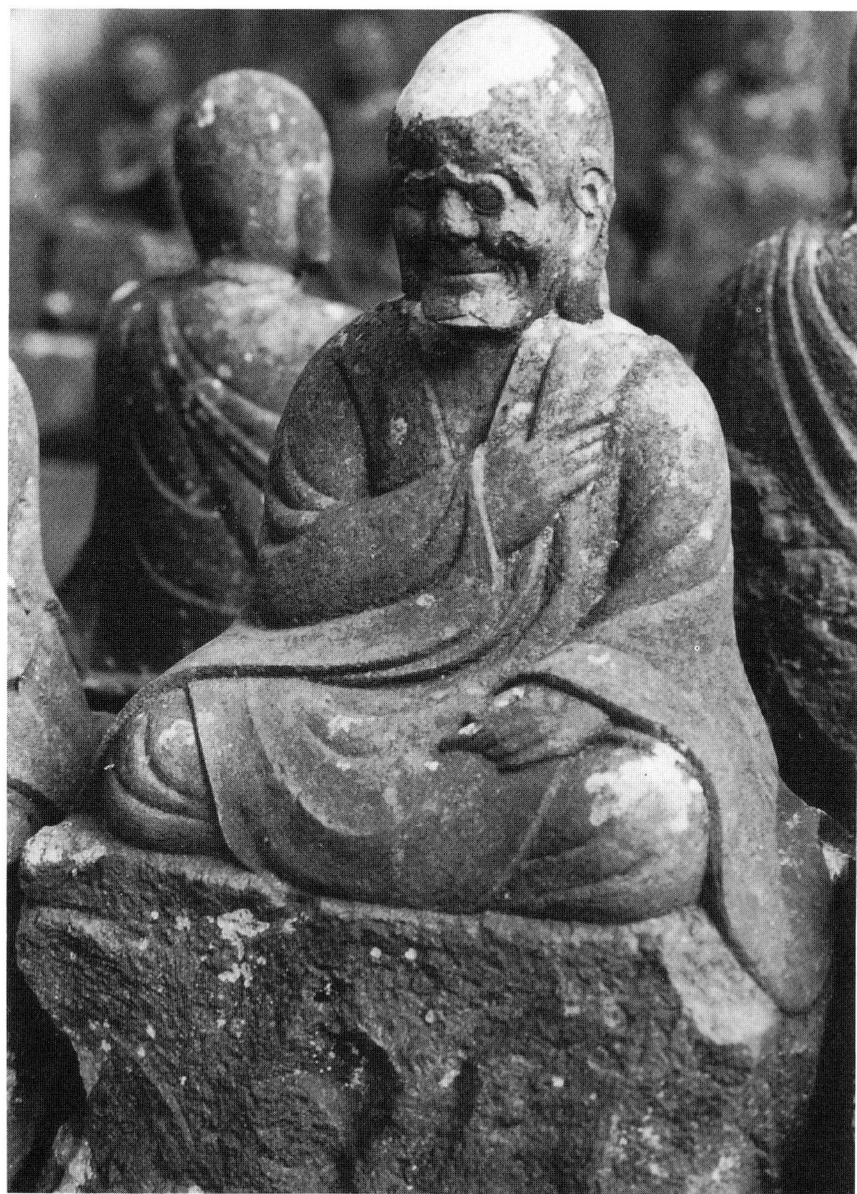

145. *Arhat,* from set of stone figures; c. 1790. Kita-in, Kawagoe. Photo: Nicole Rousmaniere.

in a loose-leaf collection of twelve assorted pages grandly entitled *Complete Illustrations of the Planets (Tenkyū zenzu),* he depicted the machine concerned and labelled it in Roman capitals, ORRERY (Fig. 146). His caption stated:

> The entire device is circular with twelve corners, a sign of the zodiac being drawn on each face. A gauge runs around the outside marked with the 360 degrees. The sphere in the centre represents the sun, and there are smaller balls radiating out from this: first Mercury, then Venus; next is Earth, which leans over at an angle, the North Pole upward, the South Pole beneath, and a sphere beside it standing for the Moon, rotating obliquely; the ring represents the lunar orbit, that is to say, the

> path of its movement; one rotation marks a day and a night, and 360 amount to a full circuit and denote a year. The next sphere is Mars, then Jupiter with its four satellites moving around it, then comes Saturn with the five lesser planets that orbit around it, and half-way up Saturn is its ring.[135]

Each orb was set in a different plate that moved independently. As the machine worked, these rotated at their own separate paces, replicating in their whirrings the deepest searches of astronomers. It was magnificent. As the essayist and politician Richard Steele wrote of the orrery in 1713: "It is like receiving a new Sense, to admit into one's imagination all that this Invention presents to it with so much Quickness and Ease. It administers the Pleasure of Science to anyone who has as much Attention as is necessary in a Man to acquit himself in the ordinary Business of any Profession or Occupation."[136] Steele believed an orrery provided such an "intelligible Method" that "any numerous Family of Distinction" should have one "as necessarily as they would have a Clock."

The orrery aspired to show in fully visible form how the entire universe worked. The name "world machine" was given it, for the clockwork or hand-cranked movements seemed to articulate everything there was to know. Kōkan stated: "An orrery is a globe illustrating the Heavens, and it was first constructed by Copernicus of Poland. The sun is in the centre, and the earth revolves around. The entire ordering of celestial space can be understood by means of it."[137] Kōkan was wrong in detail, as the machine was more recent than he supposed; although it might be called a "Copernican sphere," the instrument was invented by George Graham in about 1704 and perfected by John Rowley, who produced one in 1712 for the Earl of Orrery – hence the common name (interestingly, Rowley's instrument was covered with Chinese-style ornamentation and fifteen years later, the earl himself, an amateur *savant*, helped to sponsor publication of Kaempfer's *History of Japan*).[138] Quantities of orreries were produced in the eighteenth century for installation in the philosophical cabinets of "families of distinction" or the lecture rooms of universities.

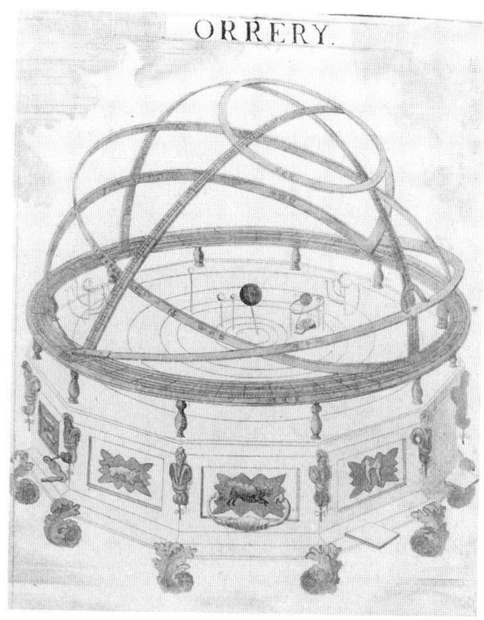

146. Shiba Kōkan, *Orrery*, hand-coloured copperplate print from his *Tenkyū zenzu*, 1796. Kobe City Museum.

Kōkan attributed his information about the device to "a Dutch book called 'Uhensukoru,' " a name that is difficult to untangle. Three years earlier, when he had first discussed the orrery, Kōkan gave his source as Egbert Buys, whose *Complete Dictionary (Woordenboek)* does indeed include an entry on the subject, identified as a *Planeet-leezer*, and defined as "an Astronomical Machine, so called from its representing the Motions, Orbits, &c of the Planets."[139] Buys's illustration is identical to Kōkan's, right down to leaf-shaped legs, symbolic markings, and lever at the side.[140] But Kōkan's orrery can be traced further. It was produced by Rowley's successor, Thomas Wright, maker to King George II; called the Great Orrery, it belonged to the Royal Academy in Portsmouth. Replicas were produced by

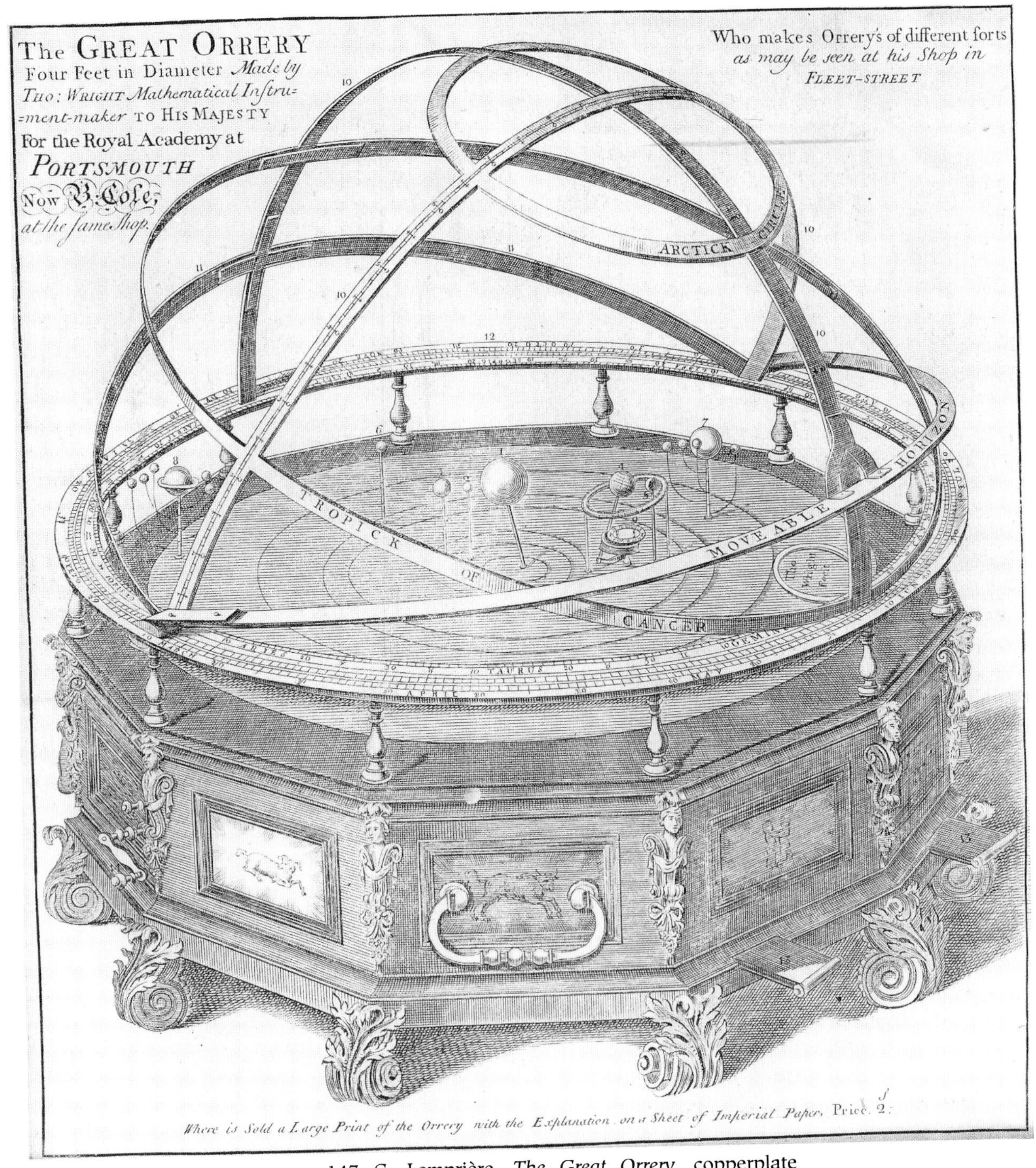

147. C. Lemprière, *The Great Orrery*, copperplate broadsheet; mid-eighteenth century. © Museum of the History of Science, Oxford University.

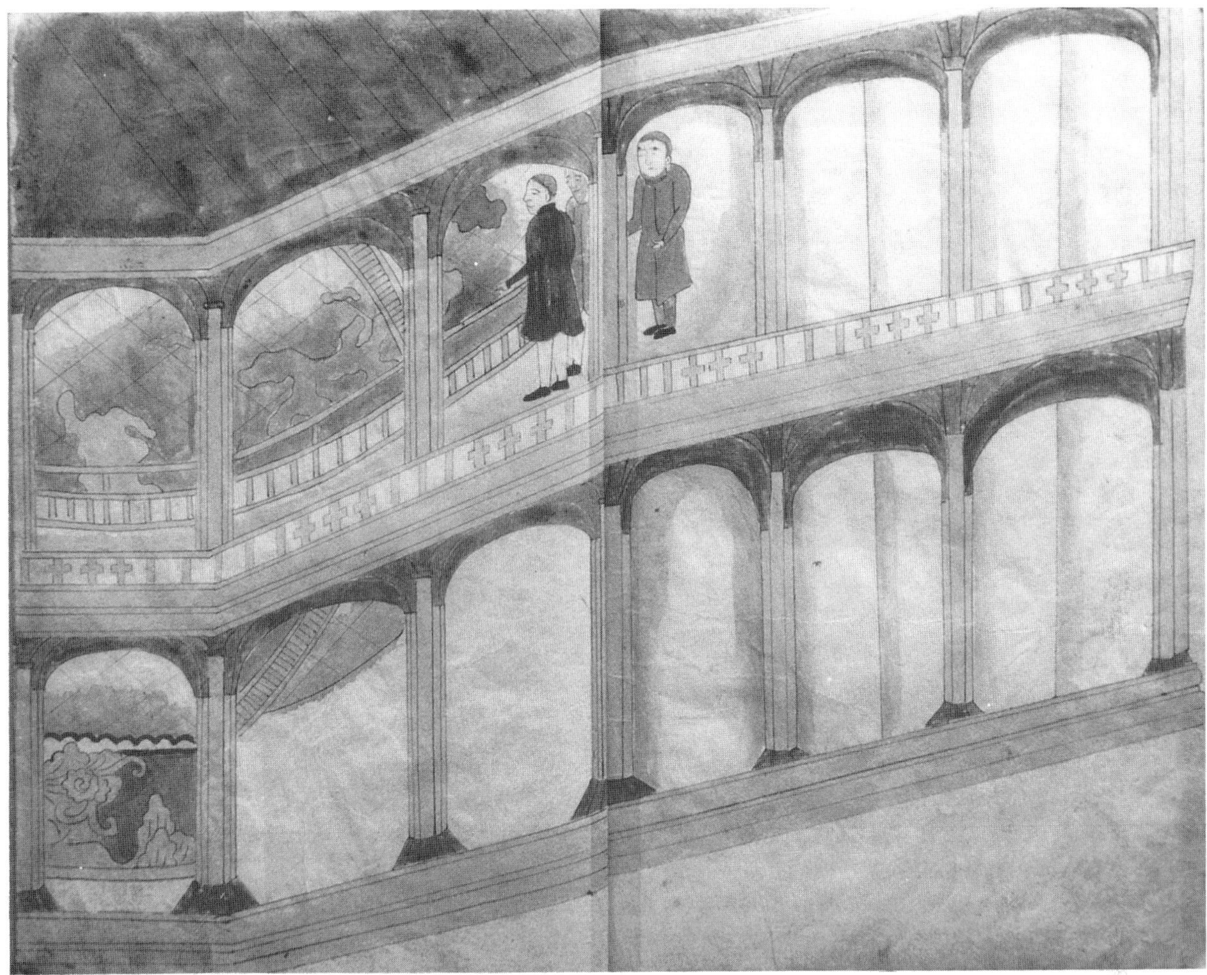

148. Unsigned, copy after Ōtsuki Gentaku & Kimura Kōgō, *Kankai ibun*; c. 1830. SOAS, University of London.

Exterior view of the St Petersburg Globe.

Benjamin Cole of Fleet Street for unspecified, though no doubt hefty, prices (orreries were never cheap: in 1764, Harvard College paid £90 for one made by Benjamin Martin, another London craftsman, who assessed it "as compleat a One as ever went from hence, & that all its Parts and Motions are perfectly true and exact").[141] The Great Orrery was also published in a broadsheet sold for just tuppence (Fig. 147).

Certain orreries were made for use in the dark, resulting in an intense theatricality that increased their dramatic impact if not their explanatory efficacy. As it was said of the Portsmouth piece, a lamp "may at any time be put in place of the *Sun* which shews the Seasons of the *Year* and Eclipses as they really appear." The use of illuminated suns expounded how shadows fall across the planets (although only up to a point, as relative sizes and distances were not respected on orreries)[142] but, more pregnantly, for the light to stand out clearly, the room had to be plunged into complete darkness. Viewers were lost to the machine, their sense of residing in routine, earthly space evaporating as they floated off among the planets, watching the spheres rotate around a shining sun.

At least one orrery was in Japan as the shogunal observatory had an "instrument of the heavenly bodies, Primitive in make," otherwise known as the "Combined Revolution Machine" (*bansei tenkai-gi/kōun-gi*), and this was illustrated in *The Book of the Kansei Calendar.* Kōkan would not have known this device, which was in any case inferior to the one he illustrated. Kōkan had access to no more than illustrations and reports. However, Tsūdayū, the castaway, was exposed directly to a splendid contrivance built in the palace of the tsar in St. Petersburg, probably some time in the 1790s, and which far exceeded the orrery, for it was a complete planetarium.[143]

Tsūdayū described how a group of guests, including himself, were taken to a six-metre circular room painted on the outside exactly to resemble the lands and seas of the earth – Tsūdayū could even make out Japan (Fig. 148). This was the successor to the famous Gottorf Globe, which worked by waterwheels and gearing, and had been built for the duke of Schleswig in 1650, but sold to the tsar in 1713; lost to fire a generation later, it was rebuilt by 1752 at twice the size of the original (if Tsūdayū is accurate) and was large enough for twelve people inside.[144]

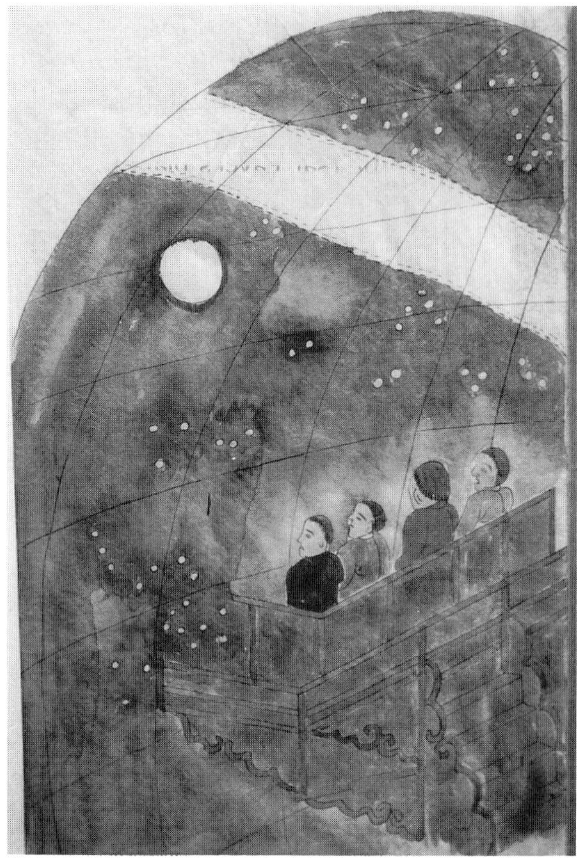

149. Unsigned, copy after Ōtsuki Gentaku & Kimura Kōgō, *Kankai ibun*; c. 1830. SOAS, University of London.

Interior view of the St Petersburg Globe.

They then went inside, and the door was shut fast behind them as they ascended to a wooden scaffold hanging in the air and jutting into the centre of the arena (Fig. 149). All was pitch-black and fully sealed. Tsūdayū watched the dome open and the stars and planets shine from the ceiling. It was as if he were looking out across the whole universe, with its celestial bodies and spaces beyond. The vision moved and shifted. The hushed observers looked on as the multifarious revolutions attested to by a discerning science were worked through smoothly in the machinery. They felt themselves heaven-borne, gazing on phenomena from outer space. Crouched on his stool, Tsūdayū was barely seeing from any point on earth.

Under interrogation from Ōtsuki Gentaku on his return Tsūdayū was at a loss to explain the sensations he received, and, striving for adequate comparisons for this total vision of the universe, what he came up with is rather telling:

in the planetarium, he said, he felt as though he were inside the body of the Great Buddha of Kamakura. Unlike the Buddha of Nara the Kamakura image could be entered for it was constructed with a door and a space within, about the size indeed of Tsar Pavel's planetary room. Visitors went in to pray or burn incense, and the interior of the holy image, where nothing could be seen but where all was infinitely known, had a profound and mystic presence. John Saris, an English captain in Kamakura in the early seventeenth century, recorded:

> This Image is much reverenced by Travellers as they passe there. Some of our people went into the bodie of it, and hooped and hallowed, which made an exceedingly great noyse. We found many Characters and Markes made upon it by Passengers, whom some of my Followers imitated, and made theirs in like manner.[145]

The insides of the enclosures of Kamakura and St. Petersburg were nuclei of fusion – cosmic and earthly, near and far, foreign and home – and they came together to alter sense drastically. Gentaku exclaimed when he heard Tsūdayū's story, "It is difficult to conceive how such things could ever have been!"[146] Indeed it was. But without a moral sense, what did such precision seeing avail?

NOTES

Where the quoted section of a work appears visibly in a Figure to the text, no note is provided here. The reader is directed to the Captions for Plates and Figures.

1: TRADE AND CULTURE

1 Takano Chōei, *Tori no nakune* (1839), quoted in Grant K. Goodman, *Japan: The Dutch Experience,* p. 205.

2 The Bansho Shirabesho.

3 For details of the school, see Itazawa Takeo, *Nichi-Ran bunka kōshōshi no kenkyū,* pp. 515–22, and Richard Rubinger, *Private Academies in Tokugawa Japan,* pp. 108–27, where the Shirandō enrollment information is tabulated p. 109, and from which it can be seen that by its demise in 1826 the school had accepted only ninety-four students; admissions were in double figures (just ten) in 1797 only. More generally, the importance of doctors – educated men with spare time – in Dutch Studies will become apparent as this book progresses. Another *Rangaku*-oriented institution to open about this time was the Seijū-kan (properly called the Igaku-kan), not a school but a meeting hall.

4 Stated in a letter to Umebo Seiryō, dated the 17th of the 8th month (year unknown, possibly 1813); see facsimile and transcription in Nakano Yoshio, *Shiba Kōkan kō,* p. 185.

5 For a table of Netherlandish national designations, see Simon Schama, *Patriots and Liberators,* p. xix.

6 The classic survey of the history of *misemono* is Asakura Musei, *Misemono kenkyū,* reworked by Furukawa Miki, *Shumin geinō: Edo no misemono;* for an English survey, see Andrew L. Markus, "The Carnival of Edo."

7 For a survey of the history of the VOC in Japan, see C. R. Boxer, *Jan Companie in Japan.* Non-VOC Dutch shipping had arrived earlier, and the company itself was incorporated in 1602 (two years after the English equivalent). For surveys of the Iberian presence, see Jurgis Elisonas, "Christianity and the Daimyo", and the English East India Company, see Derek Massarella, *A World Elsewhere,* pp. 80–130.

8 Ronald P. Toby, *State and Diplomacy in Early Modern Japan,* p. 14.

9 Engelbert Kaempfer, *A History of Japan* (1727), stated, "of foreign ships there are seldom, some few months in the winter excepted, less than thirty, most of which are Chinese Yonks," p. 255. By the end of the century, however, numbers were lower.

10 Conversely, controls were set on the quantity of metals that could be exported.

11 T. Volker, *The Japanese Porcelain Trade,* p. 51.

12 Ibid., p. 55.

13 Sugita Genpaku, *Rangaku kotohajime,* p. 479. The book is also known as *Rantō kotohajime.*

14 There are three classic late-eighteenth-century examples of *Rangaku*-inspired daimyo, all of which will be mentioned frequently below: Hosokawa Shigekata of Kumamoto, Satake Yoshiatsu of Akita, and Katsuki Masatsuna of Fukuchiyama.

15 Sugita Genpaku, *Nochimi-gusa* (1787), p. 74.

16 The theory that the assassination was to prevent an expansion in foreign trade is to be found in the writings of a leading VOC official in Japan, Isaac Titsingh (Frederick Shoberl, trans.), *Illustrations of Japan* (1822), pp. 101, 183. Titsingh returned from Japan in 1784.

17 The negative impact of the island is usually stressed by modern historians, but there were definite advantages; the Dejima compound did burn down in 1798, but was immediately rebuilt. The Chinese did not reside on an island, although from 1689 they were forced into a stockade outside town; their storehouses were on the rectangular island seen in Plate 1. For the Chinese, see Marius B. Jansen, *China in the Tokugawa World,* pp. 25–33.

18 Poste-haste would be faster and a normal business pace slower; for example, when the Dutch retinue visited Edo in 1776, it left Nagasaki on 4 March, arrived in Osaka on 8 April, and in Edo on 27 April (although this was regarded as slow); see, Charles Thunberg, *Travels,* vol. 3, pp. 95, 168. Wheeled traffic was banned from most highways as it caused damage to the surface; upper-class travellers were carried in palanquins and lower classes walked.

19 Volker, *Japanese Porcelain Trade,* p. 46.

20 Massarella, *A World Elsewhere,* p. 325. Massarella gives a vivid account of frustration in London with the Japanese factory. The English were stationed on Hirado (as the Dutch had been before moving to Dejima – originally constructed for the Portuguese – in 1641); Hirado, a *han* under the control of the Matsura family, was a sizeable natural island some 120 km from Nagasaki as the crow flies.

21 Hiroko Nishida, "A History of Japanese Porcelain and the Export Trade," p. 63. The Japanese records referred to are the *Tōban kamotsu-chō.*

22 *Oost-Indische Spiegel* (1701 and 1704), quoted without page reference in Christiaan J. A. Jorg, "Japanese Lacquerwork Decorated after European Prints," p. 57.

23 Volker, *Japanese Porcelain Trade,* p. 6.

24 Thunberg, *Travels,* vol. 3, pp. 13, 29. Thunberg is known as Charles, as his book appeared in English (F. Rimington and C. Rimington, trans.), although he would have identified himself as Carl.

25 Ibid., p. 15.

26 Ibid.

27 Ibid., p. 28.

28 The year of the appearance of the *Travels* is obscure, as a four-volume edition (the third of which relates to Japan) was published in 1795 under the title of *Thunberg's Travels,* but there is also a single-volume version with the longer title, *Charles Thunberg's Travels in Europe, Africa and Asia, performed between the years 1770 and 1779* which is undated. Pagination is the same for either work.

29 For the role and position of the Nagasaki magistrates, see Toyama Mikio, *Nagasaki bugyō,* especially pp. 53–67.

30 Thunberg, *Travels,* vol. 3, pp. 16–17.

31 Volker, *Japanese Porcelain Trade,* p. 36 (entry dated 1711).

32 Kaempfer, *History of Japan,* preface by the translator Johannes Scheuchzer, p. vii. Kaempfer, a German, was in Japan in 1690–2. For a general history of his life, see Beatrice Bodart-Bailey, "Kaempfer Restor'd." Scheuchzer was a Swiss doctor, aged twenty-five at the time of writing, and librarian to Sir Hans Sloane, and he undertook the translation only under duress (dying two years later); see also Archibald Geikie, "Biographical Note on the Scheuchzer Family." Kaempfer's original title was *Heutiges Japan.* See Bodart-Bailey, ibid., pp. 14–33. Kaempfer's subject was acupuncture, and the title of his work, *Amoenitatum exoticarum politico-physico medicarum* (1712); see G. T. Haneveld, "The Introduction of Acupuncture into Western Medicine," especially pp. 54–5.

33 Kaempfer (Scheuchzer trans.), *The History of Japan,* translator's preface, p. ii, and vol. 2, p. 74 (1906 edition).

34 Aoki Okikatsu, *Jomon jissaki* (1804) quoted in Be-

atrice Bodart-Bailey, "The Persecution of Confucianism in Early Tokugawa Japan," p. 296. Honda Toshiaki was also impressed by Kaempfer's book, see *Seiiki monogatari,* p. 40; and Matsura Kiyoshi, daimyo of Hirado, who owned a copy of it by 1782 and stated, "this book had been lost to oblivion, but finally I bought it for very little money"; quoted without source in C. C. Krieger, *Infiltration of European Civilisation,* pp. 75–6 (adapted).

35 Tachibana Nankei, *Hokusō sadan* (1795–8), p. 155. Nankei also wrote *Seiyū-ki* (1795–8), a record of his experiences *en route* to Nagasaki and back, and *Tōyū-ki* (1795–8), the diary of a trip to the East; these were amalgamated and published simultaneously as *Tōzai yūki.* I differ from Harold Bolitho, who estimates Nankei to be "credulous" and with "very little rationalism," see "Travelers' Tales," p. 493. Nankei is also known as Miyagawa Shunki.

36 Koga Jūjirō, *Maruyama yūjo to tōkōmojin,* vol. 1, p. 767.

37 Records of Western affairs were submitted via the Nagasaki magistracy under the title of *Oranda fūsetsu-gaki;* they cover the entire Edo period, see Iwase Seiichi (ed), *Oranda fūsetsu-gaki,* 3 vols.

38 Thirty-nine titles are listed under Kōsaku's name in Yasue Ryōsuke, ed., *Kokusho sōmokuroku,* q.v. For the medical school, see *ō-Edo no omoshiro yakushoku jiten,* p. 174.

39 Tachibana Nankei, *Hokusō sadan,* p. 155. Kōsaku's bath is described as having been of glass (*biiidoro*), the meaning of which is obscure, as vitreous china was not yet in use.

40 Kokan described making Kōsaku's portrait in *Saiyū nikki,* p. 124; after the painting was complete, the party retired to the Dutch room. For Kōkan's trip to Dejima, see ibid., pp. 105–6; to gain access, Kōkan was obliged to shave his head (as a doctor), probably to impersonate a visitor from Kōsaku's school. Kōkan's freedom in Nagasaki was eased by the fact he was taken as a shogunal spy (*on-mitsu*); ibid., p. 109.

41 The proportion of Chinese residents in Nagasaki can be calculated by combining Furukawa Koshōken's head count of the total population made in 1783 (51,702), see his *Saiyū zakki,* p. 161, with the 10,000 Chinese said to be in the town in *ō-Edo no omoshiro yakushoku jiten,* p. 176.

42 From 1790 trips were made only once in four years, and from 1794 this was further reduced to five.

43 Shiba Kōkan, *Saiyū nikki,* pp. 204–5.

44 Thunberg, *Travels,* vol. 3, p. 133.

45 Titsingh recounts how the mission was often delayed, see *Illustrations of Japan,* p. 126; Titsingh himself made the Edo visit three times: in 1780, 1783, and 1784. For Thunberg's trip, see *Travels,* vol. 3, p. 171.

46 *Kapitan mo tsukubawasekeri kimi ga haru;* quoted in Katsuhara Haruki, "Haikai no jūhasseiki", p. 93.

47 *Oranda mo hana ni kinikeri uma no kura;* quoted ibid. Horses were seldom used for transport within the confines of the city itself, except on this annual occasion.

48 Thunberg, *Travels,* vol. 3, p. 94; by "norimon" he means *norimono,* or palanquin.

49 Paul van der Velde, ed., *Dejima dagregisters,* vol. 3, p. 67. The shogun was referred to by Westerners as the emperor of Japan (or the *kaiser*), or sometimes as the *kubo;* this is not to be confused with the figure we today call the emperor of Japan (properly, the *tennō*), who was generally called the *dairi* (literally, "palace"); Thunberg defined him as "the country's quondam ruler now merely its pope," *Travels,* vol. 3, p. 140. The shogun was *de facto* head of state, although theoretically overlord of the daimyo and serving as the tennō's general.

50 Iwase, ed., *Oranda fūsetsu-gaki,* vol. 1, pp. 48–9. This was an annual register of reports compiled by the Nagasaki magistracy. One major gap in imparted information was the French Revolution, which was concealed from the shogunate until the assassination of Louis XVI in 1794; see ibid., p. 94.

51 For the *hatamoto* analogy, see Hirakawa Kai, *Nagasaki bunken-roku,* vol. 4, p. 10v.

52 Frederick Shoberl, translator's preface to Titsingh, *Illustrations of Japan,* p. 2. Shoberl used the present tense to refer to Titsingh, although he had died in 1812, ten years before the book appeared.

53 Thunberg, *Travels*, vol. 3, p. 256.

54 Kaempfer, *History of Japan*, noted that the Nagasaki-ya was "sufficiently remote from the street, being the upper story of a back house, to which there was no entry, but through a narrow passage which could be locked up if needful," vol. 3, p. 80 (1906 ed.); but this was not the same building as that standing at the end of the century (see note 55).

55 Van der Velde, ed., *Dejima Dagregisters*, vol. 6, p. 262; Thunberg, *Travels*, vol. 3, p. 177; for the fire, which occurred in April while the place was unoccupied, see ibid., p. 181.

56 Titsingh, *Illustrations of Japan*, p. 171.

57 Gennai had been born a samurai, but gave up his rank to study *Rangaku* in greater freedom; for his meeting with the Dutch, see Sugita Genpaku, *Rangaku kotohajime*, p. 485.

58 So far as I am aware, nothing is known of the appearance of the pre-1772 Nagasaki-ya. Hokusai's book was abbreviated and reissued in colour in 1802 as *Azuma asobi*. For the commission and its unfortunate repercussions (when the physician tried to swindle him), see Ōnishi Hiroshi et al., *Geijutsuka densetsu*, pp. 233–4. Arai Tsutomu has advanced the theory that Hokusai was a spy for the Dutch; see *Hokusai no kakushi-e*, pp. 53–74.

59 Thunberg, *Travels*, vol. 3, p. 171.

60 What became of the impressive language books made by the Jesuits in the sixteenth century is not known, but as they worked to and from Portuguese or Latin, they would have been of limited use to the VOC. Possibly such early works were concealed because of their association with Christianity, although, by contrast, Thunberg was openly shown a publication from the old Jesuit press (he did not record the title, but noted the date as 1598); see *Travels*, vol. 3, p. 186.

61 Ibid., p. 265.

62 For the members of the Katsuragawa house, see Imaizumi Genkichi, *Katsuragawa-ke no hitobito* and Tozawa Yukio, *Katsuragawa-ke no sekai;* the father, Hosan, was also a scholar of the West and had studied with the *han* doctor of Hirado (the island where the European factories had formerly been). That Chūryō and Hoshū have different surnames need not deter the reader, because most persons in the Edo period had several and altered them according to situation (modern historians are obliged to homogenise); Churyō was also known as Katsuragawa Hosai.

63 Thunberg, *Travels*, vol. 3, p. 177.

64 Katsuragawa Hoshū, *Kenbikyō yōhō* (1805). For a full list of his writings, see Yasue Ryōsuke, ed., *Kokusho sōmokuroku*, q.v.

65 Thunberg, *Travels*, vol. 3, pp. 198, 206–7.

66 For scattered minutes of Hoshū's (and others') meetings with the Dutch in the years 1794–1814, see Ōtsuki Gentaku, *Seihin taigo* (undated), partially reproduced by Mori Senzō in "Ōtsuki Bansui no Ranjin hōmon." Bansui is the same person as Gentaku.

67 Thunberg, *Travels*, vol. 3, p. 175.

68 On the use of Korean and Ryukyuan visits by the Edo shogunate, see Toby, *State and Diplomacy;* the case of the Europeans remains to be studied in depth, but see Timon Screech (Takayama Hiroshi, trans.), *Ō-Edo no injin ōrai* (forthcoming).

69 Sugita Genpaku, *Rangaku kotohajime*, p. 482.

70 Thunberg, *Travels*, vol. 3, p. 173.

71 Shiba Kōkan, *Dokushō bōge* (1810); quoted in Sugano Yō, "Kaisetsu," in *Kunmō gakai-shū*, p. 326. Kōkan particularly condemned the *Kaitai shinsho* (1774) and the *Ihan teikō* (1805), both by the authors mentioned.

72 Satake Shozan, *Gahō kōryō* (in Japanese), and *Gazu rikai* (also called *Gato rikai*, in *kanbun*); neither work was published in Satake's lifetime, although they probably circulated in manuscript. For modern editions, see Sakazaki Tan, *Nihon garon taikan*, vol. 1, pp. 99–103. Gennai's visit to Akita and his encounter with members of Satake's staff, particularly the young painter Odano Naotake, is a landmark in the history of *Rangaku*. "Shozan" was Yoshiatsu's studio name.

73 Hosan wrote the preface; for details, see Kikuchi Toshiyoshi, "Kaisetsu," in *Oranda-banashi/Ransetsu benwaku*, p. 60; Gotō Rishun refers to Hosan as Kuninori (by the same token, his son Hoshū had the name Kuniakira).

74 The preface is dated 1788, although a published version appeared only in 1799 (many Edo-period books circulated first in manuscript),

Genshō dying before the compilation was complete.

75 Morishima Chūryō, *Kōmō zatsuwa;* see pp. 469–72, 476, 454, 461, 463, 475, 480, and 467, respectively. Gennai's sexual orientation was famous, see, *inter alia,* his run-down of Edo boy prostitutes, *Edo nanshoku saiken,* in Ōta Nanpo's posthumous collection of Gennai's writing, *Hika rakuyō* (1783), p. 803; Chūryō's case is more circumstantial; see Screech, *Ō-Edo no ijin ōrai* (forthcoming).

76 Shiba Kōkan, letter dated 1813 to Koba Shunrei; see facsimile and transcription in Nakano, *Shiba Kōkan kō,* p. 45. The pupil concerned was Minwa, about whom no further information is known. Minwa referred to *sengoku,* which nowadays means the sixteenth century in Japan, but at this time normally still referred to the Chinese period of civil war, c. 403–221 B.C.

77 For an accessible assessment of the districts, see Teruoka Yasutaka, "The Pleasure Quarters and Tokugawa Culture"; for Edo in particular, see Cecelia Segawa Seigel, *Yoshiwara.*

78 This is not to deny the legitimacy of the study of sexual activity in the quarters, nor of the lives of the women who were indentured there. Unlicensed districts (*oka-basho*) offered more rudimentary action.

79 Imaizumi, *Katsuragawa-ke no hitobito,* vol. 1, pp. 145ff.

80 For a fascinating account of the Katsuragawa brothers' Floating World activities, see Haruko Iwasaki, *The World of Gesaku,* pp. 135–73.

81 *Karadehon tōjingura* has been discussed by Mori Senzō, "Kaigai chishiki de shukō o tateta kibyōshi." For the original play, see Donald Keene, trans., *Chūshingura.*

82 Onitake's biography is unclear. Takizawa Bakin named him Kurahashi Raichirō (which gives him the same family name as Harumachi), but others identify him as one Maeno Manshichirō, see Tanahashi Masahiro, *Kibyōshi sōran* vol. 1, p. 127 and vol. 3, pp. 125–33; Onitake also studied painting under Tani Bunchō, and illustrated at least one kibyoshi, see ibid., vol. 2, p. 246.

83 *Niyoro kai no miso shiru* (1788), author unknown, quoted in Inoue Takaaki, *Edo gesaku no kenkyū,* p. 200.

84 See inter alia Shikitei Sanba, *Ono no Bakamura uso ji-tsukushi,* pagination unclear, section on writing, and Takizawa Bakin, *Zeni kagami takawa utsushie* (1800), pp. 7v–8r. A pun on *Oranda* and *haranda* "given birth" was also known; see Rinshō, *Kogane no yama Fukuzō jikki,* p. 12r.

85 For the Nagasaki-ya brothel, run by one Nagasaki-ya Kohei, see Santō Kyōden, *Misuji dachi kyaku no ki ueda* (1787), p. 12v (with illustrations by the author).

86 Shikitei Sanba, *Ono no Bakamura,* pagination unclear, section on writing.

87 Santō Kyōden, *Komon gawa,* p. 104.

88 Yamanaka Kyōkō, *Suna-barai,* vol. 1, p. 55. The expression *Oranda no kana miru yō ni* is said there to date from the Tenmei period (1781–8).

89 Shikitei Sanba, *Ono no bakamura,* pagination unclear, section on writing. (Chinese characters were said to have been invented by the sage Cangxie after looking at bird footprints.) Sanba's father was a block cutter, and his two wives were both publishers' daughters; for his biography, see Robert W. Leutner, *Shikitei Sanba and the Comic Tradition in Edo Fiction,* p. 15.

90 Takizawa Bakin took the name "Crab-moving Wizard" (Kaniyuki Sennin) in reference to sideways progression; the famously wayward late eighteenth-century artist Soga Shōhaku was referred to by his nineteenth-century biographer as someone who "went sideways"; see Okada Chōken, *Kinsei etsujin shi,* cited in Tsuji Nobuo, *Kisō no keifū,* p. 88.

91 Shikitei Sanba, *Ono no bakamura,* pagination unclear, section on writing.

92 For two important general discussions, see Nakano Mitsutoshi, *Gesaku kenkyū,* and Nakamura Yukihiko, *Gesaku-ron.*

93 Among the few works to have looked closely at this question are: Iwasaki, *World of Gesaku;* Suzuki Jūzō, *Ehon to ukiyo-e;* and Inoue, *Edo gesaku.*

94 The importance to Japanese thought of "spheres" (*sekai*), and the means by which these were brought together, have been discussed by other writers (although not with reference to Holland); see, *inter alia,* Tanaka Yūko, *Edo wa nettowaku,*

and Makoto Ueda, "The Taxonomy of Sequence." This passage has benefited from discussion with Murayama Kazuhiro.

95 *Koko ni nomi tsuji wa irazu wakaruran kapitan no kiku Kokuchō no kane.*

96 The shogun, Hidetada, second in the Tokugawa line, was in office 1605–23, although the date of the donation is not recorded; see Tsunoyama Sakae, *Tokei no shakaishi*, p. 78. The bell, which still stands, was said to be too noisy for the castle whence it was moved, to be replaced there by a drum.

97 For the import of clocks and Edo-period time-telling, see below, Chapter 3.

98 Anon., *Heike monogatari*, bk. 1, chap. 1. The work is translated by Helen Craig McCullough as *The Tale of the Heike;* for the relevant section, see p. 23.

99 For an assessment of the wider question of the use of language in the eighteenth century, see Naoki Sakai, *Voices of the Past.*

100 The "first" kibyoshi is said to be Koikawa Harumachi, *Kinkin sensei eiga no yume*, illustrated by the author; for a modern edition, see Koike Masatane et al., eds. *Edo no gesaku e-hon*, vol. 1, pp. 11–30. For the duties of a *rusuiyaku*, see Sasama Yoshihiko, *Edo bakufu yakushoku shūsei*, p. 90.

101 Iwasaki, *World of Gesaku*, pp. 123–5; Iwasaki stresses the positive effects that to humorously problematise serious concerns could have on a person's career.

102 For Hokusai's written oeuvre, see Yasuda Gōzō, "Hokusai no kibyōshi"; for Kyoden's prints, see Kobayashi Tadashi, "Eshi Santō Kyōden." For Shigemosa's fiction, see Tanahashi Masahiro, *Kibyōshi sōran*, vol. 2, p. 365. For Utamaro and Harumachi's shared successor, see Shikitei Sanba, *Ukiyo-e ruikō*, supplement, quoted in Ichido Yasuhiro, "*Futari no ni-dai Kitagawa Utamaro*", p. 13, and for the Sekien connexion, see ibid. Part of one of Sekien's ghost books appears in Fig. 53 below. Chūryō's link to Utamaro is claimed in Ōta Nanpo, *Hantori-chō* (1783), see Tozawa Yukio, *Katsurakawa-ke no sekai*, pp. 149–50. Many of these bonds are questioned by modern scholars.

103 *Wakoku ni mo chinpunkan no mise arite kaite o hiki da mokuzen no kara.* A pun is intended between the name Hikida and the verb *hiku* "to pull in [custom]".

104 Shikitei Sanba, *Ukiyo-doko*, p. 289. He refers to the *Kōmō no jūri ken*, or "ten-league Red-fur gaze," although *Kōmō* is glossed as *Oranda.*

2: THE "BATAVIAN TEMPERAMENT" AND ITS CRITICS

1 I take the term "Batavian Temperament" from Simon Schama, *Embarrassment of Riches*, pp. 3–12, but whereas he uses it to refer to a Netherlandish self-image, I mean it in the reverse sense of the Japanese construction of Holland. Batavia can also here refer to new Batavia or Jakarta.

2 Of course, the Japanese assessment of Holland is not entirely dissimilar to the Dutch self-myth, but the point here is to stress that there is no priority to the latter. For the role of precision gazing in Dutch culture, see Svetlana Alpers, *The Art of Describing*, especially pp. 1–26.

3 Yoshio Kōsaku, preface to Sugita Genpaku et al., trans., *Kaitai shinsho*, p. 209. For the opposite view to Kōsaku's, see Eiko Ikegami, *Disciplining the Japanese.*

4 Furukawa Koshōken, *Saiyū zakki*, p. 167; Engelbert Kaempfer called Nagasaki-ites "the greatest debauchees and the lewdest people in the whole Empire" (*History of Japan*, p. 206) and further noted, "there are more poor people and beggars here, and more impudent than any where else" (ibid., p. 246).

5 *Kaitai shinsho* (1774) was the translation of Johannes Kulmus's *Anatomische Tabellen* (1725); for details, see below, Chap. 6.

6 Kaempfer, *History of Japan*, vol. 3, pp. 92–3 (1906 ed.); Kaempfer illustrated the event, pl. 32.

7 Quoted in Paul van der Velde, ed., *Dejima Dagregisters*, vol. 6, p. 40, vol. 7, pp. 46–7; Bockesteijn had a shock when he suddenly *was* required to perform.

8 Tachibana Nankei, *Seiyū-ki*, p. 101.

9 Hirokawa Kai, *Nagasaki bunken-roku*, vol. 4, p. 8r.

10 For their medical publications, see Yasue Kyōsuke ed. *Kokusho sōmokuroku*, q.v.

11 Morishima Chūryō, *Kōmō zatsuwa*, pp. 459–60. Hirokawa Kai mentioned three types of European institution (orphanages, hospitals, and asylums); see *Nagasaki bunken-roku*, vol. 4, p. 10r.

12 The hospital print is now in the Kobe City Museum; for a convenient reproduction, see Calvin French, *Shiba Kōkan*, fig. 38. For the Sorbonne, see *Oranda tsūhaku*, p. 534.

13 Honda Toshiaki, *Seiiki monogatari*, p. 98.

14 Several such "false etymologies" (*ateji*) became standard, although individual writers also used their own variants; for a selection, see ibid., pp. 92–3.

15 Honda Toshiaki, "Keisei hisaku," p. 68.

16 Yamamura Shōei, *Chōsei zōyaku: Sairan igon* (1802), unpaginated preface; this work was an expanded Japanese version of Arai Hakuseki, *Sairan igon* (1713), composed in Chinese. Honda Toshiaki, *Keizai hōgen* (date unknown), p. 89.

17 During the period when no ship was in port, the Dutch compound had a skeleton staff of about ten (Europeans and Indonesians), but this swelled to 100–50 when there were dockings.

18 Hirokawa Kai, *Nagasaki bunken-roku*, vol. 4, pp. 7r and 9v.

19 Tachibana Nankei, *Seiyū-ki*, p. 101.

20 Satō Narihiro, *Chūryō manroku*, p. 43. Narihiro is normally referred to as Chūryō (which was his *gō*) – hence the title of his journal – but his formal name is retained here to avoid confusion with Morishima Chūryō. As well as a period spent working in Satsuma, Narihiro was also employed in Mito.

21 For biographical details, see Tanahashi Masahiro, *Kibyōshi sōran*, vol. 3, p. 125. For the relationship to Kyōden, see ibid. vol. 1, p. 132.

The story is also known as the *Wakanran monogatari*.

22 Hokusai used a particularly large number of names, including "Kakō" from 1798–1811 and Hokusai from 1797; for a table, see Richard Lane, *Images of the Floating World*, p. 255.

23 As far as I am aware, no examples of the genre survive from this early period, but for a later one (with Hollander, Russian, and Chinese), see N. H. N. Mody, *A Collection of Nagasaki Colour Prints*, fig. 71.

24 Thunberg, being Swedish, would have pronounced his name to sound more like "Tunberry" (it is transcribed as *tsunberii* by modern Japanese historians), but while employed by the VOC he adopted a Dutch reading with a hard final "g"; see, for example, Morishima Chūryō, *Kōmō zatsuwa*, p. 454. Thunberg's book was not known in Japan until considerably later. There is probably no ironic intent in Japan being represented as a prostitute.

25 This is a multiple pun: *chinrin* means "the depths," while *chin* also evokes *chinpunkan* (Chinese nonsense, viz. "ching-chang-chong"); also evoked by the name is Haku Rakuten (Bo Jui), the Tang Chinese poet said to have come to Japan to test the Japanese skill at verse, and who came to stand for all Continental arrogance.

26 Kanwatei Onitake, *Wakanran zatsuwa*, p. 5v.

27 This interestingly prefigures what later generations were to formulate as the notional synthesis of "Western technology and Japanese soul" (*wakon yōsai*).

28 *Shin jikō-ki* (1802), reissued the following year under the revised title of *Muna-zan'yō uso no tanaoroshi*. See below, note 31.

29 *Jinkō-ki*, quoted in Satake Shōnosuke, ed., *Yanagi daru*, vol. 2, p. 111.

30 *Donjiri ni noru tōjin wa san ga take*; ibid. I interpret in the verse a play between *donjiri*, "the last person," and *shiri*, "buttocks." The original story in fact mentioned no people boarding with the elephant.

31 *Shin Jinkō-ki* was reissued the following year as *Muna-zan'yō uso tanaoroshi* (1803), see above note 28, but with the mock-scholarly subtitle "The origin of the '*Dust of Ages*' in thirty-five volumes"; see Tanahashi, *Kibyōshi sōran*, vol. 3, pp. 137 and 202. Publication of the reissue coincided with the appearance of Onitake's *Wakanran zatsuwa*.

32 *Funa-manjū*, literally a "ship's cake," was the name for prostitutes who plied their trade from boats.

33 The figure amounts to rather over 20,000 litres; the weight is given, as was normal at the time, as the cubic capacity of rice that would make the same weight.

34 For the 1597 elephant, see Bernadino de Avila Giron, *Relación* (1619), quoted in Michael Cooper, *They Came to Japan*, pp. 113–24; Avila Giron stated that the king of Cambodia had also sent an elephant to the daimyo of Bungo, "many years ago," but it did not tour the country or arouse much attention (and soon died); for the 1726 animal, see note 35 below. There is also record of the sending of an elephant by the Ming in 1574, although this may the same as the Cambodian one; see Kimura Yojiro, *Edo ki no nachurarisuto*, p. 126.

35 Kōkan referred to the elephant in a letter to Yamaryō Kazuma dated 11th of the 11th month, 1813; for a facsimile and transcription, see Nakano Yoshio, *Shiba Kōkan kō*, pp. 57–61; Kōkan also thanked the addressee for sending a picture of such a beast, which "I feel is exactly like looking at a real elephant." The bones were destroyed in World War II. For a more general account, see Ishizaka Shōzō, *Zō no tabi*.

36 *Ōei wa shokai kyōhō wa uchinajimi sankaime ni wa kaesu shinzō*; quoted in Kimura, *Edo no nachurarisuto*, p. 129. Kōkan also mentions the 1726 elephant.

37 Van der Velde, ed., *Dejima Dagregisters*, vol. 3, p. 33.

38 The series of album leaves bears an inscription dated in accordance with 1797, although doubts remain as to its authenticity; see Oka Yasumasa, " *'Bankan-zu' no shomondai*," p. 239.

39 Fukuzawa Yukichi, *Fukuō jikki*, trans. Kiyooka Eiichi as *The Autobiobraphy of Yukichi Fukuzawa*, p. 3. The date of the event is not recorded, but Yukichi was born in 1835, and he describes it as occurring when he was too small to remember, and his having only heard it from others.

40 Honda Toshiaki, *Keisei hisaku*, p. 68.

41 Fukuzawa Yukichi, *Fukuō jikki*, trans. Kiyooka as *Autobiobraphy*, p. 13. Yukichi's brother went on to study mathematics under Hoashi Banri.

42 I am endebted to Frank Dikötter for help in translating this and other Luiken verses, and to Willem Dreesman for generously supplying me with a copy of the book. It has been established that several of Kōkan's works are owing to the Luikens; see Sugano Yō, *Nihon dōbanga no kenkyū*, pp. 246–53, 275, 279–80.

43 For an overview of the cursory treatment of mathematics, see Mark Ravina, "Wasan and the Physics That Wasn't." An interesting exception may be noted in the case of Kanwatei Onitake, who as well as being a writer was an expert in *wasan* (indigenous arithmetic); see Tanahashi, *Kibyōshi sōran*, vol. 3, p. 127.

44 The Confucian school of *jitsugaku*, or practical learning, may be relevant here, but *jitsugaku* (which has be much misunderstood) was less about utility in the Dutch sense, than about extracting Confucianism from its bases in literature and art to lock it back into morality and government. See Yagi Kiyoharu, "*Keiken-teki jitsugaku no tenkai*, pp. 175–81.

45 Ravina, "Wasan," p. 207. Kaempfer's book was known by other Japanese intellectuals; see above, Chap. 1, n. 34.

46 Thunberg, *Travels*, vol. 3, p. 251 (italics his). For a useful study of the emergence of a Western-style science in Japan, see Togo Tsukahara, *Affinity and Shinwa Roku*.

47 Gotō Rishun, *Oranda-banashi*, p. 12. The argument comes in the context of a discussion of Dutch medicine, and the "evidence" referred to are the symptoms of illness.

48 Shiba Kōkan, *Oranda tsūhaku*, p. 126; Hirokawa Kai, *Nagasaki bunken-roku*, vol. 4, p. 11v; in contrast to the Iberians, to whom the Japanese had been exposed previously, the low priority paid to religious matters by the Dutch was probably a correct observation; Honda Toshiaki, *Seiiki monogatari*, p. 3.

49 *Zeigo* (1786), quoted in Grant K. Goodman, *Japan – the Dutch Experience*, p. 102.

50 Sugita Genpaku, *Rangaku kotohajime*, p. 474. The term *senko* (literally "thousand olds") occurs numerous times, e.g., p. 497.

51 See Tetsuo Najita, *Visions of Virtue*, p. 276. This is, it must be admitted, an odd term for Bantō to have used since generally *menoko zan'yō*

meant rather a rough occular assessment, or "guestimate."

52 Yamagata Bantō, *Yume no shiro hen* (1800–4), quoted in Najita, *Visions of Virtue*, p. 276 (adapted). The book he had been reading was Udagawa Genzui's *Naika sen'yō*, the translation of a treatise on internal medicine by Johannes Gotter.

53 Bernard I. Cohen, *Benjamin Franklin's Science*, p. 37; Franklin was famous for his experiments with electricity, especially the lightning conductor.

54 Tachibana Nankei, *Seiyū-ki*, p. 189.

55 Morishima Chūryō, *Kōmō zatsuwa*, p. 481. Chūryō also quotes Rishun (his father's friend) on the subject. Identification of the sitter in the picture with Hoshū is presumptive, but Chūryō stated the machine was in his family's collection, and a shaven head denotes a doctor. Unusually, Chūryō's signature appears on the image.

56 Gotō Rishun, *Oranda banashi*, p. 19. Matsudaira Sadanobu, *Taikan zakki*, p. 32. Sadanobu had surrendered most of his titles two years previously, in 1795.

57 Hiraga Gennai, *Hōhi-ron*, p. 243.

58 Ibid., p. 244.

59 Nagakubo Sekisui, *Nagasai kikō* (1805), p. 22r. Sekisui was teacher of Koshōken; see Yamori Kazuhiko, *Kochizu to fūkei*, p. 107.

60 Shiba Kōkan, letter to Yamaryō Kazuma dated 6th of 12th month, 1813; facsimile and transcription in Nakano, *Shiba Kōkan kō*, pp. 39ff.; the breeze in Osaka made it feel cooler; Kōkan added that in Edo the temperature never rose above 86 degrees.

61 Shiba Kōkan, *Oranda tensetsu* (1796), p. 32.

62 The barometer was one of a series of "primitive" (i.e., foreign) instruments (*bangi*) used to readjust the calendar in 1798; the entire equipment is illustrated in Shibukawa Kagesuke, ed., *Kansei rekisho*, vol. 19; for another piece, see below, Fig. 127.

63 Quoted in Kobayashi Yoshio, *Sekai no kenbikyō no rekishi*, p. 13. The passage is extremely laconic and other interpretations of it may be possible.

64 Buys's dictionary was known in Japan from the ten-volume edition (1769–78), but the two-volume bilingual Dutch/English edition (unillustrated) came out a year before, 1768, as *A New and Complete Dictionary of Terms of Art*. The later edition has been used in this study.

65 *Meiwa* (undated), quoted in Najita, *Visions of Virtue*, p. 142.

66 Sugita Gentaku was fond of the word; see, for example, *Rangaku kotohajime*, p. 482.

67 Kanwatei Onitake, *Wakanran zatsuwa*, p. 11v.

68 *Hiraga Kyūkei jikki*, p. 895. Kyūkei was one of Gennai's scholarly names.

69 Tachibana Nankei, *Seiyū-ki*, p. 188.

70 *Oranda kiku* is advertised as "forthcoming" in the back cover advertisements of Kōkan's *Shunparō hikki*.

71 Shiba Kōkan, *Mugen dōjin zakki*, pp. 273–74.

72 Stated at the very outset of his preface to the *Kaitai shinsho*, p. 208.

73 David Brouwer, *Diary*, quoted in van der Velde, ed., *Dejima Dagregisters*, vol. 7, p. 69.

74 Shigeru Nakayama, *History of Japanese Astronomy*, p. 167.

75 Leonard Blusse, ed., *Dejima Dagregisters*, p. 386; entry dated 26/8/1730.

76 Ōtsuki Gentaku, *Rangaku kaitei*, p. 334.

77 For the hot-air balloon, see below, Chap. 7.

78 *Tōmegane mimi ni atetaku omoi nari;* quoted in Terada Kaiyū, *Nanban kōmō jiten*, p. 50.

79 The undated picture is a single-sheet print (*hikifuda*), possibly intended as an advertisement; for a reproduction, see Sugano, *Nihon dōbanga no kenkyū*, p. 113. Egbert Buys, *Woordenboek*, *"Gehoor hoornen,"* q.v.; for a convenient illustration, see, ibid. Kōkan referred to making ear-trumpets in a letter to Eba Shunrei, dated 15th of 12th month, year unknown but probably post-1798; for a facsimile and transcription, see Nakano, *Shiba Kōkan kō*, pp. 97–107; Kōkan said he had made "six or seven" trumpets, and that, "they have become so popular I am in something of a dilemma over it" (ibid., p. 107).

80 Kyōden's full pen-name was Santō Kyōden, although the characters used were not those

which appear in Kunenbō's text; Kabe is a variant reading of the first character in the name of Hekizentei Kunenbō.

81 Hekizentei Kunenbō, *Hade mezurashiki futatsu no utsuwa*, pp. 3v–4r. Hereafter, where a quotation is inscribed on a page reproduced as a figure, no reference is given in the notes.

82 Shiba Kōkan, letter to Okano Shōgorō, dated 28th of 11th month, year unknown; for a facsimile and transcription, see Nakano, *Shiba Kōkan kō*, p. 226. Kōkan distinguished the Dutch precision picture from the Japanese genre of *saiga*, which he despised as inferior; see *Seiyō gadan*, p. 491.

83 Ōtsuki Gentaku, *Rangaku kaitei*, p. 333.

84 Gentaku refers literally to "dried meat" (*kansaku*); none of the modern commentators specify why this particular example is chosen, but possibly it stands in opposition to living bodies.

85 The *Schilderboek* was translated into many European languages: German (1729), English (1738), and French (1787). It was an unlikely source for *Ranga*, as Lairesse was opposed to the enslavement of art of science (he was criticised for his extremely beautified illustrations to Cowper's *Anatomia;* in general, Lairesse sought to discredit vulgar painters ("bambocciades"), among whom he put Rembrandt and all those who made "pictures of beggars, obscenities, a Geneva-stool [privy], tobacco-smokers, fiddlers, nasty children easing nature, and other things more filthy" (James Fitch, trans., *The Art of Painting*, p. 131). There are many references to Lairesse in *Rangaku* writings, but see, *inter alia*, Morishima Chūryō, *Kōmō zatsuwa*, p. 479; Chūryō transliterated the title as *Shikiruderubukku.*

86 Shiba Kōkan, *Shunparō hikki*, p. 413.

87 Takamori Kankō, *Seiyō gadan*, p. 357. This work is not to be confused with Kōkan's treatise of the same name of fifteen years earlier, although they often are mixed up, even by the editors of the edition used here. Kankō clearly knew of Kōkan's work and used it, but there is also a large non-overlapping area; see Nishimura Tei, "*'Seiyō gadan' no chōsha Takamori Kankō ni tsuite*"; Nishimura suggests that Hokusai may have studied under Kankō. For an example of Kōkan on a similar theme, see *Shunparō hikki*, p. 22.

88 The ancient Chinese critic Zhang Yanyuan, for example, in *Kidai minghua* (A.D. 847), dismissed the non-brushed "cloud-blown" style with the words "since the traces of the brush are not visible, it cannot be called painting," quoted in Joan Stanley-Baker, *Transmission of Chinese Idealist Painting to Japan*, p. 14 (quoting an unreferenced translation by James Cahill). *Ranga* was not the only *saiga* style seen in the latter part of the eighteenth century, and also noteworthy is the Nagasaki (or Nanpin) School, which emerged in the 1730s; many *Ranga* artists started out in the Nagasaki manner (including Kōkan, Satake Shozan, and Odano Naotake), and clearly they saw *Ranga* as in some way a fulfillment of Nagasaki postulates.

89 Shiba Kōkan, *Oranda tsuhaku*, p. 119. For Ōtsuki Gentaku on *konst*, see *Rangaku kaitei*, p. 317.

90 For example, Tachibana Nankei, *Seiyū-ki*, p. 193.

91 The two Dutch seals appear in, for example, *Chinese Bird on a Pine* and *Landscape with Mountains and Lake*, both in private collections in Japan, but conveniently reproduced in Kumamoto Kenjirō, et al., *Zuroku Akita Ranga ten*, cats. 1 and 2; for a list of Shozan's seals, see ibid., pp. 18–19.

92 Satake Yoshiatsu, *Gahō kōryō*, p. 101; for Wang Wei, see Susan Bush, *Early Chinese Texts on Painting*, p. 38.

93 Satake Shozan, *Gahō kōryō*, p. 100; Dong Qichang was a theoriser of the *bunjin* (*wenren*) movement, and Gazen (Huachan in Chinese) was his best-known name; his literary works appeared in Japan under the title of *Gazen-shitsu zuihitsu*. For Taiga's name and its dating, see Melinda Takeuchi, *Taiga's True Views*, p. 164.

94 Van der Velde, ed., *Dejima Dagregisters*, vol. 6, p. 101.

95 Shiba Kōkan, letter to Yamaryō Kazuma dated 6th of 12th month, 1813, facsimile and transcription in Nakano, *Shiba Kōkan kō*, pp. 44–5. For extant examples other than that given here, see *Shiba Kōkan zenshū*, vol. 4, pp. 259–66, and,

generally, Naruse Fujio, *"Edo jidai no yōfūga no Fuji-zu ni tsuite."*

96 Nakayama Kōyō, *Gadan keiroku,* p. 872. *Bunjin* did occasionally indulge in depicting true scenery (see Melinda Takeuchi, *Taiga's True Views*), but their output in this manner was small.

97 Rosetsu is known as an eccentric artist, although he studied for a time with the Western-inspired Maruyama Ōkyo; Rosetsu also painted much-enlarged beasts like dragons and tigers (cf. the series in the Saikō-ji, Wakayama), although they were routine themes; no minute forms painted large by him remain.

98 *Gahō yōketsu* (1689), quoted in Ueda Makoto, *Literary and Art Theories in Japan,* p. 132.

99 Motoori Norinaga, *Ga no koto,* p. 194.

100 Rosetsu provided some of the illustrations to Tachibana Nankei, *Seiyū-ki;* see Munezaki Isoo, *"Tachibana Nankei 'Seiyū-ki' to Edo kōki no kikō bungaku,"* p. 445. Other illustrations were by Maruyama Ōzui and Ōju. A portion of the diary deals with Nagasaki and Dejima, the rest with the trip there and back and general peripatations around Kyushu.

101 In 1776, Kien read *Sūdō shōdan,* a work by the *Rangaku* scholar Nishimura Tōsaku and was moved to place mathematics among the Six Arts (*rokugei*), although Kien also stated that Tōsaku's antiquarian interests were more worthy of a gentleman than his mathematical ones; see C. C. Krieger, *Infiltration of European Civilisation,* p. 66. Kien was not averse to aspects of European painting, and he inscribed a Western-style copper-plate etching (undated) by Hara Zaimei; see Oka Yasumasa, *Megane-e shinkō,* p. 143 (illustration, p. 168). For Kien and Ōkyo, see Oku Bunchō, "Sensai Maruyama-sensei den," p. 593.

102 Minagawa Kien, *Shahon Kien bunshū shōroku,* pp. 387–8. No date can be given to the verse which exists only in the later undated holograph manuscript cited here. I am grateful to Robert Campbell for assistance in translating.

103 Satake Shozan, *Gahō kōryō,* p. 100.

104 Shiba Kōkan, *Seiyō gadan,* p. 357.

105 The existence of the camera obscura in Japan had been doubted by some; for example, Henry Smith, *Hokusai: One Hundred Views of Mount Fuji,* p. 221. I find four pieces of evidence: Kōkan's writing here, Ōtsuki Gentaku's and Sugita Genpaku's writings, cited below, and, more inferentially, inclusion of the device in Buys's *Woordenboek.* For this argument, though, it is less necessary to argue for the actual presence of the instrument than for knowledge of it.

106 Shiba Kōkan, *Shunparō hikki,* p. 22, and *Oranda tsūhaku,* p. 509; see also a letter to Yamaryō Kazuma dated 16th (month and year unknown), facsimile and transcription in Nakano, *Shiba Kōkan kō,* p. 31.

107 Sugita Genpaku, *Rangaku kotohajime,* p. 482; the term Gentaku uses is *anshitsu shashinkyō,* only the latter part of which was retained by Ōtsuki Gentaku when he came to write of the instrument in *Ransetsu benwaku,* p. 45.

108 See n. 107 above.

109 Natural pin-hole cameras working without lenses had been discovered in China, and Otsuki Gentaku referred to them as the "picture-assisting" mirrors (*ringa-kyō*). I take the term "mirror" (*kyō*) in that case to mean only a generic optical effect; see *Ransetsu benwaku,* p. 45. Hokusai depicted the chance appearance of a pin-hole-camera projection in *Fugaku hyakkei* (c. 1834) and showed a man demonstrating the inverted image of Mount Fuji to visitors; see Smith, *Hokusai: One Hundred Views,* p. 31.

110 Takizawa Bakin, *Kiryō manroku,* p. 156.

111 Ibid. Bakin specified that the image cast looked like a "Dutch picture done on glass" (*biidoro-e*), for which genre see below, Chap. 5.

3: MECHANICS AND MOTIONS

1 Terajima Ryōan, ed., *Wakan sansai zue,* vol. 1, p. 245; non-mechanical items are given too, such as furs, sugar, and precious stones.

2 Tachibana Nankei, *Seiyū-ki,* p. 188.

3 Charles Thunberg, *Travels,* vol. 3, pp. 11, 25. Total tonnage is not stated, but the ship sailed from Japan with over 80,000 pounds of copper.

4 Shiba Kōkan described the ship as well as illus-

trating it; see *Saiyū nikki*, p. 117; Hirokawa Kai, *Nagasaki bunken-roku*, vol. 4, p. 10v.

5 C. C. Kreiger, *Infiltration of European Civilisation*, p. 83. Titsingh vainly recommended sending Japanese to study ship-building in Jakarta.

6 Furukawa Koshōken, *Saiyū zakki*, pp. 156–7.

7 Hirokawa Kai, *Nagasaki bunken-roku*, vol. 4, p. 9r.

8 Furukawa Koshōken, *Saiyū nikki*, p. 118. Screen paintings of Portuguese ships (*nanban byōbu*), a common theme in the early seventeenth century, frequently include acrobat-like deck-hands.

9 Ōtsuki Gentaku, *Seikyaku taiwa* (date unknown), partially reproduced (with illustration of the windmill) in Sugimoto Tsutomu, *Zuroku "Rangaku kotohajime,"* p. 56.

10 Shiba Kōkan, *Saiyū nikki*, p. 118.

11 Morishima Chūryō, *Kōmō zatsuwa*, pp. 475–6.

12 Tachibana Nankei, *Hokusō sadan*, p. 13.

13 Thunberg, *Travels*, vol. 3, p. 45.

14 Tatsukawa Shōji, *Karakuri*, p. 176 (with illustration).

15 Saitō Gesshin et al., *Edo meisho zue* (1836), vol. 1, p. 448; for further historical details of the wheel, see Kawada Hisashi, *"Edo meisho zue" o yomu*, p. 133.

16 Fluctuations in the cost of labour in Edo have been assessed by Gary P. Leupp, *Servants, Shophands and Labourers in the Cities of Tokugawa Japan*, p. 161 and *passim;* for a study of Edo-period attempts to secure market share, see Tani Minezō, *Edo no kopiiraitaa*.

17 My position here takes issue with recent revisionistic studies inclined toward enthusiasm for Edo-period mechanics; see, for example, Tobacco and Salt Museum, ed., *Edo no mekanizumu*.

18 The episode occurs in chapter 9, *Aoi* (The heart-vine); see Edward Seidensticker, trans., *The Tale of Genji*, p. 160. See also Mieko Murase, *Icongraphy of "The Tale of Genji,"* pp. 82–3 (where the event is entitled "competing carriages").

19 *Ōmori no kurama arasoi kusuridana;* quoted in Hanasaki Kazuo, *Edo no kusuri-ya*, p. 387.

20 Tachibana no Narisue, *Kokon chōmon-shū*, pp. 308–30.

21 William Coaldrake, *The Way of the Carpenter*, p. 42; Coaldrake does not, however, mention the Hida Craftsman.

22 Yasue Kyōsuke, ed. *Kokosho sōmokuroku*, q.v., lists these two works and specifies the second as not extant.

23 *Hida no takumi monogatari*. For an English translation, see Frederick Dickens, *The Magical Carpenter of Japan;* the translations used here, however, are my own. For a general account of Rokujūen's life, see Kasuya Hiroki, *Ishikawa Masamochi no kenkyū*, Masamochi being the name Rokujūen used in his poetic writings.

24 Rokujūen, *Hida no takumi monogarari*, p. 917.

25 Kanwatei Onitake, *Wakanran zatsuwa;* see above, Chap. 2.

26 *Nihon kokugo daijiten*, q. v.

27 Akisato Ritō, *Settsu meisho zue*, vol. 4 (unpaginated).

28 Ishikawa Jun, *Shokoku kijinden*, p. 11.

29 Ibid., pp. 10ff. Jotei's name, literally meaning "as if mud," was invented by his daimyo, the Lord of Matsue, and derives from a poem on drink by Huang Dingjian (1045–1105), for a translation of which, see John M. Rosenfield, "The Unity of the Three Creeds," p. 212.

30 Takizawa Bakin mentioned what appeared to have been a similar *karakuri* crab with a sake cup on its back; see *Chōsadō ichiyūwa* (1802), with illustration. For a convenient reproduction (and extant similar piece), see Suzuku Kazuyoshi, *"Edo no karakuri ningyō,"* figs. 1 and 2; neither is water-activated, however, and it is doubtful whether Jotei's really was either.

31 Rokujūen's retelling was not without its supernatural elements, but I do not consider Dickens justified in entitling his translation *The Magical Carpenter of Japan*.

32 Rokujūen, *Hida no takumi monogatari*, p. 966.

33 Ishikawa, *Shokoku kijin-den*, p. 28.

34 Akisata Ritō, *Settsu meisho zue*, vol. 5 (unpaginated), Takeda Ōmi, q.v.

35 Tatsukawa, *Karakuri*, p. 172. For Kiyomasa's Kibyoshi, entitled simply *Takeda Ō-karakuri*, see Tonahashi Masahiro, *Kibyōshi sōran*, vol. 1, p. 141. It is more a visual compendium of *karakuri* than a story; the date of publication is disputed, either 1776 or 78.

36 Takizawa Bakin, *Kiryō manroku,* p. 165. Bakin made no reference to the Osaka theatre when he visited that city, though he stated that flooding had recently wrecked many establishments on the Dōtonbori (p. 253).

37 Akisato Ritō, *Settsu meisho zue,* vol. 5 (unpaginated), Takeda Ōmi, q.v. Takeda Izumo is said to have died in 1675. Both Izumo and Ōmi, were place-names and refer to honorary titles (*jō,* "constabularies") awarded to the family; *jō,* third in the regional hierarchy was occasionally conferred upon artists and craftsmen.

38 Fukumoto Kazuo, *Karakuri gijutsu shiwa,* p. 104.

39 Shiba Kōkan, *Oranda tsūhaku,* p. 512.

40 For James Cox and Jacquet-Droz, see Richard Altick, *The Shows of London,* pp. 64–9. The terms for such devices were not standardised, and "jack" was also used; "sing-songs" referred to musical automata.

41 *Keisei yagun-dan* (author and date unknown), quoted in Mitamura Engyo, "Ningyō shibai to nō," p. 157.

42 Tani Minezo, *Asobi no design,* p. 161.

43 Santō Kyōden, *Komon gawa,* p. 46.

44 Kikuchi Toshiyoshi, *"Kaisetsu"* in *Karakuri kinmō kagami gusa,* p. 82.

45 Katsuragawa Hoshū, *Hokusa bunryaku,* p. 94.

46 Asakura Musei, *Misemono kenkyū,* p. 233.

47 Hirokawa Kai, *Nagasaki bunken-roku,* vol. 4, p. 13r. Kai illustrated a pump too, evidently the same instrument (see p. 14r) and below, note 57.

48 Suggested by Tatsukawa, *Karakuri,* p. 168.

49 Nishimura Shigenaga, *Ō-karakuri e-zukushi,* p. 14r.

50 *Bango-sen* (unpaginated). For the Mizuteppō-ya, see Sukenari, *Tengu-tsū* vol. 3 pp. 7r–8r.

51 Noël Chomel, *Dictionnaire oeconomique,* 2d ed. (1718), p. 1182. The consensus seems to be that it was the edition of 1718, expanded by Chalmot, which was imported to Japan; see Goodman, *Japan: The Dutch Experience,* p. 129.

52 Kageyasu was found to have passed a map of Edo Castle to Franz von Siebold, physician to the VOC in Japan, 1823–30, and was executed. Siebold himself was interned on Dejima after the discovery; see Grant K. Goodman, *Japan: The Dutch Experience,* pp. 185–7.

53 Twenty copper-plate engravings of the compound, the Yuanming Yuan, were made, and three sets survive in Harvard, the Bibliothèque Nationale, and a private collection in Japan. The building that had this effect was the Haiantang (Hall of Peace at Sea), and it appears in the print labelled no. 10.

54 Katsuragawa Hoshū, *Hokusa bunryaku,* p. 213.

55 The Dutch obsession with pumps is discussed by Simon Schama under the rubric of Holland's "moral geography"; see *Embarrassment of Riches,* pp. 15–51.

56 Hirokawa Kai, *Nagasaki bunken-roku,* vol. 4, p. 13r.

57 Kai's illustration of the pump is reproduced in Oka Yasumasa, "Bankan-zu no shomondai," p. 241.

58 Asakura, *Misemono kenkyū,* p. 232.

59 Kodera Gyokucho, *Misemono zasshi,* pp. 369–71.

60 Morishima Chūryō, *Kōmō zatsuwa,* p. 483.

61 Katsuragawa Hoshū, *Hokusa bunryaku,* p. 87.

62 One such fountain is extant, made in Japan in 1843, and inscribed *"honteiki": tei* means "garden"; *ki* an "instrument"; and *hon* could be interpreted as "actual." The extant device is capable of sending up a jet about 15 cm high for a period of two minutes; see Nakajima Sando, "Funsui-ki no genkei hontei-ki," p. 48.

63 Kawano Yōji, *Tōgei zakki* (date unknown); see Kikuchi Toshiyoshi, "Kiki shōshi," p. 66 (with illustration).

64 Anon., *Nichō-tsutsumi: Takeda Ō-karakuri,* pagination unclear. The original text is worn, and what the Chinese are said to be comparing is illegible. Katō Gen'etsu, *Waga koromo* (1753–1825) says Takeda Ōmi introduced a Benkei *karakuri* in 1741, which may be what is referred to here; see Tatsukawa, *Karakuri,* p. 14.

65 Anon., *Nichō-tsutsumi: Takeda Ō-karakuri* (unpaginated).

66 Dating of *karakuri* is always difficult, not least because the Takeda company tended to stress the antiquity of their pieces (rather than their novelty) out of respect for the former heads of the school. Ibid. (unpaginated) says the item was fourteen years old that year (1758?); Ak-

isato Ritō, *Settsu meisho zue,* appeared in 1798.

67 This last automaton represents a drum said to have been placed outside the palace by an ancient *tennō* for beating by subjects in time of complaint; the government was virtuous, and the unused drum eventually became a roost for birds. The theme was a generally auspicious symbol.

68 Thunberg, *Travels,* vol. 3, pp. 133 and 221. The official records of the VOC reveal several visits to the theatre in Osaka; see list in Paul van der Velde, ed., *Dejima Dagregisters,* vol. 7, p. 449.

69 *Oranda ga ashi mo kagamanu me de mireba tenchi mo ugoku Takeda karakuri;* Akisato Ritō, *Settsu meisho zue,* vol. 5 (unpaginated), Takeda Ōmi, q.v.

70 Altick, *Shows of London,* p. 57. Altick suggests that Pepys gives Cupid in mistake for Arion.

71 Hosokawa Hanzō, *Karakuri kinmō zui,* pt. 1, p. 15v.

72 Attention should be drawn to the Japanese substitution for the metallic spring of an ingenious equivalent made from whale baleen *(hige),* as recommended in Hosokawa Hanzō, *Karakuri kinmō zui,* pt. 2., p. 7r.

73 Rokujūen, *Hida no takumi monogatari,* p. 1022.

74 Nakayama Shigeru, *History of Japanese Astronomy,* p. 123. Semi-mechanical time-telling instruments such as the clepsydra existed, but it was more normal in Japan to burn a line of incense in a groove on a demarcated board, and when it reached certain points to ring a bell as public announcement.

75 For a convenient illustration, see Takanashi Seima, *Karakuri ningyō bunkashi,* fig. 3.

76 Terajima Ryōan, *Wakan sansai zue,* vol. 1, p. 245.

77 Simon Harcourt-Smith, *A Catalogue of Various Clocks, Watches Automata . . . in the Palace Museum and the Wu Ying Tien,* quoted in David S. Landis, *Revolution in Time,* p. 44; for a well-illustrated selection of still-operative pieces from the Chinese collection, see Asahi Shinbun Tōkyō Honsha, ed., *Kogū no karakuri.*

78 It should be noted that there is an almost uniform assumption among historians of clocks that Western automata barely appeared in Japan. The evidence given here (which is not found in the usual clock histories) suggests why my position differs.

79 Morishima Chūryō, *Kōmō zatsuwa,* p. 469.

80 Thunberg, *Travels,* vol. 3, p. 27.

81 Kodera Gyokuchō, *Misemono zasshi,* p. 312.

82 Inaba Tsūryū, *Soken kishō,* vol. 3, p. 113. This may be compared with the sentiment of the late seventeenth-century Chinese writer Xu Dashou that "to produce them [Western clocks] scores of ounces of silver are used, and all to no profit. . . . Are they, on the contrary, not simply a waste?" quoted in Jacques Gernet, *China and the Christian Impact,* p. 63.

83 Isaac Titsingh, *Illustrations of Japan,* p. 159. Yamaguchi Ryūji suggests that Titsingh was not being asked a fair price and points out that cheap clocks were generally to be had for about 13 *ryō,* although expensive ones might cost ten times that; see *Nihon no tokei,* p. 51.

84 The material presented here is from Ishikawa Ken, "*Kaisetsu*" in, *Dōni-ō dōwa,* pp. 5–18.

85 In 1789, the school relocated to Kanda; ibid., p. 8.

86 The first collection of Dōni's sermons was compiled by Asai Kio, a female student at the Sanzesha in 1789; Hachinomiya Itsuki, the school's head scribe, made additions in 1790–6 and published the anthology as *Dōni-ō dōwa.*

87 Hachinomiya Itsuki, ed., *Dōni-ō dōwa,* p. 29.

88 The Ninsoku Yoseba; see Herman Ooms, *Tokugawa Ideology,* p. 148.

89 Hachinomiya Itsuki, *Dōni-ō dōwa,* p. 30.

90 *Shingaku tatoe-gusa* is not extant thus its contents unknown, but Yasue Ryōsuke, ed., *Kokusho sōmokuroku,* q.v., proposes it as a serious ethical tract, not a parody.

91 Dōni did not refer to automata as such, although he occasionally referred to glove puppets or *kairai;* see below, Chapter 4.

92 The only earlier exposé (as distinct from hype) of *karakuri,* was Tagatani Kanchūsen, *Karakuri kinmō kagami-gusa,* 3 vols. (1730). For accessible reproductions and transcriptions, see Kikuchi Toshiyoshi, ed., *Karakuri kinmō kagami-gusa,* and Fukumoto, *Karakuri gijutsu shiwa,* pp. 249–88. The publishing announce-

ment at the end of that work heralds a follow-up volume (*zoku*) and a *Karakuri shinan zukai* in 3 vols., although neither work is known, and probably they never appeared.

93 Tatsukawa, *Karakuri,* see p. 18. For an English translation of Ihara Saikaku, *Kōshoku ichidai otoko,* see Ivan Morris, trans., *Life of an Amorous Man.*

94 *Shingaku tokei-gusa* contains a pun, for *gusa* means both "grass" and "rambling essays" (e.g., in the mediaeval classic *Tsurezure-gusa,* or *Essays in Idleness*); "clock grass" (properly pronounced *tokei-sō*) is passion flower. See below..

95 For a brief English biography of Jippensha Ikku, see Thomas Satchell, *Hizakurige,* pp. 13–16.

96 Tanahashi, *Kibyōshi sōran,* vol. 1, pp. 475–6.

97 Passion flower appears in Japan, seemingly for the first time, in the botanical sketches of the court noble Konoe Iehiro, *Sōboku shinsha* (c. 1730); see T. Screech, "Edo no kokoro no Rondon-dokei," p. 22 (including illustration). The plant also appears among Odano Naotake's sketches of c. 1775, see ibid. (including illustration).

98 An earlier Japanese name for the plant was *boron-gajira.*

99 *Dō kufū shite me tokei no wa a amari; Yanagi daru,* quoted in Suzuki Tei, "Tokei-zu' shōryō," p. 73.

100 The phrases *mune no karakuri* and *hara no karakuri* appear, *inter alia,* in Santō Kyōden, *Inazuma hyōshi* (1806), where the former serves as a chapter heading, p. 181, and in Rinshō, *Kogane no yama: Fukuzō jikki,* p. 8r, where the latter is invoked. For Bakin, see Tanahashi, *Kibyōshi sōran,* vol. 2, p. 568; Bakin also signed himself *"kairai-shi"* (puppet-box master); for the *kairai* box see below.

101 Where he recounts the dissection, Genpaku does not state that Hoshū was present, but he does adds it in a later passage; see Sugita Genpaku, *Rangaku kotohajime,* pp. 489 and 499. (Gentaku refers to Hoshū as "Katsuragawa-kun.") The illustrations, other than those taken from the main source, derive from such authors as Blankaart, Bartholin, and Paré, five works in all being listed; see Sugita Genpaku et al., trans., *Kaitai shinsho,* pp. 216–17.

102 This dissection became famous because of its pivotal position in Sugita Gentaku, *Rangaku kotohajime,* pp. 488–91. But Gentaku was given to self-aggrandisement, and it is not at all clear that the autopsy merits the attention it nowadays always receives.

103 Kulmus's study was intended for general practitioners, see A. M. Luyendijk-Elshout, " 'Ontleedinge' (anatomy) as underlying principle of Western medicine in Japan," p. 28. The book was imported in Gerard Dikten's Dutch translation of 1734.

104 Kōkan criticised *Kaitai shinsho* in a letter to Kaihō Seiryō dated the 27th of the 8th month (year unrecorded, probably 1813) when he called it, "awfully confused"; see facsimile and transcription in Nakano Yoshio, *Shiba Kōkan kō,* p. 186; elsewhere Kōkan complained about the needless difficulty of the book's language; see *Dokushō bōgen* (1810), quoted in Sugano Yō, *"Kaisetsu,"* in Shiba Kōkan, *Kunmō gakai-shu,* p. 326.

105 An English translation by Masanori Takatsuka and David C. Stubbs is available, entitled *This Scheming World.* It is sometimes said that Saikaku was unread in the later Edo period and could not have had any influence, but this cannot be so, as he is referred to by, for example, Hiraga Gennai in *Nenashi-gusa,* p. 62.

106 Hokusai's *Muna-zan'yō uso no tanaoroshi* is a reissue of his *Shin jinkō-ki,* discussed in Chapter 2. Sanba, *Muna-zan'yō hayawari no hō* is a section of a larger work entitled *Ono no Bakamura uso ji-tsukushi.* A pun is made on *hayawari* ("short division") and *hayakawari* ("quick costume changes").

107 For Ragorā statues in Ōbaku Buddhism, see Timon Screech, "The Strangest Place in Edo: The Temple of the Five Hundred Arthats," p. 413 (with illustrations).

108 For examples of the metaphorical use of the boat, see Rosenfield, "Three Creeds," p. 220, and Timon Screech, *Ō-Edo no ijin ōrai* (forthcoming).

109 Ōtsuki Gentaku, *Kankai ibun,* p. 584; the text was edited by Shimura Kōkyō and not completed until 1807. Tsūdayu had been wrecked in 1794; he does not name the ruling tsar, and the dating of his stay in Russia is not precise, but

Pavel was succeeded by Alexander II in 1801, possibly while Tsūdayu was there (although he does not mention it).

110 Donald Keene, *The Japanese Discovery of Europe*, p. 76.

111 Rokujūen, in *Hida no takumi monogatari*, describes how Suminawa made an automatic boat (not constructed in the Dutch style), and although he did not specify how it worked, Hokusai's illustration shows machinery which, though sketchy, is obviously intended as clockwork; for a reproduction see Dickens, *Magical Carpenter*, pl. 19.

112 Shiba Kōkan, *Saiyū nikki*, p. 118.

113 What seems to be a picture of Seishichirō's ship appears in a triptych by Utagawa Kunisada (the other two parts show a glass chandelier – Seishichirō is famous for having made one – and imported birds); for a reproduction see Nakau Ei, *Oranda-gonomi*, fig. 7. Kunisada flourished in Edo at the time Seishichirō's work was exposed; minor deviations between the prints and the written descriptions are not significant, for they are often the case in such popular works.

114 *Goten jochū to gyaman no fune wa homecha miredomo noraremai;* quoted in Furukawa, *Shūmin geinō*, p. 181.

115 Kodera Gyokuchō, *Misemono zasshi*, p. 391.

116 Kobayashi Jotei died in 1813; see Ishikawa, *Shokuku kijin-den*, pp. 19ff.

4: MACHINERY FOR PICTURES

1 Beyond prints, a second significant medium of imported works was painting done on glass, for which see below, Chap. 5.

2 The paintings were from a set of five donated to the shogun by the VOC in 1726; for a history of the temple, and of the commission and display of its pictures, see Timon Screech, "The Strangest Place in Edo: The Temple of the Five-hundred Arhats," pp. 424–8; the lost pictures are known from Japanese copies, including one by Bunchō; see ibid., figs. 14 and 15.

3 Morishima Chūryō, *Bango-sen* (unpaginated); Chūryō mentioned painting elsewhere, rendering *e* ("picture") as *shikiruderu* (*schilder*).

4 Tani Bunchō, *Bunchō gadan*, p. 189.

5 Bunchō was by no means opposed to all Western art, and he employed features of *Ranga* in his own work and discussed European art in *Bunchō gadan*, e.g., pp. 183, 132.

6 Shiba Kōkan, *Seiyō gadan*, p. 494.

7 Satake's small collection of Dutch pictures is reproduced in Hirafuku Hyakusui, *Nihon yōga no shokō;* a series of etchings mounted as a handscroll and bearing the shogunal crest is now housed in the Kobe City Museum, although which branch of the Tokugawa owned them and when the format was adapted is not clear.

8 Hiraga Gennai, *Butsurui hinshitsu*, p. 206.

9 Sugita Genpaku, *Rangaku kotohajime*, p. 478. Dodoneus's work was published in Flemish in 1554 but arrived in Japan in the Dutch translations of 1618 and 1644; Jonstonus's (Jonston's) book was originally published in Latin in 1649–53 but arrived in Japan in the Dutch version of 1660. The illustrations were not recut for the later editions, and there is therefore about a century between Dodoneus and Jonston.

10 Shiba Kōkan, *Seiyō gadan*, p. 493; Calvin French, in his translation of *Seiyō gadan*, unaccountably omits Dodoneus's name at this point; see his *Shiba Kōkan*, p. 173.

11 The question of quantity has long perplexed students of Japanese print-making. Cherry-wood blocks were hard and could produce many good impressions, although thinner lines gradually spoiled (not the case with copperplates). Some Japanese prints where "plugged" in such a way that a finely drawn section (e.g., a head) could be replaced; otherwise, individual lines could be rechiselled. The existence of these techniques suggests that publishers forced runs to the maximum when sales were good.

12 For the early history of copperplate printing in Japan, see Sugano Yō, *Nihon dōbanga no kenkyū*, pp. 69–113, and Nishimura Tei, *Nihon dōbanga shi*, pp. 45–64.

13 Morishima Chūryō, *Kōmō zatsuwa*, pp. 479–80; for the Pharmacopaeic Assemblies (organised

by Gennai) see below Chapter 5; for the history of the Seijū-kan, see below Chap. 5.

14 Shiba Kōkan, *Oranda tsūhaku,* p. 511.

15 Ibid., p. 492.

16 Shiba Kōkan, "*Seiyō gahō,*" in *Oranda tsūhaku,* p. 511. Kōkan's statement is not precise, and he states that etchings were invented by "a blacksmith in London" and that this occurred 352 years ago (i.e., in 1453), but he may intend simply book printing and be referring to Caxton. Yet Bunchō was under the impression that oil painting originated in England and claimed to have been told as much by a VOC leader, see *Bunchō gadan,* p. 232.

17 The term "perspective" ousted *veduta* as the eighteenth century progressed, but I retain the earlier designation to avoid confusion with perspective as a technique.

18 Shiba Kōkan, *Seiyō gadan,* p. 494.

19 For the most thorough analysis of Japanese *vues d'optique,* see Oka Yasamasa, *Megane-e shinkō.* Oka, however, does not entertain the possibility that non-reversed prints might have been used *ad hoc* in the *optique.*

20 Kodera Gyokuchō, *Misemono zasshi,* p. 355.

21 Shiba Kōkan, *Saiyū nikki,* p. 35 (for the fee); for Hidetake, see ibid., p. 59.

22 The gay overtones derive from the fact that the river illustrated is on Mount Kōya, a temple complex founded by Kōbō Daishi, said to have introduced *nanshoku* (man-boy love) to Japan from China in 806; the poem in the cartouche is his, and is suseptible to two interpretations, one lecherous: the last line, *oku no tamagawa,* can mean either "the river Tamagawa deep in the mountains" or "the jewelled stream [passage] up the anus." A nearly identical optique to that shown by Harunobu is housed in Kobe City Museum; for a convenient reproduction, see Oka, *Megane-e shinkō,* p. 102.

23 Inscribed on Figure 47.

24 The self-identification of Kōkan as the "first maker in Japan" appears on a copperplate of a Western artist in his studio, dated 1794, now in the Kobe City Museum; for a reproduction, see Calvin French, *Shiba Kōkan,* fig. 96.

25 The scene had formerly been assumed to depict the Serpentine in Hyde Park in London, but a print from the series *A New Display of the Beauties of England,* vol. 1 (1776), has recently been discovered and claimed as Kōkan's source; see Naruse Fujio et al., *Shiba Kōkan zenshū,* vol. 4, p. 108–9 (with illustrations). There are problems, however: I accepted that there is a close connexion between the two, but there are also differences, and so suggest that Kōkan used, not the etching (which is not reverse-printed), but a now-lost *vue d'optique* adaptation of it. No other pictures from the 1776 set seem to have had any influence in Japan.

26 So far as I have discovered, no Western *vues d'optique* on Japanese scenes exist, although China and Persia were favourite subjects.

27 Ōkyo's illustration of the Sanjūsangen-dō in Kyoto is, to my knowledge, his only view to survive in both inverted and straight froms (one copy of the former is extant, and two of the latter); for reproductions, see Maruyama Ōkyo-ten Zenkoku Jitsugyō Iinkai, ed., *Maruyama Ōkyo-ten,* pp. 11, 12, and 17.

28 The most balanced account is in Sasaki Jōhei, *Ōkyo shasei gashū,* p. 159; Sasaki notes that the pictures are too accomplished to be the work of a young man though accepting a date of early 1750. One of the surviving works, represents Shijō-Kawara in Kyoto, includes a theatrical billboard for a performance of New Year 1752, but this evidence is not conclusive as Ōkyo may be reworking an older image.

29 Julian Lee, *Origin and Development of the Japanese Landscape Print,* pp. 310–15; Lee dates Kokkadō to the early 1760s and Fuinsai to the mid-1760s (he doubts whether either artist was a bona fide pupil); but Lee's dating is based on analogy with Ōkyo's supposed *vue d'optique* period, for criticisms of which see n. 28 above.

30 Henry Smith has proposed that "floating picture" refers to the way in which distant scenes are felt to drift nearer (verbal communication).

31 The term *kubomi-e* is only attested in one source: Ishino Hiromichi, *Esoragoto* (1802), p. 274,

where he states, however, that the expression was generally current.

32 Shiba Kōkan, *Seiyō gadan*, p. 493.

33 Morishima Chūryō, *Hōgu-kago*, p. 170. Canaletto's painting of the Grand Canal was engraved for Antonio Visentini's set of *vedute* of Venice (1742; reissued 1751). Another copy (too late for our purposes) was produced by Giuseppe Battagia (1833); see Lee, *Origin and Development*, p. 317, and figs. 259–60.

34 The Chinese derivation of Japanese *uki-e* is usually stressed, and there are examples where a sequence via China can be plotted (see ibid., figs 160–70). But Lee claims a Chinese derivation also on the grounds that European toponyms are written in ideograms, not Japanese *kana* – a conclusion I reject.

35 The date of 1743 has been established by Kishi Fumikazu, *"Enkyō ni-nen no pāsupekuteibu."* The subject is an Edo kabuki theatre interior. See also note 36 below.

36 The term *uki-e kongen* is obscure because it does not follow the artist's name as a style normally would, and therefore does not necessarily indicate Masanobu was claiming that he had invented *uki-e*. For the dating of *uki-e* to the late fifth month of 1739, see Kishi, *Edo no enkinhō*, p. 4.

37 A sudden switch to *uki-e* to suggest illusory wealth is to be seen, *inter alia*, in the "first" kibyoshi, Koikawa Harumachi, *Kinkin sensei eiga no yume*, pp. 16–17, and also in Sharakutei Manri, *Shimadai me no shōgatsu*, pp. 7v–8r, illustrated by Kyōden, see here, fig. 103.

38 Hiraga Gennai, *Nenashi-gusa*, p. 77. The tale of the Wizard of the Jar is from the *History of the Later Tang*, but it became proverbial.

39 Quoted in Kishi, *Edo no enkinhō*, pp. 215 and 227. For a full translation of the play (which differs from that given here), see James R. Brandon, trans., "Sukeroku: The Flower of Edo," p. 61. See also, Kishi, "A view through a peep-hole: a semiotic consideration of *uki-e*", p. 15.

40 As well as in *Shinzō zue*, Kyōden referred to Sukeroku and *uki-e* twice: *Kyōden joshi* (1779), quoted in Yamamoto Harufumi, ed., *Santō Kyōden*, p. 161, n. 17, and *Shinpan kawarimashita dōchū Sukeroku* (1793), reproduced (with illustration) in ibid., p. 78. *Shinzō zue* uses the same categories and divisions as *Bango-sen*, although the latter is not illustrated.

41 Inscribed on Figure 47.

42 Kuwabara Shigeo, *Ai torikku hyakka*, p. 60.

43 There was a shadow theatre tradition in Japan, and shadow elements were deployed in kabuki as part of the narrative technique, often for dramatic irony; see Matsuzaki Hiroshi, *"Shōji ni utsuru kage."*

44 Yamamoto Keiichi, *Edo no kage-e asobi*, p. 140.

45 Koikawa Harumachi, *Muda iki*, p. 115 (for shadow pictures), and p. 117 (for the *honda*).

46 Yamamoto, *Edo no kage-e asobi*, p. 140.

47 Gulielmo s' Gravesande, *Physices elementa methematica*, vol. 2, p. 873.

48 Egbert Buys, *Woordenboek;* see *tover lantaarn*, q.v.

49 Sugita Genpaku, *Rangaku kotohajime*, p. 482; Genpaku also used the term "devil-conjuring lens" (*gen'yō-kyō*), ibid.

50 Otsuki Gentaku, *Ransetsu benwaku*, p. 45. The term *kyō* is problematic, as it can mean lens, slide, or mirror; any decision on how to translate must depend upon context.

51 For a reproduction and transcription of *Oranda kage-e asobi: otsuriki*, see *Edo shunjū* 4, pp. 44–6.

52 Morishima Chūryō, *Bango-sen* (unpaginated).

53 Asakura Musei, *Misemono kenkyū*, p. 242.

54 Saitō Gesshin, *Bukō nenpyō* (1850), quoted in Ono Takeo, *Edo no hakurai fūzoku-shi*, pp. 382–3; see also Kobayashi Genjirō, *Utsushi-e*, pp. 4, 61 (although Kobayashi appears to misread *ekiman-kyō* as *gyaman-kyō* ("glass lens") – surely a tautology). The grounds for believing Toraku and Yūkichi to be the same is their shared location and the fact that Toraku also used the name Yūkichi, but they had different family names (Ikeda and Kameya).

55 Yamamoto, *Edo no kage-e asobi*, p. 138.

56 Tamenaga Shunsui, *Shinshoku megumi no hana* (1836), cited in Yamamoto, *Edo no kage-e asobi*, p. 96 (with illustration). The term for the device was *"shin-kufū bakemono rōsoku."*

57 For an example of Kyōden's round-headed metacharacters representing the good and bad geniuses of his characters (called *zendama* and *akudama*) see *Shingaku hayasome-gusa* (1790);

reproduced in Koike Masatane et al., eds., *Edo no gesaku ehon*, vol. 3, pp. 251–80.

58 I have been unable to find adequate commentaries on the passage; for definitions of the terms, see *Nihon kokugo daijiten*, q.v.

59 James Legge, trans., *Texts of Taoism*, pp. 117–18 (punctuation amended). Wingtsit Chan translates *wangliang* as "shade," which significantly alters the meaning of the parable; see *Source Book in Chinese Philosophy*, p. 1980.

60 *Jikun kage-e no tatoe* is the title given in Tanahashi Masahiro, *Kibyōshi sōran*, vol. 2, p. 597, but the copy in the Kaga Bunko (of which the title page is missing) is catalogued as *Jikun kage-e no asobi*.

61 Satō Narihiro, *Chūryō manroku*, 159. For an accessible reproduction of Bunchō's two shadow portraits, Okado Tashiyuki, " 'Kage' to shōzō", figs. 2 and 8.

62 Johann Lavater *Essays in Physiognomy*, trans. Henry Hunter, bk. 2/11, p. 177; quoted in Barbara Stafford, *Body Criticism*, p. 96.

63 Saitō Gesshin, *Bukō nenpyō;* quoted in Ono, *Edo no hakurai fūzoku-shi*, pp. 382–3.

64 Tai Gongwang was often depicted as an ideological statement enjoining rulers to seek talent wherever they could find it; see Saitō Ryūzō, *Gadan jiten*, pp. 222–3. The fisherman eventually won his own kingdom of Jou.

65 Tsutaya Jūsaburō was a crucial figure in much *ukiyo-e* publishing (both literature and prints); for his life, see Matsumoto Hiroshi, *Tsutaya Jūsaburō: Edo geijutsu no enshutsu-sha*. He was commonly called "Tsutajū."

66 *Settsu meisho zue*, vol. 4 (unpaginated first page). Ikei is otherwise unknown. The text above outlines the origins of the *kairai*-box; the location is said to be in Mukō-gōri. For the character of the mountain cat (*yama neko*), see Suzuki Kuranosuke, *Yanagi-daru*, vol. 2, p. 211. The box seems to have fallen out of use in the 1780s; see Hamado Giichirō, ibid., vol. 1, p. 56.

67 *Warawase mo nakase mo senai kairaishi;* Suzuki Kuranosuke, ed., *Yanagi-daru*, vol. 2, p. 211.

68 *Kairaishi mune ni kaketaru ningyō bako hotoke dasō to oni dasō to;* Hachinomiya Itsuki, ed., *Dōni-ō dōwa*, p. 122. The same poem is cited in another sermon; ibid., p. 59.

69 *Nagasaki Oranda shōkan no nikki*, vol. 2, p. 133. A clock, teacups, and mirror were offered at the same time. Modern Japanese scholarship refers to the instrument as *tōshi-bako*, while the modern Dutch term would be *perspectifkas*. I am not aware that the term "paradise box" was otherwise used, and it seems odd that, if this was the first such box to be seen in Japan (as is usually assumed), a word for it should already have been in existence (unless borrowed from another device such as the puppet box).

70 So far as I am aware, this has previously been noticed only by Tanemura Suehiro, "*Nozoki-karakuri no toposu*," although Tanemura confuses the peepbox with the entirely different camera obscura.

71 The first known depiction of a peep-box is Enkatei Giryū, *Moji e-zukushi* (1685); for a reproduction, see Lee, *Origin and Development*, fig. 30. The precise correlation of such Japanese boxes with the imported perspective machine is difficult to fathom as evidence is so scant; there was also an additional input from China where raree shows were popular. It seems safe, though, to propose the Japanese *nozoki-karakuri* as stemming in some manner from the imported perspective box, even if undergoing subsequent adaptations.

72 Jippensha Ikku, *Kanemōke hana no sakariba* (1818), p. 5r; The anonymous print's inscription reads: *Nozoki no kisen: karakuri hitotabi nozoite atae sansen banri no Oranda ari mokuzen ni aimite sen no kata zu-shira kaeru o manman-taru kaijō hokaeru fune*. The image is now in the Chester Beatey Collection, Dublin, but for a reproduction, see Narazoki Muneshige, ed. *Hizō ukiyo-e taikan: bekkan*, pl. 98. The composition parodies the traditional *Eight Views*, one of which was *Returning Sails*, evidently the subject of one of the booth's scenes, although "returning" (*kaeru*) is punned with the homophonous "to change," i.e. to shift the sets in the booth. A second inscription in kyoka verse reads, *Hi o tenjimasuru hikure mo chikakureba nozoki mo*

yadoe kaeru shiri ni ho. It is interesting to compare the three *sen* charged here with the sixteen, or even thirty-two *mon* charged for using *optiques* (see above note 20); a *sen* and a *mon* were by and large the same amount (though subject to relative fluctuations). Hasegawa Mitsunobu, *Ehon otogishina kagami*, is quoted in Oka, *Megane-e shinkō*, p. 96.

73 For a reproduction of Mitsunobu's illustration, see Oka, *Megane-e shinkō*, fig. 11. For the arrival of elephants in Japan, see above, Chap. 2.

74 *Nanto omoshirokarō ka to nozoki ii;* Kasuya Hiroki, ed., *Yanagi daru*, vol. 6, p. 292.

75 Quoted in Lee, *Origin and Development*, pp. 56–8 (adapted). My untangling of the puns is based on Lee. *Ōtsu-e* would almost certainly not have been used with *nozoki-karakuri*, and are surely mentioned only to allow the play on words.

76 *Hana o yoku kaminasai yo to nozoki ii;* Satō Yōjin, ed., *Yanagi daru*, vol. 10, p. 68.

77 Santō Kyōden, *Komon gawa*, p. 16.

78 Kitagawa Morisada, *Kinsei fūzoku-shi;* quoted in Ono Tadashige, *Garasu-e to doro-e*, p. 66.

79 Shikitei Sanba, *Ukiyo-doko*, p. 289. The names refer to the actors better known as Sawamura Sōjurō and Ogami Kikugorō; there is no other evidence for their adoption of these styles.

80 The grammar of the passage is elliptical and the sentence structure hard to sort out. Jinbō Kazuya (editor of the Iwanami edition) assumes that the spiel contains elements of the sales hype of a telescope lender; see p. 289, n. 21. This is undeniably true (e.g.: "you can see as far as the three girls over there"), but his argument is overstated through a misunderstanding of the phrase *megane no banjō no tei*, which he takes to mean, "the shop renting glasses [telescopes] on the look-out point"; I, however, understand *tei* to mean not "shop" but a peep-show set; thus: "a scene of the look-out point for telescopes." and I take the phrase to continue on from the last, and that the look-out is in Jakarta, not, as Jinbō suggests, in Edo, "on Mt Atago or a suchlike place."

81 Santō Kyōden, *Gozonji no shōbai-mono*, p. 6r. The anonymous print (see above note 72) also carries the inscription, "*hi o tenji*," "we will illuminate it."

82 Takizawa Bakin, *Kiryo manroku;* quoted in Fukumoto Kazuo, *Karakuri gijutsu shiwa*, p. 136.

83 Jippensha Ikku, *Kane mōke hana no sakariba*, p. 5r (illustrated by Utagawa Yasuhide); a picture of the booth is provided.

84 For an example of a character with the pug-nose, see Enjirō in *Edo umare uwaki no kabayaki* (1785), pp. 149–78. For discussion of the "Kyōden nose" (*Kyōden-bana*), see ibid., p. 148.

85 Santō Kyōden, *Komon gawa*, p. 16; another joke may be intended: the peep-holes are horizontal, and as such patterns were easier and cheaper to produce than vertical arrangements, they were considered less refined.

86 Jonathan Swift, *A Tale of a Tub* (1706), p. 131 (punctuation and italicisation amended).

87 The business aspects of the Takeda company have been little investigated, and I propose them here on the basis of Takeda Ōmi's name appearing on extant pictures of peep-boxes, such as here, Figures 125, 126. Takeda also made static-electricity generators (*erekiteru*), as can be seen from his name on the box to one in Figure 6.

88 Shikitei Sanba, *Hitogokoro nozoki-karakuri*, pp. 661–3.

89 Although it is hard today to think of Hokkaido as exotic, the island was virtually unknown in the late eighteenth century; the first official expeditions were leaving Edo at just this period, a fact to which Chūryō is certainly making oblique reference. Russia was in competition for the island, and Great Britain was beginning to assess it, too; for a general introduction, see Kagawa Takayuki, *Kuzure-yuku sakoku*, pp. 109–20.

90 Kibyoshi were put out together once a year, and publishers generally used running-covers for their entire annual series (with minor particularising variations); for reproductions of the *nozoki-karakuri* covers, see Hamada Kiichirō, *Kibyōshi edaisen*, p. 37.

91 The imaginary land of the People with Pierced Chests appears in, for example, Terajima Ryōan, *Wakan sansai zue*, vol. 1, p. 228 (with illustration).

92 I have not been able to unscramble any of these

names, nor to ascertain whether they are really intended to represent real places.

93 I use the word "luxury" to convey both the sexual and opulent nuances of the original *oshiroi*. The name Chūsan is unclear, but from the mid-seventeenth century until Chūryō's writing, the Dutch state had only known *Stadholders* called Willem, Prince Willem V being the centre of court at this time. The Japanese term for all foreign rulers other than the Chinese *huangdi* was "king" (ō).

94 For a longer analysis of this image in the context of imported horology, see Screech, *"Edo no kokoro no Rondon-dokei,"* pp. 35–6.

95 The shogun Iemochi died aged 20 in 1866. He was also buried with a Japanese-made thermometer. See Suzuki Hisashi, *Zōjō-ji*, pl. 59.

5: SEEING IN

1 Tachibana Nankei, *Hokusō sadan*, p. 109.

2 Ōtsuki Gentaku, *Ranyaku teikō*, p. 379.

3 Charles Thunberg, *Travels* vol 3, p. 279.

4 Katsuragawa Hoshū, *Hokusa bunryaku*, p. 178.

5 Shiba Kōkan, *Oranda tsūhaku*, p. 516, and, *Shunparō hikki* (1811), quoted in Ono Takeo, *Edo no hakurai fūzoku-shi*, p. 251. Kōkan extenuated on the grounds that the British climate was more severe, so greater protection was required.

6 Thunberg, *Travels* vol 3, p. 41.

7 Shiba Kōkan, *Saiyū nikki*, pp. 115 and 118.

8 Nagaoka Hiruo, *Nihon no megane*, p. 63.

9 Qianglong, *Luoshan chuanji* vol. 15. I am grateful to Andrew Lo for helping me with the translation of this poem.

10 Literally "they reflect things," the poet appears to liken the window showing what ever is behind it to a mirror which shows whatever is in front; he could, however, be referring to reflections in the glass.

11 Katsuragawa Hoshū, *Hokusa bunryaku*, p. 178.

12 Asakura Musei, *Misemono kenkyū*, p. 221 (including illustration).

13 Hiruma Hisashi, *Edo no kaichō*, p. 59; again, the exact nature of the construction is not recorded.

14 Hiraga Gennai, *Nenashi-gusa*, p. 77.

15 Ōtsuki Gentaku, *Ransetsu benwaku*, pp. 199–209.

16 Ōtsuki Gentaku, *Kankai ibun*, pp. 248–50.

17 An interesting selection is given in Hirokawa Kai, *Ranryōhō* (1805), with illustrations; this was also the first Japanese book to have a copperplate frontispiece, for a convenient reproduction, see p. 209.

18 Gotō Rishun, *Oranda banashi*, p. 12.

19 Ōtsuki Gentaku, *Ranyaku teikō*, pp. 379–80.

20 Hiraga Gennai, *Butsurui hinshitsu*, p. 99.

21 The Seijū-kan was built in Kanda on land donated by the shogunate, which took over the institute in 1791 and renamed it Igaku-kan (Hall of Medicine); for details, see Ishikawa Ichiro, ed., *Edo bungaku chimei jiten* (Igaku-kan, q.v.) and Nishiyama Shōnosuke et al eds. *Edo-gaku jiten* (Kanda, q.v.). The Seijū-kan is often said to have been a centre of anti-*Rangaku* thinking, which does not square with the information presented here.

22 Hiraga Gennai, *Butsurui hinshitsu*, the objects mentioned appearing respectively on pp. 1, 5, 20, 28, 57, 76, 88 & 108. Page length of the work refers to the modern edition.

23 Shiba Kōkan, *Seiyō gadan*, p. 492; the picture of the mermaid was almost certainly that contained in François Valentyn, *Amboina* (1726); Kōkan copied it into Gentaku's *Rokubutsu shin shi-kō* (1786). For the illustrations and commentary, see Timon Screech, *Ō-Edo no ijin ōrai* (forthcoming).

24 Terajima Ryōan, *Wakan sansai zue*, vol. 1, p. 245; Ryōan does not state the purpose of spirit, and it might refer to generic liquid medicines.

25 Paul van der Velde ed. *Dejima Dagregisters*, vol. V, p. 7.

26 Ibid., vol. 7, p. 129. Nagakubo Sekisui, *Nagasaki kikō* p. 22v.

27 Hirokawa Kai, *Nagasaki bunken-roku*, vol. 4, p. 4r. Kai illustrated the statues, and they do not conform entirely to those seen in this album, but as Kai's pictures fail to match even his own textual description in many places (including here where he calls the statues nudes but shows them clad), the discrepancy is not conclusive.

28 Ōtsuki Gentaku, *Kankai ibun*, pp. 577–78.

29 *Tolong* is Chinese, literally 'iguana dragon', and

pronounced *daryō* in Japanese, although Hosokawa translates it with the more vernacular 'rain dragon', *amaryō*, that is a type of mythical beast that provoked precipitation.

30 For a discussion of this and other of Hosokawa's albums, see, Nishiyama Shōnosuke, "*Shinsha bunka shijō no Hosokawa Shigekata*", pp. 86–95.

31 I am endebted here to oral discussions with Imahashi Riko.

32 Hiraga Gennai, *Butsurui hinshitsu*, p. 102.

33 Sugita Genpaku, *Rangaku kotohajime*, p. 485.

34 Morishima Chūryō, *Kōmō zatsuwa*, pp. 454–55.

35 Thunberg, *Travels*, vol. 3, p. 206.

36 Morishima Chūryō, *Kōmō zatsuwa*, p. 455.

37 Tachihara Suiken, *Jūrin zatsuwa*, pp. 12–13; for Jūbei's life, see, ibid., "Kaishaku", p. 20. For the 1788 exhibition, see C.C. Krieger, *Infiltration of European Civilisation* p. 87 (Krieger misnames the institution Saijū-kai).

38 The undated manuscript *Honzō zusetsu* is in 195 volumes and now housed in the Iwase Bunko; the picture resembles Hosokawa's own sketch, not that which appears in Gennai, *Butsurui hinshitsu*. For a convenient reproduction, see Ueno Masuzō, *Nihon hakubutsugaku shi*, fig. 10.

39 Hiraga Gennai, *Nenashi-gusa*, p. 78. Santō Kyōden, *Gesaku mondo* (1817), pagination unclear.

40 Shiba Zenkō, *Ōchigai takarabune*, p. 7v.

41 *Biidoro no kingyō no inochi sukitōru;* quoted in, Okitsu Kaname, *Edo senryū*, p. 13.

42 Shiba Kōkan, *Oranda tensetsu*, p. 456.

43 Some doubts remain as to the authenticity of this painting, although it is usually accepted; the composition is similar to that of a print by Utamaro in the Clarence Buckingham Collection, Art Institute of Chicago.

44 Quoted in Nakamura Yukihiko, *Gesaku-ron*, p. 118. Nakamura does not name the author or date, and I have been unable to trace him. *Miso* is a bean paste stock forming the base of much Japanese cooking, and as its flavour differed from home to home, it came to stand for the preference for one's own things over other people's.

45 Gotō Rishun, *Oranda-banashi*, p. 18.

46 Kodera Gyokuchō, *Misemono zasshi*, p. 305. The text is, as usual, extremely laconic; the mirror may have been a paper-weight. For Kien's verse, see *Kien shishū*, vol. 1, p. 79. The verse is undated, but the anthology was first published in 1800.

47 Shiba Kōkan, *Saiyū nikki*, pp. 115 & 105.

48 Satō Narihiro, *Chūryō manroku* p. 75. Quite how the picture was suspended is unclear, possibly from a watch chain. The kapitan in 1798 was Gijbert Hemmij, who was older than Narihiro states: either the age or the rank of the Dutchman is wrong. For a convenient reproduction of the cover to Tsuta Karamaru (also known as Tsutaya Jūsaburō) *Jintai kaichō ryaku engi*, see *Tsutaya Jūsaburō no shigoto*, p. 1, and more generally, see Hamada Kiichirō, *Kibyōshi edaisen*, p. 133.

49 Ibid., p. 69.

50 For a discussion of this box, see, T. Screech, "Edo no kokoro no Rondon-dokei," pp. 12–13.

51 See Ōno, *Doro-e to garasu-e*, especially, pp. 140–52.

52 Kuroda Genji, *Shiba Kōkan*, p. 127.

53 Shiba Kōkan, in a letter to Yamaryō Kazuma, dated 25 of the 2 month (year unknown), reproduced in Nakano Yoshio, *Shiba Kōkan kō*, p. 27; Satō Narihiro, *Chūryō manroku*, p. 69.

54 Shiba Kōkan, *Saiyū nikki*, p. 105. Kodera Gyokuchō, *Misemono zasshi*, p. 305.

55 *Tōjin Ban nikki*, quoted in Koga Jūjirō, *Maruyama yūjo* vol. 1, p. 561. The Chinese pronunciation of the official's name would be Fan Yachi.

56 Shiba Kōkan, *Saiyū nikki*, pp. 69, 119 and 195; Kōkan does not specify whether the panes were for painting or not, but that must be what was intended. The expression *ita-biidoro* (glass pane) is used, but this should be taken to mean a pane of only a score or so centimetres across as there was not the technology for larger ones.

57 Sasaki Sei'ichi, *Nihon kindai bijutsu-ron*, p. 123.

58 Ishizaki Yūshi, *Nagasaki kokon shūran meisho zue*, (1841), preface, pp. 9–10.

59 Shiba Kōkan, *Saiyū nikki*, p. 107.

60 Nishikawa Joken, *Kaitsu shokō*, quoted in C.R. Boxer, *Jan Compannie in Japan*, p. 169.

61 Engelbert Kaempfer, *History of Japan* (1906 ed.),

vol. 2, p. 214; Kaempfer notes, "the looking-glasses they break to make spy glasses, magnifying glasses and spectacles out of them." Thunberg, *Travels* vol. 3, p. 49.

62 Narabayashi Jūbei's words were recorded by his interlocutor, Tachihara Suiken in *Jūrin zatsuwa,* p. 31.

63 Thunberg, *Travels,* vol. 3, pp. 284–85.

64 Gotō Rishun, *Oranda-banashi,* p. 18; some of the mirrors he mentions evidently had pictures on them; Takizawa Bakin, *Kiryo manroku,* p. 157.

65 Hirokawa Kai, *Nagasaki bunken-roku,* vol. 4, p. 4r.

66 Nagakubo Sekisui, *Nagasaki kikō,* p. 22.

67 Morishima Chūryō wrote here under the penname of Gekai Inshi.

68 Qianglong *Luoshan chuanji,* vol. 14. I am grateful to Andrew Lo for helping me with this translation.

69 Yūjo, *Banji,* see transcription of Sasaki Jōhei, *Ōkyo kankei shiryō 'Banji' bassui,* p. 50. The passage in datable to 1768. For other similar advice, see pp. 47–49.

70 These studies are contained in a set of scrolls dated winter 1770, *Jinbutsu shōsha sōhon,* now housed in Tenri University Library; for a virtually uncensored (though thumbnail-sized) reproduction, see Sasaki Jōhei, *Ōkyo shasei gashū,* p. 117. Pornographic pictures of masturbation were, of course, rife.

71 Ishikawa Tairō's frontispiece to *Keisei yawa* resembles a portrait by him of Genpaku now housed in Waseda University Library, dated 1812; for a convenient reproduction, see, *Genshoku Nihon no bijutsu,* vol. 25, pl. 120. Genpaku's book itself is wide-ranging, and only takes the reflected shape as the starting-point.

72 *Shunparō hikki,* quoted in Sasaki, *Nihon kindai bijutsu-ron,* p. 90.

73 Alex Wayman, "The mirror as a pan-Buddhist metaphor-simile", pp. 252ff.

74 Hachinomiya Itsuki, ed., *Dōni-ō dōwa,* p. 41.

75 As far as I am aware, the interpretation of mica as a mercury substitute has not been made before; the coincidence of the rise of mica pictures and mirrors, though, cannot be denied. A useful comparative example is a print by Utamaro of the 1790s from the series *Sugata-mi shichinin kesō,* now housed in the Tokyo National Museum, in which there is no mica background to the picture overall, but a depicted mirror is so done; for a convenient reproduction, see Roni Neuer, *Ukiyo-e: 250 Years of Japanese Art,* p. 62. Utamaro also used brass filings, stuck to the surface of the print, to make the image shimmer, for example, in the series, *Seirō jūni toki.*

76 *Nihon kokugo daijiten* q.v..

77 Hachinomiya Itsuki, ed., *Dōni-ō dōwa,* p. 41.

78 Kodera Gyokuchō, *Misemono zasshi,* p. 310. The original phrase is not in the form of question and answer, but that seems to work best in translation.

6: THE EYE AND THE LENS

1 The chaplain was Kazan; see *Heike monogatari,* bk. 3, chap. 1; the event referred to is otherwise unrecorded; see Helen Craig McCullough, trans., *The Tale of the Heike;* for this episode, see vol. 1, p. 159.

2 Kate Nakai, *Shogunal Politics,* p. 24. As a *fudai* (long-standing hereditary) lord, Nagasahige objected to submission to new men favoured by the shogun Ienobu.

3 Edo's first oculist's was run by Morita Yūki, and it opened in 1590; see Morishita Misako, *Edo no biishiki,* p. 105.

4 All mention of eye doctors is omitted in the medical section of the great Edo reference work by Terajima Ryōan, *Wakan sansai zue,* although surgeons and internal doctors, and even medical ancillaries like masseurs and acupuncturists find mention; vol. 1, pp. 102–3.

5 Sugita Genpaku, *Aran iji mondo* (1795), p. 205.

6 Ogawa Kenzaburō, *Nihon ganka gakushi,* p. 103; *Honcho ikō* is undated and described by Ogawa only as the Genroku Period (i.e., 1688–1793).

7 Ibid., p. 104; the rector was Kirifushi Dōsai, and the rules of the school drawn up in 1825.

8 Quoted in ibid., p. 103; Ogawa does not give the date of *Ganmoku meikan* and I have been unable to determine it.

9 The preface to *Ganmoku meikan* is entitled "*Ganmoku hai gozō-ron,*" quoted in ibid., p. 76.

10 See above, Chap. 3.

11 Katsuragawa Hoshū's father was Hosan; for a history of the rather extraordinary family, see Imaizumi Genkichi, *Katsuragawa-ke no hitobito*, and Tozawa Yukio, *Katsuragawa-ke no sekai*.

12 Two by-appointment oculists (called *oku on-ganka ishi*) were retained, alternating daily, and paid salaries of 200 *ryō;* see Sasama Yoshihiko, *Edo bakufu shokuyaku shūsei*, p. 319.

13 Mori Senzō, *"Ōtsuki Banzui no Ranjin hōmon,"* p. 271; Mori interprets this to mean that Hoshū had specifically requested the book.

14 Joseph Plenk *Verhandelingen over de oogziekten*, trans. M. Pruys. I am grateful to Togo Tsukahara for this information.

15 For details of the translation project, see Ogawa, *Nihon ganka gakushi*, p. 115ff.

16 Yoshida Tadashi, *Rangaku ni okeru yakugo*, p. 7. Table 4, p. 69, tabulates the various terms used in different Edo-period books.

17 Sugita Genpaku, *Rangaku kotohajime*, p. 501, outlines these three possibilities.

18 Mikumo Kanzen, *Hōyaku-in kaidantai zōzu;* Hōyaku-in was one of Mikumo's names. The dissection from which the work derives was led by Koishi Genshun and the inscriptions were by Hashimoto Shūkichi; for a convenient reproduction of the entire work, see Nihon Iji Gakkai, ed., *Zuroku Nihon iji bunka shiryō shūsei*, vol. 2, pp. 53–9. The word *oogbol* appears beside the Japanese *gankyū* (not the same *gankyū* as that used in the Plenk translation, the "jewel" radical in the latter character being omitted).

19 Charles Thunberg, *Travels*, vol. 3, pp. 25 and 60. The Japanese is given by Thunberg as *Horlanda o-me* (i.e., *Oranda-ōme*).

20 Ibid., p. 251.

21 Ōtsuki Gentaku, *Ransetsu benwaku*, p. 26.

22 Shiba Kōkan, *Saiyū nikki*, p. 115.

23 Kuki Shūzō, *'Iki' no kōzō* (1930), p. 54; Kuki intended his remarks to apply to the Kasei period (1804–28).

24 *Ki ga areba me mo kuchi hodo ni mono o iū;* quoted in Okitsu Kaname, *Edo senryū*, p. 97.

25 Kan'en gives Siebold's age as twenty-four, but in Japan at this time counting was inclusive.

26 Sakai Shizu et al., eds., *Zuroku Nihon iji bunka shiryō shūsei*, vol. 2, p. 133; the device arrived in 1827. After Siebold was compromised, Kō Ryōsai was temporarily imprisoned and had to leave his post as *han* doctor.

27 Sugita Genpaku et al., trans., *Kaitai shinsho*, p. 336.

28 As early as 1741, Konrai Tōhaku said in the *Ganmoku gyōkai* that the eye worked "exactly like a telescope lens, without which you cannot see anything"; quoted in Ogawa, *Nihon ganka gakushi*, p. 94. Ogawa dismisses the book as "pure imagination," which may be true, but the fact that such a work was written at all is remarkable. Gentaku later stated of the workings of the eye that "the principle is exactly that of a telescope"; see his *Aran iji mondo*, p. 205.

29 Shiba Kōkan, *Tenchi ridan*, p. 246 (including illustration).

30 Ibid., p. 246, and Shiba Kōkan, *Oranda tensetsu*, p. 482.

31 Jean-Jacques Scheucher, *Physique sacrée, ou histoire naturelle de la Bible* (1732–7), vol. 7, pp. 40–1; quoted in Barbara Stafford, *Body Criticism*, p. 369.

32 The Genji (or Minamoto) clan founded the Kamakura shogunate in 1185, and are not to be confused with the eponymous hero of Murasaki's *Tale of Genji*. For a translation of the nō play *Kagekiyo*, see Arthur Waley, *The Nō Plays of Japan*, pp. 123–33.

33 Danjūrō V's father was Danjūrō IV; see Lawrence Kominz, "Ichikawa Danjūrō's Golden Age," p. 79.

34 Hiraga Gennai, *Nenashi-gusa*, p. 59.

35 Iwada Shūgyō, *"Kibyōshi 'Aku shichi henme Kagekiyo' kō,'"* proposes that, throughout, Kagekiyo's eyes are drawn to resemble Danjūrō's.

36 The phrase *yome tōme kasa no uchi* is also a pun, as *yome* can mean a wife, and *tōme* means farsighted in both the figurative and medical senses.

37 It was the practice of some books (and all kibyoshi) to have running titles printed down the sides of the page; this is the only example I am aware of where a rebus is introduced instead.

Regrettably, the motif is barely visible in the figures reproduced here.

38 Jippensha Ikku, *Yome tōme kasa no uchi*, p. 1r.

39 The *Chūshingura* story existed in many forms, but for a translation of the original puppet play, see Donald Keene, *Chūshingura.*

40 The inscription reads, *"Shitoyaka ni yasashiku misete iji mo ari, sate me no uchi ni jitsu ga ari sō;* the final three graphs pun *ari sō* "has a physiognomy" with *ari sō* "would seem to have." Kunisada also produced a set of prints based on the same conceit, with the title *Tōsei sanjū-ni sō*, also written in the lens; for a convenient illustration of one, see Fukuda Kazuhiko, *Edo no shiki*, fig. 13.

41 See Nobuhiro Shinji, *Karasutei Enba nenpū*, pp. 174–5, or, for a more accessible source, Tanahashi Masahiro, *Kibyōshi sōran*, vol. 1, p. 643. Other Edo-period arts also identified "seven changes" (*shichi henge*) among their techniques, and Mekichi takes this and puns on "eyes" (*me*) to make *shichi henme.*

42 Santō Kyōden, *Komon shinpō*, p. 4r; for a facsimile with commentary, see Nobuhiro Shinji, *"Komon shinpō' eiin to chūyaku,"* pt. 2, pp. 121 and 135; the relevant illustration is on p. 121.

43 Shikitei Sanba, *Ono no Bakamura uso ji-tsukushi* (pagination unclear). Sanba intended a pun between Ono no Bakamura and the classical Heian poet Ono no Takamura; *baka*, means "stupid." The idea for the spoof dictionary and its title came from Koikawa Harumachi, *Sato no Bakamura muda ji-zukushi* (1783).

44 Mitaka Yorai, *Bankin sangyō bukuro*, p. 22v.

45 See Terajima Ryōan, *Wakan sansai zue*, where spectacles are mentioned as European twice, once under "Dutchman" (*Oranda-jin*) and once under "Glasses" (*megane*), see pp. 244 and 352.

46 Anon., *Kiyu shoran*, cited in Ono Tadashige, *Garasu-e to doro-e;* p. 264, says simply "glass" (*biidoro*), but I follow Ono in taking this to mean a lens.

47 Shirayama Sekiya, *Megane no shakaishi*, table on p. 95.

48 Shiba Kōkan, *Saiyū nikki*, p. 105.

49 I have been unable to establish any definitive connexion between the two Muranos, and it is true that Murano is a relatively normal Japanese family name. But equally, Venetian glass was held in high regard in Europe in the eighteenth century, and the VOC would unquestionably have known of it, and very possibly exported it too; Thunberg refers to Nuremburg glass as a popular good for smuggling, see above, Chap. 1.

50 Shirayama, *Megane no shakaishi*, p. 239, reproduces a list of glasses shop advertisements, from which the above information can be derived.

51 Gotō Rishun, *Oranda-banashi*, p. 18.

52 The character *gyō* of Gyōemon is written with the same as that used to write the *yuki* of Yukimachi.

53 Harumachi's first work, *Kinkin-sensei eiga no yume* is said to have begun the kibyoshi genre. The author died in suspicious circumstances in the seventh month of 1789, and Yukimachi's book was published early in 1790. See Tanahashi Masahiro, *Kibyōshi gōran*, vol. 2, pp 612–15.

54 In 1844, the idea of the moral spectacles was taken up by Mantei Ōga in *Kyōkun ukiyo megane;* a joke-book illustrated by Eisen; the title-page had an illustration of a pair of glasses.

55 Mori Senzō, *"Otsuki Banzui no Ranjin hōmon,"* p. 270; the year of the encounter was 1794.

56 Gijsbert Hemmij died on his return from the *hofreis* on 6th of 8th month, 1797; his grave, not far from Kakegawa on the Tōkaidō, became something of a tourist spot; see Timon Screech, *Ō-Edo no ijin ōrai* (forthcoming). (It was a bad spring for the VOC, for Dejima burnt down while they were away.)

57 Nagaoka Hiruo, *Nihon no megane*, p. 56. Nagaoka offers a different interpretation for the disallowing of wearing glasses in front of parents – namely, that it implied a venerable old age (i.e., seniority), and so was not tolerated on the part of juniors.

58 Koikawa Yukimachi, *Sake machi megane no toku*, p. 3v.

59 Jippensha Ikku, *Yome tōme kasa no uchi*, p. 1v.

60 Terajima Ryōan, ed., *Wakan sansai zue*, vol. 1, p. 352. The senryu reads, *nuihaku ya honda de megane kakete iru*, An 7, *ni* 3.

61 *Sanshōdayū shichinin musume* is unsigned, and Kyōden's authorship is only an attribution; see

Tanahashi, *Kibyōshi sōran*, vol. 2, p. 438; the title needs explanation: the septuplet sisters recall the Pleiades; their father is called Mimasuya, "three boxes," a plausible name, but one actually referring to the kabuki star Danjūrō's crest; all sisters have exploits linked by use of the word *tama* – in O-tsuki's case, meaning glasses. "Mimasu" can also be pronounced Sanshō which allows a pun on the name of a kabuki play, *Sanshōdayū gonin musume*.

62 *Ukiyo eshi bobo o miru no mo shigoto nari;* quoted in Hayashi Yoshikazu, *Edo makura eshi no nazo*, p. 174.

63 *Otome sugata* (anon.), is partially reproduced in Fukuda Kazuhiko, *Ukiyo-e Edo no shiki*, pp. 48–9.

64 Mitaku Yorai, *Bankin sangyō bukuro*, p. 23v; the glasses are said to reflect people coming in all directions.

65 Gotō Rishun, *Oranda-banashi*, p. 18. *Sokai megane* may have been angled opera-glasses that allowed the user to look in a direction other than the one in which they appeared to be looking, but Rinshun does not specify.

66 Edo merchants' surnames were generally the name of their shop (ending in *-ya*), but the *-ya* could be omitted, and the first syllable of the given name added instead (e.g., the publisher Tsutaya Jūsaburō was called Tsutajū). Jihinari is inconsistent, though, for the name of the protagonist here would abbreviate not as Fukutokujū but Fukutokutoku; however, as a writer Jihinari was not very careful about such things: on p. 1v, he even changed Fukutokujū's name momentarily to Fukurōbei.

67 Jihinari intends a pun, as the holiday leave is offered to the staff as a new year's present, known as a *toshi-dama*, but here, literally, *tama* (glass).

68 The sign of Fukutokujū's shop appears on p. 5v.

69 Sugita Genpaku et al., trans., *Kaitai shinsho*, p. 322.

70 Gotō Rishun, *Oranda-banashi*, p. 19.

71 Kobayashi Yukio, *Sekai kenbikyō no rekishi*, p. 19. The Lord of Tamura was a Dutch enthusiast and sponsored Nakagawa Jun'an's studies in Western surgery. Gentaku's visit is not dated, but Seian died in 1782.

72 Sugita Genpaku, *Aran iji mondo*, p. 220.

73 Morishima Chūryō, *Kōmō zatsuwa*, p. 476. Egbert Buys, *Woordenboek*, used the term "microscopium," q.v.

74 Zhuangzi, bk. 25; see James Legge, trans., *Sacred Books of Taoism*, pp. 118–20.

75 Legge, *Sacred Books*, calls the kingdoms Provocation and Stupidity. Interestingly, Primitiveness (*ban* in Japanese) was often used in reference to the Dutch, and the West generally could be called Bankoku – literally, the Kingdom (or Land) of Primitiveness.

76 Shiba Kōkan, *Mugen dōjin hikki*, p. 245.

77 Morishima Chūryō, *Kōmō zatsuwa*, p. 476.

78 Kobayashi, *Sekai no kenbikyō no rekishi*, p. 11.

79 It cannot, of course, be told to what extent Shigemasa's picture represents the real appearance of Kyōden's study, and thus whether the author really owned such a picture; I have seen no actual depictions of the theme; the scroll has what appears to be a signiture on it, but it is (presumably deliberately) illegible.

80 Jizō confers on Kyōden a seminiferous jewel, which he swallows to beget a story; for a discussion, see Hayashi Yoshikazu, 'Sakusha tainai totsuki no zu' – gesakusha uchimaku mono no tokushū – kaidai."

81 Morishima Chūryō, *Kōmō zatsuwa*, p. 476.

82 See above, Chap. 2.

83 Nakano Misao, "*Kenbikyō ni tsuite no waga kuni no saisho no bunken*," p. 1662.

84 Shiba Kōkan, *Tenchi zenzu* (unpaginated); the text appears next to the image, given here as pl. 12. For a convenient illustration, see Suntory Museum, *Nihon hakubutsu-gaku kotohajime*, p. 50.

85 Shikitei Sanba, *Hayakawari mune no karakuri* (1805), p. 647. The story mentions a microscope (*Oranda megane*) in the preface; for other comments on the book, see Timon Screech, *Ō-Edo no ijin ōrai* (forthcoming).

86 Jippensha Ikku, *Mushi-megane nobe no wakakusa*, p. 1r.

87 Jippensha Ikku, *Shinsei kobito-jima meguri gassen* (1831), quoted in Regina Johnson, *Fantasic Voyages*, p. 82 (adapted), where the expression is used in reference to midget people.

88 For gifts of microscopes, see Paul van der Velde, ed., *Dejima Dagregisters*, vol. 7, p. 441.

89 Yamagata Shigefusa, *Shigefusa kakuchō*, quoted in Nakano, "*Kenbikyō ni tsuite*," p. 1663.

90 Kodera Gyokuchō, *Misemono zasshi*, p. 298 (with illustration); I have not been able to identify the meaning of *shakushi* (written in *kana* and not given in *Nihon kokugo daijiten*); the word usually means a rice server, and possibly refers to an insect of that shape (perhaps a tadpole).

91 Technically, "insect-glasses" were simpler than microscopes, being single-lensed, but the terms were widely confused. Cf. the old French word "flea-glasses" (*lunettes à puce*).

92 The title of Kyōden's *Matsu to ume taketori monogatari* refers to the ancient *Bamboo-cutter's Tale* (*Taketori monogatari*), adapted to pun on the "Three Gentlemen" of the Chinese-inspired *bunjin* school (plum, pine, and bamboo).

93 Santō Kyōden, *Matsu to ume taketori monogatari*, pp. 861–2. The passage flows better in the original, as Japanese makes no distinction between singular and plural.

94 The link between Kunisada's illustrations, Kyōden's story, and natural-history works was first pointed out by Suzuki Jūzō, in *Ehon to ukiyo-e*, p. 117; more information was given in T. Screech, "Kunisada's Ghosts and Natural History Illustration in the Late Edo Period," pp. 101–6, new elements are also presented here.

95 Morishima Chūryō, *Kōmō zatsuwa*, p. 455.

96 It is possible that Kōkan admitted his source in an inscription on the now-lost pictures in the Katsuragawa collection.

97 The print is reproduced (without commentary) in Nonogami Keiichi, *Nagasaki ko-hanga*, fig. 66, although he does not give evidence for attributing it to a Nagasaki maker.

98 Jean Swammerdam, *The Book of Nature*, ed. and trans. Flloyd (unpaginated translator's preface).

99 The dating to the early years of the nineteenth century is suggested in Kobayashi Tadashi, *Edo no e o yomu*, p. 206.

100 *Me no sameta yō naru hana no ha ni asobu chō wa okata namaei no yume.*

101 See Legge, trans., *Sacred Books*, pp. 117–18, or Wing-tsit Chan, *Source Book in Chinese Philosophy*, p. 190.

102 The name Tsuinaoru Kitenteesu is difficult to unravel, but *tsui naoru* means something like "getting better in spite of things," while *kitenteesu* alludes to Hippocrates, cornerstone of Western medicine, who was known in Japan as "Hippokurateesu."

103 Sanō Yasusada, *Hizōshi*, last page of unpaginated volume. Yamawaki Tōyō, *Zōshi* (1759), is regarded as pivotal in the history of Japanese medicine; see, *inter alia*, Okamoto Kyō, *Kaibōgaku kotohajime*, pp. 3–31.

104 Fukuoka Sadaaki, *Ika zokudan* (date unknown), quoted in Okamoto, *Kaibōgaku kotohajime*, p. 40. Sadaaki was not an admirer of Yasusada, either; for a general discussion of those opposed to anatomy, see Okamoto, ibid., pp. 32–46.

105 Nan'a Kō, *Mushi kagami*, p. 33v. The book appeared posthumously and represents Nan'a's teaching as recorded by Kōyō Kogenryū. Two rudimentary illustrations of the device (with other types of microscope) are given.

106 Rinshō, *Kogane no yama Fukuzō jikki*, p. 2v.

107 Shikitei Sanba, *Hara no uchi gesaku no tanehon*, p. 45.

108 For Bakahito's life, see Koike Masatane et al., eds., *Edo no gesaku ehon*, vol. 1, p. 288; the fate of Shōnosuke is tantalisingly mentioned by Takizawa Bakin, *Edo sakusha burui*, quoted in ibid. A facsimile and transcription is also provided in ibid., pp. 251–80.

109 Nan'a Kō, *Mushi kagami*, p. 36v.

110 Quoted in Keith Thomas, *Man and the Natural World*, p. 167.

111 Hokusai did a second miniature set showing Lake Biwa, now in Kobe City Museum.

112 Ryūtei Tanehiko, *Edo chiri hiroi*, p. 402; Tanehiko's memory may play him false on date, and he only says the man worked "in Hōreki," i.e. 1751–61. Tani Bunchō, *Bunchō gadan*, p. 212.

113 There are other opinions concerning the reading of the title *Oranda gakyō*. Lee, *Origin and Development*, pp. 472, 498, gives not *gakyō* but *ga-kagami*, which would mean "picture mirror," and he interprets the pictures accordingly as mimicking glass paintings (finding support in the fact that they are drawn with frames

around the images). On the evidence of the style alone, though, it seems that Hokusai is replicating copperplates, and as far as I am aware the word *ga-kagami* did not exist (although *e-kagami* did, meaning a picture mirror of the kind described in Chap. 7).

114 Such small-scale *nozoki-megane* appear to have existed since the mid-century; see Lee *Origin and Development*, fig. 32B, for a box dated 1752. Utamaro made a print of one as part of the series *Fūryū-kō takara-awase* (turn of eighteenth century), showing a box, although somewhat larger, as it rests on a *go* board; the rear sign in that case also shows Ryōgoku Bridge (a copy is now housed in the Chiosonne Collection).

115 For the publishing history of the series, see Kobayashi Tadashi, *Edo no e o yomu*, p. 201. The inscription reads, *katachi yori wa sugurete adokenaku iroke arite omote ni orawazari akumade kawōrashiki sō ari.*

116 See above, Chap. 4.

7: THE VIEW FROM ON HIGH

1 Tachibana Nankei, *Seiyū-ki*, p. 189.

2 Ibid., p. 193.

3 Shiba Kōkan, *Kunmō gakai-shū* (1814), p. 3.

4 Tachibana Nankei, *Hokusō sadan*, pp. 199–200.

5 Aoki Shurin, *Kikai kanran;* quoted in Ōtsubo Motoji, *Megane no rekishi*, p. 96.

6 Mitaku Yorai, *Bankin sangyō bukuro*, vol. 3, p. 12v.

7 Terajima Ryōan, *Wakan sansai zue*, vol. 1, p. 353.

8 Mitaku Yorai, *Bankin sangyō bukuro*, vol. 3, p. 13v (p. 13r illustrates a domestic microscope).

9 Ban Kōkei, *Kanden jihitsu;* quoted in Shirayama Sekiya, *Megane no shakaishi*, p. 204. Kōkei is best known as the compiler of *Kinsei kijin-den* (1790).

10 Tachibana Nankei, *Hokusō sadan*, p. 141. Nankei identifies Iwahashi Zenbei's production as "early in the Kansei period," i.e., soon after 1789. Zenbei was son of a fishmonger but started young as a lens-grinder; ultimately, he made telescopes for the great cartographer Inō Tadataka.

11 Matthew Perry, quoted in Oliver Statler, *The Black Ship Scroll*, p. 10.

12 Charles Thunberg, *Travels*, vol. 3, p. 11.

13 For a study of the construction of political thought in the early Edo period, see Herman Ooms, *Tokugawa Ideology*.

14 Thunberg, *Travels*, vol. 3, p. 194.

15 The game was called *nonaka no ippon sugi;* it can be seen being played in Ichiba Tsūshō (Kitao Shigemasa, ill.), *Sokuseki mimi gakumon*, p. 3r, where a child is climbing on an adult's shoulders; for a convenient reproduction, see Koike Masatane et al., eds., *Edo no gesaku ehon*, vol. 4, p. 15.

16 The Golden and Silver Turrets are generally called "Pavilions" in English; the former is now a replica.

17 The Chōshū-kaku is extant, but has been removed to the Sankei-en in Yokohama.

18 Thunberg, *Travels*, vol. 3, p. 218.

19 Tanomura Chikuden, *Sanchūjin josetsu* (1813), p. 163. Chikuden chose to visit the collector and artist Kimura Kenkadō rather than ascend the pagoda (which he said he had done as a child). The temple, among the largest in Osaka, was an ancient foundation, but the pagoda was erected by the warlord Oda Nobunaga late in the sixteenth century.

20 Edo had two Kiyomizu temples, the principal one in the grounds of the Kan'ei-ji in Ueno, and a second attached to the Gongen Shrine in Nezu; for a history and illustration of the latter, see Saitō Gesshin et al., *Edo meisho zue*, vol. 3, pp. 280–4. A gantried shrine in the Kansai area was the Toyozu Inari, with its tall platform built by Toyotomi Hideyori (i.e., before 1615); for an illustration, see Akisato Ritō, *Settsu meisho zue*, vol. 3 (unpaginated), where the roofed platform is labelled as having a "fine view"; the shrine, however, was pretty inaccessible, being midway between Osaka and Kyoto.

21 For the reasons for assigning this undated work to the 1780s, see above, Chap. 4, note 28. The shortcomings of the view, however, were such that when telescopes came into fashion they were set up not at Kiyomizu, but at the Shōhō-ji above Yazaka, and Akisato Ritō showed tele-

scopes in use there, see *Miyako rinsen meisho zue* (1799), q.v.

22 Interestingly, Ōkyo also depicted the Golden Turret [Pavilion] and greatly exaggerated its height, basing the composition on a much loftier tower in China; see Julian Lee, *Origin and Development of the Japanese Landscape Print*, p. 299, and figs. 219, 220.

23 *Ichimen no hana wa goban no Ueno-yama kuromon no mae ni kakaru shiragumo;* inscribed on a print by Totoya Hokkei from the series *Kokon kyōka-sen;* a maid from an upper-class home looks off the parapet (no view visible); the work is now housed in the Genoa Museum; for a convenient reproduction, see Narazaki Munashige, *Genoba bijutsukan*, fig. 108.

24 *Kakubakari hegataku miyuru yononaka ni urayamashiku mo sumeru tsukikage;* Takamitsu's verse is contained in the late tenth-century anthology *Shūi-shū;* for citation, see note 25 below.

25 *Kakubakari medetaku miyuru yononaka o urayamashiku nozoku tsukikage;* the verse was published in Nanpo's anthology, *Medeta hyakushū ebisu uta*, but it attained greater exposure through inclusion in Ōta Nanpo et al., eds., *Mansai kyōka shū* (1782), p. 198; Takamitsu's verse is cited in ibid.

26 *Shakajū no yō ni hinomi no kao o dashi;* quoted in Isoda Giichirō et al., eds., *Yanagi daru*, vol. 4, p. 13. The card referred to is the *shaka-jū*, originally derived from the jack of the Western pack, but its picture became a Buddhist image. For the height of fire towers, see Nishiyama Shōnosuke (ed.), *Edogaku jiten* entry under "hinomiyagura" q.v.

27 For a partial reproduction of Toyokuni (ill.), *Hoya gan no koe*, see Hayashi Yoshikazu, *Edo ehon besutoserā*, p. 33. The date of the work is not known, but it parodies Takizawa Bakin's *Satomi hyakken-den* of 1814–41.

28 Watanabe Keiichi, *Kubota-jō monogatari*, p. 65; for the history and structure of Kubota Castle more generally, see pp. 70–87.

29 Ibid., pp. 97–100.

30 For the treatises *Gahō kōryō* and *Gazu rikai*, see above, Chap. 2.

31 For the banning of three-storey architecture in Edo, see Hashizume Shin'ya, *Meiji no wakagu toshi*, p. 76. Most castle towns had similar laws. Edo and other cities permitted higher building on the outskirts.

32 *Sankai ni shamisen-bori o san-sagari ni-agari miredo akitaranu kei;* quoted in *Hōseidō Kisanji nenpū*, p. 150.

33 Nagakubo Sekisui, *Nagasaki kikō*, p. 21r; the narrative was not published until 1805.

34 Tazawa Shunbo, *Nagasaki kibun* (unpaginated), includes an illustration labelled as translated here, although the platform is shown unoccupied.

35 Shiba Kōkan, *Oranda tsūhaku*, p. 515.

36 Ōtsuki Gentaku, *Kankai ibun*, p. 583.

37 Ibid., p. 566.

38 The source of Satake's stair has been identified by Kobayashi Bunji as Joseph Moxon, *Practical Perspective* (1670), pl. 35; see "*Shozan no nijū rasen kaidan-zu ni tsuite*," pp. 106–7. This interpretation has now become the standard norm; see, for example, Kumamoto Kenjirō, ed., *Akita Ranga – bessatsu*, p. 9. An image identical to Satake's is indeed included in Moxon, although that author specifically states (p. 46) he has taken it from "*Vignols* [sic] in his Book on Perspective." Kobayashi notes this, but objects that there are differences between Vignola's and Satake's illustrations, without considering the possibility of a later edition. Intrinsically, the classic text is far more likely to have been taken to Japan than an obscure English derivative. Moxon cites "*Sciamburg* in France," attributing that stair to Pietro del Bergo.

39 Hōseidō Kisanji, *Kagekiyo hyakunin isshū* (1782), illustrated by Kitao Shigemasa, pp. 4v–5r. The phrase occurs with reference to the spiral stair of the Gohyaku Rakan-ji, for which see below. Kisanji anachronistically has the mediaeval Kagekiyo ascend the stair.

40 Imai Tanito, *Edo meisho hana no shiori*, quoted in Timon Screech, "The Strangest Place in Edo," p. 422. For a general discussion of the Turbo Hall, see ibid., pp. 417–24 (with illustrations).

41 Ibid., p. 417.

42 Ibid.

43 Kakunen, *Yūreki zakki*, quoted in ibid., p. 419.

44 Morishima Chūryō, *Kōmō zatsuwa*, p. 461. The height given is impossible, even if referring to length of climb, not altitude.

45 Honda Toshiaki, *Seiiki monogatari*, p. 43.

46 Tanaka Yūko, *Edo no sōzōroku*, p. 99, stated with reference to Harunobu; Takayama Hiroshi has deployed the term in a wider context, *Kuro ni someru*, p. 16.

47 Rokujūen, *Hida no takumi monogatari*, p. 940. The building is also said to be able to sink into the ground.

48 For a collection of tales of human flight in China, see Fukumoto Kazuo, *Karakuri gijutsu shiwa* (2d ed.), pp. 197–200, but he has been able to find just one pre-1780s Japanese story (ibid., p. 201).

49 Kan Sazan, *Fude no susabi* (date unknown), quoted in ibid., p. 204.

50 Berutsu Hanako, *Ōshū taisen tōji no doitsu* (date unknown), quoted in ibid., pp. 209–10.

51 Hitomi Shōu, *Kokuten sago*, quoted in ibid., p. 211.

52 Namake no Bakahito, *Uso shikkari gantorichō*, see above, Chap. 6.

53 Rantokusai Shundo, *Karakasa no hajimari*; the Kiyomizu passage occurs on p. 5v. The author was know in his painterly work as Katsukawa Shundo.

54 Rokujūen, *Hida no takumi monogatari*, pp. 990, 991 (illustration, pp. 988–9).

55 I am grateful to Haruko Iwasaki for drawing my attention to the history of the hot-air balloon in Japan.

56 Morishima Chūryō, *Kōmō zatsuwa*, p. 460.

57 Shinoda Akira, *Kikyū no rekishi*, p. 22. There is some problem with this dating, however, as Romberg sailed from Batavia before the balloon had ascended, and it is unclear how news could have overtaken him *en route;* Shinoda speculates that Genzui misrecorded the date.

58 Ibid. A copy of another French print of a balloon was brought to Japan and copied into Ishizaki Yūshi, *Nagasaki kokon shūran meisho zue* (1841), labelled as a Dutch balloon but identified in the French original title as the ascent of Charles and Robert; for a convenient reproduction (without commentary), see Etchū Tetsuya et al., eds, *Nagasaki, Yokohama* fig. 186.

59 Quoted without source by C. C. Krieger, *Infiltration of European Civilisation*, p. 89 (adapted). The poem was written in response to a print imported in 1789. In 1787 Masatsuna published *Saiyō zenipu* on Western coins, and the following year his study of twenty years, *Taisei yochi zusetsu*. He sponsored the editor of Gentaku's *Ransetsu benwaku*, Arima Genshō.

60 Kōkan's plate is dated 1797 and is now housed in Waseda University; for convenient reproduction, see *Nihon bijutsu kaiga zenshū*, vol. 25, pl. 58. Siebold's balloon-shaped bottle is Hirado ware and now housed in the National Museum of Ethnology, Leiden; for a convenient reproduction, see Siebold Council, ed., *Yōroppa ni miru Nihon ni takara*, pl. 30. Kōkan mentioned the hot-air balloon on another occasion: see *Tenchi ridan* (1816), pp. 251–3 (with illustration).

61 Kanwatei Onitake, *Wakanran zatsuwa*, p. 12r.

62 The work is signed Hatake no Dojin Maimosuke, *Kontan teori shima*, pp. 9v–10r. The standard interpretation is that the author is Kitao Shigemasa; see Tanahashi, *Kibyōshi sōran*, vol. 2, p. 365.

63 Ōtsuki Gentaku, *Kankai ibun*, p. 570. Gentaku refers to Chūryō's account in *Kōmō zatsuwa*, and to a "single-sheet print" brought to Japan by "some Dutch captain" (ibid., p. 575); Kokan referred in 1816 to Tsūdayū seeing an ascent; see *Tenchi ridan*, p. 25 (with illustration). By the time Tsūdayū returned, miniature balloons had been sent up by the Dutch from Dejima, as Gentaku recorded in the marginalia.

64 Ibid., p. 574.

65 Ibid., p. 573.

66 Ibid., p. 574.

67 Humphrey Jennings, *Pandaemonium*, p. 81. Tsūdayu included two pictures of the hot-air balloon, and also, though they did not show the balloonists' telescope, they did show people below looking up through a lens.

68 François Valentijn, *Oud en Nieuw Oost-Indien*. For reproductions of Chūryō's two renditions of Vulture Peak, see Naruse Fujio et al., *Shiba Kōkan*

zenshū, vol. 4, pp. 114–15. For a reproduction of one of Valentijn's originals, see Calvin French, *Shiba Kōkan*, p. 125; only one of the two images published by Chūryō is signed by Kōkan. Kōkan used it again in 1793 in *Chikyū zenzu* (reproduced in French, ibid., p. 124); again in 1805 in a single-sheet negative woodblock (reproduced in Naruse, ibid., pp. 4, 299); and finally, in 1808, he wrote an *Illustrated Explanation of Vulture Peak* (*Ryōjusen zusetsu*).

69 *Naruhodo to itte mata miru tōmegane;* quoted in Isoda Giichirō et al., eds., *Yanagi-daru*, vol. 10, p. 284.

70 Saitō Gesshin et al., *Edo meisho zue*, vol. 1, p. 598.

71 Richard Altick, *The Shows of London*, p. 291. The word *heirin* does not appear in the standard modern dictionary, *Nihon kokugo daijiten*.

72 Shikitei Sanba, *Ukiyo-doko*, p. 289, mentions *Oranda no jūri-ken* at Atago. More generally, see Henry Smith, "World Without Walls," p. 16 and n. 34 (including illustration), which notes that the term for enjoying the view through a lens was *fūkei o moteasobu*.

73 *Ima ni yuku tokoro o Yushima no bōenkyō;* quoted in Okitsu Kaname, *Edo senryū*, p. 257.

74 Julian Lee, *Origin and Development of the Japanese Landcape Print*, p. 264; the two senryu quoted read, *Harasanza mite tomo ni yarn tōmegane* and, *tōmegane jiman wa moto e me ga modorū*, in the senryn corpus nos. Ten-3 chi 2 and Hō-10 ten 2 respectively. I am grateful to Kasuya Hiroki for alerting me to these verses. The daimyō of Kōriyama visited on in the second month of 1784, see Hanasaki Kazuo, "*Kinsei bungaku no nanshoku goi zuikō*, p. 63. For Russia, see Katsuragawa Hoshū, *Hokusa bunryaku*, p. 196.

75 Anon., *Kamigata koi gyoku* (c. 1813), quoted in Hayashi Yoshikazu, *Edo akura-e no nazo*, p. 183.

76 Santō Kyōden, preface to Sharakutei Manri, *Shimadai me no shōgatsu*, p. 1r.

77 Sharakutei Manri, *Shimadai me no shōgatsu*, p. 2v.

78 Ibid., p. 9v.

79 Shikitei Sanba, *Hitogokoro nozoki-karakuri* (1814), illustrated by Toyokuni; see above, Chap. 4. For the reissuing of Manri's kibyoshi, see Tanahashi, *Kibyōshi sōran*, vol. 1, p. 721.

80 Shikitei Sanba, *Ningen isshi nozoki-karakuri*, p. 3r.

81 Ibid., p. 1v.

82 Hachinomiya Itsuki, *Dōni-ō dōwa*, p. 30.

83 Watanabe Toshio, *Kinsei Nihon tenmongkushi*, vol. 1, pp. 153–8.

84 Ibid., vol. 2, p. 482–3. The building burned down in 1813, but was rebuilt and remained in use until 1869; its general appearance can be seen in an illustration in *Kansei rekisho* (unpaginated) or, more sketchily, in Hokusai, *Fugaku hyakkei*, vol. 3, p. 80; for a convenient reproduction, see Henry Smith, *Hokusai: 100 Views of Mount Fuji*, p. 51.

85 Shimozawa Gō and Hirose Hideo, "Tenmonyashiki no tatemono ni tsuite," p. 287. There were four senior astronomers, of whom two others resided elsewhere; ten manual workers were employed. The *tennō's* observatory in Kyoto was larger, although exactly half was given over to space for Shinto rituals; see ibid., p. 289.

86 Ōta Nanpo, *Ichiwa ichigon* quoted in Watanabe Toshio, *Kinsei Nihon tenmongakushi*, vol. 2, p. 494. Other *han* possessing observatories were in Sendai, Aizu, Mito, Fukuyama, and Hirosaki.

87 Shigeru Nakayama, *A History of Japanese Astronomy*, pp. 200–1.

88 Honda Toshiaki, *Seiiki monogatari*, p. 9; Ōtsuki Gentaku, *Kyōi no gen* (1794), p. 237.

89 The instruments used by the Kansei astronomers were depicted in the nineteenth and twentieth volumes of the *Kansei rekisho*, separately labelled *Gi shozu;* that section only edited by Yoshida Shirozaemon.

90 Morishima Chūryō, *Hōgu-kago* (date unknown), p. 169.

91 Kobayashi Tadashi, "Taisho e-goyomi no Harunobu to Gennai," p. 151.

92 Tachibana Nankei, *Hokusō sadan*, p. 31.

93 See above, note 89.

94 Grant K. Goodman, *Japan: The Dutch Experience*, p. 99.

95 Shiba Kōkan, *Shunparō hikki*, pp. 449–50. Kōkan stated that the daimyo had summoned "Messrs Yoshida and Yamarō and the rest of them at the

Official Observatory," but found "they know nothing about astronomy, despite being in the field hereditarily; when asked questions they cannot reply and just shrug their shoulders, bite their tongues and leave."

96 Goodman, *Japan: The Dutch Experience,* p. 95. Goodman states, of Shibukawa Harumi, "his traditionalist world-view seems to have been minimally affected by ideas from the West."

97 *Siku quanshu zongma tigao,* quoted in Jean Gernet, *China and the Christian Impact,* p. 60.

98 Sugita Genpaku, *Rangaku kotohajime,* p. 474.

99 Robert Campbell, oral communication.

100 Shiba Kōkan, *Saiyū nikki,* p. 27; Kōkan called Paul "Paulius," and he showed the painting quite openly – for example, even to a Buddhist monk called Gessen, in Ise (see ibid., p. 53). Kōkan, of course, made no reference to Paul's religious affiliation, referring to the painting only as a "portrait of a foreigner" (*ijin-zō*), but his own recreations of the Japano-Christian *Nanban* manner shows he knew well enough where it came; the *St. Paul* is lost, but see Calvin French, *Shiba Kōkan,* figs. 60–2. The tract, *Menoza* (1742), told of an Asian prince of that name said to have come to the West in search of Christian teaching. Ponteppidous was a Copenhagen theologian popular in Europe at the time; see Imaizumi Genkichi, *Katsuragawa-ke no hitobito,* vol. 2, p. 186. For a reproduction of the church, see ibid., p. 466. Imaizumi suggests Thunberg to have been the donor of the book, ibid., p. 198.

101 For examples of Iwatoya books with covers of the gods looking to earth, see Hamada Kiichirō, *Kibyōshi edaisen,* p. 99.

102 One of the books so adorned was Koikawa Harumachi, *Ware tanomu hito no makoto;* for a convenient reproduction, see Hamada Kiichirō, "Kibyoshi edaisen ichiran," p. 574. Seventeen eighty-two was also the year that the Tsuruya produced covers showing *nozoki-karakuri;* see above, Chap. 4.

103 Ichiba Tsūshō, *Tenjiku mōke no tsuji,* p. 1r.

104 Shiba Kōkan, *Saiyū nikki,* p. 60.

105 Shiba Kōkan, *Dokushō bōgen,* p. 159.

106 Senrigan and Junpuni are commented on by Tachibana Nankei, *Hokusō sadan,* p. 47; he notes that small images were kept on ships, but two of the statues he may also have seen are still housed in the Founder's Hall of the Kōfuku-ji, Nagasaki.

107 The loud-hailer, principally for casting the user's own voice, could also be used for picking up distant sound; see Morishima Chūryō, *Kōmō zatsuwa,* p. 475.

108 Shiba Zenkō, *Tōsejin tsūbutsu kaichō;* for a facsimile and transcription, see Koike Masatane et al., eds., *Edo no gesaku ehon,* supplementary vol. 1, pp. 157–86. For the historical background to the story, see ibid., pp. 187–90, and Tanahashi, *Kibyōshi sōran,* vol. 1, p. 322.

109 Shiba Zenkō, *Tōsejin tsūbutsu kaichō,* p. 2r; Koike, ibid., p. 159.

110 Jizō is always represented as a monk; it was proverbially the case that monks, who were banned by law from the pleasure districts, would dress up as doctors to sneak in. The justification for turning Jizō specifically into an oculist is the belief that another Jizō statue, the Inga Jizō in Asakusa, was effective at curing eyes, see ibid., p. 131, n. 1.

111 Sugita Genpaku et al., trans., *Kaitai shinsho,* p. 260.

112 The image is now in the Gitter Collection; for a convenient reproduction, see John Stevens, *Zenga: Brushstrokes of Enlightenment,* p. 75.

113 Matti Forrer (with text by Edmond de Goncourt), *Hokusai,* p. 204 (including illustration).

114 Ibid., p. 205.

115 Elements of the Kyoto Great Buddha were rebuilt, and its host temple, the Hōkō-ji, continues to exist. A replacement Buddha Hall burned down in 1798, and the present bust at the temple dates only to 1801.

116 The largest Buddhist image in Edo was probably a Kannon erected at the Kōgen-ji in Komagome; copied after the celebrated statue in the Hase-dera, it stood over 4.5 m high; a window in the upper part of the hall could be opened to reveal the bodhisattva's face. For a description and illustration, see Saitō Gesshin et al., *Edo meisho zue,* vol. 3, pp. 291–3.

117 Tachihara Suiken, *Yūrin zatsuwa,* p. 30.

118 Kyorori, *Haya higashi yōkan Daibutsu-mochi;* Hakusanjin Kakyō, *Azuma Daibutsu momiji no meisho,* both 1793. Both works were written to celebrate the erection of a real Great Buddha in Edo (see below). A now-dismissed theory had it that Hakusanjin was Hokusai (who also used the name Kakyō); see Tanahashi, *Kibyōshi sōran,* vol. 2, p. 372.

119 Saitō Gesshin et al., *Edo meisho zue,* vol. 1, p. 368.

120 For details of the Kaian-ji Buddha, see Asakura Musei, *Misemono kenkyū,* p. 229; Furukawa Miki, *Edo shūmin geinō,* p. 189 (which includes a misidentified illustration of the image and also misidentifies the source of its quotations). The Buddha was made to coincide with the exhibition of an image of Kannon.

121 Asakura, *Misemono kenkyū,* p. 229, quoting a kyoka on the subject.

122 Shikitei Sanba, *Ningen isshin nozoki-karakuri,* p. 2r.

123 The Great Buddha of Nara was also hyperbolically said to be 16 *jō,* see anon., *Heike monogatari;* vol. 1, p. 319. The ancient Indians were said to be 8 *shaku* and the Buddha twice that at 1 *jō* 6 *shaku,* and the Great Buddhas were thus ten times "real" size.

124 Ibid., p. 3r.

125 Nanano Mitsutoshi, "Edo no yūri," p. 136.

126 Asakura (*Misemono kenkyū,* p. 229) and Furukawa (*Edo shūmin geinō,* p. 189) specify this, quoting Kitamura Nobuyo, *Kataniwa zatsuroku (or zakkō).* Nobuyo died in 1856 at the age of seventy-three and saw the Buddha, and also remarked on Western matters; see *Kataniwa zatsuroku,* pp. 91–4. I have been unable, however, to locate the passage referring to the telescope in the editions of either Yoshikawa Kōbunkan (*Hyakka setsurin, zoku hen shitaichi*) or Iwanami (*Nihon zuihitsu taisei* 2, vol. 7).

127 Furukawa, *Shūmin geinō,* p. 188, misidentifies the source of this illustration as *Kobitoguni – sakura;* Hokusai's book does have a similar subtitle, *Kobitojima,* but *Kobitoguni – sakura* is presumably a reference to a story of 1793 by Kyōden (illustrated by Kitao Shigemasa) and is actually called *Kobitojima kokome-zakura;* that work treats a similar subject but does not mention the Great Buddha.

128 Takizawa Bakin (ill. Kitao Shigemasa), *Kujira sashi shinagawa haori.* Bakin's and Ikku's works appeared the following year, 1799. Tōshūsai Sharaku, *Ehon fumi suzuri;* for a convenient reproduction, see *Ukiyo-e* 70, p. 110.

129 The title *Nana sato fuki* seems to pun *nana sato* ("seven villages") with a different expression, written with the same characters but pronounced *shichi ri* ("seven leagues"), which was the name of a pleasure beach near Kamakura.

130 Ōta Shukki, preface to Shiba Kōkan, *Oranda tsūhaku,* p. 445.

131 Asakura, *Misemono kenkyū,* p. 229.

132 Ōtsubo Motoji, *Megane no rekishi,* pp. 193–6.

133 This legend continues to be associated with the place, although no longer put to the test. An interesting comparison is with the episode in Iharu Saikaku, *Kōshoku ishidai onna* (1686) where the female protagonist sees in the faces of Arhat statues all the men she has slept with; for an English version of Saikaku's story, see Ivan Morris, trans., *Life of an Amorous Woman;* the relevant passage is on pp. 203–8; see also illustration on p. 205.

134 Shiba Kōkan, *Dokushō bōgen,* p. 158. Nicolaus Copernicus, *De revolutionibus orbium caelestium* appeared in 1543, 266 years before Kōkan's writing. It is not clear whether Kōkan intended his phrase *chiten no setsu* to be the title of Copernicus's book; if so, it would not be an accurate rendition. I have translated otherwise.

135 Translated from an illustration of the text in *Geijutsu shinchō* Sept. 1993, pp. 64–5.

136 *The Englishman,* quoted in Henry C. King, *Geared to the Stars,* p. 154. Richard Steele founded the *Tatler* in 1709, and after his expulsion from Parliament in 1714 he returned to essay-writing (*Dictionary of National Biography,* q.v.).

137 Shiba Kōkan, *Tenkyū zenzu,* quoted in Calvin French, *Shiba Kōkan,* p. 60 (adapted). Kōkan wrote more about the orrery in *Orurerei zukai* and *Chitengi zukai* (both undated); see partial

reproduction and transcription in Kuroda Genji, *Shiba Kōkan*, pp. 254–6.

138 For a general history of the orrery, see King, *Geared to the Stars*, pp. 154–63. Rowley's orrery is extant in the Science Museum, London; for a convenient reproduction, see ibid., fig. 9.5. There was a proposal to send Rowley's second orrery (commissioned by an Indian nabob who died) to China, but it never left London; see ibid., p. 156.

139 Egbert Buys, *A New and Complete Dictionary*, "Planetarium," q.v. Buys calls the device both a planetarium and an orrery. For the list of Kaempfer's sponsoring subscribers, see front-matter to his *History of Japan* (1728).

140 *Tenchi zenzu ryakusetsu* (1793), quoted in Sugano Yō, *Nihon dōbanga no kenkyū*, p. 222. Sugano offers no suggestions on the identity of *"Uhensukoru,"* but the orrery Kōkan depicted was a famous piece (see below) and could have been found in several books and prints.

141 David P. Wheatland et al., *Early Science at Harvard*, pp. 34–5 (with illustration). The device is extant, and unlike the ones known in Japan, has a glass dome.

142 The Portsmouth orrery was made with planets "somewhat in proportion to their distances from each other"; Joseph Harris, *The Description and Use of the Globe and the Orrery* (3d ed., 1734), quoted in King, *Geared to the Stars*, p. 162. Harris's third and later editions illustrated the instrument, but not from the same angle as Buys and Kōkan.

143 Ōtsuki Gentaku, *Kankai ibun*, p. 580. Tsūdayū said the planetarium was called a *shari* (as was the balloon), because "all globes are called *shari*."

144 For the history of the Gottorf Globe (named after the site of Schleswig castle), see King, *Geared to the Stars*, pp. 104–6. The original globe was 3.1 m and was made by Adam Olearius, and the replacement (dimensions unknown other than through Tsūdayū's account), by Benjamin Scott and Philipp Tiriutin. The second globe was also lost, and a modern replica is now in its place; see ibid., fig. 6.14.

145 John Saris, from Samuel Purchas, *Purchas, his Pilgrimes*, quoted in Michael Cooper, *They Came to Japan*, p. 348.

146 Ōtsuki Gentaku, *Kankai ibun*, p. 580, with reference to the planetarium.

GLOSSARY

Ban	"Primitive"; term applied to peoples from the South, and thus to Europeans whose colonies lay in that direction. Otherwise trans lated "barbarian."
bodhisattva	"Being of Enlightenment"; those just below the Buddhas.
bugyō	Magistrate.
daimyo	One of approx. 280 rulers of a *han;* known in eighteenth-century English as the "kings and princes of Japan."
Edo	Modern Tokyo; also called Tōto, the "Eastern Metropolis."
Edo Period	1603–1868; coterminous with the Tokugawa shogunate.
haikai	Short verse form with 5-7-5 syllabic count. Now called haiku.
han	One of the approximately 280 states into which the Japanese islands were divided; ruled by daimyo. Otherwise translated "domains."
hofreis	Dutch term for the VOC trip to Edo, performed nearly annually; known in Japanese as *sanpū.*
huangdi	Chinese sovereign. "Emperor" of China.
Jizō	A popular bodhisattva, associated with children; represented as a monk.
kabuki	Song and dance theatre of the urban populace.
kaichō	Fund-raising exhibition of religious images.
Kannon	Most popular of the bodhisattvas; associated with immediate help.
kapitan	Local name for the leader of the VOC mission. *Opperhooft* in Dutch.
karakuri	Working device, contraption; automaton.
kibyōshi	Literally, "yellow-covers," short storybooks dealing humorously with contemporary themes; the short text was written over the images.
kiki	"Strange device"; often applied generically to imports.
kōmō	"Red-fur"; Dutch or, by extension, European.

kyūri	"Investigation of principles"; Confucian term coopted to denote Western science.
Kansei	Historical era, 1789–1800. Notable for the Kansei Reforms.
megane	"Glasses"; applied to any lensed instrument.
misemono	"Thing on display"; objects exhibited in public for a fee.
Nagasaki-ya	The VOC lodging in Edo; located in Kokuchō near Nihon-bashi.
Oranda	"Holland"; the modern Netherlands, by extension, Europe.
Ran	Short for *Oranda* (Holland); the West.
Ranga	Dutch (or Dutch-style) painting.
Rangaku	Academic study of Europe.
Ran'i	Western-style physician.
saiku	"Intricate work"; often applied to imported mechanics.
saiku-nin	Operator or maker of a machine.
samurai	Member of the bureaucratic-cum-military elite; some 5 percent of the population.
senryu	Humorous verse form with 5-7-5 syllabic count; derived from haikai.
Shingaku	"Heart and Mind Learning"; popular syncretic creed at the close of the eighteenth century.
shogun	Supreme governor of the daimyo, in the Edo period hereditary in the Tokugawa family. Known in eighteenth-century English as the Emperor of Japan.
Tenmei	Historical era, 1781–9.
tennō	Cultural figurehead; now known in English as the "emperor" of Japan.
Tōkaidō	Highway linking Edo (Tokyo) to Kyoto
uki-e	"Floating picture"; work done in vanishing-point perspective.
ukiyo	Floating World; culture of the brothels and pleasure districts.
ukiyo-e	Pictures of the Floating World. Most flourishing mid- to late-eighteenth century.
VOC	The Dutch East India Company.
yomihon	Novel-like books with few illustrations; popular in the early nineteenth century.
Yoshiwara	Edo's officially sanctioned brothel area.

REFERENCES

In all cases, city of publication is Tokyo, unless otherwise stated.

Edo-period books, consulted in their original editions, are not listed here (such works can be identified by citations referring to page numbers with *recto* and *verso*). The reader is directed to Yasue Ryōsuke, ed., *Kokusho Sōmokuroku* 8 vols. 2nd ed. Iwanami Shoten: 1991, for details of publication and location.

Alpers, Svetlana. *The Art of Describing: Dutch art in the Seventeenth Century.* Chicago: University of Chicago Press, 1983.

Altick, Richard. *The Shows of London.* Cambridge, Mass.: Harvard University Press, 1978.

Anon. *Heike monogatari,* ed. Kajihara Masaaki Shin Nihon bunjaku taikei Iwanami Shoten: 1991.

Anon. "Hiraga Kyūkei jikki." In *Fūrai sanjin kessaku-shū,* 837–903. Teikoku bunko. Hakubunkan, 1893.

Arai, Tsutomu. *Hokusai no kakushi-e.* AA Shuppan, 1989.

Asahin Shinbun Tōkyō Honsha, ed. *Kogū no karakuri-dokei.* 2 vols. Asahi Shinbun, 1990.

Asakura, Musei. *Misemono kenkyū.* Shibunkaku, 1977.

Bodart-Bailey, Beatrice. "Kaempfer Restor'd." *Monumenta Nipponica* 43 (1988): 1–33.

———. "The Persecution of Confucianism in Early Tokugawa Japan." *Monumenta Nipponica* 48 (1993): 293–314.

Boerhaave, Herman. "The Life of the Author." In *The Book of Nature.* John Swammerdam. 2 vols. London: 1758. Unpaginated preface.

Bolitho, Harold. "Travelers' Tales: Three eighteenth century travel journals." *Harvard Journal of Asiatic Studies* 50 (1990): 485–504.

Boxer, C. R. *Jan Compannie in Japan: 1650–1850.* 2d ed. The Hague: Martinus Nijhoff, 1950.

Brandon, James R. "Sugoroku: Flower of Edo." In *Kabuki: Five Classic Plays,* 50–92. Cambridge, Mass.: Harvard University Press, 1975.

Bush, Susan, and Shih, Hsio-yen. *Early Chinese Texts on Painting.* Cambridge, Mass.: Harvard University Press, 1985.

Buys, Egbert. *A New and Complete Dictionary of Art.* 2 vols. Amsterdam, 1768.

Chan, Wing-tsit. *A Source Book in Chinese Philosophy.* Princeton, N.J.: Princeton University Press, 1963.

Chomel, Noël. *Dictionnaire oeconomique.* 2d ed. Paris, 1718.

Coaldrake, William. *The Way of the Carpenter: Tools and Japanese Architecture.* New York and Tokyo: Weatherhill, 1990.

Cohen, I. Bernard. *Benjamin Franklin's Science.* Cambridge, Mass.: Harvard University Press, 1990.

Cooper, Michael. *They Came to Japan: An Anthology of European Reports on Japan, 1543–1640.* Berkeley, Los Angeles, London: University of California Press, 1965.

Dickens, Frederick, trans. *The Magical Carpenter of Japan.* Tokyo and Rutland, Vt.: Tuttle, 1965.

Elisonas, Jurgis. "Christianity and the Daimyo." In *Early Modern Japan,* Ed. John Whitney Hall et al. 6 vols. *Cambridge History of Japan,* 4: 301–72.

Cambridge and New York: Cambridge University Press, 1991.

Etchū Tetsuya, ed. *Nagasaki kokon meisho zue.* Nagasaki Bunken Sōsho, 1975.

Etchū Tetsuya, et al. *Nagasaki, Yokohama. Edo jidai zushi,* vol. 25. Chikuma Shobō, 1976.

Forrer, Matti, and Edmond de Goncourt. *Hokusai.* New York: Rizzoli, 1988.

French, Calvin L. *Shiba Kōkan: Artist, Innovator and Pioneer in the Westernisation of Japan.* New York and Tokyo: Weatherhill, 1974.

Fujisawa Mamohiko, ed. *Santō Kyōden, 'Ko wa mezurashiki misemonogatari' kaisetsu.* Kokon Kisho Kankōkai, 1935.

Fukuda Kazuhiko. *Ukiyo-e: Edo no shiki.* Kawade Shobō Shinsha, 1987.

Fukumoto Kazuo. *Karakuri gijutsu shiwa.* 2d ed. Fuji Shuppan, 1982.

Furukawa Koshōken. "Saiyū zakki." In *Kinsei shakai keizai sōsho,* ed. Motoki Eijirō et al., 9: 140–67. Kaizōsha, 1927.

Furukawa Miki. *Shūmin geinō: Edo no misemono.* Yūzankaku, 1983.

Geikie, Archibald. "Biographical Note on the Scheuchzer Family." In *Engelbert Kaempfer, History of Japan,* 1: vx–xix. 3 vols. Glasgow: James MacLehose & Sons, 1906.

Gernet, Jean. *China and the Christian Impact: A Conflict of Cultures.* Trans. Janet Lloyd. Cambridge and New York: Cambridge University Press, 1985.

Goodman, Grant K. *The Dutch Impact on Japan.* Leiden: Brill, 1967.

———. *Japan: The Dutch Experience.* London: Athlone, 1986.

Gotō Rishun. "Oranda-banashi." In *Oranda-banashi, Ransetsu benwaku,* 9–133, 5–19. Edo kagaku koten sōsho. Inawa Shoten, 1979. Facsimile and transcription.

s'Gravesande, Gulielmo Jacobo. *Physices elementa mathematica, experimentis confirmata.* 3 vols. Paris [Lug. Bat.], 1721.

Hachinomiya Itsuki. *Dōni-ō dawa.* Iwanami bunko, Vols. 1234–5 Iwanami Shoten, 1935.

Hamada Giichirō. "Kibyōshi edaisen ichiran: nendaibetsu, hanmoto-betsu." In *Kibyōshi, senryū, kyōka,* ed. Hamada Giichirō, 561–609. Nihon koten bungaku zenshū. Shōgakkan, 1971.

———. *Kibyōshi edaisen shū.* Yumani shobō, 1979.

———, ed. *Haifū: Yanagi-daru.* 10 vols. Kyoiku bunko. Shakai Shisōsha, 1985.

Hanasaki Kazuo. "Edo no kusuriya." In *Senryū Edo meisho zue,* ed. Hanasaki Kazuo. Kinsei Fūzoku Kenkyūkai, 1966.

Hanasaki Kazuo. "Kinsei bungaku no nanshokugoi zuikō." In *Bungaku* 6 (1995): 58–66.

Haneveld G. T. "The Introduction of Acupuncture into Western Medicine: The influence of Japanese and Dutch Physicians." In *Red-Hair Medicine: Dutch-Japanese Medical Relations,* ed. H. Beukers, 51–8. Amsterdam and Atlanta, Ga.: Rodopi, 1991.

Hashizume Shin'ya. *Meiji no wakugū toshi.* Imeiji rideingu sōsho. Heibonsha, 1990.

Hayashi Yoshikazu. " 'Sakusha taina totsuki no zu' – gesakusha uchimaku mono to tokushū: kaidai." In *Sakusha tainai totsuki no zu,* ed. Hayashi Yoshikazu, 102–10. Edo gesaku bunko. Kawade Shobō Shinsha, 1987.

———. *Edo makura-e no nazo.* Kawade Bunko, 1988.

Hirafuku Hyakusui. *Nihon yōga no shōkō.* Iwanami Shoten, 1930.

Hiraga Gennai. "Hika rakuyō." *Hiraga Gennai-shu,* 109–36. Yūhōdō Shoten, 1917.

———. *Butsurui hinshitsu. Nihon koten zenshū,* vol. 3, no. 16 Nihon Koten Zenshū Kankokai, 1928.

———. "Hōhi-ron." *Furai Sanjin-shū,* 238–56. Nihon koten bungaku taikei. Iwanami Shoten, 1961.

———. "Nenashi-gusa." *Fūrai Sanjin-shū,* 33–152. Nihon koten bungaku taikei. Iwanami Shoten, 1961.

Hirakawa Kai. "Ranryōhō." In *Ranryōhō, Ranryō yakkai,* ed. Sōda Hajime, 279–307. Edo kagaku koten sōsho. Inawa Shuppan, 1980.

Hiroyuki Shinji, ed. "Komon shinpō." *Edo bungaku* 2–3 (1990): 68–109, 119–60.

Hiruma Hisashi. *Edo no kaichō. 'Edo' sensho,* vol. 3. Yoshikawa Kōbunkan, 1980.

Honda Toshiaki. "Keise hisaku." In *Honda Toshiaki, Kaihō Seiryō,* ed. Tsukatani Akihiro and Kuranami Seiji, 11–86. Nihon shisō taikei. Iwanami Shoten, 1970.

———. "Keizai hōgen." In *Keizai shakai gakusetsu*

taikei; Honda Toshiaki shū, ed. Motoatsu Enjirō, 87–118. Shibundō, 2nd ed. 1929.

———. "Seiiki monogatari." In *Honda Toshiaki, Kaihō Seiryō*, ed. Tsukatani Akihiro and Kuranami Seiji, 87–144. Nihon shisō taikei. Iwanami Shoten, 1970.

Ichida Yasuhiro. "Futori no ni-dai Kitagawa Utamaro." *Museum* 492 (1992): 13–27.

Ikegami, Eiko. "Disciplining the Japanese: The Reconstruction of Social Control in Tokugawa Japan." Ph.D. diss., Harvard University, 1989.

Imahashi Riko. *Edo no kachō-ga: hakubutsugaku o meguru bunka to sono hyōgen*. Sukaidoa, 1995.

Imaizumi, Genkichi. *Katsuragawa-ke no hitobito*. 2 vols. Chikusaki Shorin, 1969.

Inoue, Takaaki. *Edo gesaku no kenkyū*. Shinshusha, 1986.

Ishikawa Ichirō, ed. *Edo bungaku chimei jiten*. Tōkyōdō, 1973.

Ishikawa, Jun. *Shokoku kijinden*. Chikuma Shobō, 1955.

Ishikawa, Ken. "Kaisetsu." In *Dōni-ō dōwa*, ed. Ishikawa Ken, 5–23. Iwanami Shoten, 1935.

Ishino Hiromichi. *Esoragoto*. In *Enseki jusshū*, ed. Mori Senzō et al. 6:255–75. Chūō Kōronsha, 1980.

Ishizaka Shōzō. *Zō no tabi: Nagasaki kara Edo-e*. Shinchōsha, 1992.

Itazawa, Takeo. *Nichi-Ran bunka kōshō-shi no kenkyū*. Yoshikawa Kōbunkan, 1959.

Iwada, Hideyuki. "Kibyōshi 'Akishichi henme Kagekiyo' kō." *Kinsei bungaku* 52 (1990): 64–91.

Iwasaki, Haruko. "The World of Gesaku: Playful Writers in Eighteenth-Century Japan." Ph.D. diss., Harvard University, 1984.

Iwase, Seiichi, ed. *Oranda fūsetsu-gaki shūsei*. 3 vols. Yoshikawa Kōbunkan, 1968.

Jansen, Marius B. *China in the Tokugawa World*. Cambridge, Mass.: Harvard University Press, 1992.

Jennings, Humphrey. *Pandaemonium: The Coming of the Machine, 1660–1888*. 2d ed. London: Pan Books, 1985.

Jippensha Ikku. "Oranda kage-e: otsuriki." *Edo shunjū* 4–6 (1977–7): 44–56, 18–29.

Johnson, Regina. "Fantastic Voyages: Refractions of the Real, Re-visions of the Imagined in Hiraga Gennai's 'Fūryū Shidōken-den.' " Ph.D. diss., Harvard University, 1989.

Jonstonus, Johannis. *Theatrum universale omnium animalium quadrupedum*. 4 vols. Amsterdam, 1755.

Jorg, Christiaan J. A. "Japanese Lacquerwork Decorated after European Prints." In *Kansei Daigaku Tōyōgaku Kenkyūjo Sōritsu 30-shūnen Kinen Ronbunshū*, ed. Fujimoto Katsusugi, 58–80. Nagoya: Nagoya Daigaku Shuppanbu, 1981.

Kaempfer, Engelbert. *A History of Japan together with a Description of the Kingdom of Siam*. Trans. J. G. Scheuchzer, London, 1727.

———. *A History of Japan*. 3 vols. Glasgow: James MacLehose & Sons, 1906.

Kagawa, Takayuki. *Kuzureyuku sakoku. Nihon no rekishi*, vol 14. Shūeisha, 1992.

Kasuya Hiroki. *Ishikawa Masamochi no kenkyū*. Kadokawa Shoten, 1985.

———, ed. *Haifū: Yanagi-daru*, vol 6. Kyoiku bunko. Shakai Shisōsha, 1987.

Kato, Koji. *Glassware of the Edo Period*. Trans. Tanaka Fumio, Tokuma Shoten, 1972.

Katsuhara Haruki. "Haikai no jūhasseiki: kindai Edoki, Tōkyō-ki no "naibu" kūkan." In *Edo bunka no hen'yō: jūhasseiki Nihon no keiken*, ed. Momokawa Takahito et al., 73–118. Perikansha, 1994.

Katsuragawa Hoshū. *Hokusa bunryaku*. Yoshikawa Kōbunkan, 1970.

Kawada Hisashi. *'Edo meisho zue' o yomu*. Tōkyō-dō, 1990.

Keene, Donald. *The Japanese Discovery of Europe: Honda Toshiaki and Other Discoverers, 1720–1748*. London: Routledge and Kegan Paul, 1952.

———. trans. and intro. *Chūshingura: The Treasury of Loyal Trainers*. New York: Columbia University Press, 1971.

Kikuchi Toshiyoshi. "Kaisetsu." In *Karakuri kinmō kagame-gusa, Karakuri zue*, ed. Kikuchi Toshiyoshi, 81–90. Edo kagaku koten sōsho. Inawa Shuppan, 1978.

———. "Kiki shōshi." In *Oranda shisei: Kyūri-hara, Ensei kiki-betsu, Erekiteru zensho, Oranda kiki*, ed. Kikuchi Toshiyoshi, 53–76. Edo kagaku koten sōsho. Inawa Shuppan, 1978.

———. "Kaisetsu." In *Oranda-banashi, Ransetsu benwaku*, 55–66. Edo kagaku koten sōsho. Inawa Shuppan, 1979.

Kimura Yōjirō. *Edo-ki no nachurarisuto.* Asahi Shinbunsha, 1988.

King, Henry C. (in collaboration with John R. Millburn). *Geared to the Skies: The Evolution of Planetariums, Orreries and Astronomical Clocks.* Bristol, Eng.: Adam Hilger, 1978.

Kishi Fumikazu. "A View through the Peephole: A Semiotic Consideration of Uki-e." *Monbushō kagaku kenkyūhi hojōkin kenkyū seika hōkokusho* 63/16 (1990): 20–36.

———. *Edo no enkinhō: uki-e no shikaku.* Keisō shobō, 1994.

———. "Enkyō ninen no paasupikuteibu: Okumura Masanobu-ga 'o-uki-e' o megutte." *Bijutsushi* 41 (1991): 228–46.

Kiyooka, Eiichi, trans. *The Autobiography of Yukichi Fukuzawa.* New York: Columbia University Press, 1960.

Kobayashi Bunji. "Shozan no nijū rasen kaidan-zu ni tsuite." *Bijutsushi* 88 (1973): 105–11.

Kobayashi Tadashi. "Taishō egoyomi no Harunobu to Gennai." *Yuriika* 20 (1988): 148–69.

———. *Edo no e o yomu.* Perikansha, 1989.

———. "Eshi Santō Kyōden." In *Kyōden, Ikku, Shunsui,* ed. Jinbō Kazuya et al., 69–79. Zusetsu Nihon no koten. Shūeisha, 1989.

Kobayashi Yukio. *Sekai no kenbikyō no rekishi.* Chikuma Shobō, 1985.

Kodera Gyokuchō. "Misemono zasshi." *Zoku zuihitsu bungaku senshū,* 3:285–396 4:3–55. Shibundō Shoten, 1928.

Koga Jūjirō. *Maruyama yūjo to tōkōmōjin.* 2 vols. Nagasaki: Nagasaki Gakkai, 1968.

Koikawa Harumachi. "Kinkin sensei eiga no yume." In *Edo no gesaku ehon,* ed. Koike Masatane et al., 1:11–30. Gendai Kyōiku bunko. Shakai Shisōsha, 1980.

———. "Muda iki." In *Edo no gesaku ehon,* ed. Koike Masatane et al., 1:113–48. Gendai kyōiku bunko. Shakai Shisōsha, 1980.

———. "Tōsei daibutsu kaichō." In *Edo no gesaku ehon,* ed. Koike Masatane et al., 5:157–86. Gendai kyōiku bunko. Shakai Shisosha, 1980.

Koike Masatane et al., ed. *Edo no gesaku ehon.* 6 vols. Kyōiku bunko. Shakai Shisōsha, 1984.

Kominz, Laurence. "Ichikawa Danduro IVth and Kabuki's Golden Age." In *Floating World Revisited,* ed. Donald Jenkins, 63–84. Portland, Ore., and Honolulu: Portland Museum of Art; Hawai'i University Press, 1993.

Kreiger, C. C. *The Infiltration of European Civilisation in Japan during the Eighteenth Century.* Leiden: E. J. Brill, 1940.

Kuki Shūzō. " 'Iki' no kōzō." In *'Iki' no kōzō hoka ni ten,* 11–98. Iwanami bunko. Iwanami Shoten, 1979.

———. *Le Structure de l'iki.* Trans. Toshiyuki Maeno. Paris: Maison Franco-Japonaise, 1984.

Kumamoto Kenjirō, and et al. *Zuroku Akita ranga.* 2 vols. San'ichi Shobō, 1974.

Kuroda Genji. *Edo senryū.* 2d ed. Tōkyō Bijutsu Shuppansha, 1972.

———. *Shiba Kōkan.* Tōkyō Bijutsu Shuppansha, 1972.

de Lairesse, Gérarde. *The Art of Painting in All Its Branches.* Trans. John Fitsch. London: 1783.

Landis, David S. *Revolution in Time.* Cambridge, Mass.: Harvard University Press, 1983.

Lane, Richard. *Images of the Floating World: The Japanese Print.* Oxford: Oxford University Press, 1978.

Lavater, Jean Gaspard. *Essai sur la physiogonomie* [sic] *destiné à faire connoitre l'homme et à le faire aimer.* 3 vols. The Hague, 1783.

Lee, Julian J. "The Origin and Development of Japanese Landscape Print: A Study of the Synthesis of Eastern and Western Art." Ph.D. diss., Univ. of Washington, 1977.

Legge, James, trans. *The Texts of Taoism.* Sacred Books of the East, ed. Max Müller, vols. 39–40. Oxford: Oxford University Press, 1891.

Leup, Gary P. *Servants, Shophands and Laborers in the Cities of Tokugawa Japan.* Princeton, N.J.: Princeton University Press, 1992.

Leutner, Robert W. *Shikitei Sanba and the Comic Tradition in Edo Fiction.* Cambridge, Mass.: Harvard University Press, 1985.

Luyendijk-Elshout, A. M. " 'Ontleedinge' (Anatomy) as Underlying Principle of Western Medicine in Japan." In *Red-Hair Medicine: Dutch-Japanese Medical Relations,* ed. H. Beukers et al., 27–36. Amsterdam and Atlanta, Ga.: Rodopi, 1991.

Markus, Andrew L. "The Carnival of Edo: 'Misemono' from Contemporary Accounts." *Harvard Journal of Asiatic Studies* 45 (1985): 499–541.

Maruyama Ōkyo-ten. Zenkoku Jitsugyō linkai, *Marugama Ōkyo-ten*. Hyōgo Kenitsu Rekishikan, 1994.

Massarella, Derek. *A World Elsewhere: Europe's Encounter with Japan in the Sixteenth and Seventeenth Centuries*. New Haven and London: Yale University Press, 1990.

Matsudaira Sadanobu. *Taikan Zakki*. In *Zoku-Nihon Zuihitsu taisei*, ed. Mori Senzō et al., 6:11–253. Yoshikawa Kōbunkan, 1980.

Matsuki Hiroshi. *Tsutaya Jūsaburō: Edo geijutsu no enshutsuka*. Nihon Keisai Shinbunsha, 1988.

McCullough, Helen Craig (trans.). *The Tale of the Heike*. Stanford, CA: Stanford University Press, 1988.

Minagawa Kien. *Kien bunshū*. In *Kien Shibunshū, Kinsei jūka bunshū shūsei*, ed. Takahashi Hiromi, 9: 3–56. Perikansha, 1986.

———. *Shahon: Kien bunshū shōroku*, in ibid., 9:364–444.

Mitamura Engyō. "Ningyō shibai to nō." *Mitamura Engyō zenshū*, ed. Mori Senzō et al., 11:127–328. 28 vols. Chūō Kōronsha, 1977.

Mizuno Minoru. *Santō Kyōden no kibyōshi*. Yūkō Shobo, 1976.

Mody, N. H. N. *A Collection of Nagasaki Prints and Paintings*. Tokyo and Rutland, Vt.: Tuttle, 1969.

Mootori Norinaga. "Ga no koto." In *Nihon garon taikan*, ed. Sakazaki Tan, 1:190–5. Arusu, 1927.

Mori Senzō. "Ōtsuki Bansui no Ranjin hōmon." In *Mori Senzō chōsaku-shū*, 5:266–77. Chūō Kōronsha, 1988.

———. "Kaigai chishiki de shukō o tateta kibyōshi." In *Mori Senzō chōsaku-shū*, 10:264–71. Chūō Kōronsha, 1989.

Morishima Chūryō. *Hōgu-kago*. In *Zoku-Enseki jusshū*, ed. Mori Senzō, 2: 165–79. Chūō Kōronsha, 1970.

———. "Komo zatsuwa." In *Bunmei genryū sōsho*, 1:454–86. Kokusho Kankōkai, 1913.

Morishita Misako. *Edo no biishiki: seijō suru toshi to 'onna kodomo'*. Shin'yōsha, 1988.

Morris, Ivan, trans. & intro. *Life of an Amorous Woman*. Norfolk, Conn.: New Directions, 1963.

———, trans. *Life of an Amorous Man*. London: Chapman & Hall, 1963.

Moxon, Joseph. *Practical Perspective, or Perspective Made Easy*. London: 1680.

Munesaki Isoo. "Tachibana Nankei 'Seiyū-ki' to Edo kōki no kikō bungaku." In *Azumaji no ki, Kishi kikō, Seiyū-ki*, ed. Munesaki Isoo, 437–55. Shin koten bungaku taikei. Iwanami Shoten, 1991.

Murase, Mieko. *Iconography of the 'Tale of Genji'*. New York and Tokyo: Weatherhill, 1983.

Nagaoka Hiruo. *Nihon no megane*. Tōhō Shobō, 1967.

Najita, Tetsuo. *Visions of Virtue in Tokugawa Japan: The Kaitokudō Merchant Academy*. Chicago and London: University of Chicago Press, 1987.

Nakai, Kate Wildman. *Shogunal Politics: Arai Hakuseki and the Premises of Tokugawa Rule. Harvard East Asian Monographs*, vol. 134. Cambridge, Mass.: Harvard University Press, 1988.

Nakai Shōtarō. *Shiba Kōkan*. Atoriesha, 1942.

Nakajima Sando. "Funsui-ki no genkei 'honteiki.' " *Nihon rekishi* 6 (1978): 47–9.

Nakamura Yukihiko. *Gesaku-ron. Nakamura Yukihiko chōbetsu-shu*. 2d ed. Vol. 8. Chūō Kōronsha, 1982.

Nakano Misao. "Kenbikyō ni tsuite no wagakuni no saisho no bunken." *Idan* 9 (1957): 1659–63.

Nakano Mitsutoshi. *Gesaku kenkyū*. Chūō Kōronsha, 1981.

———. "Edo no yūri." In *Kyōden, Ikkyū, Shunsui*, ed. Jinbō Kazuya, 121–39. Zusetsu Nihon no koten. Shūeisha, 1989.

Nakano Yoshio. *Shiba Kōkan kō*. Shinchōsha, 1986.

Nakau Ei. *Oranda-gonomi*. Satobumi Shuppan, 1984.

Nakayama Kōyō. "Gadan keiroku." In *Nihon gadan taikan*, ed. Sakazaki Tan, 1:842–76. Arusu, 1927.

Narazaki Muneshige. *Genoba bijutsukan. Hizō ukiyo-e taikan*, vol. 6. Kōdansha, 1989.

———. *Hizō ukiyo-e taikan, bekkan*. Kōdansha, 1989.

Naruse Fujio. *Shiba Kōkan. Genshoku Nihon no bijutsu*, vol. 25. Shūeisha, 1977.

———. "Edo jidai no yōfūga no Fuji-zu ni tsuite." In *Nihon yōgakushi no kenkyū*, ed. Arizaka Takamichi, 4:95–136. 1982.

———. "Shiba Kōkan no ukiyo-eshi jidai ni tsuite." *Ukiyo-e geijutsu* 73 (1982): 3–23.

Naruse Fujio et al. *Shiba Kōkan zenshū*. 8 vols. Yatsuzaka Shobō, 1992.

Neuer, Roni, and Yoshida Susumu. *Ukiyo-e: 250 years of Japanese Art*. London: Studio Editions, 1990.

Nihon Ishi Gakkai, ed. *Zuroku Nihon iji bunka shiryō shūsei*. 5 vols. San'ichi Shobō, 1977.

Nihon Iji Gakkai, ed. *Zuroku Nihon iji bunka shiryō shūsei*, 6 vols. San'ichi Shobō, 1978.

Niimura Shitsu. "Kaisetsu." *Nanban, kōmō shiryō*, 1:18–24. Shinbundō, 1930.

Nishida, Hiroko. "A History of Japanese Porcelain and the Export Trade." In Japan Society, *The Burghley House Porcelains*, 63–8. New York: Japan Society, 1986.

Nishimura Tei. " 'Seiyō gadan' no chōsha Takamori Kankō." *Ukiyo-e shi* 16 (1930): 2–5.

———. *Nihon dōbanga shi*. 2d ed. Zenkoku Shobō, 1967.

Nishiyama, Shigeru. *A History of Japanese Astronomy*. Harvard-Yenching Monographs. Cambridge, Mass.: Harvard University Press, 1969.

Nishiyama Shonosuke. *Edo, 3. Edo jidai zushi*, vol. 6. Chikuma Shobō, 1975.

Nishiyama Shōnosuke et al., eds. *Edogaku jiten*, 2nd ed. Kōbunkan, 1994.

Nobuhiro Shinji. " 'Komon shinpō' eiin to chūyaku." *Edo bungaku* 3 (1990): 119–60.

Nonogami Keiichi. *Nagasaki ko-hanga*. Taigendō, 1960.

O-Edo omoshiro yakushoku jiten. Rekishi Yomihon Special, 1991.

Ogawa Kenzaburō. *Nihon gankagaku shi*. 2d ed. Shibunkaku, 1971.

Ogilby, John, trans. *Atlas Japannensi: Being Remarkable Addresses by Way of Embassy from the East-India Company of the United Provinces to the Emperor of Japan*. London, 1670.

Oka Yasumasa. " 'Bankan-zu' no shomondai." In *Pari kokuritsu toshokan*, vol. 8 *Hizō ukiyo-e taikan*: ed. Narazaki Muneshige, 8:238–45. Kōdansha, 1989.

———. *Megane-e shinkō*. Chikuma Shobō, 1992.

Okado Toshiyuki. " 'Kage' to shōzō." *Nihon no bigaku* 21 (1994):132–62.

Okamoto Hiroshi. *Kaibōgaku kotohajime: Yamawaki Tōyō no hito to shisō*. Dōseisha, 1988.

Okamura Chibiki. *Kōmō bunka shiwa*. Sōgensha, 1953.

Okitsu Kaname. *Edo senryū*. Jiji Tsūshinsha, 1990.

Oku Bunmei. *Sensai Maruyama-sensei den*. In Mori Senzō, "Maruyama Ōkyo den tōki." *Bijutsu kenkyū* 36 (1934):584–93.

Onishi Hiroshi et al., trans. and supp. *Geijutsuka densetsu*. Perikansha, 1989.

Ono Tadashige. *Garasu-e to doro-e*. Kawade Shobō Shinsha, 1990.

Ono Takeo. *Edo no hakurai fūzoku-shi. Edo fūzoku shiryō*, vol. 10. Tenpōsha, 1975.

Ooms Herman. *Tokugawa Ideology: Early Constructs, 1570–1680*. Princeton, N.J.: Princeton University Press, 1985.

Ōtsubo Motoji. *Megane no rekishi*. Nihon Meganesha Kumiai Rengōkai, 1960.

Ōtsuki Gentaku. "Keiei yawa." In *Yōgaku*, ed. Numada Jirō et al., 2:245–90. 2 vols. Nihon shisō taikei. Iwanami Shoten, 1976.

———. "Kyōi no gen." In *Yōgaku*, ed. Numada Jirō et al., 1:227–90. 2 vols. Nihon shisō taikei. Iwanami Shoten, 1976.

———. "Rangaku kaitei." *Yōgaku* 1:317–71. ed. Numada Jirō et al., 2 vols. Nihon shisō taikei. Iwanami Shoten, 1976.

———. "Ranyaku teikō." In *Yōgaku*, ed. Numada Jiro and et al., 1:373–400. 2 vols. Nihon shisō taikei. Iwanami Shoten, 1976.

Ōtsuki Gentaku, and Arima Genshō. "Ransetsu benwaku." In *Oranda-banashi, Ransetsu benwaku*, 133–319, 21–53. Edo kagaku koten sōsho. Inawa Shoten, 1979. Facsimile and transcription.

Ōtsuki Gentaku, and Kimura Kōkyō. "Kankai ibun." In *Hyōryū kidan zenshū*, 22:387–694. Teikoku bunko. Hakubunkan, 1900.

Qianlong, [Gaozong]. *Luoshan chuanji dingben. Qing Gaozong yuzhi shiwen quanji*, vol. 1. Taipei: Guoli Gugong Lowuyuan, 1976.

Ravina, Mark. "Wasan and the Physics that Wasn't." *Monumenta Nipponica* 48 (1993): 205–24.

Rokujūen [Ishikawa Masamochi]. "Hida no Takumi monogatari." In *Yomihon-shū*, 915–1037. Nihon Meichō Zenshū Kankōkai, 1927.

Rosenfield, John M. "The Unity of the Three Creeds as Theme in Japanese Ink Painting of the Fifteenth Century." In *Japan in the Muromachi Age*, ed. John Whitney Hall and Takeshi Toyoda, 183–204. Berkeley, Los Angeles, London: University of California Press, 1977.

Rubinger, Richard. *Private Academies in Tokugawa Japan*. Princeton, N.J.: Princeton University Press, 1982.

Ryūtei Tanehiko. "Edo chiri hiroi." In *Enseki jisshū*, eds. Mon Senzō et al., 5:395–407. Chūō Kōronsha, 1986.

Saitō Gesshin et al. *Edo meisho zue*. 4 vols. Yūhōdō Shoten, 1927.

Saitō Ryūzō. *Gadai jiten*. 2 vols. Kokusho Kaikōkai, 1975.

Sakai, Naoki. *Voices of the Past: The Status of Language in Eighteenth-Century Japanese Discourse*. Ithaca and New York: Cornell University Press, 1992.

Sakazaki Tan [Shizuka]. *Nihon garon taikan*. 2 vols. Arusu, 1927.

Santo Kyōden. "Matsu to ume taketori monogatari." In *Zōkō Kyōden, Sanba kessaku-shū*, ed. Ohashi Shintarō, 843–921. Teikoku bunko. Hakubunkan, 1902.

———. Edo umare uwaki no kabayaki. In *Edo no gesaku ehon*. ed. Koike Masatane et al., 2:149–78. Gendai kyoiku bunko. Shakai Shisōsha 1981.

———. "Shinpan kawarimashite dochū Sukeroku." In *Santō Kyōden*, ed. Yamamoto Harufumi, 73–104. Shiriizu Edo gesaku. Ōfūsha, 1987.

———. "Mukashi-banashi inazuma-byōshi." In *Yome manjū no hajimari, Shikake bunko, Mukashi-banashi inazuma-byōshi*, ed. Mizuno Minoru, 85: 149–362. Shin Nihon koten bungaku taikei. Iwanami Shoten, 1990.

Sasaki Jōhei. "Ōkyo kankei shiryō *Banji* bassui." *Bijutsushi* 111 (1981): 46–60.

———. *Ōkyo shasei gashū*. Kōdansha, 1981.

———. "Maruyama Ōkyo no kaigaron: 'Banji' o chūshin ni shite." *Kyoto daigaku bungaku-bu bigaku bijutsushi-gaku kenkyushitsu kenkyu kiyō* 3 (1982): 1–27.

Sasaki Seiichi. *Nihon kindai bijutsu-ron: yōfū-ga konseputo to materiaru o megutte*. Ruri Shobō, 1988.

Sasama Yoshihiko. *Edo bakufu yakushoku shūsei*. 2d ed. Ozankaku, 1990.

Satake Shōnosuke, ed. *Haifū: Yanagi-daru*. vol 6. Kyoiku bunko. Shakai Shisōsha, 1985.

Satake Shozan [Yoshiatsu]. "Gahō kōryō." In *Nihon garon taikan*. ed. Sakazaki Tan, 1:100–2. Arusu, 1927.

———. "Gazu rikai." In *Nihon garon taikan*, ed. Sakazaki Tan, 1:102–3. Arusu, 1927.

Satchell, Thomas. *Hizakurige, or Shanks' Mare*. Rutland, Vt., and Tokyo: Tuttle, 1960.

Satō Narihiro [Chūryō]. "Chūryō manroku." In *Nihon zuihitsu taisei* 32:22–335. Yoshikawa Kōbunkan, 1929.

Satō Yōjin. *Haifū: Yanagi-daru*. Vol. 10 Kyōiku bunko. Shakai Shisōsha, 1988.

Schama, Simon. *Patriots and Liberators: Revolution in the Netherlands, 1770–1813*. 2d ed. New York: Vintage, 1977.

———. *The Embarrassment of Riches: An Interpretation of Dutch Culture of the Golden Age*. New York: Knopf, 1987.

Screech, Timon. "Kunisada's Ghosts and Late Edo-period Natural History Illustration." *Transactions of the International Conference of Orientalists in Japan* 34 (1989): 100–15.

———. "Ran'i to Edo no e." *Kokubungaku* 35 (1990): 64–70.

———. "Edo no kokoro no Rondon-dokei." *Edo bunkagu* 7 (1991): 12–37.

———. "The Strangest Place in Edo: The Temple of the Five-Hundred Arhats." *Monumeta Nipponica* 48 (1993): 407–28.

———. "The Meaning of Western Perspective in Edo Popular Culture." *Archives of Asian Art* 47 (1994): 58–69.

———. *Ō-Edo no ijin ōrai*, trans. Takayama Hiroshi. Maruzen Shoten, 1995.

Seidensticker, Edward G., trans. *The Tale of Genji*. 2 vols. London: Secker & Warburg, 1976.

Seigel, Celia Segawa. *Yoshiwara: The Glittering World of the Japanese Courtesan*. Honololu: University of Hawai'i Press, 1993.

Shiba Kōkan. "Shunparō hikki." *Nihon zuihitsu taisei* 11:395–467. Yoshikawa Kōbunkan, 1928.

———. "Tenchi ridan." In *Shiba Kōkan*, ed. Nakai Sōtarō, 209–53. Atoriesha, 1942.

———. "Oranda tensetsu." In *Yōgaku*, ed. Numada Jirō et al., 2:445–88. Nihon shisō taikei. Iwanami Shoten, 1976.

———. "Oranda tsūhaku." In *Yōgaku*, ed. Numada Jirō et al., 2:497–540. Nihon shisō taikei. Iwanami Shoten, 1976.

———. "Seiyō gadan." In *Yōgaku*, ed. Numada Jirō et al. 2:489–97. Nihon shisō taikei. Iwanami Shoten, 1976.

———. "Junmō gakai-shū." In *Junmō gakai-shū, Mugen Dōjin hikki*, 1–204. Tōyō bunko. Heibonsha, 1977.

———. "Mugen Dōjin zakki." In *Junmō gakai-shū, Mugen Dōjin zakki,* 205–301. Tōyō bunko. Heibonsha, 1977.

———. *Kōkan saiyū nikki.* Tōyō bunko vol. 461. Heibonsha, 1986.

Shiba Zenko. "Kappa ō-botoke ryaku engi." *Edo jidai bunka,* 17:375–80. Edo Jidai Bunka Kenkyūkai, 1927.

Shikitei, Sanba. "Hitogokoro nozoki-karakuri." In *Sanba kessaku-shū,* ed. Ohashi Shintarō, 23:661–95. Teikoku bunko. Hakubunkan, 1893.

———. "Hayakawari mune no karakuri." In *Shikitei Sanba kessaku-shū,* ed. Ohashi Shintarō, 627–59. Teikoku bunko. Hakubunkan, 1912.

———. "Ukiyo-doko." In *Sharebon, kokkeibon, ninjōbon.* ed. Jinbo Kazuya, 255–372. Nihon koten bungaku zenshū. Shōgakkan, 1971.

Shimozawa Gō, and Hirose Hideo. "Tenmon yashiki no kenchiku ni tsuite." *Rangaku shiryō kenkyū* 250 (1971): 280–9.

Shinoda Akira. *Kikyū no rekishi.* Kodansha gendai shinsho. Kōdansha, 1977.

Shirayama Sekiya. *Megane no shakaishi.* Daiyamondosha, 1990.

Siebold Council Stichting, ed. *Yoroppa ni miru Nihon no takara: Shiiboruto korekushon* (exhibition catalogue). Bungei Shunjū, 1990.

Smith, Henry D. II. *Hokusai: One Hundred Views of Mt. Fuji.* New York: George Braziller, 1988.

———. "World Without Walls: Kuwagata Keisai's Panoramic Vision." In *Japan and the World,* ed. Gail Bernstein and Haruhito Fukui, 3–19. London: Macmillan, 1988.

Stafford, Barbara Maria. *Body Criticism: Imaging the Unseen in Enlightenment Art and Medicine.* Cambridge, Mass., and London: MIT Press, 1991.

Stanley-Baker, Joan. *The Transmission of Chinese Idealist Painting to Japan.* Ann Arbor: Center for Japanese Studies, University of Michigan, 1992.

Statler, Oliver. *The Black Ship Scroll.* Rutland, Vt., and Tokyo: Tuttle, 1963.

Stevens, John. *Zenga: Brushstrokes of Enlightenment* (exhibition catalogue). New Orleans: New Orleans Museum of Art, 1990.

Stubbs, David C., and Masanori Takatsuka, trans. *This Scheming World.* 2d ed. Rutland, Vt., and Tokyo: Tuttle, 1973.

Sugano Yō. *Nihon dōbanga no kenkyū.* Bijutsu Shuppansha, 1974.

———. "Kaisetsu." In *Junmō gakai-shū, Mugen Dōjin kikki,* 313–28. Tōyō bunko. Heibonsha, 1977.

Sugimoto Tsutomu. *Zuroku 'Rangaku kotohajime.'* Waseda Daigaku Shuppanbu, 1985.

Sugita, Genpaku. "Rangaku kotohajime." In *Taion-ki, Oritaku shiba no ki, Rantō kotohajime,* ed. Odaka Toshio and Matsumura Akira, 473–516. Nihon koten bungaku taikei. Iwanami Shoten, 1964.

———. *Nochimi-gusa.* In *Nihon shōmin seikatsu shiryō shūsei,* ed. Sekiya Haku, 7:55–86. San'ichi Shobō, 1970.

———. "Oranda iji mondo." In *Yōgaku,* ed. Numada Jirō et al., 1:183–226. Nihon shisō taikei. Iwanami Shoten, 1976.

Sugita Genpaku, Maeno Ryotaku, and Nakagawa Jun'an. "Kaitai shinsho." In *Yōgaku,* ed. Numada Jirō et al., 1:207–318. Nihon shisō taikei. Iwanami Shoten, 1972.

Suntory Museum. *Nihon hakubutsugaku kotohajime: egakareta shizen.* Suntory Museum, 1987.

Suzuki Hiroshi. "Tokei-zu no shoryō." *Za Anteiku* 5 (1989): 73–7.

Suzuki Hisashi. *Zōjō-ji: Tokugawa shōgun hi to sono zuihin, zuitai.* University of Tokyo Press, 1967.

Suzuki Jūzō. *Ehon to ukiyo-e.* Bijutsu Shuppansha, 1979.

Suzuki Kazuyoshi. "Edo no karakuri ningyō: chie to gijutsu o fukugen shite." *Tobako to shio hakubutsukan kenkyū kiyō.* 3:35–52. Tobacco and Salt Museum, 1991.

Suzuki Kuranosuke, ed. *Haifū: Yanagi-daru.* vol. 3. Kyōiku bunko. Shakai Shisōsha, 1985.

Swammerdam, Jean. *Histoire générale des insectes.* Utrecht, 1682.

Swammerdam, John. *The Book of Nature, or the History of Insects.* Trans. Thomas Flloyd. Expanded ed. 2 vols. London, 1758.

Swift, Jonathan. *Tale of a Tub.* 2d ed. Oxford: Oxford University Press, 1958.

Tachibana Nankei. "Hokusō sadan." In *Tōzai yūki, Hokusō sadan,* 1–207. Yūhōdō Shoten, 1913.

———. "Seiyū-ki." In *Tōsai yūki,* ed. Munesaki Isoo, 2 vols. Tōyō bunko vols 248–9. Heibonsha, 1974.

Tachibana no Narisue. *Kokon chōmon-shū*. In *Nihon katen bungaku taikei*, eds. Nagasumi Yasuaki and Shimado Isao. Iwanami Shoten, 1963.

Tachihara Suiken. "Yūrin zatsuwa." In *Nanban kōmō shiryō*, 1:1–46. 2 vols. Shinmonkan, 1930.

Tagadani Kanchūsen. "Karakuri kinmō kagami-gusa." In *Edo kagaku koten sōsho* ed. Kimura Toshiyuki, 3:13–84, 5–12. Inawa Shuppan, 1978. Facsimile and transcription.

Takahashi Hiromi et al. *Tsutaya Jūsaburō no shigoto*. Taiyō Bessatsu: *Nihon no kokoro* 89. Heibonsha, 1995.

Takamori Kankō. "Seiyō gadan." In *Zuihitsu bungaku senshū* 2:345–72. Shōsaisha, 1927.

Takanashi Seima. *Karakuri ningyō bunkashi*. Gakugei Shōrin, 1990.

Takayama Hiroshi. *Kuro ni someru: honchō pikucharesuku kotohajime*. Arina Shobō, 1989.

Takeuchi, Melinda. *Taiga's True Views: The Language of Landscape Painting in Eighteenth-Century Japan*. Stanford, Calif.: Stanford University Press, 1992.

Takizawa Bakin. "Kiryo manroku." *Nihon zuihitsu taisei* 11:137–256. Yoshikawa Kōbunkan, 1975.

Tanahashi Masahiro. *Kibyōshi sōran*. *Nihon shoshigaku taikei*, vol. 48 (1–4). Seishōdō Shoten, 1989.

Tanaka Yūko. *Edo no sōzōroku*. Chikuma Shobō, 1988.

———. *Edo wa nettowaku*. Heibonsha, 1993.

Tanemura Suehiro. "Nozoki-karakuri no toposu." In *Hako-nuke karakuri kidan*, ed. Tanemura Suehiro, 42–56. Kawade Shobō Shinsha, 1991.

Tani Bunchō. "Bunchō gadan." *Nihon shogaen* 2:182–235. Kokusho Kankōkai, 1915.

Tani Minezō. *Asobi no dezain*. Iwasaki Bijutsu Shuppansha, 1984.

———. *Edo no kopiraita*. Iwasaki Bijutsu Shuppansha, 1986.

Tanomura Chikuden. "Sanchūjin jōsetsu." In *Chikuden garon*, pp. 40–230. Kasama sensho. Kasama Shoin, 1984.

Tatsukawa Shōji. *Karakuri*. Mono to ningen no bunkashi, vol. 3. Hōsei Daigaku Shuppankyoku, 1969.

Terajima Ryōan. *Wakan sansai zue*. 2 vols. Tōkyō Bijutsu Shuppansha, 1982.

Teramoto Kaiyū. *Nagasaki-bon: Nanban, kōmō jiten* Keisōsha, 1974.

Teraoka, Yasutaka. "The Pleasure Quarters in Tokugawa Culture." In *Eighteenth Century Japan*, ed. C. Andrew Gerstle, 3–32. North Sydney: Allen & Unwin Australia, 1989.

Thomas, Keith. *Man and the Natural World*. New York: Pantheon, 1983.

Thunberg, Charles. *Thunberg's Travels*. Trans. F. Rimington and C. Rimington. 4 vols. London, 1795.

Titsingh, Isaac. *Illustrations of Japan*. Trans. Frederick Shoberl. London, 1812.

Tobacco and Salt Museum (ed). *Edo no mekanizumu*. *Tabako to shio hakubutsukan kenkyū kiyō*. vol. 3. Tobacco and Salt Museum, 1981.

Toby, Ronald P. *State and Diplomacy in Early Modern Japan: Asia in the Development of the Tokugawa Bakufu*. 2d ed. Stanford, Calif:. Stanford University Press, 1991.

Tozawa Yukio. *Katsuragawa-ke no sekai: Edo geien no kiun*. Chikuma Shobō, 1994.

Toyama Mikio. *Nagasaki bugyō*. Chūko shinsho, vol. 905. Chūō Kōronsha, 1988.

Tsuji Nobuo. *Kiso no keifū*. Perikansha, 1988.

Tsukahara, Tōgō. *Affinity and Shinwa Roku: Introduction of Western Chemical Concepts in Early Nineteenth-Century Japan*. Amsterdam: J. C. Gieben, 1993.

Tsukamoto Manabu. "Mushi o miru me no rekishi." *Shakaishi kenkyū* 6 (1985): 37–87.

Tsunoyama Sakae. *Tokei no shakaishi*. Chūko shinsho, vol. 715. Chūō Kōronsha, 1984.

Uda Toshihiko, ed. *Mansai kyōka-shū*. 2 vols. Kyōiku bunko. Shakai Shisōsha, 1990.

Ueda, Makoto. *Literary and Art Theories in Japan*. Cleveland: Cleveland State University Press, 1967.

———. "The Taxonomy of Sequence: Basic Patterns of Structure in Premodern Japanese Literature." In *Principles of Classical Japanese Literature*, ed. Earl Miner, 63–105. Princeton, N.J.: Princeton University Press, 1985.

Ueno, Masuzō. *Nihon hakubutsugaku shi*. Kōdansha gakujutsu bunko. Kōdansha, 1989.

van der Velde, Paul, trans. and ed. *The Dejima Dagregisters: Their Original Tables of Contents*. 7

vols. Leiden: Centre for the History of European Expansion, 1990–3.

Volker, T. *The Japanese Porcelain Trade of the Dutch East-India Company after 1683.* Leiden: Brill, 1959.

Wakabayashi, Bob Tadashi. *Anti-Foreignism and Western Learning in Early-Modern Japan: The 'New Theses' of 1825.* Cambridge, Mass.: Harvard University Press, 1986.

Waley, Arthur. *The Nō Plays of Japan.* London: Allen & Unwin, 1921.

Watanabe Keiichi. *Akita-jō monogatari.* Akita: Mumeisha Shuppan, 1989.

Watanabe Toshio. *Kinsei Nihon tenmongaku-shi.* 2 vols. Kōseisha Kōseikaku, 1984.

Wayman, Alex. "The Mirror as a Pan-Buddhist Metaphor-Simile." *History of Religions* 14 (1974): 251–69.

Wheatland, David P. *Early Science at Harvard: Innovators and Their Instruments, 1765–1865.* Cambridge, Mass.: Fogg Art Museum, 1969.

Yagi Keiichi, ed. *Haifū: Yanagi-daru.* Kyoiku bunko Shakai Shisōsha, 1985.

Yagi Kiyoharu. "Keiken jitsugaku no tenkai." In *Nihon no Kinsei,* ed. Rai Kiichi, 13:175–214. Chūō Kōronsha, 1993.

Yamaguchi Ryōji. *Nihon no tokei.* 2d ed. Nihon Ryōronsha, 1950.

Yamamoto Harufumi. *Santō Kyōden.* Shiriizu Edo gesaku. Ifūsha, 1987.

Yamamoto Keiichi. *Edo no kage-e asobi.* Shoshisha, 1988.

Yamanaka Kōryō. *Suna-barai.* 2d ed. 2 vols. Iwanami bunko, Iwanami Shoten 1987.

Yamori Kazuhiko. *Kochizu to fūkei.* Chikuma Shobō, 1984.

Yasue Ryōsuke, ed. *Kokusho sōmokuroku,* 8 vols. 2nd ed. Iwanami Shoten. 1991.

Yasuda Gōzō. "Hokusai no kibyōshi, pt. 4." *Ukiyo-e geijutsu* 43 (1974): 18–29.

INDEX

[Numbers set in bold refer to illustrations.]

Akisato Ritō, 29, 44, 67, 68; *Miyako rinsen meisho zue*, 282n22; *Settsu meisho zue*, **25–26**, 29, 67, **69**, **76–77**, 77–78, 118, **119**, **218–219**
anatomy, *see* medicine
An Geikin, 167
Ando Hiroshige, *see* Utagawa Hiroshige
Aoki Shurin, 213
Arab culture, 221
Araki Gen'yū, 157
Arima Genshō, 21, **57**, 111, 225; *see also* Ōtsuki Gentaku: *Ransetsu benwaku*
Asakura Shijin, **19**
Asakusa, 29, 70, 91, 109, **112–113**, 121, 127, 130, 182, 190, 194
Asasean Eiki, 202
asobi (play), 22
astromony, 213, 235–237, 249, 284n85; in China, 237; *see also* Copernicus

Bajima School, 167
Bashō, *see* Matsuo Bashō
Brazil, 85
Buddhism, 23, 27–28, 46, 89, 109, 110, 118, 151, 158, 161, 164, 177, 192, 212, 222–224, 233, 237–238; Buddhist statues, **90**, 240–244, 247, 253, 285n106; Edo's Great Buddha, 244–246, **247**, **248**, 285n116, 286n120&127; Ōbaku, 90; parodies of, 89–90, **92–93**; Pure Land, 239–240, 242; Vulture Peak, 223–224, 228, **229**, **243**, 247, 283n69
Ban Kōkei, 213
Blaeu, Willem, 237
bunjin (literati), 54, 216, 280n92
Burgh (VOC vessel), 12
Buys, Egbert, 45, **46**, 48, 50, 53, 75, **75**, 107, 249, 262n64

calendars, 235–237; Kansei Calendar, **49**, **214**, 236, 237, 252, 284n89&95
camera obscura, 56–60, **57–69**, 172, 264n109
Canaletto, Antonio Canale, 97, 103
Catherine the Great, of Russia, 69, 134
Charles II, of England, 9, 14
China, 22, 32; Chinese, 15, 34, 46, 76; Chinese art, 103, **155**; fall of the Ming, 9; trade with Japan, 9, 68, 181, 255n17; trade with the West, 9, 11, 67, 79, 155; *see also* Qianglong
Chōkōsai Eishō, 51, **51**, 148; *Kadotama-ya Wakamurasaki*, **148**
Chomel, Noël, 71
Christianity, 9, 15, 85, 237–238, 285n100
Chūryō, *see* Morishima Chūryō
Chūshingura, 23, 126, 177
clocks, 8, 26, 47, 61, 67, 78–80, **154**, 183, **185**, 203, 224, 249; 'clock-grass', 85, **85**, 268n94&97; cost of, 267n83; first in Japan, 79; 'London' clocks, 79, 80, 131–132, 154; time telling, 26–28, 79–80, 267n74
clockwork, 66–67, 78–93, 129, 249; clockwork ships, 91–93
Cole, Benjamin, 251
Confucianism, 42–43, 46
Copernicus, Nicolaus, 149, 247, 249, 286n134
copperplate printing, 8, 89, 95–106, 154, 162, 168, 217, 220, 274n17
Crans, Jan, 142

Daikoku-ya Kōdayū, 69, 72, 75, 90, 134, 135; *see also* Russia
devil lantern, *see* viewing machines
Dodonaeus, Rembertus, 95, **96**
Dong Qichang, 54
Dutch East India Company, *see* VOC
Dutch language, *see* language, Dutch

Edo, flavour of, 21–22, 180; Edoites, 18, 32, 90; Edo Castle, 215; Edo youth, 145, 146; Edo women, 148; Great Buddha, 244–246; shrunk in size, 209, 246
England, *see* Great Britain
English East India Company, 8, 11–12, 254n7
erekiteru, see static-electricity generator

fishbowls, 145–149, **146, 147, 148**
Floating World, 22–24, 84, 89, 130, 144, 145, 162, 192, 208, 211, 236; pictures of, 28–29, 83, 104, 148, 162, 191, 232; *see also asobi*
flying machines, 224–225; *see also* hot air balloons
France, 33, 34, 67, 79, 80, 97, 103, 107, 238; Paris, 201, 225; Paris compared to Osaka, 78
Franklin, Benjamin, 44
Freith, Arend, 141
Fuinsai, 102
Fujiwara Takamitsu, 217
Fukuoka Sadaaki, 203
Fukuzawa Yukichi, 41–42, 43
Furukawa Koshōken, 62

Genji monogatari, 64, 65
George II, of England, 249
glass, 8, 29–30, 133–165, **135, 155**, 172, 182, 183, 232, 241; bottling, 137–144, **138–139, 140, 141, 142, 143, 145**; glass pictures, 30, 106, 115, **135, 156**, 152–157, 182; glass ships, 91; glass windows, 134–136, 152, 181, 220; receptacles, 136–144, **146, 147, 148, 188**; *see also* mirrors
glasses, *see* spectacles
Gotō Rishun, 21, 43, 46, 137, 152, 158, 191, 194
Gototei Kunisada, *see* Utagawa Kunisada
Graff, Nicholas de, 12
Graham, George, 249
Gravesande, Gulielmo s', 107
Great Britain, 9, 33, 34, 39, 48, 67, 79, 80, 101, 121, 134, 154–155, 228; London, 48, 79, 97, **99, 101**, 102, 103, 106, 127, 132, 134, 172, 228, 251; *see also* English East India Company, Charles II, George II, 'London' clocks
Hakuin, 241–242
Hakusanjin Kakyo, 244

Harukawa Shuzan, **189**, 190
Harunobu, *see* Suzuki Harunobu
Harvard College, 251
Hasegawa Mitsunobu, 121, 124
Hasegawa Settan, **230–231, 245**
Hasegawa Settei, **230–231, 245**
Hatake no Dojin Maimosuke, *see* Kitao Shigemasa
Heike monogatari, 27, 126, 166, 172–173
Hekizentei Kunenbō, 23, 95; *Hade mezurashiki futatsu no utsuwa*, 51–52, **51**, 240; *Hōtsuki chōchin oshie no chikamichi*, 23, 51, 109–112, **110, 111**
Hemmij, Gijsbert, 185–187, 190, 275n48, 278n56
heterosexuality, 22, 85, 124, 171, 192, 232
Hida no Takumi, *see* Suminawa
Hidari Jingorō, 64
Hiraga Gennai, 17, 20, 21, 22–23, 46–48, 53, 89, 95, 104, 136, 142, 162, 168, 174, 183, 236; *Butsurui hinshitsu*, 137, 141, **142**; *Nenashi-gusa*, 146; *yakuhin-e*, 97, 137, 141, 144
Hirokawa Kai, 33, 34, 43, 56, 61, 63, 70, 72, 141, 154, **154**, 158
Hitomi Shōu, 224
Hoashi Banri, 42, 44, 261n41
Hokusai, *see* Katsushika Hokusai
homosexuality, 21, 100, 196, 232, 233–234, 258n75
honda (hairstyle), 105, 106, 189
Honda Toshiaki, 33, 34, 42, 43, 91, 135, 223, 236
Hoogstraten, Samuel van, 119, **120**
Hōseidō Kisanji, 28, 130, 182, 222
Hoshū, *see* Katsuragawa Hoshū
Hosokawa Hanzō, 78, 82, **83**, 85
Hosokawa Shigekata, 141, 142, 150–151; *Mōkai kikan*, **140**, 141, **141**
hot-air balloons, 21, 37, 50, 225–228, **226, 227, 229**; *see also* flying machines

Ichiba Tsūshō, *Sokuseki mimi gakumon*, 281n15; *Tenjiku mōke no tsuji*, 238, **239**
Ichida Seishichirō, 91
Ichikawa Danjūrō IV, 174
Ichikawa Danjūrō V, 173–175, 180, 211, 279n62
Ichiyanagi Kagen, **14, 154**
Iemitsu (3rd Tokugawa shogun), 216
Iemochi (14th Tokugawa shogun), 132
Ieyasu (1st Tokugawa shogun), 79, 181, 237
Ihara Saikaku, 83, 268n105; *Kōshoku ichidai onna*, 286n133; *Kōshoku ichidai otoko*, 82–83; *Seken muna-zan'yō*, 89
Ike Taiga, 54
Imai Tanito, 222–223

Inaba Tsūryū, 80
Indonesia, 11, 12, **25**; Indonesians, 37, 61, 91, 170, 226
Ishikawa Tairō, 161, **161**, 169, **170**
Ishikawa Toyonobu, *see* Rokujūen
Ishizaki Yūshi, 157, 283n58
Italy, 34; Venice, 97, 103, 182
Iwasaki Kan'en, 171

Jesuits, 67, 95, 135, 237
Jinkō-ki, 38
Jippensha Ikku, 28, 29, 83, 109, 121, 126, 129, 179; as artist, **176**, **187**, **197**; *Mushi-megane nobe no wakakusa*, 196, **197**, 199; *Oranda kage-e otsuriki*, 107; *Shingaku tokei-gusa*, 84–85, **86–87**; *Taikei hōnen no mizuki*, 245–246; *Yome tōme kasa no uchi*, 176–177, **176**, 183, **187**, 189, 191
Jonstonus, Johannis, 10, 95, **96**

Kaempfer, Engelbert, 13–14, 33, 43, 157, 249, 254n7, 255n28, 256n34, 359n4
Kaitai shinsho, *see* Sugita Genpaku
Kakunen, 223
Kan Sazan, 224
Kanaoka, Kōsei no, 228–229
Kansei Calendar, *see* calendar
Kanwatei Onitake, 23, 258n82, 261n43; *Wakanran zatsuwa*, **35**, **36**, 35–37, **37**, **38**, 44, 46–48, 65, 226, **226**
Katsukawa Shun'ei, 238, **239**
Katsuki Masatsuna, 21, 225
Katsuragawa Hosan, 21, 257n62
Katsuragawa Hoshū, 18, 20, 22, 45, 69, 142, 169, 185, 194, 225; interrogates Daikokuya Kōdayū, 134, 136; *Kenbikyō yōhō*, 198; work on *Kaitai shinsho*, 88, 168, 241, 268n101
Katsushika Hokusai, 17, **19**, **35**, **36**, **37**, **38**, 35–41, 65, 202, **226**, 245; Great Bodhidharma images, 241–242, **243**; *Muna-zan'yō uso no tanaorishi*, 38–39, **39**; *Nana sato fuki*, 245–246, **247**; *Oranda gakyō*, 208–209; *Shin jinkō-ki*, 38; as writer, 29, 245, **247**
Kawano Yōji, 75
kibyoshi, definition of, 28; running covers to, 273n90
Kimura Kōgō, **251**, **252**
Kitagawa Tsukimaro, 107
Kitagawa Utamaro, 28, 29, 107, 109, 151–152, 162, 177, 180, 206, **207**, 211; *Canny One*, **188**; *Furyū-kō takara-awase*, 281n114; *'Glass' O-shima*, **151**; *Kyōkun oya no megane*, 183–194; *Woman with mini-peepbox*, **209**; *Woman with Pipe*, **178**
Kitao Masayoshi, 45, **45**, 182, **184–185**, **186**
Kitao Shigemasa (Hatake no Dojin Maimosuke), **25**, 28, 29, 89–90, **92–93**, 127, **128**, **145**, 146, **146**, **147**, 151, 182, **196**, **227**, 240, **241**; as fictionalist, 29, 227, **227**
Kō Ryōsai, 171–172, 277n26
Koikawa Harumachi, 28, 109, 182, 183, 278n53; *Kinkin sensei eiga no yume*, 104; *Muda iki*, 106
Koikawa Yukimachi, 182; *Sakaemasu megane no toku*, 182–183, 188, 190, 191
Kobayashi Jotei, 65–66, 91–93
Kodera Gyokuchō, 73, **74**, 91, 99–100, 152, 155, 164–165, **165**, 198
Kokkadō, 102
Koriki Takenobu, 242, **243**
Kubo Shunman, **29**, 29–30, 182
Kuki Shūzō, 171
Kulmus, Johannes, 89, 168, 169, 194, 241
Kunisada, *see* Utagawa Kunisada
Kunitora, *see* Utagawa Kunitora
Kurahashi Ra'ichiro, *see* Onitake
Kyōhō Reforms, 9, 10
Kyōden, *see* Santō Kyōden
kyōka, definition of, 25, 28
Kyokutei Bakin, *see* Takizawa Bakin
Kyorori, 89, 244; *Isshin muna-zan'yō*, 89

Lairesse, Gérarde de, 52, 263n85
language, Dutch, 6, 15, 17–18, 23–24; Japanese, 14, 20; Malay, 14–15; problems of translation, 169
Lavater, Johann, 113, **113**, **114**
Leeuwenhoek, Anton van, 208
literati, *see bunjin*
London, *see* Great Britain
loupe, *see* magnifying glass
Luiken, Johannes & Caspaares, 42, **43**, 72, **72**, 134, **135**, 157, **157**

machines, Edo-period attitudes to 63–64; *see also* flying machines, viewing machines, orrery
magnifying glass, 177, 181, 182, 183
Matsudaira Sadanobu, 46, 62, 81, 95, 117, 262n56
Maeno Ryōtaku, 21; work on *Kaitai shinsho*, 88, 168, 241
Martin, Benjamin, 251
Maruyama Ōju, 169
Maruyama Ōkyo, 56, 102, 159–160, 169, **221**, 216
Matsuo Bashō, 16
medicine, 15, 44, 64, 137, 175; anatomy & surgery, 37, 61, 88–89, **154**, 166, 203, 208, 211; eye medicine, 166–170, **168**, **170**, 172, 181, 241, 276n4; Hippocrates, 280n102; *kanpō*, 166–167, 203; Medicine Buddha, 241

menoko zan'yō (visual calculation), 44, 48, 261n51
Mekichi (narrator), 178–180, **179**
Mexico, 8
microscopes, 8, 21, 30, 51–52, 55–56, 172, 182, 183, 194–211, **195**, **202**, **204–205**, **207**, **208**, 212–213, 232, 240
Mikumo Kanzen, 169
Minagawa Kien, 56, 102, 153, 196, 264n101
Minamoto no Yoshitsune, *see* Yoshitsune
mirrors, 98–99, 108, 152–165, **157**, **160**, **164**, **165**, 182, 191, 232, 276n61
misemono (paying displays), 8, 61, 136, 144, 191
Mitaku Yorai, 136, **137**, 181, 213
Miura Baian, 44
Morishima Chūryō, 17, 18, 20, 21, 22, 23, 29, 45, 63, 64, 75, 79, 82, 102, 103, 130, 151, 238; *Bango-sen*, 17, 71, 94, 97, 105, 108, 167; *Hōgo kago*, 236; *Karadehon tōjingura*, 23, *Kōmō zatsuwa*, 21, 33, 45, **45**, 74, **74**, 97143, **143**, 144, 194–196, **195**, 199–201, **200**, 223, 225, 228; *Shingaku tatoe-gusa*, 81, 83–85; *Shin-Yoshitsune saiken Ezo*, 130–132, **131**; *Tora no maki*, 159, **160**
Motoki Ryōei, 237
Motoori Norinaga, 55
Murano-ya (glassware shop), 29–30, 182, 190, 194, 278n49

Nagakubo Sekisui, 47, 140, 159, 220
Nagasawa Rosetsu, 54–56, 102, 153, 196, 264n97
Nakagawa Jun'an, 18, 20, 279n71; work on *Kaitai shinsho*, 88, 168
Nakai Hidetake, 100
Nakai Riken, 195, 196
Nakazawa Dōni, 81, 82, 118, 129, 161, 162, 163–164, 234
Namake no Bakahito, 206–208, **207**, 225
Nan'a Kō, 204–205, 206
Nanpin School, 263n88
Nansenshō Somahito, 208, **208**, **210**, 211
Narabayashi Jūbei, 144, 157, 244
Nishikawa Joken, 157, 158, 235
Nishikawa Sukenobu, 83; *Woman with Clock*, **84**
Nishimura Shigenaga, 70, **70**
Nishiyama Sōkō, 229

objectivity, 172, 177, 211
Odano Naotake, **88**, 89, 168, **168**
Ōhata Giemon, *Imported automaton clock*, **80**
Ogasawara Narashige, 166
Ogawa Yoshimaru, **207**
Okumura Masanobu, 103–104
Onitake, *see* Kanwatei Onitake
optique, *see* viewing machines
orrery, 248–252, **249**, **250**, 286n137, 287n138
Orrery, Earl of, 249
Ota Nanpo, 39, 217, 220, 236, 238
Ota Shukki, 246
Ōtsuki Gentaku, 6, 21, 50, 53, 63, 134, 136, 137, 169, 171, 194, 236; *Aran iji mondo*, 277n28; *Chōtei kaitai shinsho*, 194; interrogates Tsūdayū for *Kankai ibun*, 91, 227, 252–253, **251–252**; parodied, 23, 111; *Rangaku kaitei*, 52; *Ransetsu benwaku*, 21, 23, 57, **57**, 107, 170; *see also* Shirandō

painting & drawing, Dutch-style, 20, 52–56, 94, 137, 161, 263n82; Dutch art in Edo, 94, 269n2; *see also* copperplate prints
Paré, Ambroise, 95
Paris, *see* France
peepbox, *see* viewing machines
Pepys, Samuel, 78
Perry, Commodore Matthew, 213
perspective, 97–99, 121, 125, 126
physiognomy, 113–115, **113**, **114**, 162, 177, 180–181, **180**, 191, 211; *see also* Lavater
planetarium, **251**, **252**, 252–253
Plenk, Joseph, 169
Ponteppidous, Grich, 238
pornography, 124, 156, 191, 217, 245, 276n70
private trade (*nukeni*), 12; *see also* smuggling
puppet box (*kairai-bako*), 118–119, **119**

Qianglong (Qing ruler), 67, 72, 79; on mirrors, 159, 162; on windows, 135–136

Rantokusai Shundo, 225
Rinshō, 203–206, **204–205**
Rokujūen, 65–66, 78, 84, 224, 225
Romberg, Hendrik, 225, 283n57
Rowley, John, 249
Royen, Willem van, 94, 95, 222
Russia, 16, 69, 72, 91, 134, 136, 141, 220, 221, 227–228, 252–253; *see also* Catherine the Great
Ryōgoku Bridge, 102, 104, 127, 129, 136, 191, 209, 211, 281n114
Ryōtaku, *see* Maeno Ryōtaku
Ryūtei Tanehiko, 209

saiku (precision craftsmanship), 48, 49, 52, 60, 65, 67, 70, 72, 73, 78, 91, 95, 106, 127, 191
Saitō Gesshin, 229, **230–231**, **245**
Sakaragawa Jihinari, 191–194, **192**, **193**

Sano Yasusada, 203
Santō Kyōden, 24, 28, 35, 51–52, 57, 68, 89, 109, 162, 183, 195, 227; as artist, 29, **61**, 130, **131**, 163, **164**, 172, 182, 232, **234**; *Akushichi henme Kagekiyo*, 172–176, **173**, **174–175**, 178–179, **179**; *Gesaku mondo*, 146; *Gozonji no shōbaimono*, 121, **124**, 126, 127, 130; *Hitogokoro kagami no utsushi-e* (*see Jinshin-kyō no utsushi-e*); *Jikun kage-e no tatoe*, 112–115, **112**, **114**, **115**; *Jinshin-kyō no utsushi-e*, **116**, **117**, **118**, 115–118, 129; *Kaitsū unubore kagami*, 163, **164**; *Komon gawa*, 68, **68**, 125, 126–127, 179; *Komon shinpō*, 179; *Ko wa mezurashiki misemono-gatari*, 127–129, **128**, 144–145, **145**; *Matsu to ume taketori monogatari*, 198–199, **198**, **199**, 201, 202; *Ningen sei muna-zan'yō*, 89; *Sanshōdayū shichinin musume*, 189–190, **189**, 194; *Shinzō zue*, 105, **105**; wife Yuri, 195
Saris, John, 253
Satake Yoshiatsu (Shozan), 20, 28, 53–54, 56, **75**, 89, 95, 130, 142–144, 168, **223**, 224, **224**; building projects, 218–222; *Gahō kōryō/Gazu rikai*, 20, 53, 220
Satake Yoshimasa, 224
Satō Narihiro, 35, 153–154, 260n20; *Chūryō manroku*, 113
senryū, definition of, 24–25
Scheuchzer, Jean-Jacques, 172
Seijū-kan (medical centre), 97, 137, 144, 274n21
s' Gravesande, Gulielmo, **107**
Sharaku, 245
Sharakutei Manri, 232–233, **234**
Shiba Kōkan, 7, 15, 20, 22, 33, 39, 43, 47–50, 53, 54, 56, 61, 63, 89, 91, 95, 106, 134–135, 137, 170, 181, 200, **200**, 212, 220, 228, 237, 238, 239, 252; his ceramics, 226; his copperplates, 95–97, **103**, **249**; on mirrors & glass pictures, 153, 154, 156–157, 161; *Kopperu tenmon zukai*, 149–150, **149**; *Mt Fuji seen across the Ōi*, **55**; *Mugen dōjin hikki*, 195; *Oranda kikō*, 97; *Oranda tensetsu*, 48, **49**, 150, **150**; *Oranda tsūhaku*, 97, 246; on Paradise, 239–240; *Saiyū ryōdan*, **47**, **62**; *Tenchi ridan*, 172; *Tenchi zenzu*, 196, 201; *Tenkyū zenzu*, 248–249, **249**; *Tweelandbruk*, **103**; *Yoshio Kōsaku with Symbols*, **15**; on *uki-e*, 102–103; *Vulture Peak & Hot air balloon*, **229**
Shiba Zenkō, 146, *Ōchigai takarabune*, 146–148, **146**, **147**; *Shiba Zenkō chie no hodo*, 232; *Tōseijin tsūbutsu kaichō*, 240–241, **241**
Shibukawa Harumi, 237, 285n96
Shibukawa Kagesuke, **49**, **214**, 236
Shikitei Sanba, 24, 28, 30, 196, 230, 258n89; *Hara no uchi gesaku no tanehon*, 206, **207**; *Hitogokoro nozoki-karakuri*, 129, 211; *Muna-zan'yō hayakawari no hō*, 89; *Ningen isshin nozoki-karakuri*, 233–234, **235**, 244; *Ono no Bakamura uso ji-zukushi*, 179–181, **180**; *Ukiyo doko*, 125
Shimazu Shigehide, 236
Shimokabe Ikei, 118, **119**
Shingaku, 81–87, 90, 93, 118, 129, 161, 234
Shinto, 237–238
Shirandō (Dutch Academy), 6, 23, 51, 111, 254n3
Shōun, **90**
Shunsai Eishō, 208, **208**, **210**
Siebold, Franz von, 171–172, 226, 236
silhouettes, 112–115
smuggling, 11–13, 79, 159; *see also* private trade
Soane, Sir Hans, 255n32
Soga Shōhaku, 258n90
Spain and Portugal, 8; export of clock, 79; Lisbon Earthquake, 16
spectacles, 8, 61, 172, 181–194, **184–185**, **186**, **187**, **188**, **189**, **190–192**, **193**, 232, 238; pince-nez, 247
spiral stairs, 221–224, **223**
St. Petersburg, *see* Russia
static-electricity generator, 8, 37, 44–47, **45**, **46**, 107
Steele, Sir Richard, 249, 186n136
Sugita Genpaku, 11, 15, 20, 44, 56, 88, 107, 160, 167, 176; *Kaitai shinsho*, **88**, 89, 168, **168**, 172, 194, 203, 241; *Keiei yawa*, 161, **161**; *Rangaku kotohajime*, 10, 237
Sugita Rikkyō, **170**
Sukenari, *Tengu tsū*, 108–109, **108**
Sukeroku, 104–106, **105**, 116
Suminawa, 64–66, 78–79, 224, 225
surgery, *see* medicine
Suzuki Harunobu, 100–101, 102, 183, 236, 244; *Motoura of the Yamazaki-ya in the South*, **246**
Swammerdam, Jean, 201–202, **201**; translated by Thomas Flloyd, 202
Swift, Dean Jonathan, 127

Tachibana Nankei, 14–15, 33, 34, 44–45–46, 48, 56, 60, 63, 134, 149, 154, 212, 221, 236–237, 239, 239; *Hokusō sadan*, 212–213; *Seiyū-ki*, **14**, 44–45
Tachihara Suiken, 244
Takahashi Kageyasu, 71, **71**, 82, 236
Takahashi Yoshitoki, 236
Takagi Shunzan, 144
Takamori Kankō, 53, 56
Takano Chōei, 6, 7, 171; *Tori no nakune*, 254n1
Takeda Ōmi, 46, 65, 66–67, 75–78, **77**, 82, 129, 266n37; and clockwork, 78; *Nichō tsutsumi: Takeda Ō-karakuri*, 75–76; *Ō-karakuri e-zukushi*,

70; and peeping-*karakuri*, 121, 128, 130, **131**, 211
Takehara Shunchōsai, **26–27**, 29, **69**, **77**, 77–78, **218–219**
Taki Angen, 137
Takizawa Bakin, 28, 57–58, 67, 88, 126, 158, 245, 258n90; *Kage to hinata chinmō zui*, 58; *Kiro manroku*, 57–58, **58–59**; *Satomi hyakken-den*, 282n27
Tani Bunchō, 95, 113, 209, 270n16
Tanuma Okitomo, 11
Tanoma Okitsugu, 10, 11, 22, 46, 62, 220
Tanomura Chikuden, 216, 281n19
Tazawa Shunbō, 220
telescopes, 8, 30, 50, 62, 91, 125, 159, 160, 172, 182, 183, 203, 213–214, **214**, 218, 228–232, **230**, **234**, **235**, 238, **239**, 240, 244, 245, **246**, 247, **247**, 293n80, 281n21; as symbol, 232–235
Tenmei Rōjin, **20**
Terajima Ryōan, 61, 79, 105, 137, 181, 213
Teshima Tōan, 81
Tatebe Seian, 194
Thailand, 244
Thunberg, Charles, 12, 13, 16, 17, 18, 36, 79, 134, 141, 143–144, 157, 158, 169–170, 214, 215, 216, 255n24&28, 257n60, 260n24; and Linneus, 18
Titsingh, Isaac, 14, 17, 62, 80, 255n16
Torii Kiyomasa, 203, **204–205**, 205
Torii Kiyonaga, 67, 112, **112**, 113, **114**, **115**
Toriyama Sekien, 29; *Hyakki tsurezure-gusa*, 109, **109**
Tosa Mitsuoki, 55
Tsūdayū (castaway), 90–91, 136, 141, 220, 221, 227–228, 252–253
Tsuruya Kinsuke, 130, 177
Tsuta Karamaru, *see* Tsutaya Jūsaburō
Tsutaya Jūsaburō, 89, **92–93**, 117, **118**, 130, 153, 175, 233, 238; *Jintai kaichō ryaku engi*, 90, 154

Udagawa Genzui 225, 262n52
uki-e (floating pictures), 102–106, 121, 126, 128, 209, 271n34
ukiyo, *see* Floating World
Utagawa Hiroshige, 18, **20**, 25
Utagawa (Gotōtei) Kunisada, **115**, **116**, 201, 202, 232, 269n113, 278n40
Utagawa Kunitora, **190**, 191
Utagawa Kuniyoshi, 191
Utagawa Toyoharu, 103
Utagawa Toyohiro, 58, **58–59**
Utagawa Toyokuni, 103, 109, **110**, **111**, 129, 191, **192**, **193**, 194, 217–218, 232, **235**, 233, 238
Utamaro, *see* Kitagawa Utamaro

Valentijn, François, 228
Venice, *see* Italy
viewing machines, devil lantern (magic lantern), 106–111, **107**, **108**, **110**, **111**, 129; *optique*, 98–106, **99**, **100**, **101**, **103**, 119, 182, 209, 217; peeping *karakuri* box, 8, 94, 119–132, **120**, **122–123**, **124**, **128**, **131**, 208–211, 233, 272n71&72
Vignola, Giacomo da, 222
VOC (Vereenigde Oost Indische Compannie), 9, 11, 12, **40**, 41, **41**, **47**, 54, 61, 70, 72, **73**, 77–78, 79, 91, 95, 106, 119, 125, **138–139**, 140, 153, 158, 183, 196, 220, 222, 254n7; Edo *hofreis*, 15–18, 25, 32–33, 49–50, **77**, 168–169, 171, 187

Wakan sansai zue, *see* Terajima Ryōan
Wang Wei, 53–54
Wright, Thomas, 240

Xing Linan, 167

Yamagata Bantō, 44
Yamagata Shigefusa, 198
Yamawaki Tōyō, 203
Yoshimune (8th Tokugawa shogun), 9, 10, 16, 50, 95, 166
Yoshio Kōsaku, **14**, **15**, 15, 32, 44, 49, 154, 155, 181, 220; work on *Kaitai shinsho*, 32, 168
Yoshitsune (Minamoto no Yoshitsune), 75–76, 130

Zhuangzi, 112–113, **112**, 194–195, 202